# CIVIL RESISTANCE AND POWER POLITICS

# CIVIL RESISTANCE AND POWER POLITICS
Cases covered in the chapters of this book

**EAST GERMANY**
*Civil resistance and civil society, 1989*

**CZECHOSLOVAKIA**
*From Soviet invasion to Velvet Revolution, 1968–89*

**NORTHERN IRELAND**
*Civil rights movement, 1967–72*

**UNITED STATES**
*Civil rights movement, 1945–70*

**PORTUGAL**
*Revolution of the Carnations, 1974–75*

**SERBIA**
*Civil society against Slobodan Milošević 1991–2000*

**KOSOVO**
*The struggle against Serb domination, 1990–98*

**CHILE**
*Resisting General Pinochet, 1983–88*

POLAND
*Towards 'self-limiting revolution',*
*1970–89*

BALTIC REPUBLICS
*Independence movements,*
*1987–91*

UKRAINE
*Orange Revolution, 2004*

SOVIET UNION
*Reacting to civil resistance,*
*1968–91*

CHINA
*Tiananmen*
*Square protests,*
*1989*

BURMA
*The moment of*
*the monks, 2007*

GEORGIA
*Rose Revolution,*
*2003*

IRAN
*Deposing the*
*Shah, 1977–79*

INDIA
*Gandhi and civil*
*resistance, 1917–47*

PHILIPPINES
*People Power, 1983–86*

SOUTH AFRICA
*Non-violent and violent*
*action against apartheid,*
*1983–94*

# Civil Resistance and Power Politics

*The Experience of Non-violent Action
from Gandhi to the Present*

*Edited by*
ADAM ROBERTS
TIMOTHY GARTON ASH

OXFORD
UNIVERSITY PRESS

# OXFORD

UNIVERSITY PRESS

Great Clarendon Street, Oxford OX2 6DP
United Kingdom

Oxford University Press is a department of the University of Oxford.
It furthers the University's objective of excellence in research, scholarship,
and education by publishing worldwide. Oxford is a registered trade mark of
Oxford University Press in the UK and in certain other countries

First published 2009
First published in paperback with new foreword and minor corrections 2011
Reprinted 2012

British Library Cataloguing in Publication Data
Data available

Library of Congress Cataloging in Publication Data
Data available

ISBN 978-0-19-969145-6

Printed and bound by CPI Group (UK) Ltd, Croydon, CR0 4YY

# *Foreword to the Paperback Edition: The Arab Spring*

On 17 December 2010 a 26-year-old vegetable-seller, Mohamed Bouazizi, set fire to himself in the Tunisian town of Sidi Bouzid after police had harassed him as he plied his trade. This incident set off a series of demonstrations, first locally, then across Tunisia, and then in other parts of North Africa and the Middle East. Within two months, the movements that rapidly emerged had resulted in the departure from office of two dictators—President Zine al-Abidine Ben-Ali of Tunisia on 14 January 2011, and President Hosni Mubarak of Egypt four weeks later.

These were major new episodes in the story of the growth of civil resistance as a force in politics and international relations, which is the subject of this book. In many other countries—Yemen, Bahrain, Syria among them—the demand for autocratic regimes to step down was articulated in sustained campaigns involving demonstrations, strikes, and countless other acts of non-compliance.

The Oxford University Project on Civil Resistance and Power Politics is commissioning specialist studies on several of these cases, addressing many of the questions raised in this book. Meanwhile, this Foreword presents some preliminary, tentative observations on what is clearly a major development in the centuries-old story of civil resistance. Five features of the Arab Spring seem to us to stand out. Each one of them suggests a fundamental change in the societies involved.

1. *Conditions.* The circumstances that gave rise to these movements bore some similarities to those that gave rise to al-Qaeda: awareness of the corrupt and oppressive nature of many Arab governments, which were often supported by the West, and a more general sense of the humiliation experienced under post-colonial political systems. However, in all other respects—especially in the fundamental matters of ends and means—the movements of the Arab Spring could not have been more different from al-Qaeda.
2. *Political goals.* The authoritarian and kleptocratic regimes of the Arab world were increasingly opposed by populations demanding, not some utopian society (whether communist, Islamist or other) but a decent life, the possibility of earning an honest wage, and an effectively functioning constitutional system within their own states, giving people some control over their rulers. Dignity, democracy and rule of law are at the centre of the demands.
3. *Means of communication.* In the Arab revolutions, social networking media such as Facebook and Twitter, together with satellite television channels such as Al Jazeera, and the widespread use of mobile phones, have played an important role in enabling people to mobilize and also in letting the outside

world know what was happening. They are very far from being the sole explanation of the uprisings, which continued even when, as in Egypt, internet and mobile phone services were shut down completely for several days. Without the bravery and skilful strategic thinking of the protesters, new media would have achieved nothing. Nonetheless, it is highly significant that Wael Ghonim, an Egyptian Google executive, played a vital role in the Egyptian events by organizing a Facebook page called 'We Are All Khaled Said'—named after a young Egyptian who had died on 6 June 2010 after being arrested by Egyptian police.

4. *Participation.* The movements have been both middle class and working class, with women and young people taking a major part. The role of women represented a particularly striking change from the traditionally male-dominated politics of the region.

5. *Methods.* Within the movements the emphasis has been, not on Guevarist guerrilla warfare, still less on terrorism, but on civic action. 'Peaceful, peaceful' has been a commonly used invocation. Here, as in other cases, civil resistance was not based on a presumption that authorities would not use force in response. In every country touched by the Arab Spring, some demonstrators were shot—in some cases hundreds were killed—but the movements generally carried on, determined not to let their martyrs down.

The success of the movements in early 2011 briefly encouraged the attractive idea of a rolling democratic and civil revolution, starting with Tunisia and Egypt, and leading to similar outcomes throughout the Arab world. This vision clashed with the awkward reality that there will inevitably be different outcomes to campaigns of civil resistance, depending on the local and international circumstances of each case.

Although civil resistance represents a significant break from the normal methods of power politics, that break is not complete. Hard facts of power have a bearing on the causation, the course and the outcome of campaigns. This was clear in the two cases, Tunisia and Egypt, where quick results were achieved. Both countries had authoritarian regimes that did not have a strong ideological base. These two successful revolutions involved subtle and complex interactions between non-violent demonstrators and factors of power. The demonstrators, as is normal in campaigns of civil resistance, sought consistently to discourage the armed forces and police of their countries from using force against them. They also sought to exacerbate divisions between the police and the military, or between regular soldiers and their senior officers. Despite many shootings of demonstrators and other incidents, they succeeded in securing a measure of cooperation from the armed forces. Indeed, a key slogan of the Egyptian demonstrators on Tahrir Square in Cairo was 'The army and people are one'—an unusual and paradoxical, but far from illogical, chant for a non-violent movement. (After the revolution, cracks in this unity became apparent.)

In Tahrir Square it was not only the army and police that the demonstrators had to cope with. It was also pro-regime thugs, many riding on horses and camels, who attacked the demonstrators on 2 February. In response, some in the crowd used a degree of force, including throwing stones at their attackers and arresting a number of them. By these means they succeeded in defending the square. One demonstrator tweeted that afternoon: 'I came to a peaceful protest, this is not one.' And then, eight hours later: 'I did not take part in the violence, which is a real moral dilemma for me right now, for it's the people who did who saved me.' After seeing off the thugs, the demonstrators reverted to their peaceful methods of protest. It was as if they accepted that sometimes it is necessary to use force in a defensive cause, but it should not be the main means of achieving political change.

Was the more general possibility that things might get out of hand—that peaceful protests could quickly degenerate into riots—also a factor in these events? There were certainly enough incidents of stone-throwing and looting to raise that possibility. For example, in the early days of the Egyptian revolution there was a good deal of rioting and arson, but it was significantly curtailed by the movement's leaders, not least because of concern that such violence played into the regime's hands. Indeed, in many of the Arab uprisings governments went to some lengths ( for example, sending in thugs, releasing criminals from prisons, and provoking demonstrators) to encourage violence and disorder as part of an attempt to justify repression. Whether in particular cases the possibility of violent mayhem on the streets led to a hardening of regime attitudes, or to a willingness to make concessions to the demonstrators, it is not possible to say at this stage. Overwhelmingly, however, it was the peaceful, determined character of the protests and strikes in Tunisia and Egypt that induced recognition, both domestically and internationally, that fundamental changes in the leadership and constitutional structure of the state had to be made.

There was another dimension of power politics in the Arab revolutions: the role of outside governments. Many countries and regional bodies had to address questions about whether they should actively promote change, and if so what forms any support should take: direct support for opposition movements, freezing of regime assets, withdrawal of defence cooperation, military intervention, public statements, refugee assistance or provision of aid? In their policies towards Middle Eastern states, the US and many European countries had a record of close association with dictatorial regimes, which were sometimes preferred on the grounds that they provided stability. Yet when faced with incontrovertible evidence of the unpopularity of these regimes and their repressive tendencies, both the US and Europe back-tracked. First they called for unspecified reforms, then for an eventual transition to democracy, and then for immediate change. Ultimately they put pressure on Ben-Ali, Mubarak, and others to go. The civil resistance on the Arab street was having a direct effect in Washington, London and Paris. President Barack Obama went on to embrace these movements: in an interview in May 2011 he spoke of the 'moral force of non-violence' and asserted that 'the US stands on the side of those who through non-violent means are trying to bring about a better life for themselves and their families'.

The revolutions in Tunisia and Egypt have also furnished new examples of an old problem: the need to follow up a successful campaign of civil resistance with an effective programme of governmental and societal change involving a wide range of partners, domestic and international. This is a difficult task, involving both foreign and domestic policy, and requiring different skills from the leadership of a civil resistance struggle. In both Tunisia and Egypt the outcome required cooperation with the armed forces, and also a willingness to make compromises— particularly difficult for movements that had lacked formal leadership structures and had operated primarily by networking.

In some other Arab countries the balance of outside forces, far from helping the demonstrators, made conditions tough for them. This was manifestly the case in Bahrain. There courageous citizens demonstrated repeatedly for basic democratic rights, but many neighbouring states were concerned about the possible ramifications of genuine democracy establishing itself in the Gulf, and also of the majority Shia population gaining a significant degree of control in Bahrain. Saudi forces entered the country on 14 March, under the authority of the Gulf Cooperation Council, and with the stated purpose of protecting essential facilities including oil and gas installations and financial institutions. The obvious effect of this intervention was to reduce the chances of a democratic deal between the government and the demonstrators.

In Libya, peaceful demonstrations in February made remarkable early gains. However, when they were met with violent repression by the regime of Colonel Gaddafi—some of it carried out by African mercenaries—civil resistance rapidly changed into armed uprising. These events confirmed the observations in this book, especially in the chapters on Northern Ireland and Kosovo, that repression of civil resistance can sometimes lead on to violent conflict and external military intervention. In this case the UN became directly involved almost from the beginning. UN Security Council Resolution 1970 of 26 February deplored 'the gross and systematic violation of human rights, including the repression of peaceful demonstrators'; and then, as civil war spread in Libya, with Benghazi threatened by government forces, Resolution 1973 of 17 March authorized certain member states 'to take all necessary measures … to protect civilians and civilian populated areas under threat of attack … in the Libyan Arab Jamahiriya, including Benghazi'. The NATO air campaign followed immediately. Taken together, these resolutions suggest the emergence of a doctrine that killings of peaceful demonstrators are unlawful, and when such killings lead on to civil war they may provide a legitimate pretext for an international military response. Any such doctrine is deeply problematic, not least because its application is bound to be selective, leading to accusations of double standards. At the same time, there could hardly be a more graphic illustration of the interconnections between civil resistance and power politics.

Our provisional conclusion, writing about a still ongoing story, is that the Arab Spring of 2011 confirms, but also adds significantly to, seven key propositions about civil resistance in this book:

- Civil resistance often arises because of the power of example (including in other countries), and because a few key people have had training in its basics, rather than because of a philosophical attachment to a general doctrine of non-violence.

- It has to have local roots if it is to be effective. Political ideas and forms of protest spread from one country to another, but their application in any given country depends on the interests, beliefs, and political culture of its inhabitants.
- It offers the possibility of achieving basic change even in societies that have been under apparently stable dictatorial control.
- It can occur in a wide variety of circumstances. The idea that there was little chance of activist pro-democratic politics in Arab and Islamic countries has been demolished, and there is already evidence that these events are having ripple effects in other parts of the world.
- It has a close relationship to the demand for democracy and honest elections.
- It is by no means bound to succeed. The repression of the demonstrations in Iran in 2009, protesting against a fraudulent election result, had already confirmed this point, which has since become evident in some of the Arab revolts of 2011.
- It has a complex relationship with other forms of power, and cannot be fully understood in isolation from them.

The case studies in the original edition of this book, published in 2009, suggested that the methods of peaceful resistance as practised in 1989, and in subsequent opposition movements in other states and continents, were becoming the 'default' model of how to deal with dictatorial systems and foreign occupations. With many difficulties along the route, and more to be expected, this remains our conclusion—not just for Europe, not just for the Arab world, but also more generally.

In this paperback edition we have made no changes to the original text other than a very small number of minor corrections. We repeat our gratitude to the funders of the Oxford University Project on Civil Resistance and Power Politics, details of which can be found at http://cis.politics.ox.ac.uk/research/Projects/civ_res.asp.

A.R., T.G.A.

*Oxford,*
*June 2011*

# Preface

Civil resistance has become an increasingly salient feature of international politics over the last half-century, from the US civil rights movement and Czechoslovakia in the 1960s to the so-called 'colour revolutions' in eastern Europe and Burma's 'moment of the monks' in the 2000s. We believe that the phenomenon of non-violent action deserves more study than it has so far received, and that it should be examined in a broader comparative context of international relations, politics, and contemporary history.

At the heart of this book are nineteen case studies of major historical episodes in which civil resistance played an important part. Each chapter is the work of an individual author, with his or her own distinctive approach, style and special interests. Bibliographical references and all but the most familiar abbreviations have been spelt out at first mention in every chapter, so that each can be read on its own. We have, however, gone to considerable lengths, both in the original design and in the detailed editing of this book, to try to ensure a common intellectual agenda. Carefully chosen documentary photographs are reproduced at appropriate points in each chapter. Extended captions, written by the editors in close consultation with individual authors, both explain the particular circumstances and highlight the illustrations' relevance to larger themes.

This is the first major publication of the Oxford University Project on Civil Resistance and Power Politics. We print below a list of seventeen questions addressed to contributors at the start of the project. Of course not all are relevant to or can be answered in each case, and others have emerged as research has progressed. These questions exemplify the project's concern to explore, rigorously and sceptically, the historical roles played by civil resistance, and to clarify the relationship between civil resistance and other elements of power. That relationship turns out to be more multifaceted than many proponents of civil resistance, or indeed of power politics, might have expected. Some of these connections are further teased out in the editors' introductory and concluding chapters.

A.R., T.G.A.

*Oxford,*
*March 2009*

# Acknowledgements

First and foremost we thank all our colleagues on the Oxford University project on 'Civil Resistance and Power Politics: Domestic and International Dimensions', which was established in 2006. The project held an international conference at Oxford on 15–18 March 2007. This was attended not only by academic experts on particular cases of civil resistance, but also by participants in the campaigns, journalists and writers who had reported on them, and officials who had in one way or another been involved in responding to them.

Our deepest thanks go to Dr Thomas Richard Davies, who served from January 2006 to March 2008 as Research Associate of the project, and whose contributions to the project, from the March 2006 workshop to the March 2007 conference, and then to this book, were all outstanding. Without his work, which combined efficiency, deep understanding, and helpfulness toward all involved in this enterprise, we could not have reached the finishing tape of publication so soon.

We also owe a special debt of gratitude to our fellow members of the project's Organizing Committee, Judith Brown, Peter Carey, Rana Mitter, Alex Pravda, and Jan Zielonka, all of whom played a central role in guiding the project as a whole, selecting contributors, and subsequently helping to edit the chapters in this volume.

We are indebted to Martin Gilbert for preparing the map. In the search for photographs we had talented assistance from Daniel Hemel at Oxford University, and from Steve York and Ragan Carpenter of York Zimmerman Inc., Washington, DC. While every effort was made to contact the copyright holders of material in this book, in some cases we were unable to do so. If the copyright holders contact the author or publisher, we will be pleased to rectify any omission at the earliest opportunity.

Ensuring that chapters in a wide-ranging book such as this have elements of common structure and style, and are clear to non-specialists, is no simple task. We are grateful to Kate Upshon for some exceptionally judicious subediting; to Małgorzata Gorska for invaluable assistance in commenting on and revising several chapters; to Mary-Jane Fox for rigorous comments on the Introduction and the project as a whole; and, at Oxford University Press, to our editor, Dominic Byatt, to members of the editorial staff, especially Lizzy Suffling, Louise Sprake, and Aimee Wright; and to the copy-editor, Tom Chandler.

Most of the chapters are based on papers presented at the March 2007 conference, which were always intended for publication. In this volume we have included revised texts of those papers that dealt with particular cases rather than with more general or abstract themes, and we have added a new chapter, on the events in Burma in 2007. We have also included three chapters (the first two and the last) exploring how civil resistance and power politics interact, and situating the themes pursued in this volume in the context of other literature on civil resistance and political change.

The chapters have been greatly enriched by the comments and reflections of the participants in the conference, and we would especially like to thank for their contributions the other conference speakers: Peter Ackerman, Alan Angell, William Beinart, Kenneth Bloomfield, Stephen Bosworth, Richard Caplan, Martin Ceadel, Paul Chaisty, Thomas Richard Davies, Mient Jan Faber, James Fenton, Lars Fredén, Carlos Gaspar, David Goldey, Adrian Guelke, Hydajet Hyseni, Mkhuseli Jack, Konrad Jarausch, Mary Kaldor, Mary King, Monika Mac-Donagh-Pajerová, Michael McFaul, Abbas Milani, Grazina Miniotaite, Edward Mortimer, Ghia Nodia, Lucy Nusseibeh, Bhikhu Parekh, Chris Patten, Minxin Pei, Frank Pieke, Srdja Popović, Dmytro Potekhin, Bob Purdie, Janusz Reykowski, Berel Rodal, Zita Seabra, Jacques Semelin, Gene Sharp, Patricio Silva, Jonathan Steele, Ed de la Torre, Samuel Valenzuela, Wang Juntao, David Washbrook, Laurence Whitehead, Harris Wofford, Steve York, and Zarni. For the smooth running of the conference, we are especially grateful to Denise Line of the European Studies Centre, and to Emily Speers Mears and Małgorzata Gorska, the graduate student assistants. For their participation in the preparatory workshop for the conference, we would like to thank Arshin Adib-Moghaddam, Cath Collins, Richard Crampton, Michael Freeden, Alan Knight, Teresa Pinto Coelho, William Smith, Marc Stears, and Sherrill Stroschein.

The project on Civil Resistance and Power Politics is run under the auspices of the Centre for International Studies in Oxford University's Department of Politics and International Relations and the European Studies Centre at St Antony's College, Oxford: we are very grateful for the support of the Directors of these institutions, Andrew Hurrell, Neil MacFarlane, and Kalypso Nicolaïdis. We also owe special thanks to Esther Byrom for her handling of numerous research funding applications.

Without the support of a number of generous funders, this book would not have been possible. We would like to thank particularly: Peter Ackerman and Berel Rodal at the International Center on Nonviolent Conflict in Washington, DC; Judy Barsalou, April Hall, Steve Riskin, and Trish Thomson at the United States Institute of Peace; Markus Baumanns and Michael Göring at the Zeit Foundation; Kristian Netland at the Norwegian Ministry of Foreign Affairs; Stephen Heintz and Hope Lyons at the Rockefeller Brothers Fund; Maciek Hawrylak and Jeff Senior at the Canadian Department of Foreign Affairs and International Trade; Joan Link and Matthew Preston at the British Foreign and Commonwealth Office; and the Research Grants staff of the British Academy.

# Contents

# *Illustrations*

# Contributors

**Ervand Abrahamian** is Distinguished Professor of History at City University of New York. He is the author of *Iran Between Two Revolutions* (Princeton University Press, 1982); *The Iranian Mojahedin* (Yale University Press, 1986); *Khomeinism: Essays on the Islamic Republic* (University of California Press, 1993); *Tortured Confessions: Prisons and Public Recantations in Modern Iran* (University of California Press, 1999); and *A History of Modern Iran* (Cambridge University Press, 2008).

**Mark R. Beissinger** is Professor of Politics at Princeton University, specializing in Russian and post-Soviet politics. He has written extensively on issues of national identity and nationalist movements in the post-Soviet region. His works include *Nationalist Mobilization and the Collapse of the Soviet State* (Cambridge University Press, 2002) and *The Nationalities Factor in Soviet Politics and Society* (Westview, 1990).

**Judith M. Brown** is Emeritus Professor of Commonwealth History at Oxford University and Emeritus Fellow of Balliol College, Oxford. She is the author of *Gandhi's Rise to Power: Indian Politics 1915–1922* (Cambridge University Press, 1972); *Gandhi and Civil Disobedience: The Mahatma in Indian Politics 1928–34* (Cambridge University Press, 1977); *Modern India: The Origins of an Asian Democracy* (Oxford University Press, 1984); *Gandhi: Prisoner of Hope* (Yale University Press, 1989); *Nehru: A Political Life* (Oxford University Press, 2003); and *The Essential Writings of Mahatma Gandhi* (Oxford University Press, 2008). Most recently she has co-edited with A. Parel *The Cambridge Companion to Gandhi* (Cambridge University Press, New York, 2011).

**April Carter** is an Honorary Research Fellow at the Centre for Peace and Reconciliation Studies, Coventry University. Her most recent books are: *The Political Theory of Global Citizenship* (Routledge, 2001) and *Direct Action and Democracy Today* (Polity, 2005). She also compiled (with Howard Clark and Michael Randle) *People Power and Protest Since 1945: A Bibliography of Nonviolent Action* (Housmans Bookshop, 2006).

**Howard Clark** is Chair of War Resisters' International and Visiting Research Fellow at the Centre for Peace and Reconciliation Studies at Coventry University. He is the author of *Preparing for Nonviolent Direct Action* (CND Publications, 1984) and *Civil Resistance in Kosovo* (Pluto, 2000). He compiled (with April Carter and Michael Randle) *People Power and Protest since 1945: A Bibliography of Nonviolent Action* (Housmans Bookshop, 2006) and edited *People Power: Unarmed Resistance and Global Solidarity* (Pluto, 2009).

**Richard English** is Professor of Politics and Director of the Centre for the Study of Terrorism and Political Violence at the University of St Andrews. His books include *Armed Struggle: The History of the IRA* (Macmillan, 2003), *Irish Freedom: The History of Nationalism in Ireland* (Macmillan, 2006) and *Terrorism: How to Respond* (Oxford University Press, 2009). He is a Fellow of the British Academy and a Member of the Royal Irish Academy.

**Christina Fink** is a Lecturer at the International Sustainable Development Studies Institute in Chiang Mai, Thailand. She obtained her Ph.D. in social/cultural anthropology from UC Berkeley in 1994. She wrote *Living Silence: Burma Under Military Rule* (Zed Books, 2001) and co-edited *Converging Interests: Traders, Travelers, and Tourists in Southeast Asia* (University of California at Berkeley, 1999).

**Timothy Garton Ash** is Professor of European Studies at the University of Oxford, Isaiah Berlin Professorial Fellow at St Antony's College, Oxford, and a Senior Fellow at the Hoover Institution, Stanford University. As a 'historian of the present' he witnessed a number of the episodes of civil resistance discussed in this volume. His books include *The Polish Revolution: Solidarity* (3rd edn., Yale University Press, 2002); *The Magic Lantern: The Revolutions of '89 Witnessed in Warsaw, Budapest, Berlin and Prague* (3rd edn., with a new Afterword, Vintage, 1999); *In Europe's Name* (Jonathan Cape, 1993); *History of the Present* (Penguin, 2000); *Free World* (Penguin, 2004); and *Facts are Subversive* (Atlantic Books, 2009).

**Merle Goldman** is Professor Emerita at Boston University and Associate at the Fairbank Center for Chinese Studies, Harvard University. She is the author of several books, including *Literary Dissent in Communist China* (Harvard University Press, 1967); *China's Intellectuals: Advise and Dissent* (Harvard University Press, 1981); *Sowing the Seeds of Democracy in China: Political Reform in the Deng Xiaoping Decade* (Harvard University Press, 1994); and *From Comrade to Citizen: The Struggle for Political Rights in China* (Harvard University Press, 2005).

**Carlos Huneeus** is Professor of the Institute of International Studies at the University of Chile and Executive Director of Corporation CERC. His publications include: *La Unión de Centro Democrático y la Transición a la Democracia en España* (Centro de Investigaciones Sociológicas – Siglo XXI Editores, Madrid, 1985); *Los chilenos y la política: cambio y continuidad bajo el autoritarismo* (ICHEH, 1987); *Chile, un país dividido: la actualidad del pasado* (Catalonia, 2003); *The Pinochet regime* (Lynne Rienner, 2007); and *La guerra fría chilena: Gabriel González Videla y la ley maldita* (Random House, Santiago, 2009).

**Stephen Jones** is Professor of Russian and Eurasian Studies at Mount Holyoke College. He has written over fifty articles and chapters on Georgian history and politics. His books include *Third World Countertrade: Analysis of 1,350 Deals Involving Developing Countries, 1980–1987* (Produce Studies, 1988); *Socialism in Georgian Colors: the European Road to Social Democracy, 1883–1917* (Harvard

University Press, 2002); and *Georgia: A Political Life: 1985–2007* (I. B. Tauris, forthcoming 2009).

**Mark Kramer** is Director of the Harvard Cold War Studies Project at Harvard University and a Senior Fellow at Harvard's Davis Center for Russian and Eurasian Studies. Professor Kramer is the editor of the *Journal of Cold War Studies*, published by MIT Press four times a year, and of the Harvard Cold War Studies Book Series, published by Rowman & Littlefield.

**Tom Lodge** is Professor of Peace and Conflict Studies at the University of Limerick. He has considerable personal experience of life and politics in South Africa in the last years of apartheid, having been a member of the Department of Political Studies at the University of Witwatersrand between 1978 and 2005. He is the author of *Black Politics in South Africa since 1945* (Ravan Press, 1983); *Mandela: A Critical Life* (Oxford University Press, 2006); and *Sharpeville: An Apartheid Massacre and its Consequences* (Oxford University Press, 2011).

**Doug McAdam** is Professor of Sociology at Stanford University. He is the author or co-author of eight books and more than sixty articles in the area of political sociology, with a special emphasis on the study of social movements and revolutions. His works include *Political Process and the Development of Black Insurgency, 1930–1970* (University of Chicago Press, 1982); *Freedom Summer* (Oxford University Press, 1988); and *Dynamics of Contention* (Cambridge University Press, 2001).

**Charles S. Maier** is the Leverett Saltonstall Professor of History at Harvard University where he teaches European and international history. His most recent books include *The Cold War in Europe: Era of a Divided Continent* (Markus Wiener, 1996); *Dissolution: The Crisis of Communism and the End of East Germany* (Princeton University Press, 1997); and *Among Empires: American Ascendancy and its Predecessors* (Harvard University Press, 2006).

**Kenneth Maxwell** is Director of the Brazil Studies Program at Harvard University's David Rockefeller Center for Latin American Studies and a Visiting Professor in the Department of History. His publications include: *Conflicts and Conspiracies: Brazil and Portugal 1750–1808* (Cambridge University Press, 1973); *The Making of Portuguese Democracy* (Cambridge University Press, 1995); and *The New Spain: From Isolation to Influence* (Council on Foreign Relations Press, 1994). He is a regular contributor to the *New York Review of Books*, *World Policy Journal*, and *Folha de São Paulo*.

**Amado Mendoza Jr** is Associate Professor in Political Science and International Studies at the University of the Philippines in Diliman, Quezon City. He has edited two books, *Debts of Dishonor* (Philippine Rural Reconstruction Movement, 1991) and *From Crisis to Crisis: A Historical Analysis of the Recurrent Balance of Payments Crisis in the Philippines* (National Economic Protectionism Association, 1987). He has written many articles on Philippine politics and economics.

**Adam Roberts** is President of the British Academy; Emeritus Professor of International Relations, Oxford University; and Emeritus Fellow of Balliol College, Oxford. His books include: as editor, *The Strategy of Civilian Defence: Non-violent Resistance to Aggression* (Faber, 1967); with Philip Windsor, *Czechoslovakia 1968: Reform, Repression and Resistance* (Chatto & Windus, 1969); *Nations in Arms: The Theory and Practice of Territorial Defence* (Chatto & Windus, 1976); and as joint editor, *The United Nations Security Council and War: The Evolution of Thought and Practice since 1945* (Oxford University Press, 2008).

**Aleksander Smolar** is Chairman of the Board of the Stefan Batory Foundation in Warsaw and a Senior Research Fellow at the Centre National de la Recherche Scientifique in Paris. His publications include, as editor: *La Grande Secousse: Europe de l'Est 1989–1990* (CNRS, 1990); *Globalization, Power, and Democracy* (Johns Hopkins University Press, 2000); and *De Kant à Kosovo* (Presses de Sciences Po, 2003).

**Ivan Vejvoda** is Vice President, Programs at the German Marshall Fund of the United States. In 2003–10 he was Executive Director of the Balkan Trust for Democracy, and in 2002–03 Senior Foreign Policy Advisor to Serbian Prime Minister Zoran Djindjic. He has edited several books including *Yugoslavia and After: A Study in Fragmentation, Despair and Rebirth* (Longman, 1996) and *Democratization in Central and Eastern Europe* (Continuum, 2002).

**Kieran Williams** is Instructor in Politics at Drake University. His publications include: *The Prague Spring and its Aftermath: Czechoslovak Politics, 1968–1970* (Cambridge University Press, 1997); *Security Intelligence Services in New Democracies: The Czech Republic, Slovakia and Romania* (Palgrave, 2001); and *Slovakia after Communism and Mečiarism* (University College, School of Slavonic and East European Studies, 2000).

**Andrew Wilson** is Senior Lecturer in Ukrainian Studies at the School of Slavonic and East European Studies at the University College London. His recent publications include *Ukraine's Orange Revolution* (Yale University Press, 2005) and *Virtual Politics: Faking Democracy in the Post-Soviet World* (Yale University Press, 2005).

# Initial Questions

1. Were the reasons for the use of non-violent methods derived from an absolute rejection of all political violence, or from more particular strategic, moral, cultural, and other considerations?

2. To the extent that a non-violent movement was able to operate effectively, was this in part due to particular favourable circumstances in the overall power situation, both domestic and international? How important are methods of civil resistance as opposed to the conditions within which it operates?

3. Has civil resistance demonstrated a particular value as one instrument (alongside other instruments such as external election monitors) for challenging fraudulent election processes and ensuring a free and fair outcome?

4. Can an international legal/normative regime provide a favourable background for civil resistance?

5. To what extent did the non-violent movement succeed in undermining, or threatening to undermine, the adversary's sources of power and legitimacy (military, economic, psychological, organizational, etc.)?

6. Was any force or violence used alongside non-violent methods, and if so what were its effects?

7. What has been the role of external actors of all kinds (government, quasi-non-governmental organizations, NGOs, diasporas) in assisting or attempting to influence civil resistance?

8. Is there evidence of agents provocateurs being sent in by the state, or of other efforts to discredit the movement by depicting it as violent?

9. How has the development of technologies, especially information technology (e.g. fax, email, internet), affected the capacities of civil resistance?

10. Was there any implicit or explicit threat of a future use of force or violence to carry forward the non-violent movement's cause if the movement did not achieve a degree of success, or if extreme repression was used against it?

11. If there was such a threat, was it from the leaders of the movement itself, from potential allies among its 'constituency' of support, or from outside forces such as, for example, the governments of neighbouring states or international bodies?

12. In cases where outside governments or organizations supported the movement, did they understand and respect the reasons for avoiding the use of force or violence? Should rules (possibly in the form of a draft code

of conduct) be established regarding the character and extent of such external support?

13. Was civil resistance in one country instigated or assisted by another state as a mere instrument for pursuing its own ends or embarrassing an adversary? If accusations of this kind were made, did they have any credibility?

14. Overall, can the movement be viewed as a success or failure? How adequately do these labels reflect outcomes that may be highly ambiguous, especially with the benefit of hindsight?

15. In what time-frame should the effectiveness of civil resistance be judged?

16. Has experience of civil resistance had an impact on the way in which civil society groups have subsequently operated? If they entered into government, did the leaders and exponents of civil resistance show any distinctive approach to the management and use of military and police power by their state?

17. Is there a connection between the practice of civil resistance and liberal outcomes (such as democratic government and respect of minority rights)? If yes, what is the nature of that connection, and what lessons might be learned?

These seventeen questions were drawn up in 2006–7 by the Organizing Committee of the Oxford University Project on 'Civil Resistance and Power Politics: Domestic and International Dimensions'. Authors of chapters were encouraged to select and adapt those that were pertinent to the particular subject at hand.

# 1

# Introduction

*Adam Roberts*

Civil resistance, which has occurred in various forms throughout history, has become particularly prominent in the past hundred years. Three great overlapping causes—decolonization, democratization, and racial equality—have been advanced by campaigns of civil resistance characterized by extensive use of non-violent action. So have many other causes: workers' rights, protection of the environment, gender equality, religious and indigenous rights, defence of national cultures and political systems against foreign encroachments, and opposition to wars and weaponry. Civil resistance was one factor in the ending of communist party rule in many countries in 1989–91, and hence in ending the Cold War. The world today has been shaped significantly by this mode of political action.

However, understanding exactly how civil resistance has shaped the world is a challenge. The explorations in this book are based on two core propositions. First, that civil resistance cannot be considered in isolation from all the other factors of power, domestic and foreign, civil and military, which help to determine outcomes. And second, that civil resistance, while it has had many successes, can sometimes contribute to adverse, or at least ambiguous, outcomes. The very question of what constitutes success or failure may have no immediate or obvious answer. There have been episodes—as in Czechoslovakia after the Soviet-led intervention in 1968—in which the cause could easily seem to have been lost, yet ultimately the reverberations of an apparent failure contributed, twenty-one years later and in different circumstances, to a successful transfer from communist party rule. In other cases there have been apparent successes—as in Georgia in 2003 and Ukraine in 2004—where subsequent political developments have disappointed many of the hopes of the demonstrators.

There is a large and increasingly sophisticated body of writing about civil resistance, admirably surveyed by April Carter in Chapter 2 below. One intellectual tradition within that literature has made large claims about the possible future roles of civil resistance: that it could provide an effective means of resisting all tyrannical regimes; that it could progressively replace violence in all its numerous manifestations; and that it could be the sole basis of the defence policies of states. Such claims need to be tested by a rigorous examination of the record. The chapters of this book are intended to add to the body of general knowledge about the uses of civil resistance, and to help identify some observable trends.

In its first year the Oxford University Project on Civil Resistance and Power Politics identified seventeen questions that it sought to explore.[1] These were not a rigid frame to be imposed on the contributors to this book, who were invited to focus on those questions most pertinent to the cases which they addressed. Their richly varied answers to these questions point towards the conclusion that while civil resistance can be an alternative to the use of force, the two can also have a subtle and complex relationship.

This book sets out to provide, not a theory of civil resistance, but rather accounts of its causes, courses and consequences, locating these as accurately as we could in the broader stream of history. This chapter initiates this book's exploration in five stages. First, it offers a definition of civil resistance, and suggests why it is an appropriate term to describe the phenomena under investigation. Second, it indicates how the term 'power politics' is understood in this study, and how the phenomena it describes—though often viewed as discredited—have proved enduring and have influenced the development of civil resistance. Third, it looks critically at three intellectual and political traditions that see civil resistance as replacing force in many or all of its forms. Fourth, it outlines some of the ways in which civil resistance, rather than being a total alternative to force, has had a complex relationship with it. Fifth, it discusses the hazards of 'universalism'—i.e. seeing civil resistance as a panacea, or else as a universal threat—and supports a view of it as locally rooted, but able to draw strength from international influences and norms.

## CIVIL RESISTANCE

What exactly is 'civil resistance'? This definition indicates how the term is used in this book:

> CIVIL RESISTANCE is a type of political action that relies on the use of non-violent methods. It is largely synonymous with certain other terms, including 'non-violent action', 'non-violent resistance', and 'people power'. It involves a range of widespread and sustained activities that challenge a particular power, force, policy, or regime—hence the term 'resistance'. The adjective 'civil' in this context denotes that which pertains to a citizen or society, implying that a movement's goals are 'civil' in the sense of being widely shared in a society; and it denotes that the action concerned is non-military or non-violent in character.
>
> Civil resistance, precursors of which can be found throughout history, has been used in many types of struggle in modern times: for example, against colonialism, foreign occupations, military *coups d'état*, dictatorial regimes, electoral malpractice, corruption, and racial, religious, and gender discrimination. It has been used not only against tyrannical rule, but also against democratically elected governments, over such issues as maintenance of key elements of the constitutional order, preservation of regional autonomy within a country,

---

[1] Above, xx–xxi.

defence of minority rights, environmental protection, and opposition to involvement in certain military interventions and wars.

Civil resistance operates through several mechanisms of change. These are not limited to attempts to appeal to the adversary. They can involve pressure and coercion—by increasing the costs to the adversary of pursuing particular policies, weakening the adversary's capacity to pursue a particular policy, or even undermining completely the adversary's sources of legitimacy and power, whether domestic or international. An aim of many campaigns is to bring about dissension and defections in the adversary's regime and in its basis of support. Forms of action can be very varied, and have included demonstrations, vigils, and petitions; strikes, go-slows, and boycotts; and sit-ins, occupations, and the creation of parallel institutions of government. Campaigns of civil resistance involve strategy—i.e. projecting and directing the movements and elements of a campaign.

There is no assumption that the adversary power against which civil resistance is aimed necessarily avoids resort to violence: civil resistance has been used in some cases in which the adversary has been predisposed to use violence. Nor is there an assumption that there cannot be various forms of understanding or cooperation between civil resisters and certain governments or other entities with a capacity to use force. Often the reasons for a movement's avoidance of violence are related to the context rather than to any absolute ethical principle: they may spring from a society's traditions of political action, from its experience of war and violence, from legal considerations, from a desire to expose the adversary's violence as unprovoked, or from calculations that civil resistance would be more likely than violent means to achieve success in the particular situation that is faced.[2]

The term 'civil resistance' has frequently been used in connection with some types of non-violent campaign. Gandhi used it on many occasions, including in an article in the weekly paper *Young India* in 1921—one of a series in which he set out his ideas for resisting British rule in India.[3] One post-Cold War survey of the subject was entitled simply *Civil Resistance*.[4]

Why use the term 'civil resistance' rather than one of its many near-synonyms? Civil resistance is one type of the broader overall phenomenon of 'non-violent action'. Many have seen 'non-violent action' as the over-arching concept, which famously encompasses a vast array of types of activity.[5] Other near-synonyms for civil resistance that have been used commonly have included not only those already mentioned in the definition, but also 'passive resistance', 'civilian resistance', 'civil disobedience', and 'satyagraha'. Each of these terms has its own

---

[2] This is simply one attempt at a definition. It draws on a wide variety of sources, including suggestions and published work by Peter Ackerman, April Carter, Michael Randle, Jacques Semelin, and Gene Sharp.

[3] Mohandas K. Gandhi, 'The Momentous Issue', *Young India*, 10 Nov. 1921. Reprinted in *The Collected Works of Mahatma Gandhi (CWMG)* (Delhi: Government of India, CD version, 1999), vol. 25, 76–8. On 18 Mar. 1922 Gandhi was tried for three inflammatory articles in *Young India* in 1921–2, but this particular article was not one of those singled out in the charge sheet.

[4] Michael Randle, *Civil Resistance* (London: Fontana, 1994). He defines the concept at 9–10.

[5] The classic exposition of the variety of forms of non-violent action is Gene Sharp, *The Politics of Nonviolent Action* (Boston: Porter Sargent, 1973). Based on his 1968 Oxford D.Phil. thesis, it began as a study of non-violent resistance against totalitarian regimes.

particular uses and connotations. However, 'civil resistance' is the most satisfactory general term to cover the broad range of cases addressed in this book: most cases were 'civil' in the senses that they had a civic quality, relating to the interests and hopes of a society as a whole; in some cases the action involved was not primarily disobedience, but instead involved supporting the norms of a society against usurpers; and the generally principled avoidance of the use of violence was not doctrinaire.

Definitions of all these terms leave certain questions unanswered. The most obvious problem is that certain campaigns that might on the surface appear to be non-violent in character are not necessarily perceived as such when the context is taken into account. In Northern Ireland in May 1974, the Protestant majority organized an impressive fourteen-day general strike, but the purpose, and effect, of this non-violent action was to bring down a power-sharing executive which had been established in an attempt to bring peace to the troubled province. Other examples of strikes that are non-violent in themselves, but involve a risk of violent consequences, might include a strike by hospital staff with no alternative arrangements for the patients; or a strike, without notice, by air-traffic controllers, creating immediate risks to aircraft in flight. Such possibilities prove the proposition that definitions of abstract nouns may be excellent at capturing the core of particular concepts, but always involve problems at the periphery.

## POWER POLITICS

Against the background of the carnage of the First World War, President Woodrow Wilson spoke in 1918 of 'the great game, now forever discredited, of the balance of power'.[6] He offered a vision of a world in which policies based on the pursuit of power would be replaced by policies based on justice and democracy. Attractive as his vision was, it was not borne out by subsequent events. Concerns about power and power balances—and more specifically about how to use military means to defend a social order, guard against potential dangers, or gain advantages over actual or potential adversaries—have proved to be an enduring feature of politics both domestic and international. While forms of armed conflict and military power constantly change, and much has been achieved in reducing their role in human affairs, attempts to eliminate their roles entirely have perennially run into trouble.[7]

[6] 'Address of President Woodrow Wilson at a Joint Session of the Two Houses of Congress', 11 Feb. 1918, *Papers Relating to the Foreign Relations of the United States, 1918*, supplement 1, *The World War*, vol. I (Washington DC: US Government Printing Office, 1933), 112.

[7] On evolving views of the role of power in international relations over the centuries, and the emergence of a beneficent deadlock between major powers, see F. H. Hinsley's masterly survey, *Power and the Pursuit of Peace: Theory and Practice in the History of Relations between States* (Cambridge: Cambridge University Press, 1963), esp. the conclusions at 366–7.

The term 'power politics' has long been used as a catchphrase to encompass the preoccupation of political leaders with power in its various forms. Indeed, the 'realist' school of thought identifies international relations with power politics, and places heavy emphasis on the proposition that action by states is typically self-interested, power-seeking, and even (in some versions) aggressive. In this sense, power is more than just a currency that states use in their mutual relations: it is a motive determining most if not all state action. It is not just a means, but an end.[8]

Such theories that interpret all international political developments as emanations of power politics are vulnerable to many criticisms: they ignore the extraordinary differences in the behaviour of different states and governments; they underestimate the role of international law and norms in influencing the actions of states; they have difficulty in accounting for many developments, including the Soviet Union's rapid demise and the willingness of many states to forgo expansionism and untrammelled sovereignty; and, above all, they have an excessively narrow conception of power as consisting exclusively of military power. These criticisms are serious, but they do not add up to a claim that power is of no importance: rather, they suggest that it operates in conjunction with other factors, and can assume many different forms.

A particular manifestation of great power politics that has a strong connection with civil resistance is the phenomenon often described as 'spheres of influence'. Throughout history, and for a variety of reasons, powerful states have sought to establish networks of compliant states in their region or more generally. Spheres of influence, particularly when based on authoritarian principles, tend to lead to nationalist reactions in subject-states, and often these reactions take the form of civil resistance movements. Such movements must necessarily frame their strategy with their power-political situation in mind. As the chapters in this book show, they often time their actions to coincide with changes of opinion or leadership in the dominant state. Occasionally, civil resistance movements may even benefit from the operations of the balance of power. It remains an interesting question whether, after the revolution in 1974, Portugal was saved from a serious attempt at communist party control by the wise and courageous actions of Portuguese democrats, or by a degree of Soviet acceptance that Portugal was within the US sphere of influence: both were important.

Although there is a tradition of thought that associates power politics almost exclusively with the state, many non-state entities use and pursue power as assiduously as states. Regional warlords, and leaders of guerrilla insurgencies and terrorist campaigns, are all parts of the phenomenon of power politics. The interconnections between certain non-state uses of force on the one hand, and cases of civil resistance on the other, have been varied. Civil resistance has been significant in many countries—from Portugal to the Philippines—that have also

---

[8] For classic expositions of the power politics approach, see Hans J. Morgenthau, *Politics among Nations: The Struggle for Power and Peace* (New York: Knopf, 1948); and John J. Mearsheimer, *The Tragedy of Great Power Politics* (New York: Norton, 2001).

faced guerrilla insurgencies, and has sometimes helped to establish a new political order. However, in a few cases civil resistance has played an unintentional part in the emergence of campaigns of violence, in ways indicated in the chapters on Northern Ireland and South Africa. There is often a strained and complex relationship between civil resistance and non-state violence.

Not all power involves the threat or use of armed force. Both within countries in their domestic politics, and also between countries, power can derive from authority, legitimacy, persuasion, and consent. Power can, as Joseph Nye has pointed out, involve elements of 'soft power', which is 'the ability to get what you want through attraction rather than coercion or payments'.[9] Civil resistance often depends on the power to attract, but it is not the same as soft power. A principal difference is that, unlike soft power, it can involve coercion: the peaceful withdrawal of cooperation can literally force a regime's collapse.

The idea that there can be non-military forms of power has also been reflected in perennial claims that particular states or groupings of states are 'civilian powers'. In the 1970s both the European Communities (which later became the European Union) and Japan were sometimes described as pure expressions of 'civilian power', by which was meant that they were primarily concerned with economic activity, had relatively low defence budgets, and were helping to build a world of economic interdependence. In subsequent decades the idea continued to surface periodically, especially in relation to the European Union. 'Civilian power' came to be seen as comprising four main elements: acceptance of the necessity of international cooperation; concentration on non-military, primarily economic, means to secure national goals; willingness to develop supranational structures to address key issues of international management; and civilian control over foreign and defence policy-making. Curiously, the phenomenon of civil resistance, and the extensive history of European support for it in many countries, never featured in the debates about 'civilian power Europe'—debates which are therefore of limited relevance to the present study. In any case the idea of 'civilian power Europe' has long been challenged, principally on the ground that, like other countries and regions, Europe is not an 'ideal-type', and is in fact somewhere on a spectrum between the two ideal-types of civilian and military power.[10]

In writings on non-violent forms of action there has long been recognition that civil resistance is one form of power. Indeed, the terminology and literature of civil resistance is suffused with the language of power: hence terms such as 'people power' and 'social power', and book titles in the tradition of Richard Gregg's *The Power of Non-violence*.[11] Any realistic survey of the role of civil resistance needs to take account of the role of other dimensions of power, including military power. This is not simply a matter of recognizing the con-

---

[9] Joseph S. Nye, *Soft Power: The Means to Success in World Politics* (New York: Public Affairs, 2004), x.

[10] For two excellent critical views of the concept of 'civilian power Europe' in different eras, see Hedley Bull, 'Civilian Power Europe: A Contradiction in Terms?', *Journal of Common Market Studies*, 21, nos. 1–2 (Sept.–Dec. 1982), 149–64; and Karen Smith, 'Beyond the Civilian Power EU Debate', *Politique Européenne*, no. 17 (Autumn 2005), 63–82.

[11] Richard Gregg, *The Power of Non-violence* (London: George Routledge, 1935).

tinued role of armed force in human society, but also of acknowledging the variety, and the complexity, of the interactions between classic forms of power and non-violent movements. Civil resistance is a distinct phenomenon, but it cannot be considered in isolation from other forms of power. Indeed, as the chapters in this book suggest, it often thrives in situations of great power-political complexity.

The involvement of civil resistance with power also involves negotiations with the powerful. Resistance struggles often result in a stalemate, in which the resisters can deny their adversaries legitimacy and cooperation, but they still need governmental or other assistance if they are to achieve their goals. As a result, many leaders of civil resistance movements—most notably Gandhi, Martin Luther King, and Lech Wałęsa—have engaged in negotiations with governments. The round table, as used at the opening of the critically important negotiations in Warsaw in February–April 1989, is the classic symbol. In August 1989, as a result of the Polish round-table talks and the elections that followed, a non-communist became Prime Minister—the first time this had happened in any communist country, and an epochal moment in the ending of the Cold War. This episode, with its major consequences for international relations, is one piece of evidence of the continuous interplay between civil resistance and power politics, and of the role of negotiation in that interplay.

## COMPLETE ALTERNATIVE TO FORCE?

One approach to the understanding of civil resistance has been to see it as offering an alternative to power politics. The core vision is of non-violent methods replacing political violence in many or all of its forms. This approach is found in three traditions of thought about how civil resistance relates to power politics: pacifism, 'progressive substitution', and defence by civil resistance. These are crude labels: many writers within these traditions show a strong awareness that substitutions for violence may be incomplete, and other approaches may be equally valid.

### The pacifist tradition and civil resistance

Pacifism—which can be defined as a rejection of all reliance on armed force, particularly in the realms of politics and international relations—is often best understood as part of the belief-system of individuals. When considered as a possible policy for states, it is vulnerable to three obvious lines of criticism. First, its exclusive practice by a whole country would risk leaving that country vulnerable to both internal and external forces. Second, the vulnerability of small and weakly defended countries to attack and foreign occupation can in turn increase the likelihood of major powers going to war with each other—as is evidenced by the roles of Belgium and Czechoslovakia in the outbreak of the two world wars. Third, it is an essentially negative doctrine—defined more by what it is against than by what it brings to the table.

However, there is a distinct tradition within pacifism that is more positive, seeing certain forms of civil resistance as a substitute for armed force.[12] Pacifist individuals and organizations have contributed significantly to many civil resistance campaigns, including the US civil rights movement.[13] Although the pacifist tradition of involvement in civil resistance has undeniable achievements, it has also suffered from four limitations. First, it has sometimes seen peace movements, whether campaigning against reliance on armaments generally or against particular wars, as the principal manifestation of civil resistance: less attention has been paid to movements with different aims. Second, the claim that a general belief in non-violence is a necessary foundation of campaigns of civil resistance has sometimes morphed into the narrow conclusion that any setbacks are due to a lack of principled commitment rather than to other causes. Third, a veil has often been drawn over the role of armed force in protecting certain civil resistance movements against attack, or in helping the ultimate achievement of their goals. Finally, there has been a tendency to suggest that armed force should be renounced as a matter of principle even if there remains a question as to whether the methods of civil resistance can meet a country's security needs. Above all, a problem of the pacifist tradition is that it has sometimes led, in public political debates, to civil resistance being conflated with pacifism, when actual experience suggests that it is a broader phenomenon that does not easily fit into a preconceived ideological pigeon-hole.

## The idea of 'progressive substitution'

The second tradition sees civil resistance in progressive substitution for the use and threat of force, but at the same time recognizes that force has served important functions in society—for example in policing and in defence. In this view, civil resistance needs to be developed skilfully and strategically if it is to serve the functions previously served by armed force. The hope is that it will replace reliance on force progressively in a succession of issue-areas. The central idea is that only if there is a viable substitute can force be effectively renounced. Implicitly, this tradition could be compatible with support for particular uses of armed force in circumstances where civil resistance appears impractical. Gandhi and Martin Luther King, while hard to classify tidily under one single tradition, arguably leaned toward the concept of 'progressive substitution'.

---

[12] For an account of the emergence of non-violent action as part of a revival of pacifism from the 1950s onwards, see Peter Brock, *Twentieth Century Pacifism* (New York: Van Nostrand Reinhold, 1970), 213–60.

[13] On the role of pacifist individuals and organizations in the emergence of the US civil rights movement, see Lawrence S. Wittner, *Rebels against War: The American Peace Movement, 1941–1960* (New York: Columbia University Press, 1969), 268–73.

Gene Sharp has done most to develop this tradition of thought into a coherent theory, giving it a high degree of credibility because he combined it with an analysis of political power, including that of dictatorial and totalitarian regimes. His attractive—even prophetic—vision of an expanding realm for non-violent action was stated eloquently in 1980 in the preface to *Social Power and Political Freedom*:

> The concept of replacing violent sanctions with nonviolent sanctions in a series of specific substitutions is not utopian. To a degree not generally recognized, this already occurs in various conflict situations, even on scales which affect our domestic society and international relations. Far from being utopian, nonviolent sanctions build upon crucial parts of our past and present reality. Past cases, however, are only the crude beginnings of alternative nonviolent sanctions. These could be refined and developed to increase their power potential, and adapted to meet society's genuine need for sanctions.[14]

At the end of the twentieth century, armed with the additional evidence of the impressive cases of civil resistance in the intervening twenty years, Peter Ackerman and Jack DuVall offered a vision of the historical role of non-violent struggle both as a strategic alternative to force in specific situations and as part of a progressive series of moves towards republican political systems. The final paragraphs of *A Force More Powerful* have the quality of a peroration:

> People power in the twentieth century did not grow out of the barrel of a gun. It removed rulers who believed that violence was power, by acting to dissolve their real source of power: the consent or acquiescence of the people they had tried to subordinate. When unjust laws were no longer obeyed, when commerce stopped because people no longer worked, when public services could no longer function, and when armies were no longer feared, the violence that governments could use no longer mattered—their power to make people comply had disappeared.
>
> One hundred years ago the map of the world was dominated by empires and monarchies. At the beginning of the twenty-first century, the continents are filled with republics.... Today the spirit of the old Roman *civitas* has become the universal standard—and, with a few exceptions, its enemies are gone. Gone, too, will soon be their ideas about power.[15]

Some have made even broader generalizations about the onward and upward flow of civil resistance, its intimate links with democratization, and a diminishing role for armed force.[16] Such visions were made plausible by the events in the Soviet bloc in 1989–91 and by the revolutions in Belgrade, Tbilisi, and Kiev in

[14] Gene Sharp, *Social Power and Political Freedom* (Boston: Porter Sargent, 1980), xi. His paper for the March 2007 Oxford conference reflected this vision, presenting a remarkable account of how ideas about non-violent action spread in the period since 1980, and of how some 'specific substitutions' occurred. It is hoped that a revised version of his Oxford paper will appear in a further work on civil resistance and the battle of ideas.

[15] Peter Ackerman and Jack DuVall, *A Force More Powerful: A Century of Nonviolent Conflict* (New York: Palgrave, 2000), 505.

[16] For example, Jonathan Schell, *The Unconquerable World: Power, Nonviolence, and the Will of the People* (London: Allen Lane, 2004), 388–9.

2000–4. However, these visions depend upon a set of assumptions about the relationship between civil resistance and power politics that may not do justice to the richness of the interplay between them. In particular, those countries that have experienced 'civil revolutions' have not seen a wholesale rejection of reliance on organized armed force. After the 2003 'Rose Revolution' in the former Soviet republic, Georgia's new leaders not only accepted the need for armed force and sought outside alliance with the US and NATO, but in August 2008 also authorized a use of force in the breakaway territory of South Ossetia—part of a chain of events triggering war with Russia.

## Proposals for defence by civil resistance

The third tradition of thought—which is one particular application of the second—revolves around the idea of defence by civil resistance—often called 'civilian defence' or 'civilian-based defence'. It can be defined briefly as a prepared and coordinated policy for defending a society against internal threats (e.g. *coup d'état*) and against external threats (e.g. occupation, blockade, bombing etc.) by prepared and intensive campaigns of civil resistance. This approach necessarily involves a focus on the interface between civil resistance and power politics.

Those who developed the idea from the late 1950s onwards were influenced by the dangers and moral costs of reliance on nuclear deterrence to seek an alternative defence policy. Perhaps the most prominent was the controversial critic of UK nuclear policy, Commander Sir Stephen King-Hall: his 1959 book supported unilateral nuclear disarmament by Britain, and proposed an alternative containing some reliance on conventional force plus 'a defence system of non-violence against violence'.[17] In a second book, seeking to relate his proposals to a view of power politics, King-Hall argued that the nature of power was changing in the nuclear age, but he was less clear on exactly how it was changing, and stated towards the end that 'for all practical purposes the experiences of the past are useless as a guide to our future'.[18]

Subsequently, along with many colleagues, I was involved in the attempt to look more closely at the actual experience of civil resistance with a view to exploring its potential for defence.[19] This work exposed a core problem for the idea of defence by civil resistance. It may indeed be true that when a country falls under the control of a major foreign power or is faced with a *coup d'état* by its own armed forces, civil resistance can be one means of undermining the threat. However, countries that have been through the experience of resistance to foreign

---

[17] Stephen King-Hall, *Defence in the Nuclear Age* (London: Gollancz, 1958), 145–7 & 190.

[18] King-Hall, *Power Politics in the Nuclear Age: A Policy for Britain* (London: Gollancz, 1962), 13 & 223.

[19] See esp. Adam Roberts (ed.), *The Strategy of Civilian Defence: Non-violent Resistance to Aggression* (London: Faber, 1967). The US edition was *Civilian Resistance as a National Defense* (Harrisburg, Pennsylvania: Stackpole Books, 1967). The paperback edition, with a revised and updated introduction, was *Civilian Resistance as a National Defence* (Harmondsworth: Penguin Books, 1969).

©Josef Koudelka/Magnum Photographs

**Figure 1.1** Classic confrontation of civil resistance and power politics. Prague, August 1968: a woman remonstrates with invading Warsaw Pact troops. This was among the many photos taken by Josef Koudelka that were smuggled out of Czechoslovakia and published in newspapers in western Europe.

occupation—as in the present-day cases of post-communist states in central and eastern Europe—generally want to be defended and not liberated next time.

My work on Swedish defence policy from 1969 onwards brought me face to face with the question of whether a country could make a substantial or even complete substitution. Sweden had been successful in keeping out of wars for over 150 years. Opinion there had been particularly interested in the Czechoslovak opposition to the 1968 invasion, which—although failing to prevent the return to communist orthodoxy—had indicated possibilities of effective mass opposition to invasion. In my report on Sweden's defence options, published in 1972, I stated:

> Civil resistance would be unlikely to be effective in replacing some of the functions of the Swedish armed forces—for example the defence of sparsely populated parts of the country. However, it might be the best means of resisting alien control in certain types of circumstance (e.g. total occupation by a super-power, attack by a liberal democratic state, occupation with the aim of economic exploitation; or occupation of urban and highly developed areas).
>
> Merely to add civil resistance to existing military defence could raise serious problems, as the dynamics by which the two techniques operate are very different. Civil resistance, if it was not accepted as a complete alternative,

would need to be clearly separate from military defence in place, in time, in organizational structure, and in other ways.[20]

In the course of this work in Sweden, and influenced by seeing the effects of the Soviet-led intervention in Czechoslovakia, I increasingly questioned the tradition of seeing civil resistance as being a complete substitute for force, viewing it more as a special option for special circumstances. This of course begs two all-important questions. To which circumstances is it appropriate? And if it is not a complete substitute for violence, how does it coexist with factors of force in politics and international relations?

Much subsequent work has been done on the idea of defence by civil resistance. In 1983 an independent and distinctly non-governmental body in the UK, the Alternative Defence Commission, examined the idea thoroughly and saw possibilities in it, but came out in favour of NATO countries adopting a posture of 'defensive deterrence'—i.e. deterrence based on non-nuclear weapons and strategies, including an element of military defence in depth. The underlying idea was that such an approach, to the extent that it is unambiguously defensive, would create a way out of the spiral of threat and counter-threat in which NATO and the Warsaw Pact were trapped. At the same time, the commission envisaged a role for civil resistance— mainly as a fallback policy if the UK's NATO allies refused to accept the idea of 'defensive deterrence'.[21] The Alternative Defence Commission report, although it had been published earlier in the year, played almost no part in the 9 June 1983 UK general election, in which the Labour Party's qualified advocacy of unilateral nuclear disarmament became a source of embarrassment, and, after its election defeat, led to the determination not to repeat the experience.[22]

Since the end of the Cold War the idea of defence by civil resistance has been pursued in a number of countries, including the Baltic states. However, with the partial and limited exception of Sweden, it has generally not attracted support from major political parties, and it has not been adopted as a major plank in the security policy of any country.[23] This raises a question, not about the utility of civil resistance generally, but about its capacity to be a complete substitute for military force.

[20] My first study for the Swedish Defence Research Institute, published as a paperback, was *Totalförsvar och civilmotstånd [Total Defence and Civil Resistance: Problems of Sweden's Security Policy]* (Stockholm: Centralförbundet Folk och Försvar, 1972). This summary of its conclusions is drawn from my subsequent account of this work, 'Civil Resistance and Swedish Defence Policy', in Gustav Geeraerts (ed.), *Possibilities of Civilian Defence in Western Europe* (Amsterdam: Swets & Zeitlinger, 1977), 123.

[21] Alternative Defence Commission, *Defence Without the Bomb* (London: Taylor and Francis, 1983).

[22] Adam Roberts, 'The Trouble with Unilateralism: The UK, the 1983 General Election, and Non-Nuclear Defence', *Bulletin of Peace Proposals*, Oslo, vol. 14, no. 4 (Dec. 1983), 305–12. This article contains a critique of the proposals in the Alternative Defence Commission report.

[23] On the development of the idea of civil resistance as an alternative defence, referring to developments in the Baltic states immediately after the end of the Cold War, see Randle, *Civil Resistance*, 129–30.

## CONNECTIONS BETWEEN CIVIL RESISTANCE AND FORCE

This glance at three traditions of thought raises the question as to whether non-violent action should be seen in either/or terms as an alternative to power politics. It is possible that the complete eradication of power politics is not the right aim, and that it may be more useful to see civil resistance as having a more modest role. Indeed, the tradition that sees it as progressively substituting the use of force places an excessive burden of expectation on civil resistance, which then fails to live up to the very high standard set for it. Moreover, actual cases of civil resistance show something more complex at work: a rich web of connections between civil resistance and other forms of power.

### Links in ideas: Gandhi and Martin Luther King

The first links can be found in the belief-systems of leaders of civil resistance campaigns. A seemingly general commitment to the avoidance of violence is almost always in fact selective. The history of non-violent action is full of instances of very careful discrimination in judging the phenomenon that has been the subject of so much sweeping generalization—violence. Both Gandhi and Martin Luther King recognized some modest legitimate role for force. Gandhi's views on the use of force were complex.[24] Discussing the hypothetical case of a lunatic murdering anyone that comes in his way, he openly accepted that killing a person could be justifiable: 'Taking life may be a duty... Suppose a man runs amuck and goes furiously about sword in hand, and killing anyone that comes his way, and no one dares to capture him alive. Anyone who dispatches this lunatic will earn the gratitude of the community and be regarded a benevolent man.'[25] Martin Luther King famously went to the sheriff's office and applied for a gun permit after his home had been bombed in January 1956. The application was eventually denied. It is a curious fact that the same event, the bombing of his home, which led him to think of using a gun, was also to change the entire course of the Montgomery bus boycott and the US civil rights movement.[26] This episode can partly be explained by the fact that the process whereby King became converted to Gandhian non-violence in the course of leading the Montgomery struggle of 1955–6 was slow. However, long after those events he continued to assert that violence in defence of one's own home was in an entirely different category from violence on a political demonstration.[27] These particular ideas of Gandhi and King about permissible violence related to exceptional situations rather than to the management of the campaigns of which they were leaders.

---

[24] See Judith Brown, Ch. 3 below, 47–50.

[25] Gandhi, 'Is This Humanity?—IV', *Young India*, 4 Nov. 1926. Reprinted in *CWMG*, CD version, vol. 36, 449–51.

[26] Lerone Bennett, *What Manner of Man: A Biography of Martin Luther King* (London: Allen & Unwin, 1966), 71.

[27] Martin Luther King, *Chaos or Community?* (London: Hodder & Stoughton, 1968), 27 & 55.

In practice, however, the links between force and civil resistance relate much more closely to the central aims and activities of campaigns.

## Links in practice

Leaders of civil resistance campaigns have often shown an acute awareness of power-political developments. For example, in 1989, central and east European opposition movements responded astutely to the changes in the Soviet Union, knowing that the opportunities of the Gorbachev era might not recur. Sometimes the developments to which civil resistance responds include a country's defeat in war. The 1905 revolution in Russia, following the country's setbacks in the Russo-Japanese War, is a case in point. In Argentina in 1983 the pro-democracy opposition faced the regime of General Galtieri that had been weakened by the outcome of the 1982 Falklands War; and in 2000, the campaigners for democratic change in Serbia knew that the Milošević regime had lost credibility because of its setbacks in Kosovo following the 1999 NATO military campaign.

An awareness of power-political developments is often accompanied by a lack of dogmatism—and some degree of acceptance of, even reliance on, certain uses of force. For example, the US civil rights movement in the 1960s generally welcomed the use of federal forces to protect civil rights campaigners from the wrath of police forces in the Deep South. As Doug McAdam shows in his chapter, the US constitutional framework, and the principles of equality that it embodied, played an important part in the beginnings and subsequent development of the civil rights movement, and contributed significantly to its sense of legitimacy.[28] Faced with the ever-present risk of violence from white southerners and state forces, civil rights activists generally needed a degree of armed federal protection. The great Freedom Ride of May 1961, which faced repeated violent opposition, got armed protection for parts of the journey: on the section from Montgomery, Alabama, to Jackson, Mississippi, it was escorted by twenty-two highway patrol cars, two battalions of national guardsmen, three US army reconnaissance planes, and two helicopters. This did not save the riders from being arrested in Jackson.[29] The US government provided protection partly for a power-political reason: 'The violence against the Freedom Riders was being given international press coverage and the Kennedys were concerned about their image as they prepared for an upcoming summit with Soviet premier Nikita Khrushchev.'[30] Federal protection was critically important on several subsequent occasions, most notably in connection with the Selma to Montgomery march in 1965. After the local police had assaulted two previous attempts earlier in the same month, the marchers were successful in reaching Montgomery at the third attempt, on 21–5 March, when

---

[28] Ch. 4 below, 62–5.

[29] James Peck, *Freedom Ride* (New York: Grove Press, 1962), 107.

[30] Juan Williams, *Eyes on the Prize: America's Civil Rights Years, 1954–1965* (New York: Viking, 1987), 149.

©William Lovelace/Stringer (Hulton Archive) Getty Images

**Figure 1.2** US government provides armed protection of non-violent demonstrators. Montgomery, Alabama, March 1965. Policemen watch the arrival of the civil rights march from Selma that had previously been postponed due to acts of violence against the marchers.

they were protected by troops and federal agents.[31] Civil rights leaders were generally impatient with federal agents and the federal government for being too slow to act, whether in providing protection for civil resisters or in enforcing federal legislation prohibiting racial discrimination.

The long struggles in central and eastern Europe up to 1989 provide other instances in which leaders of civil resistance, while requiring their followers to avoid any use of violence, did not see non-violent action as a general solution to the world's ills, and would have been horrified at the idea that the West should disarm completely and unilaterally in the face of Soviet power. In Czechoslovakia as elsewhere in eastern Europe, civil resistance often owed more to events, and to civil spirit, than to an overall doctrine of non-violence.[32] Václav Havel had been a skilled impresario of civil resistance in Czechoslovakia from the founding of

---

[31] Ibid. 279.

[32] The view of the resistance following the August 1968 invasion as being grounded in a determination to act honourably combined with a complete absence of any strategic plan or overall leadership was emphasized by Kieran Williams in his paper at the conference on 'Civil Resistance and Power Politics', St Antony's College, Oxford, 15–18 Mar. 2007. It was also conveyed graphically by a prominent radio journalist, Jiří Dienstbier, at a panel discussion on 'The European Way of Civil

Charter 77 in 1977 to the Velvet Revolution in 1989;[33] yet he could also, without any sense of contradiction, pay tribute to the work of the NATO alliance. In March 1991, now president of his country, he told the NATO Council:

> I am happy to have this opportunity to tell from this rostrum today the truth: the North Atlantic Alliance has been, and remains—pursuant to the will of democratically elected governments of its member countries—a thoroughly democratic defensive community which has made a substantial contribution to the facts that this continent has not experienced any war suffering for nearly half a century and that a great part thereof has been saved from totalitarianism.[34]

Often, as in this case, the military force of an outside power is important to resisters largely because it provides a defended space which their oppressors cannot control. Such space may be valuable simply because it enables the merits of freedom and independence to be demonstrated, or because it makes possible specific kinds of assistance.

A life-saving example of assistance to civil resistance from a defended space occurred in 1943 when thousands of Jews were spirited out of German-occupied Denmark and across the Sound to Sweden: this action is often and rightly upheld as an example of successful non-violent resistance to Hitler, but a crucial factor that made it all possible was that Sweden had enough of a defence system to be able to maintain at least a degree of independence from Germany—and, by 1943, could see which way the Second World War was going.[35]

Civil resistance often creates a situation in which a major power is shamed into acting—even into using military force. In the years since 1945, one notable feature of the far-flung American *imperium* has been its responsiveness to pressure from civil resistance campaigns to abandon US support of tawdry dictators. Often non-violent campaigns in a country have been able to weaken the regime of a dictator, but have not been able to bring about its final downfall. Thus in South Vietnam in 1963, the Buddhist-led popular revolt against the regime of President Ngo Dinh Diem caused a huge crisis, but was unable to resolve it. Only a mixture of US pressure on the regime, and a *coup d'état* carried out by the South Vietnamese army on the night of 1–2 November 1963 with deep US involvement, could actually depose the hated government and install a new one. The fact that this non-violent struggle erupted at the same time as the National Liberation Front (Vietcong) insurgency was gathering pace in South Vietnam may have

---

Resistance', St Antony's College, Oxford, 23 May 2008. Dienstbier published an account of the resistance of the Czechoslovak broadcasters, *Rozhlas proti tankum* (Prague: Práce, 1988), and became foreign minister of Czechoslovakia immediately after the Velvet Revolution.

[33] On Havel's role in 1989 see Kieran Williams, Ch. 7 below, 121; and Timothy Garton Ash, Ch. 22, 383.

[34] President Havel of the Czech and Slovak Federal Republic, address to the NATO Council on 21 Mar. 1991. Text in *NATO Review* (Brussels), Apr. 1991, 31.

[35] On cases of civil resistance in the Second World War generally, see Jacques Semelin, *Unarmed Against Hitler: Civilian Resistance in Europe, 1939–1943* (Westport, Conn.: Praeger, 1993). The rescue of the Danish Jews is summarized and discussed at 151–4.

© Bettmann/Corbis

**Figure 1.3** Non-violent protest against an entrenched repressive regime. Vietnamese Buddhist monks at Xa Loi Pagoda in Saigon on 18 August 1963, protesting at President Ngo Dinh Diem's discriminatory policies against the country's Buddhist majority. The signs were also in English—thereby reaching a worldwide TV and newspaper audience. In the end, it took a *coup d'état* to depose the Diem regime.

increased the pressure on the US government to sort out the political chaos by ditching its long-standing and embarrassing ally.[36] Similarly, a US change of

---

[36] On US involvement in the 1–2 Nov. 1963 coup in Saigon, see esp. US Senate, Select Committee to Study Governmental Operations with respect to Intelligence Activities, *Alleged Assassination Plots Involving Foreign Leaders* (Washington DC: US Government Printing Office, 1975), 217–23.

policy towards a discredited Asian ally appears to have been one factor in the events leading to the overthrow of President Marcos in the Philippines in 1986. As Amado Mendoza shows, US policy was not the most important factor, but it appears to have facilitated the departure of Marcos and the advent of the new regime.[37]

Some of these cases illustrate what may be a broader problem of civil resistance. Resisters may lack a clear notion of how finally to expel the government that they have succeeded in discrediting and undermining. They may thus need help from some highly disciplined authority system—whether a foreign power, the army of their own state, or a theocracy. They may indeed need support from such a body precisely because of its willingness to use force in certain circumstances. As Ervand Abrahamian's chapter suggests, this may have been roughly the situation in Iran in 1979—when Ayatollah Khomeini, after his return, established what was virtually a shadow state.[38]

So far the pattern has been of force having some role in protecting, or completing, the process that civil resistance had initiated. Yet the pattern can be the other way round. No theorist had foreseen that civil resistance could actually be in support of a military takeover: yet this happened in the 'Revolution of the Carnations' in Portugal in 1974, which was a popular and non-violent movement, a main purpose of which was to defend, and also channel in a civic direction, the military *coup d'état* that had overthrown the Salazar regime. As Kenneth Maxwell shows, these events in Portugal were deeply significant, ultimately pointing the way towards Europe's decisive rejection of autocratic systems of government.[39]

There are many tragic sides to the connections between civil resistance and violence. Richard English and Howard Clark describe civil campaigns—in Northern Ireland in 1967–72 and in Kosovo in 1988–98—which were precursors to major episodes of violence. In both cases, the assertion that non-violent methods had been tried and failed became a standard part of the justification for force. Regarding Kosovo, this claim was made by both the Kosovo Liberation Army (KLA) and the US government. On the day in March 1999 when he launched NATO air operations against Serbia, President Clinton stated:

> For years, Kosovars struggled peacefully to get their rights back. When President Milosevic sent his troops and police to crush them, the struggle grew violent.... We've seen innocent people taken from their homes, forced to kneel in the dirt and sprayed with bullets... Ending this tragedy is a moral imperative.[40]

Even when civil resistance is not followed by campaigns of violence, the possibility that things might get out of hand has been one reason why certain

---

[37] Ch. 11 below, 182, 185 & 190–1.

[38] Ch. 10 below, 174–5.

[39] Ch. 9 below, 144–6 & 160–1.

[40] President Clinton, Address to the Nation, Washington DC, 24 Mar. 1999. Full text in Heike Krieger (ed.), *The Kosovo Conflict and International Law: An Analytical Documentation 1974–1999* (Cambridge: Cambridge University Press, 2001), 415.

©PAUL J. RICHARDS/Staff. APF/Getty Images

**Figure 1.4** The 'brutal suppression' by Serbian forces of the peaceful struggle of the Kosovars is cited as one of the reasons for NATO initiating air strikes. On 24 March 1999 President Clinton announces the start of aerial bombing of Serbian targets with the stated purpose of ending the tragedy engulfing the mostly Muslim population of the province of Kosovo. From left are National Security Advisor Samuel 'Sandy' Berger, Chief of Staff John Podesta, Spokesman Joe Lockhart, and an unidentified Secret Service agent.

incumbent governments have been willing to do deals. As Martin Luther King put it: 'Nonviolence is a powerful demand for reason and justice. If it is rudely rebuked, it is not transformed into resignation and passivity. Southern segregationists in many places yielded to it because they realized that the alternatives could be intolerable.'[41]

This enumeration of interactions between civil resistance and factors of force is hardly a celebration of them, and some of the interactions sketched here are highly problematic. However, they are realities, and the chapters in this book illuminate them. Meanwhile, one conclusion that flows from this short survey is that the classic view of civil resistance as a form of action counterposed to the use of force, and the classic images of unarmed demonstrators facing armed soldiers, show only one aspect of civil resistance. Some of the conjunctions between civil resistance and factors of force can be crudely summarized:

[41] King, *Chaos or Community?*, 21.

1. Civil resistance is often a response to changes in constellations of power.[42] Sometimes such changes open up a prospect that a civil resistance movement will receive significant assistance from the government of its own country or from outside powers; or they indicate that the adversary regime lacks the will or ability to engage in sustained repression. In some countries there has been a growth of civil opposition after, and perhaps in part because of, a state's setbacks in war, whether against conventional armies or guerrillas.

2. While civil resistance is sometimes used to oppose military *coups d'état*, some campaigns could succeed in their final objective—e.g. the removal of a hated regime—only when there was the reality or the threat of a military coup to bring about the desired change. At least one non-violent campaign was in support of a military coup that had already occurred.

3. Some non-violent campaigns can be seen as reluctant or unwitting harbingers of violence. For example, if they are perceived as failures, they may be followed both by the emergence of groups using armed force and by military intervention from outside the territory concerned. The possibility of such developments can be an inducement to bargain.

4. There have also been some cases of the occasional use of force within civil resistance movements, not against their adversaries, but to maintain internal discipline.

5. When leaders of even the most determinedly non-violent movements have come to power in their countries, they have generally accepted the continued existence of armed forces and other more or less conventional security arrangements.

## INTERNATIONALISM WITHOUT UNIVERSALISM

Civil resistance is sometimes presented by its advocates as a panacea, and by its adversaries as a foreign plot. Either way, the ghost of universalism—the proposition that an idea can be applied to all societies irrespective of local conditions and traditions—haunts the subject. A brief discussion of universalist approaches leads to the suggestion that, even if universalism should be rejected, there is a role for learning across borders, international assistance, and international norm-setting.

### Civil resistance as a panacea

Advocacy of civil resistance as a panacea has a long history. One form of action, the general strike, has often been seen as a weapon with which unjust regimes

---

[42] This conclusion is consistent with the emphasis on 'framing' in the burgeoning body of literature on social movements. However, framing is generally defined in terms of the identification of a problem and a possible solution, rather than in terms of the opportunities offered by changes in constellations of power. See e.g. Hank Johnston and John Noakes (eds.), *Frames of Protest: Social Movements and the Framing Perspective* (Lanham, Md.: Rowman & Littlefield, 2005), 5.

everywhere could be brought to their knees.[43] Sometimes non-violent action has been upheld as universally applicable: for example, the Dutch pacifist, Barthélemy de Ligt, stated in the 1930s that 'the choice lies between real universal peace and universal war', and also that 'to attack social and political problems according to non-violent methods is to assure results satisfactory in every way, and at the same time to gratify the innate desire of man to expand, to radiate, and to triumph'.[44] If only!

In general, universalist approaches to politics are problematic. A germ of universalism is evident in Karl Marx's famous statement: 'The philosophers have only interpreted the world in various ways; the point is to change it.'[45] This dictum is misleading not only because it maligns earlier philosophers, who did much more than merely interpret the world, but also because its sets up a false dichotomy between interpreting and changing. To interpret and understand is a respectable cause in its own right, and advocacy of change without adequate understanding—especially of the particularities of different situations and societies—can be self-defeating or worse. Any approach that sees one form of action, or one political destination, as universally applicable risks suffering from what might be termed the 'Comintern fallacy'—the mistake of appearing to know best what is good for all other societies.[46]

This is true of civil resistance as it is of other forms of action. The most obvious challenge to universalist advocacy of civil resistance arises from legitimate doubts about its capacity to confront successfully certain systems of deeply entrenched rule. While civil resistance brilliantly helped to undermine the power of certain communist regimes that had conspicuously run out of ideological steam, and also some other dictatorial systems, it has undeniably faced setbacks against some authoritarian governments. Such contemporary cases as Burma, Darfur, Tibet, and Zimbabwe illustrate the point.

The second challenge to universalist advocacy arises from the self-evident fact that in practice civil resistance develops, in each society where it operates, different aims, types of action, and forms of organization. The chapters in this book show how it emerges from, and adapts in light of, particular social forms, historical experiences, ethics, and international circumstances.

## Civil resistance as foreign plot

Many authoritarian leaders have stated that peaceful struggle is an insidious plot cooked up by outside governments. A few weeks after the 1968 Soviet-led

---

[43] Wilfrid Harris Crook, *The General Strike: A Study of Labor's Tragic Weapon in Theory and Practice* (Chapel Hill, NC: University of North Carolina Press, 1931).

[44] Bart. de Ligt, *The Conquest of Violence: An Essay on War and Revolution,* trans. Honor Tracy (London: Routledge, 1937), 22 & 137.

[45] Karl Marx, *Theses on Feuerbach*, xi. Written by Marx in 1845, and first published as an appendix to Engels, *Ludwig Feuerbach and the End of Classical German Philosophy*, 1886.

[46] 'Comintern' was the Russian abbreviated title of the Third International, founded in March 1919 and dissolved in May 1943.

invasion of Czechoslovakia, Walter Ulbricht of East Germany sought to justify it as a response to 'the various forms and methods of the imperialist policy of expansion', claiming explicitly and repeatedly that there had been Western plots for a 'non-violent uprising'.[47] Similarly, in the first decades of the twenty-first century the governments of Burma, China, Iran, Russia, and Zimbabwe have all made public statements claiming to detect improper Western influence in movements aiming at political change in their country or region. They would say that, wouldn't they? The implications of such statements—that opposition only exists because foreigners stirred it up, and that all foreign involvement in political processes is illegitimate—are absurd. Yet such statements can sometimes resonate with public opinion and can do harm to the cause of civil resistance. In this century the Russian government in particular has had some success—at least with its own public—in presenting the 'colour revolutions' in Georgia and Ukraine in a lurid light as fomented from outside, and as a means of ushering in pro-Western regimes. This claim, effectively refuted in this volume, has negative effects: the moves towards a new authoritarianism in Russia, involving threats to key institutions such as a free press, are justified (however implausibly) on the basis of this hostile view of a pro-Western democratic tide.

The fact that conspicuous foreign influence in a campaign of civil resistance can be perceived as damaging has an obvious corollary. Sometimes civil resistance may prosper in circumstances where there is very little external power-political involvement. As Mark Beissinger's chapter shows, the Baltic states successfully regained their sovereignty in 1989–91 with much assistance from outside, and much interchange of ideas, but without the questionable benefit of explicit support from the US government.[48] Restraint on the part of outside powers may enable a civil resistance movement to get on with its work untainted by accusations of foreign interference in, or domination of, their cause.

Such restraint has been less in evidence since the end of the Cold War. The sudden and decisive collapse of many authoritarian regimes—whether in the Philippines in 1986, the Soviet-dominated world in 1989–91, Serbia in 2000 or Afghanistan in 2001—led to certain universalist conclusions. These events undoubtedly strengthened the argument that systems of multi-party democracy have wide appeal, and can be applied (with appropriate adaptations) in many previously authoritarian societies. In the post-Cold War years, some international advocacy of democracy has been skilful and effective—including much of the European effort in the post-communist countries of the 'old continent'. However, events misled some, particularly the US neo-conservatives who were influential during the administration of George W. Bush, into believing that the West had only to act decisively, including by military means, for authoritarian regimes to vanish. Challenging the sovereignty

---

[47] Walter Ulbricht, First Secretary of the East Germany's Socialist Unity Party, speech on 12 Oct. 1968, published in English as *The Role of the Socialist State in the Shaping of the Developed Social System of Socialism* (Dresden: Verlag Zeit im Bild, 1968), 8 & 13–14. On Soviet claims about Western masterminding of the Prague Spring, see also Mark Kramer (Ch. 6, 93) and Timothy Garton Ash (Ch. 22, 386 n. 27).

[48] Ch. 14 below, 245–6.

of states, and underestimating the nationalism of their inhabitants, proved problematical generally. It also presented particular hazards for certain civil resistance movements. In the case of Iran, the US advocated regime change and financed a range of activities aimed at achieving it. This heightened the risk that any attempt at popular resistance within Iran could be portrayed as the instrument of an outside power—and not just any outside power, but one that is seen as a military threat. Resistance was put in a situation of political and moral vulnerability, as some Iranian citizens were quick to point out.[49]

## Beyond universalism: learning processes, norms and organizations

To reject the simple ideas of panacea and of foreign plot does not imply a retreat into a narrow anti-universalist view of civil resistance as exclusively occurring within the confines of states, each case unconnected to any others. On the contrary, the chapters in this book show that there is much learning between cases, and a constant process of borrowing, adaptation, 'demonstration effects', and help. With civil resistance, as with other matters, there really is an international political system, albeit rudimentary in form and patchy in effects.

International norms and international organizations have an important part to play in supporting civil resistance. For example, civil resistance movements in certain central and eastern European countries found, in the Cold War years, a basis of legitimacy and support in the 1975 Helsinki Final Act, which accepted the sovereignty of all European states, but at the same time upheld a number of overarching principles in human rights and other matters. Especially in the post-Cold War period, and not confined to Europe, there has been a widely if not universally accepted norm of free and fair elections, backed by both international and local election observation missions: this normative framework has been a key basis for many civil resistance movements whose strength came from principled opposition to the stealing of elections. International organizations, including the European Union and the United Nations, have played a part in norm-setting, election observation, and other actions relevant to the role of civil resistance.

The case studies in this book are descriptive, analytical, and sensitive to local context. They are not just about democratization, nor are they prescribing the paths that different peoples should tread. They are about individual civil resistance movements over recent decades that have pursued a wide variety of goals. However, the concluding chapter again approaches the subject in a general manner. My co-editor Timothy Garton Ash explores aspects of civil resistance that emerge from the case studies: its distinctiveness as a form of power, its complex relation with violence, its role in creating a new genre of revolution, its reliance on the crowd, and the importance of the international context. He notes that it made a

---

[49] For a critique of the $US75 m. US government programme to assist democratization in Iran, including by funding Iranian NGOs, see Haleh Esfandiari and Robert S. Litwak, 'Why "Soft" Power in Iran is Counterproductive', *Chronicle of Higher Education*, 8 Oct. 2007, available at: http://chronicle.com.

significant contribution to the end of the Cold War and subsequently to the ending of various authoritarian regimes. I agree with his conclusions on all these matters. In the past I have often argued, and still believe, that civil resistance is a special option for special circumstances. This book establishes that such circumstances occur more frequently, in greater variety, and with more connections with other factors of power, than most pronouncements and writings on politics and international relations have recognized.

# 2

# People Power and Protest: The Literature on Civil Resistance in Historical Context

*April Carter*

The methods of civil resistance—including mass rallies, fasts, strikes, boycotts, political non-cooperation, and civil disobedience—have been used increasingly around the world in the past few decades. There is also now a growing awareness that civil resistance can be a successful strategy. This awareness stems from the power of example, but it has also been promoted by the growing literature on civil resistance.[1]

The civil resistance literature can be divided into the explicit exploration of non-violent struggle, and the much more extensive journalistic, historical, political, or sociological writings on movements that relied mainly (at least for a period) on non-violent methods.[2]

The main focus of this chapter is on writings specifically dealing with non-violent action. Some of these writings are by protagonists—including key figures in non-violent struggles such as Mahatma Gandhi, Martin Luther King, Kenneth Kaunda, Václav Havel, Aung San Suu Kyi, and Adolfo Perez Esquivel—justifying their cause and their methods. Other books and anthologies seek to publicize a neglected strategy, or to inspire emulation, but do not analyse in any depth the wider context or long-term effect of these campaigns. Nevertheless, significant theoretical contributions to understanding the power of non-violent action and developing a coherent strategy of civil resistance (whether as a means of toppling repressive regimes, resisting particular policies, or providing a possible element in national defence policy) have been appearing since the 1930s. This survey concentrates on the literature in English or English translation, and focuses primarily on resistance to political oppression.

---

[1] I am grateful to Howard Clark and Michael Randle for valuable advice on earlier drafts.

[2] Both types of literature are included in two annotated bibliographies: April Carter, Howard Clark, and Michael Randle, *People Power and Protest Since 1945: A Bibliography of Nonviolent Action* (London: Housmans Bookshop, 2006); updated on www.civilresistance.info; and Roland M. McCarthy and Gene Sharp, *Nonviolent Action: A Research Guide* (New York: Garland, 1997).

## GANDHI AND THE LITERATURE ON
## NON-VIOLENT RESISTANCE

The historical turning point for both the practice and the theory of civil resistance is Mahatma Gandhi, whose campaigns in South Africa in 1906–14, and in India in 1919–48, put non-violent methods on the political map. There are earlier examples of social movements using non-violent tactics and some examples of national liberation campaigns based on 'passive resistance', for example in Hungary 1849–67 and Ireland before the 1916 Easter Uprising. However, after Gandhi civil resistance became a conscious option, although guerrilla warfare often appeared the more effective or more heroic choice.

Gandhi drew inspiration from Henry Thoreau's 1849 essay 'On Civil Disobedience' and from Tolstoy's writings on non-resistance. But his own 'experiments with truth', and belief that the means determine the end, were central to his evolving philosophy and tactics. Gandhi was aware in 1906 of historical and contemporary examples of 'passive resistance'. But he soon rejected the connotations of this 'weapon of the weak', and coined 'satyagraha' ('truth force' or 'soul force') to describe the determination to resist injustice, but to avoid all violence, both physical and psychological, with the aim of 'converting' the opponent.[3]

During the 1920s and 1930s there were a few significant analyses of civil resistance: for example Clarence Case examined the sociological dynamics of non-violent coercion in 1923.[4] Richard Gregg's *The Power of Non-violence* introduced the concept of 'moral jiu-jitsu' to explain the psychological impact of meeting violent repression with non-violent resistance.[5] The Dutch anti-militarist Barthélemy de Ligt advocated non-violent struggle as the way to achieve a true revolution, and Krishnalal Shridharani emphasized the importance of Gandhi's technique of struggle.[6]

Since his death in 1948 the literature on Gandhi has mushroomed, especially in India. There have been many biographies of varying quality, and professional historians have analysed in depth the Indian struggle for independence and debated the extent of Gandhi's contribution to it.[7] The achievement of Indian independence has been the subject of conflicting interpretations—for example, as a struggle between Indian elites within the Raj, as a nationalist struggle, or as a class struggle within a nationalist movement.[8] Others have focused on factors undermining British willingness and ability to maintain imperial power, including

---

[3] M. K. Gandhi, *Satyagraha in South Africa* (1928), 2nd rev. edn. (Ahmedabad: Navajivan, 1950).

[4] Clarence Marsh Case, *Non-Violent Coercion: A Study in the Methods of Social Pressure* (New York: Century, 1923).

[5] Richard B. Gregg, *The Power of Non-Violence* (London: George Routledge, 1935).

[6] Bart. de Ligt, *The Conquest of Violence: An Essay on War and Revolution*, trans. Honor Tracy (London: Routledge, 1937); Krishnalal Shridharani, *War Without Violence: A Study of Gandhi's Method and its Accomplishments* (London: Gollancz, 1939).

[7] See esp. Judith M. Brown, *Gandhi's Rise to Power* (Cambridge: Cambridge University Press, 1972); and *Gandhi and Civil Disobedience* (Cambridge: Cambridge University Press, 1977).

[8] Bipan Chandra et al., *India's Struggle for Independence* (Harmondsworth: Penguin, 1989) 16–23; Antony Copley, *Gandhi: Against the Tide* (Oxford: Blackwell, 1987), 31–5.

its changing economic interests and relative military and economic weakness from 1945.[9]

Western studies focusing primarily on Gandhi's conception of non-violence include Joan Bondurant's 1958 *Conquest of Violence* on satyagraha as a form of social action, which examines Gandhi's ideas both in the context of Indian tradition and Western political thought.[10] Two recent books assess Gandhi in relation to campaigns inspired by him in the US.[11] Gene Sharp has studied Gandhi's campaigns and political significance in depth in order to develop his own theory of non-violent action.[12]

Gandhi's legacy, whilst providing inspiration, has also created problems. Gandhi translated concepts of non-violence and passive resistance into his Hindu culture; Western theorists have since grappled with translating them back again. In addition, Gandhi's relative success was often taken to mean (despite the bloodshed of partition in 1947–8) that Indian culture was uniquely favourable to non-violent action, and that more aggressive societies would reject non-violent methods.

Commentators on Gandhi also often stressed that the Indian independence campaign was waged against a democratic country, inhibited from ruthless repression. Whilst this argument ignored the darker side of British imperialism, there was active support for Indian independence within Britain by the 1930s, and media coverage of Gandhi's campaigns. The rise of Hitler, and the wartime Japanese threat to India, raised the question whether Gandhi's methods could work against totalitarianism, or brutal occupation. Gandhi himself had to defend non-violent protest in such situations.[13]

Gandhi's interpretation of satyagraha linked it closely to his broader conception of a non-violent society. But many subsequent advocates of non-violent methods, notably Sharp, have argued for disconnecting Gandhi's strategy of resistance from this framework.

## REINTERPRETING NON-VIOLENT ACTION: 1950s–60s

When the methods of satyagraha were used in a Western context after 1945, the preferred terms were 'non-violent resistance' or 'non-violent action'. Non-violent

[9] R. J. Moore, *Escape from Empire* (Oxford: Clarendon Press, 1983).

[10] Joan Bondurant, *Conquest of Violence: The Gandhian Philosophy of Conflict* (Princeton, NJ: Princeton University Press, 1958).

[11] Dennis Dalton, *Mahatma Gandhi: Nonviolent Power in Action* (New York: Columbia University Press, 1993); David Cortright, *Gandhi and Beyond: Nonviolence for an Age of Terrrorism* (Boulder, Colo.: Paradigm, 2006).

[12] Gene Sharp, *Gandhi Wields the Weapon of Moral Power: Three Case Histories* (Ahmedabad: Navajivan, 1960); *Gandhi as a Political Strategist* (Boston, Mass.: Porter Sargent, 1979).

[13] Gideon Shimoni, *Gandhi, Satyagraha and the Jews* (Jerusalem: Hebrew University, 1977)—though more on Gandhi's views on Zionism than satyagraha.

tactics were given prominence by the civil rights movement against segregation in the US, dramatized by the Montgomery bus boycott of 1955 and by the March on Washington and mass resistance in Birmingham, Alabama in 1963. This church-based movement, symbolized by Martin Luther King, linked civil resistance to Protestantism.[14] The rise of a militant student movement out of the 1961 sit-ins gave the civil rights movement a more secular slant, but it remained committed to non-violent methods until the mid-1960s.[15]

The US civil rights movement did not, however, rebut scepticism about the effectiveness of non-violent action against dictatorships. Although faced with socially entrenched and violent repression in the South, African Americans appealed to the US constitution, the Supreme Court, and the President. In the 1960s Congress legislated on civil rights. The movement helped to precipitate the growing responsiveness of federal institutions, but it was also assisted by that framework, including the use of federal troops. Civil rights leaders had long cultivated links to anti-colonial independence struggles, especially in Africa; their cause was significantly assisted by the growing number of African states in the United Nations and the embarrassment civil rights violations created for the US in the propaganda war with the Soviet Union.[16]

The US civil rights movement inspired other non-violent struggles. It was one inspiration for the protests in Northern Ireland, 1967–72, against discrimination and Protestant domination of the political system, although the protesters lacked a charismatic non-violent leader and non-violence was primarily tactical. The Northern Irish civil rights movement is therefore peripheral in the civil resistance literature. Bob Purdie's *Politics in the Streets* explores the dynamics and moral force of non-violent resistance, but argues that the implicit threat of violence provided the main leverage.[17] Non-violent activists became more involved later, in combating the ensuing sectarian conflict.

Others deliberately adapting Gandhi's tactics to new circumstances were pacifists resisting nuclear tests and nuclear weapons, who sailed into nuclear testing areas, obstructed missile bases and nuclear plants, and defied legal prohibitions. A less Gandhian form of non-violent resistance emerged in the later 1960s in the militant opposition to the Vietnam War, including draft resistance and support for deserters.[18]

[14] Martin Luther King, *Stride Toward Freedom: The Montgomery Story* (London: Victor Gollancz, 1958); *Why We Can't Wait* (New York: Harper & Row, 1963).

[15] Robert Weisbrot, *Freedom Bound: A History of America's Civil Rights Movement* (New York: W. W. Norton, 1990) provides a historical analysis of the movement, including federal responses; James H. Cone, *Martin and Malcolm and America: A Dream or a Nightmare* (London: HarperCollins, 1993) contrasts ideological approaches.

[16] Mary L. Dudziak, *Cold War and Civil Rights: Race and the Image of American Democracy* (Princeton, NJ: Princeton University Press, 2000), who also argues, however, that anti-communism restricted civil rights discourse.

[17] Bob Purdie, *Politics in the Streets* (Belfast: Blackstaff Press, 1990).

[18] Peter Brock and Nigel Young, *Pacifism in the Twentieth Century* (Toronto: University of Toronto Press, 1999), 254–74 provides a summary of non-violent action for peace; Michael Ferber and Staughton Lynd, *The Resistance* (Boston, Mass.: Beacon Press, 1971) on the radical wing of the anti-Vietnam War movement.

One key issue arising out of the civil rights and peace campaigns was the justification for civil disobedience in liberal democratic states. Protesters elaborated on their moral and political reasons for breaking the law, and sometimes looked back to Socrates and Thoreau.[19] The case for disobedience in a democracy also entered the mainstream of political theory in the 1960s and 1970s—the best known contribution is that of John Rawls.[20]

Advocates of non-violent resistance drew on contemporary campaigns, but also resurrected earlier examples of non-violent struggle (for example in the anti-slavery, labour, and feminist movements of the nineteenth and early twentieth centuries). Some anthologies used excerpts from earlier classic writings on non-violence.[21] Richard Gregg published an updated and elaborated version of *The Power of Nonviolence*, with a brief foreword by Martin Luther King; and several other analytical studies appeared.[22]

These publications sometimes cited recent examples from Africa, where several movements against colonialism (notably in Ghana, Malawi, and Zambia) embarked on 'positive action' in the form of strikes, boycotts, and non-cooperation to gain independence. Kenneth Kaunda engaged with the case for non-violence in Zambia's own movement and also explained why he later came to accept guerrilla tactics in Zimbabwe.[23] By far the most sustained struggle for political and social justice occurred in South Africa, where the African National Congress (ANC) was committed to non-violence from its foundation in 1910 until 1961, and launched campaigns such as the 1952 'defiance campaign' against unjust laws. Leo Kuper wrote a sociological analysis of the 1952 campaign; and Edward Feit wrote a critical assessment of protests in 1954–5, subtitled *The Failure of Passive Resistance*.[24]

Exponents of civil resistance also addressed the question whether it could be effective against a totalitarian opponent, and publicized examples of its relatively successful use under Nazism: especially in Norway, where teachers sustained their refusal to promote fascist ideology, and churches proclaimed their opposition; and in Denmark, where refusal to discriminate against Danish Jews culminated in a concerted effort to save them.[25] Other examples of non-violent protest

---

[19] Hugo Adam Bedau (ed.), *Civil Disobedience: Theory and Practice* (Indianapolis: Bobbs Merrill, 1969).

[20] John Rawls, *A Theory of Justice* (Oxford: Oxford University Press, 1972), ch. 6.

[21] Paul Hare and Herbert H. Blumberg (eds.), *Nonviolent Direct Action: American Cases. Social Psychological Analyses* (Washington DC: Corpus Books, 1968); Staughton Lynd (ed.), *Nonviolence in America* (Indianapolis: Bobbs Merrill, 1966); Mulford Q. Sibley (ed.), *The Quiet Battle: Writings on the Theory and Practice of Non-violent Action* (New York: Doubleday, 1963).

[22] Richard Gregg, *The Power of Nonviolence*, rev. edn. (London: James Clark, 1960); William Robert Miller, *Nonviolence: A Christian Interpretation* (London: Allen & Unwin, 1965); H. J. N. Horsburgh, *Non-Violence and Aggression* (London: Oxford University Press, 1968).

[23] Kenneth Kaunda, *Kaunda On Violence* (London: Collins, 1980).

[24] Leo Kuper, *Passive Resistance in South Africa* (London: Jonathan Cape, 1956); Edward Feit, *African Opposition in South Africa: The Failure of Passive Resistance* (Stanford, Calif.: Hoover Institution, 1967).

[25] Gene Sharp, *Tyranny Could Not Quell Them* (London: Peace News pamphlet, 1956). Jørgen Hæstrup, *Europe Ablaze: An Analysis of the History of the European Resistance Movements* (Odense: Odense University Press, 1978); and Jacques Semelin, *Unarmed Against Hitler: Civilian Resistance in Europe 1939–1943* (Westport, Conn.: Praeger, 1993).

occurred, for example in the Netherlands. Sceptics noted, however, that in these 'Aryan' countries German rule was relatively mild.

Predominantly non-violent resistance also emerged against Soviet rule and the excesses of Stalinism, sparked by the death of Stalin in March 1953 and Khrushchev's exposure of Stalin's crimes in the February 1956 'Secret Speech'. Mass protest erupted in East Germany in 1953, although the general strike was crushed; in Poland in 1956, where the Soviet Union stopped short of military action; and in Hungary in 1956, where Soviet troops returned to topple the new regime (at this stage they were met briefly by armed resistance).[26] When the Prague Spring in Czechoslovakia in 1968 led to the Warsaw Pact invasion, there was mass non-violent defiance.[27]

Key examples of resistance to Nazism and communist rule were assessed in the debate about civil resistance as the basis of a national defence policy, for example *The Strategy of Civilian Defence*, edited by Adam Roberts, included analysis of the 1953 uprising; and the revised edition referred to Czechoslovakia in 1968.[28]

## THEORIZING NON-VIOLENT ACTION AND THE CENTRAL EUROPEAN OPPOSITION

There was an increasingly theoretical interest in the 1970s in the potential of non-violent action to resist injustice, combat coups or contribute to national defence, for example Anders Boserup and Andrew Mack, *War Without Weapons*, which relates non-violent resistance to Clausewitzian strategic theory and stresses that 'unity' would be 'the centre of gravity'.[29] The *Bulletin of Peace Proposals* (1978) devoted an issue to the possibility of non-violent defence.[30] Moreover the Dutch, Norwegian, and Swedish governments initiated research on the possible role of civilian resistance in defence.[31]

This academic and official interest contrasted with the apparent failures of civil resistance in that period. In South Africa the escalating repression persuaded the

---

[26] Stefan Brant, *The East German Uprising, 17th June 1953* (London: Thames & Hudson, 1955); Mark Kramer, 'The Soviet Union and the 1956 Crises in Hungary and Poland: Reassessments and New Findings', *Journal of Contemporary History*, 33, no. 2 (Apr. 1998), 163–214.

[27] Adam Roberts and Philip Windsor, *Czechoslovakia 1968: Reform, Repression and Resistance* (London: Chatto & Windus, 1969). On the Prague Spring see: H. Gordon Skilling, *Czechoslovakia's Interrupted Revolution* (Princeton, NJ: Princeton University Press, 1976).

[28] Adam Roberts (ed.), *The Strategy of Civilian Defence: Non-violent Resistance to Aggression* (London: Faber, 1967); rev. edn., *Civilian Resistance as a National Defence* (Harmondsworth: Penguin, 1969).

[29] Anders Boserup and Andrew Mack, *War Without Weapons: Nonviolence in National Defence* (London: Frances Pinter, 1974).

[30] See also Johan Galtung, 'On the Strategy of Nonmilitary Defence', in Galtung, *Essays in Peace Research*, vol. 2, *Peace, War and Defence* (Copenhagen: Christian Ejlers, 1976).

[31] For details see: Alternative Defence Commission, *Defence Without the Bomb* (London: Taylor & Francis, 1983), 245 n. 6.

ANC in 1961 that resort to guerrilla warfare was necessary—although the emphasis was on sabotage. The Northern Ireland civil rights campaign was superseded by the IRA and sectarian violence. The Czechoslovak resistance to the Soviet invasion subsided when Gustáv Husák imposed 'normalization' after April 1969. In the US the non-violent civil rights movement was superseded by 'black power', stressing masculine pride and (sometimes) violent resistance. Many on the Western left also aligned themselves with the model of guerrilla warfare—a position challenged by Barbara Deming, who argued in an important essay that radical non-violent action can be an alternative.[32]

But this apparent decline of civil resistance was not the whole picture. Non-violent tactics, including civil disobedience, became more widely used and acceptable within Western parliamentary states: the 1970s saw environmental protesters experiment with new tactics and forms of organization. Non-violent methods also became more widely used in certain communist party states. In Czechoslovakia a group of intellectual dissidents launched Charter 77 in January 1977 and campaigned for human rights. More dramatically, major strikes in Poland in 1970 and 1976 forced changes in government policy.[33]

The major contribution to a theoretical and strategic basis for civil resistance was Gene Sharp's *The Politics of Nonviolent Action*.[34] Sharp drew on political and sociological theory to argue that, although there are a number of material, organizational, and psychological elements in power, ultimately the power of rulers rests on the obedience of their subjects. Since power depends on at least tacit consent, once this consent is *actively* withdrawn, a regime begins to crumble. Sharp's aim was to show that civil resistance did not require a principled commitment to non-violence. He argued for a military-style strategy, with an emphasis on discipline and organization, timing and choice of appropriate tactics. He also demonstrated that an enormous variety of non-violent methods had evolved: he listed 198.

In his discussion of the 'dynamics' of non-violent resistance Sharp reinterpreted Gregg's psychological concept of 'moral jiu-jitsu' as 'political jiu-jitsu', i.e. a change in the balance of political forces. He also distanced himself from the Gandhian emphasis on 'conversion', arguing that success could also be achieved through accommodation by the opponent, or through non-violent coercion. He later added regime disintegration as a fourth possibility.

Whilst Sharp developed a comprehensive theory of non-violent action, Hannah Arendt discovered that non-violent resistance could illuminate her theoretical explorations of political action and direct democracy. She added an epilogue to the second (enlarged) edition of *The Origins of Totalitarianism* in 1958, celebrating the workers' strikes and workers' councils which flourished in Hungary for a month

---

[32] Barbara Deming, *Revolution and Equilibrium* (New York: Grossman, 1971).

[33] H. Gordon Skilling, *Charter 77 and Human Rights in Czechoslovakia* (London: Allen & Unwin, 1981); Adam Bromke, *Poland: The Last Decade* (Oakville, Ont.: Mosaic Press, 1981).

[34] Gene Sharp, *The Politics of Nonviolent Action* (Boston, Mass.: Porter Sargent, 1973); subsequently reprinted many times in three separate paperback volumes.

after the Soviet reoccupation.[35] In *Eichmann in Jerusalem* she recorded the Danish resistance to Nazi Jewish policies, noting 'the enormous potential power inherent in non-violent action'.[36] Her most explicit discussion of non-violent action, however was *On Violence*, in which she defined instrumental violence as the opposite of power, which is based on people acting in concert, and argued that the apparent power of a supreme leader depended on popular cooperation and consent.[37]

Both Arendt and Sharp wrote primarily as observers. The Central European activists arguing the need for non-violent, rather than violent, change feared that violent protest could precipitate Soviet intervention. But their case for non-violence also had a moral dimension, including a desire to expose the systematic falsity of communist party regimes. Leading opposition intellectuals such as

**Figure 2.1** Playwright and impresario of civil resistance. Václav Havel, former President of the Czech Republic, promoting publication of his new play, *Leaving*, at a theatre in Prague in November 2007.

---

[35] Hannah Arendt, *The Origins of Totalitarianism*, 2nd edn. (London: George Allen & Unwin, 1958), 480–510.

[36] Arendt, *Eichmann in Jerusalem: A Report on the Banality of Evil*, rev. edn. (Harmondsworth: Penguin, 1965), 179.

[37] Hannah Arendt, *On Violence* (London: Allen Lane, 1970).

Adam Michnik and Jacek Kuroń in Poland, György Konrád in Hungary, and Václav Benda and Václav Havel in Czechoslovakia, exchanged ideas and developed common themes, for example the need to develop 'civil society' or a 'parallel polis' from below as a challenge to a corrupted state.[38] Kuroń urged 'Don't burn down Party Committee Headquarters, found your own.'[39] Václav Havel's much reprinted essay 'The power of the powerless' (1978), reflected on the potential of small acts of defiance, such as refusing to put a party slogan in a greengrocer's window, to undermine the system based on ideological lies. Individuals can refuse to 'live a lie' by individual non-cooperation—for example by not voting in farcical elections. Or groups can organize an open letter of protest, a concert of forbidden music, a strike or demonstration. What looks like a monolithic structure can, once exposed by non-cooperation, begin to disintegrate. 'Living in truth' is both a moral commitment and a political act.[40]

## THE RISE OF 'PEOPLE POWER' AND THE LITERATURE OF THE 1980s–1990s

'Living in truth' became transformed into a mass movement with the emergence of Solidarity in Poland in August 1980. Solidarity, which mobilized millions, not only in the trade unions, but later in the universities, the professions, and the countryside, inspired a wide-ranging literature, including assessments from the perspective of non-violent resistance.[41] Even after Solidarity was crushed by martial law at the end of 1981, it retained an underground existence, and was able to surface again to negotiate with the regime as the Soviet bloc began to crumble.

The mass exodus of East Germans in 1989 through the newly opened Hungarian border, and the fall of the Berlin Wall, followed by the 'Velvet Revolution' in Czechoslovakia, spectacularly illustrated the potential of 'people power'—even if Gorbachev's domestic and foreign policy reforms encouraged change inside the whole bloc and helped to restrain intransigent regimes. These revolutions not only inspired immediate accounts by participants, journalists and observers, but also provided considerable material for academic specialists and analysts of non-violent resistance.[42] The revolts in central and eastern Europe were followed by

---

[38] Václav Havel et al., *The Power of the Powerless* (London: Hutchinson, 1985); Adam Michnik, *Letters from Prison and Other Essays* (Berkeley: University of California Press, 1985); Gyorgy Konrad, *Anti-Politics: An Essay* (London: Quartet, 1984).

[39] Cited in Jonathan Schell, *The Unconquerable World: Power, Nonviolence and the Will of the People* (London: Allen Lane, 2004), 200.

[40] Václav Havel, *Living in Truth* (London: Faber & Faber, 1987).

[41] Jan Zielonka, 'Strengths and Weaknesses of Nonviolent Action: The Polish Case', *Orbis*, 30 (Spring 1986), 91–110; Robert Polet, *Polish Summer* (London: War Resisters' International, 1981); for wider analysis see Timothy Garton Ash, *The Polish Revolution: Solidarity 1980–81* (London: Jonathan Cape, 1983).

[42] Roland Bleiker, *Nonviolent Struggle and the Revolution in East Germany* (Cambridge, Mass.: Albert Einstein Institution, 1993); Michael Randle, *People Power: The Building of a New European Home* (Stroud: Hawthorn Press, 1991); Adam Roberts, *Civil Resistance in the East European and Soviet*

movements for national independence within the Soviet Union. The Baltic republics, which had shown signs of popular dissent for some time, seized the opportunities created by Gorbachev's reforms to try to secede. Despite attempts at harsh repression by Moscow, mass movements in which advocates of non-violence were involved led to eventual independence.[43]

Then the coup against Gorbachev in August 1991 was met by mass demonstrations in Moscow. Although commentators disagree about the impact of civil resistance, it was a new example of popular action pre-empting a *coup d'état*.[44] (Earlier examples are the 1920 mass strike against the Kapp Putsch in Germany, and the French general strike against the 1961 attempted coup by French generals in Algeria).[45]

The events of 1989–91 also provide material for comparative analysis of reasons for effective non-violent protests and of the varying outcomes of resistance, for example why initial non-violent protest in Romania rapidly turned to violence and the outcome was further repression and corruption, rather than a transition to democratic pluralism. But the most momentous 'failure' of civil resistance in 1989 occurred in China. Despite impressive student demonstrations, which were increasingly backed by worker resistance in Beijing and in other parts of the country, and divisions in the ruling politburo on how to respond, the hardliners brutally repressed dissent and reimposed old-style party control.[46]

China in 1989 can be contrasted not only with people power in Europe but with civil resistance movements in Asia—Mark Thompson covers both in *Democratic Revolutions*.[47] Kurt Schock's *Unarmed Insurrections* addresses the lack of comparative analysis and compares the ultimate failure in China with the (temporary) success of the Movement to Restore Democracy in Nepal in 1990 and the campaign against military control of government in Thailand 1991–2. Schock also covers two other important examples of people power in Asia in the 1980s–1990s,

*Revolutions* (Cambridge, Mass.: Albert Einstein Institution, 1991). An early comparative study is: Gale Stokes, *The Walls Came Tumbling Down: The Collapse of Communism in Eastern Europe* (New York: Oxford University Press, 1993). A historical study of the East German crisis using government archives and personal testimonies is: Charles S. Maier, *Dissolution: The Crises of Communism and the End of East Germany* (Princeton, NJ: Princeton University Press, 1997).

[43] Olgerts Eglitis, *Nonviolent Action in the Liberation of Latvia* (Cambridge, Mass.: Albert Einstein Institution, 1993); Grazina Miniotaite, *Nonviolent Resistance in Lithuania* (Boston, Mass.: Albert Einstein Institution, 2002).

[44] Wendy Varney and Brian Martin, 'Lessons from the 1991 Soviet Coup', *Peace Research*, 32, no. 1 (Feb. 2000), 52–68; see also Roberts, *Civil Resistance in the East European and Soviet Revolutions*.

[45] Adam Roberts, 'Civil Resistance to Military Coups', *Journal of Peace Research*, 12, no. 1 (1975), 19–36.

[46] For a scholarly overview, see: Tony Saich (ed.), *The Chinese People's Movement: Perspectives on Spring 1989* (Armonk, NY: M. E. Sharpe, 1991); from a non-violent standpoint see: Michael True, 'The 1989 Democratic Uprising in China from a Nonviolent Perspective', in M. Kumar and P. Low (eds.), *Legacy and Future of Nonviolence* (New Delhi: Gandhi Peace Foundation, 1996), 141–57. On politburo responses see Andrew J. Nathan and Perry Link (eds.) *The Tiananmen Papers* (London: Little Brown, 2001)—leaked papers generally accepted as authentic.

[47] Mark R. Thompson, *Democratic Revolutions: Asia and Eastern Europe* (London: Routledge, 2004), covers East Germany, China, and the Philippines.

©Paula Bronstein/Getty Images

**Figure 2.2** Like several other civil resistance leaders across the globe, the Burmese pro-democracy campaigner Aung San Suu Kyi is also an author. She is depicted here in 2001 at her home in Rangoon during one of her several long periods of house arrest since 1990, when the National League for Democracy, which she led, won in a general election but was prevented from taking office.

which provided a striking contrast between success and failure, the Philippines and Burma.[48] The effective non-violent movement to topple the Marcos regime from 1983–6, which eventually united Catholic nuns and priests with large sections of the population, and led to a major split in the armed forces, made the term 'people power' popular.[49] By contrast, the impressive civil resistance to military rule in Burma in 1988 was crushed;[50] as also were the demonstrations led by monks in 2007, described by Christina Fink in Chapter 21 of this book.

## COMBINING NON-VIOLENT AND GUERRILLA TACTICS AND ISSUES OF LEVERAGE: 1980s–1990s

Civil resistance in Burma highlights another problem: combining unarmed and military struggle. Burmese pro-democracy campaigner Aung San Suu Kyi is influenced by Gandhi and Havel, but ethnic minorities are also waging guerrilla campaigns. Michael Beer outlines the moves towards a resistance coalition, which recognized both types of struggle and supported their geographical separation.[51]

A very different example of combining guerrilla tactics with people power is provided by the prolonged struggle in South Africa. The ANC founded The Spear of the Nation in 1961. The existence of an armed resistance group based outside South African frontiers, but undertaking sabotage inside the country, symbolized a continued will to resist apartheid, but never moved into the stage of people's war. It has been argued that open popular protest and civic organization provided the most effective resistance in the long run.[52] There was a groundswell of civil resistance in the 1980s and the ANC itself never abandoned its belief in 'mass resistance', and turned to people power in the early 1990s when negotiations with the regime stalled.

South African mass resistance in the 1980s was far from strictly non-violent. Suspected African collaborators were killed, demonstrators often threw stones and erected barricades, and in 1985 militant youths battled with some success to

[48] Kurt Schock, *Unarmed Insurrections: People Power Movements in Nondemocracies* (Minneapolis: University of Minnesota Press, 2005).

[49] Douglas J. Elwood, *Philippines Revolution 1986: Model of Nonviolent Change* (Quezon City: New Day Publishers, 1986); Stephen Zunes, 'The Origins of People Power in the Philippines' in Stephen Zunes et al. (eds.), *Nonviolent Social Movements: A Geographical Perspective* (Oxford: Blackwell, 1999), 129–57; Peter Ackerman and Jack DuVall, *A Force More Powerful: A Century of Nonviolent Conflict* (New York: Palgrave, 2000), 369–95.

[50] Aung San Suu Kyi, *Freedom from Fear and Other Writings* (London: Viking, 1991) includes her role in the non-violent struggle; Christina Fink, *Living Silence: Burma under Military Rule* (London: Zed Books, 2001), 50–76; Justin Wintle, *Perfect Hostage: A Life of Aung San Suu Kyi* (London: Hutchinson, 2007), 225 ff.

[51] Michael Beer, 'Violent and Nonviolent Struggle in Burma: Is a Unified Strategy Workable?', in Zunes, *Nonviolent Social Movements*, 174–84.

[52] Tom Lodge (Ch. 13, below) suggests the guerrillas' main role was to offer support to the township rebellions.

create no-go areas in the townships.[53] Moreover, divisions between the ANC and the Zulu Inkatha movement resulted in serious inter-communal violence. Nevertheless, the South African struggle did overall provide an 'A to Z' of non-violent tactics.[54]

Civil resistance began to supersede guerrilla warfare as the main strategy against dictatorial rule in Latin America in the 1980s—although sometimes, as in Chile, armed and civil resistance proceeded in tandem. Trade unions and political parties were prominent, but the Catholic Church also played an important role. Non-violent strategy (*firmeza permanente*—'relentless persistence') has been promoted by Catholic activists in Service for Peace and Justice (SERPAJ) founded in 1974, which is well represented in the literature on non-violence.[55] Women have been prominent in much non-violent protest: notably in the vigil by mothers and grandmothers of the disappeared in Argentina—the Mothers of the Plaza de Mayo.[56] There was also a conscious turn towards non-violence among sections of the resistance—for example in Chile the copper miners' leader noted the influence of Richard Attenborough's film *Gandhi* and the example of Lech Wałęsa, initiator of Solidarity.[57]

The struggle of the Palestinians for an independent homeland was associated with guerrilla tactics by an external leadership, but a significant internal movement adopting civil resistance arose in 1987. The First Intifada (shaking off) began as a mass movement by all sectors of the population committed to avoiding resort to guns, despite frequent stone throwing and other occasional violence. Forms of civil resistance continued for several years. The First Intifada empowered Palestinian representatives to enter into negotiations, which resulted in the 1991 Madrid Conference and the Oslo Accords of 20 August 1993. It was also a struggle (unlike the Second Intifada) in which advocates of non-violent tactics were actively involved and retained a voice—Mubarak Awad had set up the Center for the Study of Nonviolence in the West Bank in 1983.[58]

The First Intifada has been well analysed from a non-violent perspective.[59] But it also illustrates limits to the power of non-cooperation. Andrew Rigby in *Living*

[53] Robert M. Price, *The Apartheid State in Crisis: Political Transformations in South Africa 1975–1990* (New York: Oxford University Press, 1991), 192.

[54] Dene Smuts and Shauna Westcott, *The Purple Shall Govern: A South African A to Z of Nonviolent Action* (Cape Town: Oxford University Press and Centre for Intergroup Studies, 1991).

[55] Philip McManus and Gerald Schlabach (eds.), *Relentless Persistence: Nonviolent Action in Latin America* (Philadelphia, Penn.: New Society Publishers, 1991); Adolfo Perez Esquivel, *Christ in a Poncho: Testimonies of the Nonviolent Struggle in Latin America* (Maryknoll, NY: Orbis, 1983).

[56] Jo Fisher, *Mothers of the Disappeared* (London: Zed Books, 1989).

[57] Ackerman and DuVall, *A Force More Powerful*, 291.

[58] Mubarak Awad, 'Nonviolent Resistance: A Strategy for the Occupied Territories', *Journal of Palestine Studies*, 13, no. 4 (Summer 1984), 22–36.

[59] Ralph E. Crow et al., *Arab Nonviolent Political Struggle in the Middle East* (Boulder Colo.: Lynne Rienner, 1990); Johan Galtung, *Nonviolence and Israel/Palestine* (University of Hawaii, 1989); William Vogele, 'Learning and Nonviolent Struggle in the Intifadah', *Peace and Change*, 17, no. 3 (July 1992), 312–40; Mary Elizabeth King, *A Quiet Revolution: The First Palestinian Intifada and Nonviolent Resistance* (New York: Nation Books, 2007).

*the Intifada* queries how far resisters can exert leverage when the opponent does not depend directly upon their cooperation.[60] The movement did engage in forms of non-cooperation with the Israeli state and inflicted quite serious economic damage on Israel, as Peter Ackerman and Jack DuVall argue.[61] But the rival claims by Israelis and Palestinians to the same land means that the Intifada differed both from classic examples of resistance to internal oppression and to Gandhian style anti-colonial movements, where the stakes for the colonizer were less high.

The problem of how far non-cooperation works, where the regime 'far from depending on the oppressed population . . . would rather expel it', is taken up by Howard Clark in his analysis of the civil resistance by the Kosovo Albanians in the 1990s to Serbian oppression.[62] The Kosovo struggle also illustrated how external events (the wider disintegration of Yugoslavia) can undermine the will of the ruling regime—the Milošević government in Serbia—to pursue its original policies. As in Palestine, civil resistance was superseded by a faction committed to guerrilla warfare. In Kosovo guerrilla tactics provoked counter-violence, which paved the way for military intervention by NATO.

## THE GENERAL LITERATURE ON CIVIL RESISTANCE SINCE 1980

Theorists of civil resistance have become increasingly concerned with analysing strategy. An important contribution has been made by Robert Helvey, one of a number of former military officers who have engaged with non-violent resistance, who acted as adviser to the Burmese opposition on how best to combine violent and non-violent resistance. Helvey's approach is at the opposite pole from Gandhi in stressing pragmatism rather than moral principle.[63] In similar vein, Peter Ackerman and Christopher Kruegler have examined twelve main principles of 'strategic nonviolent conflict' in relation to some major struggles of the twentieth century.[64]

Strategic issues are prominent in the later literature on civilian defence: for example Gene Keyes argues 'morale', not 'unity', is the 'centre of gravity' for non-violent resistance.[65] A sceptical analysis by Alex Schmid, *Social Defence and Soviet*

[60] Andrew Rigby, *Living the Intifada* (London: Zed Books, 1991).

[61] Ackerman and DuVall, *A Force More Powerful*, 416.

[62] Howard Clark, *Civil Resistance in Kosovo* (London: Pluto Press, 2000), 139.

[63] Robert Helvey, *On Strategic Nonviolent Conflict* (Boston, Mass.: Albert Einstein Institution, 2004).

[64] Peter Ackerman and Christopher Kruegler, *Strategic Nonviolent Conflict* (Westport, Conn.: Praeger, 1993).

[65] Gene Keyes, 'Strategic Nonviolent Defense: The Construct of an Option', *Journal of Strategic Studies*, 4, no. 2 (June 1981), 125–51. See also: Alternative Defence Commission, *Defence Without the Bomb*, 208–48; Michael Randle, *Civil Resistance* (London: Fontana, 1994); Gene Sharp, *Civilian-Based Defense: A Post-Military Weapons' System* (Princeton NJ: Princeton University Press, 1990)—includes references to his earlier writings on this topic.

*Military Power*, sets out a checklist of ten conditions needed for success, discussed critically by Clark in relation to the struggle in Kosovo.[66] A study reflecting Gandhi's influence, but also seeking to reinterpret Clausewitz, is Robert Burrowes, *The Strategy of Nonviolent Defense*.[67]

One key question about civil resistance is still how far it can succeed against extreme repression. An example often used to address that question is the uprising against the Shah of Iran in 1979. Millions took part in strikes and demonstrations despite mass shootings, and the final defection of the military toppled the Shah.[68] It could therefore be interpreted as a success for civil resistance. Since, however, the Iranian revolution resulted in the draconian regime of the ayatollahs, it also highlights problems of revolutionary transition, and is used by Sharp to illustrate this theme.[69]

Sharp's *Politics of Nonviolent Action* remains a starting point for much analysis. Detailed case studies often refer back to his strategic prescriptions or consent theory of power—see for example Zielonka on Solidarity, Clark on Kosovo, and Shock's comparative case studies.[70] Brian Martin has queried Sharp's individualistic and voluntaristic view of power from the standpoint of structuralist theories of the power embedded in capitalism or patriarchy, whilst noting that the latter also raise problems in explaining how active resistance occurs.[71] Roland Bleiker in *Popular Dissent, Human Agency and Global Politics* provides a critique of Sharp influenced by Foucault and looks at the background of East German cultural dissent before the fall of the Berlin Wall.[72] However, Jonathan Schell in *The Unconquerable World* turns to the central European theorists and Arendt in his comments on the inadequacies of the theory of power within traditional political thought.

Academics from a number of different disciplines have used them to illuminate their discussion of civil resistance. Herbert Blumberg and Paul Hare have brought social psychology to bear, for example in their previously cited *Nonviolent Direct Action*. Paul Routledge, a radical geographer, has explored the spatial components to sites of non-violent resistance in India.[73] The rise of feminist scholarship has

[66] Alex Schmid, *Social Defence and Soviet Military Power: An Inquiry into the Relevance of an Alternative Defence Concept* (Leiden: Centre for the Study of Social Conflict, 1985); Clark, *Civil Resistance in Kosovo*, 189–93.

[67] Robert Burrowes, *The Strategy of Nonviolent Defense: A Gandhian Approach* (Albany, NY: State University of New York Press, 1996).

[68] Alternative Defence Commission, *Defence Without the Bomb*, 224; Randle, *Civil Resistance*, 17, 59, 107.

[69] Sharp, *Waging Nonviolent Struggle*, 506.

[70] Zielonka, 'Strengths and Weaknesses of Nonviolent Action'; Clark, *Civil Resistance in Kosovo*; Schock, *Unarmed Insurrections*.

[71] Brian Martin, 'Gene Sharp's Theory of Power', *Journal of Peace Research*, 26, no. 2 (May 1989), 213–22.

[72] Roland Bleiker, *Popular Dissent, Human Agency and Global Politics* (Cambridge: Cambridge University Press, 2000).

[73] Paul Routledge, *Terrains of Resistance: Nonviolent Social Movements and the Contestation of Place in India* (Westport, Conn.: Praeger, 1993).

also had some impact, partly in studies highlighting the role of women in anti-war and other struggles, but also in criticism of the masculinist bias of non-violence literature and a critique of Sharp's consent theory of power.[74]

In addition, the wealth of recent examples of civil resistance has encouraged further documentation of campaigns and methods.[75] The role of non-violent action in campaigns around the world is reflected in Stephen Zunes's collection of accounts, *Nonviolent Social Movements* and Ackerman and DuVall's *A Force More Powerful.*

## PEOPLE POWER AND POWER POLITICS SINCE 2000

The inherently difficult issue of combining non-violent resistance with armed guerrilla struggle was thrown up again dramatically in Nepal. The earlier non-violent Movement for the Restoration of Democracy in 1990 (covered by Schock, *Unarmed Insurrections*) had temporary success, but corruption led to a Maoist guerrilla struggle which in turn encouraged the king to reassume absolute power. However, in April 2006 a mass civil resistance campaign by both urban and rural protesters (supported by the Maoists) succeeded in achieving the reinstatement of parliament and drafting of a new constitution. The newly elected parliament reached a peace deal with the Maoists in November 2006.[76]

The books on civil resistance have not however had time to catch up with Nepal 2006, or with the recent wave of protest against rigged elections in post-communist regimes—although Sharp's *Waging Nonviolent Struggle* and Thompson's *Democratic Revolutions* do encompass the overthrow of Milošević in Serbia in 2000. The 'colour revolutions' in ex-Soviet states since 2003 have, however, been examined extensively by academic area specialists in the *Journal of Democracy* and the post-communist studies journals.

The toppling of Milošević prompted a critical debate about the role of Western governments, which had begun to support the opposition in 1996. This critique gained momentum in response to the 'revolutions' in Georgia and Ukraine, where the regimes in power leaned towards Russia and the opposition towards the West, though some observers and participants have queried the centrality of Western funding and support.[77]

---

[74] Pam McAllister, 'You Can't Kill the Spirit: Women and Nonviolent Action', in Zunes, *Nonviolent Social Movements*, 18–35; Kate McGuinness, 'Gene Sharp's Theory of Power', *Journal of Peace Research*, 30, no. 1 (1993), 101–15.

[75] Robert L. Holmes and Barry L. Gan (eds.), *Nonviolence in Theory and Practice*, 2nd edn. (Long Grove, Ill.: Waveland Press, 2005); Roger S. Powers et al., *Protest, Power and Change: An Encyclopaedia of Nonviolent Action from ACT-UP to Women's Suffrage* (New York: Garland, 1997).

[76] International Crisis Group, Asia Report no. 115, 'Nepal: From People Power to Peace?', 10 May 2006 (www.crisisgroup.org); R. K. Vishwakarma, *People's Power in Nepal* (New Delhi: Manak Publications, 2006).

[77] Criticism of the 'colour revolutions' has appeared frequently in the *Guardian* (London) and the issue has been debated on the net, e.g. at www.openDemocracy.net. See also Andrew Wilson, *Ukraine's Orange Revolution* (New Haven, Conn.: Yale University Press, 2005).

©Paula Bronstein/Getty Images

**Figure 2.3** Events in Nepal marching ahead of the literature. On 27 April 2006 in the capital, Kathmandu, tens of thousands celebrate the ending of the period of royal rule and martial law. Earlier in the month, the widely supported '2006 Democracy Movement' had organized demonstrations and a general strike. The Maoist rebels, who had for the previous ten years been engaged in rural guerrilla insurgency, joined the unarmed civil resistance, and then focused on political and constitutional action.

Another problem with some recent 'people power' protests is that the populations are in fact bitterly divided: this is true not only of the Ukraine but of the 'Cedar Revolution' in Lebanon in 2005 and mass demonstrations against the outcome of the Mexican presidential elections in 2006.[78] So 'people power' does not always fit the 'ideal type' of a large majority pitted against a repressive elite, and the democratic legitimacy of mass protest then becomes problematic. Such divisions can also make the role of external powers tending to support opposed social groupings more salient.

## GREAT POWERS AND THE INTERNATIONAL DIMENSION

The Cold War conflict between the US and Soviet Union, and the changing balance between them, significantly structured the context of civil resistance. The Soviet political and military control over its east European satellites was an

[78] For a leftist interpretation see: Al Giordano, 'Mexico's Presidential Swindle', *New Left Review*, no. 41 (Sept./Oct. 2006), 5–27.

obvious and crucial constraint on resistance. The opening up of the Soviet and east European archives since the 1990s has, however, enabled scholars to examine the complexity of Soviet government calculations in different crises from 1956 to 1989.[79]

The less overt US role as regional hegemon in Latin America has also been critical, and its shift from backing repressive anti-communist governments to greater support for democratic oppositions assisted the toppling of military regimes. For example, in 1985 Washington began to disengage from General Pinochet in Chile.[80] By the later 1980s US attitudes were also influenced by changing perceptions of the threat from 'communism'.

The Cold War had wide ideological repercussions. For example it initially contributed to the South African government determination to suppress 'communism', and then its ending by 1990 was a factor in Pretoria's willingness to make concessions to the ANC. The South African resistance was also assisted by an unprecedented degree of international support, ranging from United Nations resolutions, international campaigns of boycotts and financial disinvestment, national governments which contributed to defence funds, the South African diaspora of activists, and demonstrators in many parts of the world. Studies of external sanctions include Mark Orkin, *Sanctions Against Apartheid*.[81] The regime's attempt in the 1980s to maintain repression but make some reforms, designed to encourage foreign investment and economic development, was undermined by further sanctions and the flight of capital in response to the mass internal resistance.[82]

## CONCLUSION

This survey has indicated that, as the number of civil resistance campaigns has increased, theorists of non-violent action have engaged in more rigorous case studies, and have begun to draw on relevant academic theories and to compare the conditions promoting success or failure. Moreover, comparative academic analyses of the spate of 'people power' protests in the last few years have begun to appear and have taken note of the deliberate adoption of non-violent strategies. The gap between the literature specifically on non-violent action and academic studies of campaigns using civil resistance has in recent years decreased. This volume is itself a contribution to bridging that gap by promoting critical analysis of the effectiveness of civil resistance strategies, and by exploring how civil resistance relates to the many other forms of power.

[79] See the *Cold War International History Project Bulletin*, Woodrow Wilson Center, and publications of the Harvard Project on Cold War Studies, directed by Mark Kramer, who has himself published extensively.

[80] Ackerman and DuVall, *A Force More Powerful*, 290. On Chile, see also Ch. 12, below, by Carlos Huneeus.

[81] Mark Orkin, *Sanctions Against Apartheid* (New York: St Martin's Press, 1989).

[82] Price, *The Apartheid State in Crisis*, 152–57, 184–6, & 220–33.

# 3

# Gandhi and Civil Resistance in India, 1917–47: Key Issues

*Judith M. Brown*

The civil resistance movements in India led by M. K. Gandhi between 1917 and 1942 are often seen as classic instances of successful civil resistance, and, as such, have had a profound ideological and practical effect on many subsequent practitioners worldwide. They raise a number of crucial and recurring issues, which are the concern of this chapter. What might constitute 'success' and 'failure' in a civil resistance movement? In what way does this form of resistance gain leverage by testing the vulnerabilities of a particular opponent? As Gandhi's campaigns are exceptionally well documented, they also permit careful historical attention to particular problems in the construction and management of mass civil resistance movements. Moreover, Gandhi was manifestly one of the greatest modern ideologues of this mode of managing human conflict. So his often troubled experience enables us to probe questions about shared ideology among leaders and also, more ambiguously, among lower levels of participants in his campaigns. The debates among leaders and participants also illuminate the perceived limits and potential of non-violent resistance.

## SURVEY OF EVENTS

Gandhi returned to India in 1915, bringing with him nearly a decade of experiments with civil resistance in South Africa. His African experience of resisting discrimination against Indians convinced him that non-violent resistance to all forms of evil (political, social, and personal) was the only moral way of conducting and resolving conflict; and he coined a new word for it, *satyagraha* or truth-force, to distinguish it from passive resistance, which he saw as a weapon for the weak rather than for the morally and physically courageous and disciplined *satyagrahi* (practitioner of satyagraha). He had become convinced that satyagraha was a broad moral force for good, transforming those who practised it as well as delivering practical results through the conversion of the opponent.[1] By 1914 he also believed that satyagraha had achieved major political improvements for Indians in South Africa. Although their situation deteriorated subsequently, the timing of his departure meant that he left for India with a conviction of the practical as well as the enduring moral significance of non-violent resistance. Back in India Gandhi conducted a number of resistance movements in the areas of Bihar and Gujarat, on restricted local socio-economic issues, in 1917 and 1918. These convinced him that it was his duty to India, and by explicit implication to a wider world, to persuade Indians on a national scale to adopt non-violent civil resistance against the British imperial ruler.

Gandhi's pan-Indian campaigns occurred through the rest of his working life, in 1919, in 1920–2, in 1930–4 (with a brief 'truce' for most of 1931), in 1940–1 and in 1942. Only the last campaign had as its goal 'Quit India', the departure of the British rulers in the particular circumstances of a possible Japanese invasion. Earlier movements were launched on specific issues, such as the government salt monopoly in 1930 or opposition to involvement in the war effort in 1940–1. Nonetheless, they challenged the very nature of British imperialism, and were designed to undermine the implicit Indian cooperation on which imperial rule rested.[2] These campaigns gathered a greater range of active participation and more passive support than had any previous political movement in India, reflecting Gandhi's own skill in interpreting independence in ways which appealed to those outside the educated elite who had previously dominated nationalist politics. It was also the result of the hospitable nature of the campaigns, which gave opportunities to many different groups to vent their particular grievances through it, and to take up aspects of it which were within their capabilities. Children could go on morning song processions in support of the cause. Women could picket shops which sold foreign cloth or liquor. Even those without education could spin, close their shops or participate in processions and illegal gatherings. While the more educated could boycott government schools and colleges, or withdraw their labour from the law courts and the legislatures.

However, Gandhi felt morally bound to call off the first two campaigns because of outbreaks of violence either against the British or against other Indians. Civil disobedience in 1930–4 eventually petered out because of official control and also the wish of most prominent leaders and second-level participants to return to

---

[1] On Gandhi in South Africa see M. Swan, *Gandhi: The South African Experience* (Ravan Press, Johannesburg, 1985; Judith M. Brown, *Gandhi: Prisoner of Hope* (New Haven & London: Yale University Press, 1989), part 1. Gandhi's own account is his *Satyagraha In South Africa*, trans. V. G. Desai (Ahmedabad: Navajivan Publishing House, 1928).

[2] Gandhi explained his understanding of the scope of civil resistance in the nationalist movement, in a pamphlet written in late 1941, *Constructive Programme: Its Meaning and Place*; also available in *The Collected Works of Mahatma Gandhi* (Delhi: Government of India, printed version, 1958–84), vol. 75, 146–66 (hereafter *CWMG*). Campaigns should be on specific issues which could be clearly understood and on which the opponent could yield, not for 'a general cause such as for independence'. Far more significant for him as the main path to independence was the campaign of moral and social reconstruction.

constitutional politics, and in particular to participate in imminent elections under a reformed constitution that would promise considerable local power to successful candidates. Gandhi had worked within and through the main political organization which claimed to speak for Indian nationalism, the Indian National Congress. But his priorities and those of most politicians within it were very different. In 1934 Gandhi bowed to reality, essentially letting Congress 'off the hook', in a situation where few agreed with his policy any more but virtually none was prepared to challenge him outright. Nearly a decade later individual protests against the war effort in 1940–1 were ineffective in the longer run and the resulting Quit India movement of 1942 was crushed by the British, who were determined to retain India and its resources in a crucial phase of the war.

In retrospect it is clear that civil resistance never made British rule impossible, although in a few exceptional situations British rule broke down temporarily.[3] More often it just made government activity difficult, for example, by filling the jails with willing prisoners, by attacking significant sources of revenue, or by pressurizing village headmen to withdraw their services. It also made government fearful for the support of many of its key collaborators such as those of the politically active or aware whom they considered more 'moderate', who were not active supporters of the Congress, but became deeply perturbed at the treatment of Gandhi and the limited nature of political change.

It was essentially the Second World War which drove the British to grant independence to the subcontinent. Indeed, in the years just before the outbreak of war it seemed as if they had successfully re-established their rule with a new constitutional framework of politics created by the 1935 Government of India Act. Between 1937 and 1939 they had very successfully yoked Congress into their new system of political collaboration. The Congress leadership had felt forced by its followers to participate in the new political system inaugurated by the 1935 Act, because of the lure of real political power in the provinces. As a result of its stunning electoral success Congress formed the government in the majority of the provinces and essentially became part of the imperial system of government. It was not surprising that the radical Jawaharlal Nehru and the moral Gandhi were both deeply disturbed by the spectacle of Congress as government, with all the compromises this involved. However, the outbreak of war led Congress into the wilderness of opposition and its leadership into jail, and broke up this collaborative nexus. When the war ended it was clear that there could be no return to the collaborative politics of 1939, and that independence was imminent.

The destructive effect of the war on the Raj had become clear as early as 1942 in the ill-starred 'Cripps Mission' when Sir Stafford Cripps went to India with a political offer designed to placate Britain's American allies and encourage

---

[3] Such temporary breakdown occurred in Malabar on the south-west coast during the non-cooperation movement of 1920–2, and in Bihar in 1942. In the latter the government had to use the Tiger Moths of the Bihar Flying Club to keep in touch with one outlying district and altogether lost touch with others. In Bombay City in the 1930–4 movement Congressmen essentially acted like traffic police in certain areas.

Congress into a wartime partnership with the Raj, on the understanding that India would gain independence after the war.[4] After this there could be no going back on the ultimate political goal for India. Moreover, by 1946 it was becoming plain that the Raj was declining in physical power and moral authority, following the Cripps offer, as India became mired in conflict among Indians about the nature of the Indian nation and the future nation state, and as the European numbers in all the key government services declined. Lord Wavell, the penultimate viceroy, was brutal in his assessment in his diary on the last day of 1946: 'The administration has declined, and the machine in the Centre is hardly working at all now, my ministers are too busy with politics. And while the British are still legally and morally responsible for what happens in India, we have lost nearly all power to control events; we are simply running on the momentum of our previous prestige.'[5]

The British also recognized that any renewed campaign of resistance, civil or otherwise, (even if Gandhi had had the will and capacity to start another after the experience of 1942) would have placed their Indian employees and allies in an intolerable position and would have needed an injection of manpower and money to re-establish the Raj for long enough to enable such people to calculate that loyalty as a viable long-term political strategy. But the British public in the throes of post-war economic and social reconstruction would never have tolerated such investment of money or British personnel. Nor would Britain's international allies have supported such a reimposition of imperial rule. It was also true that the worth of India to Britain had also declined in the inter-war period, thus making any large-scale expenditure on imperial renewal even less of an option.[6] The last viceroy, Lord Mountbatten, agreed with the sombre verdict of his predecessor at the end of 1946 and very soon after his arrival in India in March 1947 began the process of winding up the Raj as quickly as possible. Given the complexities of British calculations and of Indian politics, it seems clear that civil resistance had not made British rule impossible, or been a critical factor in the British decision to leave India. But it had been significant in building the Congress into a mass-based party which was capable of mounting both a moral and physical challenge to the Raj, and eventually forming the government of a new nation.

---

[4] See R. J. Moore, *Churchill, Cripps, and India, 1939–1945* (Oxford: Clarendon Press, 1979); N. Mansergh and E. Lumby (eds.), *Constitutional Relations between Britain and India: The Transfer of Power 1942–7*, vol. 1, *The Cripps Mission January–April 1942* (London: HMSO, 1970).

[5] Diary entry, 31 Dec. 1946, P. Moon (ed.), *Wavell: The Viceroy's Journal* (London: Oxford University Press, 1973), 402.

[6] On British decision-making see Judith M. Brown, *Modern India: The Origins of an Asian Democracy*, 2nd edn. (Oxford: Oxford University Press, 1994), 318–30; R. J. Moore, *Escape From Empire: The Attlee Government and the Indian Problem* (Oxford: Clarendon Press, 1983). On the economics of the decision to withdraw see B. R. Tomlinson, *The Political Economy of the Raj 1914–1947: The Economics of Decolonization in India* (London: Macmillan, 1979). Key documentation is to be found in the 12 vols. of Mansergh and Lumby (eds.), *Constitutional Relations between Britain and India*. Particularly illuminating are documents 35 and 94 in vol. 9.

## SIGNIFICANT THEMES

A major issue in any campaign of civil resistance, and in historical understanding of it, is that of ideology. What convinces participants that non-violence is appropriate? Is it a pragmatic response to a particular situation or a coherent moral stance in relation to all conflict? Further, a movement may contain people with many different attitudes, and if there are different ideological stances and degrees of commitment to non-violence this may make it difficult to sustain non-violence for any length of time.

Gandhi faced these issues in a particularly acute form. For him non-violence (*ahimsa*) was at the heart of his vision of morality and of the good human life. Moreover, he believed that there could be no distinction between ends and means: the right means produced moral ends, while bad means inevitably produced immoral ends. So he believed that satyagraha not only worked in the political sense of achieving visible results; but also that it transformed both parties in any conflict, protecting the integrity of each and leading both to a greater vision of truth. (Where it appeared not to do so, as in 1942, he was sure that satyagraha had not been properly observed, but tainted by violence.) It was in pursuit of the same goal—mutual integrity and agreement—that Gandhi always insisted that satyagrahis should be prepared to negotiate with their opponents on non-essentials. He was himself a willing and skilled negotiator, whether in South Africa or with representatives of the British Raj, most notably with Lord Irwin as viceroy in 1931, or in the final months of the Raj when he worked closely with Mountbatten to achieve independence speedily and mitigate the accompanying violence.

In the particular circumstances of British-ruled India Gandhi's goals were specific as well as this more general moral transformation. He recognized that British rule depended on many forms of Indian collaboration and complicity; and he hoped to educate Indians to realize this and to generate within themselves such courage and strength that they could withdraw their cooperation with the British and begin to create a new society and polity from the roots upwards. Hence his vision of real self-rule, *swaraj*, implied much more than political independence.[7]

However, there was only a tiny core of committed 'Gandhians', who shared this vision of *swaraj* and his commitment to non-violence. Many others within the nationalist movement, including some who were very close to him, such as Jawaharlal Nehru, believed that non-violence was appropriate in the context of British rule. But they did not rule out the use of violence in some situations; and they recognized that a mass movement was most unlikely always to remain peaceful. As Nehru stated the case in his autobiography, written after painful meditation in jail,

---

[7] Gandhi elaborated his vision of *swaraj* and his understanding of Indian complicity in British rule in a key pamphlet written in 1909, *Hind Swaraj*, reprinted in *CWMG*, vol. 10, 6–68.

© Central Press/Stringer (Hulton Archive) Getty Images

**Figure 3.1** Closeness and difference. Gandhi (on right) and Jawaharlal Nehru during an All-India National Congress Committee meeting, Bombay, India, 6 July 1946. Nehru, who became Prime Minister of India in 1947, never shared Gandhi's profound commitment to non-violence, though he believed that in India's particular circumstances non-violent means were the best way for the nationalist movement to confront British imperial rule.

> for the National Congress as a whole the non-violent method was not, and could not be, a religion or an unchallengeable creed or dogma. It could only be a policy and a method promising certain results, and by those results it would have to be finally judged. Individuals might make of it a religion or incontrovertible creed. But no political organisation, so long as it remained political, could do so.[8]

It was because of his anguish at the gulf in attitudes and practice between himself and his supposed followers that Gandhi called off satyagraha in 1919 and 1922 following local instances of violence. In 1934 he insisted that only he should remain a satyagrahi in order to preserve the instrument of satyagraha in its purity. Towards the end of his life he lamented that Quit India and the violence which erupted on a significant scale indicated that Indians had never really taken up satyagraha, but had only engaged pragmatically in passive resistance.

Gandhi was, nonetheless, a subtle thinker and a life-long learner, and he developed a complex and nuanced attitude to violence which in certain situations could

---

[8] J. Nehru, *An Autobiography* (London: John Lane, The Bodley Head, 1936), 84. This comment referred to Gandhi's suspension of civil resistance in 1922 after an Indian mob had burned a police station with the Indian constables inside it. The news of suspension, coming to Nehru in jail, had greatly disturbed him.

be misunderstood and laid him open to criticism. For example, he felt that for a citizen benefiting from the order which government provided it was at times morally right to support that government even by participating in war. He himself undertook ambulance work during the Boer War and Zulu rebellion in South Africa, and he actively recruited soldiers in India during the First World War. By the Second World War, although his sympathies were for the Allies and he hated what he knew of Nazi methods, his horror of global war had intensified and he felt that in these particular circumstances of multiple wrongs evil should be primarily opposed by forms of non-violence. He advised German Jews to withstand Hitler with non-violence, even to the point of death. He believed that if the British withdrew from India it was likely that the Japanese would not be interested in conquest, but that if he were proved wrong, Indians should resist by refusing to cooperate with a Japanese imperial regime. Yet he accepted that the British at home might have to fight for their freedom. He also believed that cowardice in the face of evil was worse than violence in opposing evil. It seems that this lay behind his anguished agreement to the launching of the Quit India campaign, despite knowing that violence might well break out in India in the course of it. But the alternative was supine acceptance of an imperial regime which denied Indians even the right to speak against the war effort and used Indian resources to fight a world war. Gandhi, in common with many of his compatriots, was deeply concerned about Indian masculinity and imperial criticisms of some Indian men as weak and 'unmanly'. So his fear of cowardice tapped into one of the most sensitive cultural areas of Indian responses to imperial ideology. For Gandhi real strength lay in moral and physical courage, sustained by constant physical and moral self-discipline, which found its highest manifestation in non-violent resistance to wrong.[9] But in extreme conditions he felt that violent resistance was better than cowardly inaction. Moreover in the particular circumstances of India's nationalist movement he refined his stance towards the 'peripheral violence' which might erupt as a result of his non-violent movement. Mindful of the critiques of even his closest allies, such as Nehru, who felt, after the experience of 1922, that ending a movement if there was any 'peripheral violence' would nullify it as a viable political tool, he accepted that he might have to endure seeing such violence but that his conscience would be clear if he and those at the heart of the movement remained consistent in non-violent resistance.

The complexities and ambiguities of ideological attitudes towards civil resistance in India reverberated within the cluster of problems Gandhi faced in disciplining those who 'followed' him within civil resistance campaigns—whatever 'follow' might mean in his particular context. For him and for the Indian National Congress it was essential that participants in these campaigns should maintain strict non-violence and adhere to carefully considered strategies of resistance. If this did not happen it would play into the hands of the imperial opponent and lose the movement the high moral ground—both in the eyes of watching Indians who were not directly involved, and in the eyes of international

---

[9] See Gandhi, *Hind Swaraj*, ch. 17, '*Satyagraha*—Soul-Force'.

observers and sympathisers. An example of this happening was, of course, 1942, and the outbreak of violence as a result of civil resistance, in wartime when the British empire was fighting for its life. As a result the British had no compunction about suppressing the movement and locking up the Congress leadership, including Gandhi, and knew that they would face far less external and British domestic criticism for their actions. For Gandhi, carefully staged and managed campaigns were as much about creating and manipulating images of moral resistance as about crafting strategies which in practical terms would train Indians in the qualities necessary to achieve *swaraj* and put pressure on the particular opponent in question. He grasped intuitively that civil resistance was in many ways an exercise in political theatre, where the audience was as important as the actors.

Gandhi therefore struggled to find issues on which civil resistance could be offered which would attract wide support and maintain the cohesion of the movement—no simple task in a vast country where there were such regional, religious and socio-economic differences. He always found it easier to lead and control movements where his clients and followers were small, close-knit, and homogeneous groups which shared interests and could also police themselves. This was evident in some of his local campaigns of resistance on particular local issues, as in Bihar in 1917 or in Gujarat in 1918 and 1928. His pan-Indian movements ran a far greater risk of alienating some groups of Indians. For example, landholders in northern India were profoundly alienated by the campaigns of 1920–2 and 1930–4 which attracted peasant anti-landlord movements and to an extent supported them and gave them legitimacy. More widely, Indian Muslims increasingly dissociated themselves from civil resistance after the collapse of the 1920–2 campaign, which had been partly built on supporting the cause of the sultan of Turkey, the Muslim Khalifah, in the aftermath of the war. From the 1920s onwards few Muslims were to be found in Congress, and even fewer as participants in Gandhi's satyagrahas, which seemed to them to be designed to bring about Hindu majoritarian rule in place of the imperial Raj. Interestingly, Gandhi could find no way of using non-violence to combat increasing Muslim separatism, given that he respected the moral convictions of others. His only strategy was personal example, which reached dramatic and iconic dimensions when in 1946 he insisted on walking unarmed in parts of eastern India which had been torn by communal violence, thereby bringing some peace to the area. However, this was no solution to the growth of the Muslim separatist movement. A significant number of Hindus also opposed satyagraha, believing that it emasculated what was in their eyes an essentially Hindu nation, and that armed resistance to both the British and Muslims was a more appropriate way to gain independence for a Hindu nation state.

Gandhi's attempts to craft non-violent campaigns on an all-India scale involved many levels and types of activity. He experimented with different sorts of organizational structures, making the Congress party the major stage where plans were laid and where the movements were justified in public rhetoric. Its provincial organizations became the main sinews of the movements, and local Congress leaderships his lower tiers of leadership. But he understood that within Congress there were many shades of political opinion and that these would powerfully affect the local practice of satyagraha. So he also used his own networks of ideologically committed followers, and non-political local centres as nodules for local planning, education, and discipline, as well as tirelessly deploying his personal influence and image to publicize and explain the movement. But organizations were often weak, as he discovered when he conducted an audit of Congress in the provinces in anticipation of civil disobedience in 1930; and during long campaigns they were increasingly enfeebled by lack of funds. So to control his campaigns he also concentrated much energy on choosing issues which united as many Indians as possible and gave the fewest opportunities for violence to erupt, while carefully calibrating programmes to ensure peaceful protest.

Perhaps the greatest example of this was his choice in 1930 of the government salt monopoly as a universal issue and symbol of protest. He insisted that the movement should progress in controlled stages—from protest by himself and hand-picked individuals in his famous Salt March to the coast at Dandi, western India, where he made salt on the sea shore in the full glare of international press publicity—to a more generalized ritual of making salt illegally in small quantities round the country. Motilal Nehru, father of Jawaharlal, commented with awe that the 'master mind' had hit on such a simple but effective issue. 'The only wonder is that no one else ever thought of it.'[10]

The wartime movement of individual public protest against support of the war effort was another carefully controlled drama, where the issue was unlikely to arouse violent protest, and where the players were personally selected by Gandhi for their status and their discipline. Gandhi also grappled with the issue of how his non-violent movements could be presented to a wider domestic and international public—at a time when mass communication was in its infancy. Public demonstrations of ritualized non-violence were one of his strategies of communication. So were his travels, endless speeches, and stream of journalism. He was personally hospitable to western and Indian visitors to his ashram homes and willingly gave interviews to reporters from many countries as a way of spreading his message. A cursory glance at his *Collected Works* shows the immense importance he placed on communication and political education in the pursuit of satyagraha.

Gandhi was a self-taught politician and political analyst. However, he seems to have grasped very early that one of the keys to a non-violent movement was to design ways of probing the vulnerabilities of the opponent. If the opponent was a ruling regime there could be a variety of such vulnerabilities. It might be open to challenge on ideological grounds, within its own ranks, in relation to those it ruled, or in the context of a wider world community where international players

[10] M. Nehru to M. A. Ansari, 17 Feb. 1930, Nehru Memorial Library, New Delhi, M. Nehru Papers, File No. A 15. This process of Gandhi's decision-making on this issue is discussed in a section entitled 'The dilemmas of confrontation', in Judith M. Brown, *Gandhi and Civil Disobedience: The Mahatma in Indian Politics 1928–34* (Cambridge: Cambridge University Press, 1977), 80–98. This detailed study of one civil resistance movement illuminates many of the broad issues raised in this chapter.

**Figure 3.2** Demonstration as political theatre. Gandhi on the salt march, March–April 1930, between Gandhi's ashram in Ahmedabad and Dandi on the western coast of India, where he symbolically picked up salt on the shore in defiance of the government salt monopoly. He chose the issue to start a broader civil resistance campaign because the monopoly united Indians against imperial rule and was an issue unlikely to lead to violence among the protestors. The march attracted domestic and international press attention in a new way. His woman companion was Mrs Sarojini Naidu, a prominent nationalist and poet.

with some leverage over the regime might turn against it because of its actions. Regimes can also be financially vulnerable, particularly if civil resistance can dry up sources of internal revenue or external support, or if it costs the government an excessive amount to control. Perhaps most effectively civil resistance can test the potential fault lines of a regime's structures of rule and support. It can erode

the collaboration of key supporters in the wider society and the loyalty of employees, in civil functions of government or in essential security services. Or civil
resistance may probe uneasy relationships between different levels of government
with their distinct priorities, for example between central and local government,
or in colonial contexts between the metropolitan and the colonial government.

By the time Gandhi returned to India he had realized that civil resistance had to
be carefully tailored to particular situations, and to the weaknesses of specific
opponents. This probably lay behind his insistence that satyagraha was a 'science',
and that he was an experimental scientist, trying out different strategies of
resistance and using particular symbolic issues in different contexts. He was very
aware of the peculiar vulnerability of the British in India. This was an imperial
regime which was democratic at home, where British domestic public opinion was
always significant for the way in which India was ruled. As Indian taxpayers paid
for British rule, British domestic opinion did not have the leverage it would have
had if the British taxpayer had financed the Raj. Anti-imperialism was not yet a
strong theme in British political discourse, even in the Labour Party. But there was
a powerful Christian lobby in British politics and Anglican bishops could cause
embarrassment in the House of Lords over the treatment of this Mahatma; and
Gandhi played on his connections with Christian groups in British public life,
particularly when he visited England in 1931. Moreover, he knew that Britain's
main Western ally was anti-imperial, and he took the opportunity to broadcast to
the American public in 1931 and to welcome American journalists for interviews.

Far more significant for a Raj battling to deal with civil resistance and the new
political phenomenon of a leader dedicated to non-violence, was the fact that the
Raj rested on Indian foundations which might prove precarious. For example, by
the twentieth century, Indians worked within the Raj as civilian functionaries right
up to the level of the Indian Civil Service and the top of the judicial services; they
were the backbone of its police and armed forces; they were prepared to work
within the reformed provincial and central legislatures as well as the organs of local
self-government; they were informal collaborators of many kinds, such as landholders, village headmen, and the growing numbers of professionals in public life:
they were, finally, the many taxpayers who provided the government's revenues.
If a significant number of these groups withdrew their support and labour, then
the Raj would be in dire trouble—as Gandhi had recognized in his seminal
pamphlet, *Hind Swaraj* in 1909. He encouraged his compatriots to understand
how they had the fate of British rule in their own hands, and how by throwing off
fear they could deal with their rulers on their own terms. Nehru commented on
this new sense of courage and 'a kind of intoxication' which Gandhi gave his
generation. 'Above all, we had a sense of freedom and a pride in that freedom. The
old feeling of oppression and frustration was completely gone.'[11]

Gandhi's campaigns were designed to encourage varieties of withdrawal of
cooperation—including refusal to serve in the legislatures and law courts, to buy
legal alcohol and salt (which were both government monopolies) or foreign cloth

---

[11] Nehru, *An Autobiography*, 69.

(which gave reasons for British business to support the Raj), and ultimately refusal to pay land revenue. Combined with elaborated publicity in the form of meetings and processions, this was a brilliant strategy to undermine the practical and moral foundations of British power. It was high moral theatre and a politically astute attack on the collaborative bases of imperialism. Not surprisingly, the British recognized that Gandhi posed a completely new kind of challenge to them. They struggled to handle him and his movements in ways which would not alienate the large audience of Indians and foreign well-wishers, while at the same time they sought to shore up their collaborative networks.

Gandhi's campaigns of non-violent civil resistance in India aroused more support than any previous political movement in the subcontinent. Thousands went to prison willingly and stayed there to inconvenience the government. Many more attended meetings, participated in processions and myriad other types of symbolic and practical resistance available on the satyagraha menu. Even beyond those who were activists in some sense, there were probably millions of sympathetic bystanders. Despite this novel outpouring of fervour Gandhi's satyagrahas had very diverse results; and this enables us to make more nuanced judgements about what the 'success' or 'failure' of non-violent civil resistance might actually mean. His local satyagraha movements, as in 1917–18 and again in 1928, tended to be much more 'successful' in terms of achieving the desired socio-economic or political objective. The reasons for such success tended to be common ones: the objective was clear-cut and the opponent could actually grant it; often when the opponent was part of the government, such as a local official or a district or provincial regime, he could be pressured from higher up within the imperial structure by authorities with broader visions and priorities; moreover, satyagrahis in these situations tended to be small, homogeneous, and often kin groups, who were amenable to Gandhian discipline and could largely police themselves, ensuring that no destructive violence occurred which might blunt their non-violent pressure.

By contrast the pan-Indian movements were always far more diffuse in their support and consequently far more likely to contain groups with very different motivations and priorities, however tightly Gandhi might attempt to control the personnel and the objectives. In these continental movements there was often no direct and immediate link between non-violent civil resistance and a desired outcome, so in a strict sense they could be considered as 'failures'. However, these campaigns often provided an environment in which change occurred when civil resistance was combined with other factors which put pressure on the government. So in 1946 knowledge of the support generated by past pan-Indian satyagrahas, and apprehension of what pressure renewed civil resistance might put on the imperial regime and its collaborators, was a crucial part of the environment in which the British had to make decisions about when and how to leave India. As the Secretary of State wrote to the Viceroy in November 1946, His Majesty's government agreed that there could be no question of reimposing British rule on India, given that if that were to be done it would involve staying in India for a decade or more. 'We could not contemplate anything in the nature of re-conquest and retention of India by force against nationally organised

**Figure 3.3** Gandhi insisted that a civil resister must be prepared to negotiate with the opponent and to compromise on non-essentials. He built good relationships with two viceroys, Lord Irwin and then Lord Mountbatten, with whom he is seen here at the end of March 1947. The newly-appointed Mountbatten was anxious to work with Gandhi, whose support (or at least non-opposition) was crucial to his plan for the partition of India as part of a rapid end to the British Raj.

opposition, and quite apart from the desirability of such a decision we do not believe that it would be practicable from a political, military or economic point of view.' The Labour Party and international opinion would oppose such a policy; there were not the military forces 'to embark upon the holding down of India as a whole in the face of the frustrated nationalism which would under such circumstances sway the greater part of the population'. Moreover they could not afford the cost of such a prolonged and difficult 'effort of policing'.[12]

Such calculations took place against a backdrop of growing disorder in India, which became increasingly violent and along the fault lines of religious division. The appalling loss of life and displacement of millions of ordinary people at independence, when the country was partitioned as the only apparent solution to

[12] Pethick-Lawrence to Wavell, 25 Nov. 1946, *The Transfer of Power 1942–7*, vol. 9, 174. These arguments echoed those in a blunt note by Attlee (undated) in which he also indicated that such a policy of 'reconquest' would make Britain's position intolerable at the UN, and that he even doubted whether British troops (let alone Indian ones) would agree to act in such a situation: ibid. 68. On the long-term reasons for British withdrawal see above, n. 6.

the politicians' disagreements over the future, showed only too plainly the limits of satyagraha in India. Its non-violence had been precarious at the best of times, when there was a common opponent in the shape of the imperial rule: though as we noted earlier, Muslims had increasingly withdrawn from participation in Gandhi's movements. At the point of crisis, as the British were clearly departing, violence engulfed some areas of India, as compatriots turned on each other in fearful anticipation of the future of the subcontinent independent of British rule.

Civil resistance may have unintended but significant political repercussions, recognition of which may lead to a more subtle appreciation of what might constitute 'success' in the longer term. The Indian National Congress clearly benefited from its reputation as the major party of resistance to the imperial ruler in the elections of 1936–7 and 1946, except in the seats reserved for Muslims, thus becoming the natural party of power and successor to the imperial regime. Further, Gandhi's all-India campaigns proved to be a powerful bonding mechanism for several generations of politicians who inherited power in 1947, and worked for perhaps two decades to stabilize the new regime and to reinforce assumptions about the goals of the new nation state and appropriate standards of political behaviour. Participation in these non-violent struggles, and particularly imprisonment in the course of them, also became a recognized pathway to political influence and position. Having been a 'freedom fighter' was a major factor in any personal electoral campaign or bid for party office. In India's own self-imagining satyagraha took on an iconic quality: it became the hallmark of the nationalist movement. It thus took its place in the repertoire of political action in democratic India, often in ways which would have horrified Gandhi himself.[13]

Gandhi, of course, would not have judged the success or failure of satyagraha in political terms. His goal had been a deeper moral one—to generate such strength and moral vision among Indians that they would withdraw their compliance with British rule and build for themselves a profoundly changed social and political order. Post-independence India is certainly not Gandhian in its values and practices. However, the satyagraha movements and Gandhi's incessant pedagogical role have left their mark—not least in the changing position of women, and assumptions about social equality enshrined in the constitution and increasingly driving new social and political movements among the most deprived.

## CONCLUSION

The historical evidence of India's experience of non-violent civil resistance under the over-arching leadership of Mahatma Gandhi raises crucial issues about this

---

[13] For example, Gandhi himself was well aware of the dangers of fasting as part of civil resistance. This was a way of resistance taken up by later politicians who in extreme circumstances killed themselves in an attempt to put pressure on the government. An example occurred in 1952 when an old Gandhian worker fasted to death on the issue of creating an Andhra State for Telugu-speakers.

mode of conducting conflict. Perhaps above all it shows that this is a political strategy and technique which, for its outcomes, depends greatly on historical specificities—the nature of the opponent, the characteristics and beliefs of those who seek to use it, their relations with their clientele and with a wider domestic and international audience, and the encompassing ideological and political environment. Gandhi instinctively recognized much of what I have been arguing. He tailor-made his campaigns to use to best advantage the human and ideological material he had to hand and to put the greatest pressure on the particular opponent of the day. Tragically, however, when satyagraha seemed not 'to work' in the dire extremity of the war, he did not ask himself why this should be so except in morally judgemental terms—complaining that his compatriots neither understood what he had meant by satyagraha nor practised it. He himself devoted his few remaining years to individual moral work to combat violence and create new social institutions and relations. This stance helped him avoid thinking further about the implications of the apparent failure of civil resistance in India, so that he was unable to help refine it further as part of the range of human actions for dealing with circumstances of conflict.[14] He remains, as an individual, a worldwide icon and inspiration, a profoundly creative thinker and activist. But his actual historical experience in the context of British rule in India illustrates many of the ambiguities of that experience, as well as the sorts of circumstances in which civil resistance can be a creative form of public endeavour.

[14] My historian's assessment of Gandhi and the role of his satyagrahas contrasts starkly with much early Indian writing about the independence movement, when Gandhi was in a rather simple way portrayed as the Father of the Nation. By the later 20th century, historians in India had become far more analytical and often critical of Gandhi's leadership and his views on social and political issues. However, there remains a literature which sees him as making a profound and original contribution to human thought and action but which does not engage with the historical ambiguities of satyagraha. See Joan V. Bondurant, *Conquest of Violence: The Gandhian Philosophy of Conflict*, rev. edn. (Berkeley and Los Angeles: University of California Press, 1969); D. Dalton, *Mahatma Gandhi: Nonviolent Power in Action* (New York: Columbia University Press, 1993).

# 4

## The US Civil Rights Movement: Power from Below and Above, 1945–70

*Doug McAdam*

African-American resistance to the various forms of servitude and discrimination imposed on them has been a constant of the American experience. This chapter looks at only the largest and most sustained mass movement on behalf of African-Americans to arise since blacks were first forcibly transported to American shores in the early seventeenth century. The focus of the inquiry is the US civil rights movement, starting with the onset of the Montgomery Bus Boycott in December 1955 and extending until the end of the 1960s. Since the discernible shift in federal civil rights policy that took place immediately following the Second World War is critical to an understanding of the rise of the movement, however, the historical period of interest is really 1945–70. The central question addressed here is: did the success of the movement depend primarily on the strength and resourcefulness—especially tactical resourcefulness—of civil rights forces or on changes in the broader political environment that granted decisive new leverage to the movement? A more fine-grained answer to the question will come at the end of the chapter; suffice it to say here that both factors were critically important in shaping the emergence and subsequent development of the struggle. Although the focus is on the longer period, 1945–70, the next section will be devoted to a broad brush stroke history of the mass movement years, leaving the all important period of 'state contention' over race (1945–54) for the section that follows.

### THE MOVEMENT, 1955–70

Though there were prior events that could plausibly be seen as marking the beginning of the movement, the acknowledged catalyst for the struggle was the 1955–6 Montgomery Bus Boycott. The precipitating event which triggered the boycott was the arrest of Rosa Parks on Thursday 1 December 1955 for violating Montgomery's ordinance mandating segregated seating on the city's municipal bus line. Parks's refusal to give up her seat to a white man who had just boarded the bus led, not only to her arrest, but to quick calls for a one-day boycott of city buses the following Monday (5 December) to protest against the arrest.

The rest of the story is well known. Elated at the success of the one-day protest, the decision was made to extend the boycott indefinitely. Leadership of the burgeoning movement was thrust upon a young Baptist minister, Martin Luther King, Jr, who had only recently moved to Montgomery. Under King's skilful leadership, the boycott was sustained for nearly a year, until the US Supreme Court upheld a lower court decision declaring Montgomery's segregated seating ordinance unconstitutional. With this victory, the movement was born.

The years immediately following Montgomery, however, were lean ones for the movement. The late 1950s saw the rise of 'massive resistance' within the South in response to the threat of 'the second Reconstruction'. State legislatures in the Deep South outlawed chapters of the National Association for the Advancement of Colored People (NAACP), the nation's largest civil rights organization, and enacted a flood of other segregationist bills. White Citizen Councils were formed in Mississippi to augment the work of the Ku Klux Klan in defending 'the southern way of life'. In truth, as the 1960s dawned, the movement was largely moribund.

It was the 1960 sit-in campaign that revitalized the broader struggle. Sparked by the initial sit-in in Greensboro, North Carolina on 1 February 1960, the movement spread like wildfire, encompassing the entire South (except for Mississippi) by the middle of March. Revitalized by the sit-ins, the civil rights movement entered its heyday. The period 1960–5 was marked by high levels of sustained activity, a succession of innovative tactics, and a functional division of labour involving the so-called 'Big 5' civil rights organizations. The two oldest organizations, the Urban League and NAACP, brought institutional connections, money, and legal expertise. The Southern Christian Leadership Conference (SCLC) had King's unparalleled visibility and a network of strong church-based affiliates throughout the South. Finally the Student Non-violent Coordinating Committee (SNCC) and the Congress of Racial Equality (CORE) infused the movement with tactical daring and an increasingly radical view of the 'race issue'. The period also saw a string of stunning legislative and legal victories that effectively dismantled legal segregation in the South.

The year 1965 marked a turning point in the development of the movement. With the passage of the landmark Voting Rights Act in August, the electoral underpinnings of the southern system were finally removed, paving the way for the re-democratization of voting rights in the region. Later that same month, the Watts section of Los Angeles exploded in the first major 'urban disorder' of the period. These two events symbolized the movement's great achievements in the South and the formidable challenges it would face as it sought to respond to the very different face of racism in the North. King's response to these challenges was his 1966 'open housing' campaign in Chicago. Met by angry suburban mobs, and rebuffed by the same liberals who supported his efforts in the South, King's campaign met only with stalemate. In the same year, Stokely Carmichael issued his famous call for 'black power' on a protest march through Mississippi, electrifying many young blacks and terrifying much of white America.

The late 1960s brought more of the same: stalemate in northern campaigns, a string of 'long hot summers' in America's urban black neighbourhoods, increasingly radical rhetoric in SNCC and CORE and the rise of northern home-grown black power groups, including the Black Panther Party in Oakland, California. Vietnam eclipsed civil rights as the nation's number one public issue, and the initial ameliorative response to the riots gradually gave way to a more repressive, law enforcement stance.[1] Two hugely significant events in 1968 signalled the beginning of the end of the movement. In April King was assassinated in Memphis, Tennessee, where he had gone to aid striking sanitation workers. Then in November, Richard Nixon was elected President, running on what he explicitly called his 'southern strategy'. Recognizing that the Democrats' support for civil rights had alienated white southerners—previously the most loyal of Democrats—Nixon gambled that he would be able to draw many of these 'Dixiecrats' into the Republican fold. He was right, ushering in the period of Republican dominance that lasted from 1968 until Obama's victory forty years later, and foreclosing the kind of institutional influence that moderate civil rights leaders had enjoyed with Kennedy and Johnson. With no electoral debt to blacks, Nixon (and later Republican presidents) was largely free to ignore the interests of African-Americans. Reflecting this lack of leverage, and deep divisions within the black community over the proper course of the struggle, the traditional civil rights movement wound down quickly in the late 1960s/early 70s, even as forms of black power and black nationalist activity flourished in urban America.[2]

## ON THE ORIGIN OF SOCIAL MOVEMENTS: TOP DOWN OR BOTTOM UP?

The scholarship on social movements, revolutions, and other forms of contentious politics is a bit schizophrenic when it comes to the origins of such struggles. Many observers have noted the critical importance of broad processes of change in the external political environment: when these disrupt previously stable social and political relations, they help to set in motion episodes of popular contention. Work on comparative revolutions has identified external wars or more generic economic and/or demographic strains as the usual precipitants of the kinds of state crises that normally precede revolution.[3] Scholars of ethnic conflict have also generally pinpointed a mix of demographic and economic change processes as the backdrop against which episodes of ethnic conflict and violence have taken

[1] Doug McAdam, *Political Process and the Development of Black Insurgency, 1930–1970*, 2nd edn. (Chicago: University of Chicago Press, 1999), ch. 8.

[2] William L. Van Deburg, *New Day in Babylon* (Chicago: University of Chicago Press, 1992).

[3] See Theda Skocpol, *States and Social Revolutions* (New York: Cambridge University Press, 1979) and Jack Goldstone, *Revolution and Rebellion in the Early Modern World* (Berkeley: University of California Press, 1991) respectively.

place.[4] Finally, social movement scholars have privileged one kind of environ-mental change process—'expanding political opportunities'—over all others as the proximate cause of successful mass movements.[5] And what do they mean by 'political opportunities'? 'Any event or broad social process that serves to under-mine the calculations and assumptions on which the political establishment is structured occasions a shift in political opportunities. Among the events and processes likely to prove disruptive of the political status quo are wars, industri-alization, [changes in] international political alignments, prolonged [economic problems], and widespread demographic changes.'[6]

In sharp contrast to the 'external', or environmental, focus of the aforemen-tioned literatures is the 'movement-centric' emphasis one typically finds in much of the recent scholarship on contentious politics. Two literatures, in particular, tend to embrace this perspective. With its emphasis on 'framing processes', 'strategies and tactics', 'resource mobilization', and the like, the social movement literature often tends to ignore environmental processes in favour of an emphasis on the decisions made by insurgents. This implicitly locates the source of change within the movement itself.

So too does much of the narrower literature on 'non-violence' and 'non-violent' action.[7] The suggestion in much of this literature is that adherence to non-violent principles confers great strategic advantage on those movements that adopt such tactics. In the extreme, work in this tradition implies that, through the tactical (and normative) choices they make, insurgents control their own fate. Environmental influences are elided in favour of an emphasis on internal move-ment processes.

My own view is that both of these distinct emphases within the various scholarly literatures capture an essential truth about contentious politics. Under stable environmental conditions, established regimes are exceedingly hard to challenge, let alone dislodge. Substantial movements typically benefit from prior, destabiliz-ing change processes that weaken regimes and render them more vulnerable or receptive to challenge. But this is not to posit a simple environmental determinism in the case of successful movements. Successful movements depend critically on the capacity of insurgents to recognize and exploit the opportunities afforded them by environmental change processes. Indeed, it is often impossible to clearly distinguish 'external' changes from the 'internal' movement efforts to exploit these

[4] Susan Olzak, *The Dynamics of Ethnic Competition and Conflict* (Stanford: Stanford University Press, 1992).

[5] McAdam, *Political Process*; Sidney Tarrow, *Power in Movement*, 2nd edn. (New York: Cambridge University Press, 1998); Charles Tilly, *From Mobilization to Revolution* (Reading, Mass.: Addison-Wesley, 1978).

[6] McAdam, *Political Process*, 41.

[7] Peter Ackerman and Jack DuVall, *A Force More Powerful: A Century of Nonviolent Conflict* (New York: St Martin's Press, 2000); Ronald Bleiker, *Popular Dissent, Human Agency, and Global Politics* (Cambridge: Cambridge University Press, 2000); Kurt Schock, *Unarmed Insurrections: People Power Movements in Non-Democracies* (Minneapolis: University of Minnesota Press, 2005); Gene Sharp, *The Politics of Nonviolent Action* (Boston: Porter Sargent, 1973).

changes. This more complex reciprocal dynamic was very much in evidence in the case of the US civil rights movement.


## THE MOVEMENT FROM ABOVE

To fully appreciate the significance of the destabilizing changes visited on America's racial status quo, especially following the Second World War, it is worth revisiting the stable federal/southern 'understanding' on race that held for nearly seventy-five years following the end of Reconstruction in 1876.

With the withdrawal of federal troops from the southern United States in 1876, control over southern race relations again passed into the hands of the region's political and economic elite. Predictably this reassertion of regional control over racial matters spelled the end of whatever political influence blacks had been able to exercise during Reconstruction. Despite growing strains, this 'arrangement' held until the end of the Second World War, reflecting the continuing viability of the political calculus that had given rise to it. But as Gunnar Myrdal remarked with great foresight in 1944, the arrangement never constituted a 'stable power equilibrium' and appeared at last to 'be approaching its end'.[8] Specifically, it was a series of broad change processes occurring roughly in the quarter-century 1930–54 that served to undermine the political economy of racial segregation in the southern United States. Together these processes encouraged the development of the movement by profoundly altering the 'structure of political opportunities' confronting civil rights forces.

The first cracks in the system were the product of domestic change processes, stemming from the gradual decline of the cotton economy in 1920–50. So long as cotton remained one of the central pillars of the American economy, a certain consistency of interest prevailed between the southern and northern political and economic elite. However, as early as 1915 and especially after 1930, several factors conspired to undermine the pre-eminence of 'King Cotton' and the confluence of material/political interests on which the Jim Crow system had been structured.

Among the factors weakening the cotton economy were increased competition from foreign cotton producers, the development of synthetic fibres, several boll weevil epidemics, and the collapse of the cotton market at the outset of the Depression.[9] When combined with the expanding northern demand for cheap southern labour following the cut-off of European immigration in 1920, these factors conspired to undermine the material base upon which the South's political control over 'the Negro question' had been based.

It wasn't simply the decline of King Cotton, however, that undermined the system, but other change processes set in motion by the gradual weakening of

---

[8] Gunnar Myrdal, 'America Again at the Crossroads', in Richard P. Young (ed.), *Roots of Rebellion: The Evolution of Black Politics and Protest Since World War II* (New York: Harper & Row, 1970), 35.

[9] McAdam, *Political Process*, 73–7.

the cotton economy. None of these 'other' processes was as important as the mass migration of blacks out of the South in 1910–50. In these years, some five million African-Americans (and countless poor whites) left the South. This mass exodus had major political consequences. The migrants were drawn disproportionately from states with the lowest percentage of registered black voters. So this was not so much a general migration from the South as a selective move from those areas where the political participation of African-Americans was most severely limited.

The political significance of the 'Great Migration' becomes that much clearer when we look, not just at the states migrants left, but the ones to which they moved. Nearly 90 per cent of all black out-migrants from the South in these years settled in seven key northern (or western) industrial states: New York, New Jersey, Pennsylvania, Ohio, California, Illinois, and Michigan. The electoral significance of these seven states was already well established. As William Brink and Louis Harris noted in 1963, 'no candidate for President in modern times has won without taking a substantial share of the big seven.'[10] It was the selective move to these seven states that cemented the growing political significance of the so-called 'black vote'.

By 1930 the political effects of the migration were already apparent. In that year, the NAACP, in what the *Christian Science Monitor* termed 'the first national demonstration of the Negro's power since reconstruction days', joined with other groups to block Senate confirmation of President Herbert Hoover's Supreme Court nominee, John J. Parker. These demonstrations of political influence, coupled with the continuing flow of migrants northward, had, by 1936, firmly established African-Americans as an increasingly significant electoral force. The outcome of the 1936 presidential contest only enhanced the significance of the 'black vote' by decisively shifting the electoral loyalties of most African-American voters. Up to 1936, black voters remained intensely loyal to the Republican Party, the party of Lincoln. But President Roosevelt's New Deal policies motivated most black voters to shift their party allegiance and to align themselves with the Democrats. This surprising realignment made the 'black vote' seem more volatile, thereby encouraging more party competition for the growing number of black voters.

For all the importance of these domestic changes, however, the decisive rupture of the federal/southern alignment on race came after the Second World War as a result of *international* political pressures. While the decline of King Cotton and the Great Migration certainly altered the context of racial politics in the US, it was the onset of the Cold War that changed it decisively. Consider the stark contrast in the actions of two US presidents, Roosevelt and Truman, on the matter of the 'Negro question'. In 1936 Roosevelt was elected to his second term. His margin of victory remains one of the largest in the history of US presidential politics. Roosevelt would be re-elected two more times, making him the only US president in history to serve more than two terms. He was, in short, as close to being

---

[10] William Brink and Louis Harris, *The Negro Revolution in America* (New York: Simon & Schuster, 1963), 80.

invulnerable in electoral terms as any president in American history. His New Deal reforms had been accompanied by a general leftward drift in political attitudes and had conditioned the American people to countenance assertive government action on behalf of the 'less fortunate' segments of American society. Finally, Roosevelt was himself a liberal—socially no less than politically—as was his outspoken and influential wife, Eleanor, and most other key members of his administration. Yet, in spite of all these factors, Roosevelt remained resolutely silent on racial matters throughout his four-term presidency, refusing even to come out in favour of anti-lynching legislation on the numerous occasions when such bills were brought to Congress in 1932–45.

In 1946, however, just a year after Roosevelt's death in office, his successor, Harry Truman, inaugurated a period of executive advocacy of civil rights reform when he appointed his Committee on Civil Rights and charged it with investigating the 'current remedies of civil rights in the country and recommending appropriate legislative remedies for deficiencies uncovered'.[11] Two years later, in 1948, Truman issued two landmark Executive Orders, the first establishing a fair employment board within the Civil Service Commission, and the second calling for the gradual desegregation of the armed forces. Why did Truman act when Roosevelt had not? Comparing the domestic political contexts in which FDR and Truman acted only deepens the puzzle. While Roosevelt's electoral margins left him politically secure, the fact that Truman had not been elected to office made him uniquely vulnerable to challenge as he headed into the 1948 election. Moreover, with black voters now returning solid majorities for his party, Truman had seemingly little to gain and everything to lose by alienating southern 'Dixiecrats'. And that, of course, is precisely what his advocacy of civil rights reform did. Angered by his proactive support for civil rights, southern Democrats broke with the national party in 1948 and ran their own candidate, Strom Thurmond, for president. The electoral votes of the once 'solid' South were now in jeopardy. Considering also Truman's own upbringing and attitudinal qualms about race,[12] and the 'chilling effect' the Cold War had on the American Left, one could hardly think of a less likely candidate and less propitious time to be advocating for the socially and politically progressive cause of civil rights reform.

The otherwise puzzling contrast between Truman's actions and Roosevelt's inaction, however, becomes entirely comprehensible when placed in the very different international contexts in which they occurred. The post-war world that confronted Truman exposed the US to two unprecedented sources of pressure regarding its treatment of African-Americans. One, ironically, was the anti-racist ideology the allies had espoused in waging war against the Axis powers, and which, following the conflict, was institutionalized in the founding of the UN. While all the allies had long been identified with egalitarian principles, the war effort and the boost it gave to the post-war stress on global human rights forced

---

[11] Quoted in McAdam, *Political Process*, 84.
[12] See David McCullough, *Truman* (New York: Simon & Schuster, 1992).

France, Great Britain, and the US to more scrupulously conform to these principles. For France and Britain this meant decolonization; for the US, civil rights reform.

The second source of pressure came courtesy of the Cold War. The onset of the Cold War effectively terminated the isolationist foreign policy that had, since the First World War, defined America's relationship to the rest of the world. As a result, national political leaders—especially the president—found themselves exposed to international political pressures and considerations their predecessors had been spared. Recent work by Mary L. Dudziak and Azza Salama Layton, among others, has greatly enhanced our understanding of this period by documenting the rising tide of international criticism directed at the US—by allies and non-aligned countries as well as the Soviet bloc—during the Cold War period.[13] Locked in an intense ideological struggle with the Soviet Union for influence around the world—and especially with emerging Third World nations—American racism suddenly took on international significance as an effective propaganda weapon of the communists. Viewed in this light, Truman's civil rights initiatives should be seen for what they were: not so much domestic reform efforts as a component of his Cold War foreign policy.

By the late 1940s, then, this mix of domestic and international change processes had re-nationalized the issue of race in the US and granted to civil rights forces new leverage with which to press their claims. Still it remained for those forces to recognize and exploit the opportunities these emerging political realities afforded them.

## THE MOVEMENT FROM BELOW

So was the civil rights revolution simply a product of these broader environmental shifts? No, as noted at the outset of the chapter, successful movements normally reflect a combination of favourable environmental changes and the creative efforts of activists to recognize, exploit, and indeed, *expand* the political opportunities afforded them by broader change processes. The US civil rights movement represents a textbook case of this interactive dynamic. In this sense, the extraordinary string of civil rights victories achieved in the 1950s and 1960s (and beyond) has to be accounted as owing at least as much to the creativity and courage of movement forces as to favourable environmental circumstances.

It would be impossible to identify the myriad contributions grass roots leaders and activists made to the broader civil rights revolution. Here we simply highlight two general dynamics that reflect the critical role the movement played in pushing the revolution forward.

[13] Mary L. Dudziak, *Cold War Civil Rights: Race and the Image of American Democracy* (Princeton: Princeton University Press, 2000); Azza Salama Layton, *International Politics and Civil Rights Policies in the United States, 1941–1960* (New York: Cambridge University Press, 2000).

## The social construction of political opportunity

Too often the concept of 'political opportunity' has been rendered in objective terms, as if the meaning and significance of environmental changes are transparent. They rarely are. 'While important, expanding political opportunities.... do not, in any simple sense, produce a social movement.... [t]hey only offer insurgents a certain objective "structural potential" for collective action. Mediating between opportunity and action are people and the subjective meanings they attach to their situations.'[14]

Though its significance has rarely been noted by analysts, the evidence of this creative construction/exploitation of 'opportunities' by civil rights activists is everywhere apparent in the history of the movement. It has, for example, been common for movement historians to highlight the crucial role played by an increasingly sympathetic Supreme Court in the unfolding civil rights revolution. What is less often noted is that the string of landmark rulings returned by the court after, say, 1940—culminating in *Brown* v. *Board of Education* in 1954—were the product of a carefully orchestrated legal campaign by the NAACP, who discerned in Roosevelt's court appointments a real opportunity to achieve major judicial victories.[15]

There are many other examples of this strategic interpretive work in the early history of the emerging civil rights movement. In 1941, the great civil rights leader, A. Philip Randolph, saw in President Roosevelt's increasingly strident criticism of the Nazi's 'master race' ideology a unique opportunity to press for changes in hiring in the government sponsored defence industry. Highlighting the blatant contradiction between racist hiring practices and Roosevelt's noble rhetoric, Randolph called for a July march on Washington to protest employment discrimination based on race. Faced with this embarrassing prospect, in the end Roosevelt reluctantly agreed to create a Fair Employment Practices Commission to investigate charges of discriminatory hiring in wartime employment.

Finally, US civil rights leaders were relentless in exploiting the new 'framing' opportunities afforded them by the Cold War.[16] By drawing a stark parallel between Jim Crow policies in the US and the suppression of freedom in the Soviet bloc, established leaders sought to prod a reluctant federal establishment into action by framing civil rights reform as a tool in America's struggle against communism. It was in this spirit that the NAACP attorney, Charles Houston, argued, in 1950, that 'a national policy of the US which permits disfranchisement of coloured people in the South is just as much an international issue as the

---

[14] McAdam, *Political Process*, 48.

[15] Jack Greenberg, 'The Supreme Court, Civil Rights and Civil Dissonance', *Yale Law Journal*, 77, no. 8 (1968), 1520–44; Richard Kluger, *Simple Justice* (New York: Knopf, 1976); Genna Rae McNeil, *Groundwork: Charles Hamilton Houston and the Struggle for Civil Rights* (Philadelphia: University of Pennsylvania Press, 1983).

[16] See Dudziak, *Cold War Civil Rights*, and Layton, *International Politics and Civil Rights Policies*.

question of free elections in Poland.'[17] In short, the 'political opportunities' that helped set the movement in motion were at least as much a product of the concrete efforts of civil rights leaders to exploit environmental shifts as they were the result of the changes themselves.

## Breaking the stalemate: the strategic genius of the civil rights movement

Without discounting the broad change processes that set the stage for the mass civil rights movement, it is important to recognize just how little things had changed on the eve of the movement. The broad environmental shifts noted above may have rendered the racial status quo more vulnerable to challenge, but significant change awaited the rise and active efforts of the movement.

To fully appreciate the daunting challenge that confronted the embryonic movement, we have to understand the depths of black powerlessness on the eve of the struggle. In 1950, two-thirds of all African-Americans continued to live in the southern United States. Yet, through a combination of legal subterfuge and extralegal intimidation, blacks were effectively barred from political participation in the region. Less than 20 per cent of all voting age blacks were even registered to vote in 1950. In the Deep South, the figure was many times lower.

Nor on the eve of the movement were there any signs of cracks in the 'solid South' or any diminution in the will of the region's political and economic elite to maintain 'the southern way of life'. On the contrary, the 1954 Supreme Court decision in *Brown* v. *Board of Education* set in motion a regional 'resistance movement' aimed at preserving white supremacy at all costs. Thus, on the eve of the movement, southern blacks remained barred from institutional politics and deprived of any real leverage within the region. If change were to come, it would have to be imposed from without. This, of course, meant intervention by the federal government. But with a Republican, Dwight Eisenhower, in the White House and southern Democrats exercising veto power in Congress, the movement faced a strategic stalemate at the national level as well. To break the stalemate, the movement would have to find a way of pressuring a reluctant federal government to intervene more forcefully in the South. The strategic genius of the movement was to develop and refine an aggressive 'politics of moral suasion' that in 1954–65 was responsible for most of the significant victories that it achieved. At the heart of this strategy was an interactive dynamic involving the movement, the national media, segregationists, and federal officials.

Lacking sufficient power to defeat the segregationists at the state or local level, movement forces sought to broaden the conflict by inducing their opponents to disrupt public order to the point where sympathetic media coverage and broad public support—international no less than domestic—for the movement could be mobilized. In turn, the media coverage and public support virtually compelled

[17] McNeil, *Groundwork*, 198.

federal officials to intervene in ways supportive of the movement. This last point is worth highlighting, for it helps to illustrate the complex relationship between institutional and movement politics that shapes non-violent struggles. Had the federal government remained committed to its earlier 'hands off' policy concerning southern race relations, the movement would almost certainly have lacked the leverage to compel meaningful change. Only when one set of government actors—federal officials in the executive branch—was willing to oppose another—southern elected officials—were civil rights forces granted the strategic opening they needed to leverage the great gains of the 1950s and 1960s.

Obviously, this dynamic involved an element of conscious provocation on the part of movement forces. This provocation, in turn, implies a level of tactical awareness and command on the part of insurgents that is consistent with the argument advanced here. Regardless of how favourable the broader environmental context may be, the actual pace of contention depends, overwhelmingly, on the ability of movement groups to accurately gauge the interests and likely responses of other parties to the conflict, and to then orchestrate a campaign designed to exploit these preferences.

To a greater or lesser extent, all of the major campaigns in the civil rights movement—the sit-ins, Freedom Rides, Birmingham, Freedom Summer, Selma—reflect this characteristic dynamic. But no group in the movement mastered this dynamic and exploited its possibilities more skilfully than the Southern Christian Leadership Conference (SCLC) and its leader, Martin Luther King, Jr.

Arguably the best example of King's tactical genius is his 1963 campaign in Birmingham, Alabama. In April of that year, the SCLC launched a city-wide campaign of civil disobedience aimed at desegregating Birmingham's public facilities. But why, among all southern cities, was Birmingham targeted? The answer would seem to bespeak a keen awareness of the strategic dynamic sketched above. As a chronicler of the events in Birmingham notes, 'King's Birmingham innovation was pre-eminently strategic. Its essence was . . . the selection of a target city which has as its Commissioner of Public Safety, "Bull" Connor, a notorious racist and hothead who could be depended on *not* to respond non-violently.'[18]

The view that King's choice of Birmingham was a conscious, strategic one is supported by the fact that Connor was a lame-duck official, having been defeated by a moderate in a run-off election in early April 1963. Had the SCLC waited to launch their campaign until after the moderate took office, there likely would have been considerably less violence *and* less press coverage as well. 'The supposition has to be that . . . SCLC, in a shrewd . . . stratagem, knew a good enemy when they saw him . . . one who could be counted on in stupidity and natural viciousness to play into their hands, for full exploitation in the press as archfiend and villain.'[19]

---

[18] Howard Hubbard, 'Five Long Hot Summers and How They Grew', *Public Interest*, no. 12 (Summer 1968), 5; emphasis in original.

[19] Pat Watters, *Down to Now: Reflections on the Southern Civil Rights Movement* (New York: Pantheon Books, 1971), 266.

©AP Images/PAPhotos

**Figure 4.1** Violence against demonstrators. On 3 May 1963, after two days of uncharacteristic restraint, 'Bull' Connor, the Commissioner of Public Safety in Birmingham, Alabama, used police dogs and water cannons against peaceful civil rights demonstrators. This generated worldwide outrage and gave Martin Luther King one of his most important strategic victories.

In the following passage from his 1963 book, *Why We Can't Wait*, King all but acknowledges the conscious intent of the Birmingham strategy. In describing the planning for the Birmingham campaign, King notes the 'lessons' that had been learned from an earlier, 'failed' campaign in Albany, Georgia. In Albany, SCLC used much the same tactics as in Birmingham. The difference was that Albany police chief, Laurie Pritchett, responded to King's tactics with mass arrests but without the violence and disruptions of public order so critical to sustained media attention. The result was little media attention, a lack of public awareness and no federal response. In his book King offers the following reflections on Albany:

> There were weaknesses in Albany, and a share of the responsibility belongs to each of us who participated. However, none of us was so immodest as to feel himself master of the new theory. Each of us expected that setbacks would be a part of the ongoing effort... Human beings with all their faults and strengths constitute the mechanism of a social movement. *They must make mistakes and learn from them, make more mistakes and learn anew. They must taste defeat as*

*well as success, and discover how to live with each. Time and action are the teachers.*
*When we planned our strategy for Birmingham months later, we spent hours*
*assessing Albany and trying to learn from its errors.*[20] (My italics.)

The implication of King's reflection is that a fuller understanding of the dynamic under discussion here was born of events in Albany. Without a doubt, a part of this fuller understanding was a growing awareness of the importance of segregationist violence as a stimulus to increased media attention, public support, and the all important federal intervention.

King and SCLC had learned their lessons well. After several days of uncharacteristic restraint, Connor trained fire hoses and unleashed attack dogs on peaceful demonstrators. The resulting scenes of demonstrators being slammed into storefronts by the force of the hoses and attacked by snarling police dogs were picked up and broadcast nationwide on the nightly news. Photographs of the same events appeared in newspapers and magazines throughout the nation and the world. The Soviet Union used the pictures as anti-American propaganda at home and abroad. Thus the media's coverage of the events in Birmingham succeeded in generating enormous public sympathy for the demonstrators and putting increased pressure on federal officials to intervene on behalf of the movement. The result was presidential sponsorship of a civil rights bill that, even in a much weaker form, had been described as not viable by the administration just prior to the events in Birmingham. Under continuous pressure by movement forces, the bill was ultimately signed into law a year later as the landmark Civil Rights Act of 1964.

In short, by successfully courting violence while restraining violence in his followers, King and SCLC were able to frame events in Birmingham as highly dramatic confrontations between a 'good' movement and an 'evil' system. The movement's dominant religious ideology granted this interpretation all the more credibility and resonance. The stark, highly dramatic nature of this ritualized confrontation proved irresistible to the media and, in turn, to audiences at home and abroad.

There is, of course, a wonderful irony in all of this that was not lost on the parties to the conflict. By successfully staging and framing action in this way, the movement was able to take the segregationists' ultimate weapon—violence and the threat of violence—and transform it into a liability. In so doing, they effectively broke the terror on which the system ultimately depended. In effect, any response on the part of the supremacists furthered the aims of the movement. Restraint, as in Albany, may have denied the movement its immediate need for media coverage, but it also lessened black vulnerability to, and fear of, racist violence. On the other hand, celebrated instances of violence generated media coverage, public outrage, and increased pressure for remedial federal action. In his own way, President Kennedy acknowledged the dynamic under discussion here when he offered the following ironic 'tribute' to Bull Connor. In a remark to

---

[20] Martin Luther King, Jr, *Why We Can't Wait* (New York: Harper & Row, 1963), 34–5; emphasis added.

**Figure 4.2** The chances and pitfalls of negotiation. From second left to right, front row: Martin Luther King, US Attorney General Robert F. Kennedy, Roy Wilkins of the NAACP, and US Vice-President Lyndon B. Johnson outside the White House, where they had a discussion with President Kennedy, 22 June 1963. King's ability to stage demonstrations in the South that garnered worldwide attention had gained him access in Washington. At the meeting President Kennedy questioned the wisdom of holding the planned March on Washington as it might jeopardize the passage of civil rights legislation through Congress.

Martin Luther King, Kennedy said: 'our judgement of Bull Connor should not be too harsh. After all, in his own way, he has done a good deal for civil rights legislation this year.'[21] In orchestrating the dynamic that invited overreaction from Connor and put increasing political pressure on Kennedy, it was the 'movement from below' that dictated the overall pace and specific outcomes of the civil rights revolution.

Having acknowledged the causal importance of mass mobilization in the case of the civil rights movement, it is important to reiterate the critical significance of the facilitative environmental changes that birthed the movement in the first place. There is a broader implication here. Most movements develop in the context of broader episodes of contention, involving other sets of actors. We truncate our understanding of these episodes when we focus only or primarily on the movement itself.

When applied to the broader conflict over race in post-war America, the important implication of this perspective is that analysts have long erred in seeing the Montgomery Bus Boycott as the beginning of the struggle. Given the critical importance of the Cold War to that struggle, it is more accurate to say that the broader episode of contention began soon after the close of the Second World War and certainly by the time of the Dixiecrat revolt in 1948. Montgomery then represents a crucial escalation of the conflict, but not its genesis. Indeed, rather than Montgomery making the movement, actually the reverse is true. It was the prior onset of the *national* conflict that granted the *local* struggle in Montgomery so much significance. Without its embedding in this broader national episode of contention, it is not at all clear that Montgomery would have had the kind of impact it did or that the key actors in the local struggle would have behaved in the same manner. In short, it was the *re-nationalization* of race in post-war America that transformed Montgomery from the kind of localized racial conflict that had been going on for years in the US to a movement of national—indeed, inter-national—significance.

## FINAL THOUGHTS: ON THE COMPLICATED LEGACY OF THE US CIVIL RIGHTS MOVEMENT

This chapter has addressed the question of how to explain the degree of success of the US civil rights movement, and in particular whether its achievements were due to the effectiveness of its organization and actions, or to special features of the national and international political environment in which it operated. The answer is that both were of crucial importance, and resonated with each other. In concluding the chapter, however, I cannot resist offering some final thoughts on another question: What are the movement's legacies?

[21] King, *Why We Can't Wait*, 144.

The canonical view holds that the movement was one of the most successful in US history and, indeed, one of the most influential worldwide. The international significance of the movement is beyond question, but the domestic legacy of the civil rights struggle is actually far more complicated than the popular narrative account would suggest. Obviously, the movement deserves credit for any number of domestic achievements. These include:

- the decisive end of 'Jim Crow' and its elaborate system of racial caste restrictions;
- the abolition of legal segregation in the US;
- the re-establishment of voting rights in the southern states;
- a dramatic reduction in the risk, to blacks, of extralegal white violence;
- a significant expansion in educational and employment opportunities for African-Americans.

These outcomes represent an extraordinary litany of gains for which the movement has been widely and justly praised. It is worth considering, however, the issue of movement failure. It is not far-fetched to argue that the movement has had a number of deleterious effects on the prospects for racial justice in

**Figure 4.3** Speaking truth to power. Martin Luther King at the huge March in Washington, 28 August 1963, during which he gave his 'I have a dream' speech. The next year the Congress passed the 1964 Civil Rights Act, removing certain barriers to racial equality. The Voting Rights Act followed in 1965.

America. Space constraints limit us to a discussion of only one especially damaging—if unintended—consequence of the movement.

Ironically, this particular outcome is directly linked to one of the movement's proudest accomplishments: the re-establishment of black voting rights in the South. The irony is that the restoration of these rights triggered a significant electoral realignment in the US that wound up dramatically reducing the political leverage available to civil rights forces and, indeed, ushered in the forty years of conservative Republican dominance that appears only now to be ending in America. How did this happen?

With the passage of the 1965 Voting Rights Act, the trickle of blacks who had tried to vote in the early 1960s turned into a flood. Overwhelmingly the new black voters registered as Democrats, prompting many a die-hard 'Dixiecrat' to reconsider his previous aversion to the Republican Party (e.g. 'the party of Lincoln'). Richard Nixon was the first to recognize the electoral significance of this wholesale white abandonment of the Democratic Party in the south. Running on his 'southern strategy,' Nixon prevailed in 1968 by claiming many of the electoral votes of the once 'solid (Democratic) south'. In doing so, he effectively dismantled the 'New Deal Coalition' that had allowed the liberal wing of the Democratic Party to dominate presidential politics in 1932–68 and set the stage for the rise of viable Republican Party organizations throughout the former Confederacy. George W. Bush is only the most recent beneficiary of this unintended and unexpected electoral revolution.

The social and political consequences that have followed from this electoral shift are too numerous to go into here, but they include: the wholesale assault on all manner of social programmes; the rise of the Christian right; growing opposition to affirmative action; and the exacerbation of class and racial tensions in the US. The civil rights movement cannot, of course, be blamed for these ironic outcomes, but there is a link between the re-establishment of black voting rights and the sequence of events described here. Admiration for any given movement should never blind us to the longer-term, and often unintended, consequences that follow from it.

# 5

## The Interplay of Non-violent and Violent Action in Northern Ireland, 1967–72

*Richard English*

Tommy McKearney joined the Irish Republican Army (IRA) in 1971, partly as a result of his own reading of the 1960s Northern Ireland civil rights episode, and of what he held that episode to demonstrate about the logic of Irish politics. 'Now, rightly or wrongly', McKearney told me in interview:

> I grew up with a clear perception of discrimination practised by the state against myself as part of a community. And it wasn't the type of discrimination that would be excessive in terms of, perhaps, the South African situation or some of the obscenities that are performed in south America. But there was a very, very real, tangible perception, and I would argue that it was more than a perception. . . . There was a clear perception that a very basic demand had been made for simple fair treatment and [that] it was met with the coercive end of the state rather than anything else. . . . There was an accumulation of evidence to say to me that, really, the six-county area [of Northern Ireland] is irreformable: we cannot change it.[1]

This valuably identifies the central relationship lying at the heart of this case study: the relationship between the 1960s civil rights movement (which relied on civil resistance as its chosen method of struggle) and the subsequent (and partly consequent) emergence of political violence in Northern Ireland (also called Ulster).[2] The IRA that McKearney joined thought violence to be necessary, and duly became the major agent of killing within the conflict.[3]

I am grateful to those who engaged with my arguments when a version of this chapter was presented as a paper at the Oxford Conference on Civil Resistance and Power Politics in March 2007. In particular, the comments of my fellow panel members (Kenneth Bloomfield, Bob Purdie, and Adrian Guelke) were very enlightening.

[1] Tommy McKearney, interviewed by the author, Belfast, 20 Sept. 2000.

[2] Northern Ireland—the part of the island of Ireland that remained in the United Kingdom when the rest of Ireland became an independent state in 1922—consists of six counties in the north-east of the island: Antrim, Armagh, Down, Fermanagh, Londonderry, and Tyrone.

[3] The Provisional IRA was responsible for more deaths than any other group in the Northern Ireland conflict. On its own, this organization caused 48.5 per cent of the total fatalities from the political violence. For the full range of organizations and groups responsible for Troubles deaths, see D. McKittrick, S. Kelters, B. Feeney, and C. Thornton, *Lost Lives: The Stories of the Men, Women and Children who Died as a Result of the Northern Ireland Troubles*, 2nd edn. (Edinburgh: Mainstream, 2001).

The 1967–72 period in the north of Ireland exemplified our human capacity for turning peace into war, and quiet neighbour into killer or victim. In 1967 nobody was killed in Northern Ireland as a result of political violence; in 1972, just five years later, 497 people were killed in the conflict.

In these depressing days there were illuminating Irish versions of the broader questions addressed in this volume. In situations of structural disadvantage and profound division, how effective a mechanism can civil resistance be? In sharp-edged contexts such as the Ulster of the 1960s, will civil resistance be possible without degeneration into more aggressive forms of protest or campaign? Within such settings, why do so many ordinary people turn to the use of violence? Is civil resistance deployed because of an absolute rejection of the morality of violence, or for other reasons? How does one localized campaign of civil resistance relate to other instances drawn from a variety of international cases? In what ways do the politics of civil resistance relate to the history and politics of community, of nation, and of state? And were the paths taken inevitable?

These questions cannot fully be answered in this short chapter, painted on the small canvas of Ulster. But the 1967–72 Irish case study does teach us something about them. For they are of the utmost significance. At root, what we see in Northern Ireland between 1967 and 1972 is an illustration of the central Hobbesian problem of our (and maybe any) period, which can be set out crisply in three interlinked statements: i) people on various sides of a society or community claim as good or right what is, or seems to be, in their own sectional interest; ii) they tend to argue that one opinion (their own) deserves widespread acceptance within the broad community because it is right and good and true; iii) in fact, it is not the finally decisive victory of one opinion that we will be likely to witness, but rather the persistence of different, rival, and clashing interests. Our Hobbesian challenge is to devise effective means of preventing these rival interests and views from erupting into bloody civil war. In Ulster during 1967–72 we spectacularly failed to meet this challenge; in many of the problems that we face across the globe today, failure to meet such a challenge may have far greater costs for us all.

## CHRONOLOGY OF THE TROUBLES

Though its roots went deeper, the civil rights movement formally emerged early in 1967, with the Belfast birth of the Northern Ireland Civil Rights Association (NICRA), a group agitating for a series of reforms in the north as they related to the mistreatment of Northern Ireland's Catholic minority. NICRA sought a universal franchise for local government elections (instead of one based on rate-payers and loaded by the company vote); the re-drawing of electoral boundaries with a view to removing pro-unionist imbalances; legislation to end discrimination in local government employment; a points system to ensure the fair allocation of public housing; repeal of the capacious Special Powers Act; and the disbanding of the Protestant police reserve, the Ulster Special Constabulary. Civil rights protests and marches ensued, sometimes peacefully enough (as with the August 1968 Coalisland–Dungannon march prompted by civil rights activist Austin Currie), and sometimes far more fractiously (as in Derry in early October 1968, when marchers and the Royal Ulster Constabulary (RUC)—the police force—clashed).

The comparatively emollient Northern Ireland prime minister of the time, Terence O'Neill, did preside over notable reforms. Arguably, he did all that he could have done. But such changes were seen (by many unionists) as involving too much/too soon and (by many nationalists) as embodying too little/far too late.

Protestant opinion itself was crucially divided. Some favoured O'Neillite reform, but there were those also who strongly opposed concession to the civil rights agenda, seeing this as unionists giving ground to Irish nationalists—ground which they would not later be able to regain. The stentorian voice of the Revd Ian Paisley could be heard here, and also the more violent words and acts of loyalist paramilitaries.

It seemed briefly that some reformist compromise might be reached in the final years of the decade, but avoidable events intervened. These included the deliberately provocative civil rights march of January 1969, when members of the radical People's Democracy group set out from Belfast for Derry, to be harassed by loyalists along their route and violently set upon at Burntollet Bridge, near their destination. The loyalist attackers—behaving, in distinguished civil servant Kenneth Bloomfield's evocative phrasing, 'with all the unthinking automatism of Pavlov's dog'[4]—of course did radicals and republicans a huge favour. Such episodes understandably hardened Catholic opposition to the northern state, a process reinforced when the police provided nothing like adequate protection for Catholics in the summer of 1969 during loyalist attacks on Catholic areas, especially in Belfast. After the clashes of 1969, Catholic opinion was far less amenable to moderate reform, becoming more ambitious in its demands and expectations. This became more marked still when British soldiers (brought into the province to quell the 1969 disorder) quickly developed a mutually hostile relationship with the Catholic working class, a process worsened irreparably by episodes such as the 1970 Falls Curfew in Belfast, the counter-productive introduction of internment in 1971, and the fatal tragedy of Bloody Sunday in January 1972.[5]

By 1972, new nationalist formations had emerged in the north: at the end of 1969, the more aggressive and unambiguously republican Provisional IRA (widely known as 'the Provos'); and in 1970, the constitutional-reformist Social Democratic and Labour Party (SDLP) which aimed to achieve northern reform and ultimately the end of partition. By 1972, we see something like civil war in Northern Ireland, a situation far from solved when the Belfast Stormont regime

---

[4] Kenneth Bloomfield, *Stormont in Crisis: A Memoir* (Belfast: Blackstaff Press, 1994), 102.

[5] On these episodes, see Richard English, *Armed Struggle: The History of the IRA*, 3rd edn. (New York: Oxford University Press, 2005), 136–55.

©Keystone/Stringer (Hulton Archive) Getty Images

**Figure 5.1** Protest in an increasingly violent context. This civil rights march in the Catholic Falls Road area of Belfast took place on 6 July 1970, three months after the first major confrontation between Catholics and British soldiers in Belfast, and one week after violent incidents which had led the authorities to impose a curfew on the Falls Road area. The march, protesting against the deeply unpopular curfew, was patrolled by heavily armed British troops, and was re-routed to reduce the risk of clashes.

was replaced by Direct Rule from London in March of that year. When Conservative home secretary Reginald Maudling visited Belfast in the summer of 1970, he was horrified by what he witnessed; famously, as he boarded his plane to head home for London, he ordered a large whisky and exclaimed, 'What a bloody awful country!' Less famous—but more telling in directing us to the heart of our problem in this chapter—was the response of the IRA newspaper to his remark. Yes, they said, but 'Who *made* it "a bloody awful country!"?'[6] Opinions on this have clearly and viciously varied.

## EFFECTIVENESS OF CIVIL RESISTANCE

In situations of structural disadvantage and profound division, how effective a mechanism will civil resistance be likely to prove? No neat or simple answer is likely to emerge from such a question. In Northern Ireland (as elsewhere) we have to offer an ambiguous and careful response. In part, the Northern Ireland civil

---

[6] *An Phoblacht* (Dublin), Jan. 1972.

rights initiative was the most profound and appalling of failures. For those within the 1960s movement who sought a peaceful, reformist transformation of the north of Ireland (as many genuinely did), the communal polarization, friction, and virtual civil war which were prompted by the initiative clearly represented depressing perversions of their hope and intention. Prominent civil rights enthusiasts from those days have, at times, been admirably frank about this. Nationalist politician Austin Currie, for example, has conceded that if he had then known what was to emerge from the civil rights agitation that he helped to start, he would not have started it in the first place.[7]

The problem faced by advocates of civil resistance here was essentially twofold: first, the division between the two communities in Northern Ireland was deep, pervasive, and long-rooted, so any effort to erode it would necessarily be difficult and challenging; second, the civil rights initiative focused on issues (Catholic disadvantage and experience of discrimination) which reinforced rather than dissolved people's sense of communal division, rivalry, hostility, grievance, and tension.

Moreover, the situation was aggravated by the words and actions of some (I think a minority of) civil rights enthusiasts, who were clear enough that their eagerness for 1960s civil resistance lay partly in its capacity to serve an anti-unionist purpose. This is true, in varying ways, of figures such as Eamonn McCann, Anthony Coughlan, Michael Farrell, Bernadette Devlin, and Roy Johnston, all of whom expressed views which reinforced unionist perceptions that the civil rights movement was anti-unionist and anti-partitionist. So civil rights ineffectiveness was made more likely as a result. And, from the point of view of such figures themselves, civil resistance failed in spectacular ways. Was the socialism of Eamonn McCann, or the liberal Protestant all-Irelandism of Roy Johnston, forwarded by the civil rights movement towards fulfilment? No. Both were swamped by the ethno-national carnage which has scarred Ulster since the 1960s.[8]

Yet there were aspects of success within the civil rights episode too. For those who sought to delegitimize Stormont unionism, the 1967–72 period worked terrifically well. As anyone who has taught a twenty-first-century class of Belfast students can tell you, the wrongs of Stormont have become axiomatic (and frequently exaggerated) among people who are too young to have lived under the *ancien régime*. So, in answer to our question, 'Can civil resistance undermine an enemy's legitimacy and power?', we can respond with a resounding 'Yes': devastatingly so, in fact, as the still-recycled images of civil rights marchers being assaulted by police and loyalists make clear. This is an instance of another theme of this volume: the use of new technologies to very powerful effect. Television was among the civil rights marchers' best friends, raising international

---

[7] Austin Currie, *All Hell Will Break Loose* (Dublin: O'Brien Press, 2004), 10.

[8] English, *Armed Struggle*, 83–108. See also R. H. W. Johnston, *Century of Endeavour: A Biographical and Autobiographical View of the Twentieth Century in Ireland* (Dublin: Lilliput Press, 2006); E. McCann, *War and an Irish Town*, 3rd edn. (London: Pluto Press, 1993), 79–80, 91, 102; C. D. Greaves, *Reminiscences of the Connolly Association* (London: Connolly Association, 1978), 34.

**Figure 5.2**  A leader symbolizing the fateful link between the causes of civil rights and anti-Unionism. Bernadette Devlin, seen here in Belfast on 22 April 1969, was a key figure in the civil rights movement in Northern Ireland. She participated in student protests in 1968, in the Dungannon and Derry civil rights marches of the same year, and in the Burntollet march of January 1969. On 17 April 1969 she was elected to represent the mid-Ulster constituency in the House of Commons at Westminster, becoming, at 21, the youngest-ever woman MP.

profile and blood pressure alike. For example, television coverage of the October 1968 civil rights march in Derry, with its images of policemen batoning protesters, did much to delegitimize the existing regime of Northern Ireland within wider opinion.

Civil resistance in 1960s Northern Ireland made the issue of communal equality central. It remains so today. In twenty-first-century Northern Ireland we again find everyone talking of civil rights (although 'equality' is the contemporary code-word now deployed). Even (especially?) Sinn Fein repeatedly professes itself now in favour of 'an Ireland of equals', whether speaking north or south of Ireland's border. True, one of the party's papers, *The Donegal Voice*, salutes fallen heroes from the republican past (from the 1916 rebellion, or the 1981 hunger strike) and proclaims a desire for a united Ireland at some stage in the future. But in the meantime it also concentrates attention on a very different agenda: in Gerry Adams's words, people's 'rights to a decent home, to a job and a decent wage, to decent public services like health and education, and a safer cleaner environment'. Tellingly, the paper has tended to focus, therefore, on issues such as a 'just economy', or 'dynamic public services', or a 'jobs task force'; on 'a new health system for Ireland', the creation of a 'motorway for the north west', or 'action for Donegal fisheries'.[9]

This reinforces our main conclusion concerning efficacy. Close reflection on the 1967–72 period in Ireland and its legacy demonstrates the failure of *non-civil* resistance. On the nationalist side, the failure of the Provisional IRA's style of *non-civil* resistance is striking. The Provos claimed that they would defend Catholics, that they would force British withdrawal from Northern Ireland, that they would end sectarianism, that they would inaugurate socialism—and yet none of these goals has been even nearly reached (and arguably each has been set back some distance by the Provos' own violent actions). The seeming end-point of the long Ulster crisis—the 1998-style arrangement within which we all still just about exist in the north—is in fact nearer by far to the SDLP's long-term politics and campaigns.[10]

The evidence demonstrates the extent to which the SDLP long pre-echoed the politics with which Sinn Fein would eventually achieve their greatest success. In 1974, the SDLP even prefigured a central plank of the Provos' eventual peace process strategy, with the statement that, 'The Provisional IRA can achieve nothing by carrying on their campaign of violence but they can achieve almost anything they desire by knocking it off.'[11] Twenty years passed before the IRA's ceasefire showed that the point had also (finally) dawned on them.

As to civil resistance itself, even after four decades it is perhaps too early to tell the ultimate success or failure of a political episode such as the 1967–72 Ulster story. But we can clearly see some of the key failures, and that any positive results were in the nature of an ambiguous and expensively purchased success. The 1960s episode helped to make the problem of structural disadvantage in the north more famous and urgent of redress. But it also helped to generate a conflict which made that redress much more difficult to achieve and—even now, forty years on—painfully elusive.

## DEGENERATION INTO VIOLENCE

In sharp-edged contexts such as the Ulster of the 1960s, can civil resistance occur without degeneration into more aggressive forms of protest or campaign? The Ulster answer here is far clearer. If we consider two County Tyrone Catholics already mentioned, Tommy McKearney and Austin Currie, the broad pattern is outlined. While the latter remained committed to the path of civil and constitutional mobilization, the former drew from Ulster's 1960s civil resistance the

---

[9] *Donegal Voice* (Summer 2006).

[10] G. Murray and J. Tonge, *Sinn Fein and the SDLP: From Alienation to Participation* (Dublin: O'Brien Press, 2005).

[11] SDLP Press Release, 26 Sept. 1974, Linen Hall Library Political Collection, Belfast (SDLP Box 2).

lesson that something else, something much more violent, was required. His career in the Provisional IRA reflected the view, shared by a significant minority of each Northern Irish community during the post-1960s period, that violence was necessary as a means of defending your own community and furthering its interests. In particular, this related to questions of power. The community which demanded great change (let us call it the weaker community) will usually—as in the case of the Northern Ireland Catholic-nationalist minority—lack effective power speedily to effect that change within the existing political situation; their reformist calls for change will elicit an ambiguous response from the powerful, and one which will be considered by some in the weaker community to be too belated and too minimal; but some in the stronger community will feel threatened and will feel that too much has been conceded. The end result will be that a section (in most cases, I suspect, a minority) of each community will feel that recourse to uncivil forms of action is required.

In this sense, there seems no necessary linkage between the practice of civil resistance and the eventuality of liberal outcomes. The emergence of liberal outcomes, I suggest, depends on two other factors: first, the depth of experience and inculcation of liberal-democratic norms, institutions, attitudes, and practices in the society in question; and, second, the outcome of the power relationship reached by civil and non-civil struggle alike. In Northern Ireland, as in Ireland as a whole before Irish independence in the south in the 1920s,[12] there was a lengthy legacy of parliamentary, liberal-democratic assumption and experience; and in the end the practitioners of violence on all sides in the post-1960s Northern Ireland conflict (republicans, loyalists, the state) recognized that continued violence would ensure, not victory, but rather ongoing and futile stalemate.[13] To the extent that some form of liberal-democratic outcome has emerged from Ulster's long war, it is primarily for this dual reason.

## WHY CIVIL RESISTANCE?

Is civil resistance deployed because of an absolute rejection of the morality of violence, or for other reasons? Very few people reject absolutely the morality of violence. The desire to use civil resistance as a political strategy in 1960s Northern Ireland certainly owed less to any such rejection (though this did motivate some people), than to other considerations. One was that, after the failure of traditional republican method and argument (most obviously with the feeble collapse of the IRA's 1956–62 border campaign of violence), there was a need for republicans to rethink their approach if they were to move forward. Those republican intellectuals who identified discrimination and civil rights as the weak point of unionism offered an apparently viable route. If you could

---

[12] B. Kissane, *Explaining Irish Democracy* (Dublin: UCD Press, 2002).
[13] See English, *Armed Struggle*.

mobilize northern opinion around the issue of civil rights, and highlight to other audiences further afield the deep problem inherent within the northern state, then progress could perhaps be achieved. For those of a less republican hue, but still within the nationalist family, the failure of orthodox constitutional nationalism to make headway since the foundation of the state in the 1920s also prompted a re-think in strategy. With a Belfast parliament possessing a permanent majority against you, the prospect instead of extra-parliamentary mobilization offered understandable attractions. Yet again, the *zeitgeist*—of US civil rights agitation, and European student and radical movements—pointed towards the potential success available through the kind of initiative begun in 1960s Ulster.

Was violence used alongside civil resistance? Well, the fundamental answer, as far as most civil rights sympathizers was concerned, must be 'no'. Most civil rights marchers and enthusiasts preferred and practised non-violence. But there were, as ever in the north of Ireland, exceptions. These years witnessed a variety of strategies of civil resistance, evident among different groups of activists. Some marchers did stone police, clashes with the state and with loyalists were not entirely one-sided in their aggression, and there was a small number of republicans who not only maintained a violent capacity but threatened to (and on a very few occasions, did) use such aggressive methods. Here, as in other cases elsewhere, the line between civil and uncivil demonstration and action can be far from clear in practice.

By the early 1970s, IRA violence—which should not be conflated with the civil resistance movement—had gone far beyond the civil, and civil resistance was never again to dominate political action in the ensuing decades of the Northern Ireland conflict. But the speed with which some who had been civil rights marchers became IRA killers reflects the fact that, for many, the strategy of non-violence was deployed not for reasons of absolute rejection of the morality of violence. Some within the civil rights movement unquestionably did see the politics of non-violence as positively beneficial and potentially of practical effect. However, the blurred line between constitutional nationalism and what, in Ireland, is known as the 'physical force' (or violent) nationalist tradition, is one with deep historic roots. We can see versions of it throughout the nineteenth century,[14] and the gap between civil and uncivil conflict, in Ulster at least, is a narrow one, frequently traversed.

## WHY THE TURN TOWARDS VIOLENCE?

Within such settings, why do so many ordinary people turn to the use of violence? We always have with us a minority of people who consider violence to be justified in order to achieve desirable political gain. States can do little about that. The room for affecting outcomes lies with our ability to prevent, or allow, or encourage, such minority zealotry to gain a purchase on the wider imagination within the

[14]  M. J. Kelly, *The Fenian Ideal and Irish Nationalism, 1882–1916* (Woodbridge: Boydell Press, 2006).

©Central Press/Stringer (Hulton Archive) Getty Images

**Figure 5.3** Effects on the younger generation of a descent into violence. On 12 August 1971 two children in the predominantly Catholic Markets area of Belfast re-enact the shooting of four men the day before.

relevant community or constituency. The depressing problem requiring explanation in the 1967–72 Irish case study is why so many ordinary people on all sides became capable of extraordinary and terrible violence, and so quickly. The role of those long advocating such courses of action is important, as is the contribution of external actors (in our case here, we might think of the way in which certain southern Irish politicians sought to further their own intra-party political cause by encouraging a certain line of action on the north at the end of the 1960s).[15]

[15]  See J. O'Brien, *The Arms Trial* (Dublin: Gill and Macmillan, 2000).

But these form only a part of our answer. Republican traditionalists had *long* argued the necessity of violence, and without great success. A figure such as Ruairí Ó Brádaigh,[16] a key player in the emergence of the Provisional IRA, had been arguing this for years. In 1952 and 1962 (and again, as it happens, in 2002), very few people listened to his fiercely republican-orthodox arguments. The question is why—in 1972—he had more recruits than he required for the IRA politics of his preference. Nor can this be explained purely through recourse to external actors—whether southern Irish politicians, or emigrant gun-smugglers in the US—for the role of such people was not weighty enough, in itself, to explain the shift from peace to war.

But the basic pattern of escalation in 1967–72 can be explained: it conforms to a depressingly familiar outline. There was the long-term division and tension of interest between two communities, each failed by a state which claimed its loyalty but which had not accommodated it persuasively; the call for political change (in this case, from civil rights radicals) prompted enhanced and probably unrealistic expectation on one side of this divide, and unnecessary and exaggerated fears on the other; initial and minor clashes resulted from assertive gestures or reactive moves; faced with a crisis, the state with greatest power and responsibility felt the need to act decisively, but lacked the necessary intelligence to respond subtly; in particular, heavy-handed (and at times brutal) military deployment both contained the worst of the situation and worsened crucial relationships in a lastingly disastrous fashion; the fault lines of division became deeper and wider, and each side adopted a self-comforting but implausible Manichean reading of the good and evil forces involved; violence generated counter-violence, and a process of tit-for-tat escalation ensued, as each side pursued an elusive victory, through bloody means.

At the heart of all this, one fatal process was crucially reinforced: previously marginal and simplistic arguments in favour of aggressive violence appeared to be vindicated. From the foundation of the Northern Ireland state onwards, militant IRA republicans had argued the following: the northern state is necessarily sectarian; it is irreformable; attempts to change it peacefully will fail, and efforts to engage cooperatively with it will prove futile; nationalists will be vulnerable to attack from the other community, will receive no protection from the state, and will require the IRA to defend them; the only way to end nationalists' second-class status is for the IRA to destroy the state, laying the way clear for a new, united, and independent Ireland. From the 1920s until the late-1960s, most northern nationalists largely ignored these arguments. By the early 1970s—after the attacks on Catholic areas, the batoning of civil rights marchers, the harsh actions of the British army—many had, perhaps unsurprisingly, come to be persuaded. Not only, therefore, were you prepared to use violence to hit back at the people who had hit your own community first; you also had an ideological framework providing you with justification, explanation, and a seeming hope of victory.

---

[16] See R. W. White's impressive biography, *Ruairí Ó Brádaigh: The Life and Politics of an Irish Revolutionary* (Bloomington: Indiana University Press, 2006).

In place of civil resistance was an Irish republican version of Clausewitzian argument: you used violence against your enemy (Britain) in order to make war more painful for them than it would be for them to give you what you wanted (namely, a united Ireland and Irish nationalist victory). This argument ultimately came to be recognized as flawed, even the IRA eventually acknowledging that no amount of Clausewitzian pressure on London would remove the main obstacle to a united Ireland, namely the implacably hostile opinion of so many unionists in Ulster itself. Nonetheless, this IRA argument was rendered appealing for very many by the crisis which emerged in the early 1970s.


## COMPARISONS TO OTHER MOVEMENTS

How does one localized campaign of civil resistance relate to other instances drawn from a variety of international cases? It is difficult to apply the lessons of one case study to another geographical and political arena: much of the best comparative scholarship involves an identification of difference, as much as the marking out of similarities of intention, context, or outcome. Indeed, our most important task as comparativists is, in the end, to explain the unique. If Case A is different from Case B, then why is this so? Could they have been more similar? If so, why were they not, and what were the *contingent* factors at play? If not, what were the determining *structural* factors which prevented similarity?

In relation to 1967–72 Ulster, the point can easily be made by reference to some of those places with which it is sometimes rather casually lumped together. The 1960s civil rights movement in Northern Ireland did involve a conscious glance towards civil rights in the US. However, the two cases were very different. The discrimination experienced by the Northern Irish Catholic minority was milder than that known to US blacks. Moreover, the US civil rights movement did not involve a historic battle over the legitimacy or existence of the United States itself; the Northern Irish version clearly did involve precisely such a war over state legitimacy. As already noted, key figures among those who initiated the northern civil rights agitation were undoubtedly keen on using it as a route towards the undoing of Northern Ireland, while some prominent civil rights leaders were at times emphatically and explicitly anti-unionist in their politics.

More exaggerated comparisons came to be made by those who emerged from this era into prominence as republicans (Gerry Adams amongst them), including the likening of Northern Ireland to apartheid South Africa or even to Nazi Germany. These comparisons can be easily demolished.[17] Scrutiny of the available evidence (in Belfast archives, for example) further clarifies what our opening ex-IRA man Tommy McKearney admirably stressed: that the north, for all its undoubted flaws, was *not* like South Africa.

---

[17] English, *Armed Struggle*, 367–9.

The intriguing point concerning comparison is twofold. First, in what precise ways can reflection on other situations help us more deeply to understand the uniqueness of our own, once we have looked at differences and family resemblances alike? To take obvious comparisons close to home: why did Welsh, Scottish, and English nationalisms evolve in such markedly different ways from one another, and why did all of them take such different routes through history from the Irish nationalism across the narrow water to the west? I have tried, elsewhere, to provide some answers to this question (and, in doing so, have focused more than some would like upon religion).[18] But similar questions could be set with any of the cases studied in this volume. Second, can we, in fact, provide broader lessons which transcend local context? It seems to me that we can stress the ultimate uniqueness of each setting, while recognizing that not everything is different between them. I suspect that the issues addressed in this book demand that we ask about such wider—and practical—lessons. For the interaction of legitimacy, disaffection, and grievance among national/ethnic/religious minorities will come up again and again, as will the issue of whether and why such groups might pursue violence. It could also be argued that these are the central political questions in international relations currently.[19]

## CIVIL RESISTANCE IN COMMUNITY, NATION, AND STATE

In what ways do the politics of civil resistance relate to the history and politics of community, of nation, and of state? One striking feature of Ulster civil resistance was its complex relation to the broader themes and forces of Irish history: of ethno-religious community, of nation, and of state. Put crisply, and despite the genuinely and impressively cross-communal instincts of some of those activists involved, the Northern Irish civil rights movement quickly became a movement expressing dissatisfaction on the part of one community, concerning their treatment at the hands of the other; it overlapped with national identification (Catholic-nationalist civil rights agitation versus Protestant-unionist scepticism); and it reflected the awkwardness of having a large minority of people who found themselves in a state to which, ideally and understandably, they would rather not belong.

The customary stance on all this is to say that the civil rights movement was not a nationalist movement, that it merely demanded fair treatment within the UK rather than secession from it, and that it was therefore immune to the politics of inter-communal sectarianism, nationalist sentiment, and state power. There is something in this. But such a reading seems to me straightforwardly possible only if one ignores much of the complex evidence.[20]

---

[18] Richard English, *Irish Freedom: The History of Nationalism in Ireland* (London: Pan Macmillan, 2006).

[19] Francis Fukuyama, *After the Neocons: America at the Crossroads* (London: Profile, 2006).

[20] English, *Armed Struggle*, 83–93.

It is equally unarguable, from the evidence now available, that less bellicose or militant figures also reflected something of the intersection of civil resistance, communal assertion, and nationalism versus the state. When pursuing election as a Stormont MP in 1964 Austin Currie set out his political goals, number one priority being the 'Reunification of Ireland' (addressing 'Discrimination' was number four of seven priorities). When Currie was prominent among those who, only a few years later, emerged pursuing civil rights, unionists thought that this new initiative brought with it some rather more traditional nationalist politics. This interpretation is perhaps reinforced by Currie's own claim that in the civil rights campaign he and others 'had found the Achilles heel of unionism', and that civil rights agitation formed part of the business of mobilizing 'anti-unionist opinion'.[21]

It is impossible to prove, but seems highly likely, that most 1960s Northern Irish civil rights marchers would have preferred a united Ireland rather than a partitioned one, and that their understandable desire for better treatment within the UK state was interwoven with a nationalist sense of community, struggle, and power. If asked how best to guarantee that their own individual and communal interests might be advanced, most would, I feel sure, have held that the best manner of doing this would have been to form part of the majority within a state which represented one's communal interests and culture. In this sense, the civil rights movement was indeed an implicitly nationalist one. It is not that all civil rights enthusiasts saw the episode in Trojan-horse form, as a means of bypassing the defences of unionist power and security; the civil rights movement's most accomplished historian, Bob Purdie, has been very clear about this.[22] But the arguments and logic of civil rights did relate to the broader politics of nationalism and the state in Ulster, and I think that it would be naïve to assume that it could have been otherwise.

Here it might be worth reflecting, briefly, on why such questions frequently dominate. In Ulster in the 1960s and 1970s we see a common enough problem: the existence of a significant national minority within the boundaries of a state which it considered inimical to its own national preference. The dominance of nationalism over rival forms of identification can indeed be explained by reference to the superior appeal of the nationalist politics of community, struggle and power.[23] But we need to recognize that in very many settings, the politics of civil resistance will become interwoven with (and its outcome dominated by) the politics of rival nationalisms and their associated state politics.

---

[21] Currie, *All Hell Will Break Loose*, 54–5, 79, 99.

[22] Bob Purdie, 'Was the Civil Rights Movement a Republican/Communist Conspiracy?', *Irish Political Studies*, 3 (1988); and Purdie, *Politics in the Streets: The Origins of the Civil Rights Movement in Northern Ireland* (Belfast: Blackstaff Press, 1990).

[23] English, *Irish Freedom*.

## WERE THE PATHS TAKEN INEVITABLE?

To what degree were the paths which were actually taken inevitable or contingent? One of the most intriguing features of comparative reflection lies in the realm of the counterfactual. The events between the foundation of NICRA and the bloodiest year of the Troubles in 1972 are sometimes assumed to have had an inevitability about them, as though Irish history or Anglo-Irish relations prede-termined an unavoidable growth of carnage in the north. Talented civil rights leader Michael Farrell, for example, claimed that the Belfast sectarian rioting of the summer of 1969 had a certain inevitability. For fifty years, he said, those who ruled the north had sustained a system based on privilege, through the inten-tional fostering of hatred between the two communities; sectarianism had con-sequently become such an integral part of the system that the latter's decay inevitably led to a sectarian outburst.[24]

Such views are surely misleading. Debatable and avoidable decisions on all sides were far more responsible for the north's emerging Troubles. What if Stormont had been replaced by less partial London government in 1969 (as demanded by civil rights nationalist John Hume) rather than in 1972, by which time the situation was far less open to remedy? (By late 1968 contingency plans for direct rule had indeed been prepared in London.) What if earlier and more substantial reform had been implemented during the 1960s? What if the London government had, earlier on, taken a fuller and better-informed interest in what was occurring in Northern Ireland, and had sought to address some of the inequalities there?[25] What if the Burntollet march had not taken place? What if figures such as the eye-catching Ian Paisley had adopted a less inflammatory approach? What if internment had not been introduced? What if state military action during 1970–2 had been less brutal?

And what if the Provisional IRA had itself acted differently? For just as the actions of the pre-Provisional IRA had helped to produce the sequence of events which spawned the Provisionals, so too the actions of the early Provos helped (along with the actions of others) to produce conditions within which they themselves could flourish. Timing is crucial here. Republican accounts of the birth of the IRA stress—and rightly so—the crimes committed against northern Catholics. Loyalist assaults of the 1960s, British Army actions such as the Falls Curfew in 1970 or internment in 1971, understandably etched themselves pain-fully into northern republican memory. But it is also important to examine the chronology closely. The Provisionals themselves were clear that their 'full-scaled

[24] *Irish News* (Belfast), 6 Aug. 1969.
[25] This is a point very well made in Kenneth Bloomfield, *A Tragedy of Errors: The Government and Misgovernment of Northern Ireland* (Liverpool: Liverpool University Press, 2007). The Irish govern-ment too had rather neglected Northern Ireland, and the response of Dublin to the emerging 1960s crisis was itself consequently flawed—Catherine O'Donnell, *Fianna Fáil, Irish Republicanism and the Northern Ireland Troubles 1968–2005* (Dublin: Irish Academic Press, 2007), 21.

offensive against the might of the British Army' had long preceded internment or Bloody Sunday.[26] Indeed, the IRA Army Council's January 1970 decision to pursue a sustained, offensive engagement with the British long predated even the Falls Curfew. For the Provos were revolutionaries, whose desire to engage in a war existed before, and helped to create, the conditions within which it could lastingly be fought.

The point about all of these counterfactual possibilities is that, at the time, voices were raised suggesting precisely why each of these unfortunate choices was likely to prove disastrous, and offering alternative (and almost certainly more benign) routes forward. While it is not true to claim, as does Mark Kurlansky in his recent book on non-violence, that, 'Once you start the business of killing, you just get "deeper and deeper", without limits',[27] it is true that in Northern Ireland there ensued several decades of violence at levels that could certainly have been lowered through the adoption of genuinely available alternative choices. These avoidable mistakes were made on all sides in the emerging conflict.


## CONCLUSION

The Northern Irish civil resistance campaign of 1967–72 was ambiguously effective. Civil resistance did undermine an enemy's legitimacy and power, but had counter-productive effects also. Among these was the generation of uncivil resistance which itself proved bloodily and deeply ineffective. There was an interplay between violence and non-violence in several ways: some from the violent republican movement were involved in designing and beginning the civil rights movement; some who joined the IRA (or rival groups on the other side) did so because of their reading of the logic of the civil rights movement; and the violence of the subsequent decades did emerge from the inter-communal turbulence which the civil rights initiative helped provoke. Civil resistance had not emerged from an absolute rejection of the morality of violence, and it was related to wider questions of nationalism and state power. Above all, the degeneration into civil war from civil resistance was, certainly at the high levels which emerged, avoidable and contingent rather than inevitable. It remains for readers to determine how far these Irish lessons can be duplicated and are echoed in our wider international reflections in this volume.

[26] New Year Message from the IRA's Belfast Brigade, quoted in *Republican News* (Belfast), 3 Jan. 1976.

[27] Mark Kurlansky, *Non-Violence: The History of a Dangerous Idea* (London: Jonathan Cape, 2006), 184.

# 6

# The Dialectics of Empire: Soviet Leaders and the Challenge of Civil Resistance in East-Central Europe, 1968–91

*Mark Kramer*

From the late 1960s to the early 1990s, Soviet leaders were confronted numerous times by non-violent mass protests and unofficial social movements in their sphere of influence in east-central Europe as well as in the Soviet Union itself. This chapter discusses how the leaders of the ruling Communist Party of the Soviet Union (CPSU) responded to these challenges. The aim is twofold: to show how Soviet leaders responded to civil resistance during the era of Leonid Brezhnev (General Secretary of the CPSU, 1964–82), and to underscore the drastic changes in Soviet responses to non-violent resistance after Mikhail Gorbachev came to power in 1985 and embraced a radically different agenda.

I begin by examining Moscow's reaction to civil unrest in east-central Europe (in Czechoslovakia in 1968, Poland in 1980–1, and several countries in the late 1980s), and then discuss how Soviet leaders responded to non-violent protests *within* the Soviet Union. Four key points emerge. First, the Soviet regime repeatedly tried to influence the east-central European governments' responses to civil unrest, and Soviet military power was a crucial factor in all major crises in the region. Even when Soviet troops were not deployed, the mere threat of Soviet military intervention often had a profound effect on local actors' behaviour. Second, Gorbachev's domestic political reforms fundamentally changed the way Soviet officials responded to non-violent resistance both at home and abroad. After 1986, peaceful protest actions that would have been harshly suppressed in earlier years were tolerated (if only grudgingly) and soon became routine, as disaffected groups and individuals in the Soviet Union increasingly saw that the risks of engaging in contentious politics had vastly diminished (i.e. that their political opportunity structure had greatly expanded).[1] Third, even when the central or local authorities in the Soviet Union cracked down on non-violent protests, the incipient democratization of the Soviet polity limited the scope and

---

[1] On political opportunity structures and the rise of protest movements, see Doug McAdam, John McCarthy, and Mayer N. Zald (eds.), *Comparative Perspectives on Social Movements: Political Opportunities, Mobilizing Structures, and Cultural Framings* (New York: Cambridge University Press, 1996).

success of these repressive actions. Fourth, the mostly peaceful collapse of Communism in east-central Europe and the 'demonstration effect' of mass protests there eroded Gorbachev's ability to cope with domestic turmoil. Although Gorbachev's response to civil resistance in east-central Europe did not necessarily indicate what he would do at home, the sweeping changes he set in motion— changes that quickly outpaced his expectations in east-central Europe—circumscribed his options in dealing with protests and non-violent separatist groups in the Soviet Union.

## THE SOVIET RESPONSE TO THE 1968 PRAGUE SPRING

The Prague Spring, an eight-month-long period of far-reaching political liberalization in Czechoslovakia from January to August 1968, posed a daunting challenge for the Soviet Union. Czechoslovakia had been under communist rule

©Keystone/staff (Hulton Archive) Getty Images

**Figure 6.1** Fraternal help. On 3 August 1968, less than three weeks before the Soviet-led invasion of Czechoslovakia, Alexander Dubček (left), the reforming First Secretary of the Czechoslovak communist party, with Leonid Brezhnev (right), General Secretary of the Soviet communist party, and Alexei Kosygin, Soviet Prime Minister, at a meeting in Bratislava of the leaders of six communist states. The Bratislava Declaration contained the ominous words: 'We will never permit anyone to undermine the bases of the socialist regime.'

since the Czechoslovak communist party (KSČ) came to power in February 1948. Not only did the initial pressure for reform in Czechoslovakia come mainly from above (including from the KSČ leadership) rather than below, but the whole process of political, economic, and cultural revitalization in Czechoslovakia in 1968 was peaceful throughout.[2]

The lack of any violent turmoil during the Prague Spring did not, however, prevent Soviet leaders from repeatedly drawing analogies to an event they had experienced twelve years earlier—the violent rebellion in Hungary in 1956, which was crushed by a Soviet invasion. Although Soviet officials acknowledged that no violent upheavals were occurring in Czechoslovakia ('at least not yet'), they claimed that this was purely because 'the American and West German imperialists' had 'shifted tactics' and were 'resorting to a new, step-by-step approach'. Western governments, the argument went, had been chastened by the experience in 1956 (when Soviet troops forcefully quelled the Hungarian revolution) and were therefore now adopting a subtler approach. The implication was that even if no violence erupted in Czechoslovakia, the peaceful 'seizure of power' by 'hostile forces' (supposedly 'in collusion with Western imperialists') could eventually pose the same sort of 'mortal danger' that arose in Hungary in 1956.

The significance of this new Soviet line was not fully understood in Prague until it was too late. Although Dubček was well aware that internal reforms in Czechoslovakia had sparked consternation in Moscow, he assumed that he could offset this hostility by constantly reassuring Soviet leaders about the firmness of Czechoslovakia's commitment to the Warsaw Pact and the 'socialist commonwealth'.

On 17 August the Soviet politburo voted unanimously to 'provide assistance and support to the communist party and people of Czechoslovakia through the use of [the Soviet] armed forces'.[3] On 19 August the CPSU politburo reconvened for several hours to review the military and political aspects of the upcoming operation.[4] Detailed presentations by defence minister Andrei Grechko and the chief of the Soviet General Staff, Marshal Matvei Zakharov, provided grounds for optimism about the military side of the invasion, but the political preparations received less scrutiny. Although most of the Soviet politburo members expressed confidence that the 'healthy forces' in Czechoslovakia (a group of KSČ hardliners who secretly conspired with the Soviet Union before the invasion) would carry out their plan to seize power, a few politburo members seemed more sceptical about 'what will happen after our troops enter Czechoslovakia'.[5]

[2] H. Gordon Skilling, *Czechoslovakia's Interrupted Revolution* (Princeton, NJ: Princeton University Press, 1976).

[3] 'K voprosu o polozhenii v Chekhoslovakii: Vypiska iz protokola no. 95 zasedaniya Politbyuro TsK ot 17 avgusta 1968 g.', Resolution no. P95/1 (Top Secret), 17 Aug. 1968, in Arkhiv Prezidentl Rossiiskoi Federatsii (APRF), Fond (F.) 3, Op. 45, Delo (D.), 102, List (L.) 38.

[4] 'Rabochaya zapis' zasedaniya Politbyuro TsK KPSS ot 19 avgusta 1968 g.', 19 Aug. 1968 (Top Secret), in APRF, F. 3, Op. 45, D. 99, Ll. 474–82.

[5] Comments recorded in 'Dnevniki P. E. Shelesta', in 'Rossiiskii Gosudarstvennyi Arkhiv Sotsial'no-Politicheskoi Istorii, F. 666, Tetrad' (Te.), 7, L. 213.

The Soviet High Command went to great lengths to make sure that the incoming forces would not encounter any armed resistance. When the first Soviet troops crossed the border, Marshal Grechko phoned the Czechoslovak defence minister, General Martin Dzúr, and warned him that if Czechoslovak soldiers fired 'even a single shot' in resistance, the Soviet army would 'crush the resistance mercilessly' and Dzúr himself would 'be strung up from a telephone pole and shot'.[6] Dzúr heeded the warning by ordering all Czechoslovak troops to remain in their barracks indefinitely, to avoid the use of weapons for any purpose, and to offer 'all necessary assistance to Soviet forces'.[7] A similar directive was issued by the Czechoslovak president and commander-in-chief, Ludvík Svoboda, after he was informed of the invasion—in more cordial terms—shortly before midnight.[8] As a result, the Soviet and Warsaw Pact troops faced no armed resistance at all.

Decisive as the military results may have been, they seemed hollow when the invasion failed to achieve its immediate political aims.[9] The Soviet Union's chief political objective was to facilitate a rapid transition to a pro-Moscow 'revolutionary government', as had been done in Hungary in November 1956. In Czechoslovakia, however, a pro-Moscow government failed to materialize immediately after the invasion.

Despite this setback, Soviet leaders were reluctant to abandon their initial plan, apparently because they had no fallback options. It is surprising, even in retrospect, that they would have committed themselves so heavily to such a dubious strategy without having devised a viable alternative. No doubt, this was partly the fault of Soviet embassy officials in Prague and Soviet KGB (Committee for State Security) sources who had assured the CPSU politburo that the 'healthy forces on the KSČ Presidium have finally consolidated themselves and closed their ranks so that they are now a majority'.[10]

Only after repeated efforts to set up a post-invasion government had collapsed and the invasion had met with overwhelming opposition in Czechoslovakia—both publicly and officially—did Soviet leaders get an inkling of how unfavourable

[6] Cited in 'Dnevniki P. E. Shelesta', Ll. 213–14. See also the interview with Shelest in Leonid Shinkarev, 'Avgustovskoe bezumie: K 25-letiyu vvoda voisk v Chekhoslovakiyu', *Izvestiya* (Moscow), 21 Aug. 1993, 10; and the recollections of Pavlovskii in 'Eto bylo v Prage', 5.

[7] 'Obdobie od 21.srpna do konca roku 1968', from a report by Czechoslovak defence minister General Martin Dzúr, 9 June 1970, in Národní Archiv České Republiky (NAČR), Archiv Ústředního výboru Komunistické strany Československa (Arch. ÚV KSČ), 4. oddělení (Spr. G. Husák).

[8] See the 'extremely urgent' (*vne ocheredi*) cable from Chervonenko to the CPSU politburo, 21 Aug. 1968, in Ústav pro soudobé dějiny, Sbírka Komise vlády ČSFR pro analyzu událostí let 1967–1970 (ÚSD-SK), Z/S—MID, nos. 37 and 39.

[9] The military operation itself was not wholly flawless. See Leo Heiman, 'Soviet Invasion Weaknesses', *Military Review*, 49, no. 8 (Aug. 1969), 38–45.

[10] 'Shifrtelegramma', 7 Aug. 1968 (Top Secret), from S. V. Chervonenko, Soviet ambassador in Czechoslovakia, to the CPSU politburo, in AVPRF, F. 059, Op. 58, P. 124, D. 573, Ll. 183–5. For further relevant citations from the ex-Soviet archives, see Mark Kramer, 'The Prague Spring and the Soviet Invasion of Czechoslovakia: New Interpretations', *Cold War International History Project Bulletin*, no. 3 (Fall 1993), 6–8, 13, & 54.

the conditions in Czechoslovakia were.[11] An internal Soviet politburo report shortly after the invasion conceded that '75 to 90 percent of the [Czechoslovak] population... regard the entry of Soviet troops as an act of occupation'.[12] Reports from Soviet diplomats indicated that even most KSČ members viewed the invasion in 'highly negative' terms.[13] Brezhnev and his colleagues acknowledged this point but were loath to admit that they had fundamentally misjudged the situation and had failed to take adequate precautions. Instead, they ascribed the fiasco solely to the 'cowardly behaviour' of the 'healthy forces' in Czechoslovakia and the 'lack of active propaganda work' by Soviet units.[14]

Faced with massive popular and official resistance in Czechoslovakia, the Soviet politburo decided to open negotiations on 23 August with Dubček and other KSČ officials who had been arrested on the morning of the 21st. After four days of talks, the two sides agreed to sign the Moscow Protocol, which forced the reversal of several elements of the Prague Spring but also ensured the reinstatement of most of the leading reformers, including Dubček. The decision to bring back key Czechoslovak officials did not go over well with some Soviet politburo members and with hard-line leaders in eastern Europe, who wanted to 'take whatever steps are necessary' to 'prevent rightists and counterrevolutionaries from regaining power'.[15] Warning that 'the situation in Hungary [in 1956] was better than in Czechoslovakia today', they called for the imposition of a 'military dictatorship' in Czechoslovakia. Their views were endorsed by Soviet KGB chairman Yurii Andropov, who advocated repeating what was done in Hungary in 1956 when Soviet troops invaded and installed a 'revolutionary workers' and peasants' government' that would carry out mass arrests and repression. His suggestion was backed by another candidate politburo member and CPSU Secretary, Dimitri Ustinov, who emphasized that 'we must give a free hand to our troops'.

These calls for a much more vigorous (and presumably bloodier) military crackdown were rejected by Brezhnev and other officials. Although Brezhnev was prepared, *in extremis*, to impose direct military rule in Czechoslovakia, he and most of his colleagues clearly were hoping to come up with a more palatable solution first. The task of finding such a solution was seriously complicated by the collapse of Moscow's initial political aims, but a sustained period of repression

[11] 'Shifrtelegramma', 21 Aug. 1968 (Top Secret), from Kirill Mazurov to the CPSU politburo, in AVPRF, F. 059, Op. 58, P. 124, D. 574, Ll. 184–6.

[12] 'Nekotorye zamechaniya po voprosu podgotovki voenno-politicheskoi aktsii 21 avgusta 1968 g.', 16 Nov. 1968 (Strictly Secret/Special Dossier), in Rossiiskii Gosudarstvennyi Arkhiv Noveishei Istorii (RGANI), F. 5'OP', Op. 6, D. 776, L. 137.

[13] 'Informatsiya o druzheskikh svyazyakh oblastei i gorodov Ukrainskoi SSR s oblastyami, voevodstvami, okrugami, uezdami i gorodami sotsialisticheskikh stran v 1968 godu', 20 Dec. 1968 (Secret), in RGANI, F. 5, Op. 60, D. 2, Ll. 46, 64–5.

[14] 'Záznam ze schůzek Varšavské pětky v Moskvě ve dnech 24.-27.8.1968', Verbatim Transcript (Top Secret), 24–27 Aug. 1968, in ÚSD-SK, Z/M 21; and 'Nekotorye zamechaniya po voprosu podgotovki voenno-politicheskoi aktsii 21 avgusta 1968 g.', L. 129.

[15] 'Záznam ze schůzek Varšavské pětky v Moskvě ve dnech 24.-27.8.1968', L. 3.

and 'normalization' gradually negated the defiant mood of the Czechoslovak population and consolidated the military and political gains of the invasion. In April 1969, Dubček was removed from office for good.

The implications of the 1968 crisis for Soviet responses to non-violent change and civil resistance in east-central Europe were codified in the so-called 'Brezhnev Doctrine', according to which the Soviet Union had both a right and a 'sacred duty' to preserve the 'socialist gains' of all Warsaw Pact countries.[16] The Soviet politburo therefore would be obliged to use military force not only to respond to violent outbursts—as in the case of Hungary in 1956—but also to pre-empt 'impermissible deviations from socialism', even if these were carried out through entirely peaceful means. Although a pre-emptive military option had always existed for the Soviet Union, the Brezhnev Doctrine made it explicit by proclaiming that the Warsaw Pact states would never again risk 'waiting until Communists are being shot and hanged', as in the autumn of 1956, before sending Soviet and allied troops to 'help the champions of socialism'.[17]

The Brezhnev Doctrine thus reflected the Soviet Union's profound hostility to any meaningful change in the political complexion of east-central Europe, regardless of whether such change was achieved through non-violent civil resistance or violent rebellion. But this engrained attitude did not necessarily mean that Soviet troops would intervene promptly or indiscriminately during future crises in the Soviet bloc, any more than they had in 1968. Brezhnev went to great lengths in 1968 to pursue an internal solution in Czechoslovakia that would preclude the need for a full-scale invasion. He and other Soviet officials tried for months to pressure Dubček to crack down, and it was only when their repeated efforts failed and when the dates of party congresses in Czechoslovakia were looming (congresses that would have resulted in sweeping replacements of KSČ hardliners) that the Soviet politburo finally approved the dispatch of Soviet troops. This pattern of trying every option to find an internal solution before resorting to military force was repeated during all subsequent crises in east-central Europe under Brezhnev, including those in Poland in 1970–1 and 1976.

## THE SOVIET UNION AND THE 1980–1 POLISH CRISIS

The Soviet Union played a crucial role in the imposition of martial law in Poland on 12–13 December 1981—an operation intended to crush a wave of civil unrest that had engulfed Polish society for the previous eighteen months. As Aleksander Smolar explains in his chapter in this volume, the dynamic of the crisis in Poland in 1980–1 was very different from the situation that had arisen twelve years earlier in Czechoslovakia. In Czechoslovakia the initial drive for reform in 1968 had come mainly from above, and the Prague Spring had become a 'crisis' only when

---

[16] 'Rech' tovarishcha L. I. Brezhneva', *Pravda* (Moscow), 13 Nov. 1968, 2.
[17] S. Kovalev, 'O "mirnoi" i nemirnoi kontrrevolyutsii', *Pravda* (Moscow), 11 Sept. 1968, 4.

Soviet leaders defined it as such. By contrast, in Poland in 1980–1 the pressure for change came from below, and the crisis affected every aspect of the country's polity, economy, and social system.

From the start, Soviet leaders were convinced that the rise of Solidarity posed a fundamental threat to Poland's communist system, in which the Polish United Workers' Party (PZPR) had held a monopoly of political power since 1947. They also were alarmed by the growing political influence of Poland's Catholic Church, which they regarded as 'one of the most dangerous forces in Polish society' and a fount of 'anti-socialist' and 'hostile' elements.[18] As the crisis intensified and Solidarity's strength continued to grow, Soviet leaders' condemnations of the Polish trade union became more strident, both publicly and in behind-the-scenes deliberations.

Because of Poland's location in the heart of Europe, its communications and logistical links with the Group of Soviet Forces in Germany, its projected contributions to the 'first strategic echelon' of the Warsaw Pact, and its numerous storage sites for Soviet tactical nuclear warheads, the prospect of having a non-communist government come to power in Warsaw or of a drastic change in Polish foreign policy was anathema in Moscow. Soviet foreign minister Andrei Gromyko spoke for all of his colleagues when he declared at a CPSU politburo meeting in October 1980 that 'we simply *cannot* lose Poland' under any circumstances.[19]

Quite apart from the situation in Poland itself, Soviet officials suspected—with good reason—that the crisis would have destabilizing repercussions in other Warsaw Pact countries. Soon after the Gdańsk and Szczecin accords were signed in August 1980 giving legal status to Solidarity, senior commentators in Moscow began asserting that Solidarity's 'strategy of permanent chaos' would inspire similar developments elsewhere that would 'threaten not just Poland but the whole of peace and stability in Europe'.[20] Of particular concern from the CPSU politburo's perspective was the growing evidence that turmoil in Poland was spilling over into the Soviet Union itself. From late July 1980 on, the Soviet authorities took a number of steps to propitiate Soviet industrial workers and to bolster labour discipline. These actions were motivated by an acute fear that the emergence of a free trade union in Poland would spur workers and miners in adjoining regions of the Soviet Union to press for improved living conditions, greater political freedom, and an independent labour union of their own.

By stirring Soviet anxieties about the potential loss of a key member of the Warsaw Pact and about the spread of political instability throughout eastern Europe and into the Soviet Union, the Polish crisis demonstrated, as the events of 1953, 1956, and 1968 had previously, the degree of 'acceptable' change in the

---

[18] See the many documents in RGANI, F. 5, Op. 84, Dd. 597, 598.

[19] 'Zasedanie Politbyuro TsK KPSS 29 oktyabrya 1980 goda: Materialy k druzhestvennomu rabochemu vizitu v SSSR pol'skikh rukovoditelei', 29 Oct. 1980 (Top Secret), in RGANI, F. 89, Op. 42, D. 31, L. 3.

[20] Vladimir Lomeiko, 'Kto zhe dolbit dyry v pol'skoi lodke', *Literaturnaya gazeta* (Moscow), no. 3 (21 Jan. 1981), 14.

Soviet bloc. The crisis in Poland was more protracted than those earlier upheavals, but the leeway for genuine change was, if anything, narrower than before.
Soviet leaders could not indefinitely tolerate the existence of a powerful, independent trade union in Poland. The only question was how best to get rid
of Solidarity.

With Soviet backing, the Polish authorities began planning in the first few
weeks of the crisis for the eventual imposition of martial law. Preparations for a
violent crackdown by Polish internal security commandos were launched in mid-
August 1980, and much more elaborate planning was initiated in October 1980
by the Polish general staff and the Polish internal affairs ministry. The combined
effort was overseen by the chief of the Polish general staff, Army-General Florian
Siwicki, who had long been a close friend of General Wojciech Jaruzelski, the
minister of defence (who became both prime minister and first secretary of the
PZPR in 1981). The planning was also closely supervised at every stage by high-
ranking Soviet KGB and military officials, who frequently travelled to Warsaw
and reported back to the Soviet politburo.

The constant pressure exerted by Soviet political leaders and military officers
was an enormous constraint on Stanisław Kania, first secretary of the PZPR from
September 1980 to October 1981. Even if Kania had eventually sought to reach a
genuine compromise with Solidarity and the Catholic Church, the Soviet Union
would have tried to thwart it. From the Soviet politburo's perspective, any such
compromise would have been, at best, a useless diversion or, at worst, a form of
outright 'capitulation to hostile and reactionary forces' and a 'sell-out to the
mortal enemies of socialism'.[21]

To give Kania and Jaruzelski greater incentive to proceed with a martial law
crackdown before events spun out of control, the Soviet authorities offered direct
military support. One of the first actions taken in August 1980 by the Soviet
politburo's special commission on the Polish crisis, just three days after it was
formed, was to devise plans for a two-stage mobilization of 'up to 100,000
[Soviet] military reservists and 15,000 vehicles' in order to bring a 'large group'
of Soviet tank and motorized infantry units up to 'full combat readiness...in
case military assistance is provided to Poland'.[22]

If Kania and Jaruzelski had accepted these offers of military support, the
incoming Soviet troops would have been performing a function very different
from the one they carried out in Czechoslovakia in August 1968. The 1968
operation involved hundreds of thousands of Soviet and Warsaw Pact troops
and was directed *against* the existing Czechoslovak leader, Alexander Dubček.
By contrast, in 1980–1 the idea was to use a smaller number of Soviet/Warsaw

---

[21] 'Vypiska iz protokola no. 37 zasedaniya Politbyuro TsK KPSS ot 21 noyabrya 1981 goda:
O prieme v SSSR partiino-gosudarstvennoi delegatsii PNR i ustnom poslanii t. Brezhneva L. I. t. V.
Yaruzel'skomu', no. P37/21 (Top Secret), 21 Nov. 1981, in RGANI, F. 89, Op. 42, D. 27, L. 5.

[22] 'TsK KPSS', no. 682-op (Top Secret/Special Dossier), 28 Aug. 1980, from Mikhail Suslov, Andrei
Gromyko, Yurii Andropov, Dmitrii Ustinov, and Konstantin Chernenko, in APRF, F. 83-op, Op. 20,
D. 5, L. 1.

Pact troops to *assist* the Polish regime in its battle against Solidarity. The members of the Soviet politburo seemed remarkably obtuse about the likely effect of introducing even a limited number of Soviet (and, even more, East German) troops into Poland to crack down on Solidarity. In Poland, however, the two top leaders were well aware of the pitfalls of receiving such assistance. Whenever Kania and Jaruzelski were faced with the prospect of clamping down, they warned that the entry of Soviet troops into Poland would cause a 'disaster'. Both of them sought more time for an internal solution.

Tensions escalated in early September 1981 when the Soviet Union launched its 'Zapad-81' military exercises along Poland's northern coast and eastern border—exercises involving a vast number of Soviet combat troops. Soviet officials expected that the conspicuous Soviet troop movements would have a salutary impact not only in Poland but in the West as well. On 13 September, the day after 'Zapad-81' ended, a highly secretive Polish political-military organ, the Homeland Defence Committee (KOK), chaired by Jaruzelski, reached a final decision to introduce martial law.[23] Another turning point came in mid-October 1981 when, at Moscow's behest, the PZPR Central Committee removed Kania as party leader and replaced him with Jaruzelski. The ascendance of Jaruzelski gave Soviet leaders greater confidence that martial law would soon be introduced.

In mid-November, Mikhail Suslov, a long-standing member of the CPSU politburo and the Party's leading ideologist, presented a detailed report to the CPSU Central Committee outlining the final preparations for martial law in Poland and some of the steps the Soviet Union was taking to help.[24] In particular; he stressed that the Soviet politburo was 'offering comprehensive support to the healthy forces in the PZPR', including Polish army generals, who could, if necessary, step in and impose martial law if Jaruzelski failed to do so.

As the decisive movement approached in December 1981 for the introduction of martial law, Soviet leaders remained apprehensive about Jaruzelski, who in recent weeks had seemed increasingly doubtful about his ability to sustain martial law without external (i.e. Soviet) military support. In the final days, Jaruzelski began urging the Soviet politburo to send troops to help him. Soviet leaders by this point did not want to offer any assistance to Jaruzelski, for fear that it might give him an excuse to avoid acting as forcefully as he needed to. They, unlike Jaruzelski, were fully confident that the proposed martial law operation would be successful, provided that Jaruzelski implemented it without letting up. They wanted to avoid giving him a crutch that might cause him, if only subconsciously, to refrain from cracking down as ruthlessly as possible.

The extent of Jaruzelski's continued nervousness became clear on 12 December, as the hour approached for the introduction of martial law. Jaruzelski was

---

[23] See handwritten notes by General Tadeusz Tuczapski, the secretary of KOK, 'Protokół no. 002/81 posiedzenia Komitetu Obrony Kraju z dnia 13go wrzesnia 1981 r.', 13 Sept. 1981 in Centralne Archiwum Wojskowe (CAW), Materiały z posiedzen KOK, Teczka Sygnatura 48.

[24] 'Plenum Tsk KPSS–Noyabr' 1981 g.: Zasedanie vtoroe, vechernee, 16 noyabrya', 16 Nov. 1981 (Top Secret), in RGANI, F. 2, Op. 3, D. 568, Ll. 125–45.

still urging the Soviet Union to 'provide military help'. With the fate of the martial law operation still very much in doubt just hours before it was scheduled to begin, Soviet officials made arrangements for a high-level Soviet delegation, led by Suslov, to fly to Warsaw for emergency consultations at Jaruzelski's request.[25] This visit turned out to be unnecessary after Jaruzelski placed an urgent phone call to Suslov, who sternly told Jaruzelski that no Soviet troops would be sent to help him 'under any circumstances' and that the Polish leader should proceed as scheduled.[26]

Although Jaruzelski was distraught at having been 'left on [his] own', he regained sufficient composure to launch the operation and oversee a forceful, comprehensive crackdown. The Polish security forces crushed Solidarity with remarkable speed and efficiency. Nearly 6,000 opposition leaders and activists around the country, including Lech Wałęsa, were arrested within the first few hours. With administrative and logistical support from the Polish army, the Polish security forces eliminated all remaining pockets of resistance over the next four days. The martial law operation in Poland was a model of its kind, illustrating how an authoritarian regime could quell widespread social unrest with surprisingly little bloodshed.

No one can say for sure what the CPSU politburo would have done if somehow the martial law operation had failed and widespread violence had erupted. But it seems inconceivable that the Soviet Union would simply have stayed on the sidelines and allowed the Polish communist regime and Soviet troops in Poland to come under deadly attack. Even though it seems highly likely that the Soviet politburo would have sent troops into Poland to prevent all-out civil war and the violent collapse of the communist system, it is impossible to know beyond all doubt. The members of the Soviet politburo, like almost any collective body, did not want to make a final decision about 'extreme measures' unless forced to do so by dire necessity. Because they were confident that the martial law operation would succeed if Jaruzelski cracked down vigorously, they believed they could avoid deciding in advance about an unlikely and unpalatable military contingency. This calculation was amply borne out. The striking success of Jaruzelski's 'internal solution' on 12–13 December 1981 spared Soviet leaders from having to make any final decision about the dispatch of Soviet troops to Poland.

The surprisingly smooth imposition of martial law in Poland also helped to prevent any further instances of civil unrest in east-central Europe during the years before Gorbachev came to power. The lack of any major political turmoil in the Soviet bloc from 1982 to 1985 cannot be attributed to any single factor, but the martial law crackdown of December 1981, and the Soviet invasions of Hungary in 1956 and Czechoslovakia in 1968, are undoubtedly a part of the

---

[25] Mark Kramer, 'The Anoshkin Notebook on the Polish Crisis, December 1981', *Cold War International History Project Bulletin*, no. 11 (Winter 1998), 25.

[26] This phone call has been recounted by a number of former Soviet and Polish leaders. See, for example, Witold Bereś and Jerzy Skoczylas (eds.), *Generał Kiszczak mówi: Prawie wszystko* (Warsaw: BGW, 1991), 129–30.

explanation. After the death of Joseph Stalin in 1953, the limits of what could be changed in east-central Europe were still unknown, but by the early 1980s the Soviet Union had evinced its willingness and ability to prevent or reverse 'deviations from socialism'.

## GORBACHEV, NON-VIOLENT RESISTANCE, AND THE RADICAL CHANGE IN SOVIET POLICY

The sweeping political reforms introduced by Gorbachev in the late 1980s completely altered the Soviet government's response to civil resistance both in east-central Europe and in the Soviet Union itself. Far from seeking to crack down with force on non-violent resistance in east-central Europe, Gorbachev tolerated and indeed actively encouraged sweeping political change in the region. Similarly,

©Bundesarchiv, Bild 183-1986-0421-010 / Rainer Mittelstädt

**Figure 6.2** The importance of individual leaders. It is all smiles at this early public encounter between the newly appointed leader of the Soviet communist party, Mikhail Gorbachev (left), and Erich Honecker (right), the long-time leader of East Germany's communist party, at the 11th East German party congress in East Berlin in April 1986. But change at the centre of the Soviet empire, in Moscow, would contribute decisively to the emergence of civil resistance at the periphery, on the front line with the West. Honecker, bereft of Soviet support, was swept from power in October 1989.

by the late 1980s Gorbachev had given unprecedented latitude for the formation of unofficial groups in the Soviet Union that sought to achieve their demands through civil resistance. Even when in 1989 the communist systems in east-central Europe collapsed and when the proliferation of unrest in the Soviet Union began to threaten the Soviet regime's own existence, Gorbachev declined to use force with the ruthless consistency that would have been needed to re-establish order. Hence, civil resistance, which would have been forcibly suppressed under previous Soviet leaders, contributed to the dissolution of both the communist bloc and the Soviet Union.

The real issue for Gorbachev in east-central Europe was no longer whether he should uphold the Brezhnev Doctrine, but whether he could avoid the 'Khrushchev Dilemma'. The problem was not whether to accept peaceful domestic change, as in Czechoslovakia in 1968, but how to prevent widespread anti-Soviet violence from breaking out, as in Hungary in 1956. Gorbachev would have found himself in an intractable situation if he had been confronted by a large-scale, violent uprising in Poland, East Germany, Czechoslovakia, or Hungary. On the two previous occasions when violent rebellions threatened Soviet control over those countries—in East Germany in 1953 and Hungary in 1956—Gorbachev's predecessors responded with military force. If a comparable crisis had erupted in 1989, the pressure for Soviet military intervention would have been enormous, just as it was on Nikita Khrushchev in 1956.

Hence, Gorbachev's overriding objective was to avoid the Khrushchev Dilemma altogether. He could not afford to be confronted by a violent uprising in one of the key east-central European countries. Only by forestalling such a disastrous turn of events would he have any hope of moving ahead with his reform programme. The problem, however, was that his policies, by unleashing centrifugal forces within the Soviet bloc, had already made it *more* likely that a violent rebellion would occur. One of the main deterrents to popular anti-communist uprisings in east-central Europe after 1956 was the local populations' awareness that, if necessary, Soviet troops would intervene to crush resistance and restore control. Because this perceived constraint had been steadily diminishing under Gorbachev, the risk of a violent upheaval had increased commensurately.

The record of previous crises in east-central Europe and the prospect that new crises would emerge in the near future had convinced Gorbachev's advisers (and eventually Gorbachev himself) that, as Foreign Minister Eduard Shevardnadze put it, 'if positive changes [in east-central Europe] were suppressed or delayed, the whole situation would end in tragedy'.[27] Gorbachev also was aware, however, that unless these 'positive changes' occurred peacefully, his domestic reform programme—and his own political fate—would be in jeopardy.

Mindful of that dilemma, Gorbachev and his aides by late 1988 had established two basic goals for Soviet policy in east-central Europe: first, they wanted to avoid direct Soviet military intervention at all costs. Georgy Shakhnazarov, one of Gorbachev's closest aides, had emphasized in a memorandum to Gorbachev

---

[27] E. Shevardnadze, 'O vneshnei politike', *Pravda* (Moscow), 26 June 1990, 3.

that 'in the future, the prospect of "extinguishing" crisis situations [in eastern Europe] through military means must be completely ruled out'.[28] Second, they sought to achieve a peaceful but rapid transition to a new political order in east-central Europe. By drastically modifying the region's political complexion, they could defuse the pressures that had given rise to violent internal crises in the past.

The basic problem, however, was that if most of the communist regimes in east-central Europe had been left to their own devices, they would have sought to avoid liberalization indefinitely. The hard-line leaders in Czechoslovakia, East Germany, Bulgaria, and Romania had become increasingly repressive and in-transigent as the internal and external pressures for reform grew. These regimes were heartened in June 1989 when the leaders of the Chinese communist party launched an all-out assault against unarmed protesters near Tiananmen Square. The crackdown in Beijing came less than three weeks after Gorbachev had made a landmark visit to China, the first by a Soviet leader in thirty years. (The Chinese authorities had hoped that the protests, which began in April 1989, would soon peter out and that the demonstrators would be gone from Tiananmen Square by the time Gorbachev arrived in mid-May. Far from diminishing, however, the protests—and foreign press coverage of them—increased sharply in the lead-up to Gorbachev's visit.) Televised images of the bloodshed in China in early June reinforced the widespread belief in Moscow that urgent steps were needed to forestall destabilizing unrest in east-central Europe. But the 'lesson' drawn by the leaders of East Germany, Czechoslovakia, and Romania was just the opposite—namely, that any movement toward liberalization would be dangerous and that large-scale violent repression would enable them to crush all opposition. When Soviet officials realized that the hard-line regimes in east-central Europe were willing to emulate the Tiananmen Square massacre, they concluded that the Soviet Union must actively promote fundamental change in the region, rather than simply waiting and hoping that all would work out for the best.

The decision to assume an active role is what was so striking about the reorientation of Soviet policy toward east-central Europe under Gorbachev. It was not just a question of Gorbachev's willingness to accept and tolerate drastic changes in the Warsaw Pact countries: rather, he and his aides did their best to ensure that these changes occurred and that they occurred peacefully. Unlike in the past, when Gorbachev's predecessors relied on military force to 'defend socialism' in the Eastern bloc, the Soviet Union in 1989 had to play a direct part in countering the 'unsavoury processes' that might eventually have led to widespread violent unrest in one or more east-central European countries.

The radical implications of Gorbachev's approach were evident in early and mid-1989 when drastic reforms were adopted by Hungary and Poland, culmin-ating in the formation of a Solidarity-led government in Poland in August 1989. But the full magnitude of the forces unleashed by Gorbachev's policies did not

---

[28] 'K zasedaniyu Politbyuro 6/X-88 g.', 6 Oct. 1988 (Secret), reproduced in G. Kh. Shakhnazarov, *Tsena svobody: Reformatsiya Gorbacheva glazami ego pomoshchnika* (Moscow: Rossika-Zevs, 1993), 367–9.

become apparent until the last few months of 1989. Events that would have been unthinkable even a year or two earlier suddenly happened: peaceful revolutions from below in East Germany and Czechoslovakia, the dismantling of the Berlin Wall, popular ferment and the downfall of Todor Zhivkov in Bulgaria, and violent upheaval in Romania. As the orthodox communist regimes collapsed, the Soviet Union expressed approval and lent strong support to the reformist, non-communist governments that emerged. Soviet leaders also joined their east-central European counterparts in condemning previous instances of Soviet interference in east-central Europe, particularly the 1968 invasion of Czechoslovakia. In the past, the Soviet Union had done all it could to stifle and deter political liberalization in east-central Europe; but by late 1989 there was no doubt that all the countries in the region would enjoy full leeway to pursue drastic political and economic reforms, including the option of abandoning communism altogether.

Although Gorbachev had not intended to undermine the socialist bloc and did not foresee that the changes he initiated would lead to the rapid demise of communism in east-central Europe,[29] he stuck to his policies of promoting fundamental political change while avoiding the use of military force at all costs. Originally he had hoped to preserve the integrity of the Warsaw Pact and to create favourable conditions in east-central Europe for a liberalized form of communism ('socialism with a human face') that would enable the socialist commonwealth to overcome the political instability that had plagued it so often in the past. But when the process of change in east-central Europe took on a revolutionary momentum of its own and went much further than he anticipated, he declined to interrupt it or even to try to slow it down.

In every respect, then, Gorbachev's approach to civil resistance in east-central Europe from mid-1988 on was radically different from that of his predecessors. Previous Soviet leaders had sought to maintain orthodox communist regimes in east-central Europe, if necessary through the use of military force against non-violent social movements. Gorbachev, by contrast, wanted to avoid military intervention in east-central Europe at all costs. Hence, his paramount objective was to defuse the pressures in the region that might eventually have led to violent anti-Soviet uprisings. This objective, in turn, required him to go much further than he initially anticipated. In effect, Gorbachev actively promoted fundamental political change in east-central Europe while there was still some chance of benefiting from it, rather than risk being confronted later on by widespread violence that would all but compel him to send in troops. The hope was that by supporting the sweeping but peaceful transformation of east-central Europe over the near term, the Soviet Union would never again have to contend with large-scale outbreaks of anti-Soviet violence in the region, as Khrushchev had to do in 1956. This basic strategy, of encouraging and managing drastic, non-violent change in order to prevent much more severe crises, achieved its immediate aim,

---

[29] For ample evidence, see 'Vypiska iz protokola no. 165 zasedaniya Politbyuro TsK KPSS ot 11 sentyabrya 1989 goda: O zayavlenii TASS v podderzhku Germanskoi Demokraticheskoi Respubliki', no. P165/6 (Top Secret), 11 Sept. 1989, in RGANI, F. 89, Op. 9, D. 30.

but in the process it both necessitated and ensured the collapse of the Soviet bloc in east-central Europe.

## PERCEPTIONS OF THE SOVIET REGIME'S VULNERABILITY, 1989–91

The demise of the Soviet bloc had an indirect but crucial impact on relations between the Soviet regime and the newly formed opposition and protest movements within the Soviet Union itself. Initially, most of the 'informal' (*neformalnye*) groups that emerged in Russia and the other republics of the Soviet Union were supportive of Gorbachev and perestroika, and their demands focused mainly on goals that the Soviet leader himself was pursuing. But as the leeway for change continued to expand, the objectives of these groups became much more ambitious.

By early to mid-1989, as events in Poland and Hungary were moving far beyond the limits that existed in the past, many of the unofficial groups in the Soviet Union began stepping up their demands. Coal miners in Russia and Ukraine embarked on large-scale strikes in July 1989 to seek better working conditions and greater compensation. Although the miners voiced support for Gorbachev and his reforms, the strikes were an unmistakable sign of the growing militancy of the workers' movement. Similarly, in the union-republics, where the leeway for peaceful mobilization by 1989 was vastly greater than in the past, the newly formed popular fronts and other unofficial groups were ever more willing to test the bounds of official tolerance. Despite a brutal crackdown by Soviet troops in Tbilisi, the capital of Soviet Georgia, in April 1989, nationalist groups in the Soviet Union's three Baltic republics began to sense that they could aspire not only to extensive autonomy but also to full-fledged independence. Although Gorbachev and other high-ranking Soviet officials repeatedly warned that Latvia, Estonia, and Lithuania would have to remain part of the Soviet Union, political activists in those republics increasingly viewed the Soviet annexation of the Baltic states (a 'long-endured grievance', in Tocqueville's phrasing) as 'intolerable' once 'the thought of removing it' had finally arisen.

Coming at a time of mounting political ferment in the Soviet Union, the upheavals in east-central Europe in 1989 fuelled a widespread perception in the Baltic states and other union-republics that the moment was right to challenge the Soviet regime. If Gorbachev had clamped down in east-central Europe and had used large-scale force to prevent the communist governments from collapsing, separatist groups in the Soviet Union undoubtedly would have been more fearful that attempts to defy or break away from Soviet rule would incur a violent response. Vytautas Landsbergis, who was one of the founding leaders of the Sąjūdis independence movement in Lithuania in 1988 and was elected president of the republic in 1990, later recalled that the dramatic changes in east-central Europe gave Sąjūdis greater confidence in pressing its demands for independence.

Thus the collapse of communism in east-central Europe helped to radicalize the political opposition in the Soviet Union. If Gorbachev had come to the 'defence of socialism' in 1989 by sending troops into east-central Europe as previous Soviet leaders had done, he would have drawn a line—indirectly but forcefully—for the burgeoning separatist organizations and protest movements in the Soviet Union. But by doing the opposite—by allowing and even facilitating the complete dissolution of communist rule in east-central Europe—Gorbachev inadvertently emboldened the very individuals and groups in the Soviet Union that were most intent on challenging the communist regime and breaking away from the Soviet state.

Gorbachev's unwillingness to use force in east-central Europe did not necessarily foreshadow his response to dangers *within* the Soviet Union. Until well into 1991, Stephen Kotkin argues, 'no one [in the Soviet Union] could exclude the possibility of an attempted crackdown to save the Union'.[30] Indeed, the abrupt collapse of the communist regimes in east-central Europe, and the dismantling of the secret police organs in the former East-bloc countries (especially the State Security Ministry in East Germany), prompted some high-ranking officials in the CPSU and KGB to fear that the same thing might happen in the Soviet Union unless they took forceful action to prevent it. They urged Gorbachev to use all-out violence, when necessary, to forestall or crush severe internal threats.

Although some officials in Moscow favoured a broad internal clampdown after the upheavals in east-central Europe, the drastic reorientation of Soviet–east European ties was itself an impediment to that option. The policy that Gorbachev adopted vis-à-vis east-central Europe in 1989—a policy that conspicuously ruled out Soviet military interference—inadvertently limited his freedom of action at home by making it more difficult for him to contemplate resorting to force, no matter how grave the threats he confronted. Having refrained from sending troops into east-central Europe to prevent the collapse of communist regimes, Gorbachev found it even harder than before to justify the violent suppression of peaceful groups within the Soviet Union that were seeking independence or an end to communist rule.

Gorbachev's reluctance to order violent repression at home and his decision to forgo the use of force in east-central Europe eroded the morale of the personnel and organizations in the Soviet Union that were responsible for safeguarding the integrity of the state. Soviet newspapers featured a litany of articles in 1990 about military officers who vowed they would not open fire on civilians even if ordered to do so.

To the extent that the changes in east-central Europe contributed to Gorbachev's indecisiveness about the use of force against internal threats, they weakened a central pillar of the Soviet regime. Crane Brinton observed in his study of revolution that regimes have been overthrown not when they were most repressive, but when the rulers undertook reforms and became 'more than half ashamed

---

[30] Stephen Kotkin, *Armageddon Averted: The Soviet Collapse, 1970–2000* (New York: Oxford University Press, 2001), 92.

to use force, and therefore used it badly, so that on the whole those on whom force was inflicted were stimulated rather than repressed'.[31] Gorbachev's vacillations in the Baltic republics in January 1991, when he first authorized a crackdown but then failed to complete it, reflected the diffidence and irresolution that Brinton described. The Soviet leader's Hamlet-like qualities, and his failure to use force consistently and decisively, were evident before the upheavals in east-central Europe, but they became all the more pronounced after the events of 1989.

## THE DEMONSTRATION EFFECT OF CIVIL RESISTANCE

When political crises erupted in the Soviet bloc in the pre-Gorbachev era, Soviet leaders tried to ensure that the only information available to Soviet citizens about those events was the official version approved by the CPSU politburo. During upheavals in Czechoslovakia and East Germany in 1953, Poland and Hungary in 1956, Czechoslovakia and Poland in 1968, and Poland in 1980–1, high-ranking Soviet officials exercised rigid control of the Soviet mass media and censored all coverage of external developments. By severely limiting the flow of information, they sought to minimize the spillover from east-central Europe and to prevent the crises there from becoming a catalyst of unrest within the Soviet Union itself.

By 1989, however, the top-down control of information in the Soviet Union had eroded. Glasnost (the freer flow of information) by that point had taken firm root within the Soviet media, especially in the press. The round-table process in Poland and the ferment in Hungary in 1989 were covered extensively and often accurately by Soviet journalists. When the 'winds of change' began to spread into the other east-central European countries, some officials in Moscow warned that Soviet press coverage of the escalating turmoil should be strictly limited.

These warnings proved of little efficacy. At Aleksandr Yakovlev's urging, Gorbachev not only eschewed a clampdown on the media but actually removed most of the lingering controls. On 18 November 1989 the CPSU politburo adopted a resolution calling for the 'further expansion of glasnost' and the 'elimination of all restrictions and bans [on the press] that are contrary to international law and that are not in keeping with the obligations undertaken by the Soviet Union in accordance with the all-European [human rights] provisions of the Helsinki Final Act'.[32] This resolution essentially did away with any limits on media coverage of the upheavals in east-central Europe and allowed the Soviet public to learn all about the dramatic changes that led to the demise of communism in eastern Europe.

---

[31] Crane Brinton, *The Anatomy of Revolution*, rev. edn. (New York: Prentice-Hall, 1952), 53.

[32] 'Vypiska iz protokola no. 172 zasedaniya Politbyuro TsK KPSS ot 19 noyabrya 1989 g.: O dopolnitel'nykh merakh v informatsionnoi sfere', Resolution no. P172/9 (Top Secret), 18 Nov. 1989, in RGANI, F. 89, Op. 9, D. 55, Ll. 1–5.

108 *Mark Kramer*

**Figure 6.3** Civil resistance at the heart of an empire. Boris Yeltsin (left), president of what was then still the Russian Soviet Federative Socialist Republic, part of the Soviet Union, reads a statement from atop a tank in Moscow, 19 August 1991, as he urges people to resist the attempted *coup d'état*. Seated at right is a Soviet soldier covering his face. A group of Kremlin conspirators had tried to stop any further reforms in the Soviet Union and to hold the state together, but the coup collapsed on 21 August following extensive civil resistance, particularly in Moscow. Four months later, the Soviet Union disintegrated into 15 countries and Soviet President Mikhail Gorbachev resigned, leaving Yeltsin in full control of a newly independent Russian Federation.

The unhindered coverage of events in east-central Europe had enormous implications for political stability within the Soviet Union. When Pavel Palazhchenko, who served as an interpreter and foreign policy aide for both Gorbachev and Shevardnadze in 1985–91, later sought to understand 'why the pattern of developments in East Germany, eastern Europe, and the Soviet Union was so similar [and] why it all happened almost simultaneously', he concluded that the role of 'the [Soviet] media, particularly television, [in] spreading the contagion of impatience in vivid images', was the most crucial factor.[33]

[33] Pavel Palazhchenko, *My Years with Gorbachev and Shevardnadze: The Memoir of a Soviet Interpreter* (University Park, Pa.: Pennsylvania State University Press, 1997), 177.

The succession of crises in the neighbouring Warsaw Pact countries in 1989 provided an example to separatist groups within the Soviet Union—and to leading officials in the Soviet republic governments—of the political goals to which they themselves could aspire. The upheavals in eastern Europe not only confirmed that fundamental change in the communist world through non-violent resistance was finally possible, but also offered a model for how the Soviet Union itself could be transformed. Many of the radical steps taken by the east European countries to end communist rule were soon emulated by Soviet opposition movements.

The 'demonstration effect' of the changes in east-central Europe was especially far-reaching in the Baltic states, where separatist leaders regarded the non-violent mass protests in East Germany and Czechoslovakia as a model for their own republics' path to independence. By helping to inspire newly formed opposition and separatist movements in the Soviet Union to challenge the Soviet regime through civil resistance, and by greatly reducing Gorbachev's leeway to use violent repression, the peaceful demise of communism in east-central Europe also spelled the beginning of the end of the Soviet Union.

A fitting coda to the story came in August 1991 when hard-line officials in Moscow launched a *coup d'état* to clamp down on civil unrest and restore old-style communist controls. One of the main organizers of the coup, KGB chairman Vladimir Kryuchkov, planned to send an elite KGB Al'fa unit to storm the White House, the headquarters of the Russian government headed by Boris Yeltsin. Soldiers under the command of another coup organizer, defence minister Dmitrii Yazov, were to assist in the crackdown. But when faced with the prospect of using repressive violence against a peaceful crowd that had gathered at the White House, the coup plotters backed down. As recently as December 1990, Kryuchkov had expressed his willingness to implement a violent crackdown, but when the crucial moment came in August 1991 neither he nor Yazov was willing to take responsibility for large-scale bloodshed without explicit authorization from the top. Gorbachev had refused to go along with the coup, just as he had earlier declined to use military repression in east-central Europe. As a result, the whole venture collapsed. The failure of the coup mortally weakened the Soviet regime and left Yeltsin's Russia and other Soviet republics ascendant. Within five months, the Soviet Union was dissolved.

# 7

## Civil Resistance in Czechoslovakia: From Soviet Invasion to 'Velvet Revolution', 1968–89

*Kieran Williams*

In August 1968, the Soviet Union and four other Warsaw Pact states invaded their ally, Czechoslovakia, to reverse its popular experiment in reform socialism. Rather than cow the people into submission, the invasion provoked spontaneous and widespread non-violent opposition. Practically all of the textbook tactics were utilized, coinciding conveniently with the take-off of academic interest in the subject.[1] Events in the capital were amply documented on the spot by Czech historians, who compiled a thick dossier of press clippings, statements, and eyewitness accounts, *Seven days in Prague*, which was printed in a limited run in late 1968 and soon translated into English and other languages.[2] Skilling and Eidlin also examined the resistance as part of the second wave of scholarship on 1968.[3] Today we can build on the enduring strengths of these analyses with materials made available only after the end of communist rule in 1989—itself the product of a remarkable non-violent movement.

In this chapter I revisit the resistance of 1968, treating it as technically perfect, neither a success nor a failure but largely irrelevant to the fate of reform socialism, which the invasion had sought to interrupt. New sources help us better understand what was taking place at the political-elite level, where the civil resistance was not taken into account and not used by Czechoslovak reformers to enhance their bargaining power in talks with the Soviets. Declassified documents also

The author thanks Alex Pravda for his very helpful comments on a draft of this chapter.

[1] See e.g. Adam Roberts (ed.), *Civilian Resistance as a National Defence* (Harmondsworth: Penguin Books, 1969), which was a reprint, with a new introduction, of *The Strategy of Civilian Defence* (London: Faber, 1967); and Theodor Ebert, 'Der zivile Widerstand in der Tschechoslowakei 1968', in Theodor Ebert (ed.), *Ziviler Widerstand* (Düsseldorf: Bertelsmann-Universitätverlag, 1970).

[2] *Sedm pražských dnů. 21.–27. srpen 1968. Dokumentace* (Prague: reissued by Academia, 1990). In English as Robert Littell (ed.), *The Czech Black Book* (New York: Praeger, 1969).

[3] H. Gordon Skilling, *Czechoslovakia's Interrupted Revolution* (Princeton: Princeton University Press, 1976), 775–88; Fred Eidlin, *The Logic of 'Normalization'* (Boulder: East European Monographs, 1980) and Fred Eidlin, '"Capitulation", "Resistance" and the Framework of "Normalization"', *Journal of Peace Research*, 18, no. 4 (1981).

teach us not to reduce civil resistance to *civilian* resistance, as we can now appreciate the non-violent contributions of uniformed officers of militarized institutions, such as the army and interior ministry.

I also compare 1968 with 1989, contrasting the different circumstances, methods, and impact on power politics while following the common thread of a discourse of legalism—the belief in law as an autonomous, universal mediating force in relations between citizens and the state. Starting symbolically from a symposium on the concept of the state in March 1959, convened by the Academy of Sciences' Institute of Law, until the revolution thirty years later, we can trace a sustained drive to rescue the rule of law in Czechoslovakia.[4] Young jurists worked first within the new establishment after the communist seizure of power in 1948, rose to positions of great influence during the liberalization of 1968, and then in middle age moved into the realm of dissent. Their outlook informed countless documents issued in the 1970s and 1980s, pressing the regime to honour its obligations to respect human rights and permit a true constitutionalism.[5] This legalism played an important part both in mobilizing participation and in preventing the use of violence in response to invasion in 1968 and to police brutality in 1989.

## EVENTS AND METHODS

Shortly before midnight on 20 August 1968, for reasons expertly identified by Mark Kramer in his contribution to this volume, the Soviet Union and four other Warsaw Pact states began moving thousands of tanks and hundreds of thousands of soldiers across the Czechoslovak border. They did so in such large numbers to neutralize the Czechoslovak army and allow a faction of the Czechoslovak Communist Party (KSČ) to take power and reverse a course of reforms launched earlier that year under the leadership of First Secretary Alexander Dubček. The conspiracy had banked on winning a vote in the KSČ leadership, the Presidium, on a motion to declare the country to be in crisis, request outside military assistance and sideline the best-known reformers. Instead, two secondary but still necessary conspirators in the Presidium baulked at the last minute, sided with the reformers, and voted to condemn the invasion. The text of that condemnation was then telephoned to the central radio studio, from which it was broadcast before collaborators there were in full control. The original plan fast unravelling, the Soviets had to improvise; before dawn Dubček and other reformers were arrested and eventually taken to the Soviet Union. On 23 August talks began in Moscow between the Soviets and their captives, resulting four days later in their safe return to Czechoslovakia.

[4] Vladimir V. Kusin, *The Intellectual Origins of the Prague Spring* (Cambridge: Cambridge University Press, 1971), 31–5.
[5] Zdeněk Jičínský, *Charta 77 a právní stát* (Brno: Doplněk, 1995), 94–149.

During the week that followed the invasion, Czechs and Slovaks displayed an almost unanimous opposition to gross interference in their domestic affairs. Their outrage was voiced and organized through underground media—news-papers, radio and, perhaps for the first time anywhere, television. Countless chapters and branches of every legal organization passed resolutions of refusal to recognize a communist party or government led by anyone other than the reformers whom the Soviets had abducted. Citizens also expressed their oppos-ition through graffiti, placards, petitions, jokes, songs, and poems, the compos-ition of which was often coordinated at local 'slogan centres' staffed by students, educators, artists, and actors.[6] In the first forty-eight hours after the invasion began, citizens fraternized with the soldiers to undermine their belief that a counter-revolution was taking place, and to reduce their willingness to fire on civilians. Later, as reports spread of foreign intelligence officers arriving to arrest prominent reformers still at large, radio directed residents to take down street signs, house numbers and any plaques that could identify a government building. When the invading armies' supply lines broke down, Czechs and Slovaks withheld food and water. Finally, the country came to a standstill during brief general strikes (for two minutes on 21 August, for one hour on 22 August, and again for one hour on 23 August).

For reasons relating to power politics discussed below, despite this technically magnificent resistance Czechoslovakia did not stay on the path of reform social-ism, and by the early 1970s had become one of the most oppressive regimes in the Soviet bloc. When a mass movement against it coalesced in November 1989, many of the same tactics were in evidence, such as graffiti, placards, the use of humour to diffuse tension, and a similarly brief general strike (for two hours on 27 November). Fundamentally different, however, was an emphasis on large public demonstrations in the main cities and towns, which in August 1968 were expressly discouraged by radio lest they provoke attack by Soviet units. This difference reflected a different sort of confrontation in 1989, between students, actors, workers, and intellectuals on the one hand and on the other the indigenous communist establishment backed by its own security forces, not jittery foreign armies that might overreact to the slightest provocation. Tens of thousands of Soviet troops were garrisoned in the country, but even the conser-vative KSČ leadership did not expect or seek their involvement.

The path to the breathtakingly large demonstrations of 1989, however, was not easily found and was not consciously selected in advance as the main tactic. On around thirty occasions between March 1988 and November 1989, human rights groups had called for gatherings without permission in sensitive central areas of the major cities, such as Wenceslas Square in Prague or Hviezdoslav Square in Bratislava. On half of those occasions riot police intervened harshly.[7] The

---

[6] Jindřich Pecka, *Spontanní projevy Pražského jara 1968–1969* (Brno: Doplněk, 1993), 18.

[7] Oldřich Tůma, *Zítra zase tady!* (Prague: Maxdorf, 1994), 49–50.

©Stefan Tyszko/Contributor (Hulton Archive) Getty Images

**Figure 7.1** The inventiveness of resistance. Prague, late August 1968. To prevent the invading Warsaw Pact forces from finding their way around the country, Czechoslovak citizens broke or took down road signs. A radio broadcast on 23 August, when Czechoslovak radio was still controlled by independent-minded journalists, encouraged such actions.

predictability of this outcome deterred the faint-hearted majority of citizens from heeding the call to congregate; before November 1989 not one of the attempted rallies surpassed the turnout of those in August 1969, on the first anniversary of the Soviet-led invasion.[8] Furthermore, only a certain age group had tended to take part—those between twenty-five and forty, the generation directly shaped by

---

[8] Oldřich Tůma, 'Protirežimní demonstrace v Praze', in Petr Blažek (ed.), *Opozice a odpor proti komunistickému režimu v Československu 1968–1989* (Prague: Dokořán, 2005), 153.

1968 and the subsequent restoration of one-party rule ('normalization'). Just 11 per cent were younger university students.[9]

To break out of this pattern, student organizers Monika Pajerová and Martin Mejstřík had looked for inspiration to what was happening in East Germany: so they went to observe the Monday marches in Leipzig.[10] Pajerová and Mejstřík returned from Leipzig with the idea of holding a demonstration in a more low-key area of Prague, and of getting permission to do so.[11] As the ostensible grounds for the gathering they found material in a different usable past, leapfrogging over 1968 back to the events of October and November 1939. Then, as so often in the twentieth century, Czechs had used a national holiday (28 October, Independence Day) as the first occasion to protest the occupation of their country by Nazi Germany. Many of the gestures would be replicated by future generations: the day was honoured with formal dress, black armbands and the Czechoslovak tricolour; workers downed tools; thousands of university students marched from their halls to Wenceslas Square, singing the national anthem, demanding freedom and the law. Crowds grew, were dispersed, and reassembled; in the tumult one medical student, Jan Opletal, was fatally wounded. His funeral on 15 November 1939 turned into still another protest, used by the Germans as a pretext two days later to close the universities, summarily execute nine students and dispatch 1,200 others to Sachsenhausen.[12] Czech exiles soon succeeded in making 17 November International Students' Day, and the post-war communist regime sustained an Opletal cult even though he had not been a member of the party. It was therefore plausible for the official Union of Socialist Youth (of which Mejstřík was a leading, if maverick, member) to act as a sponsor of a commemoration. There was even an appropriately out-of-the-way place to assemble, by the pathology laboratory from which Opletal's funeral procession had started out fifty years before; a march to the nearby Vyšehrad cemetery, where many giants of national culture lay buried, could easily be included.[13]

Thus was born the rally scheduled for Friday, 17 November 1989. With the city's permission, the sponsorship of the established youth union *and* the blessing of informal, quasi-dissident student networks, thousands more turned up than would have had it been either a purely official or purely unofficial event.[14] Very quickly the speakers' remarks turned from history to the present, demanding changes in the country's leadership and greater freedom of expression and association. When the approved programme had ended and a remnant of the

---

[9] Tůma, *Zítra zase tady!*, 46–7; Tůma, 'Protirežimní demonstrace v Praze', 156.

[10] See Charles Maier's discussion of events in East Germany, Ch. 16 below.

[11] Milan Otáhal and Miroslav Vaněk, *Sto studentských revolucí* (Prague: Lidové noviny, 1999), 629. Dissident groups had done something similar in Prague on 10 December 1988. That it was organized by established dissident groups, however, deterred a large turnout.

[12] Jozef Leikert, *Čierny piatok sedemnásteho novembra* (Bratislava: VEDA, 2000); Karel Hvížd'ala, 'Jediný český svátek', *Mladá fronta DNES*, 16 Nov. 2001.

[13] Bernard Wheaton and Zdeněk Kavan, *The Velvet Revolution: Czechoslovakia, 1988–1991* (Boulder, Colo.: Westview Press, 1992), 41–2.

[14] *Deset pražských dnů. 17.-27. listopad 1989. Dokumentace* (Prague: Academia, 1990), 559.

throng marched down from Vyšehrad toward the more traditional (and central) Wenceslas Square, they encountered cordons of riot police. The marchers clearly presented passive, non-threatening behaviour; the police beat them savagely.

That incident, caught on film by four western television crews, followed by unfounded rumours of a student's death (reminding many of Opletal's fate), led within forty-eight hours to a cascade of steadily bolder calls for further action. The students moved first, declaring a one-week sit-in strike at the universities and demanding an inquiry into responsibility for the police brutality of 17 November. Stage actors stepped in next, joining in a sympathy strike and offering their theatres as places of public discussion; they were the first to call for a general strike to take place for two hours on Monday 27 November. Dissidents then chimed in, framing the recent events and initial responses in their standard terms of justice, responsibility, and dialogue *within the existing order*, rather than as demands for wholesale system change.[15]

By the following Monday, 20 November, it had become clear that segments of the workforce were willing to second these objections and objectives, but within the safe confines of signing petitions, issuing statements and—in the case of journalists—overcoming self-censorship. Up to now the resemblance to forms of resistance in 1968 was strong, minus the makeshift media networks, since information could be spread with the help of widely-received Western, Polish, and Hungarian radio and television broadcasts that the regime had stopped trying to jam in late 1988.[16] Videotapes of the 17 November incident could be copied and the cassettes circulated widely, while the existence of personal computers and photocopiers, two means practically unknown in 1968, made it easy to leaflet the entire country.

The shift to riskier outdoor demonstrations is hard to pinpoint, as there was no clear summons from an authoritative body, such as the emerging conglomerates of dissidents, students, and artists known in the Czech part of the country as Citizens' Forum and in Slovakia as The Public against Violence. University students' representatives in Prague had decided on Sunday 19 November that, since it had been possible over the weekend for groups to mill about in central Prague without being dispersed, every day at 4 pm there would be a 'meeting' at the statue of patron saint Václav on Wenceslas Square. This decision, however, was not publicized in a press release or flyer; student strike committees in individual departments would spread the word by mouth. All eyes were on the general strike a week away, with agitators fanning out across the country to ensure participation. It was assumed that no political breakthrough could be achieved before a massive but brief gesture of national unity, if need be followed by a major demonstration on 10 December (Human Rights Day), leading to some sort of

---

[15] *Deset pražských dnů*, 31–8; Wheaton and Kavan, *Velvet Revolution*, 52–64. On framing during the 1989 revolution, see John Glenn, 'Competing Challengers and Contested Outcomes to State Breakdown: The Velvet Revolution in Czechoslovakia', *Social Forces*, 78, no. 1 (1999).

[16] Prokop Tomek, 'Rušení zahraničního rozhlasového vysílání pro Československo', in *Securitas imperii 9* (Prague: Tiskárna MV, 2002), 372.

high-level dialogue about the new constitution that the communists were planning to introduce, or a referendum, or...?

Instead, as daily situation reports compiled by the KSČ and secret police (StB) help us understand,[17] a shift in attitudes and tactics emerged incidentally, without conscious design, late on the afternoon of 20 November, as striking students—joined now by pupils from secondary schools—found their way to various gathering places around Prague and second city Brno to sign petitions, chant, and exchange opinions. Like their counterparts in 1939, they wore the Czechoslovak tricolour; humour was often used to diffuse tension in encounters with the police, who, apart from deflecting a march headed toward the president's seat in Prague Castle, did not intervene. The head count may have been enormous, at least 150,000 people, as even the communist party's daily newspaper admitted.[18] A major psychological barrier had been broken; with each subsequent day, crowds of ever-greater size gathered in all cities. On 24 November, even before the general strike, the despised KSČ leadership resigned.

## CONDITIONS AND PRIMING

Despite the unmistakable regional differences across Czechoslovakia, what is most striking when we look beyond Prague to what was happening in the smaller cities and towns and in Slovakia is the uniformity of the public's response, especially in 1968: the same impulses and phases of activity played out much as they did in the capital. This uniformity was a function, in part, of the media's reach, but also of the relative egalitarianism and homogeneity of Czechoslovak society, which Carter identifies as favourable conditions for non-violent resistance.[19] Differences in culture and economic development notwithstanding, no division ran so deeply between Czechs, Slovaks and the Polish, Rusyn, and Hungarian minorities that a common front could not be maintained.[20] In 1989 underlying conditions remained favourable, and perhaps had become even more so: the purge and suppression of untrustworthy professions during 'normalization' had reversed the 1960s' creep toward meritocracy. The Czechoslovak society of the 1980s was artificially levelled, with most people's status and employment out of sync with their abilities, and a pronounced gap between the party elite and

---

[17] František Koudelka, *Situační zprávy ústředního aparátu KSČ. 20. listopadu—1 prosince 1989* (Prague: Ústav pro soudobé dějiny, 1999); *Securitas imperii 6* (Prague: Themis, 2000); Pavel Žáček, *ŠtB na Slovensku za 'normalizace'* (Bratislava: Ministerstvo spravodlivosti SR, 2002).

[18] *Deset pražských dnů*, 130–6.

[19] April Carter, 'Political Conditions for Civilian Defence', in Roberts (ed.), *Civilian Resistance as a National Defence*, 319.

[20] On the social structure of the time, see Pavel Machonin, *Sociální struktura Československa v předvečer Pražského jara 1968* (Prague: Karolinum, 1992), esp. 19–22 comparing the Czech-speaking lands and Slovakia.

everyone else.[21] Owing to extensive industrialization in post-invasion Slovakia, once-considerable differences between the two constituent parts of the federation in income, education, and urbanization had been greatly reduced by the late 1980s.[22]

That the Czechoslovak public could engage in peaceful forms of resistance in 1968 with little coaching or advance planning suggests three forms of priming over the years. First, in all likelihood, they had been innocently exposed by official media to images and accounts of resistance overseas, as part of the state's anti-American, anti-imperialist discourse. That some of the first graffiti scrawled in August 1968 used the terms *pasivní resistence* and '*Rusové* [Russians] go home' suggests a familiarity with methods and catchphrases from North and South America and Asia.[23] The May 1968 events in Paris had been widely reported and closely followed in Czechoslovakia,[24] and the long French strike from mid-May into June may have inspired the immediate decision by the Prague municipal branch of the communist party to call for a general strike in response to the invasion.

Second, the communist state had also kept certain forms of peaceful protest alive at home for its own propaganda purposes, for example by getting millions of citizens to sign anti-nuclear 'petitions for peace' in 1950–1.[25] Those techniques had been rehearsed with a patriotic twist shortly before the invasion, in late July, when thousands signed declarations in support of the country's leaders as they travelled to the Slovak-Ukrainian border for talks with the Soviet politburo.[26]

Finally, by making the study of Russian language compulsory in schools, the state had created a population (especially the younger generation) able and willing to converse directly with many of the invading soldiers. One compilation of graffiti, placards, flyers, and jokes from the invasion week estimates that 8 per cent were composed in Russian.[27]

## FRAMING NON-VIOLENCE

It is important not to trivialize the incidents of violence that did occur and the possibility of their escalation. The initial reactions to the 1968 invasion were

[21] See articles by Milan Tuček and Pavel Machonin in *Sociologický časopis*, 28, no. 1 (1992).

[22] Ales Capek and Gerald Sazama, 'Czech and Slovak Economic Relations', *Europe–Asia Studies*, 45, no. 2 (1993), 214–18.

[23] *Sedm pražských dnů*, 33, 43, 82; Pecka, *Spontanní projevy Pražského jara 1968–1969*, 55.

[24] Pecka, *Spontanní projevy Pražského jara 1968–1969*, 48. At the time Czechoslovak students had carefully expressed solidarity only with the peaceful march in Paris on 13 May, not with the violent Night of the Barricades (10–11 May).

[25] Boris Titzl, 'Podpisové akce "za mír" 1950 a 1951', in *Securitas imperii 7* (Prague: Themis, 2001).

[26] Dušan Havlíček, *The Mass Media in Czechoslovakia in 1956–1968* (No name or place of publication specified, 1981), part III, 11. Publication details were deliberately obscured so the regime would not know where it was coming from.

[27] Pecka, *Spontanní projevy Pražského jara 1968–1969*, 16.

more confrontational, such as pelting tanks with rocks and bottles, using buses to erect barricades, congregating in squares near historical monuments, and sometimes forming human chains. In several instances, invading units panicked and opened fire; seventeen civilians were killed in front of the main radio studio on the morning of 21 August. Although tempers soon cooled, there was a constant, even rising tension as days passed and little news trickled out of the negotiations in Moscow. Here and there we can pick up hints of a readiness to move to methods reminiscent of partisan warfare under German occupation, if the Czechoslovak delegation did not return soon (or at all). Bolder members of the communist party's municipal committee for Prague had been thinking before the invasion about some degree of armed resistance,[28] and it was again this branch of the party that wanted to push at a clandestine meeting of delegates to the KSČ congress on 22 August for an *indefinite* general strike and perhaps armed resistance. The congress voted instead for a toned-down appeal for a symbolic one-hour strike on 23 August, although it retained a vague threat to take 'further necessary measures'.[29] Several instances have since come to light of army units

©Josef Koudelka/Magnum Photographs

**Figure 7.2** The general strike as a method of resistance against the Soviet-led invasion. Wenceslas Square, in the centre of Prague, is deserted as a one-hour general strike begins at midday on 22 August 1968. A celebrated photograph by the Czech photographer Josef Koudelka, subsequently smuggled out of the country and exhibited abroad. Koudelka asked a passer-by to stretch out his arm, with the watch showing the time.

[28] Pecka, *Spontanní projevy Pražského jara 1968–1969*, 17 n. 60.
[29] Archive of the Czechoslovak Federal Government's Commission for Analysis of the Events of 1967–1970 (hereafter, AKV ČSFR), R123, interview with Zdeněk Hejzlar, 1 October 1990.

caching weapons before they could be confiscated by the Soviets, and an embryonic partisan command post was set up at the military academy in Brno.[30]

In certain key sectors, workers went on longer strikes, with potentially great economic impact. Workers at the Dolní Rožínka and Zadní Chodov uranium mines—vital to the Soviet weapons programme—were on strike from 22 August, ready to flood or seal the shafts with explosives if invading armies tried to seize control. They also concealed weapons belonging to People's Militia, the paramilitary wing of the communist party, and ran their own radio transmitters.[31] In North Moravia, miners cut back output to below half their normal level, just enough to keep coal-fired power plants running without generating any surplus that could be exported or expropriated by Soviet or Polish troops. Workers in nearby engineering plants refused to manufacture any goods under contract to Soviet buyers.[32] Efforts to mobilize volunteers to minimize economic damage, such as to bring in the hops harvest essential to the country's brewing industry, sometimes contained hints of what might lie ahead: a flyer circulated by the Czechoslovak Campers' Association directed its members to start constructing refuges in the woods and hills to hide citizens being sought by the KGB, and as base camps for 'an underground struggle (*boj*) with the occupiers'.[33]

Several centripetal forces worked to contain the rising tension. The first was the centralism of the Leninist political model still intact at the time of the invasion. Most expressions of opposition to the invasion were natural extensions of the main form of participation in Leninist systems: the meeting of the local communist party cell or workplace collective to discuss and issue a response to a statement or document issued by the party centre. In 'normal', Soviet, conditions this was a formality to ensure compliance and surveillance; in extraordinary conditions, such as the liberalization of spring and summer 1968, it provided a framework to allow freer but still structured discourse. Even in the invasion week, the 'call and response' culture set down in the totalitarian model survived in adapted form, since the first step was taken by the communist party Presidium with its official condemnation of the invasion, issued less than two hours after foreign armies began crossing the border. Two things are noteworthy about that statement: first, it expressly disavowed armed resistance as futile, while condemning the invasion as a violation of the norms of international law.[34] That statement from the Presidium (and the abduction of its leading members) then became the focal point around which all other institutions, national and local, could mobilize their protests, parroting both the legalism of its language and its rejection of violence.

---

[30] Antonín Benčík, *Operace 'Dunaj'* (Prague: Ústav pro soudobé dějiny, 1994), 132.

[31] Prokop Tomek, *Československý uran 1945–1989* (Prague: Úřad dokumentace a vyšetřování zločinů komunismu, 2000), 40.

[32] Karel Jiřík, *Události let 1967–1970 v Ostravě* (Ostrava: Archív města Ostrava, 1991), 64–5.

[33] Jindřich Pecka, Josef Belda, and Jiří Hoppe (eds.), *Občanská společnost (1967–1970)* (Brno: Doplněk, 1995), 390.

[34] *Sedm pražských dn.*, 19.

Second, the media remained pervasive enough to reach most of the population, to discourage confrontation with the invaders, and—in combination with state and party institutions and ad hoc slogan centres—to impose a framework that constructed just going about one's normal business, living a lawful life under the legally constituted authorities, as a form of defiance, a display of respect for the pre-invasion laws and institutions of a sovereign country.[35] Congregating was expressly discouraged lest it provoke violent dispersal by Soviet forces, whom the public were advised simply to ignore. Anger at collaborators in the party leadership was channelled away from lynching into demands for formal prosecution and into petitions demanding their recall as representatives in the National Assembly. Citizens wanting to write graffiti and post placards were given detailed guidelines, often in the form of 'ten commandments', on how to formulate them for maximum emotional effect while minimizing the risk of arrest or conflict; consumption of alcohol was expressly discouraged, as was the use of Latin.[36]

Similarly in what became the 'Velvet Revolution' of 1989, an organizing framework was imposed on the public gatherings by Citizens' Forum and The Public against Violence, starting on the evening of 21 November. Their framework drew on the dissidents' legalistic discourse but also entailed elevated focal points (balconies, podiums) from which a controllable number of representatives of all the constituent parts of the opposition could speak. If StB surveillance is to be believed, the 'grown-ups' in Citizens' Forum were unnerved by the speed with which the demonstrations were growing and the impulsive moods of adolescents.[37] Once a controlling framework was safely in place, by 22 November the older dissidents were seeking the largest possible turnout of students for these now-daily demonstrations.[38]

At that very moment, the communist party came the closest it ever would during this crisis to defending itself. Although the Czechoslovak army had put about 10,000 soldiers on high alert, the most likely use of force would have been the mobilization of the People's Militia, to intimidate or disperse the demonstrators.[39] Most party leaders favoured this—they were being fed reports from the StB indicating a lack of sympathy for students among the working class—and wanted to bring in units from outside the capital on 21–2 November. As a sign of the disintegration of the political elite, the move was vetoed by the party's municipal committee for Prague.[40] Soon thereafter, the Presidium resigned en masse.

Had the party resorted to force, how would the emerging opposition movement have reacted? There is no indication in the extensive published record of strategy meetings from the period, or from later interviews, of any planning for

<hr/>

[35] This strategy was nicely summed up by Ebert as *Weiterarbeit ohne Kollaboration*—carrying on with work without collaborating. See Ebert, 'Der zivile Widerstand in der Tschechoslowakei 1968', 296.

[36] Pecka, *Spontanní projevy Pražského jara*, 18.

[37] *Securitas imperii* 6, 126.

[38] Ibid., 145.

[39] Karel Pacner, *Osudové okamžiky Československa* (Prague: Themis, 1997), 534–5.

[40] Miroslav Vaněk and Pavel Urbášek (eds.), *Vítězové? Poražení? Životopisná interview. II díl: Politické elity v období tzv. normalizace* (Prague: Prostor, 2005), 212–13.

full-scale civil resistance along the lines of August 1968. The StB alleged that some veteran dissidents sensed around 22 November the need to get the regular police (VB) on their side against the StB in the event of an assault.[41] Otherwise, all effort was invested in denouncing and renouncing violence, persuading factory workers to side with the revolution and, in a Citizens' Forum proclamation read by playwright and essayist Václav Havel to the throng on 23 November, appealing to the militia, police, and army to think of themselves as citizens and members of the people they had sworn to protect, rather than as subordinates just taking orders.[42]

## NON-CIVILIAN CIVIL RESISTANCE

It was in precisely those terms urged by Havel that men and women in uniform had viewed themselves in 1968, to an extent that only now can be fully appreciated. Declassified files reveal employees of militarized institutions, such as the Czechoslovak army, police, and sundry departments of the Ministry of the Interior, helping the resistance in three ways.

First, Soviet intelligence officers needed and actively sought the cooperation of the Czechoslovak police forces, both secret (StB) and regular (VB), but with little success; Czech and Slovak officers largely adhered to the legalism of the resistance, insisting that they would do nothing to harm citizens' rights or go against laws and orders.[43]

Second, radio was not the only means for discouraging youths from picking fights with the invaders; on the ground the police (VB) were already doing the same—gently dispersing crowds, in some towns disarming youths who had seized weapons from armouries. Officers did so all the while expressing their sympathy with the protesters and disgust at the invasion.[44] The police then intervened to protect Czechs and Slovaks caught by Soviet military patrols in the act of posting anti-invasion placards, ostensibly by taking them into custody and then releasing them at the earliest opportunity. When the Soviets caught a mobile Czechoslovak army radio transmitter relaying underground broadcasts, they wanted to shoot the soldiers on sight; Czechoslovak policemen talked the Soviets out of it.[45] So great was the new-found trust in the VB that the association representing apprentices and young workers advised its members to call the police for help if they were trying to protect someone from foreign arrest.[46]

[41]  *Securitas imperii* 6, 194.
[42]  Ibid., 182; *Deset pražských dnů*, 325.
[43]  František Koudelka and Jiří Suk (eds.), *Ministerstvo vnitra a bezpečnostní aparát v období Pražského jara 1968 (leden-srpen 1968)* (Brno: Doplněk, 1996), 233.
[44]  Ibid., 259.
[45]  Ibid., 260.
[46]  Pecka, Belda, and Hoppe, *Občanská společnost (1967–1970)*, 391.

Third, few individuals did more single-handedly to derail the attempted takeover than Colonel Oldřich Šebor, commander of the StB's seventh directorate for communications between state offices. Šebor could have used his directorate's technology to locate and disable the underground radio system; he refused, and instead directed it against pro-invasion broadcasts coming from East Germany while un-jamming Munich-based Radio Free Europe.[47] Šebor also refused to put through any calls from the Soviet embassy in Prague to Moscow and other bloc capitals.[48] Later, he set up a radio link so that pro-reform interior minister Josef Pavel could remain in charge of his department from the safety of Prague Castle, and he created a communications network for the emergency party congress.[49] Several of his subordinates allowed anti-invasion flyers to be printed on ministry presses.[50] Last of all, he liaised with sympathizers in the Czechoslovak army who put their own transmitters at the disposal of underground radio; a later investigation by military counter-intelligence identified around 590 soldiers who had aided the resistance, with 180 cases taken up by prosecutors.[51] Indeed, it seems that the only people punished for their actions in August 1968 were Šebor (sentenced in 1971 to twenty months' imprisonment), his army counterparts, and two engineers who planned to sabotage uranium mines.

## FAILURE, SUCCESS, AND POWER POLITICS

Logistically so beautiful, the resistance to the 1968 invasion is often regarded as a failure, as reform socialism was not rescued even after the safe return of Dubček and his comrades from captivity. Instead, by 1970, Czechoslovakia had become one of the most rigidly orthodox states in the Soviet bloc. To attribute this fact to some shortcoming on the part of the resistance, however, is misguided. Rather, we should see the resistance as largely irrelevant to what was happening in high politics from start to finish. Having failed to gain a majority in the Presidium on the first night of the invasion, the pro-Moscow conspirators panicked and dispersed; regrouping at the Soviet embassy, they decided to change focus, away from seizing power through the party and instead asking the head of state, President Ludvík Svoboda, to impose a 'revolutionary' government. Svoboda would have complied but for an intervention by his chief of staff, who reminded him that the constitution required a new cabinet to win a vote of investiture in the legislature. Only the prospect of asking the infuriated parliament to accept a

---

[47] Tomek, 'Rušení zahraničního rozhlasového vysílání pro Československo', 360–1.

[48] Archive of the Federal Interior Ministry of Czechoslovakia (hereafter, AFMV), f. IM, k. 5, sr. 70/2, č.j. IMČ-506/20-1969.

[49] AFMV, krab. 41, 73/7-8, č.j. IMV 003/ZO-70.

[50] Koudelka and Suk, *Ministerstvo vnitra a bezpečnostní aparát v období Pražského jara 1968*, 310.

[51] AFMV, fond VKR, A-30/412, č.j. 002174/12-71; fond A 2/3, i.j. 310, č.j. 00260/17-1970; fond A30, i.j. 408, č.j. 001783/12-1971.

© Bettmann/Corbis

**Figure 7.3** Bitter fruits of difficult negotiations. The President of the Czechoslovak Parliament, Josef Smrkovsky, explains the results of the Moscow negotiations to members of parliament during an informal meeting in Prague, 27 August 1968, the day on which the Czechoslovak delegation returned to the capital. Two days later he said in a broadcast: 'The past days were the most difficult I have ever lived through in my life.'

collaborationist government deterred the president; he otherwise showed no consideration for what the people wanted and how they would react. The transcripts released since 1989 of the negotiations in Moscow reveal Dubček and his colleagues making no use of the breadth and depth of the resistance as a bargaining chip against Soviet demands to commit to rollback of the reforms. Instead, they signed a protocol outlining the essentials of the 'normalization' that would follow their repatriation (shutdown of new political formations, dismissal of the more radical reform communists, censorship); many of these points Dubček had privately agreed to in conversations with Soviet leaders *before* the invasion.

In the ensuing months, different forms of protest were tried—demonstrations, occupation strikes at the universities, joint pledges by trade unions and students to a general strike should popular reformers lose their posts—to press the Dubček coalition to keep the country on a reform path. A student, Jan Palach, and several emulators resorted to self-immolation in early 1969 in the hope their acts would inspire the resumption of the civil resistance of August.[52] Instead of being emboldened by these displays of the public's commitment to change, more and more reformers in the KSČ Presidium drifted away from Dubček and plotted his downfall in April 1969. The final evidence of the futility of non-violent resistance came on the first anniversary of the invasion, on 21 August 1969, when thousands of Czechs and Slovaks in various cities re-enacted many of the techniques of the year before, only to be crushed, this time by the might of the Czechoslovak army.

In the Velvet Revolution of 1989, in contrast, leaders of the movement for dialogue and justice did not shy from using the massive demonstrations to gain leverage. It is true that to avoid appearing reckless in a society that valued decorum, activists pulled some punches: students volunteered to work shifts, bake bread, clean streets, and help out in hospitals, in part to minimize the economic impact of the two-hour strike on 27 November, in part to make a good

©Spectrum Pictures

**Figure 7.4** Velvet Revolution. A vast crowd gathers in Wenceslas Square, Prague, during a two-hour general strike on 27 November 1989. Compare and contrast the photo of Wenceslas Square empty during the general strike of 22 August 1968 (see p. 118). The poster on the left shows Alexander Dubček, the hero of the Prague Spring of 1968, and the sign on the statue calls for the resignation of the politburo.

[52] The first instance of this form of protest against the invasion—possibly inspired by the image of Buddhist monk Thích Quảng Đúc in South Vietnam in 1963 or of anti-war protesters in the United States in 1965—occurred in Poland on 8 Sept. 1968, when Ryszard Siwiec set himself alight at a harvest festival in Warsaw attended by Polish party leaders.

impression on their elders.[53] Citizens' Forum issued guidelines for the strike that included advice to employees in health care, transport, and 'services that meet the essential needs of towns, cities and enterprises' to indicate their sympathy without actually interrupting their work.[54] However, the men and women whom the crowds were propelling from the dissident margins to the middle of things never lost sight of the chance to convert their new authority into a power to pry open the door to talks with more pragmatic members of the KSČ and government, and to extract concessions and resignations. People power became something that could be switched on and off as negotiations required, mobilized to break an impasse and then dismissed as a good-faith gesture. That power was not at first used to gain office, but rather to manoeuvre Citizens' Forum and The Public against Violence into veto positions, following the strategy of imposing 'external control' on those communists who could be trusted to run the country. The unworkability of this arrangement—sensed more quickly by Slovak than Czech democrats—eventually led to the formation of interim coalitions governing until the free elections of June 1990.[55]

## LEGACIES

It is customary in Czech and Slovak society to look back on moments of great political passion with a certain jadedness or tristesse, to see in them the germ of the later machinations and deals that give ordinary politics its bad name.[56] No attempt has been made in Czech or Slovak historiography or philosophy to extract lessons or principles from the experiences of 1968 or 1989, as if they were not sufficiently weighty or worthy material.[57] Any evaluation of the systemic legacy of 1989 is complicated by the absence of a yardstick by which to measure what happened: how much of the credit for the relatively successful establishment of liberal democracy in the Czech Republic and Slovakia should be attributed to

---

[53] Wheaton and Kavan, *The Velvet Revolution*, 76–7.

[54] Jiří Suk, *Občanské fórum. Listopad—prosinec 1989. 2. díl—dokumenty* (Brno: Doplněk, 1998), 16.

[55] On the many switchbacks of the 1989 round-table talks, too intricate to summarize here, see Timothy Garton Ash, *The Magic Lantern* (New York: Random House, 1990), 109–24; Miloš Calda, 'The Roundtable Talks in Czechoslovakia', in Jon Elster (ed.), *The Roundtable Talks and the Breakdown of Communism* (Chicago: University of Chicago Press, 1996); Jiří Suk, *Labyrintem revoluce* (Prague: Prostor, 2003).

[56] For an example of this blue-tinted glasses effect going back to the founding of the Czechoslovak state in 1918, see Viktor Dyk's caustic novel *Můj přítel Čehona* (Prague: Šolc a Šimáček, 1925), especially the description of crowd behaviour on 125–32.

[57] Post-Communist historiography contains little reference to the techniques and skills developed during those two episodes, treating them instead as background noise in the high-politics narrative. The even fewer examples of theoretical writing on resistance and disobedience by Czech scholars make no reference to 1968 or 1989, focusing instead on foreign thinkers and on the contemporary limits of legal obligation; see Pavel Barša, 'Občanská neposlušnost v současné politické teorii', in Petr Fiala (ed.), *Politický extremismus a radikalismus v České republice* (Brno: Masarykova univerzita, 1998), and Jan Kysela, *Právo na odpor a občanskou neposlušnost* (Brno: Doplněk, 2001).

the way in which the KSČ was brought down? Here the mode of transition gets lost in the over-determined nature of post-communist development; structurally Czechoslovakia was ripe for democracy long before 1989,[58] and after 1989 the lure of the European Union kept both successor states more or less on course.[59] The mass mobilization of 1989 did not result in a subsequent politics more participatory or deliberative than elsewhere; party elites have been in the driving seat.[60] That those elites' claims to legitimacy deriving from free election trump people power was demonstrated on the tenth anniversary of the 1989 revolution, when many student leaders reunited in the Czech Republic to press for wholesale retirement of party leaders discredited by corruption, intrigue, and ineptitude. This 'Thank You, Now Leave' movement brought 100,000 people onto squares around the country, and their petition attracted 200,000 signatures; their demands were simply ignored by the parliamentary parties.[61]

Memory of August 1968 is also coloured by the conduct of elites: its power untapped by reformers too handicapped by sentiment to play hardball with the Soviet Union, in subsequent years the resistance was remembered by all yet recalled by few. As the 1970s passed, enthusiasm for the acts of allegiance to the reform communist idea and its leaders faded into a more sober embarrassment. The example of self-organization set in 1968 does not seem to have been a model or inspiration for the dissident community that coalesced in the late 1970s.[62] At most it survived as a background faith, vividly professed years later by Václav Havel, in the possible reactivation of a people that seemed to have slipped into apolitical socialist consumerism.[63] If that glimpse of a concealed potential inspired the actors of 1989 to overcome any fears or doubts, then that is probably the sole legacy of one of humanity's most impressive displays of civil resistance.

---

[58] Tatu Vanhanen and Richard Kimber, 'Predicting and Explaining Democratization in Eastern Europe', in Geoffrey Pridham and Tatu Vanhanen (eds.), *Democratization in Eastern Europe* (London: Routledge, 1994).

[59] Milada Anna Vachudova, *Europe Undivided* (Oxford: Oxford University Press, 2005). In 1992–8 Slovakia had a populist dalliance with a special 'Slovak way' under Prime Minister Vladimír Mečiar, who often presented himself as the faithful trustee of the spirit of 1989; the corruption and international isolation that resulted moved Slovak voters to displace him at the ballot box. See Tim Haughton, *Constraints and Opportunities of Leadership in Post-Communist Europe* (Aldershot: Ashgate, 2005) and Sharon Fisher, *Political Change in Post-Communist Slovakia and Croatia* (New York: Palgrave Macmillan, 2006).

[60] Magdalena Hadjiisky, 'The Failure of Participatory Democracy in the Czech Republic', *West European Politics*, 24, no. 3 (2001).

[61] The Olympian disdain of the then-chairman of the lower house of parliament for these demands drips from Václav Klaus, *Od opoziční smlouvy k tolerančnímu patentu* (Prague: Votobia, 2000), 43–5. The movement, which later played a role in persuading Czechs to vote for accession to the European Union, maintains a web presence at http://sdo.jola.cz.

[62] Conceptual texts of the human rights group Charter 77, such as Václav Benda's essay on the 'parallel polis' that emphasised cultural, economic, and educational activity outside official institutions, probably owe more to Austrian philosophical traditions than to the example set in August 1968. See Ján Pavlík, 'Philosophy, "Parallel Polis", and Revolution: The Case of Czechoslovakia', in Barry Smith (ed.), *Philosophy and Political Change in Eastern Europe* (La Salle: Hegler Institute, 1993), 67–100.

[63] Václav Havel, *Spisy 4. Eseje a jiné texty z let 1970–1989. Dálkový výslech* (Prague: Torst, 1999), 811–14.

# 8

## Towards 'Self-limiting Revolution': Poland 1970–89

*Aleksander Smolar*

While there were very significant popular protests in Poland in 1956 and 1970, the history of successful civil resistance in Poland may be dated back to a new strategy of peaceful opposition developed in the mid 1970s. In 1980, this new opposition contributed decisively to the formation of the Solidarity movement and what was aptly called a 'self-limiting revolution'.[1] This term is also appropriate to describe the culmination of a decade of struggle in the round-table talks and semi-free elections of 1989, when Poland became the first communist-ruled country to make a peaceful, negotiated transition to multi-party democracy. Solidarity was an almost entirely peaceful mass social movement, having ten million members at its height. Originally created in August 1980 by workers, and describing itself as a trade union, it soon came to include all social groups. During the sixteen months of its legal existence, the authorities tried to destroy it from inside, to demoralize its members, to isolate its leaders, and to integrate it into the institutional structures of the communist state. All this happened under rising pressure from the Soviet Union. Although the basic political structure of a communist party state was not radically changed until 1989, the extent of the party's domination over society was progressively limited.

The legal Solidarity movement was crushed, under strong Soviet pressure, by Polish military forces introducing a 'state of war'—the literal translation of the Polish term, *stan wojenny*, more usually rendered as 'martial law'—on 13 December 1981. As Timothy Garton Ash observed, 'In sixteen months this revolution killed nobody.... The first people to be killed in the Polish revolution were workers shot by armed police in the first weeks of the "war". This extraordinary record of non-violence, this majestic self-restraint in the face of many provocations, distinguishes the Polish revolution from previous revolutions.'[2]

A full-fledged communist regime was never re-established in Poland. Facing political and economic crisis, Western pressure and Gorbachev's changing policy

[1] A term coined by Jadwiga Staniszkis, *Poland's Self-Limiting Revolution* (Princeton, NJ: Princeton University Press, 1984).

[2] Timothy Garton Ash, *The Polish Revolution: Solidarity* (New Haven, Conn.: Yale University Press, 1999).

towards east-central Europe, the authorities agreed in February 1989 to the opening of round-table negotiations between their representatives and the opposition. These led to semi-free parliamentary elections on 4 June 1989, to the formation of the first non-communist government for more than forty years, and, in consequence, to the rapid, peaceful decomposition of the communist regime. It was also the forerunner of the downfall of communist regimes in the whole region, during the 'velvet revolutions' of 1989.

I shall argue that the objective of the peaceful and anti-political strategy of the opposition formed in the 1970s was to reconstruct social ties against the official policy of atomization and control. Practical solidarity with the persecuted, the fight against the lie in the public sphere, and the use of law—both international and domestic—turned out to be efficient means of resistance. The great movement of Solidarity continued this strategy but, ironically, by its very greatness undermined the possibility of equilibrium between the communist state and a society in search of liberty.

Rising economic problems, pressure from the West, and Gorbachev's position of non-intervention in the internal affairs of other countries, were major factors opening renewed possibilities for change at the end of the 1980s. The authorities understood that without an agreement with the opposition it would not be possible to introduce the economic reforms necessary to avoid another major social revolt. The relative weakness of the organized opposition, its consistent rejection of the use of violence, and its publicly declared readiness to enter into a political dialogue with the regime all contributed to the launching of peaceful round-table negotiations in February 1989. Important, but still limited, concessions accepted by the authorities triggered the rapid and soon total collapse of the communist regime.

## CIVIL RESISTANCE AND THE POLISH TRADITION

The long Polish tradition of resistance against foreign and occupying power was not at all pacific. For more than 120 years of partition between three powers— Russia, Prussia, and the Austro-Hungarian empire—Poland was the theatre of national insurrections every thirty to forty years: in 1794, 1830–1, 1863–4, and 1905. Poland regained independence in 1918 for only twenty years. The August 1944 Warsaw Uprising against Nazi occupation—but, indirectly, also against the approaching Red Army—belonged to the same tradition of military struggle for national independence. This was the characteristic pattern of Polish resistance: heroic, military, almost always tragic, and associated very much with a romantic and messianic tradition in which Poles identified their country as 'the Christ among nations'.

Armed anti-communist resistance continued in the early years of Soviet occupation after the Second World War, but was destroyed by mass repression. Most people tried to rebuild their lives in the institutional framework imposed by communist rule. Rudimentary social autonomy was limited to family circles, religious gatherings, and private farms.

The profound change in Polish political culture represented by the rejection of political violence was thus, first of all, an outcome of the Second World War, which had resulted in the decimation of the population, the destruction of the country, national exhaustion, and the feeling that there was no possible military response to Soviet domination. The tragic experience of the Warsaw Uprising played a major role in the formation of a new culture of peaceful resistance. The killing of 200,000 mostly young people and the almost total destruction of Poland's capital by the German army remained for several generations a profoundly traumatic event. Yet the legacy of armed struggle is also complex: the British historian Norman Davies is not the only observer who views the Solidarity movement as a natural child of the Warsaw Uprising, 'both in its attachment to the idea of independence and at the same time as a movement, surprisingly moderate in such a crucial historical moment, it was without doubt the result of the memory of the experience of the uprising'.[3]

The new geopolitics of the Cold War played an important role in moderating successive social conflicts in Poland. The Soviet invasion of Hungary following the Hungarian revolution of 1956, and the intervention of the Warsaw Pact armies to terminate the Prague Spring of 1968, had a profound impact on the Polish population. In such a context, it became difficult to cultivate any romantic myth of the revolt of a Polish David against the Soviet Goliath.

The internal situation in Poland also contributed to the search for non-violent ways to influence the opening of the system. Even if communism in Poland after 1956 was relatively liberal in comparison with other Soviet bloc countries, there was a dramatic asymmetry between the strength of the communist state and a largely atomized population, submitted to the violence and permanent pressure of a system that controlled most areas of public expression and association, employment, education, and travel. It was difficult indeed, if not impossible, to dream in such conditions about a liberation by revolt or by the West. The conviction that 'nothing can be done' to re-establish an independent and democratic Poland was a widely accepted lesson learned by the population. It was not the source of legitimacy of the 'New Order' of communist rule in Poland, but certainly the most important factor contributing to its stability.

However, the rejection of violent methods of social and political change among Polish elites and in society at large did not only result from political realism. This change in the Polish culture of resistance can also be traced back to the influence of the Catholic Church; to the rejection of a violent revolutionary model of social change by leading circles of the Polish opposition in favour of an alternative strategy; and to the influence of dissidents in other countries of the region.

The Catholic Church in Poland, traditionally powerful, naturally fulfilled some of the functions of an opposition, in a system based on the omnipotence of a

[3] Norman Davies, *Gazeta Wyborcza* (Warsaw), 26 July 2004.

©Cevallos/Simonpietri/Sygma/Corbis

**Figure 8.1** Solidarity before Solidarity. Vast crowds turned out to listen to the Polish Pope, John Paul II, on his extraordinary pilgrimage to his native land in June 1979. The experience of social solidarity prefigured that in the Solidarity movement, which emerged less than fifteen months later.

single party. First and foremost, the Church was an independent moral universe of free speech and free ideas. But it also presented a consistent message of non-violence, especially following the tragedy of the Second World War. In the 1950s, the hugely influential post-war primate, Cardinal Stefan Wyszyński, famously said: 'The art is not to die for the homeland; the art is to live well for it.'[4]

The authority of the Catholic Church in Poland, already very strong, was reinforced when the archbishop of Kraków, Cardinal Karol Wojtyła, became Pope John Paul II in 1978. His philosophy and his strategic vision for the transformation of Poland can be summarized in a passage often cited by him, and by Solidarity's martyr priest, Father Jerzy Popiełuszko: 'Be not overcome by evil, but overcome evil with good.'[5] Towards the end of his life, John Paul II wrote: 'If we consider the tragic scenario of violent fratricidal conflicts in different parts of the world, and the untold sufferings and injustices to which they have given rise, the only truly constructive choice is, as St Paul proposes, to "abhor that

[4] Czesław Strzerzewski, *Kardynała Wyszyńskiego wizja Kościoła* (Wrocław: Bibliotecka 'Nowego życia', 1990), 56.

[5] *Epistle of St Paul to the Romans*, 12: 21.

which is evil and hold fast to what is good".[6] As Timothy Garton Ash argued during the conference in Oxford in March 2007, in the case of John Paul II there was an absolute moral rejection of all political violence.[7]

*religious objection to use of violence*

## THE STRATEGY OF NEW SOCIAL MOVEMENTS

*opposition's view*

The new opposition formed in Poland in the 1970s did not believe in a revolutionary act of liberation as the result of a popular uprising. Revolution, as any other form of violent political change, was viewed as leading to another repressive regime. Violent political change could not only endanger the emergence of a democratic order, but might also undermine chances for the preservation of human rights. The opposition didn't believe in the communist system's capacity to reform itself either. Such illusions of the 'revisionist' intelligentsia, who had believed in the humanization, democratization, and market transformation of the Soviet-type system, belonged to the past. *new system*

*needed to be revolution*

The classic revolutionary image of the storming of the Bastille was becoming the symbol not of liberty but of the danger of people erecting new Bastilles.[8] In one of the most popular songs of the Solidarity movement, *Mury* ('The walls'), the bard of the movement, Jacek Kaczmarski, described in bitter ironic verses how the destroyed walls of prisons are preparing to rise again. Up until the declaration of the state of war in December 1981, most of the opposition was also against any conspiratorial action. Once again, Michnik was the most outspoken in warning against the dangers of conspiracy:

*movement as reflection of future political structure*

> The resistance movement must be at the same time the school of liberty and democracy; the Poland which will emerge after the state of war will be like this movement. Behind each underground there is the spectre of the 'possessed' from Dostoyevsky's novel. Any conspiracy demoralizes; in its shadow flourishes the spirit of the sect which uses its own language, which relies on circles of the initiated, on tactics that dominate everything else, on an instrumental use of the truth and on despising values not related to politics.[9]

In a seminal text of the democratic opposition, 'A New Evolutionism', Michnik rejected the alternative 'revolution or reform' and wrote: 'an unceasing struggle for reform and evolution that seeks an expansion of civic liberties and human rights is the only course that East European dissidents can take...To draw a

---

[6] For the Celebration of the World Day of Peace, 1 Jan. 2005. The text cited by John Paul II is from *Romans* 12: 9.

[7] Poland's political elites did not, however, share the Pope's condemnation of the violence associated with Polish participation in the war in Iraq.

[8] A metaphor often used by Adam Michnik. Timothy Garton Ash quoted Adam Michnik from 1984: 'any kind of terrorism necessarily leads to moral debasement, to spiritual deformation', see Timothy Garton Ash, *The Uses of Adversity: Essays on the Fate of Central Europe* (Cambridge: Granta Books, 1989), 175.

[9] Adam Michnik, 'O oporze, list z Białołęki', in his *Szanse polskiej demokracji: artykuły i eseje* (London: Aneks, 1984), 107.

parallel with events at the other end of our continent, one could say that the ideas of the Polish democratic opposition resemble the Spanish rather than the Portuguese model. This is based on gradual and piecemeal change, not violent upheaval and forceful destruction of the existing system.'[10]

The new social resistance in Poland was born with the strikes which broke out in June 1976, caused once again by price increases and the trials of hundreds of arrested workers. This time, intellectual groups initiated an open campaign in solidarity with the imprisoned workers and their families: the Workers' Defence Committee (KOR) was founded on 23 September 1976. The very creation of an organization independent from the authorities and functioning openly was a bold political act. The following months witnessed the emergence of different opposition groups, one of which was characteristically named the Movement for the Defence of Human and Civil Rights (ROPCiO), as well as the publication of illegal periodicals and books. It is estimated that between 1976 and 1980, the opposition numbered several thousand persons. It was composed overwhelmingly of the intelligentsia and students, assisted by a few individual priests and members of religious orders; the institutional hierarchy of the Church did not officially affirm its attitude towards initiatives of this sort, either for or against. Only with time did the groups in question manage to make their way—albeit on a small scale—into factories and the countryside.[11]

The strategy formulated by the leading figures of the democratic opposition, notably by Jacek Kuroń and Adam Michnik, can be summed up in a few sentences. Its first principle was Alexander Solzhenitsyn's and Václav Havel's 'live in truth'. Refusing to live in the 'Big Lie' was, in terms of a famous essay by Havel, the basis of 'the power of the powerless'.[12] Beyond the moral value of such a demand, it was a way of delegitimizing public life built on a lie and on an imposed official definition of reality. The idea of 'living in truth' became the foundation of the new opposition in the whole communist world. With the collapse of the informational monopoly of the state, the opposition started to play an ever more important cognitive, moral, and indirectly political role.

The second key principle of the new opposition was the self-organization of society. This 'civil society' strategy opposed the reconstruction of social ties to an official policy of atomization and political control of society. The new peaceful programme of social and political resistance was summed up in Jacek Kuroń's appeal to protesters: 'set up your own committees instead of burning down party

---

[10] Adam Michnik, *Letters from Prison and Other Essays* (Berkeley, Calif.: University of California Press, 1985), 142–3. As Kenneth Maxwell makes clear, Michnik's comment was somewhat unfair to the Portuguese case (Ch. 9, below).

[11] For details see the most complete book on opposition after the Second World War, and especially in the 1970s: Andrzej Friszke, *Opozycja polityczna w PRL, 1945–1980* (London: Aneks, 1994).

[12] Václav Havel, 'The power of the powerless', in Paul Wilson (ed.), *Open Letters: Selected Writings, 1965–1990* (New York: Vintage Books, 1992). Havel described how the greengrocer, in the former communist Czechoslovakia, places in his window the slogan: 'Workers of the world, unite!' The day he refuses to place the slogan among the onions and carrots, he breaks the rules of the game. 'He discovers once more his suppressed identity and dignity. He gives his freedom a concrete significance. His revolt is an attempt to live in truth'.

committees.' (In 1970–1, protesting shipyard workers on the Baltic coast had set fire to communist party offices.) He expressed the idea of a necessary self-organization of society, independent from the state and, if necessary, against it.[13] Every genuine social organization, every demonstration of mutual trust and of solidarity in society, has value in itself as a way of reconstructing a human universe. The mainstream of the opposition was deliberately and profoundly anti-political. Faced with the strategic choice described by Adam Michnik in his letter from prison,[14] the answer of the opposition was clear. The objective was not to defeat the ruling power but to progressively liberate society from its control.

The third leading principle was insistence on strict respect for the law: 'the conspicuous exercise of rights' in the words of János Kis, a leader of the Hungarian opposition. The constitution, international standards (including the 1975 Helsinki agreements), and domestic law became efficient arms of resistance. The authorities were criticized not on the basis of their own ideology—as was common in the 'revisionist' opposition of the 1950s and the 1960s—but by reference to universal moral and legal norms, which had been formally accepted by the communist authorities themselves.

The new strategy of the opposition relied on the assumption that the emergence of an archipelago of new islands of autonomy would be gradual and sufficiently limited so as not to push the communist authorities to a confrontation. It aimed at exploiting the possible interest of the authorities in tolerating the 'lesser evil' of an enlarged sphere of social autonomy, thus avoiding a perhaps bloody full-scale confrontation with the emergent opposition and its likely domestically and internationally negative effects. The dilemma facing the government was either to clamp down with all the coercive power necessary in order to eradicate dissidence, which it had all the instruments to do, or to accommodate itself to the fact that it was progressively losing control over a renascent civil society.[15]


## THE INTERNATIONAL SITUATION AND THE EVOLUTION OF THE POLISH COMMUNIST STATE

We have seen the importance of a non-violent model of change in the evolution of social resistance in Poland. The more and more open activities of the opposition were due not only to its courage and its rising influence but also to a certain tolerance on the part of a state which the opposition defined as

[13] Jacek Kuroń, in Zinaida Erard and Georges M. Zygier (eds.), *La Pologne: une société en dissidence* (Paris: Maspéro, 1978), 17.

[14] 'To be an alternative to the power, or consciously abandon such an aspiration and concentrate on limiting its impact', Adam Michnik, 'List z Kurkowej', *Aneks*, no. 38 (1985).

[15] In *Letters from Prison and Other Essays*, Adam Michnik writes about the power-holders as rational actors, 'pragmatists', capable of balancing the advantages and disadvantages of different alternatives they are facing, capable of arriving at the conclusion that it is more harmful to them to make use of 'brutal repressions' than to accommodate the forces 'struggling for pluralism'.

✳ u n p a c k

totalitarian. Ironically, the more communist power over society weakened, the more the opposition used the language of 'totalitarianism'. /

This 'repressive tolerance' was obviously not the result of a democratic choice of accepting pluralism by the communist regime. It was due to several internal and external factors. The greater flexibility of the regimes of Edward Gierek and Wojciech Jaruzelski was partly the result of Western pressure. In a situation of increasing integration into world markets, rising hard currency debt, and economic dependence on the West, the Polish authorities became more sensitive to the pressures of the developed and democratic world. Maintaining a positive image of the regime was a necessary concession in order to facilitate increasingly complicated and difficult talks about the rescheduling of a rapidly growing foreign debt. The Polish economy in the 1970s became dependent upon the West not only financially but also in the domain of technology and supplies.

The 1975 Helsinki Conference on Security and Cooperation in Europe, attended by leaders of thirty-five states representing the entire membership of NATO, the Warsaw Pact, and non-aligned countries, with the objective of forwarding the process of détente through agreements on economic and technological cooperation, security, and disarmament, also included a list of agreements concerning political freedom and human rights. Under the combined mounting pressure of internal opposition and of the West, the Polish authorities had to face new constraints on their policy.[16]

The Helsinki agreements proved to be conducive to opposition in communist states by formally committing the authorities to respect human rights. This effect of the agreements was not at all certain at that time. Zbigniew Brzeziński, then national security adviser to President Carter, later presented the mood at the White House during negotiation of the Helsinki agreements 'as one of Spenglerian pessimism'.[17] However, the approach to human rights underwent a fundamental change as a consequence of the policies both of the US presidents Jimmy Carter and Ronald Reagan and of central European dissidents. Human rights were not considered any more as 'a means of stabilizing the status quo, but as the historic inevitability of our time, the consequence of which would be a change in the status quo'.[18]

In this context the attitude of the opposition in Poland and in the whole region towards the Helsinki agreements also changed radically. Polish dissidents and political exiles typically feared that the Helsinki conference would result 'mainly, or even exclusively, in formal recognition of the division of Europe into two spheres of influence'.[19] With time, however, a conviction that the agreements

---

[16] On the importance of the attitude of the West see the political diary of a journalist close to the Gierek regime, who later became the last communist Prime Minister of Poland, Mieczysław Rakowski, *Dzienniki polityczne 1976–1978* [Political diaries] (Warsaw: Iskry, 2002).

[17] *25 years: From Solidarność to Freedom. International Conference Warsaw-Gdańsk August 29–31, 2005* (Warsaw: Solidarity Center Foundation, 2005), 24.

[18] 'Human rights for status quo—that was the devil's bargain that was being negotiated in the first half of the 1970s', in *25 years: From Solidarność to Freedom*, 24.

[19] Jan Józef Lipski, *KOR: A History of the Workers' Defence Committee in Poland, 1976–81* (Berkeley, Calif.: University of California Press, 1985), 24–5. See also an editorial in the prestigious emigré monthly *Kultura* (Paris), no. 9, 1975.

©Alain Keler/Sygma/Corbis

**Figure 8.2** Unusual alliances. Strike leader Lech Wałęsa, standing on the left, waits to make his confession to a Catholic priest during the historic strike in the Lenin shipyard in Gdańsk, in August 1980, which gave birth to the Solidarity movement. Many on the Western left were disconcerted by the spectacle of workers protesting under the sign of the cross, but this unusual alliance between workers, the intelligentsia, and the Catholic Church was one of the strategic keys to the movement's power. The communist banner over the shipyard gate says 'We thank you for your good work'.

could serve as an effective legitimating tool for the opposition became widespread, especially after the beginning of the presidency of Jimmy Carter in January 1977, and its identification of the Helsinki agreements with an agenda for promoting respect for human rights.

The strikes of August 1980 and the creation of Solidarity—the culmination of a long series of outbreaks of social anger—were the direct reaction to price increases introduced on 1 July. An inter-factory strike committee, representing hundreds of factories from the Baltic Coast, was created in Gdańsk. In their 'Twenty-one Demands', formulated on 18 August, the strikers asked for the right to form independent trade unions, the right to strike, freedom of speech, the release of political prisoners; they also articulated demands concerning economic reforms and reducing privileges for the security forces and the communist party apparatus. Economic demands did not occupy the centre stage.

The workers' demands posed fundamental problems to the regime: to the principle of the leading role of the communist party, to its monopoly of organization and of the public word, and to the crucial role of the apparatus of repression. So the problem of power was posed at the very outset. Forced to accept these demands, during the next sixteen months communist authorities tried to weaken and destroy the independent movement from inside and eventually from outside. In one case, in the so-called Bydgoszcz crisis, they almost triggered a general strike. Solidarity pressed for economic, social, and political changes but tried to avoid general confrontation. Lech Wałęsa, having signed the agreement on 31 August 1980 said: 'We got everything we could in the current situation. And we'll get the rest as well, because we have what's most important: our independent, autonomous trade unions.' *- False Walesa? more?*

In fact, Solidarity soon extended well beyond the framework of a trade union. But it was quite obvious that the anti-political strategy of the opposition of the 1970s was not adapted to the new situation. Jacek Kuroń once compared the situation to an attempt to reform traffic by changing the direction of the cars on only one side of the street. With time it became increasingly obvious that a clash would be inevitable. Bronisław Geremek was probably right that 'Solidarność was European history's greatest movement for change that did not resort to violence.'[20] But, it turned out, organized society was too strong, the communist state was too weak and not ready to accept regime change, there was no mutual trust, and the Soviet Union was pressing for a military solution. After 500 days of limited confrontation, and growing pessimism and apathy in the population, the state of war was imposed on 13 December 1981.

## FROM THE STATE OF WAR TO ROUND-TABLE NEGOTIATIONS

Having broken the back of the legal mass movement of Solidarity, the authorities felt that it was necessary to search for a degree of popular legitimacy and a certain modus vivendi with the opposition. This was reinforced by the progressive decomposition, from the middle of the 1950s, of any ideological legitimation of the communist regime. Ironically, the potential danger of Soviet intervention was becoming the only credible justification for the regime's use of force. The Solidarity movement weakened even further the legitimacy of communist power, yet the level of popular acceptance of the state of war military operation of 13 December 1981 was quite high.[21] The majority of the population believed (and still believes) in the patriotic motivations of General Jaruzelski; they also

[20] *25 years: From Solidarność to Freedom*, 20.

[21] In January 1982, 51% of the Warsaw population declared in a public opinion poll that the decision to introduce the state of war was 'justified' or 'rather justified', OBOP (Institute for Public Opinion Research) Jan. 1982. Nearly two years later, in a more complete public opinion poll, 48% disapproved of the introduction of the state of war and 43% approved it, 'CBOS (Centre for Public Opinion Research): Opinie obywateli o wprowadzeniu, trwaniu i zniesieniu stanu wojennego', Oct. 1983. Quoted from *Społeczeństwo i władza lat osiemdziesiątych w badaniach CBOS* (Warsaw: CBOS 1994), 61.

©Witold Rozmyslowicz/epa/Corbis

**Figure 8.3** Failed negotiations. In March 1981, the then Prime Minister, army general Wojciech Jaruzelski (left), and Solidarity leader Lech Wałęsa (right, with pipe), have a palpably stiff encounter at a tense moment in relations between the national movement and the communist authorities. Just over nine months later, Jaruzelski, by then communist party leader as well as head of the army, would declare a 'state of war' (also known as martial law) to crush Solidarity—and Wałęsa would be interned.

believed that crushing Solidarity saved Poland from an even bigger Soviet military danger.[22]

Although the crackdown on Solidarity was initially quite brutal, with several fatalities and at least 10,000 people imprisoned and interned, Jaruzelski's policy could nonetheless be described as a 'self-limiting counter-revolution'. Amnesties

---

[22] Twenty five years later, 60% of Poles stated they believed that the declaration of the state of war preserved Poland from Soviet intervention, and 50% that it made possible the avoidance of a civil war. At the same time, however, 53% considered that Jaruzelski's major objective was to destroy the nascent democracy. 'TNS OBOP: Stan wojenny dzieli Polaków', *Gazeta Wyborcza*, 1 Dec. 2006.

were announced in 1983, 1984, and finally in 1986, opening the door to the round-table negotiations in 1989.

It is interesting to note that such a widespread social acceptance of the state of war, the founding act of the Jaruzelski regime, actually facilitated the opening of negotiations with the opposition several years later. It was a proof for both sides that in spite of its growing weakness the communist power could be neither violently nor peacefully destroyed. In addition, two other factors played a major role in making negotiations both possible and necessary.

To what extent Moscow imposed upon the Polish authorities the military solution to the challenge posed by Solidarity remains the subject of heated debates in Poland.[23] It is clear, however, that Moscow's pressure very much influenced the imposition of the state of war on 13 December 1981. Soviet authorities exercised constant pressure on Warsaw in favour of a more radical policy towards 'anti-socialist' forces in Poland. Any attempts at searching for a modus vivendi with the opposition and with the Church were scrutinized with suspicion in the Kremlin.

With the imposition of the state of war, millions of people previously mobilized by Solidarity were forced out of public life. However, the economic and social problems which contributed to the birth of Solidarity were still there. In the second half of the 1980s the profound crisis of 'real socialism' was evident even to the authorities. They understood that without a strategy of inclusion and an agreement with at least part of the opposition, it would not be possible to introduce austerity measures and economic reforms necessary to avoid another major social revolt.[24] From the middle of the 1980s, public opinion polls indicated a worsening public evaluation of both the political and the economic situations.[25]

With the election of Mikhail Gorbachev as general secretary of the central committee of the Communist Party of the Soviet Union in March 1985, Moscow became more open to changes in central Europe. The gradual abandonment of the 'Brezhnev Doctrine' by Gorbachev dramatically altered the perception of the range of possibilities, and with that the strategies of the political actors in Poland. Wojciech Jaruzelski soon exploited the new possibilities opened by Moscow. A new wave of strikes in 1988 was perceived by the authorities as the last warning before a catastrophe. We can get a sense of the urgency with which people around Jaruzelski accepted negotiations with the opposition from a memorandum written by three top advisers to Jaruzelski in August 1988, government spokesman Jerzy Urban, central committee secretary Stanisław Ciosek, and vice-minister of internal affairs General Władysław Pożoga: 'Soviet support is the main asset of our team. But it will become weaker and weaker, or will even disappear, if our

---

[23] See Mark Kramer, Ch. 6 in this volume, and Garton Ash, *The Polish Revolution: Solidarity*, 410–12 & 417.

[24] Antoni Dudek, *Reglamentowana rewolucja. Rozkład dyktatury komunistycznej w Polsce 1988–1990* (Warsaw: Arkana 2004), 110–20.

[25] *Społeczeństwo i władza lat osiemdziesiątych w badaniach CBOS*, 268.

actions turn out to be ineffective. During this autumn, Moscow's disappointment may seal our end.'[26]

Since the mid-1980s, the communist authorities had adopted a strategy of inclusion which relied on a tacit acceptance of 'living with the opposition' rather than inflaming social tension by its persecution. Ironically, this moderate policy contributed to even stronger pressure both from the internal opposition and from Western governments and non-governmental actors. This is another example supporting Alexis de Tocqueville's famous observation that the most dangerous moment for a bad government is when it tries to reform.

The new wave of strikes in 1988 reinforced the authorities' willingness to start negotiations. The participation of a widely respected third party in preparing the negotiations (i.e. the Catholic Church), contributed to the building of trust on both sides. Political changes were facilitated not only by the strikes and the negative attitude of public opinion but also by the relative weakness of the organized opposition. Towards the end of the 1980s, the heroic period of the mass Solidarity of 1980–1 seemed far away. Active opposition was once again limited to a few thousand activists. Consequently, the authorities were less afraid of the opposition; indeed, they underestimated its potential influence upon the population. Without such helpful illusions, Jaruzelski and his collaborators would probably never have accepted the semi-free elections of 4 June 1989 agreed upon in the round-table negotiations earlier that year.

The concept of a round-table negotiation was mentioned for the first time by General Jaruzelski in June 1988.[27] The acceptance of a negotiated agreement implied that there would be neither a Soviet intervention nor Polish domestic repression of the 13 December 1981 type. But the readiness of the communist power-holders to respect the negotiated solution was not yet evident. The oppressive apparatus of the party-state was still powerful and there were forces within the regime ready to use violence to save state socialism. However, General Jaruzelski himself and his close associates, including the head of the internal security forces, an army general called Czesław Kiszczak, were prepared not only to renounce the use of force, but also to act politically to prevent violence. The paralysing fear of both domestic and external reactions helped them to neutralize hard-liners. Gorbachev's declared policy of non-intervention meant, in reality, active support for Jaruzelski and his strategy.

The realistic attitude of the leaders of Solidarity also contributed very much to the launching of peaceful round-table negotiations. In spite of the very difficult conditions of underground activity, prison, and everyday repression, workers' leaders such as Lech Wałęsa, Zbigniew Bujak, and Władysław Frasyniuk, and their intellectual advisers, such as Bronisław Geremek, Tadeusz Mazowiecki, Adam Michnik, and Jacek Kuroń, had been developing for many years the idea of a necessary compromise between both sides in Poland's civil 'cold war'. They not

[26] Włodzimierz Borodziej and Andrzej Garlicki (eds.), *Okrągły stół. Dokumenty i materiały*, vol. 1 (Warsaw: na zlec. Kancelarii Prezydenta Rzeczypospolitej Polskiej, 2004), 172.

[27] *Trybuna Ludu* (Warsaw), 14 June 1988.

why is Anna not included in this account at all?

only consistently rejected the use of violence but also publicly declared their readiness to enter into a political dialogue with the regime in order to prevent violence. Many times they expressed their conviction that avoiding violence was in the common interest: they were concerned about both violent repression by the regime and the threat of an explosion of popular anger, emphasized by the wave of strikes in 1988.

The idea of a 'crisis agreement' between the Polish regime and the Solidarity movement was floated in 1988 by Bronisław Geremek in an interview given to an official monthly, four months before Jaruzelski spoke of a round table.[28] The idea of entering into a dialogue on political change with the authorities to prevent political violence was not new; but it was new to publish in an official journal demands for social and trade union pluralism—which in practice meant the re-legalization of Solidarity—and for the presence of the opposition in a second chamber of the parliament. Geremek declared at the same time the will to respect the existing constitutional order, including 'the leading role' of the ruling communist party.

## ROUND-TABLE NEGOTIATIONS AND THE FALL OF COMMUNISM

Round-table negotiations started in Poland on 6 February 1989, and ended on 5 April 1989. Most of the real negotiating happened in three groups: economy and social policy, political reforms, and trade union pluralism. About 450 people took part in the negotiations, from the official side, from the opposition, and from the Catholic Church. The underlying assumption of the negotiations was that the communist party would maintain control of political power through an election law which would secure the majority (65 per cent of seats in the lower house) for it and two small satellite parties, and through control of presidential elections. The opposition obtained the recognition of independent trade unions (i.e. legalization of Solidarity), partly free elections—representation in the lower house up to 35 per cent of seats—and entirely free elections to a new upper house (the Senate), an increased pluralism of media (although still with censorship in place), and a promise that the elections in four years' time would be free.

These were important but still limited concessions by the communist regime. However, they triggered its rapid collapse. The pursuit of a 'lesser evil' strategy by the regime showed its revolutionary dangers when the people were ready to push its consequences much further than the formal agreement implied. The results of the elections of 4 June 1989 were disastrous for the authorities. Many of the most prominent figures of the regime were not elected to parliament. Solidarity won all the seats available to it. It was important that not only the satellite parties started to seek a new alliance with Solidarity from one day to the next, but even many

[28] *Konfrontacje* (Warsaw), Feb. 1988.

©Kok/Gamma/Eyedea, Camera Press, London

**Figure 8.4** The importance of a round table. From February to April 1989, Poland pioneered the 'round table negotiations' which resulted, following the semi-free election of 4 June 1989, in the appointment of the first non-communist prime minister since the imposition of Soviet-type communism in central and eastern Europe more than forty years before. This photograph shows the large round table ready for the televised formal opening of negotiations. It was specially made for the occasion. Most of the real negotiating took place in smaller groups at other tables, but the 'round-table' model would be emulated elsewhere.

new parliamentarians of the communist party displayed their democratic instincts. On 19 July 1989 parliament elected Jaruzelski president of Poland, as a result of a tacit understanding on both sides, but with a majority of only one vote.[29] He was not, however, able to impose the formation of the government by the communists. On 3 July Adam Michnik had published a famous article on the front page of a newly formed opposition paper, *Gazeta Wyborcza* (literally, 'Election Gazette'). Its headline was a political programme in itself: 'Your President, our Prime Minister'.[30] On 24 August 1989 Tadeusz Mazowiecki became the

[29] Interestingly, Jaruzelski had external support not only from Gorbachev but also from US President George Bush, who describes in his memoirs how on 10 July 1989 he tried to convince Jaruzelski to be a candidate for the presidency. Jaruzelski was considered by both sides as a guarantee of the stability and predictability of the political process. George H. W. Bush and Brent Scowcroft, *A World Transformed* (New York: Alfred A. Knopf, 1998), 117.

[30] Adam Michnik, 'Wasz prezydent, nasz premier', *Gazeta Wyborcza*, 3 July 1989.

first non-communist prime minister in the whole communist world. The government consisted of Solidarity and the two former satellite parties, although two generals—both allies of Jaruzelski—controlled defence and internal affairs. Communist power was thus symbolically reduced to its essential core. Its practical influence, however, was diminished from one day to the next. A year later, the communists were not in the government any more.

## CONSEQUENCES

The evolutionary model of transition from dictatorship to democracy makes it difficult to define the crucial moment of change. Was it the round-table negotiations in February–April 1989? The semi-free elections of 4 June 1989? The formation of a new government with Tadeusz Mazowiecki as prime minister in August and September 1989? Was it the election of Lech Wałęsa as president in general elections in 1990? Or maybe the first entirely free parliamentary elections in 1991?

The communist regime fell in ruins within a couple of months after the round-table negotiations. But the Polish transition which started as the first one in the Soviet bloc took quite a long time to be completed. Although there was an obvious connection between the practice of civil resistance, the chosen strategy of change, and its democratic and liberal outcomes, even some twenty years later the leaders of Solidarity of that time were still being violently criticized by some participants of the pre-1989 opposition. Today the critics are represented notably by Lech and Jarosław Kaczyński: respectively the president of Poland from 2005 and its prime minister from 2005 until 2007.[31] These accusations, and the emotional atmosphere surrounding such debates, indicate that the peaceful model of transition—with a safe place reserved for members of the old regime—was not and still is not accepted as something self-evident by the whole population, and especially by part of the political elite.

The Polish round-table negotiations had an enormous impact on political developments in the whole communist world, and beyond. They gave a signal to millions of people and to the ruling elites in the region that there was a peaceful way out of communism. As a result of the Polish changes, the perception of the relative balance of forces in other countries of east-central Europe changed dramatically. Those changes also confirmed that the Red Army was not there any more to support local regimes. Gorbachev's position of non-intervention in the internal affairs of other countries was further reinforced. After the Polish negotiations it also became possible elsewhere to agree on the legalization of the opposition, free speech, and freedom of association, to have and win elections; and

---

[31] See the exposé presented at the Heritage Foundation in Washington on 14 Sep. 2006 by Prime Minister Jarosław Kaczyński: 'The Fall of Post-Communism: Transformation in Central and Eastern Europe', www.heritage.org/Press/TheFallofPostCommunism.cfm.

for the power-holders from the old regime peacefully to accept a humiliating defeat. While the opposition formed a new government, those who were losing power retained personal security and even a privileged social and economic position. That was the deal.

One year after the formation of the first non-communist government in Poland, nearly all the former communist countries of the region had held some form of free or semi-free elections. They subsequently moved far away from the communist past. Poland's home-grown model of peaceful self-limiting revolution, as it evolved from the seminal opposition re-thinking of the mid 1970s to the pioneering round-table talks of 1989, thus contributed decisively to the peaceful end of communism in Europe, and the transformation of world politics that followed.

# 9

## Portugal: 'The Revolution of the Carnations', 1974–75

*Kenneth Maxwell*

On 25 April 1974 the Portuguese military—or, more precisely, the younger members of the officer corps—led a revolt against the authoritarian government which had prevailed in Portugal since 1926. The coup took Europe and the US by complete surprise. It also led almost immediately to the collapse of the regime. There had not been demonstrations before the coup, and the coup leaders urged citizens to stay in their homes. However, within hours the streets filled with multitudes of Portuguese celebrating the military's action, appealing to pro-government forces not to resist the coup, and festooning with red carnations the often-bewildered soldiers who had taken part in the coup. These flowers were to give the coup its lasting name, the Carnation Revolution.[1]

The dictatorship in Portugal had its own peculiar characteristics. Even though it had begun as a military regime in the 1920s, it soon became a civilian right-wing authoritarian system, under the prime ministership of Antonio Salazar from 1932 to 1968, and then headed by Marcello Caetano. By 1974, Portugal faced a political and economic impasse, aggravated by the long wars that ensued from its determination to hang on to its African colonies. Portugal had resisted the decolonization wave of the 1950s and '60s. Thus, as French and British colonies became independent, the Portuguese stood alone and grew increasingly isolated internationally. The strain on a relatively small population (less than ten million) became intolerable as Portugal struggled to sustain a military force of over 150,000 in Africa. The junior officers who engineered the military coup of April 1974 that ended the Portuguese dictatorship were committed both to political change within Portugal (including the legalization of political parties) and to rapid decolonization.

The coup of April 1974 ushered in a year and a half of revolutionary turmoil which eventually resulted in Portugal's acceptance of democratic politics essential

---

[1] An inventory of many of the documents, newspapers, and subject files which provide the sources for this chapter can be found in the collection which I gave to the Special Collections Division of the Princeton University Library and are available on microfilm from Thomson Gale. I also provide a comprehensive bibliographic guide and essay in my book *The Making of Portuguese Democracy* (Cambridge: Cambridge University Press, 1995), 201–35.

©Henri Bureau/Sygma/Corbis

**Figure 9.1** Unusual alliances: civil resistance in support of the military. Huge crowds fill the streets of Lisbon in celebration of the young military officers who had overthrown one of Europe's longest lasting dictatorships in a *coup d'état* on 25 April 1974. Soldiers, many of whom had been drafted to fight the unpopular colonial wars in Mozambique, Angola, and Portuguese Guinea, were festooned by the population with red carnations, which gave the Portuguese revolution its lasting name.

to its integration into the European Community. In this process, both civil resistance and power politics played significant parts. The events encompassed civil resistance in an unusual context, however: popular mobilization in support of a military *coup d'état* and, even more remarkable, a military coup which, as soon became evident, was one from the Left. In this period, civil resistance was a significant factor in containing any tendencies towards violence in general, and, especially in the summer and autumn of 1975, prevented both a right-wing counter-coup and a communist putsch intended to consolidate the power over the state of the Portuguese Communist Party (PCP). The mobilization of the population—along with the very considerable covert and overt intervention by the European powers and the US—helped save Portugal from a potential civil war, and led to the acceptance of democratic politics and to a future integrated into the European Community. This was, for the period, an unexpected and remarkable development. In the mid-1970s, there was a tendency to expect the extremes to dominate in such a chaotic situation. But in Portugal at that time, new political parties were emerging, elections took place, and the people were able to express their views in favour of a constitutional, European-style democracy. They did not favour a return to an authoritarian system of the Right, nor did they embrace an authoritarian system of the Left as was proposed by the powerful PCP and its allies.

Yet contemporary Portuguese democracy rests on the obfuscation of this conflictive experience. Most foreign observers found the coup of 1974 hard to categorize. It took the Harvard political scientist Samuel Huntington to place Portugal at the centre—or at least at the beginning—of what he called the 'third wave' of democratization.[2] Huntington recognized Portugal's precociousness. How to interpret this precocity is another question. One major problem with the idea of the 'third wave', or at least the way it developed into an academic industry, is that it has flattened out and homogenized the Portugal case into a comparative framework and thus obscured many vital elements in Portugal's process of democratization.

But why has the 'flattening out' of this critical episode in twentieth-century European history occurred? Those on the Portuguese Right have de-emphasized the history of the Revolution and at times even deny that a revolution occurred. They have also, in effect, demilitarized this period and stripped it of its African dimensions. Yet the military and decolonization were central components of the Portuguese crisis. One cannot understand April 1974 through November 1975 without recognizing the intimate connections between the independence of the former Portuguese colonies and political developments within Portugal itself.

On the Left a similar process of obfuscation has taken place. During the 1980s, the PCP appropriated to itself 'the defence' of what the party called the 'gains of the Revolution': the expropriation of the large businesses, banks, and rural landholdings in 1975, and the socialist clauses in the 1976 Portuguese constitution which declared these nationalizations and land expropriations 'irreversible'. This rearguard action in the defence of these measures by the communists helped to disguise the fact that the nationalizations and expropriations of land and property in 1975 were prompted as much by the absence, or collapse, of state authority as by a communist plot. The radicalism of the upheaval of 1974–5 also explains why political parties in Portugal still retain designations rhetorically to the left of their actual position on any traditional European left–right political spectrum.[3]

In fact, the communists after the coup of 1974 pursued a policy of subverting the upper levels of administration—seizing the so-called 'levers of power' within the bureaucracy, the press, the military, and the unions. Problematically, these 'levers of power' did not work in the very fluid anti-authoritarian atmosphere following 25 April 1974. No one in Portugal was paying much attention to orders from above. Deference, authority, and discipline all disintegrated, and the communists found themselves challenged by many activists to their left. The communist leadership, which was tightly disciplined, closely attuned to Moscow, and hardened but isolated by decades of clandestine activity, did not understand this

---

[2] Samuel P. Huntington, *The Third Wave: Democratization in the Late Twentieth Century* (Norman, Okla.: University of Oklahoma Press, 1991).

[3] For example, the Partido Social Democrata (PSD) is actually conservative rather than social democratic, and the Partido Socialista (PS) is in practice social democratic.

phenomenon and thus miscalculated the political dynamics of the revolutionary situation they were facing.

Portugal, in fact, saw the emergence by late 1974 of a chaotic, aggressive, largely uncoordinated popular movement composed of students, soldiers, landless workers, and homeless people in the cities, as well as opportunists who seized and occupied empty apartments, many belonging to immigrants. At the grass-roots level, this movement took the initiative into its own hands, forcing the pace of change between January and November 1975. In many cases the communists did not want such a radical turn so soon. This was particularly the case with the large-scale land seizures which took place in the Alentejo, the most revolutionary of the actions of 1974–5.[4]

The great disadvantage of the historical amnesia on Left and Right is to obscure some of the dynamics vital to understanding the role of popular participation in the emergence of Portuguese democracy. Agonizing choices were faced by many Portuguese in 1974 and 1975, on matters of politics, faith, civil rights, freedom of the press, the role of political parties, and the institutional structures of democracy itself. Obscuring the centrality of these choices also hides the sources of the strength of Portuguese democracy, which flows from the fact that it was born of struggle and conscious choices at critical moments by Portuguese men and women of all classes, all regions, and all levels of educational attainments.

When the people were allowed to vote, they turned out in overwhelming numbers to show they valued the right to participate. The election to the Constituent Assembly in April 1975, held exactly one year after the coup, became a *foundational* event. The elections also revealed that Portugal was a deeply divided nation. The conservative, Catholic north and centre valued private property, as opposed to the south, where the communists were strongly entrenched. The Constituent Assembly election results proved that large sectors of the country were not willing to support a radical reordering of society and the economy. This in turn showed the United States and western Europe whom they needed to support in Portugal and where their potential allies were located. This was not an insignificant revelation, as Henry Kissinger, then the powerful US Secretary of State, had come to the conclusion that Portugal was as good as lost to a communist power grab.

## A *COUP D'ÉTAT* FROM THE LEFT, AND ITS CONSEQUENCE

The intense confrontations which took place in Portugal of 1975 were played out in the coalescence and disintegration of military and political alliances. The

---

[4] These popular movements are well documented in Sections II and IV of the Princeton University collection and in Nancy Gina Bermeo, *The Revolution within the Revolution: Worker's Control in Rural Portugal* (Princeton, NJ: Princeton University Press, 1986). See also John L. Hammond, *Building Popular Power: Workers' and Neighborhood Movements in the Portuguese Revolution* (New York: Monthly Review Press, 1988).

tumultuous period after the collapse of the old order in a coup from the Left in 1974 and before the crystallization of the new in 1976 saw intense popular mobilization on both sides of the political spectrum, in both the north and south, and in both the major cities and the countryside. There were victims. It is important to remember this: people were imprisoned (many without formal charges) or driven into exile; others lost property and jobs. Yet the institutional break was total. This was not a 'transition' of power. The Salazarist institutional structures were jettisoned. A provisional government was set in place by a military junta. Provisional constitutional law incorporated the programme of the Armed Forces Movement directly. The single political party of the old regime was abolished.[5]

After five decades of dictatorship, it was perhaps inevitable that political society was under-organized or not organized at all. Some dissidents had emerged in the early 1970s but these civilian opposition groups bore no

©Henri Bureau/Sygma/Corbis

**Figure 9.2** Dealing with the secret police. While the military coup met minimal resistance, members of the secret police of the old regime were a partial exception. They were responsible for the only fatalities on 25 April 1974—less than half a dozen—when they held out briefly at their headquarters in Lisbon. The offenders were quickly rounded up and imprisoned by the military. We do not know the exact story of the suspected secret policeman in this photograph.

[5] Decree-Law No. 203/74 (15 May 1974).

responsibility for the regime's overthrow. Civil society was taken almost completely by surprise when the coup occurred. It is very important to recognize that popular mobilization in Portugal took place *after* the regime had fallen, not before. Unlike later cases of regime transitions in eastern Europe, no non-violent movement played a role in the demise of the Salazar/Caetano dictatorship.

The scale of popular response after the coup, the mobilization of workers, and the huge chanting crowds in the streets took the military by surprise.[6] The high schools were thrown into chaos after April, and students spent the rest of the academic year purging the faculties of 'fascists' and forming short-lived administrative committees of students, teachers, and maintenance personnel. Here Portugal belatedly followed the paradigmatic example of 1968 France, and many Portuguese students living in France returned to stir things up. Faced with the impossibility of holding examinations, the government accepted all high school students in their final year into the universities, creating in the autumn of 1974 an incoming class of 28,000. The universities' inability to absorb so many students forced the government to cancel the entire freshman class, sending thousands of mostly middle-class young people onto the streets with nothing to do but demonstrate, attend endless meetings, and engage in increasingly violent and intolerant internecine disputes. Many attached themselves to a plethora of small Marxist-Leninist, anarchist, and Maoist parties far to the left of the PCP.[7]

To be sure, some organized opposition movements operated in Portugal prior to 1974. The most prominent was the PCP, led by Álvaro Cunhal. The PCP had been founded in 1921 and Álvaro Cunhal had assumed leadership of the party in 1943. Party organization followed strict Leninist lines: small cells, tight discipline, members kept unaware of each others' identities, and decisions handed down from above. Cunhal himself spent thirteen years behind bars in Portugal and another fourteen in exile in eastern Europe and Moscow. The party was therefore a classic cadre party, dependent on and subservient to Moscow. It did possess, however, a strong base in the Alentejo, the grain-producing lands south of the Tagus River—a region of great landed estates with strongly implanted party support among the anticlerical, landless rural labourers. By 1970 the communists were strongly entrenched in the metallurgical unions, and increasingly influential among lower middle-class white-collar workers, especially the bank workers' unions in Lisbon and Oporto. The Socialist Party (PS), on the other hand, was founded only a year before the coup and in West Germany, where it had developed strong ties with Willy Brandt and his Social Democratic Party (SPD). The PS, led by Mário Soares, the Lisbon lawyer and oppositionist, became affiliated with the Socialists International. This proved to be an important link for Soares, because at that time Social Democrats governed the United Kingdom, Sweden, and West Germany. Unlike the communists, the socialists had a minimal organizational base in Portugal.

---

[6] On labour disputes after the coup see Maria de Lourdes Lima Santos, Marinus Pires e Lima, and Vítor Matias Ferreira, *O 25 de abril e as lutes sociais nas empresas* (Oporto: unknown publisher, 1976) and José Pires, *Greves e o 25 de abril* (Lisbon: Edições Base, 1976).

[7] On schools see Ben Pimlott and Jean Seaton, 'How Revolution Reached the Schools of Portugal', *New Society* (London), 9 Dec. 1976, 508.

Another factor is vital to understanding how civil resistance developed in Portugal after the coup. Over the so-called 'hot summer' of 1975, resistance emerged and found its voice and organization largely on the right. Many were unprepared for this phenomenon, and it requires explanation. Although Salazar had adopted by the early 1930s many of the trappings of European fascism, the regime functioned much more as a Catholic authoritarian system and did not seek, unlike the Germans and Italians, to mobilize the population for support. In fact, the regime discouraged any populist engagement.

Thus, when political parties were legalized after the April coup, the more conservative, intensely traditionalist segments of the population—which had passively supported the previous regime—found themselves without spokesmen, or organization, or international political connections. The conservative Catholic rural peasantry of the north and in the Azores archipelago nevertheless constituted a potentially important political constituency.[8] Two new parties emerged after the coup and attempted to harness these conservative forces: the Popular Democratic Party (PPD) and the Democratic and Social Centre Party (CDS). The former was founded in May 1974 by Francisco Sá Carneiro, a lawyer from Oporto, and Francisco Pinto Balsemão, a newspaper proprietor and editor from Lisbon. The CDS, founded by a young Lisbon law professor, Diogo Freitas do Amaral, who had been Caetano's favourite student and protégé, aimed to create a Christian Democratic option in Portugal.[9] But both parties came very late to the game. The urban middle class, the civil servants, and white-collar employees, who might have formed these parties' popular base, were, in this period, among the most vociferous 'leftists'. An embittered Marcello Caetano, in exile in Brazil, acidly summed up the situation in which the Portuguese middle class found itself: 'The truth is', he wrote, 'that the Portuguese bourgeoisie, used to enjoying a climate of peace during half a century, under the protection of so many police institutions, which acted as their shield, had no combative spirit and did not know how to act in defence of the principles they said they professed.'[10]

## THE 1975 ELECTIONS AND THE CHANGED POLITICAL LANDSCAPE

The question of the political legitimacy of the post-coup leadership became a matter of intense dispute in 1975. The struggle involved the military as well as

[8] For a useful compendium of articles and documents published at the time on the role of the Church, see 'The Church and Revolution', *International Documentation on the Contemporary Church*, I (New York: IDCC, 1976).

[9] See comments by Caetano in Joaquim Veríssimo Serrão, *Marcello Caetano: Confidências no exilio* (Lisbon: Verbo, 1985), 334–5. An important source for the new political class was SEDES (Association for Economic and Social Development), founded in 1970.

[10] Marcello Caetano, *Depoimento* (Rio de Janeiro: Distribuidora Record, 1974).

civil society, electoral outcomes and massive street demonstrations, the threat of violence and, in some cases, violence itself. A dispute between the communists and the socialists was the most dramatic political manifestation of this struggle. The conflict reached beyond mere party factionalism because it paralleled, and to some extent intersected with, major divergences emerging within the military Left.

The first major crisis occurred in September 1974, when provisional president General Spínola attempted to mobilize what he called the 'silent majority' in opposition to a perceived growth in communist influence. The communists blockaded Lisbon, and Spínola resigned the presidency. His replacement, General Costa Gomes, had always been more acceptable to the leftist junior offices behind the coup. In March 1975, Spínola was tricked into believing that an anti-communist putsch might succeed but when, on 11 March, he arrived at the Tancos air base, ostensibly to take command of the revolt, he instead found a shambles. He barely escaped arrest before boarding a helicopter and fleeing across the border to Spain. The radical elements within the military, with communist support, used this occasion to purge and sometimes imprison their more moderate colleagues as well as leading members of the old oligarchy.

They then moved quickly to establish, on 12 March, a 'Council of the Revolution', which became the supreme authority in the state. It was joined by an assembly of 240 men, representing the three services, which met on 11–12 March to impose a series of drastic measures, the most critical being the nationalization of the banks and insurance companies. Because of the close interlocking nature of the Portuguese oligarchy and its control of major sectors of the economy, the nationalization of the banks put into the hands of the state the major part of privately owned Portuguese industry.[11] The banks also directly owned or held mortgages on virtually every Portuguese newspaper. The state thus seized financial control of much of the communications media—all the Lisbon morning dailies and weekly magazines. An exception was the evening paper *República*, owned by 3,500 small shareholders and edited by Raúl Rego, a leading socialist. It had been one of the few voices of criticism during the long dictatorship. The Council of the Revolution also threatened a major land expropriation of all estates over 500 hectares, a measure intended to destroy the power of the great *latifundiários* of the south. These nationalizations immediately placed Portugal among the most radical of European states. On 11 April 1975, the Council of the Revolution forced the political parties to sign a pact guaranteeing military supremacy for at least three years and relegating the provisional government to a subordinate position in the new hierarchy of power.

The Constituent Assembly elections, however, had been an integral part of the original programme of the coup-makers and the provisional constitutional documents had promised that they would take place exactly one year after the coup—in other words, on 25 April 1975. As the political dynamics had moved

---

[11] For a text of decrees see Orlando Neves (ed.), *Textos históricos da revolução*, 3 vols. (Lisbon: Diabril 1975–6), vol. 2: *A revolução em ruptura*.

leftward, the more radical military, as well as the communists, had wanted to abandon this commitment; but to do so would have been a direct affront to the Portuguese people, who, after fifty years of manipulated electoral contests and a narrow franchise, were itching to vote. The Constituent Assembly election thus became an event of enormous political importance. In one of the highest turn-outs ever recorded in a national election (91.7 per cent), Mário Soares's PS took 37.9 per cent of the vote; Sá Carneiro's PSD gained 26.4 per cent; Álvaro Cunhal's PCP, on the other hand, received a mere 12.5 per cent nationwide; and Freitas do Amaral's CDS got 7.6 per cent.

The constituent election returns showed decisively that a majority of the Portuguese people wanted change, but only by democratic means.[12] Equally significant, the election demonstrated Portugal's division over two crucial issues: religion and land ownership. These two elements underpinned the struggle that was about to begin.


## OUTSIDE INTERVENTION

The election also revealed a geography for counter-revolution. Outside interven-tion and power politics in fact played an important role in the Portuguese crisis. Portugal is a founding member of NATO, and the NATO dimension became a matter of contestation almost immediately after the coup of 1974 when General Spínola, in one of his first decisions as provisional president, invited the com-munists into the provisional government. He hoped that by placing a communist in the Ministry of Labour and bringing Cunhal into the cabinet as a minister without portfolio, he could moderate and restrain labour militancy. As it turned out, however, Spínola badly miscalculated the consequences of his invitation.

The PCP's strategy in the aftermath of the coup was to act 'with moderation', whatever its position in or outside the new government. The Chilean experience of 1973, when Salvador Allende, an elected Marxist president, was overthrown in a bloody military coup, figured heavily in the minds of the Portuguese Left in 1974 and made communists wary of the kind of military and civilian support that had made General Pinochet's coup possible. But the shocked reaction of NATO to the presence of the first communists in a western European government since the beginning of the Cold War, and especially with a leader as orthodox and as close to the Soviet Union as Cunhal, meant that Spínola's attempt to buy social peace at home bought him only the hostility of Portugal's allies abroad.

On 18 October 1974, over lunch at the State Department in Washington, Henry Kissinger made his misgivings abundantly clear to visiting President

---

[12] For election returns and analyses, see Jorge Gaspar and Nuno Vitorino, *As eleições de 25 de abril: Geografia e imagem dos partidos* (Lisbon: Livros Horizonte, 1976). Also see analysis by John Hammond in Lawrence S. Graham and Harry M. Makler (eds.), *Contemporary Portugal: The Revolution and its Antecedents* (Austin, Tex.: University of Texas Press, 1979); and Ben Pimlott and Jean Seaton, 'Ferment of an Old Brew', *New Society* (London), 24 July 1975, 202.

Costa Gomes and Foreign Minister Mário Soares. Kissinger complained of communist penetration of the institutions, media, and trade unions in Portugal and warned Soares that he would become a Portuguese Kerensky. Soares said: 'But I don't want to be Kerensky.' And Kissinger replied: 'Neither did Kerensky.'

To back up his concerns, Kissinger sent to Lisbon a high-powered new embassy team recommended by General Vernon Walters, deputy director of the CIA and an old Portugal hand; it included Frank C. Carlucci III as ambassador, Herbert Okun as his deputy, and Colonel Robert Schuler as defence attaché. All three spoke fluent Portuguese and had worked with Vernon Walters on the 1964 American-backed coup against Brazilian President João Goulart. They had a clear mission in Lisbon as far as Washington was concerned: to remove the communists from the government and keep them out. The western Europeans were no less opposed to the communists but took the more practical approach of infusing Portuguese political parties and unions with foreign cash. Soares and the PS had received substantial subsidies from the West Germans via the SPD and that party's foundation, the Friedrich-Ebert Stiftung.[13]

The task of 'taming' Portugal, however, was not easy. Over a short period of time, this country of less than ten million was forced to absorb a series of disruptive challenges: an ill-led and increasingly undisciplined army, with tens of thousands of soldiers returning from an unsuccessful and unpopular war; half a million destitute former colonial settlers forced to flee to Portugal from Africa; unemployment figures approaching some 400,000; more than four hundred large rural estates taken over by their workers and expropriated; worker control in the factories; 'people power' in the urban neighbourhoods and 'peasant power' in the countryside. Taken together, these elements gave Portugal's revolution its chaotic character. Europe had seen nothing like it in decades.

Ambassador Carlucci and the US embassy, however, soon came to doubt Kissinger's dire predictions. 'The pressures and forces that have been unleashed must be tempered, they cannot be stuffed back into the tube,' he told Washington. Herbert Okun developed an efficient polling operation in anticipation of the Constituent Assembly elections, accurately predicting the results. And Colonel Schuler cultivated the younger members of the officer corps, working with General Alexander Haig, the NATO commander, to incorporate selected Portuguese officers in NATO training programmes, among them an obscure colonel called António Ramalho Eanes. 'A boy scout for democracy' was how Okun described Eanes. But the task of combating the communists proved only slightly less arduous for Carlucci than confronting the presuppositions of Henry Kissinger in Washington. When Carlucci argued that Mário Soares was the 'only game in town', Kissinger shouted at his staff: 'Whoever sold me Carlucci as a tough guy?' But Kissinger found that the Europeans would not accept his alarmist

---

[13] Thomas Bruneau, 'As dimensões internacionais da revolução portuguesa: apoios e constragamentos', *Análise Social*, no. 18 (1982), 885–96; and Carlos Gaspar, 'International Dimensions of the Portuguese Tradition', Instituto Português de Relações Internacionais, http://www.ipri.pt/prog_invest/tema.php?idt=5.

predictions. Much less would they accept a 'Chilean solution'.[14] The West Germans argued strongly for Soares. But Kissinger was not convinced. He told President Ford on 1 May 1975: 'The election was a popularity contest with no significance. There has been no change in direction because of the election. Algeria is their model. The Europeans are ecstatic. But we could face in ten years a Socialist Europe whose cement is anti-Americanism.'[15]

By the summer of 1975, the struggle in Portugal had become a major concern for both the Right and the Left throughout Europe. Though the Carnation Revolution preceded the age of the fax and the Internet, the way that it was interpreted internationally had important political implications.[16] The issues that most caught foreign attention were freedom of the press and freedom of religious expression, the former focusing on the old opposition newspaper, *República*, and the latter on the Catholic Church's radio station, Rádio Renascença. Both were seized in late spring 1975 by radical workers with the acquiescence of the communists. Each case served to point up sensitive concerns, especially in France, that lay just beneath the uneasy alliances between social democrats and communists.[17] Since June 1972, the Parti Communiste Français (PCF) had been allied with the socialists in a common programme resembling the strategy that had ended in disaster in Chile. The Partito Communista Italiano (PCI) had gone even further and opted for a 'parliamentary road to socialism', much as Allende had in Chile. Both the French and the Italian communists had much to lose from the Leninist tactics adopted by the PCP; their differing responses to developments in Portugal in the summer of 1975 led to an unprecedented public quarrel. The French refused to condemn the PCP but the Italians publicly criticized the Portuguese communists for analysing events from a 'third-world' perspective and for allying themselves too closely with the military. Only later on did the French intellectual Jacques Fremontier retrospectively comment that 'the African or third-world illusion' had done much 'to cause the Portuguese Revolution to go off the rails'.[18]

---

[14] 'Portugal als Lehrbeispiel der Demokratisierung; 25 Jahre nach der Nelkenrevolution', *Neue Zürcher Zeitung*, 4 Apr. 1999. Cited by Jens-Ulrich Poppen, 'Soft Power Politics: The Role of Political Foundations in Germany's Foreign Policy', Ph.D. thesis, London School of Economics.

[15] 'Meeting with President Ford', 1 May 1975 (*Digital National Security Archive*, KT01608, ProQuest), 2.

[16] Following Portugal at the time, I was struck by the importance of the way in which the international media interpreted events. Afterwards I organized two conferences to discuss this phenomenon: see, for example, Kenneth Maxwell (ed.), *The Rebirth of Iberian Democracy* (Westport, Conn.: Greenwood Press, 1977). Also in the documents at Princeton are the complete transcripts of a major conference on the role of the media in the transitions to democracy in Portugal and in Spain, which involved participation by major political and media actors in both countries.

[17] For a good account of the complicated *República* and Rádio Renascença cases see Phil Mailer, *Portugal: The Impossible Revolution?* (London: Solidarity, 1977).

[18] Jacques Fremontier, *Portugal: Les points sur les i...* (Paris: Éditions sociales, 1976). For an excellent account of the different reactions of the French and Italian communist parties to events in Portugal see Alex Macleod, *La révolution inopportune: les parties communistes française et italienne face à la révolution portugaise (1973–1975)* (Montréal: University Press of Montréal, 1984).

©Henri Bureau/Sygma/Corbis

**Figure 9.3** The importance of independent media. Portuguese soldiers (one sniffing his carnation) read a newspaper in late April 1974 to find out the latest on the 'Revolution of the Carnations'. Freedom of expression became a matter of intense controversy after radical workers with communist support took over the independent socialist newspaper *República* and a radio station belonging to the Catholic Church.

## POPULAR MOBILIZATION IN 1975

Popular mobilization and civil resistance were central to the events of the 'hot summer' of 1975, and it was a civil resistance that crossed the political spectrum. In particular, it came as a considerable surprise to most observers in Lisbon and overseas when the intensely traditionalist Catholic, small landowning majority in the north and centre of Portugal rose up and chased the communists out of much of the countryside and small towns. The petite bourgeoisie, as Cunhal defined these small proprietors, proved more resilient than had the great family cartels and the large landowners of the south. The 'inevitability of history' did not impress them once they perceived there to be threats to their livelihoods, religion, and property.

As the land seizures took place in the south, a strong reaction was developing in the north and centre of the country where even many industrial workers owned land or had access to small plots. The landless rural workers of the Alentejo had been quickly organized by the communists (and other leftist groups) into collective and cooperative farms throughout the region, thus preventing the break-up of old estates. But the smaller landowners of the north and centre were also mobilizing into the newly established Portuguese Confederation of Farmers (CAP), just as small businessmen joined the Portuguese Confederation of Industrialists (CIP) in droves. The Catholic Church was growing increasingly outspoken. Priests in countless villages throughout the interior were ending their sermons with the prayer 'God save us from the communists', to which the anxious congregations responded with fervent 'Amens'. The *dinamização cultural* teams, sent in by the army to promote the Revolution, were totally counterproductive. Far from winning over the devout peasants, these leftist military 'dynamizers' irreversibly alienated them.

The disenchantment with the Left outside Lisbon and the south opened up avenues for the purged factory owners and the Church to re-enter the process. The Portuguese immigrant communities soon linked up with anti-communist elements at home. Violent clashes broke out between communist union organizers and those workers who feared losing their employment and wanted to see the old bosses return. By August 1975, these workers had adapted the revolutionary slogans to their own purposes: 'Friend boss: the people are with you. Out with the union committee, death to the communists!'[19] The intensity of these regionally based popular movements, and their identification with the Right in the north and the Left in the south, brought Portugal very close to civil war.

In this highly volatile and dangerous situation, the communists were surprised to find that the Western powers did not follow the usual Cold War policy, especially in Latin America, of supporting anti-communist military coups. US Secretary of State Henry Kissinger remained unconvinced that the alternative approach advocated by the Europeans and by the American Embassy in Lisbon

---

[19] For the struggle within one family-owned textile enterprise in the north, see *O caso dos 17 da textil Manuel Gonçalves: um documento para a história da luta dos trabalhadores* (Oporto, 1976).

would work. He complained angrily to his chief adviser on Soviet affairs, Helmut Sonnenfeldt, on 30 April 1975: 'I just can't seem to get through [to the Europeans] the idea that it is much worse to have the present situation in Portugal than a straight takeover on the Czech model. If this were Latin America and we had that kind of situation, we would have a little more time for maneuver but with Portugal and NATO...'[20]

Instead of a 'Latin American solution', Europe (with the reluctant support of the US) reverted to the strategy employed in the immediate aftermath of the Second World War in Italy and France. Here, with the memory of fascism very fresh in their minds, Western leaders threw clandestine support behind the political parties of the centre, be they Social Democratic or Christian Democratic. Since Portugal in 1975 lacked a serious Christian Democratic alternative, the preferred choice became Mário Soares and the Socialist Party.

The West did not support the far right, arrayed in a clandestine grouping behind General Spínola. The Movimento Democrático da Liberação Portuguesa (MDLP) and the more radical Exército da Liberação Portuguese (ELP) committed some terrorist bombings in Portugal in 1975 and had cells organized in Salamanca, Madrid, and Brazil, as well as among the Portuguese immigrant communities in the United States and Venezuela. But official government policy in both the US and Brazil repudiated them. Here, Ambassador Frank Carlucci and his deputy, Herbert Okun, played a critically important role in steering clear of the far right. Unusually for an American ambassador, Carlucci was able to circumvent Kissinger and get his views directly to President Ford via the influence of his old Princeton college friend and wrestling mate, Donald Rumsfeld, then the White House Chief of Staff. The embassy urged Washington to support the middle course and argued that the Constituent Assembly elections had clearly demonstrated the resonance that such a position enjoyed among the Portuguese people. The United States thus steered clear of Spínola in exile and the Brazilian government did likewise.[21]

No less dangerous was the relationship between revolutionary Portugal and Francoist Spain. Although the Spanish government was very concerned about events in Portugal, its response was generally cautious. On 13 March 1975, just two days after General Spínola's failed coup attempt in Portugal, General Franco told the US ambassador that 'no purpose would be served whatsoever in Spain intervening in any way in Portuguese events'.[22] At a meeting a few days later Carlos Arias Navarro, the last Spanish prime minister to serve under Franco, expressed to the US ambassador 'his deep concern over what was occurring in Portugal since "Spínola's last insane act"'. Portugal was a serious threat to Spain

---

[20] 'European Affairs', 30 Apr. 1975 (*Digital National Security Archive*, KT01602, ProQuest), 6.

[21] Carlos Dugas, *MDLP-ELP—que são? A verdade sobre os dois movimentos clandestinos* (Lisbon: Afragide, 1976).

[22] US Ambassador to Spain Robert Ingersoll, after presenting his credentials to General Franco, secret message to Kissinger, 13 Mar. 1975, para 4. Available at: http://aad.archives.gov/aad/createpdf? rid=45624&dt=1822&dl=823.

not only because of the way the situation there was developing, but because of foreign support it might ultimately receive which could be hostile to Spain.'[23] The prime minister's statements at this meeting have been interpreted as indicating an intention to wage war on Portugal.[24] However, the evidence for this is not conclusive. What is clear is that there was some dangerous Portuguese provocation of Spain. On 27 September 1975, in reaction to the execution of five anti-Franco militants by the Spanish authorities, mobs attacked and burnt the Spanish embassy and consulate general in Lisbon and the consulate in Oporto. The Portuguese armed forces and police provided no protection. Fortunately, no one was hurt, and in the event the government in Madrid behaved with unexpected moderation. Any Spanish military intervention would have been disastrous for both countries, damaging Spain's post-Franco transition to democracy and potentially inciting a nationalist reaction in Portugal, among the Right and the Left, against their traditional enemy.

The Soviet Union's role through this entire period of turmoil was very ambiguous. Although heavily invested in the PCP, the Soviet Union was divided about the value of supporting a communist coup in western Europe. President Ford, seeking to engage with the Soviet Union in a policy of détente, had nevertheless issued to General Secretary Leonid Brezhnev warnings about the dire consequences for US–Soviet relations if the communists seized power in Lisbon. In any case, the Soviet leadership now had its eye on Angola, whose future, in November of 1975, was being decided largely as a result of an unexpected military intervention by Cuba.

At the Oxford Conference on Civil Resistance and Power Politics, Zita Seabra gave testimony about how the PCP felt let down by the Soviet Union in 1974–5. Herself at the time a member of the PCP's Political Commission, she described the PCP view that the April 1974 coup was the equivalent of the February 1917 revolution, destined to be followed later by a Portuguese 'October revolution'. She stated that shortly after the decisive failure of the 25 November 1975 leftist uprising she took part in a delegation to Moscow, meeting with the leading Soviet ideologist and Politburo member Mikhail Suslov, who gave no assurances of Soviet support.

As Carlos Gaspar has shown, there was a major split in Moscow between ideologues such as Suslov, who had seen in the Portuguese situation an unexpected opportunity for the communists in western Europe, and the more pragmatic Soviet leaders who feared that an aggressive Soviet role in Portugal would bury détente. In the aftermath of the 1974 coup, Cunhal had believed that the PCP could make alliances with the small landowners against the oligarchy, and also with the military. By summer 1975, however, he believed that a second stage had been reached and these alliances could be sacrificed in the interest of a real

[23] Ingersoll, after meeting with the prime minister, secret message to US Secretary of State Kissinger, 18 Mar. 1975, para 3. Available at http://aad.archives.gov/aad/createpdf?rid=45560&dt=1822&dl=823.

[24] Ingersoll's message of 18 Mar. was the basis for a report in *El Pais* (Madrid), 3 Nov. 2008, asserting that Carlos Arias had sought at the meeting to garner support for a war on Portugal.

revolution. Ironically this was at precisely the moment the West had come to believe the anti-communist resistance in Portugal was a serious factor and was moving to shore up Soares and the socialists.

The precise relationship between the PCP and the Soviet leadership in October–November 1975 remains obscure. For example, how much the Soviet leaders knew about, or were involved in, the Cuban intervention in Angola is a matter of dispute. Zita Seabra's testimony suggests that they were not prepared to support a communist coup in Lisbon in November 1975; yet at this point the PCP, which rarely acted without Soviet approval, entered into an alliance with far left forces they were well known to despise in order to promote a coup.[25] Were these diversionary tactics to cover the build-up of Cuban forces in Angola? The current view is that Cuba acted alone, but I am not convinced. The Cuban forces arrived in Angola equipped only with light arms, which in Angola were to be matched up with Soviet materiel brought in by a massive Soviet airlift. The Americans, with their attention focused on what the communists were up to in Lisbon in November, entirely missed the initial Cuban build-up in Angola. More archival research on the linkages between Moscow, Lisbon, Havana, and Luanda is required before a definitive judgement can be made.

During these critical months in late 1975, the centre and the democratic right in Portugal also acted with great restraint, far beyond what the communists might have expected, considering past experience. As far as one can tell, the anti-communist military in Portugal was scrupulous in keeping a distance between themselves and those nostalgic for a return to the old regime. On several occasions when large-scale violence might have discredited and split the anti-communist alliance now forming between socialists and moderates in the military, cautious voices prevailed.

The most dangerous moment occurred on 13 November 1975, when a large crowd of construction workers—perhaps 100,000 strong—besieged the Constituent Assembly and members of the government, including the prime minister, in the parliament building in Lisbon. Ben Pimlott, an English political scientist who was trapped inside the building with the deputies, was told by a journalist that 'the Assembly with the prime minister's residence attached would be a symbolic Winter Palace as a place to storm'. It was obvious to all that the government lacked any authority, not least over the military. Within a week, the government declared itself to be 'on strike', and finding a political solution to the crisis of authority grew more unlikely each day.

The military by now was itself totally divided, each unit defining itself politically. The commandos in fact had wanted to go in and clear the crowd from the square in front of the parliament building, but they were held back by President Costa Gomes. Despite his own very equivocal behaviour during this period, he was not prepared to see Portugal plunged into civil war, which any bloodshed at this critical moment might have provoked. His backbone was strengthened by a

---

[25] Zita Seabra, Oxford, 16 Mar. 2007, in her comments on my paper.

forceful démarche delivered personally by Ambassador Carlucci on behalf of the US and by Ambassador Fritz Caspari on behalf of the West Germans.

The defensive strategy of the non-communist military paid off when officerless radical soldiers in the paratroop corps in Lisbon led a 'leftist' uprising that provided the excuse for the anti-communist military under the command of Colonel Ramalho Eanes to crush them on 25 November 1975.[26] Significant retribution was minimized. The communists were instead encouraged to partici- pate in the democratic process. Naturally, Kissinger and the State Department viewed the repression of the uprising favourably, but the US had been much less directly involved in Portugal than in Angola.[27] The decisive defeat of the military radicals on 25 November 1975 was essentially a Portuguese affair, and was of great significance for the future. It became a foundational moment for the new democratic regime.

## OVERCOMING RIGHT AND LEFT

The constitutional regime inaugurated in 1976 thus inherited two distinct historical legacies which strongly affected the attitudes of those who had to work within its rules. One legacy came from the reaction against half a century of right-wing dictatorship, but no less important was the legacy which came from the traumatic encounter with the authoritarian left. The politicians, especially the socialists, entered the constitutional regime with as clear a view of the threat to them represented by the communists as they did of the threat from the far right. Civil resistance and power politics were intimately involved in producing these outcomes.

In fact, the strength of the Socialist Party leader Mário Soares's popular appeal very much derived from his ability to capitalize on his opposition to both Salazar before the Revolution and communism after it. He exemplified the Western and

[26] See Ramiro Correia, Pedro Soldado, and João Marujo, *MFA e luta de classes* (Lisbon: Ulmeiro, 1976). For Pimlott's eyewitness account of the siege of the Constituent Assembly and government see Ben Pimlott, *Frustrate their Knavish Tricks: Writings on Biography, History, and Politics* (London: HarperCollins, 1994), 262–8. Also for this period see José Freire Antunes, *O segredo do 25 de novembro: O verão quente de 1975 e os planos desconhecidos do grupo militar* (Lisbon: Publicações Europa-América/Mem Martins, 1980). The 'moderates' and their Western backers were not fully confident of victory on 25 November. Plans had been made to establish a government in the north of the country in the event that Lisbon was lost to the far left; this was the 'commune of Lisbon' scenario. Groups in the Azores were also poised to declare independence from Lisbon in this eventuality.

[27] For the reaction of Kissinger and his closest colleagues to the events of 25 November 1975, see the recently declassified 'Memorandum of Conversation', 25 Nov. 1975 (*Digital National Security Archive*, KT01835, ProQuest), 1–4. Even after the victory of 25 November in Lisbon, Kissinger remained committed to having US advisers in Angola to support the National Front for the Liberation of Angola (FNLA) in the civil war there. In the US this was an inflammatory position to take in the year South Vietnam had fallen. Predictably, the news leaked, and led directly to the congressional ban on this US military assistance. For a detailed account of the Angolan episode, see Walter Isaacson, *Kissinger* (New York: Simon & Schuster, 1972), 673–85.

European alternatives to the dual legacies of the recent past. He became the essential interlocutor between the civilian democratic forces in Portugal and the political and governmental forces in western Europe and the United States.

In many respects the most remarkable feature of the emergence of democracy in Portugal was this political triumph of the 'moderates' such as Soares. And there can be little doubt that the broad mobilization of civil society over the period of 1974–5 had been a decisive factor. In the extremely volatile situation that developed after April 1974, those who in the end triumphed were the practitioners of the messy art of democratic politics, not those who made utopian promises.

In the mid-1970s such victories were far from certain. Alistair Horne, whose brilliant book on the bitter struggles of French decolonization in Algiers, *A Savage War of Peace*, reflected informed opinion at the time, noted 'the lesson of the sad, repeated failure of the moderates, or a third force to compete against opposing extremes'. This lesson, Horne continued, 'is one of constant relevance to the contemporary scene, be it in Northern Ireland, South Africa or Latin America'. He concluded that in modern revolutions the extremist triumphs, not the moderate. But he was wrong. Portugal broke this pattern decisively. By 1976 the Portuguese had been able to create a representative and pluralistic system of government, fully comparable to the western European mainstream, and they did so without bloodshed.

This outcome was crucially important. In the mid-1970s many considered political parties moribund, elections no more than 'beauty contests', and liberal democracy itself a sham. But on 25 April 1975, the election to the Constituent Assembly showed all these assumptions to be erroneous. New political parties could and did arise. No less important, the results demonstrated categorically that popular support for authoritarian solutions, especially that proposed by the communists, was limited.

In 1975, Henry Kissinger had told Mário Soares he was 'doomed' to become a Kerensky. But in the context of the Portuguese Revolution, Kerensky, not Lenin, survived; Soares, not Cunhal, triumphed. Even Kissinger conceded later that he had been wrong. In a recently declassified conversation with Mário Soares held on 26, January 1976, he said: 'I must tell you that what you have done surprised me. I must admit this. I don't often make mistakes of judgment.'[28] The Portuguese people's navigation of these turbulent months made their country into a precocious forerunner of the largely peaceful transitions from authoritarianism to democracy that followed in southern and eastern Europe and in Latin America. It was a remarkable historical achievement.

[28] 'The Secretary's Meeting with Mário Soares', 26 Jan. 1976 (*Digital National Security Archive*, KT01888, ProQuest), 6.

# 10

# Mass Protests in the Iranian Revolution, 1977–79

*Ervand Abrahamian*

'I had never admired the Iranian people as much as in the past few months. Their courage, discipline, and devotion to the cause of overthrowing the monarchy had been amazing.'

Anthony Parsons, British Ambassador in Tehran[1]

Revolutions have been depicted as rude interferences of the masses into high politics. This is especially true of the Islamic Revolution in Iran. The popular revolution against the Shah's rule started in October 1977 with university protests. It picked up pace with seminary protests in January 1978 and with forty-day mourning commemorations through the early part of that year. In the latter part of the year, it developed dramatically with mass rallies estimated to have involved as many as two million people. The Shah left the country on 16 January, and two weeks later Ayatollah Khomeini returned after fifteen years of exile. The revolution reached a climax in February 1979—sixteen months after the first demonstrations—with vast numbers pouring into the streets to immobilize diehard elements in the armed forces. These protests were backed with petitions, open letters, work stoppages, and general strikes. It is often said that the midwives of revolution are catastrophic wars, financial meltdown, economic depression, food shortages, and peasant uprisings. In Iran none of these were present. What was very much present was the central role of street protests. As the MI6 man in Tehran wrote, 'the revolution triumphed' mainly because of a 'mass popular movement' with its 'force and fury, language and imagery'.[2] What is more, these crowds were on the whole peaceful, orderly, and non-violent—on rare occasions when they resorted to violence, they targeted not humans but specific types of property and symbols of authority. They behaved much like those described by George Rudé in his *The Crowd in History* and *The Crowd in the French Revolution*—perhaps even more so.[3] Since the revolution was televised

---

[1] See reference in n. 38.

[2] Desmond Harney, *The Priest and the King: An Eyewitness Account of the Iranian Revolution* (London: Tauris, 1999), 1.

[3] George Rudé, *The Crowd in History, 1730–1848* (New York: John Wiley, 1964); *The Crowd in the French Revolution* (New York: Oxford University Press, 1959); *Ideology and Popular Protest* (New York:

worldwide, it had some influence on subsequent events in other parts of the world, especially in eastern Europe.

The aim of this chapter is to analyse not the causes of the revolution but the reasons why the revolution took the shape it did—that of peaceful demonstrations. This can be described as an outstanding case of a revolution through civil disobedience. Despite the final outcome, its main dynamics would have won the admiration of not only George Rudé but also that of Rosa Luxemburg and even Mahatma Gandhi. In answering this central question, the chapter will describe the role of the crowd—its ideology, aims, slogans, aspirations, targets, faces, casualties, and organizational components. It will also explain why ordinary civilians armed with only slogans were able to bring down a vast, well heeled, and impregnable-looking state. On the eve of its collapse, the American president had hailed Iran as 'an island of stability in a sea of instability'.[4]

Conventional explanations for why crowds played such a pivotal role in the Iranian Revolution invariably cite the supposedly all-encompassing role of Islam—especially Shi'i Islam. According to this explanation, since the vast majority of Iranians are Shi'is, they see the central event in world history and in their calendar to be the martyrdom of their main saint, Imam Hussein, at the battle of Karbala in the month of Muharram in the year AD 680. This seventh-century battle supposedly determines how contemporaries perceive present-day politics. According to a prominent anthropologist, the revolution was a re-enactment of the 'Karbala paradigm'.[5] The entire process from beginning to end is seen as a religious movement—starting with seminary protest, picking up pace with clerical denunciations (especially by Ayatollah Khomeini), developing into an Islamic Revolution, and, inevitably, producing an Islamic Republic. Such narratives begin with January 1978—in Iran, as elsewhere, chronology can be highly tendentious. They argue also that the crowds became larger and more radical as people realized that the authorities were not willing to crack down hard. According to one American political scientist, 'Iranians were more likely to participate in revolutionary events if they felt that many others would do the same.'[6] He adds that the revolution was the 'largest protest event in (world) history'.

To fit the revolution into the conventional narrative, one needs to ignore much, iron out inconvenient details, and, most important of all, reinterpret Karbala into a story of unarmed civilians marching into martyrdom. In fact, Imam Hussein and his cohorts had marched forth into Karbala not as unarmed civilians baring their chests and ready to speak truth to power, but as hardened soldiers with drawn swords ready to kill as well as to be killed. Imam Hussein had very much

Pantheon, 1980); Harvey Kaye (ed.), *The Face of the Crowd: Selected Essays of George Rudé* (New Jersey: Humanities Press, 1988).

⁴ Soroush Research Group, *Taqvim-e Tarekh-e Enqelab-e Islami Iran* [Calendar of the Islamic Revolution of Iran] (Tehran: Soroush Press, 1991), 53.

⁵ Michael Fischer, *Iran: From Religious Dispute to Revolution* (Cambridge: Harvard University Press, 1980), 13.

⁶ Charles Kurzman, *The Unthinkable Revolution in Iran* (Cambridge: Harvard University Press, 2004), 122 & 170.

**Figure 10.1** The force of numbers. A crowd estimated at one million marches through the streets of Tehran in January 1979, demanding the return from exile of Ayatollah Khomeini, whose image they carry, and expressing their opposition to the government of Prime Minister Shahpour Bakhtiar. The government fell soon thereafter.

been a prophet armed. His true heirs were not the mainstream opposition—led by Khomeini—that refused to declare *jihad* (crusade) and instead insisted on using non-violent means to undermine the regime. Rather, his true heirs were the various guerrilla groups—especially the Mojahedin and Fedayin—that had emerged first in the early 1970s but by the mid 1970s had been so decimated by executions and shootouts that they had no presence outside the prisons.[7] Their survivors even toyed with the idea of giving up the armed struggle for more traditional forms of political activity such as labour organizing. The Mojahedin had initially described Imam Hussein as Che Guevara's forerunner and Karbala as an eternal inspiration for armed struggles throughout the Third World. Such reinterpretations had not sat too well with the clerical hierarchy. In fact, Khomeini deemed the Mojahedin to be at best confused eclectics; at worst, Marxists masquerading as Muslims.

---

[7] Ervand Abrahamian, *Tortured Confessions: Prisons and Public Recantations in Modern Iran* (Berkeley: University of California Press, 1999), 103.

## CROWDS IN IRANIAN HISTORY

The main contention of this chapter is that Iranians resorted to street protests not because of religious culture but because of national history. Demonstrations, strikes, petitions, and taking of sanctuary (*bast*) were all deemed to be integral parts of the national experience. They were as Iranian as apple pie is American. Iranians did not have to study theories of civil disobedience to appreciate the power of the street. Even school children with limited familiarity with the stock histories—such as those of Ahmad Kasravi on the Constitutional Revolution— knew that crowds had played major roles in the recent past.[8]

In 1891–2, street demonstrations, together with mosque meetings and bazaar strikes, forced the Shah to cancel a monopoly for the sale and export of tobacco he had sold to a British entrepreneur. It was said that even the Shah's wives observed the general strike and refused to handle his pipe. This Tobacco Protest was a dress rehearsal for the 1906 Constitutional Revolution. In 1905, the shooting of a demonstrator led some 14,000 to take *bast* in the British Legation and to demand a written constitution. One journalist later wrote that experience verified Rosa Luxembourg's theory that the general strike is the best means for bringing about political revolutions.[9] In 1919–20, protests prevented the government from ratifying an Anglo-Persian Agreement which would have in effect incorporated Iran into the British empire. In 1924, crowds, this time led by conservative clerics, scuttled schemes to establish a republic—as in Turkey.

In 1951–3, mass meetings provided Muhammad Mossadeq, the prime minister, with the clout both to nationalize the Anglo-Iranian Oil Company and to challenge the Shah over constitutional powers. On 20 July 1952 (30 Tir according to the Iranian calendar) mass demonstrations forced the Shah not only to retain him as premier but also to hand him the Defence Ministry. Some twenty demonstrators were killed in Tehran, and 30 Tir remains sacred in the nationalist calendar. Elizabeth Monroe, the British historian, claimed that the 'mob' was the key for understanding Iran: 'Provide Tehran with a political stir and out pours the mob from its slums and shanty towns no matter what the pretext for a demonstration.'[10] Mossadeq remained in power until the CIA coup of August 1953. Soon after the coup, on 7 December, three Tehran University students were shot protesting against the visit of Vice-President Nixon, 7 December became—and remains to the present day—the unofficial student day throughout the country. In 1967, when Mossadeq died after years of house imprisonment, he left on his mantelpiece a statue of Gandhi and photographs of these three students. He also left a will requesting to be buried alongside the 'martyrs' of 30 Tir. Needless to say, his request was not granted.

---

[8] Ahmad Kasravi, *Tarekh-e Mashruteh-e Iran* ('History of the Iranian constitution') (Tehran: Amir Kaber Press, 1981).

[9] Hassan Arsanjani, 'Anarchism in Iran', *Darya*, 17 July 1944.

[10] Elizabeth Monroe, 'Key Force in the Middle East—the Mob', *New York Times*, 30 Aug. 1953.

Crowds also played a major role in June 1963 when Khomeini appeared on the national scene for the very first time. He denounced the Shah for reviving nineteenth-century imperialist 'capitulations' by granting American military personnel immunity from Iranian laws. Other ayatollahs also took the Shah to task for launching the 'White Revolution'—especially land reform and women's suffrage. During Muharram, angry crowds attacked government buildings in downtown Tehran. The military retaliated by shooting into the crowds and killing thirty-two demonstrators.[11] June 1963 is now celebrated as the beginning of the Islamic movement. Crowds carry such mystique that royalists did their best to depict the 1953 coup as a movement of the dispossessed masses. They billed 19 August (28 Mordad according to the Iranian calendar) as the 'Shah-People Uprising'.

## THE CROWD IN 1976–9

The Islamic Revolution began to unfold not in February 1978—as convention would have it—but in late 1977. In the course of 1975–6, the issue of human rights violations in Iran came under increasing scrutiny in the West. Mainstream papers such as the *Sunday Times* ran exposés on 'Torture in Iran'.[12] Amnesty International, the International League of Human Rights, and the highly respected International Commission of Jurists published scathing reports. The former went so far as to describe Iran as having 'the highest rate of death penalties in the world, no valid system of civilian courts and a history of torture which is beyond belief'.[13] Congress heard testimonies depicting Iran as 'a one bullet' state with no free press, no right of assembly, and no due process of law.[14] What is more, Jimmy Carter, during his 1976 presidential campaign, mentioned Iran as a country where the US should do more to protect human rights. Although Khomeini supporters later denied that this had in any way helped their revolution, Mehdi Bazargan—Khomeini's first premier—admitted in 1980 that Carter made it possible for Iran to 'breathe once again'.[15] His party, the Liberation Movement, described Carter's election as a milestone on the long road to revolution.[16] Similarly, his foreign minister acknowledged that Carter's human rights campaign, although designed for the Cold War, had unforeseen but important repercussions for Iran.[17]

[11] Cyrus Kadivar, 'A Question of Numbers', *Ruzegar-e Now*, 8 Aug. 2003.

[12] Paul Jacobson, 'Torture in Iran', *Sunday Times*, 19 Jan. 1975.

[13] Amnesty International, *Annual Report for 1974–75* (London, 1975).

[14] US Congress House of Representatives Committee on International Relations Subcommittee on International Organizations, *Human Rights in Iran* (Washington DC, 1977), 23–5.

[15] Mehdi Bazargan, 'Letter to the Editor', *Ettela'at*, 7 Feb. 1980.

[16] Liberation Movement, *Showray-e Enqelab va Dowlat-e Movaqat* ('Revolutionary council and provisional government') (Tehran: Liberation Movement Press, 1982), 12.

[17] Ibrahim Yazdi, *Akherin Talashha dar Akherin Ruzha* ('Last struggles in the final days') (Tehran: Rashdieh Publications, 1984), 10.

©Wally McNamee/Corbis

**Figure 10.2** Greeting the saviour. Iranian women show support for Ayatollah Khomeini at Tehran University, two days after his triumphal return to Iran on 1 February 1979. Women were conspicuous in the huge rallies that welcomed Khomeini. At that time, wearing the hijab was still voluntary.

Responding to these pressures, the Shah instructed SAVAK, his secret police, to stop torturing prisoners. He opened prisons to the Red Cross; and amnestied 280 religious prisoners including five who had assassinated his prime minister in 1965. Leftists, deemed to be the main threat, were not released. He also promised that in future political detainees would have hearings within twenty-four hours, would be tried in civilian courts, would be able to choose their own attorney, and that these attorneys would be protected from state prosecution.[18] He gave these concessions in part because he was concerned about his image in the West; in part because he did not want to weaken his special relations with Washington; but in most part because of over-confidence. The recent quadrupling of world oil prices had brought him a windfall. The Resurgence Party—founded in 1974—had created a formidable-looking one-party state. The expansion of the armed forces had equipped him with the fourth largest military in the world. What is more, the White Revolution had supposedly put finishing touches to the Shah-People Uprising. By 1975 he was lecturing foreign journalists on how he outdid all

---

[18] International Commission of Jurists, *Human Rights and the Legal System in Iran* (Geneva: International Commission of Jurists, 1976).

168 *Ervand Abrahamian*

other historic figures in enjoying a 'dialectical relationship with his people'. 'No people', he boasted, 'has given its ruler such a carte-blanche.'[19] The terminology, as well as the boast, revealed much about him at the height of his power—some would say his megalomania.

The relaxation of controls had unforeseen consequences. Old organizations— the Liberation Movement, Mossadeq's National Front, the communist Tudeh Party, the Writers Association, the Association of Teachers, and Society of Bazaar Merchants and Guilds—reappeared. And new organizations—the Committee for the Defence of Political Prisoners, the Committee for the Defence of Human Rights, the Group for Free Books and Free Thought, the Association of Iranian Jurists, and the National Organization of University Teachers—appeared. Some began to publish open letters and their own manifestos and circulars.

In October 1977, the Writers Association took the ground-breaking step of organizing ten poetry-reading sessions in Goethe House near Tehran University. These were so successful that they continued for the rest of the month in the nearby Industrial University. There they became larger and more vociferous eventually overflowing into the streets. According to eyewitnesses, some five thousand marched out shouting 'Death to the Shah', 'Equality, Worker's Author-ity', and the traditional student slogan 'Unity—Struggle—Victory'.[20] Some fifty were arrested; an unknown number injured and killed. The first blood had been spilled. The *Washington Post* reported that after years of relative quiet the streets were now being disrupted on almost a daily basis.[21] The demonstrators had no real organizational links but identified vaguely with the Mojahedin, Fedayin, National Front, Tudeh, or other Marxist groups. The crisis was compounded first by a nationwide university strike on 7 December; second, by the televised scene of the Shah on the White House lawn wiping tears from his eyes—the Washington DC police had used tear gas to break up an Iranian student demon-stration; and third, by the lenient treatment meted out by the courts to the fifty arrested after the poetry-reading sessions. This sent a clear message to others.

On 7 January 1978, the semi-official newspaper *Ettela'at* ('Information') pub-lished a scurrilous article on Khomeini.[22] It smeared him as a 'black reactionary'— clerics wore black clothes; as a foreigner—his grandfather had lived in Kashmir; as a tool of British and 'red imperialisms'; and, to top it all, as a licentious layabout— he was rumoured in his youth to have written sufi poetry praising wine, women, and song. This article is deemed to be the bombshell that sparked off the

[19] 'Interview with the Shah-in-Shah', *Kayhan International*, 10 Nov. 1976.

[20] Nasser Pakdaman, 'Reflections on the Coming of the Iranian Revolution', *Cheshmandaz*, no. 1 (Summer 1986), 61–94; Nasser Pakdaman, 'Ten Nights of Poetry-Reading: An Evaluation of an Event at the Beginning of the Iranian Revolution', *Kankash*, no. 12 (Fall 1995), 125–206; and Revolutionary Organization of the Tudeh Party, *Zendebad Jonbesh-e Tudeh-ye Aban va Azar 56* ('Long live the mass movement of October–December 1978') (Rome: Red Star Publication, 1977), 1–20.

[21] William Branigin, 'Iranian Riot Police Cash with Student Protest March', *Washington Post*, 18 Nov. 1977.

[22] Editorial, 'Iran and the Black and Red Reactionaries', *Ettela'at*, 7 Jan. 1978.

revolution. In fact, the Shah had been making similar attacks ever since 1963. This time they had disastrous consequences.

The next morning a procession of seminary students proceeded from home to home of the senior ayatollahs in Qom urging them to speak out against this article.[23] The following day they were joined at the central mosque by shop assistants and high school students who had closed down the bazaar and the schools. Once the mosque meeting adjourned, they marched to the police station on the way throwing stones at the Resurgence Party offices and chanting 'Death to the Shah', 'Long Live Khomeini', 'Long Live the Unity of the Seminaries and Universities', and 'Down with Yazid's Regime'—Yazid was the Caliph responsible for Imam Hussein's martyrdom. As they surrounded the police station, military reinforcements fired. According to the government, two demonstrators were killed. According to the opposition, seventy were. Throughout the revolution, the two issued drastically different casualty figures. Also throughout the revolution, the public, deeply distrustful of the regime, readily accepted the higher ones. The police added insult to injury by chasing a demonstrator into the home of Grand Ayatollah Shariatmadari—the leading liberal cleric. Shariatmadari, backed by the main opposition groups, asked the country to respect the dead by attending peaceful services at their local mosques on the fortieth day of their deaths (forty-day memorials are common throughout the Middle East). His message was disseminated widely through cassettes, underground circulars, and foreign broadcasts, especially the BBC—to this day royalists hold the latter responsible for the whole revolution. Thus began the five cycles of forty-day crises.

The first cycle came on 18–19 February. Services were held in most cities. In Tabriz—Shariatmadari's home town, the day turned violent when thousands marched from the central mosque into downtown attacking royal statues, police stations, luxury hotels, movie houses showing Hollywood films, stores owned by the royal family, and the offices of the Resurgence Party, the Iran-American Society, Pepsi Cola, and the Sadarat Bank—the latter two were owned by Baha'is—Baha'ism being a nineteenth century offshoot of Shi'ism deemed heretical by mainstream Shi'is. Bank cash was left untouched. The London *Times* noted that the 'rioters choose their targets carefully'.[24] The *New York Times* reported that 'the huge mob' was not dislodged until the following day when the military came with full force.[25] The opposition claimed hundreds were killed. After the revolution, the new regime placed the number at nine.[26] Most of the 650 arrested rioters turned out to be college students, high school pupils, bazaar apprentices, and workers from small factories.[27] The Shah declared martial law and dismissed many of the local officials. The Tabriz uprising does not fit well

---

[23] Liberation Movement, *Qiyam-e Hamaseh-e Qom va Tabriz* ('The Epic uprising of Qom and Tabriz') (Belleville, Ill.: Liberation Movement Press, 1978), 1–139.

[24] *The Times* (London), 11 May 1978.

[25] Paul Hofmann, 'Behind Iranian Riots', *New York Times*, 4 Mar. 1978.

[26] Anonymous, 'The Bloody Uprising of Tabriz', *Ettela'at*, 17 Feb. 1981.

[27] Anonymous, '650 Arrested in Tabriz', *Iran Times*, 3 Mar. 1978.

into the conventional narrative claiming that the movement became radical only in the very last stages. Immediately after the uprising, the opposition called for another round of forty-day commemorations—this time for the Tabriz dead.[28]

The second cycle fell on 27–30 March. The worst incidents this time were in Yazd, Isfahan, and Kerman. The third came on 6–7 May. Many cities—especially Mashed—experienced some bloodshed. The fourth fell on 18 June with the worst incidents in Yazd again. The fifth fell on 28 July. The worst clashes erupted in Isfahan leading to the declaration of martial law in that city. To prevent the situation spinning further out of control, the opposition, including the clerical leaders, placed a moratorium on forty-day commemorations. Instead they called for peaceful celebrations on 4 September for the festival of *Aid-e Fetr* (Day of Sacrifice).

On that day, rallies were held in most large towns. The one in Tehran began at dawn from four corners of the city and ended in the vast Shahyad Square in mid afternoon. The *Financial Times* described it as the largest demonstration in twenty-five years and estimated it in the 'tens of thousands'.[29] The main slogans were 'Independence, Freedom, Islamic Republic', 'We want the Return of Khomeini', 'America out of Iran', 'Free Political Prisoners', 'Long live Palestine', 'Brother Soldiers, Why do you Shoot Brothers', and 'We are not against Women, We are against Corruption'. Voices were lowered as they passed hospitals so as not to disturb the patients. Florists distributed carnations so that demonstrators could hand them out to soldiers.[30] The leader of the National Front told French reporters that the rally should be seen as a national referendum. *Time* reported:

> They marched, tens of thousands strong, defiant chanting demonstrators surging through the streets of Tehran, a capital unaccustomed to the shouts and echoes of dissent. The subject of their protest was the policies of Iran's supreme leader, Shah Mohammad Reza Pahlavi. Some carried signs demanding his ouster. Others called for a return of long denied civil and political liberties... The crowd, at times numbering more than 100,000, was a colorful, sometimes incongruous cross section of Iranian society: dissident students in jeans, women shrouded in the black chador, the traditional head-to-foot veil, peasants and merchants, and most important, the bearded, black robed Muslim mullas.[31]

Diverse elements organized the four processions ending at Shahyad Square on the western road out of Tehran. College students marshalled the two from the university campus nearby and from the modern middle-class neighbourhoods in the north-east. Apprentices and shop assistants coordinated the eastern one starting at Jaleh Square—a lower middle-class district walking distance from

---

[28] Revolutionary Organization of the Tudeh Party, *Javedan Bad Khaterat-e Qiyam-e Khonen-e Tabriz* ('Long live the memory of the bloody Tabriz uprising') (Rome: Red Star Publications, 1978), 1–44; Mojahedin Organization, *Qiyam-e Khonen-e Tabriz* ('The bloody uprising in Tabriz') (Yemen: Mojahedin Publications, 1978) 1–16.

[29] Andrew Whitley, 'Tehran Demonstration', *Financial Times*, 8 Sept. 1978.

[30] 'Huge Rally began from Four Places', *Kayhan*, 5 Sept. 1978.

[31] 'The Shah's Divided Land', *Time*, 18 Sept. 1978.

the central bazaar. High school students organized the southern one starting at the railway station in the midst of the working-class districts. Further south were some of the worst slums. Emad Baqi, who later became prominent as a liberal gadfly journalist, reminisces that as a high school kid in these slums he and his classmates took active part in street demonstrations.[32] They also distributed cassettes, duplicated manifestos, and tried to politicize the Hojjatieh Society—a conservative group permitted to function so long as it focused its attacks on the Baha'is. Baqi, like many, joined the Hojjatieh because it was the only organization in town. He writes that eventually he and his friends formed their own ad hoc group separate from the local mosque since the resident preacher could not tolerate subversive ideas. He adds that most preachers did not join the movement until late in the day. The outspoken preachers in the bazaar appear to have been the exception. He remarks caustically that he was surprised to see on the final day of the revolution his local cleric toting a pistol and inciting demonstrators to violence. Baqi admits that the formative influences on him were Ali Shariati, a radical sociologist denounced by conservatives as an 'unbeliever' (*kafer*), and his school teachers, some of whom turned out to have been secret Marxists. In the preface to his memoirs, Baqi complains that conventional history fails to look at the past from below. As far as he is concerned, the revolution was made by street folk—not by leaders and centrally coordinated organizations.

Three additional blows added to the crisis thereby drawing larger numbers into the movement. In August 1978, on the anniversary of the 1953 coup, unknown arsonists burned down a cinema in Abadan, incinerating over 430 people including many women and children. The public—knowing well that in that past SAVAK had bombed homes and offices—automatically blamed the regime.[33] After a mass burial, some 10,000 relatives and mourners marched into Abadan shouting: 'Burn the Shah. End the Pahlavis. Soldiers, you are Guiltless. The Shah is the Guilty One.' The *Washington Post* commented that the demonstration conveyed one clear and simple message: 'The shah must go.'[34] The *Financial Times* was surprised that so many people, even those with vested interest in the regime, pointed fingers at SAVAK.[35] It added that 'at heart of the problem is lack of public trust. The public is unwilling to give the Shah benefit of the doubt.'

The fire was soon overshadowed by a massacre. On 8 September, immediately after Day of Sacrifice, the regime tried to regain control by imposing martial law on eleven cities. The general responsible for June 1963 and known as 'Butcher of

[32] Emad Baqi, *Tarekh-e Shafah-ye Enqelab* ('Oral history of the revolution') (Tehran: National Library, 1982), 1–145.

[33] Shayda Nabavi, 'Abadan, 19th August, Cinema Rex', *Cheshmandaz*, no. 20 (Spring 1999), 105–27. An official investigation launched after the revolution at the insistence of family members found that the arsonists were a handful of religious fanatics working on their own. In a blatant non-sequitur, the investigating judge concluded that the crime was so horrendous that the perpetrators could not have been Muslims and therefore must have been Marxists. For the religious background of the arsonists, see report of the court trial, *Iran Times*, 12 Sept. 1980.

[34] William Branigin, 'Abadan Mood Turns Sharply against the Shah', *Washington Post*, 26 Aug. 1978.

[35] Anthony McDermott, 'Peacock Throne Under Pressure', *Financial Times*, 12 Sept. 1978.

Tehran' was appointed military governor of the capital. He ordered troops to use force to disperse ad hoc crowds that tended to gather early in the mornings at the main squares chanting anti-Shah slogans. At Jaleh Square, they fired into a crowd perpetrating what became notorious as Black Friday—reminiscent of Bloody Sunday in 1905 Russia. The regime placed the number of dead at eighty-seven.[36] The opposition placed it as high as 4,000–8,000. Within hours, youths from the southern slums were attacking government offices and commercial banks but leaving cash untouched.[37] Anthony Parsons, the British Ambassador with an in-depth knowledge of the country, was impressed by their 'discipline' and 'selectivity'.[38] European correspondents reported that Jaleh Square resembled a firing squad, that the military left behind 'carnage', and that the day's 'main casualty' was the possibility of any compromise.[39] Desmond Harney, the MI6 man, concluded that the gulf between Shah and the public was now unbridgeable since the latter held the former personally responsible for both Black Friday and the Abadan fire.[40] It was soon clear that these strong-arm tactics had failed. Strikes spread from universities, high schools, and bazaars to government offices, newspapers, railways, factories, and the vital petroleum installations. Oil workers declared they would not produce for export until they had had exported 'Ali Baba and His Forty Thieves'. By the fortieth day after Black Friday the general strike had ground the whole economy to a halt. The *Financial Times* concluded that 'the dam has burst'.[41]

The third cycle of crisis—known as 'the day Tehran burned'—came on 4–5 November. Baqi writes that he and his classmates would make daily trips to the Tehran University where—within the sanctuary of the campus—they would attend impromptu meetings, listen to speeches, chant slogans, and entice soldiers from across the street to join them.[42] On 4 November, an officer fired on a defecting soldier and instead hit a demonstrator. Angry students poured out of the campus burning the usual targets and ransacking the nearby British Embassy. Harney wrote that the intruders were 'boyish, prankish, rather than terrifying' and uninterested in either looting or harming embassy officials. The city, he added, looked as if it had suffered the Blitz.[43] The *Christian Science Monitor* reported that the campus shooting—rumoured to have taken over thirty lives—led 'rampaging mobs' to 'set ablaze' Tehran: 'I have never seen anything like it. Block after block of burned-out shells. It looked like a war had been and gone.'[44] The Shah tried to give more clout to martial law by naming a general as his prime minister and packing his cabinet with top brass. This merely added more fuel to

[36] Foreign Broadcasting Information Services (FBIS), 11 Sept. 1978.
[37] *The Times* (London), 11 May 1978.
[38] Anthony Parsons, *The Pride and the Fall* (London: Jonathan Cape, 1984), 98 & 126.
[39] Jean Gueyras, 'Liberalization is the Main Casualty', *The Guardian*, 17 Sept. 1978.
[40] Harney, *The Priest and the King*, 25.
[41] Andrew Whitley, 'The Shah Struggling to Retain his Grip', *Financial Times*, 13 Oct. 1978.
[42] Baqi, *Tarekh-e Shafah-ye Enqelab*, 64–8.
[43] Harney, *The Priest and the King*, 63.
[44] Tony Allaway, 'Uprising in Tehran', *Christian Science Monitor*, 6 Nov. 1978.

the crisis. Harney stressed that by mid November the 'hatred and discontent of the people'—which had been simmering for over twenty years—was now 'terrifying'.[45]

In an attempt to cool the situation, the Shah reversed direction and negotiated with Ayatollah Taleqani, a left-leaning nationalist who had just been released from prison. He agreed to permit Muharram processions on condition the demonstrators did not mock him and did not venture into the very northern parts of the city where the royal family resided. This paved the way for the vast rallies on 10–11 December commemorating the climactic days of Tusu's and Ashura during Muharram. The rally was coordinated from Taleqani's home where his extended family had strong links not only with university students but also with the Liberation Front, the National Front, the Writers Association, the Society of Bazaar Merchants and Guilds, the Mojahedin, and even Marxist guerrillas (his sons had been active in such groups). The *Financial Times* wrote that the rally 'brought in all social classes' and numbered nearly one million.[46] General Qarabaghi, the Shah's last chairman of the joint chiefs of staff, estimated it as two million.[47] As on the Day of Sacrifice, four processions made their way from parts of the city to Shahyad Square. In addition to their earlier slogans, they chanted: 'Every Day Ashura, Every Month Muharram, Every Place Karbala'; 'Abadan, Abadan, the Shah Committed a Crime'; 'Shah Commits Treason, Carter Supports Shah'; and 'Iran is our Country, Soldiers are our Brothers'. Harney commented that the key to this success was 'discipline'.[48] At Shahyad Square, the crowd ratified by acclamation resolutions calling for the return of Khomeini, establishment of an Islamic Republic, delivery of 'social justice' to the 'deprived masses', expulsion of 'imperial' powers, and extending a hand of friendship to the armed forces.[49] The *Washington Post* concluded that 'the disciplined and well organized march lent considerable weight to the opposition's claim of being an alternative government.'[50] The *New York Times* wrote that the message was loud and clear: 'The government was powerless to preserve law and order on its own. It could do so only by standing aside and allowing the religious leaders to take charge. In a way, the opposition has demonstrated that there already is an alternative government.'[51] Similarly, the *Christian Science Monitor* reported that 'a giant wave of humanity swept through the capital declaring louder than any bullet or bomb could the clear message: "The Shah must go".'[52] Similar rallies were held in most towns. It was rumoured that the Shah had stopped reading

[45] Harney, *The Priest and the King*, 76.

[46] Andrew Whitley and Simon Henderson, 'Million in Peaceful Protest March against the Shah', *Financial Times*, 11 Dec. 1978.

[47] Abbas Qarabaghi, *Haqayeq darbareh Behran-e Iran* ('Truth concerning the Iranian crisis') (Paris: Sahil Publications, 1983), 87.

[48] Harney, *The Priest and the King*, 58.

[49] 'Resolution Passed by Acclamation in the Ashura Rally', *Khabarnameh*, 15 Dec. 1978.

[50] Jonathan Randall, 'In Iran, a Throng Votes No', *Washington Post*, 12 Dec. 1978.

[51] R. W. Apple, 'Reading Iran's Next Chapter', *New York Times*, 13 Dec. 1978.

[52] Tony Allaway, 'Iran Demonstrates', *Christian Science Monitor*, 12 Dec. 1978.

national newspapers, having been insulted by the fact that they now referred to him as simply 'the shah'.

He left Iran five weeks after 'the day Tehran burned' having appointed as premier Shahpour Bakhtiar, a former member of the National Front who, although widely respected and a long-standing critic of the Shah's regime, was not seen by the crowd as a credible long-term head of a successor government. In its thirty-six days' existence the Bakhtiar government sought in vain to move towards a secular and democratic order in Iran, while at the same time permitting the return of Khomeini.

Some speculate that the Shah left at the urging of the White House.[53] But a far more likely reason was that he realized he had lost control not only of the streets but also of the military. Soldiers were refusing orders, deserting, fraternizing with demonstrators, handing over weapons to them, and even firing on gung-ho officers.[54] Qarabaghi writes that field commanders were highly critical of Bloody Friday and after that day did not dare to issue live ammunition to tank officers for fear that such lethal weapons could easily fall into wrong hands.[55] The *New York Times* reported that the main reason the Shah pulled troops off the streets during Muharram was the 'fear that young soldiers, nearly all conscripts, would not follow orders and shoot'.[56] The day he departed, an estimated one million celebrated in the streets of Tehran. Some carried the blunt newspaper headline 'Shah Gone'. The correspondent for the *Christian Science Monitor* reported that he had 'never seen such a vast gathering'.[57]

Khomeini returned on 1 February—seventeen days after the Shah left. He was greeted by some two million exuberant well-wishers blocking the streets and forcing him to take a helicopter from the airport to his first stop, the cemetery of Behesht-e Zahra (Zahra's Paradise), where he paid respects to the 'martyrs of the revolution'. Four days later, he named Bazargan as his prime minister, denounced the Shah's prime minister as 'illegitimate', and thus forced the country to choose. Crowds again played key roles. They prevented ministers from gaining access to their offices. They blocked army contingents attempting to move towards the capital. They took over many provincial cities including Isfahan, Qom, and Shiraz. They surrounded armouries, barracks, and military bases in Tehran. And on 10–11 February, crowds—supported by remnants of the Mojahedin and Fedayin—broke into armouries, distributed weapons, and, fought pitched battles with the Imperial Guards—the sole segment of the armed forces that had remained loyal. The final blow came when the chiefs of staff announced that the armed forces were 'neutral' in the conflict between the two prime ministers.

---

[53] Qarabaghi, *Haqayeq darbareh Behran-e Iran*, 161–70. See also Gary Sick, *All Fall Down* (New York: Penguin, 1985), 153; and William Sullivan, *Mission to Iran* (New York: Norton, 1981), 202.

[54] Simon Henderson, 'Shah's Imperial Guards Kill Officers in Mutiny', *Financial Times*, 14 Dec. 1978.

[55] Qarabaghi, *Haqayeq darbareh Behran-e Iran*, 126 & 429.

[56] R. W. Apple, 'Shah's Army is Showing Stresses', *New York Times*, 18 Dec. 1978.

[57] Geoffrey Godsell, 'Tehran's Joy—and Grim Resolve', *Christian Science Monitor*, 22 Jan. 1979.

©Alain Keler/Sygma/Corbis

**Figure 10.3** Power politics and human rights. US President Jimmy Carter on a brief visit to Tehran, 31 December 1977. Demonstrations against the Shah had begun earlier in 1977.

According to the *Financial Times*, these final two days were the 'bloodiest' in the whole revolution.[58]

Soon after the revolution, one of Khomeini's colleagues declared that the Islamic Revolution had been 'nourished by 63,000 martyrs'.[59] This has become the official figure. The real figure was far more modest. Two sociologists in

[58] Andrew Whitley, 'Iran Slides towards Anarchy', *Financial Times*, 13 Feb. 1979.
[59] Ayatollah Lahuti, 'The Islamic Revolution produced 67,311 Martyrs', *Ettela'at*, 29 May 1979.

America, working with data collected by a student researcher in Tehran, estimate the total to be near 3,000–2,500 of whom were killed in the final two months.[60] Baqi, who, after the revolution, worked in the Martyrs' Foundation compensating relatives, placed the total at 2,781—this probably included the Abadan fire.[61] Figures released by the Bazargan government are even more modest. Right after the revolution, the new government published an illustrated 830-page 'book of martyrs'.[62] Even though the book casts a wide net, reaching back to 1952–3, it identifies only 578 as having been shot and killed in the streets during these sixteen months: 12 in late 1977; 314 in 1978; 52 in January 1979; and more than 160 in February 1979—many in the final two days. In terms of age, 28 had been in their early teens, 114 in late teens, 212 in early twenties, 76 in late twenties, 44 in early thirties, 26 in late thirties, 24 in early forties, 20 in late forties, and 19 in their fifties. The victims included seven children and five senior citizens. In terms of location, all but 31 had been killed in large urban centres: 147 in Tehran; 36 in Qom; 109 in Persian-speaking cities of central Iran; 36 in Azerbaijan; 34 in Kurdestan; 58 in the oil towns; 29 in Khurasan; 44 in the Caspian provinces; and 19 in the Gulf ports. In terms of occupation, the book listed fifty-two high school students, forty-four professionals and white collar employees, thirty-seven workers, twenty-eight college students, nineteen from the bazaars, fourteen conscripts, six clerics, and five seminary students. Many others were probably recent high school graduates without fixed occupations. None were identified as farmers or peasants. Even though women had been conspicuous in the large rallies they totalled no more than ten. In short, the typical protestor was a young urban male.

## CONCLUSION

The Iranian Revolution is a rare example of a non-violent revolution without any articulated theory of civil disobedience. The actors were influenced not so much by theories of non-violence—later events showed that they were not averse to using mass violence against opponents—but by their national history where demonstrations and strikes had often changed course of events. Although guerrilla groups did exist and some activists did favour the 'armed struggle', the revolution as a whole, especially Khomeini, was consistent in shunning violence, in refusing to declare jehad, and in advocating non-violent means. This strategy was highly successful not only in mobilizing the masses but also in immobilizing

---

[60] Ahmad Ashraf and Ali Banuazizi, 'The State, Classes, and Modes of Mobilization in the Iranian Revolution', *State, Culture and Society*, 1, no. 3 (Spring 1985), 3–40.

[61] Emad Baqi, 'Statistics on those Sacrificed in the Revolution', *Iran Emruz*, 30 July 2003. See also Cyrus Kadivar, 'A Question of Numbers', *Ruzegar-e Now*, 8 Aug. 2003.

[62] Society for Islamic Charity, *Lalehha-ye Enqelab: Yadnameh-e Shaheda* ('Tulips of revolution: martyrs' memorial') (Tehran: Society of Islamic Charity Publication, 1979), 1–830.

the armed forces—prompting conscripts to desert, junior officers to refuse to shoot, and senior officers to confine troops to their barracks. This abdication meant that the revolution—unlike many others—did not produce a civil war.

The strategy also helped to small extent in persuading the Carter administration to resign itself to the fall of the Shah. In actual fact, the administration had no other choice since the constant barrage of general strikes, nationwide demonstrations, and mass meetings had pulverized the old regime. Carter did not cause the revolution. Nor did he bring it to a successful conclusion. But his human rights campaign did help in opening up the political system, and, thereby, permitting the release of deep-seated resentments that had been pent up for over twenty-five years. In short, external forces did not cause the revolution, but they did contribute towards making it possible.

The revolution began with street protestors wanting drastic changes but the majority of the public probably wanting merely reform and return to the 1906 constitution. The revolution ended with the vast majority of the public as well as the protestors demanding root and branch changes. This is reflected in the diverging fortunes of Khomeini and Shariatmadari. Until the Abadan fire and Bloody Friday, Shariatmadari and his call for the return of the 1906 constitution was deemed to have a running chance. After the catastrophes, Khomeini's demand for an Islamic Republic won hands down.

The Iranian Revolution—like many others—'came' from below rather than was 'made' from above. There were no statewide parties, no systematic networks, and no coordinated organizations mobilizing the mass protests, meetings, and strikes. On the contrary, the crowds were often assembled by ad hoc groups, grass-roots organizations, and, at most, informal networks: classmates in high schools, colleges, and seminaries; teenagers in the slums; guild members, shop assistants, and, occasionally, mosque preachers in the city bazaars. Khomeini did not set up central bodies—a Revolutionary Council to supervise Bazargan's Provisional Government and a Central Komiteh (Committee) to coordinate the many local volunteer groups that had sprung up throughout the country—until very late in the day. He succeeded in part because his radical pronouncements were in tune with public sentiments; in part because mosques provided a modicum of protection; and in part because he had an informal network of former students, who, in turn, had their own former students ensconced in local mosques. They did not make the revolution. But they were well placed enough to be able to harvest the fruits of that revolution. They, unlike others, started the crisis with a semblance of a nationwide informal network.

The Islamic Revolution, coming without a nationwide organization but with a national history rich in crowd participation, has led some to expect similar 'regime change' in the near future. Events in eastern Europe have further fuelled these expectations. Such expectations, however, are unwarranted for a number of interrelated reasons. First, the Islamic Republic, unlike its predecessor and despite many shortcomings, continues to enjoy widespread support. It came into existence not through a foreign coup but a mass uprising—so much so that the new constitution gives important concessions to the electorate meshing theocracy with democracy, vox dei with vox populi, religious authority with popular sovereignty. It even enshrines the right to assemble, protest, and demonstrate. If there are any parallels between Iran and eastern Europe it is not between the Islamic Republic and the People's Democracies, but between the Pahlavi monarchy and the communist regimes. The Shah had been brought to power by the CIA; the latter by the Red Army. Second, the leaders of the Islamic Republic—unlike the Shah—are unconcerned about their image in the West. They do not fret about how European journalists are going to treat them in press interviews. Third, the Islamic Republic wields an effective mass army known as the Revolutionary Guards. Recruited selectively and hardened by the eight-year Iraqi war, this new army is capable of crushing the opposition. It has proven this capability on a number of occasions. Fourth, the regime—in contrast to its opponents and the previous regime—uses language, symbols, and images that resonate well with the general public. Fifth, the Islamic Republic, unlike the Shah, has effectively extended the tentacles of the state into the larger society. It has brought electricity, roads, schools, clinics, piped water, and television into the countryside. It has also brought under its supervision local mosques, seminaries, religious foundations, and bazaar guilds. Grass-roots organizations that had been able to play a role in the revolution are now very much under state supervision. Finally, the lead figures of the opposition now call not for revolution but for reform, not for the overthrow of the regime but for its opening up, not for a new upheaval but for the creation of a 'civil society'. If in the near future they resort to public protest it will be not for the overthrow of the Islamic Republic but for its democratization.

# 11

## 'People Power' in the Philippines, 1983–86

*Amado Mendoza Jr*

The non-violent removal of Ferdinand Marcos in February 1986 through a mass uprising that had started in 1983 was a landmark event both in the Philippines and internationally. It introduced the term 'people power' into academic and journalistic discourse and was used as a model for subsequent civil disobedience movements in Asia and the Soviet bloc. It raises many questions regarding the relationship between civil resistance and other forms of power, and the difference between short-term and long-term success.

After his unprecedented re-election as president in 1969, Marcos declared martial law in September 1972 to keep himself in power. Moderate opposition forces were neutralized as he closed the legislature and gagged the press. For a number of years, as the country enjoyed a modicum of political stability and economic growth, the only opposition was offered by communist and Muslim secessionist insurgencies. By the early 1980s Marcos's legitimacy was eroded by a souring economy, corruption, and widespread human rights abuses. Moderate opposition to the regime was revived when a revered leader, former senator Benigno Aquino Jr, was assassinated at Manila international airport in August 1983. His death sparked a vigorous civil resistance movement. This attracted broad political support, surpassing the armed insurgencies. After years of pressure, the embattled Marcos took a gamble and called for snap presidential elections, held on 7 February 1986. Not intending to lose, he resorted to violence and blatant fraud that further stoked the fires of civil resistance. Politically isolated and rapidly losing his grip on the levers of power, he fled the country on 25 February 1986, never to return.

It might have been expected that the Marcos regime would be overthrown violently by the ongoing communist insurgency or a military coup. Scholars of regime change have long argued that neo-patrimonial dictatorships are particularly vulnerable to violent overthrow by armed opponents.[1] The peaceful

I acknowledge the useful comments made by Peter Carey, Donald Emmerson, Carolina Hernandez, and Maria Stephan on previous drafts.

[1] Richard Snyder, 'Explaining Transitions from Neopatrimonial Dictatorships', *Comparative Politics*, 24, no. 4 (1992), 379–400; Richard Snyder, 'Paths out of Sultanistic Regimes: Combining Structural and Voluntarist Perspectives', in H. Chebabi and J. Linz (eds.), *Sultanistic Regimes* (Baltimore: Johns Hopkins University Press, 1998), 49–81.

**Figure 11.1** An act of violence sparks a campaign of civil resistance. On 21 August 1983 the Filipino opposition leader Benigno Aquino Jr lies dead on the tarmac at Manila Airport. A soldier dragged him to a military van moments after he was fatally wounded in the head and neck. His suspected assassin lies dead beside him. The assassination of Aquino was widely seen as having been approved by the Marcos regime.

outcome in the Philippines is therefore a puzzle. Thompson argued that Marcos's removal was the result of moderate forces successfully out-manoeuvring the different armed groups.[2] Boudreau acknowledged the competitive and complementary relationship between the armed and unarmed anti-dictatorship movements, but believed that the creation of an organized non-communist option that regime defectors could support was decisive.[3]

Analysis of non-violent resistance in the Philippines is still incomplete. This chapter attempts to fill this gap by offering reflections on the use of non-violent methods in the Philippine context. The first section offers a historical overview of the uneven democratization process from the early 1970s to the flawed election of 2004. The second section, which is in several parts, addresses questions relating to the role of civil resistance in political change. It considers the reasons for the adoption of non-violent strategies, and the ways in which the coexistence of

[2] Mark Thompson, *The Anti-Marcos Struggle: Personalistic Rule and Democratic Transition in the Philippines* (New Haven: Yale University Press, 1995).

[3] Vince Boudreau, *Resisting Dictatorship: Repression and Protest in Southeast Asia* (Cambridge: Cambridge University Press, 2004).

armed struggles in the Philippines influenced the adoption and effectiveness of non-violent methods. It shows how particular circumstances, especially the regime's shameless electoral fraud, contributed to the movement's success. It looks briefly at the role of international power balances generally and the US in particular. Various criteria are suggested for the evaluation of the success and failure of the civil resistance movement during the Marcos and immediate post-Marcos years. The concluding section draws out the links between the practice of civil resistance and democratization, and suggests some lessons which can be learnt from the Philippine example. In particular the conclusion asks what post-authoritarian governance in the Philippines since 1986 shows about a possible connection between the practice of civil resistance and liberal outcomes.

## AUTHORITARIANISM AND DEMOCRATIZATION SINCE 1972

Marcos declared martial law on 21 September 1972 in order to maintain his rule after his term's expiration in 1973. To justify authoritarianism, he exaggerated the threat of the communist and Muslim insurgencies. American support was crucial here.[4] Accusing elite political rivals of allying with the communists, he seized their assets and either imprisoned or exiled them. He also disbanded the legislature and muzzled the press. While martial law was initially welcomed by big business and the Catholic Church in the interests of political order, Marcos soon exhausted political capital by his regime's blatant corruption and repression. By the late 1970s, the regime was morally bankrupt. The communist insurgents, after some difficult years, steadily gained strength. Observers claimed Marcos was the guerrillas' best recruiter.[5] By contrast, mainstream oppositionists were either silenced or co-opted and their political parties rendered ineffectual.

Through limited liberal reforms and parliamentary elections in 1978, Marcos assuaged the human rights concerns of US president Jimmy Carter and prevented the formation of a moderate–radical coalition against him. Elite oppositionists, including his most famous political prisoner, senator Aquino, participated in these elections. To their consternation, electoral participation helped consolidate Marcos's political position. The dictator made sure his followers 'won' in the polls. In frustration, some moderate oppositionists resorted to arson, bombing, and the establishment of guerrilla armies.[6] Crippled by arrests and organizational failures, they won no concessions from Marcos. They were blacklisted as terrorists by the US government.

---

[4] Raymond Bonner, *Waltzing with a Dictator: The Marcoses and the Making of American Policy* (New York: Times Books, 1987).

[5] Ibid. 359; Gregg Jones, *Red Revolution: Inside the Philippines Guerrilla Movement* (Boulder, Colo.: Westview, 1989), 7.

[6] Thompson, *Anti-Marcos Struggle*, 81–95.

In 1981, Marcos was sufficiently confident to lift martial law, but he retained decree-making powers. Many elite oppositionists and the communists boycotted the June 1981 presidential elections, allowing Marcos to 'run' against a weak opponent. This was the apogee of Marcos's political power. From then on it was all downhill. There were various reasons for this. Steady growth of the communist insurgency in rural areas prompted wider state-sponsored repression and human rights violations. Foreign loans were squandered on wasteful projects. Cronyism and corruption flourished. Following the 1979 oil shock, the economy stalled and former allies in the business community and the Catholic Church became outspoken. Meanwhile, Marcos's August 1982 illness raised succession concerns. A committee that was established to lead the country in the event of his death became an arena where rivals attempted to outflank each other. Eventually the president's politically ambitious wife, Imelda Marcos, together with Armed Forces of the Philippines (AFP) chief, General Fabian Ver, eased defence minister Juan Ponce Enrile and Philippine constabulary head General Fidel Ramos from contention, opening serious rifts within the regime.[7]

Exiled to the US in 1980, Senator Aquino returned in August 1983 hoping to persuade an ailing Marcos to step down and allow him to take over. His brazen assassination at Manila international airport unleashed a broad civil resistance movement which eventually outstripped the communist insurgency in terms of media coverage and mass mobilization. The Catholic Church, led by Cardinal Jaime Sin, played an active role in bringing together the non-communist oppos- ition and Manila's business elite. Pro-opposition mass media outlets were opened and a citizens' electoral watch movement was revived. Aquino's death also prompted US State Department officials to assist political moderates and pres- sure Marcos for reforms. Marcos tried to divide the opposition anew through the 1984 parliamentary elections. While some moderates joined a communist-led boycott, others (supported by the widowed Corazon Aquino) participated—and won a third of the contested seats despite widespread violence, cheating, and government control of the media.[8]

Emboldened moderates consequently spurned a communist-dominated anti- dictatorship alliance in 1985 to form their own coalition. When Marcos called for 'snap' presidential elections, they united behind Mrs Aquino's candidacy. The communists, hoping to worsen intra-elite conflicts, called for another boycott. Military officers associated with Enrile formed the Reform the Armed Forces Movement (RAM) and tacitly supported Aquino's candidacy while preparing for an anti-Marcos coup. Faced by a vigorous opposition campaign, Marcos resorted to fraud and systematic violence. The combination of a now unmuzzled press and the presence of election observers sparked large-scale civil disobedience. The Church declared that Marcos had lost the moral right to rule.

---

[7] Boudreau, *Resisting Dictatorship*, 177–8.
[8] Jennifer Franco, 'Elections and Democratization in the Philippines' (Ph.D. thesis, Brandeis University, 1997), 172–9.

©Sipa Press/Rex Features

**Figure 11.2** Election campaign to defeat an authoritarian ruler. Cory Aquino, widow of Benigno, campaigning on 21 January 1986 for the presidential election held on 7 February.

The end-game was precipitated by a RAM coup attempt.[9] Pre-empted by loyalist forces, rebel officers led by Enrile and Ramos defected to Aquino on 22 February 1986 and recognized her as the country's legitimate leader. These events led to an internationally televised standoff between loyalist troops and millions of unarmed civilian protesters who had gathered to protect the rebels. As the regime came under increasing pressure, it lost the will to survive. Defections mounted and the Reagan administration finally withdrew its support. On 25 February 1986, the Marcos family and entourage were airlifted to exile in Hawaii.

The government of Mrs Aquino was an uneasy coalition between anti-Marcos civilians, military rebels, and 'reformists'. Critical of Aquino's initial moves—which included freeing prominent communist leaders and conducting peace talks with the insurgents—military rebels and Marcos loyalists repeatedly tried to topple her government.[10] These attempts went on until December 1989, with Enrile and his military allies attempting to seize power. The US government opposed talking with the communists and worried that Aquino would close key US military bases in the country. Meanwhile, the communists scored significant

---

[9] Alfred McCoy, *Closer than Brothers: Manhood at the Philippine Military Academy* (New Haven: Yale University Press, 1999), 237–8.

[10] Thompson, *Anti-Marcos Struggle*, 168–70.

propaganda gains through daily media exposure during the peace talks, raising fears of an eventual leftist takeover. The killing of several peasant demonstrators near the presidential palace by the government's security forces in January 1987 ended peace negotiations and renewed the anti-insurgency drive.

Besieged by insurgents and military rebels, Aquino adopted the policy preferences of her key political opponents and foreign patrons. The resumption of anti-insurgency operations pleased the US government and eroded the basis for military coups. Despite her earlier pronouncements, Aquino eventually favoured retaining the American military bases. Business groups and landowners were placated by a watered-down agrarian reform law and the dismissal of her labour minister and other left-leaning cabinet colleagues.[11]

The move from 'revolutionary' to regular constitutional government in 1987–8 involved ratification of a new constitution, establishment of a legislature, and reconstitution of local governments. This enabled previously disenfranchised politicians to return to power at the national and local level. The peaceful assumption of the presidency by Ramos in 1992, and by the erstwhile movie actor, Joseph Estrada, in 1998 marked the high point in the consolidation of Philippine democracy. However, problems began to emerge during Estrada's increasingly contested administration (1998–2001). In January 2001, a less acclaimed reprise of 'people power' successfully ousted Estrada and installed his vice-president Gloria Macapagal-Arroyo as chief executive.[12] Arroyo survived an uprising of Estrada's followers in May 2001 and a military mutiny in July 2003.[13] In 2004, she ran for president, the first time an incumbent had done so since the Marcos era, the 1987 constitution having imposed a single-term limit on the supreme executive office. Her shameless use of government resources gave rise to a widespread perception that she had cheated to 'win' the elections.[14] Indeed, in mid-2005, wiretapped conversations between Arroyo and a high-ranking election commissioner seemed to indicate that she had indeed ordered the padding of the vote count to ensure her victory.[15] While her government has survived subsequent political challenges, questions regarding her legitimacy still linger and have contributed to ongoing political instability. These developments raise serious doubts about the progress of Philippine democratization since February 1986.

[11] James Putzel, *A Captive Land* (Quezon City: Ateneo de Manila University Press, 1992), 220, 259–81.

[12] Carl Lande, 'The Return of "People Power" in the Philippines', *Journal of Democracy*, 12, no. 2 (2001), 88–102.

[13] Patricio Abinales and Donna Amoroso, *State and Society in the Philippines* (Pasig City: Anvil Publishing, 2005), 277–8.

[14] Benjamin Muego, 'The Philippines in 2004: A Gathering Storm', in *Southeast Asian Affairs 2005* (Singapore: Institute of Southeast Asian Studies, 2005), 293–312.

[15] Eva-Lotta Hedman, 'The Philippines in 2005: Old Dynamics, New Conjuncture', *Asian Survey* 46, no. 1 (2006), 187–93.

# THE ROLE OF CIVIL RESISTANCE IN THE POLITICAL CHANGES

## Principled or strategic considerations?

Was the recourse to civil resistance from 1983 onwards derived from a principled rejection of violence, or from particular strategic, moral, and cultural consider-ations? All played a part in the moderate political forces arrayed against the dictatorship. The use of violence was rejected by the Catholic Church as well as other smaller religious groups, the bulk of big business, the middle class, and members of the under-classes newly mobilized by the Aquino assassination. But this must be qualified. Certain key members of the Catholic hierarchy clearly condoned violent methods. Some Jesuit priests had links with guerrilla armies. Others were involved in arson and bomb attacks. Christian lower-level clergy and laity defied their superiors and either joined outright, or at the very least sympathized with the communist-dominated National Democratic Front (NDF).[16] This Christian–Marxist partnership against the dictatorship was institutionalized in the Christians for National Liberation (CNL), a key organization within the NDF.[17]

Before 1983 political violence had been part of the standard repertoire of Filipino politicians as they vied for electoral posts. After Marcos's re-election in 1969, key opposition politicians allied with communists, Muslim secessionists and student activists to resist the would-be dictator. From his declaration of martial law in late 1972 up to Aquino's assassination in August 1983, in conjunc-tion with some businessmen they supported a botched bombing campaign by social democrats. When that failed, they allied with the communists to launch a series of electoral boycotts.

Strategic considerations essentially dictated the anti-Marcos elite's adoption of non-violence after 1983. Aquino's assassination afforded the moderate opposi-tionists a chance to enhance their political strength and credentials vis-à-vis the three key elements in Philippine politics: the dictatorship, the armed opposition forces, and the US government. They realized that if they embraced armed struggle against the regime they would be playing second fiddle to the armed opposition. Suspicious of the communists, they saw non-violence as a demarca-tion line. The escalation of armed violence and the resulting political polarization would, in their view, benefit only the communists and diminish US support for their cause. A diverse group of actors all saw eye to eye on this issue. These included the US government, the RAM military rebels and other regime defect-ors, the Catholic Church hierarchy, the local Christian democrats, and big

---

[16] Boudreau, *Resisting Dictatorship*, 137–40; Thompson, *Anti-Marcos Struggle*, 72.

[17] Edicio De La Torre, 'EDSA 1986: the struggle for interpretation', discussion paper, Conference on Civil Resistance and Power Politics, Oxford, 15 Mar. 2007; Dennis Shoesmith, 'The Church', in R. May and F. Nemenzo (eds.), *The Philippines after Marcos* (London: Croom Helm, 1985), 70–89.

business. All wanted to keep the communists at bay. They therefore cooperated to marginalize the communists during the turbulent end-game which marked the closing months of the Marcos dictatorship. In fact, the communists isolated themselves through their ill-conceived boycott of the 1986 'snap' presidential elections. Even if they had not done so, it is certain that the non-communist forces would have sought to exclude them from any post-Marcos settlement.[18] Ironically, the failed military coup attempt in February 1986 opened the possibility for anti-communist forces to oust the dictatorship by non-violent means. Marcos's failure to crush the handful of military defectors holed up in Camp Aguinaldo during the night of 22 February was also fatal. By dawn on the following day, the initiative had shifted decisively to the Church and the moderate opposition who were able to summon a million-strong crowd to cocoon the rebels.

## Civil resistance and the armed struggle

The emergence of a civil resistance movement came much later than the development of armed opposition to Marcos. The communist insurgency kicked off in 1969. Islamic secessionism, which began in 1968, was less important to the anti-Marcos resistance because its armed operations were limited geographically to the majority Muslim districts of Mindanao. Up to the early 1980s, while most of the non-violent political forces were quiescent and some business interests profited during the early years of martial rule, fringe elements in the Christian churches, the intelligentsia, and a few opposition politicians allied themselves with the communists. This alliance between anti-Marcos politicians and the communists, however, was essentially tactical and was marked by a high degree of distrust and opportunism on both sides. Oppositionist politicians were looking to harness the communists' armed clout and urban mass following to their advantage, while the communists were mainly interested in the material resources which oppositionist politicians could bring to their cause. The communists believed that dalliance with oppositionist politicians would worsen splits within the ruling elite. However, distrust of the communists was so pervasive that even the armed non-fundamentalist Muslim secessionists did not ally with them strategically though both shared a common enemy.

In addition to its armed component, the communist-led movement had an unarmed component—the National Democratic Front (NDF). The relationship between the two was not problem-free. In theory, the armed component took precedence, while the unarmed wing was there to support and complement it. The unarmed campaign was largely carried out in the country's urban centres and abroad in areas with large Filipino diasporas such as North America. The NDF also established an international office in the Netherlands. The NDF's unarmed

---

[18] Kathleen Weekley, *The Communist Party of the Philippines 1968–1993: A Story of its Theory and Practice* (Quezon City: University of the Philippines Press, 2001), 145–8.

**Figure 11.3** Ridicule as a weapon of opposition. On 3 February 1986, four days before voting in the presidential election, demonstrators gather around effigies of President Ferdinand Marcos and President Ronald Reagan. After the 7 February vote, Marcos was fraudulently proclaimed the winner, leading to widespread criticism of his dictatorship at home and abroad.

activities included propaganda, fundraising, collection of war materiel, establishment of underground cells, and alliance with non-communist political forces.

The Filipino communists were forthright about their identities and programmes—their 'honesty' possibly contributing to their isolation when civil resistance took root. The NDF was limited to organizations that accepted communist leadership. Innovative leaders such as Horacio ('Boy') Morales and

Edicio de la Torre attempted to moderate the NDF programme in the early 1980s to broaden its political appeal.[19] Among the significant changes they introduced were provisions for a mixed economy and a democratic coalition government that included all anti-dictatorship forces. Their arrest in 1982 by government troops and replacement by doctrinaires reversed this trend. In the open political arena, these developments were mirrored in the refusal of political moderates to join the communist-dominated anti-dictatorship alliance. The key issues preventing strategic radical–moderate alliance at this level included party leadership, the US military bases, and elections. While radicals accepted party leadership, boycotted elections, and favoured the unconditional closure of the bases, moderates distrusted the party, kept their options open with regard to the bases, and showed themselves ready to participate in elections even under authoritarian auspices.

That the communist movement had a non-violent component did allow some moderates, including elements within the Church hierarchy, to offer their support. As far as the regime was concerned, the Church was the only institution with credibility, a nationwide presence, and substantial independent resources. While the Church hierarchy initially adopted a 'critical collaboration' stance vis-à-vis the regime, many lower echelon elements opposed the dictatorship from the start.[20] Churches, seminaries, and convents were made available to radicals (both communist and non-communist) for meetings. Anti-Marcos propaganda was printed there and sick and wounded comrades given medical treatment. Beyond offering material resources, more radical Church elements adopted 'liberation theology' and organized Basic Christian Communities (BCCs) among the poor. Through these BCCs, they were able to develop and mobilize mass bases independent of the communists.[21]

The division of labour within the communist movement also contributed to the viability of non-violent opposition. While local communists sought to gain every advantage in their tactical alliance with anti-Marcos politicians, the latter also benefited from the relationship. As the communists supplied the muscle in urban mass actions after the Aquino assassination, anti-Marcos politicians participated and gained greater political stature. If the communists had neglected the urban mass movement and eschewed tactical alliances, concentrating instead on the rural armed struggle, moderate politicians would not have enjoyed the same degree of political exposure. The Church and the US State Department—interested in ending the Marcos dictatorship, but concerned about post-Marcos arrangements—were uneasy about this marriage of convenience between moderates and communists, and thus sought to wean the former away from the latter.

How important were non-violent methods in the conditions within which they operated in the Philippines? The viability of civil resistance was clearly

[19] Thompson, *Anti-Marcos Struggle*, 99–100, 106; Weekley, *Communist Party*, 121–6.

[20] Abinales and Amoroso, *State and Society*, 220–3.

[21] Kurt Schock, *Unarmed Insurrections: People Power Movements in Nondemocracies* (Minneapolis: University of Minnesota Press, 2005), 72.

demonstrated only after Aquino's assassination. Notwithstanding the declared human rights focus of the Carter presidency (1976–80), the US government had remained squarely behind Marcos. The trend was a polarization between the regime and the insurgent forces, foreclosing non-violent methods of political change. The downturn in the world economy in 1979, however, created the conditions for a non-violent strategy. The steep economic slowdown and the bail-out of crony firms ordered by Marcos enraged non-crony economic interests and brought white-collar employees and their bosses into the anti-dictatorship struggle. The broadening social base of the moderate opposition also strengthened non-violent possibilities and preferences.

While complementary and cooperative at times, after August 1983 the violent and non-violent anti-dictatorship movements increasingly competed with each other. Until the Aquino assassination in August 1983, the elite opposition's willingness to condone violent methods had resulted in the alienation of the US government. At the same time, the opposition had been steadily depleted through arrests, deaths, and exile. The off–on alliance with violent movements had proved deeply frustrating to many. However, the traditional politicians and their allies carefully avoided violent methods after August 1983. They thus gained a moral advantage vis-à-vis the dictatorship and the armed opposition, winning broad support that compensated for their lack of armed strength. The failure of the military coup contemplated for early 1986 and the communist boycott of the snap elections allowed non-violent forces to claim victory against Marcos in February 1986. The key figure here was the martyred Aquino—likened to the national hero, José Rizal (1861–96), or even to Jesus Christ. Neither the dictatorship nor the insurgents had any equivalent.

### Civil resistance, electoral fraud, and regime legitimacy

Civil resistance and election monitors clearly demonstrated their value in challenging the fraudulent process of the snap elections held on 7 February 1986. However, on their own they were insufficient to ensure a free and fair outcome. Given the groundswell of popular support for Mrs Aquino, the dictatorship was determined to cheat even with the presence of a bipartisan US monitoring team, an 'army' of local and international journalists, and hundreds of thousands of National Movement for Free Elections (NAMFREL) volunteers.

A critical episode was the televised walk-out staged by Commission on Elections (COMELEC) computer technicians in protest against the fraudulent count.[22] This was part of a pattern of civil resistance that eroded the legitimacy of the Marcos government and helped turn domestic and international public opinion against it. The US monitoring team helped catalyse the process of the Reagan administration's disentanglement from Marcos and paved the way for the dictator's flight to Hawaii.

[22] Ibid. 77.

Had the non-violent movement acquiesced in the officially declared electoral outcome, Marcos might have been able to stay in power and convince the US and the outside world of his new mandate. However, earlier political debacles had also helped undermine government credibility. A commission formed to investigate the Aquino assassination was rejected by the democratic opposition for its lack of independence. The eventual dismissal of charges against General Fabian Ver in connection with the assassination was seen as another instance of Marcos's perfidy.

The activation of hitherto inert 'middle' forces—including the business elite—now helped convince international bankers to withhold credit and limit the government's access to financial resources. The almost daily political rallies in the country's main business district were an unmistakable sign of political crisis. An economic crisis had preceded the Aquino assassination, but the political crisis which it engendered greatly exacerbated it. The depth of the twin crises and the demonstrable inability of the dictatorship to resolve them convinced all domestic political forces that the dictatorship had to be ended. This realization was reached within the non-violent movement through the *Tagumpay ng Bayan* ('Victory of the Nation') civil disobedience campaign launched on 16 February 1986 when an estimated two million gathered at the Luneta Park—site of Rizal's execution at the hands of the Spanish colonialists some ninety years earlier—to hear Mrs Aquino. Her call for a boycott of pro-Marcos newspapers, banks, and companies showed signs of success: stock markets slumped, banks reported runs, and orders for products from crony firms were cancelled.[23]

The split within the military reflected the splits within the ruling circles as the Imelda–Ver and Enrile–Ramos camps mirrored the succession struggles of the early 1980s. RAM's core was formed by officers associated with Enrile serving as his counter-force against Ver. Under cover of military reform, RAM prepared an anti-Marcos coup. The non-violent movement had no role in fomenting these splits within the Marcos 'camp'. Nonetheless, the RAM officers recognized the political worth of the non-violent opposition and entered into a tactical alliance. These liaisons have remained largely opaque and undocumented.[24] It is also unclear whether the US embassy played any leading role in facilitating political dialogue between military rebels and moderates even as the US government approved of RAM's reformist thrusts.

## Civil resistance and external actors

The US government was vital though it did not adopt a monolithic approach to the Philippine question. President Reagan and senior White House aides personally supported Marcos to the end, while pragmatic elements in the State Department and the US embassy in Manila cultivated relations with the moderate opposition. Nevertheless, all the main players in the dramatic end-game of the Marcos regime—Reagan, the 'pragmatists', and elite Filipino politicians—sought

---

[23] Thompson, *Anti-Marcos Struggle*, 154.      [24] Ibid. 155–8.

to prevent a communist victory over the dictatorship. Thus, the anti-communist forces adopted an electoral strategy against Marcos, slowly building political strength by winning more and more electoral posts while the US government pressured Marcos to ensure fair elections or agree to share power with traditional politicians. The US goal was a post-Marcos arrangement that would protect American interests in the country—particularly its military bases.

US government officials involved in the formulation of its Philippines policy were not predisposed to non-violence as a matter of principle. Several sources have noted US support for RAM.[25] While there may have been US sympathy for RAM's reformist and professionalizing ethos, American officials were probably aware that it was preparing an anti-Marcos coup.[26] The US government supported civil resistance in the Philippines in pursuit of its own ends, and although Reagan was visibly on Marcos's side up to the last moment, the role the US government was perceived as playing in Marcos's removal deflected the opprobrium of having been one of the strongest props of the dictatorship.

How about other foreign actors? There is as yet no clear evidence that socialist and Christian democrat politicians in the West were prepared to assist their Filipino counterparts. However, 'protected sources' indicate that western European Social Democrats, Greens, and other leftists provided political and material support for the NDF: Christians for National Liberation members helped generate these funds from international social action and Church-related donor agencies.[27] Such monies from non-state actors were however insufficient for the insurgency to achieve pre-eminence vis-à-vis all other anti-dictatorship forces. In addition, the estrangement of local communists from the Soviet bloc, the changed attitude of the People's Republic of China (PRC) after the establishment of diplomatic relations with the Philippines in 1975, and the repeated bungling of arms smuggling operations in the 1970s all restricted communist gains relative to other oppositionists.[28]

## Success or failure?

If the goal was the removal of Marcos, then the anti-dictatorship struggle can be seen as a success. However, it is moot whether this success can be claimed either in part or in whole by the non-violent component of the anti-dictatorship movement: other factors contributing to the defeat of Marcos in 1986 need to be considered, and the mixed record of democratization in the Philippines since then reinforces doubts about calling the struggle a success.

---

[25] Bonner, *Waltzing with a Dictator*, 368, 409; Sterling Seagrave, *The Marcos Dynasty* (New York: Harper & Row, 1988), 398, 407–12.

[26] Seagrave in *The Marcos Dynasty* (407–8) claims the Americans gave the green light for the RAM coup attempt against Marcos. Bonner in *Waltzing with a Dictator* (436) reports that the Americans provided intelligence support, fuel, and ammunition for the military rebels.

[27] Abinales and Amoroso, *State and Society*, 220.

[28] Jones, *Red Revolution*, 71–83; William Chapman, *Inside the Philippines Revolution* (New York: Norton, 1987), 20–2.

An under-discussed aspect of the Philippine story is the inexplicably lame and non-violent response of the dictatorship during the key days (22–5 February 1986) which decided its political fate. None of the accounts have so far told the side of the principal losers—Marcos himself, his family, and his temporarily banished cronies. Why did not Marcos crush or neutralize the military rebels during the first day of the uprising when the latter were most vulnerable—that is, before a protective civilian cocoon had been mobilized to protect them? Since Marcos never told his side of the story, even in embittered exile in Hawaii, one can only speculate about his reasons. The former dictator may have wanted to avoid worsening the split within his camp. Alternatively, he may have wanted to negotiate a settlement with the renegades, or consolidate his constituency amongst his loyalists first before going on an offensive. Marcos's hand might have been stayed because of a credible threat of even greater violence. A bloody internecine struggle within the AFP sparked by an attempt to crush the RAM could only have benefited the communist and Muslim insurgents.

Had Marcos resorted to violence, the timing and events might have been very different, but the outcome would most likely have been the same. By crushing the military rebels, Marcos would have further strengthened the moral position of the non-violent opposition, isolated the dictatorial clique, and worsened the splits within his own camp. Reportedly, he had been warned by the US against attacking the military rebels with heavy weapons. Some maintain that he had been told that such an attack would mean an immediate cut-off in US military assistance.[29] Be that as it may, probably an even greater reason for Marcos's passivity was the great advances made by the non-violent anti-dictatorship movement in 1986. Magno asserts that an insurrectionary situation was evident from the night of the 7 February snap elections when the fraudulent electoral process and its tense aftermath placed the Marcos clique on the defensive: they were now 'prone to commit more blunders and deepen fissures within their own ranks'.[30] Despite communist gains, the non-violent movement represented the greater threat to the dictatorship's continued existence. By their own admission, the communists were not poised to win power in early 1986.[31] As a result of their election boycott, they had been pushed aside by the non-violent mass movement and had lost the political initiative. With the communists on the sidelines and the non-violent opposition in the ascendant, Reagan was finally forced to drop Marcos.

On the other hand, it is incorrect to undervalue the contribution of armed movements to Marcos's downfall due to their end-game errors. If that radical pole had not existed Marcos might have been able to inflict greater physical harm on his more moderate political rivals. They may have even survived because Marcos turned his attention to the greater threat—the Muslim secessionists in 1972–7 and

---

[29] In the March 2007 Oxford conference on civil resistance, former US ambassador to the Philippines Stephen Bosworth said he telephoned Marcos and warned him against attacking the military rebels.

[30] Alex Magno, 'The Anatomy of a Political Collapse', in A. Magno, C. de Quiros, and R. Ofroneo, *The February Revolution: Three Views* (Quezon City: Karrel, 1986), 9.

[31] Author's interview with Rodolfo Salas (Chairman, Communist Party of the Philippines, 1977–89; and commander-in-chief, New People's Army, 1977–85), conducted in Quezon City, 18 Sept. 2006.

the communist insurgents thereafter. In the 1970s the communists could sneer at the puny numbers of moderate oppositionists but, given the spectacular growth of a mass non-communist movement, they could no longer do so after August 1983.

With hindsight, the labels 'success' or 'failure' are misleading. Final closure regarding the dictatorship has not yet been achieved. There is no Filipino equivalent of the truth and justice commissions organized elsewhere to pinpoint responsibility and prescribe ways to heal a divided and brutalized society.[32] The AFP, torturers, and security personnel involved in human rights abuses were all absolved of their violations during the dictatorship. By a sleight of hand, they were able to distance themselves from their now exiled commander-in-chief by

©AP Images/PAPhotos

**Figure 11.4** On the edge of violence. A Filipino youth slashes an oil painting of Philippine dictator Ferdinand Marcos with a stick as looters stormed the Presidential Palace in Manila, Philippines in February 1986. The riots followed the resignation of Marcos on 25 February, forced to flee after the People Power Movement uprising.

[32] The South African case is acknowledged to be the most successful one. James Gibson, *Overcoming Apartheid: Can Truth Reconcile a Divided Nation?* (New York: Russell Sage, 2005); James Gibson, 'The Truth about Truth and Reconciliation in South Africa', *International Political Science Review*, 26, no. 4 (2005), 341–61.

donning the uniform and insignia of the New Armed Forces of the Philippines (NAFP). The same held true for the US government. Their joint culpability was not even whispered about during the heady days after Marcos's exit. The Aquino government eventually allowed the re-entry and political rehabilitation of most of the regime stalwarts after Marcos's death in 1989. The accommodations and compromises reached after February 1986 suggest that the democratic transition was more of a pacted settlement than a revolutionary rupture or the 'insurgent path' taken in South Africa and El Salvador.[33]

The democratic institutions established after 1986 were improvements over the dictatorship.[34] The effectiveness of non-violent resistance in ending authoritarianism is clear. However, civil resistance could not be reasonably burdened with the task of consolidating democracy in the Philippines and elsewhere.[35] The rather distasteful compromises with the military and regime stalwarts during the Aquino administration (1986–92) may have been necessary to ensure the survival of a fledging democracy besieged by military rebels and communist insurgents alike. Better an imperfect democracy than a return to authoritarianism.

## CONCLUSION

The Philippine case of civil resistance is unusual in several respects. One is that, occurring alongside armed resistance, the non-violent movement managed to out-manoeuvre the pre-existing armed movements against the Marcos dictatorship, and engineer its demise. The case thus illustrates the potency of civil resistance against authoritarianism.

Recourse to civil resistance did not stem from a principled rejection of political violence but from strategic political considerations. What are the implications? A principled commitment to non-violence may not be needed to oust a dictator, but it may be important for democratic consolidation. Elite political actors who resort to non-violence as a political expedient may subsequently resort to violence if deemed necessary, as when the Aquino government unsheathed the 'sword of war' against the communists in 1987. In the process, democratic principles and civil political dialogue may be seriously compromised. A key problem in this case was how a democracy, which had been restored by a broad political coalition which included an anti-revolutionary albeit reformed military, would deal with

[33] Elisabeth Jean Wood, 'An Insurgent Path to Democracy: Popular Mobilization, Economic Interests, and Regime Transition in South Africa and El Salvador', *Comparative Political Studies*, 34, no. 8 (2001), 862–88.

[34] Mark Thompson, 'Off the Endangered List: Philippine Democratization in Comparative Perspective', *Comparative Politics*, 28, no. 2 (1996), 179–205.

[35] Michael McFaul warns that democracy can only solve 'small' problems and is not good at resolving 'boundary' and 'property redistribution' issues ('Causes of Democratization', Presentation at the 2nd Fletcher Summer Institute for the Advanced Study of Nonviolent Conflict, Fletcher School of Law and Diplomacy, 25 June 2007).

the ongoing communist insurgency. It is quite clear that the democratic credentials of any government, in particular that of Aquino, would be put to a severe test.
Continuing human rights violations by the Philippine military from 1987 up to
the Arroyo presidency are among the worst aspects of post-Marcos governments.
Thompson reminds us, however, that 'such crimes committed by an otherwise
democratic government in the context of a civil conflict are not exceptional'.[36]

These difficulties recall the most important prerequisite identified by Rustow
in his seminal work on democratic transition—that the 'boundary' question is
resolved.[37] That was not and is not the case in the Philippines. Armed Muslims
want to secede and armed communists and military rebels share no consensus
with regard to elections and representation. In other democratization cases, this
question was settled more emphatically. The Soviet Union was broken up into
several smaller states and Czechoslovakia was split in two.

There is another problem in the Philippines: how can a restored democracy
make its military accountable for its authoritarian past without running the risk
of a military backlash? The blanket absolution of the AFP, especially of the RAM
leaders, was essentially wrong yet was politically necessary at the time. The failure
to pursue military accountability was further compounded by the kid-glove
treatment of the anti-Aquino military putschists by her defence officials, including soon-to-be president, Ramos. Indeed, during his first years in office Ramos
bought tactical peace through a political settlement with military rebels. The
shortcomings of this appeasement policy became apparent in the role played by
the military in the removal of President Estrada in January 2001, and the repeated
coup attempts against President Arroyo thereafter.

The Philippine experience underscores the difficulties faced by a restored
democracy as it attempts to consolidate itself. It was burdened by the legacies
of authoritarianism and underdevelopment, including widespread poverty and
social inequity, a weak economy, a highly politicized civilian and military bureaucracy, weak or non-existent political institutions, the continued existence of
maximalist forces, the shallowness of its elite democracy, and an unresolved first-
order 'boundary' question.

Since the overthrow of Marcos, the record of democratic commitment has been
mixed. The political elites and 'yellow' forces in the Philippines subsequently
failed to sustain their democratic credentials.[38] A reprise of 'people power' in
January 2001 failed to impress true democrats. Albeit deeply corrupt, President
Estrada had been democratically elected.[39] In this case, 'people power' may have

[36] Thompson, 'Off the Endangered List', 197.

[37] Dankwart Rustow, 'Transitions to Democracy: Toward a Dynamic Model', *Comparative Politics*,
2, no. 3 (1970), 337–63.

[38] After the Aquino assassination, the non-violent anti-dictatorship activists donned yellow shirts
and ribbons to distinguish themselves from the communist 'reds'.

[39] In a provocative lecture that compared the removal of President Estrada and Prime Minister
Thaksin Sinawatra, Thompson argued that the commitment of Filipino and Thai elite and middle forces
was primarily to 'good governance' rather than democracy ('The Role of Middle Forces in Social
Movements in the Philippines and Thailand', lecture at the UP Third World Studies Center, 23 Jan. 2007).

stunted the growth of the country's political institutions rather than enhanced them. These same elites apparently turned a blind eye to a prima facie case of systematic cheating by President Arroyo during the May 2004 elections to prevent a populist Estrada-like presidency from perpetuating itself.[40] While expedient in 2001 and 2004, the failure to uphold democratic principles lies at the root of current political instability. Questions regarding the legitimacy of Arroyo's mandate have inspired subsequent imitations of people power—including uprisings, military mutinies, and attempted coups. While styled as a referendum on her continued rule, the May 2007 mid-term elections failed to settle the legitimacy issue.

Notwithstanding the less than pristine basis of civil resistance in the Philippines, it did depose the Marcos dictatorship. What is more important—the overthrow of the dictatorship or the principled commitment to non-violent means of resolving conflict? Upholding the democratic mandate of a venal chief executive or a preference for good governance? Should irregular politics be frowned upon since they undermine existing institutions or should non-institutional deviations be tolerated or even encouraged given institutional inadequacies? If these difficult questions find resonance and engage analysts of civil resistance and democratization, then this chapter will have served its purpose.

[40] The strongest rival to Arroyo for the Philippine presidency in the 2004 elections was another movie actor, Fernando Poe Jr (now deceased). He was also Estrada's closest friend.

# 12

## Political Mass Mobilization against Authoritarian Rule: Pinochet's Chile, 1983–88

*Carlos Huneeus*

Chile's transition to democracy in the 1980s is widely regarded as a case of peaceful regime change through consensus politics among elites, with no consideration given to the dynamics of mass politics. It was, however, a more complex process. Mass mobilization from 1983 until 1988 severely weakened the legitimacy of General Augusto Pinochet's authoritarian regime, led to his defeat in a plebiscite on its continuation in October 1988, forced the regime to accept the result, and culminated in a transition to civilian rule in March 1990. This political process, involving mass civil resistance, helps to explain the commitment of the government of President Patricio Aylwin (1990–4) to a policy of truth and justice for the crimes committed during Pinochet's dictatorship (1973–90).

Social and political mobilization and confrontation between the regime and the opposition was intense from 1983 to 1988. This created a risk of the polarization sought by the Communist Party (PC) and by Pinochet who wanted to prevent the emergence of a democratic alternative bringing together centre political parties—the Christian Democrat Party (PDC) and the Radical Party (PR)—and left represented by the Socialist Party (PS), which joined together to form a new coalition, the Alianza Democrática. Pinochet's aim was to perpetuate his power by provoking the type of political confrontation seen in Central America, particularly in Nicaragua with its Sandinista revolution and the armed overthrow of the Somoza dictatorship in 1979.

The opposition's strategic decision to seek a peaceful transition to democracy within the institutional framework established by the dictatorship allowed it to stave off polarization while maintaining the pressure from below that strengthened its own power and weakened the regime's legitimacy. The opposition mobilized in three ways. First, it organized street protests and mass demonstrations to show that it had the support of the majority of the population; secondly, it reorganized the parties and actively participated in elections in student

I am indebted to the Alexander von Humboldt Foundation, and Dr Günter Buchstab, director of the Scientific Services/Archive for Christian Democratic Politics. I also thank Rodrigo Cuevas, Ruth Bradley, and Alan Angell.

federations and professional associations, all of which it won; and thirdly, it mounted an active campaign encouraging voters to register for the plebiscite held on 5 October 1988 on Pinochet's continuance in power. The success of these initiatives explains the opposition's victory in the plebiscite and in the presidential and congressional elections that followed in December 1989 in which the candidate of the Concertación por la Democracia, Patricio Aylwin (PDC), was elected as Chile's first post-dictatorship president. On 11 March 1990 the new congress was installed, and Aylwin became president. Pinochet's regime finally ended.

The mobilizations that produced this outcome were triggered by an economic crisis that erupted in 1982, which abruptly ended Chile's 'economic miracle' of 1979–81. During this crisis, there was mass unemployment, the income of poor and middle-class families fell and poverty increased dramatically.[1] Thanks to its well-organized parties, which had strong roots in society and had survived the repression, the opposition was able to take advantage of the crisis to exert pressure for a return to democracy.

Chile also had a relatively strong trade union tradition with close ties to the parties.[2] With politically experienced leaders and grassroots organization, it was able to play a major role against the Pinochet regime.

Mindful of the collapse of democracy in 1973 (when the military overthrew the leftist government of President Salvador Allende (PS), 1970–3) and the subsequent repression during Pinochet's authoritarian rule, PS and PDC leaders put past differences behind them, cooperating to recover democracy.[3] Similar cooperation was also seen among trade union leaders. Had it not been for the political resources of the parties and trade unions, the economic crisis would not have had its enormous impact.

The crisis was a serious blow for General Pinochet's regime because economic success was a key element in its bid for legitimacy and because of the scale of the protests in poor and middle-class neighbourhoods. In the latter, women protested by banging saucepans which was symbolically important because this was also the way they had protested against the Allende government during the 1972–3 economic crisis.

The government reacted to the protests that the economic crisis generated with three closely interrelated types of policies. First, the armed forces and the police took extremely repressive measures against the protests. However, this failed to contain opposition mobilization and had damaging consequences for the regime. Serious differences occurred between the army and the police force on how to

---

[1] Ricardo Ffrench-Davis, *Economic Reforms in Chile: From Dictatorship to Democracy* (Ann Arbor: University of Michigan Press, 2002).

[2] Alan Angell, *Politics and the Labour Movement in Chile* (London: Oxford University Press for Royal Institute of International Affairs, 1972).

[3] The formation of these ties is explained in the memoirs of former president Patricio Aylwin, *El reencuentro de los demócratas* (Santiago: Ediciones Grupo Zeta, 1998).

deal with the protests and members of both institutions committed horrifying acts of repression that had a tremendous impact on public opinion.

Secondly, the regime adopted a policy of liberalization—the so-called *apertura*—implemented by Sergio Onofre Jarpa, a politician of long-standing experience. Appointed as interior minister on 11 August 1983, he launched a dialogue with the opposition with a view to reaching agreement to move towards democracy. Under this policy, many exiles were allowed to return. Press freedom also increased and new weekly magazines appeared. Radio emerged as a highly influential form of mass communication: broadcasters became active in providing information. The opposition took effective advantage of the *apertura*, developing an enormous capacity for organization and mobilizing hundreds of thousands of Chileans in the two mass demonstrations organized by the Alianza Democratica in Santiago that were permitted by the regime (1983 and 1984).

Thirdly, the regime introduced more pragmatic neoliberal economic policies implemented by Hernán Büchi, its finance minister (1985–9). These included stricter bank regulation, selective increases in import tariffs, subsidies, and renegotiation of the debts of small businesses. It also sharply reduced social spending with a marked impact on the poverty rate, which reached 40 per cent in 1987 when five million Chileans were below the poverty line. These policies dismantled a relatively advanced welfare state, with an education system dating back to the nineteenth century and healthcare services that had been developing since the beginning of the twentieth century.

This chapter is organized as follows. In the first part, the context in which the protests took place is discussed and then the political process of the *apertura* and the protests is described. In the second part, two key issues are analysed: the repression's political effects and the influence of international factors, with particular reference to the role of Germany which was important but has not been studied.

## CONTEXT AND DEVELOPMENT OF THE PROTESTS

### The political background

In order to understand their political impact, the protests should be viewed in the context of the Pinochet regime[4] established after a military coup on 11 September 1973, which ended a long period of democratic stability.[5] Since the nineteenth century, Chile had experienced sustained democratic development and only one military dictatorship, that of General Carlos Ibáñez (1927–31).

In one of the main characteristics of the 1973–90 dictatorship, power was highly personalized in Pinochet who was, at the same time, head of state, head of

---

[4] This section draws on Carlos Huneeus, *The Pinochet Regime* (Boulder, Colo.: Lynne Rienner, 2007).
[5] Simon Collier and William F. Sater, *A History of Chile, 1808–1994* (Cambridge: Cambridge University Press, 1996).

the government, and commander-in-chief of the army.[6] He carried out these three functions with similar energy, although it was clear to him that his power rested on his control of the army.[7]

Secondly, the military participated in all spheres of government both as institutions and individuals, and controlled legislative power through the Junta de Gobierno (formed by the commanders-in-chief of each of the three services—navy, air force, and a representative of the army[8]—and of the general director of the police). As ministers, under-secretaries, regional governors, etc., hundreds of military officials worked alongside civilian professionals, including the two main civil power groups within the regime: its economic technocrats—the so-called 'Chicago boys'—and the young graduates from the Catholic University who were known as *gremialistas*.[9] There was great cohesion within the government and the ruling elites, and no minister or under-secretary deserted to the opposition.

Thirdly, the regime suffered from a basic contradiction: it was highly repressive, especially during its initial phase—over its whole period, it was responsible for some 3,000 deaths[10]—yet it also sought to bring about a profound and ambitious transformation based on economic freedom and individual initiative that was designed to achieve political objectives as well as GDP growth. These neoliberal policies had both short-term aims—recovery from the economic crisis that existed at the time of the 1973 coup—and the long-term goal of modifying the state's role in society, shifting towards a market economy that would benefit particularly the regime's civil supporters.

The main organ of terror was the DINA (National Directorate of Intelligence), founded in 1973, which had great autonomy and committed crimes in Chile and abroad. In 1977, the DINA was transformed into the CNI (National Centre for Intelligence) which existed through to 1990. Although responsible for fewer deaths than the DINA, the CNI used violence selectively against journalists, trade union leaders, and students.

The repression prompted a courageous defence of human rights in which the Catholic Church's Solidarity Pastoral Office, founded by the Archbishop of

---

[6] This marked an important difference with contemporary dictators in Argentina, Peru, and Brazil who did not maintain command of the army.

[7] After the transfer of power, Pinochet stayed on as army commander-in-chief for a further eight years and then took up a life Senate seat on 11 Mar. 1998. However, his political career was halted during a visit to Great Britain where he was detained at the request of the Spanish courts on 16 Oct. 1998 and was held under house arrest in London for 503 days. After his return to Chile, he was stripped of immunity from prosecution by the Supreme Court and subsequently had to resign his Senate seat.

[8] General Pinochet, who was commander-in-chief of the army, was not a member of the Junta de Gobierno. The army was represented by his second-in-command (*vicecomandante en jefe*).

[9] Carlos Huneeus, 'Technocrats and Politicians in an Authoritarian Regime: The "ODEPLAN boys" and the "Gremialists" in Pinochet's Chile', *Journal of Latin American Studies*, 32, no. 2 (May 2000), 461–501.

[10] For details of these deaths, see the *Informe de la Comisión Nacional de Verdad y Reconciliación*, 3 vols. (Santiago, Feb. 1991). An English translation was published by Notre Dame University Press in 1993.

Santiago, Cardinal Raúl Silva Henríquez, played a key role.[11] An extraordinary man who, from the beginning of the dictatorship, spoke out strongly against the violation of human rights, he was also supported by the vast majority of bishops and an important group of laymen and laywomen.[12] In its antagonistic posture towards the dictatorship, the Church in Chile was an exception within Latin America and was more similar to the Church in Poland than that in Spain which supported the Franco dictatorship until the end of the 1960s.[13] The Catholic Church implemented an extensive and well-organized programme of help for the poor, which was possible thanks to the significant resources provided by European charities, particularly from Germany, Holland, and Belgium, and by the European Community.[14]

Another feature of the Pinochet regime was that it was supported by a significant part of the population which had opposed the socialist and communist Popular Unity government of Allende, had welcomed the coup and still remembered the political conflict and economic difficulties of those years. This support was reflected in the plebiscites that the regime called to strengthen its legitimacy (1978 and 1980) as well as in mass rallies and in the electoral support obtained by Pinochet in the 1988 plebiscite. However, as from 1983 it remained largely passive after the opposition took the initiative with its political demands.

In its use of violence, its insistence that the previous democratic system had been decadent and weak in the face of Marxism, and its ambitious neoliberal reforms, the Pinochet regime represented a radical rupture with Chile's democratic and social traditions. However, it was unable to break the country's powerful legal tradition[15] and issued laws to justify its decisions and wrote a constitution with a strong emphasis on the doctrine of national security designating the armed forces as the guardian of the limited form of democracy that would replace the regime. It was this legal tradition that led the armed forces to recognize their defeat in the 1988 referendum and to transfer power to civilians in 1990.

## The economic crisis and subsequent mass protest

The economic crisis, which was already apparent in 1982 when GDP fell by 14 per cent, became acute in early 1983 when the banking system was brought to the

[11] Pamela Lowden, *Moral Opposition to Authoritarian Rule in Chile, 1973–90* (London: Macmillan, 1996).

[12] For his very interesting memoirs, see Cardinal Raúl Silva Henríquez, *Memorias* (Santiago: Ediciones Copigraph, 1992), 3 vols.

[13] Stanley G. Payne, *Spanish Catholicism* (Madison: University of Wisconsin Press, 1984).

[14] The Oficina Coordinadora de Asistencia Campesina (OCAC), which was created in 1974 and helped several of the country's main bishoprics with their social programmes, received some $US51 million, of which only $US5.1 million came from the US while the rest took the form of donations from European institutions. I am indebted to Iván Radovic, OCAC's executive director since its foundation, for this information provided in an interview on 26 Mar. 2007.

[15] Robert Barros, *Constitutionalism and Dictatorship: Pinochet, the Junta, and the 1980 Constitution* (Cambridge: Cambridge University Press, 2002).

verge of collapse by excessive borrowing and lending among companies within the same business group. The government took over five important banks and some other financial institutions and, over a period of several years, spent the equivalent of 35 per cent of GDP—or the education budget of a decade—on bailing out the system.[16]

The bankruptcy of so many companies left thousands of workers and white-collar employees jobless and, in Greater Santiago, unemployment reached 31.3 per cent in mid-1983 when 15 per cent of the city's economically active population was registered in one of the emergency job programmes created by the government. However, workers, who were hired through the municipalities, demonstrated against these programmes and, as a result, they were cut back.

Opposition mobilization began among workers. Before the 1973 coup, Chile's trade union movement had a strong presence in the manufacturing sector and copper mining.[17] As well as the Central Unica de Trabajadores (CUT), an umbrella organization controlled by the PC in which PS and PDC leaders also played an important role, there was an influential public sector union—the Asociación Nacional de Empleados Fiscales (ANEF)—led by members of the PR, accompanied by Socialists and Christian Democrats.

The dictatorship repressed the trade union movement and sought to weaken it institutionally through a labour law reform in 1979 that permitted the formation of more than one union in the same company. As from the late 1970s, opposition trade union leaders took the first steps towards the creation of a federation that would permit cooperation between Communists and Christian Democrats, a process in which Manuel Bustos (PDC) played a vital role. The most significant progress towards unification was achieved in the Confederation of Copper Workers (CTC), which was decisive in launching the protests against the dictatorship.

Led by Rodolfo Seguel (PDC), the CTC called the first protest on 11 May 1983, after a list of demands was agreed at a national meeting of union leaders. The protest was backed by the National Workers' Command (CNT), some of whose leaders were members of opposition parties, particularly the PDC and the PC.[18] Seguel, a young and charismatic leader, obtained the support of other political and union leaders and, helped by a group of journalists who advised the CTC, was able to publicize his union's activities.

The action of trade unionists was particularly courageous because the regime was determined to prevent the formation of an autonomous trade union movement. A year earlier, in 1982, DINE (Dirección Nacional de la Inteligencia del Ejército), the army intelligence unit, had brutally assassinated ANEF president Tucapel Jiménez when he was attempting to organize a united workers' front.

The success of the first protest persuaded its organizers to call one for the 11th of every month. Support for the protests increased among poor Chileans but so

---

[16] I am indebted to Ricardo Ffrench-Davis for this information.
[17] Angell, *Politics and the Labour Movement in Chile.*
[18] From an interview with Rodolfo Seguel on 10 Nov. 2006.

**Figure 12.1** Use of tear gas against protestors. On 18 November 1983, a riot policeman in Santiago fires tear gas at demonstrators as passers-by cover their heads after a column of protesters tried to march on the Presidential Palace, following a massive rally called by opposition parties to demand an end to the military government of President Pinochet.

did social conflict because, in poor neighbourhoods, the PC encouraged young people to participate in an attempt to radicalize the political process, strengthen its own weakened following among workers and challenge the leadership of the parties of the Alianza Democrática. In addition, CNI agents provocateurs infiltrated worker and student assemblies, encouraging them to step up their demands and clash with the security forces, or kidnapping or beating up their leaders.

A number of factors contributed to the scale of citizen participation in the protests. First, grassroots organizations had been created in poor neighbourhoods by the parties, by the Catholic Church—which, with international support, ran programmes such as soup kitchens and childcare centres—and by the NGOs helping those sectors most affected by the economic crisis.

Secondly, the opposition and, particularly, the PDC which had been the country's most important political party since 1961, had a countrywide structure and a presence among workers, students, and professionals that it rapidly activated once the protests provided an opportunity. Leaders of the PDC and other opposition parties formed a united coalition which bore fruit first in 1978 when the Grupo de Estudios Constitucionales (Constitutional Studies Group) was created to draft an alternative to the regime's proposed Constitution, and then in 1983 when the Alianza Democrática was formed. The PC neither participated in these initiatives nor was subsequently invited to do so.

Thirdly, and very importantly, the active role of the press during the *apertura* ensured that the opposition's activities were known to the population at large. Greater press freedom was rapidly taken advantage of by weekly magazines, such as *Análisis* and *Hoy* (both launched in 1977); and by three radio broadcasters, particularly *Cooperativa* (owned by prominent members of the PDC), and the Catholic Church's *Chilena* with stations in the different regions of the country that were owned by the corresponding dioceses, and radio *Santiago*. Other new magazines, notably *Cauce*, and a newspaper, *Fortín Mapocho*, were also launched. This, in turn, encouraged the work of journalists who, with courage and skill, gathered information about the political process, including the repression.

One distinguishing characteristic of the *Cooperativa* and *Chilena* radio broadcasters was that they were non-profit-making, giving them greater independence to withstand the economic pressure of the regime's control of advertising. Both were able to attract leading journalists who produced excellent work out of their commitment to re-establishing democracy. The case of *Cooperativa* is particularly interesting because it had a long history and had been purchased specifically to serve as a cross-party opposition voice and not as a business.[19]

The regime underestimated the influence of radio and was convinced that television, which it controlled,[20] and particularly TVN, the state-owned channel, was sufficient to keep the population informed. However, TVN was favoured by only a minority of 29 per cent as compared to the 53 per cent audience rating of *Universidad Católica* channel, which was more inclined to report opposition activities.[21] At a time of rapidly moving events, radio had the advantage that it could be listened to at any time and any place, allowing it to influence the population in general and the elites with enormous speed.

## SIGNIFICANT ISSUES

### The limitations of coercion and conflicts among repressive organizations

During the protest of 11 August 1983, the fourth called by the CTC together with political parties and social organizations, 18,000 soldiers patrolled the streets of

[19] Interviews with Carlos Figueroa and Luis Ajenjo, president and general manager of *Cooperativa* during this period, Jan. 2007.

[20] There was TVN, a state-owned channel, and three university channels, of which the most important was Canal 13 of the Catholic University, which was controlled by the *gremialistas*.

[21] CERC poll, July 1988, conducted by the author. (Centro de Estudios de la Realidad Contemporánea, Centre for the Study of Contemporary Reality, an independent research centre organized by the Academia de Humanismo Cristiano in Santiago.)

Santiago as they had done for the coup itself, acting with great violence especially in poor neighbourhoods. Twenty-six people died while hundreds were injured and thousands arrested. In his often-repeated phrase 'we are at war, gentlemen', Pinochet found a justification for creating a climate of confrontation that he thought would work to his advantage. In this stance, he was backed by the 'Chicago boys' and *gremialistas* who dismissed the protests as organized by the PC.

Justification for Pinochet's policy of confrontation was also provided by the armed resistance of the Movimiento de Izquierda Revolucionaria (MIR) and the Frente Patriótico Manuel Rodríguez (FPMR). The MIR, which had some presence among students and workers of a small number of companies in Santiago before the 1973 coup, was dismantled by the DINA between 1974 and 1976. It regrouped abroad and, after receiving military training, dozens of its members returned to Chile and used acts of violence, such as bank hold-ups, to raise funds and achieve a public impact. On 15 July 1980, it assassinated Colonel Roger Vergara, director of the Army Intelligence School and subsequent acts of violence included the assassination of Santiago's regional governor, Carol Urzúa, a retired major general, on 30 August 1983.[22]

The FPMR, the armed wing of the PC, had been organized in 1980 and, when it opted for armed resistance, chose as its target the police, who had been energetic in repressing protests in poor areas.[23] Its armed resistance began in 1983 with the sabotage of public lighting in poor neighbourhoods and, in the ensuing months, it attacked the police, killing several. It went on to mount its assassination attempt on Pinochet in September 1986, killing five of his bodyguards while losing none of its own members, and to smuggle several thousand arms into Chile, which were discovered that same year.

The attempt on Pinochet's life allowed the regime to argue that there was a terrorist offensive requiring a military response, thereby reaffirming Pinochet's confrontational approach. However, the opposition categorically condemned the assassination attempt, reaffirming its commitment to a peaceful and early return to democracy and questioning the use of violence as grist to the mill of Pinochet's policy of confrontation.

In order to combat the FPMR, the director general of the police force, César Mendoza, created the Police Communications Directorate (DICOMCAR), without the knowledge of the Junta de Gobierno. On 30 March 1985, this organization kidnapped three members of the PC, including José Manuel Parada who worked for the Solidarity Pastoral Office and whose parents were leading figures in the arts. All three men were killed by having their throats cut.

This atrocity received extensive media coverage and had a tremendous impact on public opinion, eliciting unanimous condemnation. The Church saw it as a direct attack on one of its organizations and the new archbishop of Santiago,

---

[22] Almost all the leaders of 'Operation Return' were killed by the military in 1983 and 1984. See Julio Pinto, '¿Y la historia les dio la razón? El MIR en Dictadura, 1973–1981', in Verónica Valdivia et al., *Su revolución contra nuestra revolución* (Santiago: LOM Editores, 2006), 153–205.

[23] On the PC during this period, see Carlos Bascuñán, *La izquierda sin Allende* (Santiago: Planeta, 1990).

Mgr. Francisco Fresno, responded by inviting leaders of the opposition parties and those that supported the regime (the Independent Democratic Union declined the invitation and only the National Union Party accepted) to reach agreement on a peaceful return to democracy. After several meetings, the National Agreement for the Transition to Full Democracy was signed. This was rejected by the government, General Pinochet, and the *gremialistas*, but provided important support for the opposition's call to advance peacefully towards a genuine democracy and not the restricted type of democracy favoured by Pinochet.

The DICOMCAR's action also damaged the government by causing conflict with the CNI, which considered it counterproductive. The CNI, which monitored the DICOMCAR's activities, provided the judge investigating the assassinations, José Cánovas, with evidence of the organization's participation and, in early August, in a ruling that was published in the press, he charged the DICOMCAR's senior officers, causing great public commotion and shocking the regime's supporters.

This caused a crisis in the police force where senior officials feared that Pinochet would take control of the institution as he had done the air force in 1978 during a power struggle with its commander-in-chief, General Gustavo Leigh. In that incident, most air force generals had been forced to retire and, in order to pre-empt a similar situation in the police force, Mendoza resigned and appointed General Rodolfo Stange as his successor.

Stange took drastic measures to improve the institution's image, removing seventeen of its twenty-one generals as well as dozens of colonels, disbanding the DICOMCAR and reorganizing other units. In addition, he decided that the police would no longer participate in acts of coercion, leaving repression and its costs to the army. Greater military involvement in repression led to a number of atrocities of which the most horrifying occurred during the protest of 2 and 3 July 1986 when two young demonstrators were burnt alive by an army patrol. Rodrigo Rojas, a US citizen and the son of a Chilean exile, died while Carmen Gloria Quintana survived, but with severe burns. During the Assembly of the Inter-Parliamentary Union, held in Santiago in May 1986 at the time of a national strike called by the CNT, the city was occupied by soldiers and small military tanks patrolled the streets, surprising and shocking overseas delegates.

As also seen under Brazil's authoritarian regime in the 1970s, the autonomy acquired by the repressive organizations resulted in acts that harmed the regime, strengthening the argument that the armed forces should return to their barracks. This view also began to be shared by some sectors of the elites that supported Pinochet. In other words, coercion ended up damaging the regime because it failed to stop the opposition while having a negative effect on the regime's image in the eyes of the population at large.

## International context

In a feature that is not new in Chile, the international context had an enormous influence on the political process analysed in this chapter. Since the 1940s,

Chilean Christian Democrats and Socialists were active internationally, maintaining contact with political leaders in western Europe and other Latin American countries. The last two democratic governments—that of Eduardo Frei Montalva (PDC) (1964–70), which promised a 'revolution with freedom' and that of Salvador Allende with its 'socialist revolution within the law'—attracted great international interest. The 1973 coup, with its pictures of planes bombing the La Moneda presidential palace and the repression that followed, also had an enormous international impact that was reflected in a wide variety of help, seen first in the refuge given to thousands of Chilean exiles by European countries.[24] The political and financial support received by the opposition, particularly from European organizations, was greater than that provided to other Latin American countries under military dictatorships. Trade union leaders were also given support by the International Confederation of Free Trade Unions (ICFTU), an organization based in Europe, and by the American Federation of Labor and Congress of Industrial Organizations (AFL-CIO).

Academics who were expelled from universities but decided to stay in Chile received help to set up private research centres, some of which operated under the wing of the Catholic Church.[25] These centres were active in drawing up ideas and designing policies in preparation for the first democratic government and also helped party leaders, contributing to the modernization of the parties' policies and operations.

Thanks to the presence in Chile of foreign correspondents, the opposition was able to publicize its activities and communicate information about the scale of repression. Visits from European politicians also had repercussions in their home countries because they were accompanied by journalists who not only covered their activities but also reported on the state of the country.

Trade union leaders found a particular echo in Chile because of the popularity attained by Polish trade union leaders. Their activities were regularly reported in the Chilean media and the strikes of August 1980 in Gdańsk received wide coverage because, in line with its anti-communism, the dictatorship was anxious to draw attention to this crisis in a communist country. During August 1980, *El Mercurio*, Chile's main newspaper which identified with the regime, reported daily about the strikes and on nine occasions put them on its front page. Rodolfo Seguel was seen as Chile's Lech Wałęsa.

The international support afforded to the opposition was in marked contrast to the dictatorship's international isolation. With the exception of the Carter administration (1977–81), the US government had supported Pinochet, but was the only country to do so and its stance changed in 1985 when the Reagan

---

[24] Alan Angell, 'International Support for the Chilean Opposition, 1973–1989: Political Parties and the Role of Exiles', in Laurence Whitehead (ed.), *The International Dimensions of Democratization. Europe and the Americas* (Oxford: Oxford University Press, 2001, expanded edition, originally published in 1996), 175–200.

[25] Cardinal Silva created the Academia de Humanismo Cristiano, which made possible the operation of a number of research centres.

**Figure 12.2** The much-criticized relationship between the Pinochet regime and the US government. General Pinochet, who had come to power in a *coup d'état* in 1973, welcomes US Secretary of State Henry Kissinger on a visit to Santiago on 8 June 1976. At a meeting there of the Organization of American States, Kissinger criticized Chilean abuses of civil liberties, but stopped short of taking any action against Pinochet. Later, US policy shifted towards more support for democracy.

administration, faced with the violence of the repression and the risks of polarization, backed progress towards democracy. This shift was reflected in the transfer of Ambassador Harry J. Barnes, a distinguished diplomat, from India to Santiago. Barnes actively supported a transition to democracy, incurring the anger of Pinochet. His presence, alongside dozens of young PC activists waving party flags, at the mass funeral of Rodrigo Rojas, who had been burned by a military patrol, was a particularly striking event.

## Germany's role

For several years, European Community countries had been supporting the opposition's efforts to achieve a peaceful transition to democracy. In order to illustrate this support, I will refer to the case of Germany, which had close political, cultural, and economic ties with Chile dating back to the colonization of the south of the country by German immigrants in the 1850s. German political foundations had played a very active role in Chile since the 1960s.[26] The German government, political parties, parliament, and Catholic and Evangelical charitable organizations gave very early support to the opposition; and the Catholic Church, particularly, established close relations with leaders in both countries that were of great use during the *apertura*. Members of parliament, particularly from the Social Democratic Party (SPD) and the Christian Democratic Union (CDU), visited Chile during the dictatorship, especially from 1983. However, the government's foreign policy was cautious because, unlike other European ambassadors, those appointed to Santiago by the Ministry of Foreign Relations, which was controlled by the liberals (Free Democratic Party), did not make contact with opposition leaders.

The arrival of Helmut Kohl (CDU) as federal chancellor in October 1982 helped the Chilean opposition. Unlike his predecessor Helmut Schmidt (SPD), Kohl was acquainted with leading Chilean politicians. He had been elected president of his party three months before the 1973 coup[27] and, in the party conference of November 1973 in Hamburg, he met and got on well with Patricio Aylwin, who was then president of the PDC and had been invited to speak at this event through the Adenauer Foundation. Subsequently, Kohl also met former President Eduardo Frei Montalva when he was invited to Germany. Kohl followed political developments in Chile with interest, committing the CDU to support the PDC. On 5 May 1983, a week before the first protest, he received Gabriel Valdés, the new PDC president, and the meeting was publicized by the CDU's press office.

Under Kohl, Chile held a prominent place in the CDU's active international policy. Kohl feared a polarization similar to that seen in Central America and, in this policy, he had the support of different CDU organizations, particularly university groups (Ring Christlich-Demokratischer Studenten, RCDS), the party youth (Junge Union)[28] and its worker organization (Sozialausschüsse), which supported the PDC in Chile from the mid-1970s. Leading CDU politicians such as Norbert Blüm, Minister of Labour (previously secretary-general of the Sozialausschüsse) and Heiner Geissler, Minister of Youth and Family and party secretary-general, were very active in supporting Chile's return to democracy and both visited Chile twice.

Kohl was supported by the CDU's Office for International Affairs (Büro für Auswärtigen Beziehungen, BAB), which he himself had created a few months

---

[26] Stefan Mair, 'Germany's Stiftungen and Democracy Assistance: Comparative Advantages, New Challenges', in Peter Burnell (ed.), *Democracy Assistance: International Co-operation for Democratization* (London: Frank Cass, 2000), 128–49; Ann L. Phillips, 'Exporting Democracy: German Political Foundations in Central-East Europe', *West European Politics*, 6, no. 2 (Summer 1999), 70–98; Michael Pinto-Duschinsky, 'Foreign political aid: The German political foundations and their US counterparts', *International Affairs*, 67, no. 1 (1991), 33–63.

[27] For an analysis of his political career, see Carlos Huneeus, 'How to Build a Modern Party: Helmut Kohl's Leadership and the Transformation of the CDU', *German Politics*, 5, no. 3 (Dec. 1996), 432–59.

[28] Matthias Wissmann, president of the Junge Union, was very active in helping the PDC and visited Chile several times, publicly criticizing violations of human rights. See Matthias Wissmann, 'Chiles Militärjunta is mit ihrem Latein am Ende', *Die Entscheidung* (Bonn), 10 (Oct. 1976).

before becoming chancellor and which was headed by a CDU diplomat. Chilean politicians communicated with the CDU through the BAB which was also responsible for preparing their visits to Bonn and those of CDU politicians to Chile.[29] It carried out this task in close collaboration with the Adenauer Foundation, the CDU, the office of Kohl,[30] and of the party's secretary general, and co-ordinated the visits of German politicians to Chile with the Ministry of Foreign Relations. Its memoranda and the minutes of meetings in Bonn and Santiago that it prepared were read with interest by Kohl as demonstrated by the notes he made on them.

In supporting the Chilean opposition, the CDU also had its own political interests because it sought to rival the Social Democratic Party in its defence of human rights, arguing that the latter only criticized right-wing dictatorships while keeping silent about left-wing dictatorships. However, this stance was controversial within the CDU since it put it in conflict with its sister party, the Christian Social Union, whose leader Franz-Josef Strauss explicitly supported Pinochet and had visited Chile in 1977.


## CONCLUSIONS

A combination of domestic and international factors of an economic and political nature resulted in massive citizen protest that changed the balance of power between the Pinochet regime and the opposition. However, because of his military support, this did not endanger Pinochet's hold on power. In the short term, repression worked to his advantage, but it was detrimental in the medium term because the atrocities committed by military personnel and the police were rejected by the population at large, including some sectors of his support, and because it caused conflict between the CNI and the police.

It is to the credit of the opposition leadership that it prevented the development of the climate of polarization promoted by sectors of the far Left and by Pinochet. The opposition's decision to accept the institutional framework established by the dictatorship to ensure its own continuance after 1988, and to participate in the plebiscite that took place on 5 October 1988, was an intelligent strategic move in that it provided an institutional channel for regulating conflict and gave legal legitimacy

---

[29] It was important that, between 1981 and 1984, the BAB's director was Peter Hartmann, who had been posted to Buenos Aires as cultural attaché in the late 1970s. He spoke perfect Spanish, understood the idiosyncrasies of Chilean politics, had a clear vision of the strengths of the PDC, and maintained very good relations with its leaders. In 1989, at the time of the fall of the Berlin Wall, Hartmann was deputy director of the federal chancellor's international office while the director was Horst Teltschik. The BAB's close relations with the PDC continued under Hartmann's successors.

[30] His secretary in the CDU, Michael Roik, both as a student at Bonn University and as RCDS leader, had previously been very active in supporting the PDC from the very beginning of the dictatorship. He translated and edited important documents of the Chilean political process. See Michael Roik, *Chile nach Pinochet: Dokumentation* (Bonn: RCDS-Bundesvorstand, 1976).

to progress towards democracy. Pinochet and his supporters did not expect the opposition to form a solid electoral coalition and were convinced that, by mounting an anti-communist campaign, they could produce polarization between a left-wing Marxist minority and the majority of the country, creating a situation in which the centrist vote would carry him to victory.

The solidity of the PDC and the policy of the democratic left prevented this outcome and, in a unique event in authoritarian regimes, Pinochet was defeated, taking 43 per cent of the vote compared to 54.7 per cent for the 'No' camp and 2.3 per cent which were blank or spoiled votes. The remarkable fact that the armed forces recognized their defeat and transferred power to a civilian government is explained by Chile's long and solid tradition of elections and respect for their results as well as by the legal force of the 1980 Constitution. This had envisaged the possibility of a defeat and established that, in this case, a presidential election would be held within a year. As in the case of the Franco dictatorship in Spain, the regime's plans for its succession proved to be a boomerang.[31] The violent actions

©Reuters/Corbis

**Figure 12.3** Civil resistance vindicated by victory in the polls. On 6 October 1988 demonstrators in Santiago celebrate Pinochet's defeat in the plebiscite held on the previous day. Pinochet had called the plebiscite to continue in office as president of Chile for a further eight years. Following his defeat, a new president was elected democratically in December 1989, and on 11 March 1990 Pinochet relinquished the presidency.

[31] Carlos Huneeus, *La Unión de Centro Democrático y la transición a la democracia en España* (Madrid: Centro de Investigaciones Sociológicas, Siglo XXI Editores, 1985); 'Autoritarismo, cuestión sucesoria y transición a la democracia: España, Brasil y Chile', *Opciones* (Santiago), 8 (1986), 138–80.

of the FPMR also strengthened the opposition's decision to seek the peaceful restoration of democracy.

Pressures from below in the form of protests by workers, poor people, and the middle class were extremely important in shaping the peaceful transition from authoritarianism to democracy. This confirms Rustow's model in which a transition is preceded by a stage of intense political conflict posing great dangers that the elites decide to avoid by advancing towards democracy. Democracy was possible because of the combination of pressure from below, the opposition's organizational capacity, and the army's respect for Chile's legal tradition.

A long and solid tradition of democracy in Chile, which is considered by Sartori to be 'the most significant (Latin American) country in terms of democratic tradition and structural consolidation of the party system',[32] allowed the opposition to emerge as a powerful government alternative. Its organizational capacity was demonstrated by the millions of Chileans who registered to vote in the plebiscite of 1988 in which Pinochet was defeated.

The social mobilization that began in 1983 also had an effect on the country's new democracy in that it left part of the population without the energy to continue participating actively in the political process. This apathy, which has also been seen in other new democracies, such as those of Spain and in eastern Europe, is a result of this process of hyper-mobilization that brings about the end of an authoritarian regime.

As a result of the intense conflict of the period analysed, the population preferred a policy of accommodation between the *Concertación* government and the opposition formed by the Independent Democratic Union (UDI) and the National Renewal Party (RN). This had its drawbacks because it undermined the democratic government's capacity to reform the country's economic system and important parts of its political system. The fact that General Pinochet stayed on as army commander-in-chief for eight years after 1990 represented a potential risk to the stability of the new democracy that further encouraged consensus politics.

The severity of the repression meant that truth and justice as regards the regime's human rights violations were urgently required: this was the main priority of President Aylwin. The Rettig Commission (1991), which investigated and reported on cases of repression resulting in death, was a key event in this process and, in 2004, was followed by the Valech Commission on the use of torture, appointed by President Ricardo Lagos. The courts condemned perpetrators of these crimes who included many high-ranking army officials, some of whom received prison sentences. This is an area in which Chile took very important steps as compared to other new democracies.[33]

---

[32] Giovanni Sartori, *Parties and Party System: A Framework for Analysis* (Cambridge: Cambridge University Press, 1976), 173.

[33] See Julio S. Valenzuela, 'Los derechos humanos y la redemocratización en Chile', in Manuel Alcántara and Leticia M. Ruiz Rodríguez (eds.), *Chile: Política y modernización democrática* (Barcelona: Ediciones Bellatera, 2006), 269–312.

# 13

## The Interplay of Non-violent and Violent Action in the Movement against Apartheid in South Africa, 1983–94

*Tom Lodge*

Between 1983 and 1994 South Africans participated in an uprising that ended with the replacement of the long-entrenched system of white minority government within the Republic of South Africa. The main organizations in this rebellion were the exiled African National Congress (ANC) and an internal movement, the United Democratic Front (UDF). In addition to guerrilla warfare and more generalized violence, millions of people participated in various kinds of non-violent activism.

The key question addressed in this chapter concerns the effectiveness of the non-violent dimensions of this struggle. How important were the non-violent politics of the rebellion to its success? Were they hindered or strengthened by the violence? Was non-violence significant in enlisting support for the rebellion outside South Africa, and did the use of non-violent tactics help shape the outcome of the conflict: the adoption of liberal democracy?

### BACKGROUND

South African civil disobedience dates back to 1906 when Mohandas Gandhi began organizing resistance amongst Indians against restrictions on immigrants. From 1950, the ANC embraced civil disobedience in its opposition to the recently elected Afrikaner nationalist government's programme of apartheid. Mass 'defiance' climaxed in 1960 when a breakaway group, the Pan-Africanist Congress (PAC), urged Africans to surrender themselves without passes outside police stations. On 21 March 1960, crowds of PAC supporters assembled without their passes. Police fired into these crowds and at Sharpeville killed sixty-nine people. Initially the government conceded a temporary suspension of the pass laws, but on 8 April the ANC and the PAC were banned.

In mid-1961, ANC leaders and communists agreed to sponsor an armed wing, Umkhonto we Sizwe. Certain ANC principals, including Nelson Mandela, one of the architects of the 1950s defiance campaign, had been considering the use of violent tactics for several years. For many, though, the repression of a three-day strike called by the ANC leadership and its allies for May 1961 was decisive. Large-scale non-violent protest seemed impossible.

Umkhonto was intended to lead a sabotage campaign. The saboteurs attempted to avoid bloodshed. Within the ANC and the communist party there remained disagreements about violence. While some hoped that sabotage would induce reforms, most Umkhonto commanders understood sabotage as simply a preparatory stage for guerrilla warfare. However, by the end of 1963 most Umkhonto leaders, including Nelson Mandela, were either in prison or had fled into exile. For the next ten years, the ANC's presence in South Africa would be very limited.

In 1976 however, protests by schoolchildren reignited rebellion. African advance into semi-skilled manufacturing had given labour new leverage. Strikes in 1973 helped constitute a combative trade union movement. Mass literacy nurtured a new generation of political organizations, inspired by the American black power movement and led by the expanding numbers of graduates from the segregated universities. The collapse of Portuguese colonialism in Angola and Mozambique supplied militant inspiration. In an education system under increasing strain the racially assertive Black Consciousness Movement drew ready adherents. The enforcement of a regulation that half the curriculum should be taught in Afrikaans provoked demonstrations on 16 June 1976 in Soweto. The police fired into a crowd of 15,000 children. In a tumultuous year at least 575 protesters died. Several thousand refugees from the uprising crossed South Africa's borders to join the ANC, which had set up arrangements to receive the refugees in several nearby countries. In responding to the 'Soweto Uprising', the government mixed repression with reform. In 1979 legislation conceded collective bargaining rights and official recognition for black trade unions. Other measures attempted to solicit support from urban Africans.

By the 1980s, though, urbanized Africans were more likely to acknowledge the authority of the ANC exiles. In exile the ANC had constructed a formidable bureaucracy including an army based in Angola. It was still led by the generation who had predominated in the 1950s, a mixture of elite professionals such as the ANC president, Oliver Tambo, an urbane lawyer who had once shared an attorneys' partnership with Nelson Mandela, and working class militants from the trade union movement, many of them communists. Within the organization, the communist party shaped the ANC's strategic ideas.

What were these ideas? Communists understood themselves to be engaged in a struggle for 'national democracy', itself a transitional phase in the advance to a fully socialist society. They understood national liberation as a profound systemic alteration of a kind that could only follow their seizure of power. How to achieve this objective became clearer in 1979. Up to then the ANC had expended most of its efforts on recruiting, training, and deploying guerrilla fighters. Events in

Soweto suggested fresh prospects for the kinds of legal activities that had seemed impossible in the mid-1960s. A visit to Vietnam underlined the importance of building an organizational base through a non-violent political struggle in which the general population could participate. In turn, later, this political movement would provide a platform for a 'people's war'. So, for the time being, the ANC should foster a broad front from existing legal organizations to promote the widest kinds of political struggle.

Meanwhile Umkhonto's 'armed propaganda' made the ANC visible. After 1980, the guerrilla campaign became more conspicuous. Operations were directed at targets chosen for their psychological impact on the general population, not just those groups most likely to support the ANC. On the whole, the campaign was concentrated in the Johannesburg–Pretoria area and in Durban. A successful rocket attack on the Sasolburg synthetic fuel refinery in June 1980 represented Umkhonto operations at their most elaborate and dramatic.

Despite such spectacles the warfare was essentially symbolic. Between 1976 and 1982, Umkhonto attacks numbered less than 200. Command structures remained external and there were never more than 500 Umkhonto soldiers deployed inside South Africa. The insurgents' conduct reflected the nature of their training. In particular, cadres were warned of the dangers of 'militarism', the isolation of military from political activity. ANC leaders opposed indiscriminate terrorism and up to 1984 the basic intention of Umkhonto's activity was not to represent a serious military challenge but rather to enhance the ANC's popular status and win for it a loose mass following. By the end of 1983, the formation of a 'United Democratic Front' suggested that Umkhonto's 'armed propaganda' had succeeded in its essential objective.

## THE FORMATION AND DEVELOPMENT OF THE UDF

It was reforms that prompted the establishment of the United Democratic Front. In 1982 the Black Local Authorities Act instituted elected African municipalities. The following year a new constitution replaced the existing exclusively white House of Assembly with a 'tri-cameral' legislature in which coloured and Indian voters would be represented in separate chambers. Africans remained excluded from central government.

On 8 January Oliver Tambo announced 1983 to be 'The Year of United Action'. All democratic forces, Tambo urged, should merge 'into one front for national liberation'. Two weeks later, in Johannesburg, the Reverend Allen Boesak, president of the World Alliance of Reformed Churches, delivered a keynote address. Here he advocated a 'politics of refusal' in which a 'united front' should oppose the government's constitutional measures. Eight months later, the UDF assembled itself at a well-publicized launch.

Campaigning began with electoral boycotts. In 1983 the UDF sponsored an offensive against the Black Local Authorities' elections, featuring open air meetings, extensive door-to-door visits and the distribution of half a million leaflets. UDF leaders perceived the low turnouts as evidence of success. They then directed an even more elaborate undertaking to persuade coloured and Indian voters to abstain. During this first phase, the UDF's performance deliberately evoked the mass politics of the 1950s: songs, slogans, and speeches extolled Nelson Mandela and other ANC heroes. As with the movement the ANC mobilized in the 1950s, leadership was multiracial, though, as in the 1950s, supporters were mainly African. Elderly veterans from the 1950s Congress Alliance were conspicuous within the UDF's leadership.

Appearances were deceptive. Although the UDF's style seemed to echo the ANC repertoire of thirty years before, the movement was significantly different. The Front was a federation of many different organizations and authority and initiative were dispersed. Initially, UDF leaders were preoccupied with opposing the parliamentary elections for Indians and coloureds. Hence, with respect to its African base, in the next two years local activists would determine and in so doing radicalize the Front's programme. They would draw their symbolism from more modern sources. The activists' *Toyi-Toyi* dance was a striking instance of this, imported into the townships from the goose-stepping parade drill used in ANC training camps.[1]

At dawn on 3 September 1984, pickets halted buses entering the townships around Vereeniging. The picketers represented the Vaal Civic Association. The VCA was directing its opposition at new rent increases, counting on a rising tide of public anger at the venal behaviour of the new councillors. By noon most of the shops and public buildings in Sebokeng and Sharpeville had been burned down. The deputy mayor, Kuzwayo Dlamini, was dead, killed in Sharpeville, burned alive by members of the enraged crowd after his bodyguards had opened fire on a procession of demonstrators. Thirty more members of the Lekoa council would die during the next week.

This insurrection spread to Soweto on 17 September and became national with its extension to the townships of the Eastern Cape in November. Soldiers moved into the Vaal area in late September, the first army deployment in quelling civil unrest since 1961. On 5 November in the Transvaal a two day 'stay-away' was called by trade unions: a million workers participated, the first of dozens of such strikes trade unionists would mobilize between 1984 and 1994. This was a rebellion without historical precedent. How was this movement organized and sustained?

The UDF claimed the adherence of about 700 affiliates. Its impact across regions varied. The Front was especially strong in the Eastern Cape, in Johannesburg, the Vaal, around Pretoria, in the West Rand, and in the coloured suburbs of Cape Town. It was weaker in the townships of the East Rand, a centre for the new trade union movement, and only superficially organized in African townships around Durban and Pietermaritzburg. Its relative strength in the Eastern Cape was a

---

[1] See Ronnie Kasrils, *Armed and Dangerous: From Undercover Struggle to Freedom* (Johannesburg: Jonathan Ball, 1998), 192.

©Bernard Bisson/Sygma/Corbis

**Figure 13.1** The role of women. At a funeral on 7 September 1985 (see also picture on p. 224) members of the UDF-aligned United Women's Organization serve as a guard of honour. They are giving the clenched-fist ANC salute, in use since the 1960s. Note the uniforms, first worn by the ANC Women's League in the 1950s. Their paramilitary style predated the ANC's turn to violent politics and helps to illustrate how in South African nationalist politics the distinctions between non-violent and armed resistance had been blurred for a long time.

consequence of several factors including compact urban geography which made it easier for local activists to organize, long-standing regional loyalty to the ANC, and African ethnic homogeneity. Weakness in Natal partly reflected tensions between African and Indian UDF leaders but was also a result of hostility from Inkatha, the ruling party of the Kwa-Zulu homeland. Inkatha's association with the Zulu royal house helped it build extensive networks of support among hostel-based migrant workers in the main cities. Violence between UDF and Inkatha supporters began in 1984, beginning when UDF leaders opposed an administrative takeover of townships outside Durban by the Kwa-Zulu authorities.

The way the UDF represented its own constitution was misleading. In theory, affiliated bodies could be ideologically diverse, united only in their opposition to the government's new political arrangements. In practice, in many African townships the Front functioned as an ideologically homogeneous movement with individuals popularly perceived as simultaneously UDF and ANC supporters. In most localities, a basic triumvirate emerged that supplied the UDF with its most active following: a civic or a community organization, a women's group, and a 'youth congress'. At its base amongst its main urban and rural following, amongst working-class Africans and unemployed school-leavers, affiliation to the Front usually required acknowledgement of the ANC's claims to political primacy, admiration for the armed struggle, and almost millennial expectations of revolutionary change.

The movement's explosive energy was attributable to structural developments: the combined forces of inflation and unemployment generated by a recession that had gripped the national economy from 1982. Eighty per cent of black 18–26 year olds were unemployed in 1986 and inflation was accelerating. The economic downturn fatefully coincided with the government's efforts to introduce devices to legitimize its authority amongst black South Africans to a greater extent.

The Front's strength depended not so much upon sophisticated leadership and coordinated organizational structures, but rather on the vitality of its township based affiliates. External resources helped sustain the movement. Money mainly from Dutch churches and Swedish trade unions—totalling R2 million in 1987[2]—provided the support needed to maintain full-time political organizers, to underwrite community newspapers, to pay for the posters, publicity, and T-shirts, to equip this movement with a common vocabulary and a collective iconography that gave it a shared sense of purpose.

As the ANC's strategists had hoped, the UDF's activist culture was informed by a rediscovery of ANC traditions and inspired by the martial theatre of Umkhonto we Sizwe. Of course, though loyalty to the ANC was a core component of the UDF's ideology, what the ANC represented and how its programme could be interpreted varied considerably according to constituency. At the African base of the movement, however, an explicit commitment to a rough and ready Marxist vision of socialism was pervasive, especially in those centres in which trade unions were strong. The sentiments expressed by Comrade Bongani, from the Tumahole Youth Congress, reflected this vision:

> *Question*: What do you understand by capitalism?
> *Answer*: It is a system of private ownership by certain individuals who own the means of production. My parents, from Monday to Friday, can make a production of R1,000, but he or she is going to get, say R50. So our parents are being exploited so that certain individuals can get rich. That's why I prefer socialism, because the working class will control production.[3]

As well as their socialism, these activists brought into the movement their susceptibility for really brutal violence. From March 1985, this included the 'necklacing' with burning tyres of people whom the activists believed to be informers and collaborators. The first victim of 'this highly symbolic method of

    [2] Ineke van Kessel, *Beyond Our Wildest Dreams: The United Democratic Front and the Transform-ation of South Africa* (London and Charlottesville: University of Virginia Press, 2000), 55.
    [3] 'Talking to a comrade', *Financial Mail* (Johannesburg), 31 Oct. 1986, 53.

**Figure 13.2** On the edge of violence. At a Cape Town funeral on 1 July 1985, Bishop Desmond Tutu pleads with the crowd to spare the life of a suspected police informant whose car had just been set alight. By this stage, activists across South Africa had begun to kill people they believed to be working for the police, identifying them at public meetings and setting them alight after hanging around their necks a petrol-filled tyre—a practice known as 'necklacing'.

purging evil forces'[4] was Tamsanqa Kinikini, a councillor who refused to renounce his position in KwaNobuhle in the Eastern Cape.

When South African Defence Force (SADF) soldiers moved into the townships in the wake of the September 1984 rebellion, the UDF became a movement galvanized by local initiatives, with civics and youth congresses organizing a remarkable series of consumer boycotts to compel white city councils and businessmen to negotiate on their behalf the withdrawal of troops, the release of local leaders under detention, and the redressing of local grievances. The negotiations were undertaken as local initiatives and were sometimes criticized as reformist in ANC polemics but modest local victories considerably enhanced the popular moral credentials of civic leaders.[5] In a geographically limited State of Emergency between July 1985 and February 1986 the police detained 8,000 people. In reaction, surviving local leaders called afresh for consumer boycotts

---

[4] Van Kessel, *Beyond our Wildest Dreams*, 35.
[5] Ibid. 29.

and formed street committees that could evade emergency restrictions on mass meetings.

The authorities' failure to contain resistance, the increasing incidence of armed confrontations between the occupation forces and increasingly militarized 'comrades', sometimes trained and equipped as Umkhonto auxiliaries, and the succession of local victories won through consumer boycotts all served to stimulate a euphoric conviction concerning the state's vulnerability and the imminence of national liberation. Motivated mainly by the pragmatic need to regulate the disorder resulting from the collapse of township administration and the absence of routine policing, but inspired also by an almost apocalyptic expectancy, civics and youth movements began to construct an alternative institutional framework of 'people's power'.

In particular, local UDF affiliates assumed judicial functions in their efforts to cope with the consequence of a vacuum of authority. 'People's courts', though, were often inspired by an egalitarian and redemptive conception of their social mission. 'The people's court is not simply a bourgeois court taking place in a back room in a ghetto,' insisted a pamphlet circulated in Atteridgeville in Pretoria. 'Unlike the present legal system, it should not be biased in favour of the powerful.'[6] The courts' main aim, a Mamelodi activist explained, was 'rehabilitation. To re-educate the wrong-doer and make him a better person.'[7] In several recorded instances courts fell short of such exalted ideals, providing summary tribunals in which harsh retribution could be imposed upon both political opponents and the socially marginalized.[8] The language employed by UDF officials and ideologues to explain the workings of these agencies was significant despite these shortcomings in practice because of the aspirations it expressed. 'People's power' was not liberal democracy. As a contributor to *New Era*, a publication affiliated to the Cape Town UDF, noted:

> Democracy means, in the first instance, the ability of the broad working masses to participate in and to control all dimensions of their lives. This for us, is the essence of democracy, not some liberal, pluralistic, debating society notion of a 'thousand schools contending'.[9]

A constant refrain in UDF speeches and statements was that democracy should be the politics of popular participation, that leaders were merely the bearers of the popular mandate, and that as delegates they were accountable directly to the organization's membership, a notion borrowed from recent South African trade union experience with its strong emphasis on shop-steward accountability. In this vein leaders could advise and inspire but they could not prescribe. During the Soweto consumer boycott, for example, trade unionists on the boycott committee objected to the youths stoning the wholesalers' trucks that were replenishing the township shops

---

[6] Raymond Suttner, 'Popular Justice in South Africa', paper delivered at the Sociology Departmental Seminar, University of the Witwatersrand, Johannesburg, 5 May 1986, 12.

[7] Kumi Naidoo, 'Internal Resistance in South Africa: The Political Movements', in Shaun Johnson (ed.), *South Africa: No Turning Back* (Bloomington and Indianapolis: Indiana University Press, 1989), 184.

[8] Van Kessel, *Beyond Our Wildest Dreams*, 207–9.

[9] 'Sowing Confusion', *New Era* (Cape Town), 1, no. 1 (Mar. 1986), 38.

that were allowed by the boycotters to remain open. However, they and other regional UDF leaders were reluctant to rein in the youngsters: 'It is not our duty to tell them not to stone or burn the trucks. We can only tell them why.'[10]

Though on this occasion their views went unheeded, within the UDF the influence of trade unionists was often decisive. Labour politics itself was complex and for many trade unionists the ANC's directives were not necessarily authoritative. In the first half of the decade black trade unions were sharply divided. They disagreed over whether to register under the new official labour dispensation. The Federation of South African Trade Unions (FOSATU) favoured registration. A number of UDF-aligned unions rejected the government's collective bargaining regime. The FOSATU group held back from political alliances, as its leaders maintained that links with the ANC had destroyed an earlier generation of black unions in the 1960s when their shop stewards joined Umkhonto. Unions should concentrate on shop-floor issues for if they became involved in wider struggles, then working-class interests might be compromised. Their critics argued that in a context in which workers had no democratic rights, workers' organizations should take up a wider range of issues than simply workplace concerns; they should acknowledge that workers were members of wider communities. A series of industrial strikes that were backed by consumer boycotts helped convince the FOSATU leadership of the merits of this argument as did its own formation of regional shop-steward councils, bodies that brought together trade unionists from different factories to enable them to identify common concerns: inevitably these concerns were political drawing FOSATU into confrontation with the authorities.

In December 1985 the formation of the Congress of South African Trade Unions (COSATU) brought the UDF unions and the more politically independent FOSATU affiliates together in a single federation representing around half a million workers in which all senior officials recognized the 'basic truth'[11] of the inseparability of 'the struggle on the shop floor... from the wider political struggle'.[12] COSATU itself remained outside the UDF but in a visit to the ANC's headquarters in Lusaka in April 1986, COSATU officials acknowledged the ANC's senior status in the liberation struggle. At its 1987 conference, COSATU adopted the ANC's Freedom Charter 'as a guiding document'.[13] Ostensible recognition of the ANC's political seniority did not imply complete agreement with the ANC's strategic orientation. For example, not all trade unionists agreed with the UDF's and the ANC's advocacy of sanctions and disinvestment. More generally, COSATU's independence was indicated by its

---

[10] 'Tactical Differences', *Work in Progress* (Development Studies Group, Johannesburg), Oct. 1985, 23.

[11] Jay Naidoo quoted in Robin Smith, 'The Black Trade Unions: From Economics to Politics' in Jesmond Blumenfeld (ed.), *South Africa in Crisis* (London: Croom Helm, 1987), 97.

[12] Cyril Ramaphosa, quoted in Gregory Houston, *The National Liberation Struggle in South Africa: A Case Study of the United Democratic Front* (Aldershot: Ashgate Publishing, 2000), 173.

[13] Congress of South African Trade Unions, *COSATU Resolutions* (Johannesburg: Art Printers, 1987), 3.

particular take on the ANC's Freedom Charter; by representing it as a set of 'minimum democratic demands', trade unionists were suggesting that liberation might extend beyond the 'national democratic' goals of the Charter.[14]

By mid-1986, 'national democracy', however understood, must have appeared a more distant prospect than it had appeared to UDF activists one year previously. A national state of emergency imposed in June 1986 ended the rebellion's most Jacobin phase. Much fiercer press restrictions, a record deployment of soldiers, and 25,000 detentions affected even the most junior layers of leadership, driving the movement off the streets. Though support for the movement continued to be manifest in a widespread rent boycott, in contrast with the movement at its peak, the assertiveness of UDF politics diminished, and it became the clandestine activity of committed enthusiasts.

In the trials of the activists and leaders associated with these events, public prosecutors tried to prove that the defendants were participants in a conspiracy directed by the ANC. This claim was only partly true. The degree to which the UDF's principals were conscious participants in a revolutionary strategy varied sharply and different groups mobilized during the course of the rebellion were animated by their own preoccupations and were quite likely to resist any direction from above. Neither Allen Boesak, the UDF's most prominent 'patron', nor Popo Molefe, the Front's general secretary, believed that the ANC's vision of a revolutionary capture of power was plausible. Especially within the relatively more conservative coloured and Indian communities, Front leaders used a politically restrained, rights-based vocabulary, emphasizing the Front's significance as 'the last mass non-violent effort' to induce the government to concede change peacefully. Such language would have reflected tactical circumspection but it could also reflect the preferences of particular UDF leaders.[15]

Even among its more committed supporters within the UDF's senior echelons, it was very difficult for the ANC to impose its authority. An internal ANC report written from inside South Africa in 1986 details 'problems of a subjective nature' that had beset the Front, arising from 'different, opposing groupings' within its leadership. As the report's author noted: 'There is no central "Congress Organization" which would be the core of the UDF etc.' It continues:

> Most of the leadership of the mass democratic movement considers itself Congress but they do not belong to movement structures to which they can account and be given collective assistance. Our discussions with the leadership of the mass democratic movement tend to be suggestive; we do not assert our positions clearly and unambiguously.[16]

In fact the Front functioned in much the fashion that was forecast in the ANC strategic review, with a significant degree of autonomy from the ANC's networks.

---

[14] Anthony W. Marx, *Lessons of Struggle: South African Internal Opposition* (New York: Oxford University Press, 1992), 205.

[15] Jeremy Seekings, *The UDF: A History of the United Democratic Front* (Cape Town: David Philip, 2000), 113–14 & 133.

[16] 'Nkukheli', unpublished typescript document, 1986, 12. Author's possession.

Even so, ANC strategists were encouraged by the willingness of the UDF's constituents to acknowledge the ANC's authority. Within the townships, ANC strategic thinkers noted in 1985, there were emerging 'organs of self government'. These had the potential to develop both as sources of 'alternate power' to the state and as 'organs of insurrection'. 'Uprisings' had 'become a permanent feature of our struggle'.[17]

## STRATEGIC REALIGNMENT: FROM PEOPLES' WAR TO NEGOTIATED TRANSITION

At the ANC's 'Third Consultative Conference',[18] held in Zambia in June 1985, ANC leaders announced it was time to move to a 'Peoples' War' that would conclude in the 'seizure of power'. Now, 'the risen masses' would be turned 'into organised groups of combatants' while an externally trained 'core' would function as an 'officer corps'.[19]

In the next eighteen months following the conference, Umkhonto stepped up operations.[20] In 1986 guerrillas struck 228 times. Almost 160 guerrillas were killed or captured, one-third of Umkhonto losses since 1977. The escalation probably reflected wider weapon distribution: at the beginning of 1987 for example, 'comrades' protecting rent boycotters often possessed side arms, evidence that guerrillas were indeed training and equipping local 'mass combat units'. This may help to explain the growing incidence of attacks on targets such as shopping arcades. In October 1988, however, the ANC released a statement forswearing attacks on civilians. Umkhonto operations continued, though, the number of attacks nearing 300 in 1989. Even at their peak, however, Umkhonto's activities scarcely represented a serious threat to South African security.[21] In October 1986, the ANC circulated to its national command centres a soberly critical assessment. 'Despite all our efforts,' it argued, 'we have not come anywhere near the achievement of the objectives we set ourselves.' ANC structures inside South Africa remained too weak to supply reliable support for Umkhonto cadres. Umkhonto units still largely operated largely in isolation from 'mass combat groups'.[22] The ANC had had its organization dismantled in Mozambique,

---

[17] 'Political Report of the National Executive Committee', in *Documentation of the Second National Consultative Conference* (Lusaka: ANC, 1985), 18.

[18] At the time the ANC referred to this meeting as its second such conference. During its exile three consultative conferences were held, at Lobatsi, Botswana, in 1962; at Morogoro, Tanzania, in 1969; and at Kabwe, Zambia, in 1985.

[19] Quotations in this paragraph are from ANC, *Documentation of the Second Consultative Conference*, 10–12, 18, & 44.

[20] Kasrils, *Armed and Dangerous*, 279.

[21] For a comparative assessment of the threat represented by political violence in South Africa in the late 1980s see Jeffrey Herbst, 'Prospects for revolution in South Africa', *Political Science Quarterly*, 103, no. 4 (Winter 1988–9), 674–6.

[22] '1987: What Is To be Done?', document distributed by the ANC Politico-Military Council to regional command centres, Oct. 1986. Circulated by the South African police at a press conference in Nov. 1986. Document in author's collection.

©Bernard Bisson/Sygma/Corbis

**Figure 13.3** The imprisoned myth. South Africans at a funeral on 7 September 1985 for nine people who had died during riots in Guguletu, a black township in Cape Town, on 28 August. During the UDF's rebellion, funerals served as political assemblies in which eulogies to the dead alternated with exhortations to the living. At such meetings, Nelson Mandela's name would often lead a litany of heroes and martyrs from the history of 'the struggle'. His portrait is of the younger man, since no photographs of the long-time political prisoner Mandela were available.

Lesotho, and Botswana. Detentions under the state of emergency had depleted the ranks of the comrades whom the Umkhonto commanders hoped to enlist as guerrilla auxiliaries. South African police continued to anticipate with precision the arrival of trained guerrillas from across the border—an indication of their success in infiltrating Umkhonto command structures, especially in Swaziland.[23] In the field the average survival period for guerrillas was six months, according to an Umkhonto officer's estimate.[24] Meanwhile South African threats and actual 'destabilization' of neighbouring countries made it increasingly difficult for the ANC to maintain supplies and reinforcements.

From 1986 onwards, ANC spokesmen began to refer more frequently to the prospect of a negotiated accession to power. In September 1985, a meeting

[23] Stephen Ellis and Tsepo Sechaba, *Comrades against Apartheid: The ANC and the South African Communist Party in Exile* (London: James Currey, 1992), 168–9.

[24] Howard Barrell, *MK: The ANC's Armed Struggle* (Johannesburg: Penguin, 1990), 60.

between ANC leaders and leading South African businessmen in Zambia signalled that powerful interests inside South Africa were willing to contemplate a change of regime. Here ANC officials explained the ANC's nationalization policies to the South African visitors: monopoly capital, including the press would be under public control but 'beyond that private capital would exist'. Nationalization might be on the Zambian model, with a 51 per cent state holding, leaving plenty of room for big companies.[25]

Contacts between the ANC and representatives of different interest groups proliferated. From prison, Nelson Mandela launched his own schedule of talks with members of the government. In mid-1986, ANC leaders offered a qualified endorsement of a negotiation proposal developed by the British Common-wealth's Eminent Persons Group. By 1988 the ANC was beginning to qualify its own expectations about the future. A set of constitutional guidelines and eco-nomic principles published by the ANC in mid-1988 suggested a substantially reorganized political system, certainly, but a polity that would retain existing laws and personnel. The economic prescriptions omitted any specific commitments to nationalization. Several months earlier, the ANC's national executive released a statement 'reaffirming' the ANC's commitment to a negotiated transition. The statement announced the ANC's acceptance 'that a new constitution could include an entrenched bill of rights to safeguard the individual'.[26]

Changes in ANC strategy were matched by a turnabout in South African government policy. The withdrawal of South African soldiers from Angola in 1988, followed in December by an internationally brokered agreement by Pretoria to cease supplying and reinforcing Angolan rebels in return for the removal of ANC bases from Angola, was a catalyst in this change.

South African military setbacks in Angola were compounded by continuing domestic political and economic failures. South African total external debt in mid-1989 stood at $US21 billion; the urgency of rescheduling 1990/1 repayments was probably one of the sharpest inducements favouring the appearance of nego-tiations on the government's regional and domestic agenda.[27] For by 1989 the government was in severe financial trouble. Twelve per cent of its expenditure in 1987 and 14 per cent in 1988 was simply directed at debt repayment. In 1989, increased budgets for the military and for education (the two single largest items in the government's projected expenditure) and a general 21 per cent increase in the overall total were to be funded by raising taxation; and by 1989 individual mainly white tax payers were supplying 60 per cent of government revenue. Government spending increases contrasted with falling growth rates—in the first three months of 1989 economic growth fell to 1.5 per cent per annum. South Africa's gold and foreign exchange reserves were actually worth less than its short-term debts.

[25] Oliver Tambo quoted in 'Notes of a meeting at Mfuwe Game Lodge, 13 September, 1985', 21. Unpublished typescript, author's possession.

[26] 'Statement of the National Executive Committee of the ANC on the Question of Negotiations', 9 Oct. 1987. Typescript fax in author's collection.

[27] Dan O'Meara, *Forty Lost Years: The Apartheid State and the Politics of the National Party, 1948–1994* (Randburg: Ravan Press, 1996), 355.

**Figure 13.4** It always takes two to negotiate. Frederik Willem de Klerk (left), the former South African president, shaking hands with his successor, President Nelson Mandela (right), in January 1994. Without de Klerk's readiness to negotiate with Mandela and the ANC, South Africa's transition to democracy would almost certainly have been far more difficult and bloody. He, like Mikhail Gorbachev, belongs to a select group of what the German writer Hans Magnus Enzensberger has called 'the heroes of retreat'.

That year, the replacement of P. W. Botha by F. W. de Klerk, first as leader of the National Party and later as state president, sharply diminished the influence that military strategists had exercised over cabinet decision-making during the Botha era. On 2 February 1990 F. W. de Klerk opened parliament with a speech he had written out by hand, consulting only his closest advisers. The government would legalize all prohibited organizations, he announced. Political prisoners not guilty of violence would be freed. The authorities would release Nelson Mandela without conditions. Nine days later Mandela walked through the gates of Victor Verster prison, hand in hand with his wife.

Over the next four years, South Africans would negotiate a political settlement that would establish a constitutional liberal democracy. To many observers their achievement appeared a miraculous reversal of an inevitable trajectory towards a full-scale civil war. The detailed dynamics of the negotiations are beyond the concern of this chapter but what needs to be underlined are the ways in which both violent and non-violent kinds of activism contributed to a successful outcome.

Though the ANC suspended its guerrilla operations after Nelson Mandela's release violence escalated. Between 1990 and the end of 1994 16,000 people died, mainly the victims of hostilities between ANC/UDF supporters and Inkatha adherents. Certainly this was a conflict to which covert police and military agencies contributed as agents provocateurs and, for the most part, Inkatha allies; but ANC and UDF followers also participated in armed raids on communities perceived to be supporters of their political adversaries. Though the political violence nearly derailed the constitutional negotiations, it also helped to induce willingness to compromise: both the ANC and the government offered substantial concessions to each other during the later stages of the settlement. Arguably, the ANC extracted more than it conceded, especially with respect to the very temporary character of the power-sharing arrangements that were put in place in the 1994 constitution.

Polling evidence suggested that political violence generally had reduced public support within its own constituency for the National Party: hence its leaders' eagerness by 1993 to settle quickly. The ANC's ability to mobilize its increasingly evident support was also a critical factor in its leaders' success in negotiation. COSATU had been relatively unaffected by the militarized suppression of township organization in 1986–9, and trade unionists played a very important role in rebuilding the ANC's branch level organization, and in demonstrating disciplined popular support for the positions ANC negotiators adopted. In addition, the ANC's evident ability to lead and control its following was a critical factor in its ability to persuade opponents that it was negotiating in good faith. Strong leadership and loyal supporters are very important if negotiators are to abandon disciplined intransigent 'positional' approaches. Such leadership would not have been available without the activism of the preceding decade.

## CONCLUSION

Many of the tactics employed in this rebellion were not new. The ANC and the communist party had employed passive resistance, boycotts, and industrial action in mobilizing African protest since the First World War, especially during the 1950s. Making the movement in the 1980s different was its scale, its duration, and the willingness of its participants to maintain the rebellion when confronted with violent state repression. What had changed, of course, was the setting. By 1984 a substantially organized semi-skilled African industrial workforce existed with the will and the capacity to close down whole sectors of the economy for extended periods. In the 1950s African labour organization was very confined, and striking African workers could be easily replaced. By the 1980s a substantial African professional middle class existed, possessing the resources needed for political leadership. Mass literacy was the consequence of more than a decade of almost total school enrolment. Daily tabloid newspapers under black editors and directed at a popular African readership represented a crucial medium through which the UDF, and indeed the ANC, could reach their followers. Even state television reported the rebellion quite extensively until the 1986 emergency. Resource flows from outside South Africa enabled the UDF to maintain a substantial number of full-time officials whereas earlier political organizations at best had employed a handful of staff. The 1980s rebellion received unprecedented international attention, much of it sympathetic. In the US among university students and African-American civil rights activists the rebellion inspired a powerful social movement that succeeded in prompting widespread withdrawal of investments in South Africa.

Did non-violent forms of political opposition to apartheid make the major contribution to bringing about South Africa's transition to democracy? One difficulty in answering this question is that the popular rebellion that the avowedly non-violent UDF headed was quite frequently violent. If the UDF had confined itself to the kinds of activism that had preceded the 1983/4 electoral boycotts—pamphleteering, meetings, and door to door canvassing—it would have hardly represented a significant challenge to the authorities. It was the rebellion against the local councils in the townships that was decisive in turning the UDF into a popular insurgency. Violent attacks by activists on perceived collaborators were important in prompting an administrative collapse in African local government and in creating the political space in which local UDF leaders could exercise authority. To a degree—and this varied considerably between different areas—the movement's authority itself could be coercive if not violent. Examples of this included the brutal punishments inflicted upon people and the beatings administered by the more retributive people's courts. Moreover, the political culture that motivated and sustained the UDF's young African following was nurtured by the ANC's guerrilla warfare. Notwithstanding the limited scope of Umkhonto operations, for activists the 'armed propaganda' represented the achievable possibility of apocalyptic change and appeared to demonstrate the state's vulnerability.

Even so, as noted above, it was the sheer scale of the rebellion by the UDF that made it unprecedented, and this scale was most evident in protests that were essentially non-violent. These included the tumultuous processions and crowds that assembled before television cameras, particularly at the funerals of activists killed by the police. Repetitive national stay-away strikes—stoppages by millions of workers that closed down whole cities—became the most obvious form of protest after the declaration of the 1986 emergency. Boycotts were also a key tactic, in the 'Tricameral' and Black Local Authority elections in 1983 and1984, but also, and more importantly, when the UDF called upon African city-dwellers to withhold rents and service charges, denying the authorities a substantial source of local revenue. It was these events—and the state violence that engendered them—that created the impression of public disorder that was so indispensable in undermining internal and, more importantly, external confidence in the regime. South Africa's fiscal crisis was partly the consequence of an international sanctions campaign but it was also a consequence from 1985 of international banks increasingly perceiving the country as a bad credit risk. The non-violent dimensions of the protest were critical in eliciting international solidarity: it is difficult to imagine North American and European churches mobilizing comparable support for a predominantly military movement.[28] Inside South Africa, legal non-violent protest allowed better prospects for building well-structured mass organization.

To a degree, the movement the UDF commanded drew strength from particular kinds of insurgent violence, and it benefited from the anger and the moral revulsion prompted by the state's violence. The ANC's heroic stature among street-level activists was principally an effect of its guerrilla operations. These operations were, to a degree, directed at targets that were the focus of civic campaigning, rent offices in townships for example. The ANC accumulated political authority during the decade and this was a key resource it brought to negotiations. By 1990 it had a unique capacity to bestow legitimacy on the inevitable compromises that would accompany any political settlement.

How central and indispensable was violence in this rebellion? Organized guerrilla warfare, whether by externally trained guerrillas or their local auxiliaries, remained on a modest scale. Umkhonto's guerrilla operations were concentrated around the Witwatersrand and in Durban because these two urban complexes were well within reach of external supply lines; by contrast, there was comparatively little Umkhonto activity in the Eastern Cape, by far the best organized UDF region. As for activist violence of a less organized kind, increasingly, towards the end of the decade, this became geographically concentrated, especially in Kwa-Zulu Natal where it certainly weakened the ANC and the UDF. Violence was an inevitable accompaniment to the rebellion of the 1980s. In its early stages activist violence may have enhanced the authority of local UDF leaders, but a more violent movement might not have won such a wide following—or as many admirers outside South Africa. State violence and state coercive capacity was also important, for it limited the revolt and by 1988 had deflected it from its original insurrectionary course. ANC leaders shifted strategic direction at the end of the decade partly because of the state's success in containing the armed revolt, though for the state this was a very costly achievement.

The extent to which the rebellion was non-violent had important long-term consequences. The ANC's vision of a 'people's war', even if it had succeeded in forcing the government into conceding a settlement, would have been unlikely to have produced a robust democracy. The UDF's tactical repertoire invited popular participation and helped nurture a political culture that favoured debate, consensus, and accountability—though it was also true that many UDF activists were contemptuous of liberal procedural democracy. African trade unions emerged from this period as formidably strong organizations, able to imprint their own programmatic concerns on the political settlement, strengthening its democratic content. A more militarized insurgency would have been most unlikely to have produced a democratically structured movement, and in that case the ANC

---

[28] See Donald R. Culverson, 'The Politics of the Anti-Apartheid Movement in the United States, 1969–1986', *Political Science Quarterly,* 111, no. 1 (1996); Janice Love, *The US Anti-Apartheid Movement: Local Activism in a Global Context* (New York: Praeger, 1985); Renate Pratt, *In Good Faith: Canadian Churches against Apartheid* (Waterloo, Ont.: Wilfred Laurier University Press, 1997).

leadership's commitment to the liberal rights entrenched in 1994 might have been much weaker.

How important was the rebellion as a whole in causing change? Could change have happened without it? Would South Africa have reformed its institutions democratically without an insurrection? For President F. W. de Klerk, an important consideration in releasing Mandela and allowing the ANC's return from exile was the fall of the Berlin Wall. This effectively ended any further prospect of Soviet support for the ANC's armed insurgency. De Klerk believed that without its eastern European allies a domesticated ANC would be much weaker.[29] Events in eastern Europe occurred independently of any South African political trajectory. Even without the financial difficulties posed by sanctions, disinvestment, credit withdrawal, and government borrowing, all of these direct or indirect consequences of the insurgency, it is just possible that an intelligent conservative administration might have tried to impose its own version of a liberal settlement. What brought stability to South Africa in 1994, though, was the degree to which the settlement was not imposed but was rather the product of cooperation by parties willing to acknowledge each other's power. That situation was the product of an insurrectionary movement, largely non-violent but extensively violent as well, and it could not have existed without such a movement.

[29] See Adrian Guelke, *Rethinking the Rise and Fall of Apartheid* (Basingstoke: Macmillan, 2005), 162–3.

# 14

# The Intersection of Ethnic Nationalism and People Power Tactics in the Baltic States, 1987–91

*Mark R. Beissinger*

It is often said that ethnic nationalism contains a particular propensity for violence rooted in its emotional charge and in the ways in which it simulates the emotional bonds of kinship, infusing nationalist conflict with a passion that few other social relationships match. Violence, however, is not the only sphere in which political passion manifests itself. Indeed, non-violent civil resistance can also be considered a form of passionate politics, one that draws on deep-seated emotions and beliefs about the nature of just community.

This chapter explores the circumstances under which civil resistance can be-come the preferred strategy of ethnic nationalist movements. It focuses on the struggles for self-determination in the Baltic states (Estonia, Latvia, and Lithu-ania), which achieved independence from the Soviet Union after almost a half-century of occupation.[1] In the first part, I outline the main events leading to the achievement of independence in 1991, and then, in an analysis of these events, I identify six conditions that help to render civil resistance a potent choice for ethnically defined nationalist movements: (1) appropriate goals of liberation; (2) political opening; (3) extreme imbalance in the means of coercion; (4) strong and broadly shared identities; (5) weak counter-movements; and (6) significant sup-port from external allies. These circumstances reflect many of the same factors that render civil resistance strategically effective irrespective of whether resistance is framed in ethno-nationalist terms or assumes some other form. Here, I do not mean to imply that movements mechanically choose tactics as a result of goals or circumstances. Some movements choose violence because they are oriented towards it, or non-violence because they value non-violence. Some choose strat-egies that are inappropriate for the circumstances that they face. But aims and contexts make particular tactics more or less effective as choices. In what follows, I explore why ethnic nationalism manifested itself in successful civil resistance in the Baltic popular fronts of the late 1980s and early 1990s. As the Baltic cases show,

---

[1] Estonians, Latvians, and Lithuanians are sometimes referred to collectively as 'Balts'.

non-violence and passionate ethnic identity need not be incompatible. On the contrary, their intersection can, under particular circumstances, be quite power-ful, rendering the emotional bonds that have often made ethnic nationalism prone to violence into effective resources for peaceful mass resistance.


## THE BALTIC PATH TO INDEPENDENCE

The Baltic independence movements represent highly successful examples of civil resistance. The popular fronts (Sąjūdis in Lithuania, the Latvian Popular Front, and the Estonian Popular Front) mobilized hundreds of thousands of followers on repeated occasions, using the pressure generated from the street to place politicians sympathetic to them in power, pressure the state to recognize the independence cause, gain direct control over government, and prevent efforts by the Soviet regime to reimpose its authority by force. Compared with national liberation struggles elsewhere, the number of victims was minimal: from January 1987 through August 1991, 25 people were killed and 935 people injured in the Baltic independence campaigns—with all of the deaths occurring in 1991. More-over, the Baltic popular fronts inspired numerous attempts at emulation throughout the former Soviet Union, acting as a catalyst that transformed the political landscape and helped to trigger the break-up of the Soviet state.

   That non-violent resistance would become the dominant strategy of Baltic independence struggles would not necessarily have been predictable from the past record of Baltic resistance. What are today Latvia and Estonia had been the site of significant violence during the 1905 Revolution, and from 1918 to 1920 the Baltic was a chaotic military battleground in which Bolsheviks, White Russians, Ger-mans, Poles, and Baltic nationalists fought for control. The memory of these struggles remains a central element in Baltic nationalist narratives to this day. Peace treaties in 1920 with Soviet Russia ushered in two decades of independence, only to be cut short by the Molotov–Ribbentrop Pact in 1939, Soviet invasion in 1940, German invasion in 1941, and the re-entry of the Soviet army into the region in 1944. The Soviet occupying authority unleashed a campaign of terror and intimidation, collectivizing the countryside and imposing Stalinist political and social organization. In response, Baltic resistance assumed predominantly violent form, as guerrilla movements known as Forest Brotherhoods waged a hit-and-run battle against Soviet authorities. The Soviet regime deployed brutal force in retaliation. In Lithuania alone up to 20,000 partisans were killed, 140,000 people sent to concentration camps, and 118,000 people deported.[2]

   There is some truth to the observation that non-violent resistance in the Baltic 'was the last stage of resistance, when, due to its suppression, armed resistance . . .

---

[2] Nijolė Gaškaitė-Žemaitienė, 'The Partisan War in Lithuania from 1944 to 1953', in Arvydas Anušauskas (ed.), *The Anti-Soviet Resistance in the Baltic States* (Vilnius: Genocide and Resistance Research Centre of Lithuania, 2000), 23–45.

©Andrey Solovyov/AFP/Getty Images

**Figure 14.1** Symbolic rejection of a hated power-political deal. At the 'Baltic Chain' demonstration on 23 August 1989, placards symbolizing the Molotov–Ribbentrop Pact, concluded exactly fifty years earlier, are burned in Tallinn capital of Estonia. The Pact had been the basis of two secret protocols of August and September 1939 specifying a carve-up whereby certain territories, including the three Baltic republics, would be forcibly consigned to the Soviet Union's sphere of influence, while others, including most of Poland, would fall under German control.

turned out to be impossible'.[3] With the defeat of the Forest Brotherhoods, opposition to Soviet rule assumed more diffuse forms ranging from participation in underground groups to refusal to conform to official norms. Sporadic acts of protest continued. But the vast majority of Balts accommodated themselves to the Soviet system—in the words of one Estonian writer, believing it to be 'unpleasant' but 'inevitable and eternal'.[4] A significant number joined local communist parties, forming a nativized party elite that would play a critical role in the independence movements of the 1980s. At the same time, a vibrant nationalist subculture persisted, helping to explain why Baltic nationalisms emerged so quickly once a political opening materialized.

The first manifestations of Baltic nationalisms under glasnost assumed the form of environmental protest. Outrage over a series of industrial projects was

    [3] Heinrihs Strods, 'The Nonviolent Resistance Movement in Latvia (1944–1958)', in Anušauskas (ed.), *The Anti-Soviet Resistance in the Baltic States*, 162.

    [4] Jaan Kaplinski et al., 'Resistance, Scepticism and Homo Sovieticus', in Jean-Jacques Subrenat (ed.), *Estonia: Identity and Independence* (New York: Rodopi, 2004), 158, 161.

fuelled not only by their ecological impact, but also by the large numbers of Russians expected to flock to the region to build and operate them. This was a sensitive issue in Estonia and Latvia, where the proportion of the native population had declined from 94 per cent and 83 per cent respectively in 1945 to 62 per cent and 53 per cent by 1985 as a result of Russian in-migration to the region.[5] In early 1987 Gorbachev's release of political prisoners infused a network of dissident nationalists into the region. However, in none of the Baltic republics did dissident groups lead the eventual drives to independence. Rather, that role was played by the Baltic popular fronts, whose activist base consisted primarily of intellectuals working within official institutions.

In spring 1988 the Baltic intelligentsia, through the official cultural unions that had once suffocated it, began to press for a revision of official history. Their championing of historical truth, attacks on local bureaucrats, and criticism of excessive centralization in Moscow paralleled closely Gorbachev's assaults on bureaucracy at the time. External events played a key role in triggering Baltic mobilizations. The Nineteenth Conference of the Communist Party of the Soviet Union, in June 1988, at which Gorbachev unveiled a plan for major political reforms, constituted a watershed in the diffusion of contention throughout the Soviet Union, and brought into being 'popular fronts' in support of perestroika across the country. In the Baltic, popular fronts developed at an astounding pace, fed by workplace, family, and friendship networks. Within six weeks of its founding the Estonian Popular Front already claimed a membership of over 40,000 in 800 localities.[6] Communists were disproportionately represented in the leaderships of these movements. Almost half of the 106 members of the leadership of the Estonian Popular Front were party members, while 30 per cent of the participants in the founding congress of the Latvian Popular Front were communists—far beyond the 5–6 per cent of the Latvian population consisting of party members.[7]

This early stage of Baltic independence movements was characterized more by consensus than conflict due to significant support within the halls of government and direct intervention from Moscow on their behalf. Efforts by the Estonian party leadership to stack the Estonian delegation to the Nineteenth Party Conference evoked an outpouring of criticism in the official media, just at the moment when the annual Tallinn song festival, attended by 60,000 people, convened. The festival turned into an orgy of nationalist expression—the beginning of the so-called 'Singing Revolution'. The local party leadership panicked, requesting military intervention from Moscow to prevent a large rally planned by the Popular Front. Instead, Moscow removed the leader of the Estonian communist party and appointed a successor sympathetic to the front—reflecting Gorbachev's belief at the time that the popular fronts were allies in his reformist efforts. On 17 June a crowd of up to 150,000 celebrated the leadership change and pressed further

---

[5] Romuald J. Misiunas and Rein Taagepera, *The Baltic States: Years of Dependence, 1940–1990* (Berkeley, Calif.: University of California Press, 1993), 112, 282.

[6] *Vesti iz SSSR* (Munich, Germany), no. 12, 20 June 1988, 41.

[7] *Sovetskaia Estoniia*, 14 Jan. 1989, 3; *Sovetskaia Latviia*, 26 Jan. 1989, 1.

demands for Estonian 'sovereignty'. When the Estonian communist party endorsed establishment of Estonian as the state language in September 1988, 300,000 people (one out of every three Estonians of all ages) gathered to express their support. With this, writes Rein Taagepera, 'the Singing Revolution reached its grand finale'.[8] Obviously, independence had not yet been achieved, nor had the Popular Front formally come to power. Nevertheless, with the informal capture of the state by a pro-nationalist coalition, the Estonian independence movement became a movement for deepening sovereignty and for defence of the Estonian state. Already in November 1988 the Supreme Soviet of Estonia, under the influence of the front, passed a constitutional amendment affirming Estonian sovereignty and the power of the republic to veto any decision by Moscow that affected its territory—the opening act of what would become known as the 'parade of sovereignties'. Moscow disputed the validity of the declaration, setting off a 'war of the laws' over which government—the republic or the union— exercised ultimate authority. Analogous declarations of sovereignty were adopted by Lithuania in May 1989 and Latvia in July 1989.

In Lithuania the popular front, Sajūdis, organized its first major rally in July 1988. With banners supporting perestroika and pictures of Gorbachev floating in the crowd, the demonstration called for legalization of the interwar Lithuanian flag, resignation of the republican party leadership, and 'sovereignty' for Lithuania. Fearing the movement would escape party control, the Lithuanian party leaders sent 'panicky characterizations' of Sajūdis back to Moscow and called for intervention.[9] In response, Gorbachev dispatched his deputy Aleksandr Yakovlev to investigate. Yakovlev shocked his local hosts by publicly supporting the popular fronts against local party bureaucrats, making it impossible to harass, censor, or ignore the movement any longer. On 23 August, the forty-ninth anniversary of the Molotov–Ribbentrop Pact, Sajūdis organized a wave of demonstrations across Lithuania, attracting up to 200,000 people in Vilnius alone. A broad array of speakers, including some communist officials, denounced the secret protocol of the Molotov–Ribbentrop Pact that had consigned Lithuania to Soviet control and called for its publication and renunciation by the Soviet government. In September local party leaders made an attempt to re-establish control by targeting unauthorized rallies. The move backfired, leading Moscow to remove the local party leader and appoint Algirdas Brazauskas, a supporter of Sajūdis, in his place.

The Latvian Popular Front emerged later than its Estonian and Lithuanian counterparts. Only after Yakovlev's visit to the Baltic in August, the massive protests in Estonia and Lithuania, and the selection of a new party leadership sympathetic to the front, did it begin to operate on a significant scale. At its founding congress in October the front organized a mass demonstration of 200,000 people in which Anatoly Gorbunovs, the newly elected chair of the Latvian Supreme Soviet, lent official support to the movement. The front echoed

---

[8] Rein Taagepera, *Estonia: Return to Independence* (Boulder, Colo.: Westview, 1993), 133–6, 142.

[9] Alfred Erich Senn, *Lithuania Awakening* (Berkeley, Calif.: University of California Press, 1990), 86–92 & 102.

themes that had found expression elsewhere in the Baltic: sovereignty within a confederal Soviet Union, the assertion of Latvian cultural rights, and the removal of bureaucratic domination and privilege.

Beginning in early 1989 politics in the Baltic polarized, as the popular fronts openly embraced the independence cause and minority groups (Russian-speakers in Latvia and Estonia and Poles and Russian-speakers in Lithuania) engaged in counter-mobilizations against newly enacted language laws and to halt the fronts' growing influence. Already in February 1989 Sąjūdis declared independence to be its ultimate goal, and similar declarations were made by the Estonian Popular Front in April and the Latvian Popular Front in May. As Baltic fronts took up the independence cause, the secret protocols of the Molotov–Ribbentrop Pact naturally came to the fore. Moscow denied their very existence, while Baltic fronts sought to obtain recognition of their illegality. This conflict coincided with a broader destabilization of the Soviet state, as nationalist mobilization spread to the Caucasus, Ukraine, and Moldova, and significant violence broke out in Karabakh, Abkhazia, and Central Asia. Within Russia itself a shift in attitudes toward the centre was taking shape, as hundreds of thousands of coal miners, incensed over

©Andrey Solovyov/AFP/Getty Images

**Figure 14.2** Transnational solidarity. Inhabitants of Tallinn hold hands as part of the 'Baltic Chain', held on 23 August 1989—the fiftieth anniversary of the hated Molotov–Ribbentrop Pact. This demonstration was approved by the ruling communist parties of Estonia, Latvia, and Lithuania, all of which were then still formally republics inside the Soviet Union. Involving about two million participants along a 520-kilometre path, it symbolized solidarity both within and between the three republics as they sought independence from the Soviet Union.

shortages of soap and other necessities, went on strike. In this situation of ferment and instability, the Baltic fronts engaged in one of the most spectacular civil disobedience campaigns ever mounted. On 23 August 1989, the fiftieth anniversary of the signing of the Molotov–Ribbentrop Pact, a 600-kilometre, two-million-strong human chain stretching from Tallinn to Vilnius—known as the Baltic Way—brought the issue of the involuntary incorporation of the Baltic states into Soviet and international public attention. In the wake of this campaign at least one of Gorbachev's advisers had privately concluded that the departure of the Baltic republics had become 'inevitable'.[10] This opinion became increasingly widespread within the Russian intelligentsia over the ensuing months.

By the autumn of 1989 the nationalist revolts against the Soviet state flowed over Soviet borders to eastern Europe; in turn, the end of communism in eastern Europe further radicalized and diffused the nationalist revolts inside the USSR. The effects were compounded by the elections of 1990 in the republics forming the Soviet Union: these institutionalized the power of popular fronts in each of the Baltic republics, as well as bringing opposition movements to power in Russia, Moldova, Armenia, Georgia, and portions of Ukraine. In March 1990 the Lithuanian Supreme Soviet, now under direct Sajūdis control, formally declared independence, only to be forced to issue a temporary moratorium several months later after a campaign of intimidation by Moscow. Soon, however, the governments of Estonia, Latvia, Moldova, Georgia, and Armenia declared their intentions eventually to secede. The final stages of the Baltic struggle for independence thus took on the character of struggle between governments, with Moscow increasingly under the control of hardliners intent on using force to preserve the union and the mutinous republics mobilizing their supporters in defence of their sovereignty.

In this phase repression by the Soviet government intensified in an effort to overthrow the elected Baltic governments and replace them with pliant clients. In Vilnius in January 1991 the Soviet government precipitated a false crisis by organizing demonstrations by local Poles and Russians against price increases and sending in troops on the pretext that the republic had slipped into chaos. Large crowds of unarmed Lithuanians mounted a makeshift defence, and 14 people were killed (some crushed by tanks) and 165 wounded when KGB troops stormed the republic's broadcasting tower on 13 January. What was dubbed 'Bloody Sunday' in Vilnius evinced a huge backlash against the Soviet government throughout the Soviet Union and played an important part in the events leading to the final collapse. As General Yevgenii Shaposhnikov, an important actor in the failure of the August 1991 coup that sought to overthrow Gorbachev, later recalled, 'After Vilnius and the television scenes that I saw of our soldiers beating civilians with the butts of their automatic rifles, I understood that a decisive and final end had to be put to this.'[11] Although the decision by the State Emergency Committee to overthrow Gorbachev was profoundly conditioned by

[10] A. S. Cherniaev, *Shest' let s Gorbachevym* (Moscow: Kultura, 1993), 296.
[11] Yevgenii Shaposhnikov, *Vybor* (Moscow: Pik, 1995), 19.

**Figure 14.3** Lithuanian defences against Soviet military intervention. The parliament building in Vilnius, the Lithuanian capital, is protected by concrete and barbed-wire barricades, 18 January 1991. The barricades had been erected in response to interventions by Soviet paratroopers: on 13 January, 'Bloody Sunday', fourteen Lithuanians seeking to stop Soviet forces from entering the TV station and tower were killed, and several hundred injured. After the Soviet occupation of the TV station it was feared that parliament would be next, and many demonstrators had gone there. The barricades stayed in place for two years.

Moscow's inability to contain the nationalist revolts facing it, the Baltic republics were a minor theatre in the drama. The main events unfolded on the streets of Moscow in August 1991. However, Estonia and Latvia utilized the confusion surrounding the Moscow coup to declare independence, and Lithuania renewed its earlier declaration. The Russian Federation recognized Baltic independence within days of the failure of the coup, with a number of European states following. The final step occurred on 6 September when Gorbachev, temporarily restored to diminished power in Moscow, recognized what he could never bring himself to accept earlier: Baltic independence.


## NATIONALISM AND CIVIL RESISTANCE

Why was civil resistance so successful in the Baltic in the late 1980s and early 1990s? And how did ethnic nationalisms that once had been strongly associated with protracted violence come to be so closely associated with civil resistance?

One set of common explanations is value-based, revolving around the role of deeply held beliefs in underpinning non-violence. A strong commitment to democratic values has at times been cited as an explanation for why Baltic independence struggles remained peaceful, for democratic dedication to individual rights and the rule of law promotes antipathy to violence. But it is difficult to sort out whether a value-commitment to democracy sustained non-violent resistance in the Baltic, or whether the experience of non-violent resistance sustained commitment to democracy. There is little evidence that Balts learned these tactics through exposure to non-violent philosophies; access to Gene Sharp's classic work on non-violence, for instance, did not occur until late 1990.[12] Nor was the use of violence completely ruled out by Baltic movements. The Sąjūdis government openly disobeyed directives from the Soviet government that the population should be disarmed, and while Sąjūdis strove to avoid violent confrontation with Moscow, it was prepared to engage in defensive violence as a last resort.[13] More important in conditioning the choice of non-violence were three factors: (1) Soviet television coverage of European peace movements, which brought non-violent tactics to the attention of the Soviet public; (2) the memory of earlier failure of violent resistance to the Soviet state; and (3) the widespread belief that violence against the Soviet state would be a losing strategy.

Values thus present a mixed picture. One cannot dismiss their role entirely. But it is clear that they are an insufficient explanation for why Baltic non-violence prevailed. Accordingly, I focus instead on the strategic context of mobilization. In particular, six conditions helped to render civil resistance attractive for Baltic movements: (1) appropriate goals of liberation; (2) a political opening; (3) an extreme imbalance in the means of coercion; (4) strong and broadly shared identities; (5) weak counter-movements; and (6) significant support from external allies.

## Appropriate goals

There is a relationship between the objects of a movement and relevant political tactics. Non-violent resistance involves the deployment of large numbers in peaceful acts of protest for inducing social and political change. Its power derives not merely from the disruption typical of all protest, but more importantly from the moral pressure that large numbers exert, fostering defections and ultimately undermining the coherence of ruling coalitions. Historically, of the many purposes to which non-violent resistance has been applied, three stand out: racial integration, decolonization, and democratization. What unites these spheres is a common grievance—domination, defined by Pettit as 'having to live at the mercy

---

[12] Grazina Miniotaite, *Nonviolent Resistance in Lithuania: A Story of Peaceful Liberation* (Boston: Albert Einstein Institution, 2002), 58.

[13] Vytautas Landsbergis, *Lithuania: Independent Again* (Seattle: University of Washington Press, 2000), 244–8.

of another, having to live in a manner that leaves you vulnerable to some ill that the other is in a position arbitrarily to impose'.[14]

The relevance of non-violent resistance to the Soviet situation had very much to do with 'living at the mercy of another'. It was not only a matter of the dictatorial character of the Soviet party-state. Equally important was the imperial dimension of Soviet rule—the overwhelming sense of foreign domination attached to it. The Baltic fronts viewed themselves as decolonization movements, not simply democratization movements, and used the language of decolonization to represent their struggle. The grievance of empire transcended the Baltic and was a rallying cry for east Europeans attacking Soviet control over their states and for non-Russian nationalists seeking autonomy and independence. Among Soviet nationalities the Balts were unique in that, aside from the Tyvans, they were the only groups to have experienced prolonged independence in the twentieth century—an experience that better positioned them to draw upon international norms against conquest and colonization.[15] Indeed, in 1989 the fronts issued appeals directly to the United Nations in an attempt to rally international support for their cause. The goal of transcending domination made non-violent resistance a relevant tactic. However, it did not necessarily make it an attractive tactic. For that, other conditions were necessary.

## Political opening

In the Baltic (as was true throughout the Soviet Union and Soviet bloc) glasnost was a necessary precondition for wide-scale civil resistance. This was so not only because of the political space that glasnost provided for those seeking to mount challenges. In a regime in which the fiction of public support had long been a central narrative of reigning ideology, glasnost created a new set of vulnerabilities for the Soviet state. Large-scale protest punctured the regime's central legitimating myths, such as the claims that it had 'solved' the nationalities problem or represented the interests of 'toilers'. Even if located thousands of miles from Moscow, protest violated long-standing norms of behaviour in Soviet politics, exposed the weakness of the Soviet state, and created tensions within governing circles. In a context of press liberalization, its effects were not spatially confined, but followed the lines of information flows within and across republics. Thus, civil resistance exploited two fundamental weaknesses of a semi-liberalized Soviet state: it attacked the gap between the regime's pretence that it represented genuine public will and the reality of widespread antipathy to Soviet rule; and it exploited the new information milieu in which criticism of a once secretive and infallible regime had become normalized.

---

[14] Philip Pettit, *Republicanism: A Theory of Freedom and Government* (Oxford: Clarendon Press, 1997), 4–5.

[15] Tyva, which had been nominally independent of Russia since 1921, was incorporated into the Russian Federation in 1944 as an Autonomous Republic.

Glasnost also functioned as a major constraint on repression by the Soviet regime. Fear of the political fallout from any significant use of violence came to be referred to as the 'Tbilisi syndrome'—named after the April 1989 massacre in Georgia that generated the first broad-based cross-national opposition to Soviet deployment of massive force. In the wake of the Tbilisi events, the Soviet military came under enormous public criticism. As a result, many generals grew increasingly uncomfortable with the role of gendarme into which they were being cast. Certainly, one of the important factors holding back repression was Gorbachev's personal distaste for violence, although eventually even Gorbachev consented to a campaign of intimidation to bully the Balts into giving up their independence drives. Beginning in 1990 national monuments were mysteriously blown up across the Baltic, local minorities were mobilized into protests and occasional brawls and riots, and bombs were detonated in Soviet installations in an attempt to generate the appearance of chaos. Gorbachev was aware of these actions, though he publicly denied such knowledge, and certainly did nothing to stop them. After the Lithuanian declaration of independence in March 1990, Soviet tanks entered the city of Vilnius. As Vytautas Landsbergis notes: 'Clearly I recognized that they had the power to crush us at any time, but . . . we were convinced that the present government of the Soviet Union would neither wish nor dare to adopt Stalin's methods.'[16] Landsbergis was correct. As would occur again a year later in Vilnius, the Soviet government backed down, largely because Gorbachev feared the international and domestic reactions that any attempt to crush the Lithuanians forcefully would generate. Thus, liberalization established an atmosphere that undermined Soviet capabilities for repression, further making civil resistance an attractive tactic to pursue.

## Extreme coercive imbalance

If glasnost undermined Soviet capabilities to repress, an extreme imbalance in the means of coercion between government and opposition also pushed opposition activity away from violence. One of the surprising patterns of mobilization during the glasnost period was how little violence was directed against the Soviet state—not only in the Baltic, but elsewhere as well. Practically all movements that engaged in mobilization against the Soviet government did so non-violently, often in sharp contrast to the violent struggles that emerged against other targets of mobilization by these very same movements. Only 10 per cent of mass violent events in the USSR as a whole during glasnost were directed against Soviet authorities, as opposed to 49 per cent directed against republican and local government and 76 per cent against members of another ethnic group. This contrasts with the 42 per cent of all non-violent demonstrations that were directed against the government of the Soviet Union during this period, the 20 per cent directed against republican and local government, and the 7 per cent

---

[16] Landsbergis, *Lithuania: Independent Again*, 75, 178.

directed against members of another ethnic group. Georgian, Armenian, and Moldovan nationalist movements, while engaged in significant violence aimed at republican and local governments or against ethnic minorities in their republics, generally did not mobilize violently against the Soviet government.

The main reason for this was the severe imbalance in the means of coercion between the Soviet state and its opponents. It was widely understood that violent resistance against the Soviet state would be a losing strategy, provoking an overwhelming coercive response and providing the pretext for political crackdown. As one study notes, resistance in Latvia under glasnost assumed a non-violent character primarily because 'any violent means would have been doomed to fail in the hopelessly unequal conflict with the USSR'.[17] Even when volunteer armed forces were organized (as was true in Lithuania in January 1991), the expectation was that these forces would be wiped out in any battles that might have occurred and that armed resistance would have been a purely symbolic act. Indeed, in the one case of major armed insurrection against Soviet power during these years (the Azerbaijani revolt of late 1989 and early 1990), opposition was put down with brutal force, and this repression enjoyed overwhelming public support in the Soviet Union (in contrast to the public rejection of attempts to crush Lithuanian non-violent resistance in January 1991).

The awareness that violent struggle by nationalist movements against the Soviet state was doomed to failure and merely justified repression helped to contain those who might have entertained thoughts of achieving independence violently. Baltic movements consciously sought to avoid violent confrontation with the Soviet regime. The Lithuanian government, for instance, called on its supporters 'to behave peacefully at all times and not to resist the army whatever the provocation', and Lithuanian border guards loyal to the Sąjūdis government were instructed that their weapons were not to be used to defend themselves against any attacks, lest their return fire become an excuse for sending in Soviet troops.[18] By contrast, the Soviet government sought to provoke violent reaction from independence forces for precisely this purpose. Thus, at the same time as glasnost undermined Soviet capacity to repress non-violent resistance, the extreme coercive imbalance between the Soviet state and its opponents rendered violent resistance against Moscow impractical.

## Strong identities

Successful non-violent resistance requires intense and widely shared commitment to a collective cause. These movements rely on the ability to mobilize large numbers of people to generate moral pressure on rulers, disrupt the normal operations of an ongoing order, and foster defections from the ruling elite.

---

[17] Olgerts Eglitis, *Nonviolent Action in the Liberation of Latvia* (Cambridge, Mass.: Albert Einstein Institution, 1993), 41.

[18] Landsbergis, *Lithuania: Independent Again*, 175, 178, 244–6, 274–5.

Without a thickly shared sense of identity within target populations, movements are unlikely to mobilize large enough protests for achieving these objectives and are more vulnerable to repression. Among nationalist movements in the Soviet Union, the Baltic movements stood out for the speed and extent to which they mobilized populations. Senn referred to the initial Baltic mobilizations as a 'primordial explosion'[19] due to the speed with which massive waves of protest materialized. In Latvia the mood of the enormous crowds was 'euphoric': in the words of one participant, 'it was togetherness—a power one is suddenly aware of, Latvia's power'.[20] There were moments in the Baltic (such as the Baltic Way protests of August 1989) when the number of people participating in protest acts approximated the size of the able-bodied adult population of the Baltic nations, so that the crowd as simulated nation approached the actual dimensions of its claimed community.

All this could not have been done without a very strong sense of identity. Strong identities reduced the role of movement organization to that of facilitator rather than persuader, blurred the distinction between institutional and non-institutional politics, and minimized the degree of violence involved in the affirmation of once politically marginalized ranges of discourse. Statistical analysis of patterns of mobilization during the glasnost era shows that, controlling for other factors, identity processes (the degree to which a nationality was linguistically assimilated) were associated with the timing, frequency, and resonance of mobilization, so that more assimilated groups mobilized later, less often, with lower turnouts, and with less success. Moreover, the inability to mobilize large numbers of followers significantly increased the likelihood that a movement would be subjected to repression, and groups with higher rates of linguistic assimilation were less capable of generating backlash mobilization when faced with repression.[21] Thus, the strength and scope of identities make a significant difference in the outcomes of civil resistance because they are strongly related to the ability to mobilize large numbers, which in turn affects the ability of movements to pressure regimes and weather repression.

## Weak counter-movements

One of the key counterfactuals of Baltic independence was why minority counter-movements did not play the spoiler role that many in the Soviet government had hoped. They could have subverted independence by driving these struggles in a more violent direction, undermining political order, forcing Baltic governments to temper independence demands, and creating an atmosphere conducive to imposition of martial law. This is indeed what hardliners in Moscow wanted.

[19] Alfred Erich Senn, *Gorbachev's Failure in Lithuania* (New York: St Martin's Press, 1995), xv.

[20] Juris Dreifelds, 'Latvian National Rebirth', *Problems of Communism* (July–August 1989), 85.

[21] Mark R. Beissinger, *Nationalist Mobilization and the Collapse of the Soviet State* (Cambridge: Cambridge University Press, 2002).

Moscow's encouragement of minority counter-movements in Georgia and Moldova as a counterweight to secessionist mobilizations led to ethnic violence, with Moscow forced to intervene to contain these conflicts. The potential that civil resistance in the Baltic could have evolved into violent conflict, as in Georgia and Moldova, was real, and Baltic independence movements were well aware of this threat. At first minority counter-movements seemed well-positioned to fulfil such a role. In early 1989, after the passage of language laws, minority counter-movements organized a wave of protest that attracted fifty to sixty thousand participants in each of the Baltic republics. But in contrast to Georgia and Moldova, where minority mobilization intensified as the break-up of the USSR grew imminent, the mobilizational capacity of minority counter-movements in the Baltic deteriorated over 1990 and 1991, with smaller numbers participating in strikes and demonstrations. Logically, one might have expected the reverse—for minority resistance to grow more significant as the prospect of independence grew nearer.

The explanation is rooted in these counter-movements' weak base of support. Their followers were considerably older than the nationalist movements they opposed, and as Anatol Lieven noted, pensioners are simply 'not the stuff of which successful counter-revolutions are made'.[22] In Abkhazia and Ossetia local governments had been established within the ethno-federal system to represent embedded minorities, and in Moldova a similar federal unit had once existed in Transnistria in the interwar period. These units and their already existing boundaries became natural foci for minority separatism. By contrast, in the Baltic no such units existed, making it more difficult to mount separatist challenges. Minority communities in the Baltic were strongly divided over independence. The higher standard of living in the Baltic in comparison with Moscow encouraged attachment to the region, even among those who opposed independence. A significant number of Russian-speakers in Latvia and Estonia supported the independence cause. An April 1990 poll indicated that 58 per cent of non-Estonians in Estonia supported independence, and another 27 per cent said that they would not oppose it if it materialized. Eventually, in the March 1991 referenda on independence up to a third of non-Estonians in Estonia and half of non-Latvians in Latvia voted for independence.[23] In Lithuania the events of January 1991 and vocal support of Lithuania by neighbouring Poland pushed a large part of the Polish minority over to the independence cause. For all these reasons, minority separatism was considerably muted in the Baltic in comparison with Georgia and Moldova, defusing the potential for violence and undermining Soviet attempts to utilize minorities for re-imposing control over the region.

---

[22] Anatol Lieven, *The Baltic Revolution: Estonia, Latvia, Lithuania and the Path to Independence* (New Haven, Conn.: Yale University Press, 1993), 197.

[23] Taagepera, *Estonia: Return to Independence*, 141 & 194; Kristian Gerner and Stefan Hedlund, *The Baltic States and the End of the Soviet Empire* (London: Routledge, 1993), 110; Rasma Karklins, *Ethnopolitics and Transition to Democracy: The Collapse of the USSR and Latvia* (Washington, DC: Woodrow Wilson Center Press, 1994), 101.

## External allies

One of the important conditions of Baltic success lay in the presence of external allies. The Baltic émigré communities of Europe and North America, though not directly involved in the popular fronts, had long provided resources and informational networks critical to nationalist opposition in the region. America's lack of recognition of Baltic incorporation into the Soviet Union also played a symbolic role. Nevertheless, it would be wrong to place too much emphasis on the role of Western states and émigré networks. While the United States, as the Soviet Union's Cold War rival, championed human rights in the Soviet Union, it took a decidedly cautious approach to Baltic independence. In December 1990 the prime minister of Lithuania, Kazimira Prunskienė, was forced to enter the White House through a back door for fear of sending the wrong signal to Moscow about American desires to see the Soviet Union dissolve. European officials continually cautioned Baltic independence leaders to temper their demands.

Rather, the most important allies for the Balts lay within the Soviet state and Soviet bloc. The Baltic popular fronts would not have developed without intervention on their behalf by Gorbachev, who refrained from repressing them at their initial stage and even facilitated their rise to influence. East Europe also played an important role, as the revolutions of 1989 radicalized nationalist movements throughout the Soviet Union, undermined further the legitimacy of the Soviet state, and provided moral and some logistical support for the Baltic movements. Especially significant was the cooperation across the Baltic republics themselves. Each of the popular fronts saw their situations as linked and coordinated extensively with one another. This began early on and was subsequently manifested in the spectacular Baltic Way demonstration and in a common struggle against Soviet efforts to reimpose authority over the region. Baltic fronts also consciously sought to extend their influence across the Soviet Union, both out of philosophical and strategic considerations, forging a cross-national alliance with nationalist movements throughout the Soviet Union. The Balts pioneered the sovereignty frame that eventually gutted the Soviet state in 1990 and 1991, as group after group (and even some cities and islands) declared their sovereignty vis-à-vis the Soviet government. But perhaps the most important external allies for the Baltic fronts were Russian liberals in Moscow. When Boris Yeltsin became an advocate of Russian sovereignty vis-à-vis the Soviet government, he was borrowing from the Baltic repertoire. Indeed, as politburo member Vadim Medvedev had warned the Soviet leadership, 'To make Russia sovereign is the golden daydream of the Balts,'[24] for Russian sovereignty justified Baltic independence and undermined the existence of the central Soviet government. The issue of Baltic independence could not have been resolved in the Baltic alone: ultimately it could be settled only in Moscow. Indeed, for many movements the locus of protest and the locus for resolving issues diverge, so that transnational

---

[24] *Soiuz mozhno bylo sokhranit'* (Moscow: Aprel'-85, 1995), 64.

and transcultural influences are critical in determining outcomes. Had Baltic popular fronts engaged in their struggles against the Soviet state alone, in isolation from one another and from other movements, and had Russia not demanded sovereignty in imitation of the Balts, it is doubtful that the Soviet Union would have collapsed or that the Balts would have gained independence.

## CONCLUSION

The Baltic cases suggest a broader logic to civil resistance. The factors underlying the success of Baltic civil resistance—goals of liberation, political opening, coercive imbalance, strong identities, weak counter-movements, and external allies— were fundamentally structural in nature; they imply a rationality to non-violent resistance that is conditioned by circumstances, not simply a values-based choice. As these cases also suggest, the ethnic passions often associated with violence can, under the proper circumstances, become effective resources for civil resistance. Indeed, successful civil resistance requires strong identities, for without them movements cannot generate the public support necessary for these tactics to work. The Baltic cases were success stories of civil resistance not only because civil resistance gained mass resonance. Their success lies as well in the important role played by civil resistance in precipitating and consolidating stable democratic outcomes. Civil resistance was critical in the development of Baltic democracy not only because of its efficiency in overcoming Soviet rule. It also allowed Baltic states to avoid the ethnic civil wars that enveloped some former Soviet republics; and it activated civil societies, providing a basis for the emergence of civic life so crucial to democratic development. Thus, civil resistance in the Baltic left lasting legacies that helped to define the quality of democratic life in its aftermath.

# 15

## The 1989 Demonstrations in Tiananmen Square and Beyond: Echoes of Gandhi

*Merle Goldman*

Between 15 April and 4 June 1989 there was a series of demonstrations in China, especially in Tiananmen Square in Beijing, demanding reforms to the system of communist party rule that had existed in China since 1949. This chapter will address the issue as to whether there are any similarities between the methods used by China's protesters during the Tiananmen demonstrations in 1989 and Gandhi's methods of civil disobedience and non-violent group resistance used against British rule in India to 1947. At first glance, an historian of China would say there are none and would point to the deeply rooted Confucian tradition of moral remonstrance as the major influence on the 1989 Tiananmen demonstrators. A Confucian scholar could and did criticize officials, and even the emperor, if they did not live up to Confucian ideals. It was also his duty to speak out against anyone, including the emperor, who did not live a moral life or engaged in oppressive practices. Yet the Confucian scholar would criticize as an individual or with a small number of like-minded people; unlike the 1989 Tiananmen demonstrators, Confucian scholars did not organize others in a mass movement of civil disobedience or passive resistance against the government.

Historically, mass movements in China usually occurred towards the end of a dynasty, when the regime had become repressive, corrupt, and unable to maintain the country's economic infrastructure. Such movements were generally peasant rebellions that ultimately led to the violent overthrow of the dynasty. Nevertheless, post-dynastic China in the early decades of the twentieth century does have instances of peaceful protests, even ones of organized dissent. The most well-known is the 4 May movement of 1919 protesting against Western imperialism and calling for 'democracy and science'. It began initially as a student movement and then spread throughout the urban population. Though there was some violence, generally it was a relatively peaceful movement. Thus, China is not without precedents of peaceful protests of mass disobedience in its immediate past.[1]

---

[1] Jeffrey Wasserstrom, 'Student Protests and Chinese Tradition', in Tony Saich (ed.), *The Chinese People's Movement: Perspectives on Spring 1989* (Armonk, NY: M. E. Sharpe, 1990), 3–24.

The goal of Gandhi and his non-violent followers in India, however, was very different than that of the participants in the 1989 Tiananmen demonstrations. Gandhi's movement was motivated mainly by nationalism which sought to rid India of British imperial rule. In contrast, the 1989 student demonstrators sought to reform China's authoritarian party-state. Moreover, even though Gandhi's movement may have hastened Britain's departure, the British ultimately left India due to the Japanese entry into the Second World War and England's post-war reconstruction and withdrawal from its colonial territories. The economic and social costs forced the British to grant independence to India. Still, Indian civil resistance helped to create the atmosphere in which Britain's democratic government and civil society, for both moral and economic reasons, felt that it must withdraw from India in the immediate post-Second World War period.

Despite the facts that China has no tradition of non-violence and civil disobedience in a philosophical sense and that the goals of the Indian demonstrators against British rule and those of the 1989 Tiananmen demonstrators differed, interviews with a number of the 1989 Tiananmen student leaders revealed that Gandhi's methods did have some influence on their strategies and thinking at the time.[2] Although they were not well-grounded in Indian history or even particularly knowledgeable about Gandhi, several of China's student leaders had read works by Gandhi and/or had seen the 1982 film on Gandhi's life. In addition, they also had some knowledge of the methods of civil disobedience used by Martin Luther King, a follower of Gandhi, and were particularly impressed with King's 'I have a dream' speech. They believed that King's methods of non-violence and civil disobedience had helped the blacks win civil rights in the United States. They were also impressed by King's interaction with American presidents in that effort, which offered them a model to follow when they requested a meeting with China's leaders during the Tiananmen demonstrations.

The 1989 student leaders were also attracted to Gandhi's non-violent methods. In attaching great importance to public communication in presenting their demands for political reforms, they believed that Gandhi's strategy of peaceful demonstration would attract public attention at home and abroad and would help spread their ideas and mobilize support. In reality, peaceful protest was their only viable option because China's one party state banned public expression of dissident ideas and the establishment of independent political organizations. Moreover, in the late 1980s the Internet had not yet been introduced into China. With official channels being closed to them, and violent resistance lacking any serious appeal, for those who wanted to express their views openly peaceful action was the only choice.[3]

The most important explanation for the Tiananmen demonstrators' use of non-violent methods and civil disobedience, however, was the fact that the Chinese communist party completely controlled the police and military power. Furthermore, because of the public reaction against the violence and turmoil of

---

[2] Interviews with Wang Dan, Wang Juntao, and Wang Youcai.

[3] Colman McCarthy, 'Nonviolence and the Process of Change in China', *Washington Post*, 28 May 1989, F4.

the Mao era, non-violent and peaceful methods were the most likely to win wide popular support. So, for the student organizers, these methods were the most rational strategies for achieving their goal of political reform. Furthermore, they had also been influenced by the peaceful methods and slogans used by the student demonstrators in South Korea in the 1980s to bring about a democratic government and the Philippine demonstrators against Ferdinand Marcos, which they had viewed on television. These movements ultimately succeeded in establishing democratic governments in those countries.[4]

In addition to these foreign examples, the peaceful approach of the 1989 Tiananmen demonstrators can also be attributed to a belief that China's post-Mao regime was capable of reform from within.[5] Throughout the 1980s, a number of China's public intellectuals had called for political reforms in articles in China's mainstream media and in speeches.[6] Perhaps unrealistically, the demonstrators believed that communist party leaders sought political reforms as well as economic reforms. Not only did China's constitution of 1982 stipulate freedom of speech, assembly, and association,[7] but the Chinese communist party in the 1980s was led by two reformist leaders. Hu Yaobang (1980–7) rehabilitated virtually all the people whom Mao had condemned during his rule and talked about political reforms.[8] After Hu Yaobang was purged in January 1987, he was succeeded by Zhao Ziyang (1987–9), who though he was primarily focused on economic reforms, in the late 1980s called for the separation of the party and state, a separation that would in effect dilute the party's power.[9] Zhao also talked about interest groups, pluralization, and the rule of law. Equally important in explaining the use of non-violent methods is the fact that the 1989 Tiananmen demonstrators believed that China's paramount leader, Deng Xiaoping, who had appointed Hu and Zhao, was in favour of political reforms. In a speech given on 18 August 1980, Deng explained that it was the political system that had given China's top leader so much power, which had led to Mao's political and economic disasters.[10] These views gave the leaders of the Tiananmen demonstrations confidence that the party leadership would be responsive to their demands.

There had also been a precedent for the 1989 peaceful Tiananmen demonstrations in 1986, at the University of Science and Technology in Hefei, Anhui.[11] There the astrophysicist Fang Lizhi had attempted to foster an atmosphere of academic freedom, leading to demonstrations at the university that called for

---

[4] John Pomfret, 'Tiananmen Square, Symbol and Battleground', Associated Press, 22 May 1989.
[5] 'A New Kind of Intellectual Activist', in Merle Goldman, *Sowing the Seeds of Democracy in China* (Cambridge, Mass.: Harvard University Press, 1994), 338–60.
[6] See e.g. Su Shaozhi and Wang Yizhou, 'Two Historic Tasks of Reform', *Renmin ribao*, 5 Mar. 1988, 5.
[7] Jonathan Spence, 'Introduction', in Han Minzhu, *Cries for Democracy* (Princeton: Princeton University Press, 1990), xv.
[8] Goldman, *Sowing the Seeds of Democracy*, 28.
[9] Zhao Ziyang, 'Speech at the Thirteenth Party Congress', *Beijing Review*, 9–15 Nov. 1987, xvii.
[10] 'On the Reform of the System of Party and State Leadership', *Selected Works of Deng Xiaoping*, vol. 3: *1975–82* (Beijing: Foreign Languages Press, 1984).
[11] Goldman, *Sowing the Seeds of Democracy*, 199–203.

more freedom and political rights, and quickly spread to other campuses and other provinces. The students' slogans such as 'Democratic rights are not bestowed as a favour' and 'only rights won by ourselves are dependable' were echoed on campuses throughout China.[12] Although the party quickly suppressed the protests and purged Fang Lizhi, these demands and peaceful methods used by the 1986 demonstrators provided a model for the 1989 demonstrators. In both instances, the demonstrations began spontaneously, but were quickly coordinated by student leaders of informal discussion groups on campuses. The organizers then contacted friends and colleagues at other universities.[13] Some of the 1986 slogans, such as 'give me liberty or give me death,' and the repeated singing of the 'Internationale' would also be used during the 1989 demonstrations.

Unlike the 1989 demonstrations, however, the 1986 demonstrations did not win wide support outside the universities. Urban residents and workers did not participate to any degree, and the students kept the non-students at arm's length because they knew that the Chinese leadership most feared the joining together of workers and intellectuals in political action, such as that which had occurred in eastern Europe, particularly Poland in the early 1980s, and had spelt the beginning of the end of the communist states in eastern Europe. The link-up in Poland between intellectuals and the labour movement, Solidarity, was a scenario that China's leaders wanted to avoid at all cost.[14] Also, in 1986 inflation was not as high nor was corruption as widespread as they were to become in 1989. Therefore, the 1986 demonstrations remained primarily a student movement without the participation of other classes.

In contrast to 1986, the 1989 Tiananmen demonstrators, like Gandhi and King, sought broad participation in their movement. In addition to calling for political reforms, they demanded a crackdown on corruption and control of China's accelerating inflation, which by the late 1980s was increasingly affecting major segments of China's urban population.[15] Also like Gandhi, they solicited support from international public opinion and civil society. As Gandhi sought help from those circles in Great Britain which were embarrassed by their country's repression of his non-violent movement, so did the leaders of the 1989 movement seek help from sympathizers in Western countries to bring pressure on the Chinese government. They were not totally unrealistic in their belief that China's leaders would respond to outside pressure. Unlike Mao, who did not care about his image in the outside world, China's post-Mao leadership wants China to be considered a respected member of the international community. As a result, it is not immune from outside pressure.[16]

Similarly, like Gandhi and his colleagues, the 1989 Tiananmen demonstrators engaged in a variety of street theatre to attract not only sympathetic Chinese

[12] Edward Gargan, 'Protests by Students Spread to Beijing', *New York Times*, 24 Dec. 1986, A3.

[13] Goldman, *Sowing the Seeds of Democracy*, 201.

[14] Daniel Southerland, 'Chinese Politburo See Set to Oust Moderate Party Chief', *Washington Post*, 25 May 1989, A1.

[15] Andrew Higgins, '1989: The Year of Revolution', *The Independent* (London), 27 Dec. 1989, 13–16.

[16] Merle Goldman, *From Comrade to Citizen: The Struggle for Political Rights in China* (Cambridge: Harvard University Press, 2005), 18.

political leaders, intellectuals, and urban bystanders, but also a wide domestic and international audience. They debated, held banners, sang songs, recited poems, and bellowed speeches through loudspeakers in order to capture people's attention. To mark the death of Hu Yaobang on 15 April 1989, which sparked the march to Tiananmen Square, the demonstrators carried a huge portrait of Hu into the square and hailed him with banners that called him 'a fighter for democracy'. At one point towards the latter stage of the demonstration, they made a replica of the American Statue of Liberty that they brought to the Square to capture the attention of the United States as well as China's own population. They also made great use of phones and copy and fax machines to spread the news of the demonstrations at home and abroad.

As Gandhi had used the foreign media, especially the media in democratic countries, to spread word of his movement and win widespread support, so did the student organizers. China's own media and newspapers did not cover the demonstration until a week or more after it began and then only in a distorted way. But due to China's opening to the outside world in the 1980s, students had access to journalists from the foreign media, particularly the BBC and Voice of America, as well as the Hong Kong media, that beamed information about the demonstrations back into China, thus helping the Tiananmen demonstrators garner support at home as well as abroad. In fact, as the foreign coverage spread news of the Tiananmen demonstrations back into China, it ignited similar demonstrations in virtually every large city in China.

## MULTI-CLASS DEMONSTRATIONS IN 1989

What also made the 1989 Tiananmen movement different from the earlier 1986 demonstrations and more like Gandhi's demonstrations in India was that it attracted a variety of different classes. Like the 4 May movement, it was a multi-class demonstration led by students. Initially, workers seeking to join the 1989 demonstrations were kept at arm's length because of the traditional Chinese scholars' elitist attitudes towards workers and because the leaders knew that China's leadership feared such an alliance. Yet, as the accelerating inflation and spreading corruption activated the urban population to join the student movement, workers, business people, and ordinary citizens by early May had formed their own groups and literally pushed themselves into the Tiananmen demonstrations. Consequently, the multi-class nature of the 1989 demonstrations resembled Gandhi's movement in India, although both movements had considerable dissension and differences of ideological direction within them. This new departure in China was not so much a result of emulation as a result of the inability of the student leaders to prevent the participation of the other classes.[17]

---

[17] Tony Saich, 'When Worlds Collide', in Saich (ed.), *The Chinese People's Movement*, 37–8.

©Baldev Kapoor/Sygma/Corbis

**Figure 15.1** Drawing on other traditions. On 13 May 1989 a student in Beijing's Tiananmen Square wears the US civil rights movement's classic slogan, 'We Shall Overcome'. He was among thousands of students staging demonstrations and a hunger strike against the Chinese government's hard-line policies opposing democratic reform and freedom of speech. This demonstration was two days before the widely publicized visit to Beijing of the reforming Soviet leader Mikhail Gorbachev.

Among the participants were members of China's growing entrepreneurial class. In addition to the growing inflation and corruption, they were also protesting the leadership's unwillingness to define property and legal rights. They ranged from the Flying Tigers motorcycle brigades of small business people who sped through Beijing delivering messages among various groups to street vendors who provided participants with free food and clothing. Before the 1989 demonstrations, members of China's private sector had not joined in demonstrations. Their participation in 1989 revealed that some members of China's new business class were beginning to work for political reforms and were using their personal and financial resources to support such reforms.

Though most of China's newly rich entrepreneurial class stayed clear of the demonstrations for fear of harming their connections with local officials, a private computer company, the Stone Group, was a major participant in the movement. It provided advanced communication networks, photocopiers, computers, and fax machines; and Wan Runnan, the head of the company, joined in the Tiananmen demonstrations. He was a member of the Red Guard generation who had successfully made the transition from revolutionary to entrepreneur. Whereas during the Cultural

Revolution, Wan Runnan had rebelled against the party in the name of Mao's utopia, in the post-Mao period he challenged the party in the name of democracy. He too wanted property rights, but he also believed that economic reforms could only be secured when they were accompanied by political reforms.

Another indication of the multi-class nature of the demonstrations was the support of the various workers' organizations. Zhu Houze, secretary of the official All-China Federation of Trade Unions, was one of the few reform officials to become directly involved in the 1989 demonstrations. By mid-May, as workers and other urban groups had literally pushed themselves into the demonstrations, both official and non-official workers' groups joined in. The unofficial Beijing Workers Autonomous Federation, established during the demonstrations with 20,000 members, was headed by a 27-year old railway worker with a high-school education. This federation was the first independent labour organization to be formed in the People's Republic. It posed a much greater threat to the party than the student demonstrators: the establishment of this independent labour organ-ization directly challenged the party as representative of the workers. By May 1989 autonomous workers' federations emerged in other major cities as well. Many of their members were unemployed workers or small shopkeepers. Despite the known fear of the party leadership of such a growing alliance of intellectuals and workers, it appeared to be forming during the demonstrations.

As the Tiananmen demonstrations continued to gather more and more parti-cipants, by late May, they attracted virtually all segments of the urban population in China's major cities. The reasons for the participation of these social groups were diverse: workers, entrepreneurs, and ordinary citizens were more concerned with economic issues; students and intellectuals were more concerned with political issues. But, for the most part, all of the demonstrations remained non-violent. A unifying call that linked the various participants together was the outcry against the accelerating inflation and the corruption of party officials and their children who had used the economic reforms to serve their own interests.

In both India under British colonial rule and post-Mao Zedong China under communist party rule, there were some political reforms. In India in the 1920s there was a greatly expanded legislature directly elected in Delhi and the prov-inces, and members of the Legislative Assemblies were gaining great clout as the voice of local interests and as intermediaries between local people and the state. In the late 1980s, China began elections for village heads and village councils that spread to most of China's villages. Nevertheless, in both countries, protesters found these channels inadequate for their purposes. Consequently, they turned to non-violent demonstrations, parades, posters, and slogans to express their views.

## HUNGER STRIKE

Another feature of the Tiananmen demonstrations that resonated with Gandhi's strategy was the use of a hunger strike. Although Gandhi engaged in fasting as an act of individual moral protest, China's students in 1989 carried out a hunger strike to capture the attention of the Chinese leadership as well as the world community. On 13 May, after failed efforts to conduct a meaningful dialogue with the political leadership, about 3,000 student demonstrators began a hunger strike in Tiananmen Square to focus public attention on their efforts. Their hunger strike captured the attention of the international media, which recorded the strike and beamed it back into China and to the rest of the world. Whether Gandhi's methods sparked the hunger strike is not clear, but one of his strategies did have a direct impact on the hunger strikers' behaviour. On the third day of the strike, their teachers recommended that they drink milk because they said that when Gandhi went on a hunger strike he drank milk. Actually, Gandhi drank only salted water, but several of the hunger strikers who drank milk said that it made it possible for them to survive for two weeks without any other food. On 18 May over a month into their protest, the leaders of the Tiananmen demonstration were finally able to arrange a brief meeting with Prime Minister Li Peng, but it ended in a hostile stand-off. Their dramatic gesture of self-sacrifice may have captured the attention of outside observers and gained the support of the Beijing populace, who rushed to the square to lend their support to the hunger strikers, but it did little to change the Chinese leadership's refusal to engage in meaningful dialogue or be responsive to the strikers' demands.

During the hunger strike, the party elders held meetings in which they concluded that the student demands for political reforms and greater freedom would lead not only to the party's dissolution, but also to the end of their own power. Deng Xiaoping was reported to have heard shouts of 'Down with Deng Xiaoping', which evoked the slogans shouted against him during the Cultural Revolution, when Mao had labelled him 'the number two capitalist-roader in the party'. He and the party elders became increasingly fearful that the demonstrations, in particular the participation of ordinary workers along with the students, would result in a repeat of the Cultural Revolution, when they were the targets of attack.[18] On 19 May, Zhao Ziyang went to the Square to try to convince the hunger strikers to return to their campuses, but to no avail.

The spread of demonstrations to China's major cities and the spectre of increasing cross-class support for the demonstrators led to the party elders' decision to impose martial law, which was done on 20 May. This action re-energized the multi-class alliance that was emerging during the hunger strike. Consequently, when tanks and military columns entered Beijing from their army barracks in the suburbs, a human wall of peaceful protesters attempted to stop them. These actions continued and expanded until the night of 3–4 June when, following a decision made by Deng Xiaoping, force was used against the remaining protestors in the square. As troops and tanks moved toward Tiananmen Square, many of Beijing's residents as well as students were killed trying to flee. Yet, even after the violent crackdown on 4 June, the protestors' rhetoric did not call for violence or for the overthrow of the party. The students and their urban

---

[18] Jonathan Kaufman, 'China in Focus: "Interesting Times"', *Boston Globe*, 28 May 1989, 77.

©Bettmann/Corbis

**Figure 15.2** Heroic gesture against violence. On 5 June 1989, after the People's Liberation Army crackdown on the demonstrators in Tiananmen Square on the night of 3–4 June, a lone demonstrator seeks to block the path of a tank convoy leaving the square. He was eventually pulled aside and taken away by secret police.

sympathizers still engaged in passive resistance. They remained firm in their commitment to the principle of non-violence and dialogue even as the troops used force to repress them violently.

## CONTINUANCE OF CIVIL DISOBEDIENCE: THE TIANANMEN MOTHERS' MOVEMENT[19]

After the 4 June crackdown, non-violent methods continued to be used in what has come to be called the 'Tiananmen Mothers' Movement'. Whether or not the mothers knew anything about Gandhi, they engaged in a strategy that resonated with Gandhi's methods of passive resistance. The Tiananmen mothers were the parents of those killed or wounded in the military crackdown on 4 June. Even more than the 1989 Tiananmen demonstrations, the mothers' efforts to change the designation of the 1989 demonstrations from what the party called a

---

[19] Goldman, *From Comrade to Citizen*, 68–78.

'counter-revolutionary' movement to a 'patriotic' movement resembled Gandhi's movement of civil disobedience. Their peaceful movement set a moral tone and expression of anguish over the deaths of their children that the party could not completely suppress. Family members of those killed became vocal critics of the party's violent actions. More importantly, calling for accountability, they organized and sustained a peaceful movement that after 4 June publicly continued to challenge the party's view of the 1989 demonstrations as 'counter-revolutionary'.

Their actions were unprecedented in the People's Republic. During the Mao era, when an individual or a group was singled out for attack in a political campaign, their families, friends, and colleagues did not defend them and some even denounced them for fear that if they did not, they and their families would also be persecuted. Yet, despite the threats of arrest and harassment, parents, wives, siblings, relatives, friends, and even individuals unacquainted with the mostly young people slain on 4 June organized peaceful efforts calling for an official reassessment of the 1989 events.

They staged demonstrations and made contact with the international community, the foreign media, and the UN Commission on Human Rights. The continuing ability of the Tiananmen mothers to challenge the party and defend their loved ones was due to the party's seeming reluctance to crack down too harshly on families grieving for their slain loved ones. In this respect, their civil disobedience seems to have caused shame among the Chinese leadership, perhaps similar to the embarrassment felt by segments of the British leadership over its actions in India. Like the participants in Gandhi's movement, they made contact with the foreign media and journalists. Consequently, their movement of civil disobedience in honouring the dead on the yearly anniversaries of 4 June was reported on and beamed all over the world, bringing further shame on China in the international community.

The Tiananmen mothers' movement was initiated and organized by Ding Zilin and her husband, Jiang Peikun, both professors at People's University, whose only son, Jiang Jielian, a junior at the high school attached to the university, was killed on 3 June on his way to Tiananmen Square. Despite persistent government harassment, Ding launched a one-woman campaign to find out the names of those killed and wounded during the military crackdown and to determine who should be held responsible for what had happened. Even when she and her husband were put under close government surveillance, they continued their efforts. Gradually they were joined in this endeavour by other families that had also lost their loved ones on 4 June. Ding Zilin depicted this movement as 'a group of common citizens brought together by a shared fate and suffering'.[20] Despite escalating threats of repression, members of Ding's group did not relent in their efforts. Over time, some of them also became public advocates of the political causes of the 1989 demonstrators.

---

[20] Ding Zilin, 'Hardship Years', trans. Sophie Bearch, *China Rights Forum* (Summer/Fall 2000), 27. Available at www.hrichina.org.

Initially, Ding gathered various victims' families to talk about their pain and grief, but in April 1991 prior to the Qingming Festival that honours the dead, she decided to tell the story of her son's death to the outside world. Together with another mother, she gave an interview to a Hong Kong newspaper.[21] In May 1991, in an interview with the American television network ABC, she not only condemned the military crackdown on 4 June, but she also denounced Premier Li Peng's explanation that the crackdown was necessary in order to maintain order.[22] She demanded that the government reveal the number of people killed in the crackdown and provide a list of their names. She also called on people of conscience not to forget those who had lost their lives. The Tiananmen mothers' movement even inspired those, who had not lost loved ones, to join them.

In the manner of Gandhi and the Tiananmen demonstrators, the mothers carried out public peaceful activities that sought to focus public attention on their cause and solicit support. Despite the party's efforts to suppress their activities, a few dozen parents of those killed meet together annually on the anniversary of 4 June. On the seventh anniversary in 1996, thirty-one relatives jointly submitted a petition to the Standing Committee of the National People's Congress, China's rubber-stamp congress, demanding the formation of a special committee to conduct an independent investigation into the events of 4 June.[23] On 28 September 1998, as China was about to sign the UN Covenant on Civil and Political Rights in October, Jiang Peikun drafted and circulated two declarations which went beyond demanding an accounting of what had happened on 4 June and called for civil and economic rights.[24] These declarations differed from earlier efforts in that instead of merely appealing to the authorities for redress as they had in the past, they called on all Chinese citizens to take the initiative to realize their fundamental rights.

Like Gandhi and his followers, despite continual rebuffs, warnings, surveillance, intimidation, and brief detentions, the Tiananmen mothers' movement continued their campaign of civil disobedience. They did so into the twenty-first century, persisting in commemorating the events of 4 June among themselves on the yearly anniversary of that event. Ding Zilin's apartment is turned into a mourning hall and candles are lit in memory of the deceased. They continue to speak out publicly, petition the government, and call for a reassessment of the 1989 Tiananmen events. Their civil disobedience is an unofficial grassroots movement that takes place without party permission. The party has not yet suppressed it, perhaps because of its moral nature and the fear of reviving images of the military crackdown on 4 June.

[21] Goldman, *From Comrade to Citizen*, 71.

[22] Ibid.

[23] Gilles Campion, 'Dissidents, Families of Tiananmen Dead Petition Parliament', Agence France-Presse, 29 May 1996.

[24] 'Call for Civil Rights as China Prepares to Sign International Covenant', Agence France-Presse, 29 Sept. 1998.

## GANDHI'S CONTINUING INFLUENCE IN CHINA

Despite the party's repression of the 1989 Tiananmen demonstrators, the methods of civil disobedience and peaceful resistance still exert influence in China. While the Tiananmen mothers' movement did not attribute their methods directly to Gandhi, participants in other acts of civil disobedience in the post 1989 Tiananmen period have cited Gandhi's influence. An example occurred in the village of Taishi in Guangdong in 2005, when the villagers sought redress against corrupt officials who did not compensate them adequately for their land confiscated for modern development. The Taishi villagers asked a rights defender lawyer, Guo Feixiong, to help them get rid of their corrupt village head and open the village's financial records to public scrutiny. Guo arranged for the villagers to watch the movie of Gandhi's life to give them new ideas about how to fight for their rights. As exemplified in Taishi village, the film helped spread the idea of civil disobedience beyond an intellectual elite. Yet, despite their use of Gandhi's methods—petitions and peaceful protests—the local officials used force against them. Another example of Gandhi's influence can be seen in the experience of an ordinary farmer, Lu Banglie, in Baoyuesi village in Hubei. He too had seen the film about Gandhi and advocated Gandhi's methods of dialogue, learning, and petitions to campaign against the land seizures, corruption, and rising health care costs in the countryside. In 2005, he campaigned against the village head, whom he charged with corruption, and he was popularly elected head of Baoyesi village.

Yet, in Taishi and Baoyesi villages as well as in the 1989 Tiananmen demonstrations, non-violent movements have yet to succeed in China. No matter how well-trained or peaceful the participants, the leaders of China's party-state have been unresponsive to acts of civil disobedience. Yet, peaceful resistance was and is the only pragmatic strategy available to the Tiananmen protesters, the Taishi villagers, and others seeking redress against corrupt, repressive officials because of the overwhelming military and police forces arrayed against them. Moreover, without the use of peaceful resistance, the demonstrators would not be able to enlist the support of other people who fear violent methods and ensuing chaos. Defections from the military and police can be a decisive factor in a non-violent struggle, but there is little indication, either in 1989 or in the first decade of the twenty-first century, of such defections or any weakening of party control over the police and military.

Although Gandhi's methods may have had some influence on the leaders of the 1989 Chinese demonstrations, public intellectuals, and rights-defending lawyers as well as a small number of villagers and workers, for the general public, including those who participated in the 1989 movement, the Chinese tradition of moral remonstrance—which seeks to exert moral pressure on political leaders to live up to their enunciated ideals—played an even greater role. The participants did not seek to overthrow the existing government or the Chinese communist party. Like their Confucian predecessors, they saw themselves as loyal followers, appealing to the authorities to live up to their promises. Nevertheless, as seen in the subsequent Tiananmen mothers' movement and other protests in China after 1989, a number of protests have engaged in a range of peaceful strategies. Their methods may be based on Gandhi, Chinese tradition, cool calculation, or a combination of all these strategies. The underlying motive for such activities in the post-Mao period has been to seek redress and to promote political reforms. Whether these peaceful protestors and movements of civil resistance will some day succeed in China will depend not only on continuing pressure from below, but also, as occurred with the British government in India, on an acceptance in time by the political leadership of the legitimacy of the demands and the methods of civil disobedience.

Unlike India under British rule, China has its own government. Moreover, in the last two decades of the twentieth and first decade of the twenty-first century, this government has presided over an extraordinary period of economic growth. Its economy grew at 9–10 per cent for almost thirty years and the number of people living below the poverty line was reduced from 30–40 per cent to 5 per cent. At the same time, China's rising middle class has been co-opted into the party. Consequently, despite the violent crackdown on the 1989 Tiananmen demonstrators and the worldwide dismay that the crackdown occasioned, China's government has been able to maintain its legitimacy. As long as China continues its economic growth and maintains stability, it will be difficult for a movement of civil disobedience to have much impact on China's political system.

# 16

Civil Resistance and Civil Society: Lessons from the Collapse of the German Democratic Republic in 1989

*Charles S. Maier*

'The fall of the Wall' remains, more than any other perhaps, the world's most famous image of the triumph of civil resistance. Televised in colour as crowds of young people danced atop its once lethal ramparts, the breached Berlin Wall became the overwhelming image of the end of the Cold War, just as for twenty-eight years, photographed in black and white, it had served as the iconic artefact of communist repression. Few observers would have predicted that the German Democratic Republic (GDR)—perhaps the most quiescent and controlled of the Soviet 'satellites' in central and eastern Europe since the 1950s—would become a major arena for the peaceful demonstrations that would convulse the region from 1989 to 1991. Understanding the ideals and the calculations that led people into the streets is one of the historical challenges for assessing the mass mobilization. But it is not the only one. To understand its successes and limits, the historian has to pay equal attention to the overwhelming contextual influences that impinged from outside the small rump republic of 17 million people. Because of the presence of a larger and wealthier West German state next door, because, too, of the Soviet leaders' decision not to intervene in East German events, the story of civil resistance in the GDR is a special one and raises particular questions. Of all the countries casting off communist rule, only East Germany was in a position simply to merge into a larger established democracy.

This chapter is not about the process of unification: it concentrates on East Germany's internal transformation before November 1989. Still, the influence of West Germany over GDR developments had grown since the emergence of *Ostpolitik*, initiated by Chancellor Willy Brandt but sustained by his Social Democrat and Christian Democrat successors.[1] The success of East German civil resistance depended in part on the beckoning influence of the Federal Republic just next door, even if many GDR opposition leaders hoped to avoid having to accept the capitalist economic principles of the other Germany. It was

[1] For this two-decade policy see Timothy Garton Ash, *In Europe's Name: Germany and the Divided Continent* (New York: Random House, 1993).

also crucial that the GDR was only one of many societies caught up in the terminal crises of the state socialist world at the end of the 1980s. In effect, Chancellor Helmut Kohl and President Mikhail Gorbachev were major architects of East German developments alongside the civic movements of 1989. To evaluate the role of civil resistance in the GDR, the historian cannot write about East Germany alone.

On the other hand, many political scientists (and West Germans) later decided that the internal resistance played no significant role. This is also short-sighted: civil resistance from within forced the attention of the external actors. This chapter seeks to show the relationship. It begins with the most contingent developments, in the streets, and works outwards from there. It then considers the relationship of the mass mobilization of autumn 1989 to the longer-term pattern of dissidence, examines the crucial balance between the local and the contextual or systemic, and finally asks what continuing contribution civil resistance and the East German civic movements made to post-unification Germany.

## THE FRAGILITY OF NON-VIOLENCE

The evening of Monday 9 October 1989 in Leipzig now seems to belong to a closed and remote-feeling past epoch. In this rather compact city of 600,000, a crowd of perhaps 70,000 marched around the Leipzig Ring—the perimeter of squares and streets that circumscribes the historic centre—without provoking the beatings they were prepared to encounter. They were watched warily by armed soldiers and armed factory militia men who answered to the ruling Socialist Unity Party (SED). This was not the first but rather the third major demonstration since Monday 25 September, but it was by far the largest to date and fraught with a sense of climax and decision. A week earlier there had been clashes near the churches. A violent confrontation appeared a real possibility, ready to explode either through calculated strategy on the side of those who had the guns, the clubs, and the water cannon, or by a simple loss of control. Anxious to forestall violence that evening of 9 October, six eminent citizens, including conductor Kurt Masur, Pastor Peter Zimmermann and three party secretaries, issued a public appeal for 'dialogue'.[2]

---

[2] For these events see among the many assembled reports and interviews, Christof Wielepp, 'Montag abends in Leipzig', in Thomas Blanke and Rainer Erd (eds.), *DDR-Ein Staat Vergeht* (Frankfurt am Main: Fischer Taschenbuch Verlag, 1990). Wolf-Jürgen Grabner, Christian Heinze, and Detlev Pollack (eds.), *Leipzig im Oktober: Kirchen und alternative Gruppen im Umbruch der DDR—Analysen zur Wende* (Berlin: Wichern-Verlag, 1990). The 2 October clashes are described in Wielepp, 'Montag abends', 71–8, and from the police viewpoint in Armin Mitter and Stefan Wolle (eds.), '*Ich liebe euch doch alle!' Befehle und Lageberichte des MfS Januar-November 1989* (Berlin: BasisDruck, 1990), 190–1—a still invaluable collection of Stasi reports. See also Neues Forum Leipzig, *Jetzt oder Nie—Demokratie: Leipziger Herbst '89* (Leipzig: Forum Verlag, 1989; and Munich: C. Bertelsmann Verlag, 1990). When not otherwise cited I draw also on material documented in my own study: Charles

But suppose a rowdy or inebriated marcher had thrown a rock; a militia man was struck in the head and his nose began to bleed, his colleagues began to panic and a gun went off; demonstrators surged forward, there was more firing, a dozen demonstrators were dead or wounded, the rest fleeing, generals did their duty... No agent provocateur or fixed orders would have been required for a spark to fly. Erich Mielke, the minister for state security, had ordered the police reinforced with party reservists and loyal factory *Kampfgruppen* (workers' shock troops). Ambulances and blood plasma had been readied. After all, four months earlier in the face of demonstrations in a far vaster public square and a far bigger country—China—the ruling communist party had decided not to flinch and had violently dispersed student demonstrators.

©Bundesarchiv, Bild 183-1989-1023-022/ Friedrich Gahlbeck

**Figure 16.1** From peace prayers to revolutionary marches. After prayers for peace at St Nicholas's Church in Leipzig, demonstrators calling for peaceful change inside the German Democratic Republic would march around the city's inner ring road—here on 23 October 1989. The Leipzig marches were in many ways the icebreaker for peaceful protest in the rest of East Germany. Only after the fall of the Berlin Wall did the chants of 'Wir sind das Volk' (We are the people) turn to 'Wir sind ein Volk' (We are one nation).

S. Maier, *Dissolution: The Crisis of Communism and the End of East Germany* (Princeton: Princeton University Press, 1997), esp. ch. 3. See also Elizabeth Pond, *Beyond the Wall: Germany's Road to Unification* (Washington DC: Brookings Institution, 1993) and a reflective memoir by a then leading GDR historian: Hartmut Zwahr, *Ende einer Selbstzerstörung: Leipzig und die Revolution in der DDR* (Göttingen: Vandenhoeck & Ruprecht, 1993).

Two months later in Romania, protestors could not complete the overthrow of the Ceaușescu regime without bloodshed and lynching the leader and his wife.

Indeed, up to a few days before 9 October, there had been potentially serious clashes. Peace prayer meetings had already resumed in Leipzig on 4 September after the August vacation. There for the first time, demonstrators called out, '*Wir bleiben hier.*' (We are staying here'—that is, not going to the West, as were those trying to flee into the West German embassy in Prague and to Austria, suddenly accessible through Hungary after 11 September). On 4 October, police had dispersed 10,000 demonstrators in Dresden and on 7 October, 30,000, as they crowded around the railroad station where GDR citizens who had crowded into the West German embassy in Prague were being conveyed to the West. Between 4 and 9 October, demonstrators had spilled out of the large red-brick churches of East Berlin after peace prayers to be set upon by the police and carried away in paddy wagons.[3] It was because they were so aware of the explosive potential that those six prominent citizens—including the pastor of the church that served as a centre for prayers by demonstrators—called so emphatically for civic peace. Now the peace held, and for a few hours the demonstrators could march unchallenged through Leipzig's public squares. A month later, between 4 and 9 November (when the Wall was opened almost inadvertently), far larger demonstrations of several hundred thousand demonstrators crowded the central squares of East Berlin as spokesmen for the new protest organizations called for reforms and the SED surrendered one asset of its long power after another, including the closed frontier regime that had buttressed its rule for twenty-eight years.[4]

Of course, even had the Leipzig 'demo' turned violent, the final outcome might have been the same. The politburo—already divided between aging hard-liners and frustrated middle-aged functionaries, such as Günter Schabowski and the rather mediocre Egon Krenz, who believed the GDR should follow Mikhail Gorbachev's programme of glasnost and perestroika—might have sought to restore civil peace and made concessions that accelerated into regime change. On the other hand, the old guard—Erich Honecker, Erich Mielke, Günter Mittag, and others—might have prohibited peace prayers in the Lutheran churches of Leipzig and the capital city. After all, the student Left in West Berlin in 1967–8 had not been able to shatter a regime after demonstrations became violent. Just as unforeseen events can determine a wartime clash, so the civic battlefield becomes the site of contingency;

Nevertheless, even had the aging East German hard-liners decided to emulate the Chinese model and imposed a hard-line policy on wavering security forces, over the longer run, whether a few months or another decade, they probably

[3] On Berlin events, the feisty *taz* or *Berliner Tageszeitung* published a collection of its reportage on the autumn days as *taz: DDR Journal zur Novemberrevolution: August bis Dezember 1989*, 2nd enlarged edn. (Berlin, 1990); also *Schnauze: Gedächtnisprotokolle 7. und 8. Oktober 1989, Berlin, Leipzig, Dresden* (Berlin: Berliner Verlags-Anstalt Union, 1990). See also, Ulrike Breach et al. (eds.), *Oktober 1989: Wider den Schlaf der Vernunft* (Berlin [East]: Neues Leben and West Berlin: Elefanten Press, 1989).

[4] On the opening and later dismantling of the Wall, see Hans-Hermann Hertle, *Chronik des Mauerfalls: Die dramatischen Ereignisse um den 9. November 1989* (Berlin: Ch. Links-Verlag, 1996).

could not have enforced their own power: East Germany was not China. The communist regimes were renouncing power throughout central and eastern Europe. The Russian leadership was set on a reform course under Gorbachev. Following round-table talks the Poles had already installed the first non-communist prime minister in eastern Europe for more than forty years.[5] The Hungarians, to Honecker's consternation, were defecting from the Warsaw Pact phalanx outright. For years they had let workers run their factories on profit-making principles after hours and they were propping up their maverick party rule with infusions of West German aid. Whether in return for a special grant of West German aid or from an understanding that their future lay with the West, the Hungarian leadership had agreed in September to open the country's frontier with Austria to East Germans and thus breach the so-called 'iron curtain'. These changes transcended the dramatic confrontations on the Leipzig Ring, and would probably have precluded a counter-revolution. Most fundamental, Moscow had decided not to resort to repression by violence. They would not intervene as they had in Berlin in 1953, Budapest in 1956, and Prague in 1968. Still, if violence had exploded inadvertently, if urban fighting raged, could their troops have remained on the side-lines?

## THE LOCAL AND THE SYSTEMIC

Success of the civic movements, including the explosive growth of the im-promptu reform group who announced the formation of the New Forum in mid September, involved intensely local confrontations. The contestation of a bounded public space, initially in Leipzaig and then in Berlin, was critical. This sort of spatialized focus is characteristic of protest and upheaval. From the storming of the Bastille to the freedom marches of the American civil rights movement to the confrontations of 1968, to Moscow 1991 and beyond, both non-violent protest movements and many armed resistance struggles build on the dramaturgy that is possible on the local stage. Non-violent demonstrations entail great theatricality. Even under the conditions of modern politics, democratic or authoritarian—indeed especially under the conditions of modern politics, car-ried out through the media—the control of public space is crucial. This was the lesson of the Tet offensive, of Paris and Prague in 1968, of Mexico City and the American university confrontations in the same years, of Tehran in 1979, of

---

[5] For the Polish situation in the late 1980s, Bartlomiej Kaminski, *The Collapse of State Socialism: The Case of Poland* (Princeton: Princeton University Press, 1991); David Ost, *Solidarity and the Politics of anti-Politics: Opposition and Reform in Poland since 1968* (Philadelphia: Temple University Press, 1990); Grzegorz Ekiert, *The State against Society: Political Crises and their Aftermath in East Central Europe* (Princeton: Princeton University Press, 1996), 215–304; on the origins of Solidarity: Timothy Garton Ash, *The Polish Revolution: Solidarity* (Yale: Yale University Press, 2002); and Roman Laba, *The Roots of Solidarity: A Political Sociology of Poland's Working-Class Democratization* (Princeton: Princeton University Press, 1991).

Tiananmen Square, of Leipzig and Berlin, all in 1989. If state authorities cannot demonstrate that they can preclude others from claiming the same sensitive acreage, the regime they represent, whether in power or seeking power, will not prevail. Conversely, protesters will fail if they cannot maintain their insurrectionary presence.

Nonetheless, resistance cannot be analysed apart from the widest geographic conjuncture of political action. Resistance is local, but the local is necessarily embedded in a wide spatial context and the local and systemic reciprocally determine success or failure. Ultimately the global balance of economic, political, and military trends helped shaped what was unfolding in Leipzig and the GDR, but changes at the centre were crucial to the developments on the periphery—at least as long as the conditions of non-violence prevailed. Without the opening of the Hungarian border and the ability of East Germans to leave, first through Hungary, then from the embassies in Prague, those who wanted to fight for reform at home would not have raised their voices so clearly. *Wir bleiben hier* resounded in Leipzig from the first large demonstration on, but as a rallying cry it testified that as of September there was an alternative. To use Albert Hirschman's famous distinction, the 'exit' option enabled the 'voice' option, and soon thereafter the voice option vastly widened the exit option.[6]

Just as fundamentally, without the Soviets' recalculation of what their real interests were in central and eastern Europe and at home, non-violence would have been a non-starter. The necrosis of communism did not progress just in East Germany; it was a system-wide decay that followed from Soviet, Czech, and Polish dissenters' unwillingness to accept continued repression and from the evidently inferior economic performance of central planning as a means of coordinating modern economies. Still, such difficulties could have been met with increased doses of repression. Mark Kramer's contribution to this volume explains in detail why under Mikhail Gorbachev the Soviet leadership embarked on a decisively different course, unaware of how far it might lead but determined not to revert to traditionally applied repression. As he suggests, Gorbachev's commitment to glasnost ended the Russian willingness to intervene with force that had marked 1953 and 1968. At the same time, the successful transformations abroad limited his capacity to resist democratization at home.

From one perspective the civic movement emerged quickly; it nurtured itself as crowds grew with explosive vitality. The public protests did not rest on long preparation and power. Indeed its protagonists, such as the leaders of the New Forum in Berlin, had no clear idea of how far their reform movement might be carried. Public protest, we can say, pulled itself up by its own bootstraps. As in

---

[6] Albert O. Hirschman, *Exit, Voice, and Loyalty: Responses to Decline in Firms, Organizations, and States* (Cambridge, Mass.: Harvard University Press, 1970). For Hirschman's application of the typology to the GDR see his 'Exit, Voice, and the Fate of the German Democratic Republic', now in Hirschman, *A Propensity to Self-Subversion* (Cambridge, Mass.: Harvard University Press, 1993), 9–44. For a reapplication of Hirschman's categories see Stephen Pfaff, *Exit-Voice Dynamics and the Collapse of East Germany: The Crisis of Leninism and the Revolution of 1989* (Durham, NC: Duke University Press, 2006).

space, so in time: civil disobedience is both generated on the spot, and bears a relationship to the long-term weighing of imagined (or utopian) alternatives. We can always find ideological origins, but they alone cannot ensure success. At the same time, however, their staging and their success depended upon a far wider and longer sequence of events.

Compared to Poland, where dissident intellectuals and working-class activists had briefly compelled a certain pluralist accommodation on the part of the regime in 1981, there was no equivalent mass movement. Poland, after all, had been a leader both because it had intellectuals plugged into a new labour movement based in the Baltic shipyards and the new working class and because it continued to have pre-industrial collective forces—namely the uncollectivized peasantry and a strong Catholic Church. The regime had not eliminated, indeed had compromised with, these central residues of the pre-war republic. A Polish pope elected in 1978 provided renewed prestige and energy to the Polish Catholic Church. Czech Catholicism retained less of a strong political presence. The federation of East German Lutheran churches (the Evangelischer Kirchenbund) had negotiated a sphere of relative autonomy, but until the crisis had a relatively small base in a secular society.[7] In eastern Germany the old forces of Social Democratic unionism had been crushed after 1933; the communist cadres, strong in Saxony in the Weimar period, returned from exile or emerged from the camps and prisons to join the regime of the comrades who arrived from Moscow in 1945. Christian Democrats and centrist liberals who re-emerged under the Soviet occupation were pressed into political groups that had little choice but to become compliant coalition partners in the new 'people's democracies'.

## NUCLEI OF RESISTANCE

What sources of civil resistance might have survived the ensuing forty years of Stalinist and post-Stalinist administration? The tolerated but emasculated political parties outside the SED no longer offered any real opposition, although the West German parties would quickly rush into the open political landscape of autumn 1989. But in the early and mid-1980s, it was the Protestant ministry that provided natural leaders of opposition. Theological studies were one of the only university curricula that did not require SED membership. While a generation of Protestant ministers had reached a modus vivendi with the regime, by the early 1980s many churchmen, along with other dissidents, such as Robert Havemann, grew impatient with this temporizing. Pastor Rainer Eppelmann had organized a Berlin Appeal in February 1982, which called for removal of nuclear weapons from both Germanies, and sympathizers wore 'Swords into Ploughshares' badges

[7] For a comparison of national communist outcomes that goes beyond its focus on education see John Connelly, *Captive University: The Sovietization of East German, Czech and Polish Higher Education 1945–1956* (Chapel Hill, NC: University of North Carolina Press, 2000).

until the more compliant church authorities grew uneasy. GDR authorities initially tolerated such activities since they seemed to aim primarily at the NATO decision to respond to Soviet missile upgrading with new Cruise and Pershing rockets. Peace seminars emerged as did such groups as 'Doctors for Peace' and 'Women for Peace'. These ephemeral groups involved only tiny circles of activists. Still, the peace movement quickly came to channel a wider discontent with the ideological constraints imposed by the regime. Prayers for peace were necessarily prayers for an end to Cold War divisions, and perforce some rapprochement between systems, hence a dismantling of old communist structures. By 1987 a so-called 'Church from Below' challenged the official consistory structure of the Protestant Church.

Surveying the possible centres of resistance in May 1989, the Ministry for State Security listed about 160 hostile church groups and ten coordinating committees agitating on behalf of ecology or peace.[8] This was hardly a formidable number, especially a decade after the Helsinki Accord had encouraged human rights activism in Czechoslovakia, Poland, and Russia itself. Some of the leading clergy were already caught up in a tissue of conversations with the Stasi that had learned how to co-involve them in the providing of information. Some of these clergymen possessed a natural political vocation, but most would learn politics on the job later. What motivated them through the 1980s was an ethical earnestness that an American observer might find among his own Protestant ministers as well. These leaders no longer represented the generation of ministers influenced by Karl Barth or Bishop Dibelius who sought to preserve the apolitical autonomy of an independent Church amidst totalitarian pressures. Such older ministers tended to distrust political activity, including the peace movement. Rather, the new younger Church activists remembered Bonhoeffer more than Barth; they believed in an engagement for lofty social and political goals, including disarmament, and they radiated an aura of reformist sincerity that was familiar to those who had seen American pastors active in the civil rights struggle.[9]

This meant that the Protestant Church was divided; indeed one can cite the two great churches a few hundred metres apart in the Leipzig city centre as emblematic. The Nikolaikirche had a deacon friendly to an emerging peace movement, mobilized, as in West Germany, with the upgrading of nuclear arms in the early 1980s. The other church, St Thomas's, was led by a more apolitical or

---

[8] Stasi report of 1 June 1989 in Mitter and Wolle, '*Ich liebe euch doch alle*', 46–71. For dissidence in general, see Mary Fulbrook, *Anatomy of a Dictatorship: Inside the GDR 1949–1989* (Oxford: Oxford University Press, 1989).

[9] For the Churches see Detlev Pollack (ed.), *Die Legitimität der Freiheit: Politisch alternative Gruppen in der DDR unter dem Dach der Kirche* (Frankfurt am Main: Peter Lang, 1990); also Pollack, 'Religion und geselllschaftlicher Wandel: Zur Rolle der evangelischen Kirche im Prozess des gellschaftlichen Umbruchs in der DDR', in Hans Joas and Martin Kohli (eds.), *Der Zusammenbruch der DDR* (Frankfurt am Main: Suhrkamp, 1993). For the relations of the churches to the regime see Gerhard Besier and Stephan Wolf, '*Pfarrer, Christen und Katholiken', Das Ministerium für Staatssicherheit der ehemaligen DDR und die Kirchen*, 2nd edn., rev. (Neukirchen-Vluyn: Neukrichener Verlag, 1992).

conservative minister, Hans-Wilhelm Ebeling, who rejected political involvement and sought to limit peace prayers to a part of the communion service.[10] Children whose parents were notable dissenters found their way into the choir school barred. For many pastors throughout East Germany the idea of politicization was upsetting. Not necessarily approving of the regime, they believed that enrolling the Church in politics was at odds with its real mission. After all, the Protestant Church had reached a sort of accommodation with the godless regime: it would remain the Church *in* socialism—*Kirche im Sozialismus*—autonomous, but not resistant. The state in return would allow whatever criticism was uttered within the church interiors without outright intervention, so long as exercised congregants did not spill into the streets. But that line had been breaking down in 1987–8, as peace-prayer participants had over-crowded the churches and had to stand in the surrounding squares. In their dozens, later hundreds, of frail, flickering flames against cold and damp nights, potential resistance had formed the barest embryo of public resistance. But it was a resistance that had no real political programme for the GDR, but rather wanted an overarching framework that was no longer locked into the deep freeze of the second Cold War, that understood its national government to be frozen into power by the transnational confrontation of the two blocs. There was no real plan for elections or pluralism or the negotiations between workers and state that Polish Solidarity had attempted and no real formula for self-limiting protest as its leaders such as Adam Michnik and Jacek Kuroń had sought to theorize.

The non-Church forces for protest were even more fragmented before they expanded vertiginously during the final crisis. In January 1986 the 'Initiative for Peace and Human Rights' had announced its formation; the next September the Berlin Environment-Library was founded, as was the so-called 'Working Group: Renunciation of the Principle and Practice of Exclusion'. The latter would lead to the civic movement of 'Democracy Now' in the fall of 1989, a potential rival to the really successful foundation of that fall: New Forum, led by biologist Jens Reich and Bärbel Bohley. In January 1988, the 'Green Network: Ark' appeared. By June 1989, the group 'Democratic Breakthrough—social, ecological' emerged, as did an East German Social Democratic Party initiative in July.[11]

Intellectuals as such hardly presented a problem for the regime. They policed themselves and applied a collective self-censorship through their Writers' Association, which periodically rebuked and cajoled its members in what Wolfgang Templin termed a dialectic of threat and reward.[12] Publication of work by a state

---

[10] On the Leipzig churches see Grabner, Heinze and Pollack (eds.), *Leipzig im Oktober*; also Hans-Jürgen Sievers, *Vom Friednsgebet zur Demonstration: Die Kirche in Liepzig in den Tagen der Revolution 1989: Das Stundenbuch einer deutschen Revolution* (Zollicon: G2W-Verlag and Göttingen: Vandenhoeck & Ruprecht, 1990).

[11] Karl Bruckmeier, 'Vorgeschichte und Entstehung der Bürgerbewegungen in der DDR', and 'Die 'Burgerbewegngen der DDR im Herbst 1989', in Bruckmeiner and Gerda Haufe (eds.), *Die Bürgerbewegungen in der DDR und in den ostdeutschen Ländern* (Opladen: Westdeutscher Verlag, 1992).

[12] See the Enquete-Kommission, 'Aufarbeitung von Geschichte und Folgen der SED Diktatur in Deutstchland', II, I, p. 124.

publishing house required a process of dialogue with censors who believed they were helping to bring socially constructive literature to the public, and could guide would-be authors in shaping their narratives. Censorship was not brutal but rather construed almost as therapeutic. Trials and prison became unfashionable options by the 1970s, but for those authors who insisted on satire or protest that seemed really subversive, preventing their return from a trip to West Germany remained a recourse as well. Let them dissipate their disloyalty abroad.[13]

The bottom line was that, as of the summer of 1989, these circles of dissenters, and other small groups officially unregistered, could hardly trouble the regime, which in any case had infiltrated most of them with Stasi collaborators. Pre-existing oppositional groups had hardly achieved a troubling profile. The German Democratic Republic remained a state and society with a highly organized group life. Teams, factory associations, musical and hobby groups thrived. Honecker bragged to Gorbachev that three quarters of the East Germans were joiners. These associations were not organized to contest the regime, but to live in partnership with it. The most that can be said is that a sense of disaffiliation, of opting out, of cynicism was growing—especially after the spring 1989 electoral results showed evident signs of rigging. Set against this potential for disintegration, however, were the remaining inner sources of stability. These included the capacity to mobilize youth and organize official campaigns based on anti-fascism or peace; to rely on official party youth rites, including the communist version of a Protestant confirmation ceremony (*Jugendweihe*); to rely on the long generation that had come of age in the 1950s and had constructed their lives within the system and could hardly disavow it, such as the Modrows and other reformist loyalists. Moreover, the Stasi's role of subverting social protest remained significant. No other secret police claimed such assistance from unofficial collaborators—the Stasi had a sense of dissent: it monitored the opposition, debriefed them, elicited their collaboration, sowed distrust. It was a panopticon without walls. Indeed its pervasiveness served those later who had not resisted as a sort of alibi for their compliance. Coercion remained an instrument, frightening interrogation and cold jail cells a real possibility. Nevertheless, 'soft coercion' allowed a more functional guidance of the citizenry: denial (or facilitating) of vacations, of educational opportunity for children, of promotion.[14]

Günter Gaus famously described the GDR as a niche society, a sort of cosy socialism. The term, though, tended to obscure the public cost and underplay the

[13] On censorship and the writers' conferences see Manfred Jäger, 'Das Wechselspiel von Selbstzensur und Literaturlenkung in der DDR', in Ernst Wichner and Herbert Wiesner (eds.), *'Literaturentwicklungsprozesse': Die Zensur der Literatur in der DDR* (Frankfurt am Main: Suhrkamp, 1993); also Jäger, *Kultur und Politik in der DDR, 1945–1990* (Cologne: Wissenschaft und Politik, 1995); Robert Darnton, 'The Viewpoint of the Censor', *Berlin Journal, 1989–1990* (New York: Norton, 1991), 202–17.

[14] For the long generation of communist lives see the interviews in Lutz Niethammer, Alexander von Plato, and Dorothee Wierling, *Die volkseigene Erfahrung* (Berlin: Rowohlt, 1991). Cf. for a general analysis of state and society, Sigrid Meuschel, *Legitimation und Parteiherrschaft in der DDR: Zum Paradox von Stabilität und Revolution in der DDR, 1945–1989* (Frankfurt am Main: Suhrkamp, 1992).

pervasive corruption of privilege, just as Western market liberal rhetoric obscures the slow corrosion of civil life through increasing inequalities. Let me suggest provocatively that civil society, as the term might be applied to the unions or the Catholic Church in Poland, or to the private sectors of the Hungarian economy, was not a concept that really made sense in the East German context. Surveillance and privilege became the attributes of the public sphere; the search for accommodation became the preoccupation of the private sphere—these 'spaces' flowed into each other and pre-empted what commentators from the West kept hoping to find, believing they must find: civil society. Such a system of reciprocal state-societal corruption undermined the state as well as distorting civic culture.

The deepest threat to the regime derived from an arrogantly self-confident and aging leadership that underestimated the momentum of the Soviet changes (as did Gorbachev himself).[15] Honecker had angered the Soviet leader. Moreover, the party provoked widespread anger by evidently falsifying the electoral results of May 1989, inflating the affirmative vote that party candidates allegedly received even in a single-party state. Even as his generals understood the deep disaffiliation that those fleeing through Hungary or Czechoslovakia represented, Stasi leader Erich Mielke remained convinced that ultimately government force would remain decisive. Perhaps if the GDR had been a single massive country, a wager on force would have prevailed. But if East Germany was the machine-tool powerhouse for the eastern bloc, it was still dependent on mutual policing and collective enforcement of the 'iron curtain'. Ulbricht and his colleagues knew that Hungary was on a treacherous course of approaching the West; they had reason to suspect that the Czech leadership, though apparently loyal, was demoralized. What they did not realize was how devastating these defections could be for East Germany. When Hungary opened its frontier, East Germans could escape through Hungary. In Prague, East German citizens besieged the Western embassies for visas, and the GDR had to agree to let them transit back through Dresden to the Federal Republic.

This meant that when the opening of the Hungarian frontier provided a spark for emigration abroad or protest at home, the self-organization of protestors rapidly spilled beyond the small nuclei of protest organized during the previous

---

[15] In retrospect it became apparent how profoundly vulnerable the regime had become in economic terms. Günter Mittag's Potemkin policy of heavy social spending and expensive public building in the showcase capital ('The unity of social and economic policy', acclaimed by the 8th Party Congress) imposed a heavy burden, even if it could be alleviated by the flow of West German credits that Ostpolitik encouraged. The leadership long felt it must respond to the pressure of consumerism that the televised proximity of that wealthy society helped to encourage. East German communists claimed until the end productivity results comparable with the West, which was patently false. Observers could see what they wanted—whether the costly spiffing up of East Berlin for the 1987 Luther anniversary that East and West both commemorated, or the seedy disrepair of side streets away from the centres of Berlin or Leipzig—bad plumbing, scarce cars, crumbling stucco—and the ten to twenty year gap in living standards with the West that seemed to be widening not narrowing. On these issues see Jonathan R. Zatlin, *The Currency of Socialism: Money and Political Culture in East Germany* (Washington DC: German, Historical Institute, and New York: Cambridge University Press, 2007).

©AFP/Getty Images

**Figure 16.2** Which one is Judas? Reformist Soviet leader Mikhail Gorbachev, left, embraces Erich Honecker, the unreconstructed East German communist leader, during the celebration of the fortieth anniversary of the German Democratic Republic's creation in East Berlin on 7 October 1989. It was on this visit that Gorbachev famously declared: 'Those who come too late are punished by life itself.' But change in East Germany— Honecker was deposed as party leader on 18 October—did come too late, and a year later the GDR had ceased to exist. See also Figure 6.2 (p. 101) showing an earlier encounter.

seven years. The spectacle of those departing encouraged those not ready to flee to stand and fight for rights at home in late September and October. While the Church dissidents had defended the rights of civil resistance, the people who got together in Berlin in mid-September to sign the manifesto for New Forum called for a set of broad institutional reforms—the rights of political association, an end to violence and secret policing, entrepreneurial independence but without Western-style competitive capitalism. New Forum provided the organizational network that excited previous fence-sitters and prompted an explosion of political meetings and organization. New Forum talked the sociological language of 'dialogue', not the older Lutheran rhetoric of conscience. The major charismatic organization for change, for carrying forward the impetus of the demonstrations from Leipzig to Berlin, was thus a product of the self-emancipation already underway. The impetus of events overtook the long-term commitments of the reformers. At the same time, the demoralization of many of the ruling elites allowed the process to take place without armed resistance. Peaceful revolutions entail the discouraged capitulation of those no longer confident in the justice of the order they have been defending.


## INSTITUTIONAL LEGACIES AND LESSONS

The breaching of the Berlin Wall on 9 November became the great symbol of regime change—but it was almost inadvertent. What the collapse of the Berlin Wall did was to let West Germans flow in, as well as East Germans flow out. It denied the capacity for decision to what remained of the East German regime. The protesters of 1989 opened a civic space, they enabled the apparent triumph of what we call civil society, but they did not continue to prevail. What happens when the magical moment of civic transformation has passed; when the fraternity of the Leipzig Ring, the Gdańsk shipyards, or Timothy Garton Ash's Magic Lantern in Prague has dissipated? Students of religious movements and sociologists since Durkheim have analysed the interval between two plateaus of stability as a suspension of the everyday. It is the moment that Victor Turner identified as the triumph of antistructure, or Franco Alberoni called *Lo stato nascente* ('the formative moment'). But eventually it yields to a new everyday.[16] The New Forum and other groups, allied together as Alliance-90 won only about 3 per cent in the last and finally free elections to the GDR's *Volkskammer* (People's Chamber) in the spring of 1990 and could not really reverse course thereafter. The equivalent movements in Poland and Czechoslovakia split in the years after 1989 into quarrelling components, some carrying on the reformist mission that Western observers had applauded, others becoming more neo-liberal, still others reverting to a more traditionalist or populist stance. Such a development, revealingly, has not been an outcome unique to post-1989 Europe. The Resistance movements of the Second World War could not organize successfully after 1945 despite their dreams of a new politics or political renewal. In Belgium, France, and Italy—not even considering the outcomes in central and eastern Europe—such Resistance parties (Combat in France, Azionisti in Italy) rarely won more than 2 per cent of the electorate. Newspapers last better than parties.

Alliance-90 or the civil movements (*Bürgerbewegungen*), incorporating New Forum and other smaller groups, had perhaps an even more difficult task than Civic Forum in Czechoslovakia or Solidarity in Poland. The hopes of those who led the protests of autumn 1989 had been to achieve a reformed GDR. With the rare exception of some of the church leaders, they had not inscribed reunification as a goal. But neither the Krenz nor the Modrow regime could stabilize their small

---

[16] Victor Turner, *The Ritual Process: Structure and Anti-Structure* (New York: de Gruyter, 1995); Francesco Alberoni, *Movement and Institution*, Patricia C. Arden, trans. (New York: Columbia University Press, 1984). On social movements in general see Sidney Tarrow, *Power in Movement: Social Movements, Collective Action, and Politics* (Cambridge: Cambridge University Press, 1994).

state given the power and the wealth of the Federal Republic. As Stefan Heym said, there was no *raison d'être* for an independent GDR if it was not to persist as a socialist state. Chancellor Kohl conducted a masterly diplomacy in late 1989 and 1990, envisaging continuing fusion, but knowing that he had to assure both the Russians and his Western allies that this result would not restore Germany as an overbearing power in Europe. He was successful in part because the first Bush administration firmly believed that German unification and continued German affiliation in NATO would be a great victory for its own aspirations of half a century. But Kohl also convinced Gorbachev to concede unification on the West's terms. In fact, Soviet policy makers and diplomats had given up on Honecker's stubborn resistance to reform since the mid-1980s, and were convinced that West German economic vitality was their own best hope of helping to finance perestroika.

The fact that after the fall of the Wall, the residual GDR was surviving on life support became visible in mid-January 1990, when further serious demonstrations shook the state at a moment it appeared that the Modrow government might try to restructure rather than simply dissolve the Stasi apparatus. Thereafter the major contest became one between the West German Social Democrats' Brandt-inspired vision for a unity based on quasi-parity and a new constitutional compact, and Kohl's promise of quick absorption of the old GDR and a revaluation of its peoples' savings. After many years of relative privation vis-à-vis the West and the chance to escape from austerity, the outcome should not have been surprising—save for the fact that history can always surprise.

Still, the failure of the reformist GDR forces to stabilize a democratized East Germany presents an explanatory challenge. Part of the explanation may be the power and wealth of Kohl's West Germany, indeed just the beckoning opportunity to reconstruct the united Germany that had existed before 1945. But in addition, the movements generated in the course of civil protest may be ill suited for the routines of power sharing in a day-to-day modern democracy. Once their common opponent has yielded power, they fragment according to divergent interests and beliefs. Their adherents become disillusioned; the forces of the old order—central and eastern European politics provides ample evidence—often know, better than the idealists of the moment, how to exploit the politics of bureaucracy and capitalist transition to construct a new neo-liberal corporatism. This is no cause for despair; the Germans constructed and renewed decent institutions after 1989 as they did after the much more challenging moment of 1945. Public life, after all, is conducted by means of institutions. The interval in which some dissolve and others are created to take their place comes rarely and, as we can see in the case of earlier upheavals, is usually brief, whether lasting days, as in 1968, or months as in 1848, or even years, as in 1789. For a wonderful moment those who take to the streets enjoy the illusion that public life can be conducted without constraining institutions; the present crowds out past and future, as in the opening months of a great love affair. But these liminal moments, as Victor Turner calls them, must dissipate. The challenge for the reformists, the revolutionaries, or just the protesters of a Monday night is not to perpetuate a moment that cannot be perpetuated, but to create new institutions that will be more open, liberal, democratic, and responsive, and conversely less rigid, bureaucratic, arrogant than their predecessors. The protesters of 1989 throughout central and eastern Europe did succeed in that aspiration.

The nostalgia or *Ostalgie* or even perfectionism that would deny their achievement is inappropriate. 'We wanted justice and we got the *Rechtsstaat* (rule of law state),' Bärbel Bohley would later lament. In fact this was a great achievement. Subsequent disillusion has its own reason for being; the bitter aftertastes of power are the results of failures of exercising power, not of seizing it. Still, the movements themselves often dissolve with their own achievement and we must ask why. 'History to the defeated,' Auden wrote, 'May say Alas but cannot help or pardon.' But what does history say to the victorious? This is the question that the East German citizens' movements found it difficult to answer after their peaceful demonstrations helped to bring down the communist regime. Indeed by the time that the process of democratization for which they had marched concluded with their absorption into the united Federal Republic of Germany, many felt more disappointed than victorious.

## CONCLUSION

Historical outcomes resist generalization—but some conclusions can be derived from the East German case.

*First*, resistance and solidarity matter. Because of the sudden crystallization of opposition, the lack of an adversarial face-off for years or decades, the absence of social formations (Church, persisting peasantry, independent trade unions) that might challenge the regime, many observers characterized the events of 1989 as an 'implosion'. True enough, as in 1848 or in 1919 central European bureaucratic authority seemed to collapse from within, leaving a power vacuum. Nonetheless, it is wrong to label what happened in East Germany in 1989 as a mere implosion. Even if it did not develop over a long era of dialectically generated opposition, citizens organized themselves quickly and summoned their courage to take to the streets. Their crowd action in the key urban spaces revealed that the regime was not able or willing to use force to re-establish its authority. Successful crowd protest depends in turn upon solidarity: the conviction that to make a difference, protesters must act together and alongside fellow citizens. This is not to diminish the heroism of such solitary dissenters as Andrei Sacharov in Russia or Robert Havemann in the GDR, but their contribution is more to inspire and orient those who can act together.

*Second*, protest builds upon itself and its success—or even conflict—in the street. Contestation of power in public places, violent or non-violent, really matters. If repressive regimes cannot control public space, they are shown to possess neither efficacy nor legitimacy. If day after day protesters claim the streets with impunity, no regime can survive intact. This does not mean the state cannot regroup and recover, which is precisely what happened in 1848 and in 1968 (in East and West). But there is a real interval, where earlier authority is impotent and recovery hinges upon the divisions among those who inherit power. And not every regime recovers.

Violent movements, of course, can also bring about this transformation. But the hopeful message of 1989 was that non-violent protest could fell a system of dictatorship most Westerners had believed unshakeable. Still, non-violence was not guaranteed and part of the reason that the leaders could preserve non-violence was that the Soviet leadership and many other communist leaders had become convinced that their method of rule must change fundamentally. The non-violent movements were met at least half-way.

*Third*, the impact of resistance in the street may bear little relation to the period of long preparation and building of a formal movement. Pre-revolutionary societies may be vulnerable because of fiscal crises or battlefield setbacks, but few suspect how close they are to collapse. As de Tocqueville wrote about the French Revolution, no event seemed more unlikely before the fact and none so inevitable

©Chris Niedenthal/Time & Life Pictures/Getty Images

**Figure 16.3** The moment of individual liberation. On 10 November 1989, East Germans queue up to pass through the Wall to West Berlin—usually for the first time in their lives. The evening before, on 9 November, in response to rising mass protests and a wave of emigration, an East German leader, Günter Schabowski, had announced that citizens of the GDR would be free to travel to the West. Hearing the news on television, large crowds of East Germans had gathered at the Wall, and were finally let out to the West, thus turning a planned concession by the regime into a spontaneous triumph of people power.

afterwards. The historian should not abandon the search for long-term or structural vulnerability, but neither should he or she forget that the *journée*, or at least the repeated *journée, and* the *place* are the decisive theatres for radical upheaval. In physics and in the social sciences, sudden changes of state, discontinuities, bursts of self-organization are fundamental challenges to explanation. Every smooth curve or continuous function potentially decomposes into jagged fragments at potentially any point.

*Fourth*, context may not be all, but for small countries integrated into the web of larger alliance systems, the international context counts for a lot. Even in large countries such as India or the United States, the context of larger events affects the potential for civil disobedience—the experience of the Second World War and British wartime defeats in nearby Southeast Asia in the case of India; their experience in the Second World War and thereafter the decisions of the Supreme Court for the US African-Americans who began their mass protests in 1960.

*Fifth*, a lesson learned from central and eastern Europe and Russia more than from united Germany, where the presence of West German forces determined so much: the old communist elites might not be able to reconstruct their old party-states, but could adjust to the new regimes and find their footholds in new parties and economic fiefs. They were aided in this quest by the rapid return of politics—not of the old regime, but of the everyday business of group competition.

It may not be possible for those who made what Timothy Garton Ash has called the 'refolutions' of 1989[17]—that combination of reform and self-limiting transformation—to perpetuate the mood of exhilaration and emancipation. But they must continue to fight within the newly stabilized institutions for their reforms. They cannot rely on civil society alone to win that struggle but must recover the skills of party politics. History need not reinstate dictatorship, but it will not let political participants escape the work of negotiation and competition. Thus to apply Christa Wolff's question, not to the old regime, but to the very protest movements that helped dissolve it: *Was bleibt?* What remains—not of the discredited Biedermeier utopia of a small socialist regime, but of the revolutionary fervour of 1989? 'Bliss was it in that dawn to be alive'—the young author of those famous words, William Wordsworth, became an old man who could write appalling sonnets in praise of the hangman. Those who study civil resistance need to examine not only the happy achievement of bloodless emancipation but the post-revolutionary transition from successful protest to stabilization. Civil resistance is powerful and heartening but when it is successful it leaves those who organized it to carry on in the post-heroic world of party politics. That requires a different sort of courage.

---

[17] Timothy Garton Ash, *The Magic Lantern: The Revolution of '89 Witnessed in Warsaw, Budapest, Berlin and Prague* (New York: Vintage, 1999).

# 17

## The Limits of Prudence: Civil Resistance in Kosovo, 1990–98

*Howard Clark*

In the early 1990s, while the republics of Slovenia, Croatia, and Bosnia-Herzegovina fought wars to leave Yugoslavia, Albanians in the autonomous province of Kosovo took a different path.[1] Warnings that war was imminent in Yugoslavia were sounded from 1989 onwards when the Serbian leader Slobodan Milošević set about effectively abolishing the status of autonomy that Kosovo (population around 2 million) had been accorded under the 1974 Yugoslav constitution.[2] The situation in Kosovo was not promising for any form of resistance, yet a movement was active in 1990–8 that sought not only to defend the rights of the Albanian majority population in Kosovo and to avoid war: it also demanded independence for Kosovo. Prudence was a major factor determining the choice and character of non-violent action in Kosovo: however, this strategy became too passive and, ultimately, failed to avert war. Armed hostilities began in Kosovo in 1998 and concluded with the NATO military campaign against the Federal Republic of Yugoslavia (FRY) in 1999. Although international bodies had ruled out independence as an option for Kosovo in 1991–2,[3] international military intervention, when it eventually came in 1999, was not neutral but in reality ended Serbian rule in Kosovo and paved the way for a 'managed process' of independence, including the February 2008 Declaration of Independence.

Neither the criminal nature of Milošević's project of 're-Serbianization', nor the determination of close to 90 per cent of Kosovo's population not to live under

---

[1] The use of the anglicized term 'Kosovo' implies no position on its status. The Albanian majority in the territory call it 'Kosova'.

[2] Until 1991 the Socialist Federal Republic of Yugoslavia comprised six republics: Bosnia-Herzegovina, Croatia, Macedonia, Montenegro, Serbia, and Slovenia. The 1974 constitution had recognized Kosovo (and also Vojvodina) as autonomous provinces within the republic of Serbia. Although Kosovo and Vojvodina thus constituted entities within one republic, they participated directly in the federal presidency alongside the six republics of Yugoslavia. In the early 1990s Slovenia, Croatia, Bosnia-Herzegovina, and the republic of Macedonia broke away from the federation, leaving only Serbia and Montenegro as the republics comprising the Federal Republic of Yugoslavia (FRY). Following Montenegro's independence in 2006, the remaining state was called simply 'Serbia': the term 'Yugoslavia' was no longer in official use.

[3] It was because Kosovo did not have the status of a republic that the European Community's Badinter Commission ruled in its report of 11 Jan. 1992 that Kosovo had no right to secede.

Belgrade, induced a change of international policy until there was armed conflict. This chapter therefore centres on the widespread perception—especially dominant in Kosovo itself—that armed struggle succeeded where civil resistance failed. In particular it asks:

- What were the achievements and limitations of civil resistance?
- In a situation where non-cooperation had little leverage, what was the potential for 'active non-violence'?

## HISTORICAL SURVEY

### Nationalisms on the rise

The largest non-Slav ethnic group in Yugoslavia consisted of Albanians.[4] Most of them lived in Kosovo: they comprised about two-thirds of the population of Kosovo from 1948–61 (rising to perhaps 90 per cent by 1991). From 1969 onwards, President Tito, apologizing for previous anti-Albanian discrimination, introduced Albanian-language secondary and university education and granted Kosovo the status of 'autonomous province'. This raised Albanian expectations whilst provoking Serbian reaction. Although enjoying a 'cultural renaissance', Kosovo Albanians complained about Kosovo's poverty; their conditions remained worse than those of Kosovo Serbs. When their frustration erupted in 1981, federal troops cracked down. Henceforth Kosovo Albanians were under suspicion of 'irredentism'.[5]

Repression of Albanians did not assuage Serbian resentment of 'Albanization'.[6] Serbian nationalism made Kosovo its central symbol, denouncing the 'expulsion' of Serbs and 'cultural genocide' while vilifying Albanians as 'rapists'.[7] Furthermore, Kosovo's autonomy epitomized the 'weak Serbia, strong Yugoslavia' line attributed

---

[4] In this chapter, all references to Albanians are to the Albanian population of Kosovo, not to the citizens of the neighbouring state of Albania.

[5] 'Irredentism' means a policy of seeking the reunion to one country (in this case Albania) of a region (e.g. Kosovo) currently subject to another country, and was regarded as 'treason' in former Yugoslavia. There were and are tendencies in Kosovo that ultimately aspire to the 'reunification' of all Albanians—those from former Yugoslavia and from Albania—in one political entity. However, few have seen this as a practical political option. Since the disintegration of Yugoslavia, there has been a broad consensus among Kosovo Albanians in favour of 'independence within the present borders'. Opinion polls for the UN Development Programme in 2006 and 2007 indicate up to 96% of Kosovo Albanians support this status, as against no more than 3.5% supporting unification with Albania. See successive issues of *Early Warning Report Kosovo* at http://www.ks.undp.org/ews.

[6] 'Albanization' as viewed by Serbs encompassed changed demographic balance, bilingualism in public administration, Albanian publishing and broadcasting, Albanian street names and statues, and use of the Albanian flag. An authoritative account of this controversial period is the study by Momčilo Pavlović on 'Kosovo Under Autonomy 1974–1990' (Feb. 2005) which can be found in the section on the Former Yugoslavia Scholars' Initiative on the website of the Salzburg Seminar's Institute for Historical Justice and Reconciliation, http://www.salzburgseminar.org/ihjr/index3.cfm.

[7] Wendy Bracewell, 'Rape in Kosovo: Masculinity and Serbian Nationalism', *Nations and Nationalism*, 6, no. 4 (Oct. 2000), 563–90, discusses Serbian 'rape panic'.

to the 1974 Yugoslav constitution.[8] Milošević took control in Serbia in 1987–9 by allying himself with this rising nationalism. Kosovo's autonomy was dismantled in 1989 and 1990 and a host of anti-Albanian regulations introduced, with a promise to 're-Serbianize' Kosovo. Measures such as imposing the Serbian language and curriculum were accompanied by an effort to redress the demographic balance: offering incentives to Serbs to settle while harassing Albanians to leave.

## The beginnings of non-violence

Kosovo Albanians did not adopt strategic non-violence until 1990. However, even before that the miners were steadfastly non-violent in defending Kosovo's autonomy—first their 'long march' from the pitheads to Prishtina, the capital of Kosovo, in the snow of November 1988, and then their six-day stay-in strike in February 1989. These inspired spontaneous mass demonstrations both inside Kosovo and also in Slovenia and Croatia.

Briefly, there flickered a hope that the organized strength of industrial workers could defeat Milošević, especially when his newly appointed provincial leaders resigned to end the six-day strike in February 1989. Instead, Milošević rejected the resignations, convinced the federal presidency to impose a state of 'exception', and arrested suspected ringleaders. This provoked other strikes that were snuffed out by sending every striker a letter threatening arrest or dismissal. It later became plain that Milošević did not need Albanian labour and was prepared to let economic production in Kosovo collapse. Eventually, more than 80 per cent of employed Albanians would lose their jobs.[9]

On 23 March 1989, the Kosovo Assembly, surrounded by the armoured vehicles of federal security forces and with armed men intimidating deputies inside the chamber, voted for constitutional amendments annulling key aspects of Kosovo's autonomy. For the rest of 1989 protests repeatedly degenerated into clashes between armed police and protesters throwing stones or petrol bombs or sometimes using firearms. At least thirty-two protesters were killed in January 1990. The turn to non-violence would require greater organization and a persuasive methodology of action.

In 1990–2, Serbian acts of violence convinced Kosovo Albanians that Milošević wanted to provoke war. In March 1990 there were reprisals against local Serbs after the most emotive episode—the alleged poisoning of 7,600 school pupils.[10]

---

[8] For instance, under the 1974 constitution the votes of the two 'autonomous provinces'—Kosovo and Vojvodina—outweighed that of their 'parent' republic, Serbia, on the nine-member federal presidency.

[9] The figures compiled by BSPK, the independent trade union federation formed in 1990, indicate that of a total of 164,025 Kosovo Albanians employed in 1990, 146,025 were dismissed. Miners were especially seriously hit—all but 300 were dismissed. *National and Social Discrimination of the Albanian Workers in Kosova* (mimeo, no date, collected from BSPK office, Prishtina, Nov. 1997).

[10] Pupils reported symptoms of 'neuro-intoxication'—fainting, spasms, nausea, drowsiness—caused, believe Albanians, by a chemical weapon such as Sarin. The authorities and Serbs in general dismissed this as at best 'mass hysteria', at worst a politically orchestrated sham. Beliefs about this are reviewed in Julie A. Mertus, *Kosovo: How Myths and Truths Started a War* (Berkeley, Calif.: University of California Press, 1999), 187–98.

However, in this explosive situation, an alternative strategy emerged. The miners' actions of 1988 and 1989 offered an example of struggle without arms: when Serbian media were dominated by anti-Albanian 'hatespeak', they communicated 'we are not as you present us'. The 1989 'velvet revolutions' elsewhere in eastern Europe suggested that maybe the West would be favourable to non-violence, 'the modern European preference'. Many Kosovo Albanians—especially the young and urban—aspired to be modern Europeans and targeted 'backwardness' in campaigns against blood feuding and women's illiteracy. Not least there was an assertion of pluralist values after the years of communism.

New Kosovo-wide organizations were formed in December 1989—the non-party Council for the Defence of Human Rights and Freedoms (CDHRF) and the Democratic League for Kosova (LDK). The CDHRF, chaired by Adem Demaçi, became the main monitoring centre on human rights violations and police maltreatment; the LDK became a national movement claiming hundreds of thousands of members and led by Ibrahim Rugova. Initially the LDK did not advocate non-violence, but soon there was a transformation in popular attitudes. 'Non-violence imposed itself.'[11] It was not pacifism (principled rejection of lethal force) but strategic non-violence, a practical alternative to war or submission.

The new organizations took charge—principally the LDK, but also the CDHRF, the independent trade union federation, and a circle (including the Youth Parliament), generally known as the 'Kosova Alternative'. A voice for pluralism, the Kosova Alternative continually sought to raise issues that went beyond 'the national question'. This increasing degree of organization of the non-violent movement, and the negative experience of violent protest, convinced people that violence would be catastrophic. Inside Kosovo (but not in the diaspora), the tiny Marxist-Leninist/Enverist sects became isolated, especially when their most emblematic figure, Adem Demaçi (the 'Albanian Mandela', first imprisoned in 1958), declared his support for 'non-violent resistance and the democratic option'.[12]

The crucial first step in shifting to non-violent methods was 'naming the violence' of the regime, collecting and publishing evidence, and developing forms of 'semi-resistance', especially to mark killings—through actions such as lighting candles or 'homages' (five-minute work stoppages). Above all, after an incident such as police raiding a village, organizers went to collect evidence, show solidarity and explain why it was important to avoid a violent response. Two campaigns deepened the non-violence:

1. The petition 'For Democracy, Against Violence', published in January 1990. In June, Rugova and the petition's initiator, Veton Surroi, presented 400,000

---

[11] Shkëlzen Maliqi, *Kosova: Separate Worlds—Reflections and Analyses* (Prishtina/Peja: MM Society and Dukagjini, 1998), 101.

[12] *Ibid.*, 32. The term 'Enverist' identifies these groups with Enver Hoxha (1908–85), the leader of the ruling Albanian Party of Labour from 1944 to 1985, although these groups were repudiated by him and his successors in the government of Albania.

signatures (nearly 40 per cent of the adult population) at the UN in New York, establishing Kosovo's non-violent credentials internationally.

2. The Campaign to Reconcile Blood Feuds, which began in February 1990. Students searched out feuds, and then older leaders would arrive to persuade families to participate in public ceremonies of forgiveness 'in the name of the people, youth and the flag'. Within two years, 2,000 feuds were reconciled.[13]

Initially a counsel of realism, non-violence became, said Rugova, 'not only a necessity but also a choice':

> By means of this active resistance based on non-violence and solidarity, we 'found' ourselves. Today, we have succeeded in touching this point of the spirit of the Albanian people...Oppressed, but organized...this is the first time [Kosovo Albanians] feel that they have a power...that they feel citizens despite the occupation.[14]

## Self-determination

As Yugoslavia disintegrated, Kosovo Albanian demands evolved, from defending autonomy (1988–9) to demanding to become 'an equal unit in Yugoslavia' (July 1990). Finally, after Slovenia and Croatia declared secession, Albanian members of the Kosovo Assembly met clandestinely in Kaçanik, near Macedonia, and on 22 September 1991 issued a Declaration of Independence. This was promptly endorsed by a self-organized referendum, taking place between 26 and 30 September, in which virtually the entire Albanian electorate of Kosovo voted in favour of independence. They saw their future as outside rump-Yugoslavia (i.e. Federal Republic of Yugoslavia—Serbia and Montenegro); they were entitled to govern themselves. This stance could not be abandoned prior to negotiations, although—as LDK vice-president Fehmi Agani indicated—there was room for manoeuvre if the essential point was recognized that they should not live under Serbian domination.

Invariably after meeting diplomats, Rugova reported international concern for human rights and respect for Kosovo's non-violence, never mentioning the flat rejection of independence or complaints that children's education was being sacrificed for an impossible goal. Rather, Kosovo Albanians proceeded with the strategy of 'political as if'.[15] They were acting as if they had their independent state in order to bring it about.

In May 1992 a parliament and a president (Rugova) were elected. However, the main symbol of the independent state was the parallel school system with, at its peak, more than 20,000 teachers and 350,000 students from primary to university

---

[13] Howard Clark, *Civil Resistance in Kosovo* (London: Pluto, 2000) includes more detail on non-violent initiatives mentioned in this chapter.

[14] Ibrahim Rugova, *La Question du Kosovo: Entretiens réalisés par Marie-Françoise Allain et Xavier Galmiche* (Paris: Fayard, 1994), 119, 130, & 175–6.

[15] Noel Malcolm's phrase in *Kosovo: A Short History* (London: Macmillan, 1998), 348.

level. Backing this was voluntary tax collection, levying funds from businesses and families inside and outside Kosovo.

## Leadership

Although the non-violent struggle is identified with Rugova and the LDK, others played a vital role in the turn to non-violence; and the parallel education and health structures were originally largely self-organized. However, following the May 1992 'parallel' elections, Rugova's style of leadership became less collegiate and the LDK ceased to be a forum for strategic discussion.

In 1994 prime-minister-in-exile Bujar Bukoshi publicly criticized Rugova's 'passivity', while the 'political prisoners' faction'—headed by Demaçi outside the LDK and Hydajet Hyseni inside—bemoaned the struggle's 'stagnation'. Meanwhile Veton Surroi, intent on challenging LDK hegemony through publishing a weekly magazine *Koha* (and later the daily *Koha Ditore*), re-entered the fray.[16] To their intense frustration, Rugova rarely answered his critics, assuming greater authority through being 'above debate'. Increasingly remote, he depended on two or three unelected advisers plus the hard-working and approachable Agani.

When the Dayton negotiations (November 1995) focused on Bosnia and did not 'reward' Kosovo's non-violence, criticism of Rugova spread. The term 'active non-violence' gained currency, promoted by figures such as LDK co-vice-president Hydajet Hyseni, but more widely discussed outside the LDK, including by Demaçi who in 1996 entered party politics as leader of the Parliamentary Party. Most tangibly this meant resuming protests (suspended in 1992), convening the parliament and reclaiming school buildings.

After the 1992 suspension, the first protest to be held was a candlelit demonstration in April 1996 by the LDK Women's Forum, defying their own party, to mark the random shooting of an Albanian student in Prishtina. Then in September 1996, the university students' union (UPSUP) proposed demonstrations to reopen education buildings, but were dissuaded by Rugova who had just signed an education agreement with Milošević. A year later, however, it was a different story.

In September 1997, to test feeling, UPSUP urged students to join Prishtina's evening promenades. Many did, sparking enthusiasm about the planned march to 'reclaim' university buildings. Rugova again asked UPSUP not to proceed, but—while politely showing respect for his presidential authority—they insisted on their rights both to education and to protest. Soon UPSUP received the most high-powered delegation yet to visit Kosovo—diplomats from twelve countries headed by the ambassadors of the US, Britain, and the Netherlands (as EU President of turn): they urged postponement, inadvertently confirming UPSUP's analysis that the world pays more attention to protest than passivity.

---

[16] Surroi had resigned as Kosovo Youth Parliament leader in 1992.

**Figure 17.1** The dynamism of students. Ethnic Albanian students hold banners saying 'Kosova university now—tomorrow will be late' in Prishtina, the capital of Kosovo, 29 October 1997. About 10,000 ethnic Albanian students held a peaceful, one-hour rally as a follow-up to a march on 1 October which Serbian riot police had violently broken up. These protests challenged the LDK's five-year moratorium on demonstrations, expressing student frustration not only with their exclusion from proper educational facilities but also with the passivity of the LDK leadership.

The first student demonstration was a model non-violent confrontation. On 1 October, the start of the university year, wearing white shirts and with a non-violent code of discipline, 15,000 students marched towards the university. Stopped by police, the front line remained standing to receive baton blows while those behind sat down. And then the police attacked. This drama became world news, foreign diplomats feted UPSUP while Belgrade students—veterans of daily anti-Milošević demonstrations in winter 1996–7—sent solidarity messages and some came to Prishtina to support the November protest.

This glimpse of an alternative non-violent strategy came too late to change the course of events. On 28 November 1997 UÇK (Kosova Liberation Army) soldiers 'appeared' at a village funeral, scotching the denial of their existence by Rugova and others. 'To give political forces a last chance', Demaçi proposed a three-month UÇK ceasefire—but in vain. Skirmishes escalated until the Drenica massacres in 1998 (see below), after which thousands of recruits flocked to the UÇK. Foreign journalists set out to track down 'the army of the shadows'. More than 400,000 people were displaced during 1998, although there was no fighting in the main cities where the regime—after initial repression—tolerated the repeated demonstrations, perhaps as a safety valve.

Although international pressure brought a ceasefire in October 1998, all sides expected a reconflagration in spring 1999. When the presence of the Organization for Security and Cooperation in Europe's (OSCE's) Kosovo Verification Mission (KVM) and the Rambouillet conference (February–March 1999) failed to forestall this, NATO began what turned out to be a seventy-eight-day bombing campaign against targets in Kosovo and throughout FRY, while UÇK fought on the ground in Kosovo. Kosovo Albanians welcomed the NATO intervention despite the fact that, in the short term, the war provided an environment convenient for 'ethnic cleansing' to proceed against them.

The war ended in June 1999 when Serbia agreed to withdraw its forces and Kosovo was placed under the UN Interim Administration Mission in Kosovo (UNMIK). Many Serbs had already fled; thousands of those remaining were subjected to eviction, or worse, by returning Albanians in the post-war law-and-order vacuum of summer 1999.[17] When the situation was sufficiently 'normalized' for elections to proceed, the LDK won the 2000 municipal and the 2001 Kosovo Assembly elections: Rugova was still the politician most trusted by Kosovo Albanians. However, the killings of three key advisers—including Agani—rendered his post-war leadership even less dynamic than before, and UNMIK officials considered him the party leader least helpful on 'minority issues'.[18] Of the Serbs (and other non-Albanians) who fled Kosovo in 1999, only a small proportion have returned (about 8,000 Serbs)—and Serbs living in Kosovo continue to complain of lack of security and freedom of movement inside the territory.

## Military options

In the early 1990s, Kosovo Albanians were publicly 'on message' in support of non-violence. Yet not everyone was convinced. Some left, some fought in Bosnia or Croatia (including future UÇK general and prime minister Agim Çeku). Others stayed, accommodating themselves to non-violence while preparing for war.

In 1991 Croatia's President Tudjman urged Kosovo to open a 'second front' against Serbia, and formed special Croatian army units with 400 Albanian soldiers for deployment there.[19] They were disbanded when this patently self-interested 'offer' was rejected as suicidal. However, Rugova's policy was not pacifist: rather, he was courting more powerful allies. In December 1991 the Bush administration threatened to meet Serbian aggression with bombing—a

---

[17] There is no reliable independent estimate of the number of non-Albanians who fled Kosovo in 1999. Belgrade government figures of around 200,000 are widely used but might well be exaggerated in view of Serbia's political interests and refusal to accept UN help in revising its register of displaced people.

[18] Iain King and Whit Mason, *Peace at any Price: How the World Failed Kosovo* (London: Hurst, 2006), 207.

[19] Tim Judah, *Kosovo: War and Revenge* (New Haven: Yale University Press, 2000), 113–14.

threat repeated in February 1992 under Clinton—apparently guaranteeing the non-violent strategy armed protection.

Despite public denials, Rugova himself countenanced military preparations. One local analyst remarked in private that, looking at Bosnia, Rugova would have been negligent not to have a contingency plan. In 1993, former army officers were arrested and imprisoned for 'organizing a parallel Ministry of Defence'. They denied charges, but in 1999 their leader, Hajzer Hajzeraj, confirmed that he had indeed been minister of defence in 1991–3, authorized by Rugova and meeting periodically with Agani.[20] The former provincial head of Territorial Defence, Hajzeraj's role was to revive these structures for 'self-protection'. Upon Hajzeraj's imprisonment, prime-minister-in-exile Bukoshi continued the planning, ultimately forming the FARK (Armed Forces of the Republic of Kosova), which

©AP Images/PAPhotos

**Figure 17.2** The familiar boot of repression. Serbian police beat ethnic Albanians during demonstrations in Prishtina, 2 March 1998, just two days after the killings at Drenica. Thousands of ethnic Albanians protested as inter-ethnic violence escalated, with both Albanian and Serb victims. But the Serb-Yugoslav state still had most of the instruments of force.

[20] *Zëri Digest* (Prishtina), no. 1709, 2 Oct. 1999.

emerged belatedly in 1998 offering an alternative to the UÇK. FARK was eventually absorbed into the UÇK.[21]

The UÇK was not established to protect civilians but to instigate a general uprising. Founded by small diaspora groups cooperating with people inside Kosovo, including the Jashari family, the UÇK also had members in both the LDK and the CDHRF.[22] From 1996 to mid-January 1998, the UÇK claimed to have killed twenty-one people, eleven Albanian 'collaborators' and ten Serbs (five police). It comprised perhaps 300 trained members.[23]

The massacres in the Drenica region in central Kosovo ended non-violent struggle in the villages and made the UÇK a central player. On 28 February 1998, Serbian special forces in helicopters and armoured vehicles attacked Likoshane village without warning, killing twenty-six people, including eleven unarmed men in the Ahmeti household.[24] The Ahmeti men, as advised during the non-violent struggle, waited inside, helpless but with nothing to hide. They were taken outside, beaten, then executed. UÇK involvement is unclear, although police claimed to be 'pursuing terrorists'. In contrast, a week later, the Jasharis of Prekaz became folk heroes. Their men died fighting Serbian forces, a girl survivor remembering her uncle Adem singing patriotic songs to the last. Some fifty-seven people died in the attack on their family compound, but the UÇK now had a legend of epic martyrdom.

The LDK corporately—and its president personally—entered into a period of acute political paralysis, while the UÇK had more recruits than it could handle. 'We are all UÇK' was the new slogan. Rugova's rivals competed with each other to become its 'political voice'. Despite the antipathy between the LDK and UÇK leaderships, most Kosovo Albanians 'saw no contradiction between supporting both Rugova and the [UÇK]'.[25]

## ACHIEVEMENTS AND LIMITATIONS

For Tim Judah, 'passive resistance' was 'an extraordinary experiment' that failed.[26] James Pettifer, acknowledging the earlier 'power and value' of non-violence, believes 'the willingness of the [UÇK] soldiers ... to die had achieved

---

[21] Andreas Heinemann-Grüder and Wolf-Christian Paes, *Wag the Dog: The Mobilization and Demobilization of the Kosova Liberation Army* (Bonn: Bonn International Center for Conversion Brief 20/Friedrich Naumann Stiftung, 2001), 10–12. Some post-war killings between UÇK factions relate back to quarrels between the FARK and the UÇK.

[22] Two prominent 'sleepers' who emerged as UÇK field spokespeople in 1998 were Jakup Krasniqi (elected to the LDK board in February 1998 after years of local leadership) and Shaban Shala (elected CDHRF vice-president in 1997).

[23] Clark, *Civil Resistance in Kosovo*, 172–3 & 250–1.

[24] *Humanitarian Law Violations in Kosovo* (New York: Human Rights Watch, 1998), 20.

[25] Judah, *Kosovo: War and Revenge*, 146.

[26] Ibid. 59.

more in two years than the [LDK] had in ten'.[27] Such judgements, however, need measuring against other factors—objectives, costs, options, possibilities.

The policy of non-violence was relatively successful in pursuing three interim objectives.

1. *Maintaining the Albanian community and way of life in Kosovo.* Kosovo Albanians demonstrated a social solidarity not seen earlier (or since). 'The cause of schooling', comments Kostovicova, 'turned Albanians into a community of solidarity.'[28] Health was another critical area, especially as half Kosovo's Albanian physicians were sacked. The parallel medical network expanded continuously, eventually maintaining ninety health clinics and a gynaecological unit.

2. *Preventing war when it was most dangerous.* By not threatening violence, Kosovo Albanians let the anti-Albanian frenzy of 1989–90 abate. War weariness took its toll in Serbia, while leading nationalist intellectuals (including former FRY President Ćosić) began to see the attempt to 'reclaim' Kosovo as self-defeating. Refusing provocation also created space for international measures to prevent war. The huge disproportion between the meagre resources applied to prevention before 1998 and the major amounts consumed by NATO and the international post-war operation is a damning comment on the world security agenda. Kosovo saw a striking contrast in governmental attitudes to 'interference'—between governments' unwillingness to support social programmes associated with non-violent struggle, and their readiness to overcome qualms about assisting armed groups. When NATO needed a ground ally, there was little hesitation in helping the UÇK become more effective.

3. *Winning international support against the regime.* Lobbying on human rights brought international pressure against Serbia (the 'outer wall of sanctions' maintained after Dayton) and some disposition to 'protect' Kosovo, especially by the US (military threats, plus opening the US Information Office—a quasi-embassy in Prishtina—in 1996).

These three achievements, however, still left Kosovo under rule from Belgrade. International diplomacy tended to view Kosovo in terms of 'containment', urging Albanians to settle for full autonomy within FRY. A year of armed conflict and Serbian atrocities changed that. By the time of Rambouillet, Fehmi Agani was already talking about Serbia's defeat:

> the real defeat of Serbia was a political defeat, and this was achieved by the LDK. It was not enough, but the [UÇK] emerged at a time when Serbia had already become a strange presence in Kosovo. The ground was prepared for them.[29]

Thus civil resistance could be justified as a *phase* preparing more favourable conditions for armed struggle, achieving vital objectives at a time when armed struggle would have been disastrous.

---

[27] James Pettifer, *Kosova Express: A Journey in Wartime* (London: Hurst, 2005), 48 & 202. Comparatively few UÇK members died. Pettifer notes (190) that in the rout at Malisheva, July 1998, the UÇK 'lost much territory, but few fighters'.

[28] Denisa Kostovicova, *Kosovo: The Politics of Identity and Space* (Abingdon: Routledge, 2005), 112.

[29] Interview with Anthony Borden, *Institute for War and Peace Reporting Balkan Crisis Bulletin*, 32, 13 May 1999.

**Figure 17.3** The search for international legitimacy and support. Ibrahim Rugova (right, with his trademark Paisley scarf), the long-time leader of Kosovar Albanians' civil resistance, meets UN Secretary-General Kofi Annan on 1 June 1998, at UN headquarters in New York. By this time, Rugova's non-violent strategy was being overwhelmed by violence, and there was a growing stream of refugees from Kosovo. NATO emphasized its concern in a statement on 11 June 1998, and a UN Security Council Resolution on 24 October expressed alarm at 'the impending humanitarian catastrophe'.

The more complex comparison between achievements of civil resistance and armed struggle is about the situation after the stagnation of civil resistance. Claims that the UÇK 'empowered' the population should be treated with caution. Theirs was a 'victim' discourse: UÇK members on trial denied rather than defended their politics.[30] It is often claimed that the UÇK's main achievement was engineering NATO intervention by provoking Serbian forces to commit atrocities.[31] However, three comments are in order. First, that NATO intervention was *not* the declared intention of the UÇK. Their rhetoric was of 'liberation struggle' and 'popular uprising'. Elements of the UÇK even lacked the strategic sense to desist from attacking the OSCE's KVM. However, ultimately the UÇK

---

[30] Nait Hasani—the most prominent of a group of seventeen defendants—told the court: 'I maintain that the peaceful approach . . . is still the best.' *Kosova Information Centre Daily* (Prishtina), 16 Dec. 1997.

[31] James Gow, *The Serbian Project and its Adversaries: A Strategy of War Crimes* (London: Hurst, 2003) offers a different reading: Milošević decided in February 1997 to prepare a military campaign in Kosovo, implementing longstanding plans for ethnic cleansing. The UÇK merely provided a pretext. Ultimately, the 'practical relevance' of the UÇK—bearing in mind, its incoherence, weakness, and its lack of 'independent capacity'—was as a 'limited ground complement' to NATO.

acceded to the longstanding consensus on the need for outside help in ending Serbian rule and gladly cooperated with NATO.

Second should be noted the willingness of the UÇK to put unarmed Albanians at risk. Agani commented that of the roughly 2,000 Albanians killed in 1998, probably only 5 per cent were UÇK members. Fred Abrahams of Human Rights Watch has observed:

> The KLA's [UÇK's] disregard for ethnic Albanian civilians is also striking. Villages declared 'liberated' by the KLA were often smashed shortly thereafter by the Serbian security forces, who vented their anger on the civilians who did not retreat into the hills with the KLA. Ambushes of police or army checkpoints often provoked a response against the nearest village, if the KLA was based there or not. The pattern of KLA behavior suggests that the rebels, relying on the predictable aggressiveness and brutality of the Serbian forces, may have deliberately provoked attacks against ethnic Albanian civilians, since innocent victims would promote their cause.[32]

The UÇK not only targeted 'collaborators' but also practised intimidation: on a number of occasions, village leaders were punished for pleading with the UÇK to stay away, recognizing that their presence would provoke attack without offering protection.[33] Third, the UÇK undid some of the gains of civil resistance, it is arguable, especially through its record of serious human rights violations. Immediately after the war, when the UÇK was the only armed body capable of stopping 'revenge violence', its members played a leading role in the expulsion of Serbs.[34] The subsequent lack of safety of Serbs in Kosovo strengthened the Serbian case, if not for partition then for major concessions in UN envoy Ahtisaari's plan of March 2007 for the 'supervised independence' of Kosovo. Ahtisaari also indicated concern about the role of UÇK cadres by recommending the disbanding of their symbolic post-war stronghold—the Kosovo Protection Corps (a civil emergency corps formed mostly of UÇK veterans).[35]

## A CASE FOR 'ACTIVE NON-VIOLENCE'

'Prudence' and 'patience' were Rugova's watchwords. They served well when prudence was combined with action—finding spaces for 'semi-resistance': noise-making at curfew, brief work stoppages, wearing armbands. The decision to organize their own schooling was prudent: daily protests (and daily police

---

[32] Fred Abrahams, *Under Orders: War Crimes in Kosovo* (New York, Human Rights Watch, 2001), 53.

[33] The most publicized occasion was the UÇK's 'arrest' of two LDK officials in Malisheva on 31 Oct. 1998. Elsewhere families were evicted by the UÇK or opponents simply 'eliminated'.

[34] Interviews with abducted Serbs who survived reveal arguments within the UÇK: some commanders restraining and others leading the torture and extra-judicial killing. See *Abductions and Disappearances of non-Albanians in Kosovo* (Belgrade: Humanitarian Law Center, 2001).

[35] See 'Report of the Special Envoy of the Secretary-General on Kosovo's future status', UN doc. S/2007/168 of 26 Mar. 2007, Annex on 'Main Provisions of the Comprehensive Proposal', para. 9.

violence) at schools were unsustainable. However, towards the end of 1992—days when the US was sufficiently alarmed to threaten air strikes—the LDK suspended street demonstrations. A temporary moratorium might have offered a useful strategic lull: this permanent risk avoidance, however, produced a profoundly demoralizing quiescence. Without the outlet of more assertive action, resentment and frustration simply accumulated, making the situation more explosive.

In contrast the 1997 UPSUP protests made parents proud of their student offspring, found allies even in Serbia, and showed that following the advice of foreign diplomats was not necessarily the way to gain an international hearing. UÇK soldiers were not the only people willing to die for Kosovo: at a time when police and paramilitary harassment was widespread, activists such as local human rights reporters and the 1,000 voluntary tax collectors raising money for the parallel education system were especially in danger. However, the UPSUP protests were the only occasions when non-violent Kosovo Albanians consciously courted violence in order to dramatize their situation. Could a strategy of 'active non-violence' have challenged Serbian domination more effectively and created better conditions for peaceful coexistence?

Civil resistance against occupation is a 'battle of wills', suggests Robert Burrowes, paralleling Clausewitz on war: 'the strategic aim of the defence is to consolidate the power and will of the defending population to resist the aggression'. Some would say the counter-offensive's strategic aim is 'undermining the power' of the regime but Burrowes is more precise: 'to *alter the will* of the opponent elite to conduct the aggression', recognizing that undermining power might be one means for this.[36] Kosovo Albanians had little hope of undermining Milošević: far from depending on them, he wanted them to leave and was even willing to abandon Kosovo's industry. This was a profound weakness for civil resistance. Their strength, however, was in their own will, the resilience and solidarity of the community. 'The Serbs tried to kill our society, but we woke up instead', commented a sacked radio journalist who threw herself into organizing women's literacy programmes. As well as the schools and health clinics, so many small businesses—mainly retail—had opened that by 1994 Kosovo was better stocked than sanctions-hit Belgrade.

However, by 1994, this initial sense of empowerment was wearing thin. The problem was not Serbian ruthlessness. Milošević never seriously interfered with the operations of the LDK nor even tried divide-and-rule tactics. Rather, the problem was a lack of strategy, both to maintain their own momentum and to alter the regime's will.

'Active non-violence' was never spelt out as a coherent alternative policy. The common points among its advocates were preparing selected non-violent confrontations and greater mobilization of community resources. If non-cooperation had only symbolic purchase, then other forms of action needed to be pursued with more energy. To this might be added, controversially, two other approaches that

---

[36] Robert Burrowes, *The Strategy of Nonviolent Defense: A Gandhian Approach* (Albany, NY: State University of New York, 1996), esp. ch. 8, 125–34.

could have yielded results: first, greater contact with the opposition in Serbia; and second, greater flexibility on goals—a point on which Demaçi isolated himself by proposing a re-federation with three equal republics (Kosovo, Serbia, and Montenegro).

Diplomats found Rugova exasperatingly stubborn in his demand for independence—despite his flexibility from 1993 onwards in proposing an interim UN protectorate. His local critics, however, perceived him as being far too compliant on methods. A more assertive approach was typified first by the journalists' hunger strike, led by Demaçi in 1993 and gaining internationally negotiated concessions, and later by the UPSUP protests of 1997.

The obvious non-violent confrontation that Rugova eschewed was to convene parliament. Electing their parliament in 1992 had felt empowering for Kosovo Albanians; its failure to meet for six years was absolutely the reverse. The risk would have been confined to 130 elected leaders—surely people who should be in the front line—presenting Milošević with the dilemma 'let our parliament function, or show the world how you deny democracy'. As UPSUP's experience demonstrated, engaging in non-violent confrontation could have accelerated the learning process of foreign diplomats who failed to understand the Serbian project or who thought that Albanians might resign themselves to being subordinate to Serbia.

If the LDK would not stage confrontations at least it should have mobilized constructive activity. Establishing the parallel schools and university provided a base. However, instead of encouraging further initiatives, the LDK reined in youth—even denying its own youth organization a seat in the party's council. Meanwhile, on the central question of the economy, laissez-faire ruled. The self-proclaimed 'Republic of Kosova' was haemorrhaging money to Serbia: an estimated $US1 million per day was spent on importing food products from Serbia to Kosovo.[37] There were no coordinated efforts to reduce this dependence. Starting micro-enterprises to process locally grown food would have provoked some police vandalism and harassment. However, if 'prudence' is to be useful, it means not *avoiding* risks but *assessing* and *managing* them, putting possibilities to the test. Too often initiatives were blocked by a self-victimizing attitude that something was impossible because of 'the Serbs'.

To change Serb opinion, the LDK strategy relied on two types of leverage: attrition and international pressure. Attrition was exerted simply by staying put. Milošević, far from attracting new settlers, could not stop Serbs leaving Kosovo. Leaders in the 1980s anti-Albanian mobilization—the Serbian Academy, the Orthodox Church, and some Kosovo Serbs—began to look for compromise. Rugova reasoned that, provided Milošević was not given some excuse to attack, international pressure and demographic realities should bring independence. Such 'prudence', however, left the population not relying on their own efforts, but waiting for somebody else and 'enduring'.

---

[37] *Economic Activities and Democratic Development of Kosova Research Report* (Prishtina: Riinvest, 1998), 39.

Kosovo Albanians expected international concern for human rights to overrule Serbian claims on Kosovo. They were sceptical about their own capacity to influence Serbian opinion or cultivate Serbian allies. Hence Rugova, having announced in 1994 the planned opening of a Kosovo bureau in Belgrade, decided that even this would be counter-productive.

Various Kosovo Albanians maintained contacts in Serbia, even arranging public talks with opposition spokespeople, but saw little prospect of gaining leverage. In general the concept of building 'a chain of non-violence'—in which one circle of connections leads to another and a growth of influence—was missing.[38] There were signs of movement in Serbia, and reason to hope for more—although, realistically, not enough to make a decisive difference in 'the battle of wills'. However, the 'chain of non-violence' is not a concept confined to non-violent struggle: it also helps to prepare sustainable coexistence with neighbours. In struggle against an ethnic adversary, non-violence cannot simply aim to 'win'. Cross-community linkages should be valued in themselves, not just as points of leverage or ways of seeking allies, but also as laying the ground for shared understandings and relationships that can restrain escalation to war and help prepare a reasonable settlement.

Some people understood this well. However, it was an unpopular approach that at one point marginalized Surroi and Maliqi (already considered 'too Yugoslav'). Demaçi and Hyseni had similar attitudes but—as long-term political prisoners—different credentials: the first Serbs they publicly praised were those who had helped them endure prison. Then in 1993 when Belgrade opposition leader Vuk Drašković was publicly beaten by Milošević's thugs, Demaçi sent him a message of sympathy. In 1996, he sent another message, supporting Belgrade's anti-Milošević demonstrators. The LDK-aligned newspaper *Bujku* mocked this, although at the 16 December rally Drašković did something previously unimaginable in Belgrade, calling a minute's silence for the latest Albanian death in police custody in Kosovo. Ethnic blinkers, such as those of *Bujku*, were widespread, even shared by most UPSUP leaders: when Patriarch Pavle condemned Serbian police brutality against the students, UPSUP's response predictably focused on his suggestion that they should accept Serbian rule. Then the Belgrade paper *Naša Borba* awarded UPSUP its Prize for Tolerance 1997 without any objectionable comments, yet still the students declined to collect it. Ethnic polarization increasingly vitiated the prospects of non-violence, both in terms of strategy and in terms of future coexistence, obstructing efforts to expand any zone of goodwill between the two communities in Kosovo, or even between Kosovo Albanians and Belgrade oppositionists.

---

[38] On 'chain of non-violence' see Johan Galtung, *Nonviolence and Israel/Palestine* (Honolulu: University of Hawaii Institute for Peace, 1989), ch. 2. Informed Albanians appreciated the work of various groups in Serbia, but regarded them as 'marginal'. The 'chain' image, however, suggests that even 'marginal' groups have links.

## CONCLUSION

When Kosovo Albanians turned to non-violence, some tried to invest the goal of independence with a democratizing content of pluralism and reforming patriarchal traditions. A decade before the UN invited Kosovo to achieve certain *standards* before the question of *status* could be resolved, many Kosovo Albanians took the attitude that in order to gain independence they would show themselves worthy of it, practising the values proclaimed in their own constitution, especially respect for minority rights. Many local and sectoral leaders were scrupulously 'correct' towards ordinary Kosovo Serbs, seeking to serve as role models and reassuring Serbs that they would have a place and rights under independence. Perhaps with greater international engagement at an earlier stage, this attitude could have been maintained, escalation to war prevented and the prospects for multi-ethnic coexistence improved. However, the experience of repression propelled popular feeling in a different direction.

The situation generated hatred. Some local Serbs had been activists fomenting anti-Albanian feeling since the 1980s; some became paramilitaries. Others were at least beneficiaries of Milošević's policies, had not protested when Albanian colleagues were sacked or children shut out of schools, and might serve as police reservists, taking part in dawn raids on villages. The educational segregation imposed by Serbs created breeding grounds for 'prejudice, charged with animosity and inviting revenge'.[39] While the parallel schools helped stabilize Albanian society, the growing frustration of pupils and students within the parallel system plus the content of the teaching contributed to the explosive potential of the situation.[40]

Rugova's counsel of 'self-restraint', based more on fear than on hope, was increasingly disconnected from practising the values of a desired future. Thus, while it postponed the outbreak of physical hostility, it could not combat the hardening of ethnic polarization. Kosovo Albanians began to feel that their 'self-restraint' was being taken for granted. There were predictions of war from 1988 onwards, yet only when the conflict escalated into war did powerful international actors apply themselves to devising new responses—such as the Kosovo Verification Mission improvised after the 1998 ceasefire—but too late to have much effect.

Kosovo Albanians remained grateful that NATO drove out the Serbian occupying forces. However, by 2007, after almost a decade of UN administration, most citizens believed that Kosovo's new institutions were corrupt.[41] Organized crime

---

[39] Denisa Kostovicova, 'Albanian Schooling in Kosovo 1992–1998: "Liberty Imprisoned"', in Kyril Drezov et al. (eds.), *Kosovo: Myths, Conflict and War* (Keele, Staffordshire: Keele European Research Centre, 1999), 15.

[40] Kostovicova, *Kosovo: The Politics of Identity and Space*, ch. 5, based on a study of textbooks, suggests that the history as taught strengthened a 'victim' nationalism that was ambivalent about non-violent resistance.

[41] *Early Warning Report Kosovo*, no. 17 (Apr.–June 2007), 30–1. Available at www.ks.undp.org/ews.

was endemic. The main political parties were not democratic, had little vision beyond 'independence', and readily resorted to intimidation. The 'Unity Team'— the Albanian negotiating team in the talks up to 2008 on Kosovo's future status— was all-male. Most Kosovo Albanians still depended on remittances from abroad and spent this money mainly on imports. With unemployment over 40 per cent, much young talent had simply left or had plans to emigrate.[42]

Faced by a deadlock in negotiations on the status of Kosovo, in February 2008 the Kosovo Assembly passed a new Declaration of Independence, more than sixteen years after the first. This time, however, while the objections of Russia and Serbia deny UN membership to Kosovo, the self-proclaimed independence has wide recognition—including from the US and most members of the European Union—and promises of practical support. Nevertheless the real challenge is not to attain the status of independence, but to restore values and revive hope.

The case of Kosovo shows civil resistance functioning when other forms of resistance would have been disastrous. However, it then shows the need for civil resistance strategy to renew itself, to build on the basis established, to innovate in its own community and to pose new challenges to the adversary. In hindsight, civil resistance appears now to have been a phase through which Kosovo Albanians survived repression and succeeded in convincing the world of the injustice and inhumanity of Belgrade's politics. Finally and belatedly, once armed struggle was underway, the Kosovo Albanian patience was 'rewarded' with an unprecedented military intervention by NATO and later by the unprecedented recognition of an independence that for years they had been told was inconceivable.

---

[42] *Early Warning Report Kosovo*, no. 17 (Apr.–June 2007), unemployment, pp. 34–5, and intention to emigrate, p. 31. While the 'unemployment rate' has been calculated at 41.4%, this is in a context of low participation—especially of women—in the labour market. The 'employment rate' among working-age people in Kosovo is only 28.5%. Among the 18–24 age group, nearly 47% of Kosovo Albanians and more than 53% of Kosovo Serbs say they have plans to emigrate.

# 18

## Civil Society versus Slobodan Milošević: Serbia, 1991–2000

*Ivan Vejvoda*

Serbia is a quite specific case of post-communist transition. By comparison with the 'velvet revolutions' of central Europe, the violent break-up of Yugoslavia in the last decade of the twentieth century was an aberration. Serbia, the largest of the six republics comprising the Socialist Federal Republic of Yugoslavia (SFRY)—a communist 'federation'—went in the opposite direction to central Europe in the 1990s. As a consequence of its rulers' actions, it came under international sanctions, experienced world-record-breaking inflation—about 363,000,000,000,000 per cent at its peak in December 1993—and finally was bombed for seventy-eight days in 1999 in NATO's first major and sustained use of force.[1]

In this disastrous decade Serbian political life was dominated by Slobodan Milošević, who was not only leader of the Socialist Party of Serbia (SPS) from its foundation in 1990, but was also President of Serbia (1989–97), and then President of the Federal Republic of Yugoslavia (FRY) from 1997 until his removal in the remarkable events of September–October 2000. The FRY was created in 1992 after the collapse of the SFRY due to the secession of four of its six constituent republics, and existed until 2003. It consisted of the two remaining republics, Serbia and Montenegro. Serbia, far the largest and most populous of the two, contained (in addition to Serbia proper) the two 'autonomous provinces' of Vojvodina and Kosovo.

During the regime of Slobodan Milošević, a regime of power politics, Serbia saw the rise of its civil society. By civil society, I mean in the first place the non-governmental organizations (NGOs) and associations that originated in Serbia from existing groups of intellectuals and individuals who had already been active in the 1970s and 1980s defending human rights and freedom, and opposing censorship and authoritarian regime practices. Citizens began to learn and acquire the tools of peaceful protest, self-organization, association, and resistance. The last decade of the past century is a story of how Serbian civil society and pro-democratic politicians endeavoured against all odds to end the regime's

---

[1] Tim Judah, *The Serbs: History, Myth and the Destruction of Yugoslavia* (London: Yale University Press, 1997), 267. Also Mladjan Dinkić, *Ekonomija destrukcija: velika pljačka naroda* [The Economy of Destruction: The Great Robbery of the People] (Belgrade: VIN, 1995).

downward spiral of neglect and devastation, including four wars and the crim-
inalization of state and society. The fruit of this labour was achieved between 24
September and 5 October 2000, through elections which were then defended in
the streets of Belgrade and other cities in Serbia. The result was the peaceful
toppling of Slobodan Milošević, who ended his days in 2006 at the International
Criminal Tribunal for the former Yugoslavia (ICTY) in The Hague. It was only in
2000 that Serbia began in earnest a democratic and economic reform process—
ten years after others in post-communist Europe had embarked down that road.

This chapter will start by showing why Serbia took a path opposite to other
countries of the post-communist world. It will then describe the birth and growth
of civil society and civil resistance, in the midst of nationalism and war, during
the authoritarian regime of Slobodan Milošević; the slow, imperceptible political
weakening of the regime and the steady recovery of society against the authoritarian state; and the final non-violent, electoral victory of democracy over power
politics—a 'revelection'.[2] Europe, in both its geopolitical and democratic value-
based guise, will be a key factor in explaining why the Serbian political and social
dynamic produced the outcome that we know.[3]


## HISTORICAL BACKGROUND

The period under consideration is the 1990s, but to understand how this came to
be a decade of decline and rebirth in Serbia it is important to understand the run-
up to this decade. Yugoslavia, positioned during the Cold War inbetween the
Warsaw Pact and NATO, a communist country 'in-between' West and East, with a
free travel regime for its citizens and with developed trade and economic relations
with the European Community, was in the 1980s seen as the most likely candidate
to first join the European Community (now European Union) and NATO.
Constituted of six republics (states) and two autonomous provinces, this communist 'federation' broke apart, as did the other two communist 'federations',
namely Czechoslovakia and the Soviet Union. Yet Yugoslavia, in comparison to
the other two, suffered a more systematically violent breakdown, taking many
tens of thousands of lives, creating havoc and destruction, displacing hundreds of
thousands of people.

The disappearance in 1989 of the 'cement' of communist ideology and rule left
Yugoslavia as a weak shell harbouring six proto-states in search of a new regime.
Some were seeking immediate independence, others were in search of a demo-
cratic third Yugoslavia (after the first as a monarchy, 1918–41, and the second as a

---

[2] Timothy Garton Ash, 'The Last Revolution' [Serbia], *The New York Review of Books*, 47, no. 18, 16
Nov. 2000.

[3] For a detailed account see Ivan Vejvoda, 'Yugoslavia 1945–1991—from Decentralisation without
Democracy to Dissolution', in D. A. Dyker and I. Vejvoda (eds.), *Yugoslavia and After: A Study in
Fragmentation, Despair and Rebirth* (London, New York: Longman, 1996).

communist state, 1945–90), but all of the former communist elites in each of the republics were in power-retention mode. Attempts at a peaceful resolution of the differing aspirations were unsuccessful and violence ensued. Lack of accountability and responsibility, and democracy *tout court*, meant that extra-institutional forceful, violent 'solutions' were contemplated and implemented by the ruling elites. The inability of the communist leaders of the six republics to find a compromise on the way forward created the space for fear and uncertainty among the population. Violence erupted in the Serb-inhabited areas of Croatia especially in the spring of 1991 (although already in the summer of 1990 in the Krajina region protests were ongoing). The Yugoslav People's Army intervened on behalf of the Serbs, with Croatian police and territorial defence forces (the kernel of the future Croatian Army) counter-attacking. But it was the ten-day war in Slovenia in June 1991 that unexpectedly lit the powder-keg that was to spread the war fully to Croatia, later to Bosnia and Herzegovina, and finally to Kosovo. War and conflict thus formed the backdrop of the 1990s in Yugoslavia, and in the former Yugoslav republics that were in turn gaining independence through a process organized by the International Conference on the Former Yugoslavia (ICFY) led by Lord Carrington. A commission appointed by the ICFY, and chaired by the French constitutional judge Robert Badinter, laid down the rules for recognition of independence for the new emerging states. This was the European Community's first major foreign policy challenge and it was wholly unprepared for it—which led to many flaws in its approach.

Elections were held in all six Yugoslav republics during 1990. In December, last in line, Serbia held elections in which Milošević's party, renamed from the League of Communists of Serbia to the Socialist Party of Serbia, won with the slogan: 'With us there is no uncertainty.' His main opponent Vuk Drašković—later to become a democratic leader, and the survivor of two assassination attempts by the Milošević regime—was advocating a strongly nationalist policy, close to war-mongering. Ironically enough, the people who voted for Milošević thought that he would not lead them to war.

Being by far the biggest of the six republics, Serbia was, with Croatia and Bosnia and Herzegovina (hereafter: Bosnia), at the geographical core of the conflict. The Yugoslav People's Army (JNA) sided with the Milošević regime and thus gave Milošević's power politics an edge in pushing forward the policies of trying to conquer parts of Croatia and Bosnia where majority Serb populations were living. Milošević's message during the whole of this period was 'Serbia is not at war with anyone'. War crept in through the back door. There was no official announcement or proclamation of war, but there was a call-up for military service in the army—the draft in May 1991.[4]

---

[4] For an account of the role of political, social, religious, and academic actors in Serbia's descent into war see Nebojša Popov and Drinka Gojković (eds.), *The Road to War in Serbia: Trauma and Catharsis* (Budapest: Central European University Press, 2000). (Original full Serbian edn., Nebojša Popov (ed.), *Srpska strana rata: Trauma i katarza u istorijskom pamćenju* (Beograd-Zrenjanin: Republika, 1996.)

The beginning of civil resistance to Milošević's power politics can be traced exactly to 9 March 1991, the day that thousands of citizens of Belgrade went into the streets to demand the resignation of the head of the national television because of the hate and war-mongering language announcing what was to come.[5] This demonstration was in fact a call for the demise of Milošević. That was openly asked for several days later by the students of Belgrade University, when Milošević agreed to visit it. In strong and courageous speeches, students came to the roster one by one asking Milošević to leave because it was clear to them, they said, that he was leading the country the wrong way. On the evening of 9 March 1991, before any conflict had begun on the territory of what was then still Yugoslavia, Milošević, in agreement with the federal presidency of Yugoslavia, brought out into the streets of the capital the army and tanks against the citizens of Serbia. Vuk Drašković, then the key opposition figure, was immediately arrested. This was a clear announcement of harsher, more brutal power politics to come.

Milošević had first come to power as communist party secretary for Belgrade in 1983, his wife Mira Milošević taking, in parallel, control of the strong and influential communist party secretariat of the University of Belgrade. They both started a hard-line ideological policy. Milošević took over full command through a coup inside the communist party of Serbia in December 1987, displacing his friend and ally Ivan Stambolić, whose abduction and assassination he would subsequently instigate and order in the run-up to the September 2000 election. (This has been proven by the supreme court of Serbia in a case against the assassins, who were part of the special operations unit of the state security service.[6])

Milošević was thus a known political quantity, although few could surmise that he would lead the country to war. The March 1991 demonstrations in Belgrade continued after the 9th, with an 'occupation' of the main square, Terazije. There was a permanent 'happening' around the clock, the 'Terazije Parliament' as it came to be called. A fledgling small radio station, B92, which was supporting the democratic demands, was shut down by the regime. Radio B92 was to become the flagship broadcast medium of the civil resistance, and a civil actor in its own right—courageous, innovative, and technologically cutting-edge, using the Internet as a space of public freedom.[7] After spending ten days in the centre of the city

---

[5] The state-run media, broadcast in particular, were the instigators of violence to come. See Mark Thompson, *Forging War: The Media in Serbia, Croatia & Bosnia and Herzegovina* (London: Article 19, 1994); and Svetlana Slapšak et al., *The War Started at Maksimir: Hate Speech in the Media 1987–1991* (Belgrade: Medija Centar, 1997).

[6] The testimony of Radomir Marković, Milošević's head of secret services from the end of 1998 until the beginning of 2001, amply confirms this: 'Milošević mi je rekao da Stambolića treba ukloniti' [Milošević told me that Stambolić must be eliminated], *Danas* (Belgrade), 18 Jan. 2005, 14. Marković is now serving a long prison sentence for his role in these events, as well as a forty-year sentence for his role in the attempted assassination of Vuk Drašković, which resulted in the killing of four of Drašković's associates.

[7] For a full account of B92's role see Matthew Collin, *Guerrilla Radio: Rock 'n' Roll and Serbia's Underground Resistance* (New York: Thunder's Mouth Press/National Book, 2001); also Dušan Mašić,

resisting and protesting, the citizens and students came out partially victorious: the head of state TV was dismissed, and Vuk Drašković was released, but the regime remained in place and further strengthened its grip on power.

An important but rarely recalled aspect of civil resistance to this power politics of the regime was the opposition to the draft in 1991 and in the ensuing years.[8] In Belgrade itself, close to 90 per cent of draftees resisted the call. In cities and towns throughout Serbia, the percentage was lower but equally impressive due to the fact 'everyone knows each other' and the peer pressure was greater. Many who agreed to go to war and reached the frontline did so only to turn back and throw away their weapons in disgust at what they saw. This led the regime to substitute the draft resisters with paramilitaries recruited from the 'lumpenproletariat' and jails of Serbia. Yet military action continued unabated in spite of this civic resistance.

The year 1991 also saw the birth of the first non-governmental organizations or civil society organizations in Serbia. Among these the Centre for Anti-War Action, Women in Black, and the trade-union Independence were the most prominent. Largely a Belgrade phenomenon at first, this birth of NGOs progressively spread to cities throughout Serbia.[9] A 'pre-parliament' gathered intellectuals and activists from all over Yugoslavia in Sarajevo, to debate 'how to prevent total war'.[10] Women played a key role in all of these organizations. Peace activities and 'peace caravans'—consisting of buses with activists that went around Yugoslavia trying to convince citizens not to let themselves be led into a war—were often led by women activists, and women's networking through the former Yugoslavia played a crucial role.[11]

The shelling of Dubrovnik in 1991 by the Yugoslav People's Army brought out several hundred citizens in front of the presidential office in Belgrade. The lengthy siege of the Croatian town of Vukovar led among other things to a petition by Serbian citizens demanding that Milošević resign. It garnered close to 900,000 signatures. On 2 April 1992, 50,000 young people were in the streets again for a concert for peace under the slogan 'Don't Count on Us'. The Belgrade Circle of Independent Intellectuals was founded in March 1992 and began a series of

*Talasanje Srbije: knjiga o radiju B92* [Rocking Serbia: A Book about Radio B92] (Belgrade: Samizdat B92, 2007).

[8] See Ivan Vejvoda, 'Not Our War', *New Internationalist* (Oxford), no. 256 (June 1994). See also: *Oči boje fronta* [Eyes Colour of the Frontline: A Project of the Center for Anti-War Action about Draft-resisters during the NATO Intervention in FR Yugoslavia] (Belgrade: Centar za anti-ratnu akciju, 2000).

[9] For a chronology of the civil resistance see Obrad Brusin, 'Chronology', in Velimir Ćurgus Kazimir (ed.), *The Last Decade: Serbian Citizens in the Struggle for Democracy and an Open Society 1991–2001* (Belgrade: Medija Centar, 2001), 182–205.

[10] *Predparlament Jugoslavije: Kako sprečiti totalni rat* (Belgrade: Republika, 1991).

[11] Lina Vušković and Zorica Trifunović, *Ženska strana rata* [Women's Side of the War] (Belgrade: Žene u crnom, 2007); for an exhaustive list of civil resistance peace initiatives see Ružica Rosandić, Nataša Milenković, and Mirjana Kovačević, *Teži put: mirovne akcije na tlu bivše Jugoslavije* [The Harder Way: Peace Activities on the Territory of Former Yugoslavia] (Belgrade: Centar za antiratnu akciju, 2005).

activities and weekly gatherings under the title 'Another Serbia'.[12] In May 1992 there was a demonstration with one hundred thousand citizens to protest the siege of Sarajevo and voice support for the victims of the war in Bosnia. The University of Belgrade was occupied for a month and a half in the summer of 1992, with demands for the resignation of Milošević, permanent events, panels, discussions, and cultural activities.

Two Serbias were confronting each other. The civic Serbia was, at the beginning of the 1990s, weak and concentrated principally in Belgrade. Milošević had managed to garner strong public support for strengthening Serbia's position, including by undertaking military action. The tide of nationalism was rising, stoked by Milošević's policies and by state-controlled television and newspapers. He had also unleashed the Serbian Radical Party as the spearhead of actions of hate, intolerance, and violence toward non-Serbs in Serbia. In the spring of 1993 this had reached such proportions that even Milošević's acolytes in the SPS began criticizing some of these actions. Probably a good half of the Serbian public, if not more, was carried away by this nationalist tornado. Polling data from the time show Milošević's overwhelming popularity as a leader. He was seen by a large part of Serbian public opinion as righting the wrongs of the past done to Serbia under Tito's rule, for example the fact that Serbia was the only one of the six Yugoslav republics not to have a unified territory but one with two autonomous provinces Vojvodina and Kosovo that both had substantial institutional prerogatives beyond Serbia's control. His whole policy was perceived as a redemption of Serbian dignity.[13] Most of those who were on the opposite side were in a state of silent discontent and opposition. It was a vocal and active minority who were on the streets of Belgrade and speaking out in the available broadcast and print media outlets, anticipating the catastrophic outcomes that all this was going to lead to.

It was only during the three-month-long mass protests of 1996–7 that the silent opponents began to join more fully in the struggle for freedom in Serbia. Serbia had lost three wars by then: in Slovenia, Croatia, and Bosnia. The Dayton peace agreement in November 1995 had led to the end of the war in Bosnia and to a feeling that the drama was moving towards closure—although everyone knew that it would only ultimately end in Kosovo, where the whole dynamic had begun in the late 1980s. Public support for Milošević had slowly begun to erode.

[12] Ivan Čolović and Aljoša Mimica (eds.), *Druga Srbija* [Another Serbia] (Belgrade: Beogradski krug, 1992); and *Intelektualci i rat* [Intellectuals and War] (Belgrade: Beogradski krug, 1993).

[13] Polling data by a number of independent Belgrade-based institutions demonstrate Milošević's popularity and loss of it. See Srećko Mihailović, 'Legitimnost političkog sistema treće Jugoslavije: Kako građani evaluiraju politički sistem' [Legitimacy of the Political System of the Third Yugoslavia: How Citizens evaluate the Political System], in S. Mihailović (ed.), *Između osporavanje i podrške: Javno mnenje o legitimitetu treće Jugoslavije* [Between Contesting and Support: Public Opinion on the Legitimacy of the Third Yugoslavia] (Belgrade: Institut društvenih nauka i Friedrich Ebert Stiftung, 1997), 7–41. Also Srećko Mihailović, 'Ima li nade za promene' [Is there Hope for Change?], in S. Mihailović (ed.), *Javno mnenje Srbije: Između razočaranja i nade* [Public Opinon in Serbia: Between Disillusion and Hope] (Beograd: Centra za proučavanje alternativa, UGS 'Nezavisnost' i Udruženje za unapređivanje empirijskih istraživanja, 2000), 189–208. This is an opinion poll conducted in the immediate aftermath of the NATO bombing in 1999 indicating the potential for political change.

©Brian Rasic/Rex Features

**Figure 18.1** Students in the vanguard again. For three months in the winter of 1996–7, Serbian students marched every day through the streets of Belgrade to demand that Slobodan Milošević recognize the victory of democratic opposition parties in the local elections of November 1996. Here, on 27 December 1996, students face the police cordon on Knez Mihajlova Street, as they did most days. The students are holding up their red student record books, and the banner says 'Hey man in blue, follow your heart not your orders!'

A continuous series of smaller or larger civic resistance activities culminated in the winter of 1996–7 when, after the November 1996 municipal elections, Milošević falsified the results to deny the victory of the democratic parties in 55 per cent of all major Serbian cities. The whole country exploded in civic and student protest that would last for over three months with permanent 'promenades' (*šetnje* in Serbian) every day, this time in all cities and towns where the democratic opposition won. The whole civic protest movement had thus spread beyond Belgrade in a major way. Despite a massive police presence, the atmosphere of these 'promenades' (often under snow and rain, sometimes in extreme cold) was festive, with whistles, a large effigy of Milošević in a convict's uniform and speeches by political figures.

The former Spanish prime minister, Felipe Gonzalez, was called in by the Organization for Security and Cooperation in Europe (OSCE) to mediate between Milošević and the democratic opposition. On 27 December 1996 his mission concluded that the democratic opposition had won the elections. Milošević himself ultimately recognized the victory of the opposition with a 'lex specialis' on 4 February 1997, thus conceding power to an alliance of democratic parties called 'Zajedno' (Together). Zoran Djindjić became the first democratic-ally elected mayor of Belgrade.

This would be the (then as yet unrecognized) springboard for the non-violent, electoral victory against Milošević in 2000. The mere fact that the opposition gained real power at the local, municipal, and city levels gave it a firm political foothold to organize for future political struggle. Equally important was that local media in these cities and towns became independent outlets with a strong influence on public opinion. An Alternative Network of Electronic Media (ANEM) brought all of these outlets, principally radio stations, together into a civic-professional association.

Milošević never won an election in Belgrade itself—a little known fact. Nationally, his vote steadily declined throughout the 1990s, after his first victory in December 1990. Through the use of electoral laws, electoral fraud, and the coalition-building schemes with smaller political parties in the parliament he was able to maintain power, switching himself in July 1997 from the position of president of Serbia to that of president of the FRY. Milošević, though, respected the electoral calendar through-out the 1990s, following the regular schedule of parliamentary and presidential elections. After the bombing of 1999, it was clear that he had lost even more support among the voters in the south of Serbia, where until then his supremacy had been uncontested. The democratic opposition and civil society were waiting for him to call elections, which he did in July 2000. At that moment he changed the constitu-tion so as to be elected by universal suffrage, not by an election in the parliament. His plan was to shore up his tattered legitimacy, weakened by the lost war against NATO. Democratic Serbia knew this was the moment of reckoning. The election would be a vote on the Milošević regime itself.

## WHY AND HOW DID SERBIA CHOOSE CIVIL RESISTANCE AGAINST POWER POLITICS?

Belgrade, Serbia, and Yugoslavia as a whole had had its 1968 student demonstra-tions. Although different from those in Paris, Berkeley or Warsaw, nonetheless the spirit of the 1960s had entered this country that had broken away from Stalin in 1948. Tito had opened the borders in the mid-1960s to resolve a growing unemployment problem, thus allowing Yugoslav citizens to travel freely and find jobs as migrant workers ('gastarbeiter') throughout Europe. Intellectuals around the 'Praxis' group of philosophers based in Zagreb and Belgrade were in intense contact with the Frankfurt school of critical theory but also with Polish, Czech, and Hungarian dissidents. Belgrade was a city in which Václav Havel's plays were staged throughout the 1970s and 1980s. The Dubrovnik Inter-University Centre had become a hub for many an intellectual debate between East and West.

The intelligentsia that would come to form the backbone of the democratic political party movement in Serbia from 1989 onwards was thus bred on the ideas of the 'warm current of Marxism' and on those of east European dissidents, exemplified in Adam Michnik's idea of a 'new evolutionism',[14] and on his understanding that the change away from communism did not entail in the present day the revolutionary storming of Bastilles or Winter Palaces.[15] It meant the creation of a 'parallel polis', a 'second society', an oasis of freedom and civil society, the struggle for human rights and independent institutions.[16] This would be the driving theoretical and practical political idea in the struggle against Milošević's power politics.

Throughout the 1970s and then 1980s a fledgling human rights movement appeared, resembling in form and methods those in other communist countries. A movement of 'petitionists' emerged, involving the signing of petitions against arrests and curtailing of freedom by the regime. Some of the ground was thus already laid for what would come in the 1990s. The intention was clear from the outset in both civil society and democratic political opposition circles: non-violent, peaceful, institutional means were to be the way to break the authoritarian backbone, because that was the only way to create firm and sound pillars of a future democracy.

There was of course a parallel revival of nationalism and chauvinism, spurred on by both politicians and the intelligentsia.[17] The nationalist intelligentsia sided with and gave grounding to Milošević's violent policies and use of the army. His power retention strategy was backed by an ideological legitimation given by nationalist intellectuals with a desire to right historical wrongs on the basis of ethnic principles. An 'ethnification of politics' had been introduced that had its origins in the history of Yugoslavia. This was a dangerous exacerbation that had contributed to the downward spiral of violence.[18] Communist and aspiring nationalist leaders of 1990 Yugoslavia grasped ethnicity and identity politics as their key legitimating tool in the struggle to retain or gain power.

The European Community in 1991 had dismally failed in stopping the violent breakdown of Yugoslavia. Yet it was the 'return to Europe' of other post-communist countries that eventually also inspired Serbia. It was the European context coupled with specific political, social, and economic developments that defined the reasons

[14] See Adam Michnik, 'A New Evolutionism' [1976], in his *Letters From Prison and Other Essays* (Berkeley, Calif.: University of California Press, 1985). See also Aleksander Smolar, Ch. 8 above.

[15] See 'Towards a Civil Society: Hopes for Polish Democracy: Interview with Erica Blair (John Keane)', in Adam Michnik, *Letters from Freedom: Post Cold-War Realities and Perspectives* (Berkeley, Calif.: University of California Press, 1998), 96–113. Originally published in *Times Literary Supplement*, London, 19–25 Feb. 1988.

[16] H. Gordon Skilling, 'Introduction: Parallel Polis, or an Independent Society in Central and Eastern Europe: An Inquiry', *Social Research*, 55, no. 1–2 (Spring–Summer 1988), 211.

[17] See Jasna Dragović-Soso, *'Saviours of the Nation': Serbia's Intellectual Opposition and the Revival of Nationalism* (London: Hurst, 2002).

[18] For a detailed account of the role of nationalists and the state, social, cultural, and religious institutions in the road to war see Popov and Gojković, *The Road to War in Serbia*. On the 'ethnification' of politics: Claus Offe, *Varieties of Transition: The East European and East German Experience* (Oxford: Polity Press, 1996).

for the choice of non-violent methods. Europe was the favourable and enabling geopolitical and economic environment. Milošević's repressive policies toward Kosovo, beginning in the late 1980s and leading to the de facto abolition of Kosovo's autonomy in 1990, were an indication of his approach to 'solving' challenging issues. Milošević strengthened his rule politically through his dealings with Kosovo, a province of Serbia that had been an unresolved issue under Tito's regime, with recurring protests by Kosovo Albanians in 1968, 1970–1, and 1981. This Kosovo policy heightened the nationalist tone already in 1987, with Milošević's repressive and highly authoritarian approach highlighted by his speech at Kosovo Polje in 1989 on the occasion of the sixth centenary of the Battle of Kosovo. What came later grew out of these beginnings.

The conditions which Milošević inherited—including a well-organized state administration (Belgrade having been the capital of a country of twenty million people was now a capital for about eight million) with some nascent elements of the rule of law, and a certain degree of media freedom—continued to exist throughout, even though Milošević's power politics trampled on all of these at certain moments in time with very brutal means. For those who wished to act and to speak up there were meagre spaces open: Radio B92 and Radio Index in the capital, the daily *Naša Borba*, the weekly *Vreme*—small and weak compared to the state-run media outlets, yet nonetheless existent. Public panels were organized throughout the early 1990s by the Belgrade Circle of Independent Intellectuals, where opposition was explicitly voiced; NGOs began their actions and artists, actors, dramatists, and film-makers were equally active.

Milošević used a number of proxies for his power politics. The Serbian Radical Party of Vojislav Šešelj, whom he once termed 'his favourite opposition leader', is a case in point. Šešelj was engaged in the rhetoric of hate as well as actions against non-Serbs and was the clearest advocate of a Greater Serbia (the name of one of his party's publications), a policy whose intention was to occupy the parts of Croatia and Bosnia where Serbs lived. Šešelj was also allegedly commanding his own paramilitaries in operations in Croatia in the early 1990s. A number of smaller parties were also included by Milošević as part of this policy.

Milošević respected certain key stipulations of the constitution while abusing and disregarding others. It was thus possible to predict certain outcomes and not others. The backdrop of the war and the violent breakdown of Yugoslavia loomed large over internal developments in Serbia. Contacts from an early stage with European actors, and with European and American donors, were a significant source of support and solidarity for NGOs and independent media. But it was the fundamental energy and internal dynamic of Serbian society that drove the process of resistance forward. Without it, all the support and help would not have amounted or led to a democratic outcome. The enormity of the challenge confronting civil society mobilized its deepest resources.

The way to civil resistance was led initially by a combination of actors from the critical intelligentsia involved in oppositional activities under communism, and then progressively joined by a new generation of activists spurred to action by the Milošević regime's autocratic and war-mongering policies. The key element in the ultimate success of civil society's resistance against the power politics of the regime lay in the learning process and the progressive accumulation of building blocks along the path to the final electoral victory. Each failure was a step forward, often invisible to the actors immediately involved. The first half of the 1990s was a minority activist struggle against a regime backed by strong public support. But as the regime began accumulating defeats in wars so public opinion began awakening slowly to the dire consequences of Milošević's catastrophic policies. The activists would stumble, beaten by the regime, but would stand up again, regroup, and carry the baton a few steps further. New actors, in particular the students and youth, joined at every stage. This was especially true in the smaller cities and towns where individuals began organizing human rights groups, or social self-help groups, and young people swelled the ranks of the new youth movement Otpor and other NGOs.

## THE INTERNATIONAL ENVIRONMENT AND THE DIGITAL DAVID

Among the complexities of the Serbian/Yugoslav case was that the political, economic, and social dynamic occurred in a country that was disintegrating, through war and conflict, and in a changing Europe. 'The hour of Europe has come' were the proud words of the foreign minister of Luxembourg who, as president of the European Community's foreign ministers' council, headed the European crisis management efforts at the beginning of the Yugoslav crisis in June 1991.[19] This turned out to be an empty and fatuous boast which not only did not impede the violent breakdown of Yugoslavia but in certain instances aggravated the situation. Europe was consumed by its next integrative move. The Treaty of Maastricht 1992 was a key step in the deepening of the EU at the very moment that the flames of war were being fanned inside former Yugoslavia. The recognition of the independence of Slovenia, Croatia, and Macedonia (which had also received a green light from the Badinter Commission, but was vetoed by Greece) became bargaining chips in the European (Franco-German) debate about how to get a consensus on the Maastricht Treaty.

Notwithstanding the failure of EC/EU external policy in the early 1990s, the geopolitical embeddedness of Serbia in Europe, a post-1968, and a post-Helsinki Europe in which human rights and the rebirth of civil society had become guiding principles of struggles against communist dictatorship—all this was the normative backdrop against which Serbian civic actors engaged in the 1990s, opposing war as a method and favouring non-violence as the political basis of the future.

Election monitoring was a key part of the process of change. From the outset Serbia had an EU monitoring mission, and as an OSCE member it also received

---

[19] Stefan Lehne, 'Has the "Hour of Europe" come at Last? The EU's Strategy for the Balkans', in *The Western Balkans: Moving on* (Paris: Institute for Security Studies, Chaillot Paper no. 70, Oct. 2004), 111.

OSCE election monitors. But it was not until a home-grown domestic organization, the Centre for Free Elections and Democracy, appeared in 1996, that real
efficiency of monitoring of elections occurred as the watchdog arm of the civil
resistance. Milošević was able successfully to manipulate elections through the
first half of the 1990s. The local elections of 1996–7 were the first major defeat for
the regime and the precedent for more effective monitoring of subsequent
elections. Again, it was the domestic effort that was fundamental in ensuring
true results, although external support was helpful in aiding the technical efforts
and in representing an anchor of solidarity.

It is in the sphere of media that the interplay of creative approaches by local
actors, technological innovations, and international support gave especially substantive results, which the regime's powerful interventions constantly tried to
undermine. Radio B92, the ANEM network, and B92's subsequent website
'Opennet', launched in 1995, were to prove invaluable in carrying the message
of the civil resistance domestically (to the initially small number of some 10,000)
and internationally. The B92 radio was a rallying point. It was shut down in 1991
and in December 1996. 'When B92 was shut down, it immediately began publishing news bulletins over the internet, short-cutting the censorship and appealing directly to the outside world. Its RealAudio sound files were picked up by the
BBC and Voice of America and beamed back into Serbia; ironically, its connection had just been installed by the state phone company.'[20] New information
technology was thus instrumental in the communication strategy of the civil
resistance. Another radio station, Radio Index, would pick up the radio waves at
moments when B92 was banned, if it was not banned at the same time. This story
of a digitally savvy David against a seemingly almighty Goliath caught the
attention of the international media and an international public. International
support groups started to appear in a show of solidarity with the Serbian civil
resistance through radio and Internet B92.

There was an anachronism in Milošević's politics of war and violence.
A prominent member of the Belgrade 'Praxis' group of philosophers, Mihailo
Marković, who made a 180 degree shift and joined Milošević's party as an
ideologue, said during the early 1990s that it was no wonder that the young
generation did not want to go and fight in the war because they had been brought
up in their urban apartments listening to rock music. Some observers have even
characterized the wars in former Yugoslavia as an 'urbicide', as wars of the rural
against the urban.[21]

The major problem was the surprise of war in a European country for this
urban generation—old and young. Rather than 'voice' or 'loyalty'—in Albert
O. Hirschman's famous triad—many chose 'exit'.[22] A massive brain-drain from
Serbia ensued, estimated at about 300,000 mostly younger people fleeing this
European tragedy. Some younger people who remained went into hiding to avoid

---

[20] Collin, *Guerilla Radio*, 114.

[21] e.g. Bogdan Bogdanović, *Grad i smrt* [The City and Death] (Belgrade: Beogradski krug, 1994).

[22] Albert Hirschman, *Exit, Voice and Loyalty: Responses to Decline in Firms, Organisations and States*
(Cambridge, Mass.: Harvard University Press, 1970).

being drafted. Others, not numerous at the beginning, took up the struggle and fought back. Very few had expected to see a war in the country, many wanted to follow where other post-communist countries were leading, yet at the same time the nationalist grievances stoked by the regime led astray those desires for normalcy and prosperity in the name of a promise to reclaim national pride through violent means. That is why it took a decade for a broad-based social stratum to awaken, to come out of an apathetic, passive stance, organize, and create a large scale movement.

Milošević's policies had whipped up strong nationalist feelings and created a political following among a good half of the population who believed that he was righting the wrongs of history done to the Serbian nation. Numbers of citizens of Belgrade threw flowers at tanks that were on their way to the Croatian battlefield in 1991. He had won the elections in December 1991 with 48 per cent of the vote. It was the loss of the successive wars in Slovenia, Croatia, and Bosnia, and ultimately the war against NATO over Kosovo in 1999, which showed the majority that these policies were leading Serbia into a dead end without hope for a European, prosperous future. Also the successful policies of transition to democracy and advance towards European and NATO integration in neighbouring countries were a clear sign that Serbia was lost in transition, and had to regain the main road on which others were well ahead of it. As we shall see, in the late 1990s the Serbian opposition learned directly from the experience of those neighbours.

## 'HE'S FINISHED'—OTPOR AS INSPIRATION

The 1996–7 protests were a turning point: they marked the beginning of the end of the Milošević regime. Milošević was to stay in power for another three and half years, but there was a sense of the vulnerability of the regime and the limits of the regime's capacities for total control. The 'winter of discontent' was a massive, protracted three-month-long uprising of Serbia during which every single day citizens and students came out into the streets of all key Serbian cities and towns.[23] Students and the universities played a cardinal role. Many of those students are today democratic political leaders, or in positions in government. It was a school of protest and leadership. The learning curve was extremely steep during the events for both civil society and democratic politicians who endeavoured together to see the right of their vote upheld. Zoran Djindjić, Vesna Pešić, and Vuk Drašković were the leaders of the political 'Zajedno' (Together) movement.[24] After the victorious outcome (Milošević recognizing the local elections result) but with the concomitant defeat (Milošević more than ever in full possession of power at the national level,

---

[23] Mladen Lazić, *Protest in Belgrade: Winter of Discontent* (Budapest: Central European University Press, 1999).

[24] Vojislav Koštunica, the candidate who beat Milošević in the 24 September 2000 elections, had been conspicuously absent along with his party from the winter 1996–7 protests.

cracking down on the prerogatives of local government and on media) deep disillusionment set in among the rank and file of the civil resistance. However, NGO, political, and student leaders (especially those who had led the 1996–7 movement) regrouped and picked up the pieces and again started planning for non-violent action, without knowing exactly when the opportunity would occur.

Many academics were ousted from the university at this time for siding with the protesters. As a reaction they set up the Alternative Academic Educational Network (AAEN, or AAOM in Serbian) which was in essence a parallel university. Funded by external donors it quickly established itself as a hub of academic excellence and a gathering point for students and professors. But it was the students and other young people who themselves came to the idea of creating Otpor (Resistance) which would fully implement strategies of civil resistance.[25] This was a true breath of fresh air after what seemed to be the shrewd return of Milošević to power, even while he conceded defeat in the local elections. Otpor, which appeared in October 1998, chose a non-hierarchical, horizontal organizational structure with no strong visible individual leaders, but a collective invisible leadership. It would attract apathy-ridden and disillusioned youth, especially through a series of regime-mocking actions throughout the country.[26]

It was the fearlessness of the activists that drew early attention to them in 1998. The first arrest of a group of three Otpor activists in Belgrade by the police ended after a couple of days. They emerged from the prison cell and went directly into a press room to state exactly what had happened to them and the maltreatment that they had undergone, as well as who the policemen were, if they had heard their names. They said that their aim was to rid Serbia of an unpopular regime, thus opening the road to a European, democratic future. This openness, this absence of fear in the face of an authoritarian regime, galvanized public opinion, and in particular opposition-oriented citizens. István Bibo, a Hungarian historian, wrote in 1947: 'Being a democrat means, primarily, not to be afraid.'[27] Otpor exemplified this.

The Otpor movement grew and its ranks swelled to about 18,000 members throughout the country, at its peak in 2000. As activists became more forceful and skilful over the last years of the regime, the police were arresting them and beating them. Interestingly, a grandparents' support group appeared to protect their Otpor grandchildren, so one could on occasion see senior citizens defending young protesters under attack from the police. All this contributed to an image of pervasive civic resistance which became extremely potent. More importantly this

[25] Srdja Popović, Andrej Milivojević, and Slobodan Djinović, *Nonviolent Struggle 50 Crucial Points: A Strategic Approach To Everyday Tactics* (Belgrade: Center for Applied Non-violent Action and Strategies, 2006).

[26] 'Popular Movement Otpor (Resistance): Chronology of Actions 1999–2000', in Ćurgus Kazimir (ed.), *The Last Decade*, 374–80.

[27] István Bibó, 'The Misery of Small European States' in István Bibó, *Democracy, Revolution, Self-Determination* (Boulder, Colo.: Social Science Monographs, distributed by Columbia University Press, 1991), 42.

significant gathering of thousands of young people clearly spelt out a *fin-de-régime* atmosphere as the country entered the year 2000.

The imagery and slogans of Otpor were crucial in creating the 'brand' and in making it visible and popular. The fist was the image of defiance vis-à-vis Milošević, who had ignored the voice of students back in March 1991 when they first asked him to resign. The slogan 'Gotov je' (He's finished) was a powerful, courageous message that became a pervasive sticker (white bold letters on a black background) on walls, lamp-posts, and lifts in apartment buildings. Monty Pythonesque mini-theatrical shows in town squares, sports playgrounds, and university settings attacking the regime with ridicule, added to the sense that the regime's power politics had no real response, other than violence and arrests. Otpor also appeared at political rallies of the opposition parties as the elections of 24 September 2000 drew closer, to act as a catalyst and watchdog of the parties sticking together.

Meanwhile, the regime clamped down ever more viciously on the independent media. Daily newspapers were fined exorbitant amounts of money for criticizing regime politicians or their actions. The Serbian Radical Party, which held the Ministry of Information in the Milošević coalition government, played a particularly blatant role in this repression of free speech.

© Kontos Yannis/Corbis Sygma

**Figure 18.2** The self-confidence of a civil revolution. 'He's finished!' is the slogan being confidently stuck on a policeman's riot shield outside the Belgrade parliament, 5 October 2000. Milošević was indeed finished. By that evening, his disastrous eleven years in power had effectively ended.

## NATO BOMBING, THE CONFLUENCE OF PRO-DEMOCRACY FORCES, AND THE BRATISLAVA PROCESS

Milošević's repressive, violent, and discriminatory policies in Kosovo, and his refusal to continue in his role as 'peacemaker'—achieved in Dayton, Ohio, in November 1995 when he was a key player in the negotiations that ended the war in Bosnia—led to the NATO bombing of the FRY. This seventy-eight-day military intervention, from 24 March to 10 June 1999, signified that Milošević had lost touch with reality.[28] His own policies had turned society against him and the regime that had led the country into a cul-de-sac, devastated its economy and criminalized its institutions. Serbia was in a typical *fin-de-regime* situation. The de facto capitulation of FRY (in effect, Serbia) on 9 June in Kumanovo, Macedonia, with the signing of a military-technical agreement between the International Security Force (KFOR) and the governments of the FRY and the Republic of Serbia, opened the final fifteen months of the life of the regime of Slobodan Milošević and his acolytes.

Every oppositional actor and grouping began reflecting on the way forward. There were illusions as to the possible rapidity of the end of the regime, some believing that it would happen before year's end. Others understood that society had to come out of the trauma of the bombing, regroup and organize itself. Political parties began working on overcoming the divisions that had plagued the democratic opposition throughout the 1990s. In September 1999, pro-democracy political parties initiated a process that led to the creation of the united Democratic Opposition of Serbia (DOS). Civil society organizations likewise began turning to each other and to experiences that could be learned from other international precedents. G17, a group of economists that came together in 1997 to prepare the economic reforms that would be necessary once democratic forces came to power, organized in August 1999 the first post-1999 war rally and announced the forming of a broader based 'G17+' civil society organization. This would be another spearhead of the civic mobilization. The independent media were also mobilizing with the understanding that a concerted effort was needed to support these coalition-building endeavours in an adverse situation, when the regime felt vulnerable and thus much more nervous and volatile in its repressive reactions. Cracking down on independent media outlets became the rule.

In July 1999 a meeting took place in Bratislava, Slovakia, under the auspices of the Slovak NGO and governmental circles and the EastWest Institute from New York, with the participation of Serbian democratic parties, NGO leaders, union and

---

[28] In an interview in *Odbrana* (Belgrade), 15 Oct. 2007, the president of Serbia, Boris Tadić, said: 'This was the only time in Serbia's history that it did not have an ally while entering a war against virtually the whole world. This is a unique case in history—a fact for Ripley's Believe It or Not!—but also offers an insight into the devastating policy choice that was then made in the name of our country... The consequences of such a policy could only be catastrophic: for the citizens, infrastructure, economy, army and ultimately the future of our country. We are still healing and shall be healing the effects of that policy choice.'

independent media personalities. This led to the creation of the so-called 'Bratislava Process'. This was an enabling structure that would meet on a regular basis during the next fifteen months, helping to build a broad coalition of all relevant democratic actors in Serbian society and friends from the international donor community. It was the political element of this broad coalition, the Democratic Opposition of Serbia, that was the central actor that was going to deliver the victory over the regime. The seventeen political parties of this coalition were in constant contact with European parties of similar orientation and with EU and US officials. Funders—public and private, European and US—were working in concert to help the efforts of parties, civil society, actors, and media. There was a clear understanding that Serbian society had moved towards a willingness for change and that change needed to be supported. Peace and stability in the Balkans were at stake.

An additional crucial learning experience began. The Slovak example of electoral victory over the Vladimír Mečiar regime in November 1998 was the single most enlightening case of mobilizing voters. The lessons would be applied both in Croatia in January 2000, contributing to the defeat of Franjo Tudjman, and in Serbia. The model of the mobilization of the electorate through a 'get out the vote' campaign was an essential lesson. Meanwhile Otpor continued to grow and become bolder by the day.

An essential element of the success of the movement was to be found within the structures of the state. After the 1996–7 events, and in particular after the 1999 NATO intervention, a number of middle- and higher-ranking police and army officers realized that Milošević was taking the country down a dead-end street. They made secret pacts with the democratic opposition and helped the movement forward. Lines of contact were established between democratic opposition parties and officers in both police and the military, who informed them on the internal dynamics of these institutions. An internal opinion poll on attitudes of the army after the NATO bombing campaign, made public by a courageous journalist who was condemned and sent to prison because of his action, showed that a significant number of officers in the army were disillusioned with Milošević and did not trust his leadership.[29]

## 5 OCTOBER 2000

The 24 September 2000 election produced a victory for the democratic opposition candidate who won 50.24 per cent of the vote as opposed to Milošević's 37.15 per cent. Turnout was extremely high, at 71 per cent. The choice of candidate was of the essence. Vojislav Koštunica was able to rally a broad spectrum of democratic-minded voters from left to right. At no point was there any doubt about who would be the best choice. It was then a question of putting

[29] Miroslav Filipovic, 'Serbs Officers Relive Killings', *Balkan Crisis Report* (London: Institute for War and Peace Reporting), no. 130, 4 Apr. 2000, www.iwpr.net/?p=bcr&s=f&o=247641&apc_state=henibcr2000.

the campaign together. Zoran Djindjić was the campaign manager and G17 + prepared the *White Book on Milošević's Regime* depicting the devastating consequences of his time in office.[30] They also prepared a detailed road map for the actions of the future democratic government.

The groundwork had been laid over the previous decade, through civic, political, electoral struggles, defeats and victories. A 'get out the vote' campaign of massive proportions was mounted. In February 2000 a group of thirty NGOs started preparing a strategy that would lead to Exit 2000 (Izlaz 2000) a joint campaign of numerous Serbian NGOs which would be another building-block in this effort.[31]

The support of outside governments and organizations was a most significant form of solidarity in technical and political terms. There was finally a coordinated effort overall that had been lacking in previous years. A Donors' Forum had been created at the beginning of July 2000.[32] A key element in this outside support was that the EU decided to give support directly to those cities and towns in which the democratic opposition to Milošević had been in power since 1997. This was a demonstration of a direct and concrete form of European support to those in Serbia who saw their future in Europe. A series of three projects—with the unusual names Asphalt for Democracy, Oil for Democracy, and Schools for Democracy—delivered goods, mended roads, and improved schools in an extremely efficient manner in democratically led municipalities throughout the country. Many European member states and the US gave significant support to these efforts. Switzerland and Norway in particular made a notable effort to help Serbian democratic actors.

The use of force was contemplated by the regime in preparation for 5 October 2000, which was to be the day on which the would-be democratic Serbia was going to defend the electoral victory that Milošević was trying to steal from it. At least half a million people congregated in Belgrade, from all over Serbia, to defend their vote against a decade of devastation by Milošević's power politics. The question that loomed large was whether Milošević would give the order to the special police forces and the army to shoot at the crowd gathered in front of the parliament. Milošević did give the order but it was disobeyed. Zoran Djindjić, in an effort to avoid bloodshed, decided to speak to the head of the police Unit of Special Operations (JSO), Milorad Ulemek, 'Legija',[33] so as to convince him to not follow Milošević's orders. Although two people lost their lives that day—one by

---

[30] *Bela Knjiga Miloševićeve vladavine* [The White Book on Milošević's Regime] (Belgrade: G17 +, July 2000).

[31] Jelica Minić and Miljenko Dereta, 'Izlaz 2000: An Exit to Democracy in Serbia', in Joerg Forbrig and Pavol Demeš (eds.), *Reclaiming Democracy: Civil Society and Electoral Change in Central and Eastern Europe* (Bratislava: German Marshall Fund of the United States, 2007), 79–99.

[32] Ibid. 89–90.

[33] In 2006, he was condemned to forty years in prison, after a three-year trial, for technically organizing the assassination of Zoran Djindjić.

accident under the wheels of the 'revolutionary' bulldozer, and another shot by a stray bullet—the feared bloodshed did not occur.[34]

Some very limited force was used by the opposition on 5 October to seize the parliament building and the national TV station. It revealed the seriousness of secret preparations for the historical date. A huge yellow bulldozer—which would become the symbol of 5 October—privately owned and driven by the owner, who came from the suburbs of Belgrade, manoeuvred along with the demonstrators to help them in their non-violent but forceful actions. It seemed that this limited use of force was necessary to prove that the pro-democracy movement was not leaving anything to chance. Confronted with the possible destructive violent power of the dying Milošević regime, the opposition leaders had prepared a scenario whereby

©AFP/Stringer/Getty Images

**Figure 18.3** The symbolic bulldozer. This bulldozer, seen here in front of the Yugoslav Federal parliament building in Belgrade on 5 October 2000, the day the building was occupied and Slobodan Milošević compelled to resign, became a symbol of the Serbian revolution. Like the convoy of heavy vehicles from the provincial town of Čačak, and like the burly men who used their physical bulk and sharp elbows to enter the parliament building, this bulldozer illustrates how the Serbian breakthrough involved a show of physical strength very close to the actual use of force.

[34] Dragan Bujošević and Ivan Radovanović, *5 Oktobar: Dvadeset četiri sata prevrata* [5 October: Twenty Four Hours of Revolution] (Belgrade: Medija Centar, 2000), 258. This 'instant history' book documents some of the preparations for use of force in a variety of scenarios that the democratic opposition made in the run-up to 5 October 2008.

they would, if need be, forcefully defend the electoral victory that was clearly coming. The leadership of the Democratic Opposition of Serbia prepared a plan in secrecy, whereby they would first defend the electoral victory in the streets with the support of the citizens, and secondly take over that same evening and in the following day or days the key state institutions and media outlets. Thus B92 was able to re-enter its premises from which it had been ousted the previous year, and Vojislav Koštunica could appear on state TV that same evening interviewed by an opposition journalist. All the opinion polls indicated that the people would vote massively against Milošević, which suggested in itself that the silent abstainers would also turn out to vote for a future without the regime. The opposition had secretly planned its actions to take over the parliament and other key institutions on the night of the victory. The regime was on its knees but was capable of striking back. Rumour spread that several army generals' sons and daughters were among the protesters and that they would thus refrain from any major violence. The regime was disintegrating from the inside.

Vojislav Koštunica, the president-elect, stood on the balcony of Belgrade City Hall at 6:30 pm that evening, opposite the parliament building, and pronounced Serbia a free country. He promised to endeavour soon to make it a 'boring' country. The inauguration of the new president occurred on 7 October, and a few days later Koštunica was standing in Biarritz, at an EU summit with the leaders of fifteen EU member states.

## CONCLUSION: THE SERBIAN *LONGUE DURÉE* AND *LONGUE JOURNÉE*

The Serbian experience of civil resistance led to a liberal outcome that is still in the making, with many a challenge still lying ahead. The convincing victory of the pro-European, democratic block of parties in the parliamentary elections of 11 May 2008, following as it did the re-election in February of Boris Tadić as president of Serbia, was a confirmation of the choice of future that Serbia had made in autumn 2000.

The civil resistance in Serbia was an emphatically home-grown movement that underwent a long but eventually deep learning process. This is the story of the survival and self-preservation of a European society struggling to find its rightful European place in circumstances in which the pull of retrograde forces, war and decline, was immense. At the moment of a general 'return to Europe' in the post-1989 world, Serbia under Milošević had strayed away from a possible future democratic course. In the late 1980s and early 1990s it had been mesmerized by Milošević's use of nationalist promises of the redemption of Serbdom, when in fact his concern was with personal power retention. In the process Serbia lost four wars and ten unredeemable years of development, came under international sanctions from 1992–2000, became impoverished, lost a generation of mostly

© Kontos Yannis/Corbis Sygma

**Figure 18.4** Revolution to reverse a fraudulent election outcome. A demonstrator waves a banner bearing the slogan 'Who TODAY speaks in our name? Koštunica of course!' on the steps of parliament in Belgrade, 5 October 2000. On the same evening opposition leader Vojislav Koštunica declared his victory, pronouncing Serbia a free country. Two days later he was formally inaugurated as president, replacing Slobodan Milošević.

younger professionals now scattered around the world, and suffered a loss of image and credibility.

Thus the victorious outcome, to the disbelief of so many, stands out as a particularly significant one. As Thomas Carothers has written: 'In short, it was the ideas, persistence, courage, and actions of Serbian politicians, civic activists, and ordinary citizens that brought down Milošević. US and European support made real contributions in broadening and deepening that opposition, but the aid campaign was a facilitator of change, not the engine of it.'[35]

The name of the late, assassinated, prime minister of Serbia, Zoran Djindjić, stands out as one of the key architects, along with all the actors and organizations mentioned above, of the final electoral and political *longue journée*. This leadership, audacity, and determination to see Serbia into the modern democratic age was instrumental in the victory over the power politics of the Milošević regime. It is he who launched Serbia on the liberal-democratic road after 5 October 2000.

---

[35] Thomas Carothers, *Ousting Foreign Strongmen: Lessons from Serbia* (Washington DC: Carnegie Endowment for International Peace, Policy Brief no. 5, May 2001), 4.

Society adapted to the new post-October 2000 situation and moved from the role of civil resistance and opposition into one of critical constructiveness. This was not a linear seamless process. A number of civil society organizations played a key role in transferring their acquired experience, methods of action, and knowledge abroad to other societies fighting for their freedom, most prominently in Ukraine and Georgia, but also elsewhere. This invaluable repository of civil resistance is still being used. Otpor as a movement disappeared and blended into diverse political and civic streams, as well as carrying forward its methods and spirit to other parts of the world.

The institutional, economic, and social devastation left by the Milošević regime has proven to be an immense challenge. There was no democratic Arcadia behind the crumbled façade of Milošević's regime. After the 'annus mirabilis', came the 'annus realismis' and the 'annus desillusionis'.[36] Serbia has advanced by fits and starts. The assassination of Zoran Djindjić on 12 March 2003 dealt a huge blow to the fledgling democracy, but the gauntlet of the retrograde past was thrown back. Post-October Serbia had a full agenda of transition challenges but also an unresolved union with Montenegro (independent since May 2006), a definition of statehood challenge with Kosovo (self-proclaimed independent on 17 February 2008) and the need to comply fully with the ICTY in the Hague. (To date forty-three Serbian high-ranking officials have been or are being tried in the Hague; three more cases are outstanding).

With ebbs and flows Serbia has advanced, but is still—at this writing—near the back of the EU enlargement pack. The electoral victory of pro-European democratic forces in 2008 seemed to give a significant edge to the modernizers in their struggle with the traditionalists. Embedded in the south-eastern flank of Europe, a 'belated nation' (Helmut Plessner), Serbia came of democratic age in 2000. The legacy is one of citizens' power, an accomplished desire for what Machiavelli called the *vivere libero, vivere civile*. Citizens in Serbia are alert and watchful of politicians' actions. No one in Serbia, or in the Balkans for that matter, wishes a return to the catastrophe of the 1990s. Politicians throughout the region are mindful of this. Civic and non-governmental organizations have finally gained a position comparable to that of similar organizations in other transition countries. It took Serbia and its citizens a decade to awake fully from the nightmare into which Milošević had plunged them. And yet Serbia, with its electoral revolution of 2000, did prove itself capable of a grand moment. That event, the culmination of a painful, decade-long learning process, demonstrated the capacity of a society to bring together all relevant political and social actors in a peaceful, electoral 'tyrannicide'.

[36] A quote from a lecture by Elemér Hankiss in 1994.

# 19

## Georgia's 'Rose Revolution' of 2003: Enforcing Peaceful Change

*Stephen Jones*

Watching the theatre, heroism, and glory of the Rose Revolution in the cold and rainy streets of Tbilisi in November 2003, Georgian parents trembled with fear. Newspapers announced that trains transporting soldiers from the north to the capital of Tbilisi were blocked by villagers dragging logs onto the tracks. The State Chancellery warned of a 'second civil war'.[1] Georgian parents recalled similar challenges to the state in 1956, 1989, and 1991 which led to bloody climaxes and dead teenagers. Western leaders were also concerned. Earlier in 2003, Senator John McCain, John Shalikashvili (former chairman of the Joint Chiefs of Staff), and Strobe Talbott visited Georgia. In July James Baker III flew to Tbilisi to mediate honest elections. Lynn Pascoe, Deputy Assistant Secretary for European and Eurasian Affairs arrived on 18 November, a few days before the final confrontation. Why such attention? Georgia was a vital ally in the 'cold peace' being fought with Russia over energy pipelines, and a violent breakdown would have unpredictable consequences for US marines stationed in Georgia. It would end the hope of a successful pro-Western transition in the region and reinforce the arguments of the US's domestic critics of wasteful spending on democratic experiments. Fortunately, the crisis in Georgia turned out to be non-violent. The climactic storming of the Georgian parliament ended with one smashed window and yet another political patriarch slinking off the political stage.

Many Western observers saw the Rose Revolution as a vindication of US and European policies of civic and democratic development. Richard Miles, the US ambassador at the time, sighed with relief that 'finally in Georgia there was something you could look at and say, "it worked"'.[2] But despite the triumphal rhetoric blasted through megaphones in Tbilisi's Freedom Square, and the rationalizations

I thank Gia Tarkhan-Mouravi, Lado Papava, Tedo Japaridze, Mamuka Tsereteli, and Zurab Karumidze for their comments on a draft of this chapter.

[1] *The Daily Telegraph* (London), 12 Nov. 2003, www.telegraph.co.uk/news/main.jhtml?xml=/news/2003/11/12/wgeor12.xml.

[2] David Anable, *The Role of Georgia's Media—and Western Aid—in Georgia's Rose Revolution* (Cambridge, Mass.: Joan Shorenstein Center on the Press, Politics and Public Policy, Working Paper Series, 2006 no. 3), 28. Available at http://www.hks.harvard.edu/presspol/research_home.htm.

in Western capitals, this revolution, like most others, hung on a thread. It had no
script, and was unexpected and mostly unwanted by the opposition leaders themselves. The sober revolutionary, Leon Trotsky, reminds us: 'People do not make
revolutions eagerly any more than they do war.'[3] This was not a carnival despite rock
groups and parades, and it could have ended in catastrophe.

The Rose Revolution—along with its companions in Serbia (2000), Ukraine's
Orange Revolution (2004–5) and Kyrgyzstan's Tulip Revolution (2005)—has
added to the scholarly debate on revolution as well as to the successful record
of non-violence against corrupt, often repressive, governments. First, it showed
that speculation about the end of revolution after the triumphs of 'liberal
democracy' in 1989–91 was premature.[4] Second, it proved the effectiveness of
non-violent strategies. Political violence would have been the Rose Revolution's
undoing. Third, despite the values it shared with the 1989 revolutions, the Rose
Revolution made no demands for major economic, social or systemic change. It
revealed a new model of post-communist revolution. The slogan of the Rose
Revolution's leadership was 'revolution without revolution'. There was no ideological innovation, no 'anti-politics' or 'living in truth,' no social or peace
movement, and no expectation of socio-economic transformation. Non-violence
was a strategy, not an ideological goal. In terms of ideas, the revolution was
poorer than its eastern European predecessors. Based on its ideological content,
'colourless' is the best adjective. It sought to improve market democracy and
return to liberalism's constitutional principles. It was, as Ghia Nodia put it, a
'catch-up revolution' which wanted to join the mainstream, not abandon it.[5]

Yet the scale of protest, the rapidity of change, the disintegration of ruling
elites, the abandonment of President Shevardnadze by the armed forces, the
passionate speeches in front of the State Chancellery, and the call for renewal
and national unity—all these characterized a revolutionary situation. The Rose
Revolution was a classic example of structural disintegration from the centre, a
process Sir Lewis Namier described as the 'corrosion of the moral and mental
bases of government'.[6] But despite the important generational change in leadership, the 'emancipation' from corrupt elections and oligarchs, and claims for the
Rose Revolution's global significance, in goals and outcome the Rose Revolution
was an anti-revolutionary revolution.[7] It rejected absolutism and millenarianism

---

[3] Leon Trotsky, *The Russian Revolution: The Overthrow of Tzarism and the Triumph of the Soviets*,
trans. Max Eastman (New York: Doubleday, 1959), 304.

[4] See in particular the debate between Jeff Goodwin, 'Is the Age of Revolutions Over?', and Eric
Selbin, 'Same as It Ever Was: the Future of Revolution at the End of the Century', in Mark N. Katz (ed.)
*Revolution: International Dimensions* (Washington DC: CQ Press, 2001), 272–97.

[5] Ghia Nodia, comments on my paper as discussant at the Conference on Civil Resistance and
Power Politics, St Antony's College, University of Oxford, 15–18 Mar. 2007.

[6] Sir Lewis Namier, *Vanished Supremacies: Essays on European History 1812–1918* (London: Hamish
Hamilton, 1958), 22.

[7] For an assessment of the relationship of the 1989 revolutions to revolutionary theory, see Richard
Sakwa, 'The Age of Paradox: the Anti-Revolutionary Revolutions of 1989–1991', in Moira Donald and
Tim Rees (eds.), *Reinterpreting Revolution in Twentieth Century Europe* (New York: St Martin's Press,
2001), 159–76.

©David Mdzinarishvili/Reuters/Corbis

**Figure 19.1** Turning the security forces. Interior ministry servicemen greet opposition leaders in the parliament yard in the Georgian capital Tbilisi, on 23 November 2003. A few days earlier they still appeared loyal to Georgian president Eduard Shevardnadze, but Shevardnadze had just signalled his readiness to negotiate on opposition demands.

in favour of normalcy and legality. The victors moved rapidly to have the November election results dismissed by the Supreme Court and new legal elections take place. This revolution was about moral regeneration, clean government, joining the world, and sticking to the rules, not about creative destruction or the building of a new society. Yet the non-violent struggle was passionate. It resulted in the complete and sudden removal of the old political elites.

The fame of the Rose Revolution rests in part on its primacy. It was the first successful assault in the former Soviet Union on what the scholarly field calls 'competitive authoritarian states'. All such states—Georgia, Armenia, Azerbaijan, Ukraine, and Kyrgyzstan—were (and most still are) led by Soviet-trained former *apparatchiki*. These leaders were publicly committed to democracy including elections, a degree of press freedom and toleration of organized public dissent.[8] But all presided over regimes which had metamorphosed into peculiar post-Soviet capitalist hybrids, distinguished by presidential strongmen ruling through corrupt client

---

[8] Steven Levitsky and Lucan Way, 'Elections Without Democracy: The Rise of Competitive Authoritarianism', *Journal of Democracy*, 13, no. 2 (2002), 51–65.

networks and semi-privatized state structures over fractured societies. The duality of fantasy ('democracy') and reality (popular powerlessness), when combined with corruption, economic decline, and ineffectual state structures, produced in these regimes significant vulnerabilities which Georgian dissenters were the first success-fully to exploit.

More important than its pioneering feature (which only applied to the post-Soviet space) was the Rose Revolution's bloodless consummation—this in a country which over the last fifteen years has experienced a civil war, two seces-sionist wars and at least two assassination attempts on its president. How was it that this peaceful liberal revolution—what Timothy Garton Ash in another context has called 'refolution'—confounded the expectations of many of us who concluded it could only end in bloodshed like the Georgian protests of 1956 and 1989, and 1992 (the overthrow of President Gamsakhurdia). Was it an innovative model of peaceful change or blind luck that no one was sacrificed on the barricades? Was it a regional model of revolution based on post-Soviet legacies and shared mobilization strategies—the Serbian youth organization Otpor's Slobodan Djinović declared that Shevardnadze was ousted 'according to the Yugoslav scenario'[9]—or was the peaceful outcome due to Georgia's own political context? And finally, to what degree did the West, and its support of civil society institutions and democracy-building programmes, contribute to the bloodless victory?

## THE CONTEXT: THE POST-SOVIET LEGACY IN GEORGIA

After the overthrow of President Gamsakhurdia in January 1992, Western gov-ernments saw Shevardnadze as the best political bet for the transition to liberal democratic state building in Georgia. But despite restoring central government and stabilizing the economy between 1992 and 1995, Shevardnadze's government failed to establish its authority or democratic credentials. It was constructed from the roof downwards and although democratic scaffolding was in place, its core was a tradition-based patrimonial authority which ruled by custom, threat, private dispensations, and privileges granted by the president. The state facili-tated private networks that dominated the country's economic life and which deprived it of the proper political and economic revenues needed to function. The state was effectively privatized, in part by Shevardnadze's family. It had no monopoly of violence in vast areas of the country which were either independent or ruled by regional overseers accountable to a chief executive who, after thirty years of almost uninterrupted leadership, had slipped into routine and passivity. Shevardnadze relied on familiar personnel, traditional networks, and ad hoc advisory bodies such as the National Security Council and the regionally

---

[9] *The Hindu* (Chennai), 31 Dec. 2003, www.hindu.com/2003/12/31/stories/2003123101161000.htm.

appointed governors to maintain his power, rather than on accountable institutions and popular authority. The council of ministers was a rag-bag of officials with no collective identity or political influence and parliament's power was undermined by ineffective parties, fixed elections, and powerful unelected regional governors. Clientelism and informal channels of power were the hallmark of Georgian politics under Gamsakhurdia and Shevardnadze.[10]

Lucan Way argues that a major feature of this soft authoritarianism is 'the inability of incumbents to maintain power or concentrate political control by preserving elite unity, controlling elections and media, and/or using force against opponents'. The source of this 'pluralism by default' as he calls it, is 'incumbent weakness', 'ineffective elite organization', and 'a widely popular national identity' which together undermine the incumbent's political capacity even where civil society is weak.[11] Georgia under Shevardnadze was not in the same authoritarian category as Russia and Belarus, but the fragmentation of the state, deepened by centrifugal forces among Georgia's national minorities and competition among criminalized elite networks within the ministries and security bodies, led to a dilemma for Shevardnadze. How to remain a 'democrat' without democracy? Splitting power at the top and permitting dissent from below gave an impression of pluralism and competition, but it disguised the fact that Shevardnadze, though not quite a dictator, was not much of a democrat either. When the crisis came, he was unable to unite political elites to defend his 'democracy' or to appeal to popular sentiment against rebellious former ministers. Poor constitutional design, which worked against collective responsibility in the cabinet, and poor supervision of parliament and the executive added to his troubles. When the time came to defend the regime, the long-standing competition and antagonism among Georgia's post-Soviet elites made a coherent government response impossible. Most important of all was Shevardnadze's status as a lame duck president. With seventeen months left of his term, there was little point in defending him. The lame duck, in the days and weeks of November, became a visibly dead duck. This is what primarily separates 2003 from the violent experiences of 1956, 1989, and 1990–1 when the state had the ability—and took the initiative—to suppress the opposition violently. In November 2003, by contrast, Shevardnadze had been abandoned by all.

The fragility of the *ancien régime* is only part of the story. Revolutions are complicated, often inarticulate sequences of events that are shaped by ideological frameworks, leadership errors, popular participation and, in many cases, external involvement. In the Georgian case, the catalyst for years of popular discontent was the 2 November parliamentary elections. Since 1990 Georgians have participated in thirteen nationwide elections but before 2003, only two (in October 1990

---

[10] For an assessment of the Shevardnadze era, see Jonathan Wheatley, *Georgia from National Awakening to Rose Revolution: Delayed Transition in the Former Soviet Union* (Aldershot: Ashgate, 2005).

[11] Lucan Way, 'Authoritarian State Building and the Sources of Regime Competitiveness in the Fourth Wave: The Cases of Belarus, Moldova, Russia, and Ukraine', *World Politics*, 57, no. 2 (Jan. 2005), 231–61.

and arguably October 1992), led to any real change in power. Georgian elections since 1992 have been peaceful, but marred by party boycotts and poor electoral design, including vast disparities between the numbers of voters in each electoral district, inadequate mechanisms for ensuring transparency, and a party list system which marginalized national minority representation. The falsified election in Georgia in November 2003, as in Serbia in 2000 and Ukraine in 2004, was a perfect tool for the Georgian opposition to underline the illegitimacy of the regime, maintain popular attention, mobilize citizens, and invite international attention.[12]

In the lead up to the November 2003 parliamentary elections, there was hope that new legislation incorporated into the Unified Election Code, would end government manipulation of the vote. There was for the first time a real choice of parties beyond those compromised by deals and alliances with the government. Amendments provided for parallel tabulation of votes, a new marking system to prevent repeat voting, the eradication of supplementary voting lists, and the open tabulation of precinct election results. Electoral commissions, which had been in the hands of the ruling parties, were revamped to give the opposition better representation. But despite $US2.4 million from the US government to help Georgia prepare for the November ballot and the presence of 5,000 electoral observers from the Organization for Security and Cooperation in Europe (OSCE), the National Democratic Institute for International Affairs (NDI), the International Republican Institute (IRI), and indigenous NGOs—and regardless of exit polls pointing to quite different results—Shevardnadze's unpopular coalition 'For a New Georgia,' secured first place in the 235 seat house with 21.3 per cent of the vote (57 MPs). The Union of Democratic Revival, led by Aslan Abashidze, came second with 18.8 per cent (39 MPs). Abashidze ruled Achara, an autonomous republic in Georgia's south west, as a personal fiefdom, and free elections had not taken place there for over a decade. In the November 2003 election, his party won 96.7 per cent of the vote in Achara, with a Soviet-style 97 per cent turnout. The United National Movement, led by the youthful and popular Mikheil (Misha) Saakashvili, came in third with 18.1 per cent (36 MPs) despite leading in the exit polls and in the parallel tabulation of votes.[13]

---

[12] For a review of Georgian elections in 1992–5, Darell Slider 'Democratization in Georgia', in Karen Dawisha and Bruce Parrott (eds.), *Conflict, Cleavage, and Change in Central Asia and the Caucasus* (Cambridge: Cambridge University Press, 1997), 156–98. For the 2003–4 elections, see Stephen Jones 'Presidential and Parliamentary Elections in Georgia, 2004', *Electoral Studies*, 24, no. 2 (June 2005), 303–11; on the November 2003 parliamentary elections, see *Georgia, What Now?* (Tbilisi/Brussels: International Crisis Group, Europe Report no. 151, 3 Dec. 2003), www.crisisgroup. org/library/documents/europe/caucasus/151_georgia_what_now.pdf.

[13] Some of this material, including statistics on the election results in November 2003 is in my 'Presidential and Parliamentary Elections'. See also Jean-Christophe Peuch, 'Georgia's Parliamentary Elections: Democracy in the Making', *Caucasus Election Watch* (Washington DC: Center for Strategic and International Studies, 27 Oct. 2003); for more detail, see *International Election Observation Mission: Parliamentary Elections, Georgia—2 November 2003* (Tbilisi: OSCE/ODIHR Election Observation Mission, 3 Nov. 2003), 9, www.osce.org/press_rel/2003/pdf_documents/11-3659-odihr1.pdf.

Given expectations of change and the crude falsification of the vote, the November result led to mass indignation. The opposition, in particular strategists in the Liberty Institute, knew the methods and techniques that had made 'electoral revolutions' in the Philippines (1986), Chile (1988), Slovakia (1998), and Serbia (2000) so powerful, and over the month of November, using a combination of patriotic rallies, marches, boycott of parliament, painted slogans, T-shirts blazoned with anti-Shevardnadze catchphrases, and concerts, focused on maintaining high numbers of demonstrators on Rustaveli Prospect, the main thoroughfare, effectively paralysing the government. The planning, discipline, and organizational capacity of the opposition (helped by cell phones and the Internet) was a crucial departure from previous revolts in Georgia since independence, but it was the bitter popular disappointment with a regime that had failed to end the population's economic misery that led them to the streets.

## AN INNOVATIVE MODEL OF CHANGE?

On 10 November, in televised comments, Shevardnadze declared he was 'elected by the Georgian people, and I do not intend to resign at the demand of individual politicians and a few dozen young people waving flags'.[14] He thought, as he later confirmed, that it would all blow over. But this time was different. First, the opposition was organized with an artful 36-year-old Mikheil Saakashvili at its head, backed by a supreme strategist, the former Speaker of parliament and Shevardnadze's erstwhile campaign manager, Zurab Zhvania. Before 2003, like other governments in the Commonwealth of Independent States (CIS), the Georgian administration had faced little organized political resistance in parliament. Georgian political parties, despite their colourful posturing and occasional successes, were not formed by grass roots organizations but were creations of the state or powerful kingpins. They belonged to what Scott Mainwaring calls 'weakly institutionalized' party systems—volatile, poorly rooted, weak in legitimacy, and possessing few resources with indistinguishable programmes.[15] The formation of the United National Movement in October 2001 by Saakashvili changed the political landscape. Saakashvili, an effective populist, exalted 'the people' and displayed unabashed patriotism. He resembled the best media-savvy American politicians, and after his resignation as Justice Minister in the fall of 2001, as newly elected Chair of the Tbilisi City Council, he relentlessly exposed government corruption. His party, though dependent on

[14] *The Guardian* (London), 10 Nov. 2003, www.guardian.co.uk/international/story/0,,1081370,00. html.
[15] Scott Mainwaring, 'Party System in the Third Wave', in Larry Diamond and Marc Plattner (eds.), *The Global Divergence of Democracies* (Baltimore, Md.: Johns Hopkins University Press, 2001), 185–99.

Saakashvili's personality, was more modern and more successful than any other in reaching out to the regions, to disillusioned students and to marginalized pensioners. It was the first really post-Soviet party, one that Shevardnadze was unable to tempt with sinecures and access to state resources. It was led by sophisticated urban youth, many of whom had been educated in the West, had worked in Western NGOs in Georgia, or had participated in Western-funded indigenous NGOs such as the Liberty Institute, which promoted media freedom, religious tolerance, and human rights.

Second, the united opposition had a strategy. Benefiting from networks of European civil society activists and electronic access to international media, the National Movement, the United Democrats, and other smaller allied parties quickly absorbed the lessons of non-violent movements elsewhere. The influence of the Serbian opposition including the youth movement, Otpor (Resistance), which had helped oust Slobodan Milošević in October 2000, was important. Giga Bokeria, the National Movement's most influential ideologue, along with Levan Ramishvili, a founder of the influential Liberty Institute, met with Otpor and other Serbian activists in Belgrade in spring 2003. In the summer of 2003, Otpor trainers travelled to Tbilisi to instruct Georgian youth. The Georgian youth organization 'kmara' (Enough), established in the spring of 2003 and a noisy battalion in the Rose Revolution, replicated the tactics of Otpor.[16] Its organizational model, like Otpor's, was horizontal and decentralized. Its confrontational tactics included the establishment of youth groups, outreach to traditionally apolitical sections of the population through graffiti, rallies, and theatre, including the co-option of rock groups and media personalities. In mid-November, as kmara activists mobilized demonstrators by email and cell phone in the Liberty Institute—its walls decorated with Serbian resistance posters including the clenched fist of Otpor—the independent TV channel, Rustavi 2, showed the film *Bringing down a Dictator*, a documentary about the fall of Milošević.[17] Ivane Merabishvili, general secretary of the United National Movement and by all accounts the organizational genius of the Rose Revolution, later declared that 'all the demonstrators knew the tactics of the revolution in Belgrade by heart because they showed...the film on their revolution. Everyone knew what to do. This was a copy of that revolution, only louder.'[18]

The ideas of the National Movement, as it became known, were not Gandhian. There was no clear code of conduct defining passive resistance, no condemnation of force. The fiery symbol of the revolution, Mikheil Saakashvili, was irascible and emotional, threatening revenge and retribution. But the lessons of the Serbian experience were clear: renounce armed struggle which had proved too costly in

[16] On the role of kmara in the Rose Revolution, Giorgi Kandelaki, *Georgia's Rose Revolution: A Participant's Perspective* (Washington DC: US Institute of Peace, Special Report 167, July 2006).
[17] Anable, *Role of Georgia's Media*, 5.
[18] Ibid. 11

Georgia in the early 1990s; mobilize crowds onto the streets to prevent retaliation; ensure international media coverage; fraternize with the police and army; maintain a unified political opposition and establish an alternative source of authority. Nino Burjanadze, Speaker of the Parliament, for example, was persuaded to announce herself interim Georgian president the day before Shevardnadze's resignation. The decision to create a Civil Disobedience Committee, also known as 'Art Committee' (*Artcom* for short) because of the large number of artists, film directors, and writers in its leadership, was an echo of the Serbian campaign. Its strategy of disruption included sit-down demonstrations at regional administrative offices, occupations of universities, chains of people around the State Chancellery, strikes (some teachers responded), and synchronous horn blowing by Tbilisi's cars, a sound which eerily echoed the whistle blowing of striking factories in 1917.[19]

The effect of the Serbian movement should not be exaggerated; its impact in Georgia depended on the right local conditions, among them weak incumbency, an electoral crisis, and a united opposition—but it illustrates the importance of two phenomena in the Rose Revolution: first, what Mark Beissinger calls 'modular action', or revolutionary waves as one revolutionary opposition emulates another.[20] Our electronic world permits rapid communication between what Margaret Keck and Kathryn Sikkink call 'transnational advocacy networks'.[21] These international networks consist of democracy activists who have access to significant funding from international foundations and Western governments. The Liberty Institute, kmara, the Georgian Young Lawyers Association (GYLA), and other NGOs—important influences on the course of the Rose Revolution—benefited from information, training, and advice from these international alliances. Second, the ideas of these advocacy networks reflect not only democratization and a moralization of politics, but a renewed practice of non-violence and grass-roots mobilization. Leaving aside for now whether this establishes a new 'soft power' of Western hegemony, it has led to the creation of a network of 'professional revolutionaries' (or 'consultants' if they get paid), supported by Western states, transnational organizations, and international NGOs.[22] Their activity stretches as far as Lebanon and Zimbabwe. The ideas, methods, and success of the Rose Revolutionaries, who participated in these networks from the 1990s on, showed them to be adept learners.

[19] Interview with David Zurabishvili, one of the leaders of the Liberty Institute, in Zurab Karumidze and James V. Wertsch (eds.), *'Enough': The Rose Revolution in the Republic of Georgia, 2003* (New York: Nova Science Publishers, 2005), 66.

[20] Mark Beissinger, 'Structure and Example in Modular Political Phenomena: The Diffusion of Bulldozer/Rose/Orange/Tulip Revolutions', *Perspectives on Politics*, 5, no. 2 (June 2007).

[21] Margaret Keck and Kathryn Sikkink, *Activists Beyond Borders: Advocacy Networks in International Politics* (Ithaca, NY: Cornell University Press, 1998).

[22] Nicolas Guilhot in *The Democracy Makers: Human Rights and the Politics of Global Order* (New York: Columbia University Press, 2005), suggests that these advocacy networks have become a new instrument of Western powers and their strategic and economic goals in developing countries.

## A NEW GEORGIAN PATH

Mark Beissinger suggests that without the Serbian 'Bulldozer' revolution, there would likely have been no Rose Revolution at all.[23] His proposition underlines the impact of ideas, emulation, and international advocacy networks over structure, culture, and history as sources of Georgia's Rose Revolution. Other analyses of post-communist stagnation and weak statehood emphasize the legacies of the Soviet era and national political culture. Jadwiga Staniszkis, Ken Jowitt, and Katherine Verdery are some of the best-known scholars who have thought about the complexities of path dependence in communist and post-communist states.[24] Their ideas suggest the best clues to the genesis of the coloured revolutions is in national-Soviet legacies.

In answering why the Shevardnadze regime was defeated and why it went peacefully, structural explanations, focusing on the weakness of the *ancien régime*, are convincing. But they cannot be disconnected from national legacies and political culture.[25] There are four specific Georgian contexts to the Rose Revolution. First, twentieth-century Georgian history is littered with bloody revolutions and counter-revolutions (or attempted revolutions and coups, depending on your definition): 1905, February 1917, February 1921 (the Red Army invasion of Georgia), the end of communist rule in 1989–90 and the overthrow of President Gamsakhurdia in 1992. The non-violent Rose Revolution in this historical context is exceptional, yet its peaceful outcome was, in part, conditioned by the country's history of violence. Zurab Zhvania, in an interview on the November 2003 events, declared:

> People were not looking for a revolution... The new generation in Georgia has experienced what civil unrest means [in the civil war and war in Abkhazia in the early 1990s]. They have experienced how turbulent events can affect every family.[26]

The Georgian population was severely chastened by the civil war of 1991–3, which ended in the destruction of Tbilisi's city centre, the division of families, and hundreds of dead and wounded. The bloody failure of Gamsakhurdia's

---

[23] Beissinger, 'Structure and Example', 25.

[24] See Jadwiga Staniszkis, *The Ontology of Socialism* (Oxford: Clarendon Press, 1992); Ken Jowitt, *The New World Disorder: The Leninist Extinction* (Berkeley, Calif.: University of California Press, 1992); and Katherine Verdery, *What was Socialism, and What Comes Next?* (Princeton, NJ: Princeton University Press, 1998).

[25] Classic examples of structural interpretations of revolution, which because of their emphasis on peasant societies, have less relevance to the Georgia case, are Theda Skocpol, *States and Social Revolutions: A Comparative Analysis of France, Russia, and China* (Cambridge: Cambridge University Press, 1979); Barrington Moore Jr, *Social Origins of Dictatorship and Democracy: Lord and Peasant in the Making of the Modern World* (Boston, Mass.: Beacon Press, 1966); Jack Goldstone, *Revolution and Rebellion in the Early Modern World* (Berkeley, Calif.: University of California Press, 1991).

[26] Karumidze and Wertsch, *'Enough'*, 35.

radical revolution in 1991–3 contributed to a popular mood which rejected violence and excessive militancy. In an IRI survey in May 2003, six months before the Rose Revolution brought thousands onto the streets, 75 per cent disapproved of 'demonstrations without permission' and 78 per cent condemned the 'occupation of buildings and enterprises'.[27] This mood was reinforced by the position of the Georgian Church. Consistently the most respected institution among Georgians in opinion polls, it warned against violence in its sermons, in the patriarch's epistles, and at decisive moments on Georgians' path to independence, such as the Patriarch's call to abandon public protest in April 1989 just before demonstrators were slaughtered by Soviet troops. The Shevardnadze government exploited this anxiety and warned of the dangers of 'one more civil confrontation'.[28] In this context, any attempt to use arms would have damned the National Movement and have made victory less likely, less legitimate, and less popular.

Second, although the Serbs provided a systematic strategy for civil resistance, non-violent strategies were not new to Georgians. In the last decades of Soviet rule in Georgia, rallies, petitions, hunger strikes, and appeals to international forums took place. Some, like the 1978 protest in central Tbilisi demanding the retention of Georgian language status in the constitution, were successful demonstrations of public resistance. At the same time, the bloody denouements to public rallies in 1956 and 1989 added to the heroic virtues of defiance. After the collapse of the Soviet Union, Georgian politics was an intoxicating mix of civic protests, boycotts, occupations, sit-ins, mass rallies, and vigils. Although they were overshadowed in the Western media by reports of violence, parliamentary fistfights, and attacks on religious minorities, these civic strategies were successful weapons against state arbitrariness. They brought Gamsakhurdia's government to power, and they helped bring it down. In November 2000, non-violent rallies led to the resignation of the government and in October 2001, to the resignation of a number of powerful ministers. There was a strong and fruitful tradition of direct action and civil resistance to draw upon in Georgia. The Serbian model incorporated civic protests into an overall strategy, but Georgian activists were experienced organizers.

Third, the Rose Revolution was a revolution of national and moral regeneration. Its complaints focused on Georgian domestic troubles such as state and judicial corruption, unemployment, disreputable political parties, and healthcare. But underlying this concern for practical improvements in their lives was a yearning among Georgians for a lost identity, pride, and national renewal. Saakashvili in a later interview declared the Rose Revolution 'was all about morality and restoring morality in the government'.[29] The absence of the Georgian Patriarch at the opening of the new—and to most people illegitimate— parliament on 22 November under Shevardnadze's jurisdiction, was an endorsement of the opposition's claims for the moral high ground. Just as Gandhi's

---

[27] International Republican Institute/Georgia, 'Georgian National Voter Study May 2003', 15, available at www.iri.org/eurasia/georgia/pdfs/2007–05–10-Georgia-Poll.ppt.
[28] Nodar Ladaria in *'Enough'*, 116.
[29] Mikheil Saakashvili in *'Enough'*, 26.

328 Stephen Jones

© Gleb Garanich/Reuters/Corbis

**Figure 19.2** Bring out more flags. Georgian opposition supporters wave national flags as they stand on an armoured vehicle, celebrating the resignation of President Eduard Shevardnadze outside his residence. Shevardnadze announced on TV: 'I see that all this cannot simply go on. If I was forced tomorrow to use my authority it would lead to a lot of bloodshed. I have never betrayed my country and so it is better that the president resigns.'

spinning wheel symbolized a return to an idealized past of community and simplicity, the new Georgian flag of five crosses which fluttered in thousands at every rally, represented a return to a lost past of Christian morality and a repossession of Georgia's 'special place within European civilization'.[30] Georgians' enthusiasm for integration into Europe, their ardent support of Western interests from NATO to US troops in Georgia, the participation of Georgian youth in Western educational exchange programmes (Saakashvili was educated at Columbia University), all contributed to dense connections with European (and North American) governments, NGOs, and international financial organizations in the

---

[30] See Mikheil Saakashvili's inaugural speech as newly elected president in Jan. 2004. 'Sakartvelos preszidentis Mikheil Saakashvilis mier tsarmotkmuli sitqva inauguratsiis dghes' [Inaugural speech by President Mikheil Saakashvili], in Makhaz Matsaberidze (ed.), *Sakartvelos prezidemteebis sainaugur-atsio sitqvebi—1991–2004—tsleebi: krebuli* (Tbilisi: Sh.P.S. Publishing Analytical Centre 'akhali azri', 2007), 45–6.

1990s. Much more than in neighbouring Azerbaijan and Armenia, this contributed to a small, but exceptionally sophisticated Third Sector which as the Shevardnadze era dragged on became increasingly politicized and oppositionist.

Finally, there is Eduard Shevardnadze. The personality of leaders can make or break revolutions. Shevardnadze was shaped by his long experience with public resistance in the Soviet Union and post-Soviet Georgia. He learned, before the debacle of Gamsakhurdian excess, that government violence in Georgia, even in tough situations, rarely gains support. It is a sure way to undermine government legitimacy. This understanding, combined with his helplessness as power ebbed away from his office, and an awareness that bloody denouements result in retribution, led in the end to the inevitable decision to resign without a fight despite a final feeble attempt to declare a state of emergency.

## CIVIL SOCIETY AND THE WEST

One of the more popular theories used to explain the peaceful outcome of the Rose Revolution is the growth of Georgian civil society. Laurence Broers suggests that 'it was civil society, rather than warlord armies, that emerged as the major force behind the revolution'.[31] Valerie Bunce in her work on comparative youth and electoral revolutions agrees that post-communist revolutions were 'built on the long-term development and organizational capabilities of civil society'.[32] David Anable points to the media, an important instrument of civil society, as the crucial factor.[33] Underlying all these arguments is the implication that Western governments and organizations, by funding democracy-building programmes and the media, played a crucial role in preparing the conditions for a peaceful Rose Revolution.

The impact of the West on Georgian civil society development was powerful. Between 1995 and 2000, the US government spent over $US700 million on direct aid to Georgia. The US blanketed Georgia with civic and democracy-building programmes through USAID, NDI, the World Bank, the Eurasia Foundation, and a myriad of other smaller programmes. The EU was not far behind. Between 1991 and 2003, it contributed total grant aid valued at more than €385 million and this did not include contributions from separate member states.[34] Shevardnadze's tolerance of the process—an acknowledgement of his pro-Western orientation and support of his claims for Western credits—led to the largest Third Sector in

---

[31] Laurence Broers, 'After The Revolution: Civil Society and the Challenges of Consolidating Democracy in Georgia' (unpublished paper), 2.

[32] Valerie Bunce and Sharon Wolchik, 'Youth and Electoral Revolution in Slovakia, Serbia, and Georgia', *SAIS Review*, XXVI, no. 2 (Summer–Fall 2006), 55–65.

[33] Anable, *Role of Georgia's Media, passim.*

[34] *Country Strategy Paper 2003–2006 & TACIS National Indicative Program 2004–2006, Georgia* (Brussels: European Commission, 23 Sept. 2003), 5. http://ec.europa.eu/external_relations/georgia/docs/index_en.htm.

the Caucasus. In 2005, 9,000 NGOs were registered with the Ministry of Justice, although not all were active. Shevardnadze later regretted his indulgence—he threatened at one stage to expel the Soros Foundation from Georgia—for he realized, as Thomas Carothers, Michael McFaul, and others have pointed out, that it is precisely such political space that gives the opposition its opportunity.[35] Despite the waste, inefficacy, poor coordination and one-sided understanding of civil society among Western funders—trade unions as defenders of labour rights were completely neglected, for example—a Westernized, educated, and youthful 'labour aristocracy' was nurtured and sustained. The privileged leaders of the Georgian Third Sector in Tbilisi, paid in dollars and driving imposing looking Land Rovers, were often resented by the general population, but they promoted norms of democracy and civil rights in legislation, in the media, and in the universities.

The Georgian Third Sector was elitist and weak: it had poor representation in the provinces, was dependent on Western funding, and its penetration of Georgian society was shallow. Yet it had a disproportionate influence on the Rose Revolution and its peaceful outcome. First, Georgian NGOs, loosely coordinated by Western-funded organizations such as the International Society for Fair Elections and Democracy (ISFED) and GYLA, mobilized thousands of monitors and established a system of parallel voting tabulation and exit polls in a number of constituencies. Forty-three monitoring organizations were registered with the Central Election Commission, and ISFED alone claimed it had 2,500 monitors.[36] This exercise proved that a cynical electoral swindle had nullified the popular will. Whether the parallel voting tabulations and the exit polls were accurate did not matter. The popular perception was that they were, because they differed from government tallies. Second, NGOs had the equipment and training to mobilize the population and coordinate demonstrations throughout November. Saakashvili in his own assessment of the Rose Revolution admitted 'the mobile phone was very important'.[37] Third—and more important than the cell phone—was the NGO movement's close association with the media and its ability to generate interest in the West. The Liberty Institute, which took a leading role in November 2003 and helped establish kmara, was created in the mid-1990s by two employees (Levan Ramishvili and Giga Bokeria) of Rustavi-2, an independent TV channel highly critical of the government. During November, Rustavi 2 was the most important tool for mobilizing the public—Ghia Nodia called it the 'revolution television'.[38] Rustavi 2 later dubbed itself the 'TV of the Victorious People'.

Western governments and their money played a vital role in keeping the Third Sector alive in the 1990s. The media assistance programmes from the Eurasia

---

[35] Thomas Carothers, *Critical Mission: Essays on Democracy Promotion* (Washington DC: Carnegie Endowment for International Peace, 2004), esp. 167–217. Michael McFaul, 'Transitions from Communism', *Journal of Democracy*, 16, no. 3 (July 2005), 5–19.

[36] *International Election Observation Mission: Parliamentary Elections, Georgia—2 November 2003*, 9.

[37] Mikheil Saakashvili in *'Enough'*, 25.

[38] Cited in Anable, *Role of Georgia's Media*, 9.

Foundation, USAID, and Internews (an international media development organization based in California), were critical in the early stages of Georgia's media development. In the lead-up to the November elections, the international community created an Ambassadorial Working Group (AWG) and a Technical Working Group (TWG) to help ensure proper elections. The International Research & Exchanges Board (IREX), a US agency concerned primarily with exchange programmes, helped organize political debates for regional and Tbilisi-based media. Western money helped transform the November election into an open and technically sophisticated referendum on Shevardnadze's record. Western governments' multiple linkages to Georgian society and business, and their crucial role in Georgian economic and military security, significantly hindered Shevardnadze's ability to use force. An important turning point in the November events was the US withdrawal of support for Shevardnadze's conduct of the elections. On 20 November, the US State Department declared that 'the results do not accurately reflect the will of the Georgian people, but ... reflect massive vote fraud'.[39]

The Western contribution to the Rose Revolution was ambiguous. Western governments supported Shevardnadze for years when it was clear that reform and democratization had stalled. They—and in particular US ambassador Richard Miles—discouraged the Rose Revolutionaries from radical action, preferring negotiations and the preservation of the Shevardnadze regime until its term officially ended.[40] On this, they were at one with the Russian government. At the same time, their democracy-building programmes created a frustrated and educated constituency for change. In November, Western governments were confused. They wanted both stability and change. However, their pressure on Saakashvili and Shevardnadze to refrain from violence was an important calculation for both contenders. The first to use violence would tilt Western support in favour of his opponent.

External intervention can have a crucial impact on revolutions. But in this case, overall US support for Shevardnadze or Saakashvili had marginal influence. The same applies to Russia. Its government was as baffled as its Western counterparts. Russian foreign minister Igor Ivanov, dispatched to Georgia on 23 November, was, according to Zurab Zhvania, 'shocked' at the speed of events. After greeting protestors and briefly trying to affect some compromise, he departed for Achara.[41] This was a Georgian revolution made by Georgians in Georgian conditions. The man in charge was a Columbia-educated lawyer which strengthened the view of Shevardnadze and Russian officials that Western governments were behind the revolt, but they were not and gave no surety of influence either. Pol Pot, after all, was educated in Paris.

---

[39] 'Washington says Georgia election results reflect "massive vote fraud"', *Agence France Presse*, 21 Nov. 2003.

[40] David Zurabishvili in *'Enough'*, 65.

[41] Zurab Zhvania in *'Enough'*, 38–9.

### CONCLUSION: A BIT OF LUCK AND A LOT OF PLUCK?

Was the non-violent outcome luck? The answer is yes and no. Peaceful revolutions—characterized by groups that challenge an existing power-holder, that are backed by large-scale popular participation, and that seek compressed and unconstitutional political change—are often a matter of 'luck and pluck'. But much depends on the authorities, the strategies of the opposition, the role of outsiders (what if Russia had provoked violence in Abkhazia?), and the local political culture (attitudes towards guns, for example). In November there seemed to be a lot of luck. A shoot-out in Samegrelo, West Georgia, during the election campaign, was quickly controlled; club-wielding Acharans stationed outside the parliament under the orders of Aslan Abashidze never used them; the police never put up any serious resistance to the large crowds as they stormed parliament; and the army, despite Shevardnadze's last ditch attempt to introduce a state of emergency, stayed in its barracks.

But it was not *blind* luck. First, the bad luck that brings violence was fettered by Georgian conditions. This is what made 2003 a peaceful revolution compared to the bloody tragedies in 1956 and 1989. By mid-November, it was clear—unlike 1956 and 1989—that the state had lost its governing capacity. Shevardnadze was powerless. He had alienated reformers, initiated the disintegration of his own party—the Citizens Union of Georgia—and had failed to create a coherent government. He had long lost the media, which considered itself victimized by the government, and students (who in September 1993 had begged on their knees that he withdraw his resignation). He alienated many in the Georgian Church, both his Western and Russian allies, lost touch with vital regional constituencies, and most importantly of all, failed to secure the loyalty of an impoverished army and a corrupt police force. The police had not been paid for three months prior to November 2003.

Second, the opposition by mid-November was united—with some exceptions such as the Labour Party and the party of New Rightists—behind a charismatic leader who promoted a non-violent strategy. This included fraternization with the police (providing police guards with sandwiches and sending women to place flowers in their gun barrels), the paralysis of government by overwhelming numbers on the streets, clever stage-managed images of popular support for Western cameras, mobilization of the provinces, and finally a heroic storming of the last corrupt bastion of the *ancien régime*—the parliament—with roses in their hands. The role of Saakashvili was fundamental. Revolutions need their leaders and Saakashvili's commanding style—brash, risky, energetic—was in line with Georgian cultural expectations. The mild mannered Zhvania and the neatly coiffured Nino Burjunadze, his colleagues in the triumvirate which emerged from the revolution, did not fit the bill.

The November events reflected Lenin's two conditions for revolution: ' "lower classes" [who] do not want the old way, and . . . "upper classes" [who] cannot

©David Mdzinarishvili/Reuters/Corbis

**Figure 19.3** The sweet smell of victory. Georgian opposition leader Mikheil Saakashvili after a meeting with President Eduard Shevardnadze in the president's residence. Shevardnadze announced his resignation on Sunday 23 November 2003, bowing to opposition protesters who stormed parliament and declared a 'Rose Revolution' in the former Soviet republic.

carry on in the old way'.[42] Civil society, the media, Western governments and the opposition—all had a role in establishing propitious conditions for a peaceful transfer of power in November 2003. But all were secondary to the most significant agent of the non-violent revolution—a disarmed, illegitimate, and morally compromised government unable to control its own armed forces. This, combined with a united, popular, and well-led opposition reduced bad luck's capacity to turn the revolution into a bloody one.

However, the practice of non-violence in November 2003 was a strategic decision. This explains, as does Georgia's unstable regional environment and the demands of state-building, why Georgia's Rose Revolutionaries have spent their energies since 2003 on the creation of a powerful army. Georgia in 2007, where the ideas of civil resistance along with the influence of civil society have

[42] Krishan Kumar (ed.) *Revolution: Readings in Politics and Society* (London: Weidenfeld & Nicolson, 1971), 165.

been marginalized by a government-inspired martial patriotism, suggests the legacy of successful civil resistance on a state's administrative practice and foreign policy is a limited one. This was confirmed forcefully by the violent events in November 2007 when President Saakashvili, the Rose Revolution's fabled leader, crushed peaceful demonstrations against his government and declared a state of emergency. Peace and 'normal politics' have since been restored, but the Rose Revolution's strategy of non-violence turned out to be a short-lived one. The government's militant rhetoric on South Ossetia set the scene for the tragic conflict with Russia in August 2008.

# 20

## Ukraine's 'Orange Revolution' of 2004: The Paradoxes of Negotiation

*Andrew Wilson*

Ukraine's 'Orange Revolution' is normally timed at seventeen days. A presidential election on 21 November 2004, rigged in favour of the then prime minister, Viktor Yanukovych, provoked massive street protests. Numbers may have topped 500,000 in the capital Kiev by the time it became difficult to count. The world's media filled with telegenic images of peaceful crowds dressed in seas of orange, the campaign colours of the 'defeated' challenger Viktor Yushchenko, Yanukovych's more liberal predecessor. The authorities were initially caught off guard; an aborted attempt to clear the streets by force on 28 November being too little, too late. The Supreme Court broke the deadlock on 3 December, when it ruled the election fraudulent and ordered a rerun. Nevertheless, further compromise was necessary. On 8 December 2004 parliament agreed a package of constitutional reform that meant any incoming president would only enjoy full powers until 1 January 2006, in exchange for changing the election law and election commission in order to allow a free and fair repeat vote on 26 December; this Yushchenko duly won by 52 per cent to 44.2 per cent.

I will argue that the choice of non-violent methods in Ukraine in 2004 was over-determined—that is, it resulted from a confluence of many factors pointing in the same direction. There was an important 'learning effect' from previous 'colour revolutions' in Georgia in 2003 and Serbia in 2000, and also from the Slovak experience in 1998; there were intellectual influences from Gene Sharp and others; and some consequent international tutelage. More important, however, were the domestic lessons learnt from the failed 'Ukraine without Kuchma' campaign in 2001. Incipient divisions in the authorities' ranks also meant that non-violence would likely gain leverage.

Non-violence also clearly worked, at least in the short term. Arguably, however, the sheer number of demonstrators meant that the Revolution's aims became increasingly diffuse, and the protests culminated in an elite compromise that largely prevented an 'electoral revolution' from spreading its effects elsewhere, although not before certain key sectors, particularly civil society and the mass

The author would like to thank the following: Dmytro Potekhin, Valentin Yaukushik, Olexii Haran', and Rostyslav Pavlenko.

media, had been profoundly transformed. Ukraine's 'Orange Revolution' was therefore a curiously self-limiting affair.


## WHAT WERE THE REASONS FOR THE USE
## OF NON-VIOLENCE?

Some have argued that non-violence is ingrained in Ukrainian political culture. At least in recent history, both Ukrainian elites and public have consistently opted for compromise over confrontation. Ukraine avoided the civil strife that Russia suffered in October 1993, despite similar tensions at the same time between president and parliament. Unlike Russia, an agreement that both should be subject to early elections in 1994 was adhered to, despite the president's private plotting.[1] Potential conflict in the Crimea has, at this writing, yet to become actual. Pacts of varying degrees of formality and finality were negotiated in October 1990 (to end student hunger strikes), August 1991 (to usher in independence), June 1995

©Joe Klamar/AFP/Getty Images

**Figure 20.1** Orange revolution. Thousands of orange balloons cover supporters of Ukraine's opposition presidential candidate Viktor Yushchenko during a rally in Kiev's Maidan square, 2 December 2004. The colour had been carefully chosen for the autumnal season by the opposition parties' campaign advisers.

---

[1] Leonid Kravchuk, *Maiemo te, shcho maiemo. Spohady i rozdumy* (Kiev: Stolittia, 2002), 227–9.

and June 1996 (to enact the constitution), December 2004 (at the height of the Orange Revolution), and August 2006 (the National Unity 'Universal'). One article in the wake of the Orange Revolution satirized this as a different 'aesthetic of revolution', a preference for 'tents over tanks'.[2]

Although it changes but slowly, political culture is not a fixed variable.[3] Not so long ago, Ukraine had a tradition of armed struggle embodied by the Organization of Ukrainian Nationalists (1929), and the wartime Ukrainian Insurgent Army (1943).[4] In the 1960s, however, the local dissident movement decisively rejected this tradition, and not just because of the apparent stability of the Soviet state.[5] Dissidents were forced to rethink the self-limiting narrowness of Ukrainian ethno-nationalism, and, as elsewhere in the Soviet Union, turned towards working within Soviet law and within the 'original' ideology of Marxism–Leninism. The main dissident organization of the 1970s called itself the Ukrainian Helsinki Group, in an attempt to encourage the Soviet authorities to live up to their formal commitments in the 1975 Helsinki Final Act. In the Gorbachev era there were no major groups that preached anti-regime violence. The main opposition movement, Rukh, was always lukewarm about boycott and civil disobedience tactics, even at the most dangerous moment for its cause, Gorbachev's referendum on the preservation of the Soviet Union in March 1991.[6]

The tents that would become Ukraine's political trademark were first pitched in the 'Maidan', or 'square', the main open space and transport intersection in downtown Kiev, in October 1990. At the time they sheltered student hunger strikers, who forced the resignation of the Soviet Ukrainian government headed by Vitalii Masol, although other concessions, in particular the promise of early multi-party elections, were subsequently not delivered. Elections had been held in March 1990, but simultaneously with the abolition of the communist party's 'leading role'. Arguably therefore, one of the lessons of 1990 was not learned as well as those of 2001—namely the importance of winning an enforceable agreement. Nevertheless, several of the leaders of the 2004 protests were veterans of 1990.

## 'Ukraine without Kuchma': non-violence as principle

Many of the lessons learned in the 1960s and in 1990 were soon unlearned. The most important precedents shaping behaviour in 2004 were the mistakes made in

---

[2] Oles' Donii, 'Ïkhnim tankon na nash namet', *www.pravda.com.ua*, 4 Dec. 2004, http://ua.pravda. com.ua/ru/news/2004/12/4/14328.htm.

[3] Stephen Whitefield (ed.), *Political Culture and Post-Communism* (Basingstoke: Palgrave Macmillan, 2005).

[4] For recent analyses of a highly controversial period, see Stanislav Kulchyts'kyi et al., *OUN i UPA: istorychni narysy* (Kiev: Naukova dumka, 2005); Yaroslav Hrytsak, 'Tezy do dyskusiï pro UPA', in his *Strasti za natsionalizmom; istorychni eseï* (Kiev: Krytyka, 2004), 90–113.

[5] For the debates of the time, see Heorhii Kas'ianov, *Nezhodni: ukraïns'ka intelihentsiia v rusi oporu 1960–80-kh rokiv* (Kiev: Lybid', 1995).

[6] Andrew Wilson, *Ukrainian Nationalism in the 1990s: A Minority Faith* (Cambridge: Cambridge University Press, 1997), 125–6.

the previous campaign against the authorities in 2001, when more radical elements succumbed to the temptation of violence, or allowed regime *provocateurs* to create the impression of violence; and the campaign had failed disastrously. This time, the lessons learned went deep: they became a matter of strategic first principles for most, but they followed from a rethink of tactics over only three years, from 2001 to 2004.

The 1990s were largely a time of political demobilization in Ukraine. The original national-democratic opposition had its teeth drawn in 1991, when it made a 'grand bargain' with the communist *nomenklatura*. Former communists could stay in power so long as they supported independence. Rukh split in 1992 and 1999, and many of its leaders were co-opted into government. Politics was dominated by former bureaucrats. Power changed hands within the elite in 1994, from the first president, Leonid Kravchuk, a former party ideologue, to Leonid Kuchma, a former 'red director'. Kuchma proved to be more skilled in the arts of political manipulation, splitting, reinventing, and largely neutering the opposition at the elections of 1998 (parliament) and 1999 (his re-election as president).

The last was a pyrrhic victory. In November 2000, a headless corpse was found in woods outside Kiev. The corpse was widely assumed to be that of the missing journalist Hryhorii Gongadze, who had founded Ukraine's first investigative web site 'Ukrainian Truth'. Oleksandr Moroz, leader of the opposition Socialist Party, used parliamentary privilege to read out extracts from secret tapes supposedly made in Kuchma's office by a disaffected security guard, Major Mykola Mel'ny-chenko. On these tapes the president was implicated in Gongadze's kidnap— although he was not heard to order his actual murder.

After a false start due to political bickering, during which important momentum was lost, demonstrations against Kuchma began in earnest in February 2001.[7] As in October 1990, a tent city was set up on the edges of the Maidan, where it adjoins Kiev's main shopping street, Khreshchatyk. Demonstrations of support attracted a maximum of 20,000 to 30,000 in February, but opposition politicians were divided. The organization closest to the Maidan, 'Ukraine without Kuchma', was little more than a slogan. According to Vladyslav Kaskiv, later leader of one version of the student-based opposition movement Pora, '"Ukraine without Kuchma" wasn't a campaign as such. It had no management. It was just a wild uprising [*dykyi bunt*].'[8] Younger activists set up the rival 'For Truth!' movement. Both were cold-shouldered by the then Prime Minister Viktor Yush-chenko, who, under pressure from Kuchma, even signed a notorious letter accusing the protestors of representing 'a Ukrainian brand of National Socialism'. (Longer-term, however, this encouraged many younger activists to strike out on

---

[7] On the events of 2001, see Yaroslav Koshiw, *Beheaded: The Killing of a Journalist* (Reading: Artemia Press, 2003); Paul D'Anieri, 'Explaining the Successes and Failures of Post-communist Revolutions', *Communist and Post-Communist Studies*, 39, no. 3 (Sep. 2006), 331–50; Andrew Wilson, *Ukraine's Orange Revolution* (New Haven, Conn.: Yale University Press, 2005), 58–60.

[8] Pora actually had two wings, 'Black Pora', which operated more underground, and 'Yellow Pora', which was more mainstream. Author's interview with Vladyslav Kaskiv, leader of Yellow Pora, 31 Oct. 2006.

their own).[9] Yushchenko's deputy Yuliia Tymoshenko helped to organize yet another group, a 'National Salvation Committee' after she was fired from government on 19 January 2001, but she was in prison by 13 February.

The government propaganda machine went into overdrive, exploiting the agenda created by 'anarchist' and 'nationalist' *provocateurs* from fake parties secretly funded by government supporters in the Yanukovych's Party of Regions, and in the so-called Social Democratic Party of Ukraine (united) which was actually a front for Kiev's business elite.[10] The first artificial disturbance was staged on 6 February, when 300-odd surprisingly muscular 'students' from the faux-nationalist organization 'Trident' (secretly funded by the security services, the SBU), infiltrated the crowds and staged provocations with leftists. The authorities now had the excuse they needed to clear the tent city, but waited for the media furore to die down and caught demonstrators unawares during the morning rush hour on 1 March.

The denouement came on 9 March, the birthday of Taras Shevchenko, Ukraine's national poet, when hundreds of activists were due to arrive in Kiev from west Ukraine for the formal founding conference of the 'For Truth!' movement. Nationalist groups, some real, some fake, were also determined to stop Kuchma laying the traditional wreath at Shevchenko's statue. The plan to use 'two waves' of activists, first students who then stood aside for 'tougher', often skinhead, militants,[11] was a recipe for disaster. *Provocateurs* from the Ukrainian National Assembly made sure the regime had the pictures it needed, both at Shevchenko Park and later outside the presidential administration on Bankivs'ka Street, where Molotov cocktails were allegedly thrown. Just to make sure, the L'viv students were arrested at Kiev railway station, before they could get to the park. Two hundred and five arrests were made, and fifty serious sentences handed down. Thirty-six police were allegedly hospitalized. One irony, however, is that the over-use of *provocateurs* in 2001 made the tactic more difficult to use in 2004.

## The 2002 elections and 'Arise Ukraine!'

The authorities had temporarily won control of the 'narrative'. The campaign against Kuchma never officially ended, however. The 'For Truth!' movement eventually became one branch of Pora. Both Yushchenko, who was forced out of office in April 2001, and Tymoshenko, who was released from her supposedly 'prophylactic' prison term on 27 March 2001, belatedly founded or refounded their own political parties. The regime had survived, but had tottered precariously, and new parliamentary elections were due within months, in March 2002. Moreover, the new opposition was empowered when Kuchma's protestations of

---

[9] Author's interview with Dmytro Potekhin, leader of Znayu, a campaign to inform and activate voters, 30 Oct. 2006.

[10] Andrii Duda, '"Natsyky" z Bankovoï', www.tribuna.com.ua/politics/2004/05/17/9843.html.

[11] Author's interview with Kaskiv.

clean hands led him to permit an unprecedented domestic and foreign election monitoring operation. A large-scale exit poll limited the possibilities for feasible fraud. Public opinion, aided by the economic successes of the Yushchenko government in 1999–2001, had belatedly rallied behind the newly minted moderate opposition, if not behind the more radical protestors. Yushchenko's 'Our Ukraine' won 23.6 per cent of the vote, the Tymoshenko block another 7.3 per cent and the Socialists 6.9 per cent, easily outscoring in total the 18.1 per cent won by the two main pro-government forces.

The opposition's success allowed it to reclaim some public space—if not to win control of parliament. The techniques used in 2002 had an ambiguous long-term effect on the next elections in 2004. On the one hand, groups like Freedom of Choice (i.e. freedom of voting choice) had gained valuable experience in election monitoring. On the other hand, the authorities took note of the success of the exit poll and would try to confuse voters by 'cloning' it in 2004. Fraud had been reduced in comparison to 1999, but other types of 'administrative' pressure had still effectively reversed the voters' verdict. Many activists were convinced the next step must be a more active engagement with the administrative machine itself.

Extra-parliamentary protest continued after 2002, although Yushchenko in particular was usually reluctant to join it. A new 'Arise Ukraine!' campaign began on the anniversary of Gongadze's disappearance on 16 September 2002. Numbers were, again, not large—a maximum of 30,000 in Kiev—but the protests were notable for reconnecting with the leadership of the nominally united new opposition, including Tymoshenko, the socialists, periodically Yushchenko, and even temporarily the communists. The 'Arise Ukraine!' campaign was also notable for debuting satirical and theatrical tactics to mock the authorities,[12] although much of this satire was too black to attract a wider audience. A public mock trial of Kuchma, with the former chief procurator Viktor Shishkin and former justice minister Serhii Holovatyi providing an air of mock formality, ended with Kuchma predictably sentenced to life imprisonment and the burning of his effigy.

The campaign continued into spring 2003. Smaller demonstrations were again held on the third anniversary of Gongadze's disappearance in September 2003. If the initial reaction to the Gongadze scandal had been muted in 2000–1 because it came at a psychological and organizational low-point, with the opposition demoralized after the elections of 1998 and 1999, the 2004 elections would now take place amidst a powerful upswing of activism.

## 2004: CULMINATION OF A LEARNING PROCESS

In 2004 Ukraine had a united opposition, characterized above all by its variety. It had a rapidly developing NGO sector, a well-tested system of election and media

---

[12] On the 'Arise Ukraine!' campaign, see 'Opposition Launches Anti-Kuchma Protest Campaign', *RFE/RL Poland, Belarus and Ukraine Report*, 4, no. 35, 17 Sep. 2002; Yaroslav Koshiv, *Gongadze: Ubiistvo, kotoroe izmenilo Ukrainu* (Moscow: Prava cheloveka, 2005), 190–2.

monitoring, a campaign to inform and activate voters (Znayu), an independent exit poll consortium, a new youth movement (Pora), and a rapidly expanding Internet which was mostly one step ahead of governmental control. The political opposition and the various civic movements kept their distance from each other, however, despite overlapping in parts. Unlike Georgia after the Rose Revolution in 2003, this has meant limited NGO influence on government since 2004, but the NGO sector has at least kept its independence. According to Dmytro Potekhin, the leader of Znayu, 'the traditionally political and the "non-political" met at a certain point—the election—and this made the change possible. But civic and political campaigning shouldn't mix directly. We were trying to do different things, and reach a different audience.' This, however, was not true of all groups; others, such as Yellow Pora, 'had stronger links to political players'.[13]

Both the civic and the political tendencies were agreed on non-violence, but with subtle differences. Older groups like the Freedom of Choice umbrella or the Committee of Voters of Ukraine confined themselves to analysis and reporting. Znayu and initially Pora saw themselves as leading an 'informational-educational campaign'.[14] Over time, Pora especially saw its role more in terms of Gene Sharp's principles of 'strategic non-violence': engaging the regime's weak points and undermining the will and capacity of repressive organs. Both were also drawn towards street theatre and situationist tactics designed to mock the authorities and dispel the fear of repression, but both avoided satirical excess.

## Non-violence and 'electoral revolution'

The 2004 election vindicated the tactic of assembling a broad hinterland of social support. Pora wanted to begin protests immediately after the first round of voting on 31 October.[15] The politicians were less sure, so Pora activists went ahead and organized their own prototype protest camp, already using the eventual winning formula of tents and entertainment, down the hill in Kiev's lower town, opposite the Kiev-Mohyla Academy (UKMA), Kiev's main independent, and independently minded, university.

A head of steam was therefore already building up before the second round, but out of sight of international and most local media. However, the speed with which protestors poured onto the Maidan on the day after the second round of the election surprised everybody—10,000 to 20,000 by breakfast time on Monday 22 November and 100,000 by the afternoon. Numbers held up over a cold night, and by midday the next day exceeded 200,000.[16] If the authorities were to have cracked down, the time to have done so would have been early on the Monday morning, or possibly on election night itself (the Sunday), after an initial early

[13] Author's interview with Potekhin.
[14] Author's interview with Kaskiv.
[15] Author's interview with Kaskiv.
[16] Author's interviews with participants: Feb. 2005, July and Oct. 2006.

rally had largely dispersed; but this would have been to prejudge even the authorities' fraudulent result. The relatively muted protests after the first round of voting had also lulled some in the regime into a false sense of security. It has also been argued that elite 'signalling' allowed protestor numbers to grow,[17] but this was probably at the secondary accumulation phase from day three onwards, when numbers climbed to over half a million.

Mood was just as important as numbers for the success of the Orange Revolution. In private discussion in the summer of 2004, 'there were propositions to make the protests more dramatic'.[18] Ideas that were floated included hunger strikes, either of youth activists or of prominent Ukrainian intellectuals,[19] and protestors chaining themselves to public buildings. But carnival was better. 'It was planned, from the start, to have less drama than in the Georgian case, even.' The practice rallies that began in Kiev in July 2004 and moved on to regional cities were a show of strength, but were also designed to show that any protests in November 'would be peaceful, fun, and, above all, safe'.[20] That said, there were some accidental elements. The authorities had turned the Central Election Commission into a fortress after sporadic protests that followed the first round—so the focus shifted downtown to the Maidan.

Carnival was also telegenic. The organizers of what came to be known simply as 'the Maidan' skilfully exploited the world media's appetite for positive pictures and symbolic events. Even the fact that the militia were placed close to the Maidan in full view of the cameras allowed the demonstrators to show their peaceful purpose in the interface between the two, giving out flowers to the militia and placing folk groups to entertain them in no-man's-land. Entertaining the crowd with so much music was also astute: it obviously advertised non-violent intent, the programme itself was deliberately wide and inclusive, and it helped reassure the militia that the crowd would remain stationary. The Maidan also began and ended every day with a multi-denominational religious service, to emphasize inclusivity and peaceful intent.

## Non-violence and the temptation of force

The authorities were clearly foxed by the sheer numbers simply staying put on the Maidan and elsewhere. But progress was slow. On several occasions the demonstrators contemplated more radical measures, although these did not necessarily involve violence. The next step advocated by some was usually occupation of, rather than mere encirclement of, government buildings—although these were of course heavily guarded. The leaders of Yellow Pora admit that they had already shifted from 'Plan A' to 'Plan B' at the start of the protests, from 'an information-educational

---

[17] D'Anieri, 'Explaining the Successes and Failures of Post-communist Revolutions', 344.

[18] Author's interview with Rostyslav Pavlenko, Kiev political scientist, 30 Oct. 2006.

[19] Author's interview with Oleksii Haran', political scientist from UKMA, 30 Oct. 2006.

[20] Author's interview with Pavlenko.

campaign' to 'active resistance' 'in the face of mass falsification', though the latter 'was necessarily a work in progress'.[21]

On the night of 23 November, two days into the protests, Pora led its 3,500-strong self-styled 'Guard (*Varta*) of the Revolution' from the Maidan towards the presidential administration. There were some ill-thought out plans to climb over the militia with ladders, and also amongst some the hope that the men in uniform might simply disperse or stand aside—some hoped to replay the capture of parliament in Georgia's Rose Revolution. A more concrete plan involved chaining the members of the Guard together in groups of five. The plan was then to lock them all together on arrival, creating one big immoveable mass outside Kuchma's office. However, Yuliia Tymoshenko arrived independently and urged the column to go home, given a real risk of bloodshed, claiming she had seen 'with her own eyes' Russian snipers stationed nearby.[22]

On later occasions Tymoshenko seems to have been the one calling for more radical measures, once her prominent role on the Maidan had encouraged her to think she might take charge. On 30 November, after parliament revoked its earlier censure of the election commission and talks appeared to be breaking down,[23] several demonstrators broke into parliament, but were pushed back by none other than Yushchenko himself.

The temptation was not great. The opposition knew that the first side to use violence risked losing the battle for public and international opinion, although the former was of primary importance. Significantly, even the SBU statements against the use of force warned more specifically against a 'first strike'.[24] More-over, if the opposition lost discipline, it would allow the regime's 'political technology' narrative (the nationalist 'threat', the use of *provocateurs*) to gain traction. The revolution's opponents were making a strong case before the Supreme Court that the demonstrators' tactics, in particular the blockade of government buildings that supposedly made their work impossible, and the actual takeover of at least three such buildings around the Maidan (the House of Trade Unions, Ukrainian House and the October House), were already in breach of Ukrainian law and the constitution.[25]

---

[21] Author's interview with Kaskiv.

[22] Author's interview with Kaskiv. A similar account is given in Dmitri Popov and Ilia Milstein, *Julia Timoschenko: Die Zukunft der Ukraine nach der Orangenen Revolution* (Cologne: Dupont, 2006), 305–7.

[23] See Ihor Guzhva, Oleksii Popov and Oleksandr Chalenko, 'Maidan's Secrets', *Segodnia*, 21 Nov. 2005, as translated for *The Ukraine List*, no. 371, available at www.ukrainianstudies.uottawa.ca/ukraine_list/ukl371_12.html.

[24] See the key SBU statement on 22 Nov. 2004, warning all participants to stay 'within the law' and use 'only peaceful steps', and citing as its main aim, 'the preserving of civic peace and accord (*zlahoda*) in society', available at www.sbu.gov.ua/sbu/control/uk/publish/article?art_id=41775&cat_id=39575.

[25] Author's interview with Valentin Yaukushik of UKMA, who helped put Yanukovych's case to the Supreme Court, 24 Feb. 2005; Yakushik, 'The 2004–2005 Ukrainian Revolution: Basic Characteristics and Manifestations', in Geir Flikke and Sergiy Kisselyov (eds.), *Beyond Recognition? Ukraine and Europe after the Orange Revolution: Conference Proceedings* (Oslo: Norwegian Institute of International Affairs, 2006), 79–86, available at www.dfc.ukma.kiev.ua/books/beyond_recognition_eng_text.pdf.

**Figure 20.2** Style statement and branding. Fashion-conscious millionairess and politician Yuliia Tymoshenko—here talking at a press conference on 26 December 2004 in Kiev—was a fiery and popular leader of the Orange Revolution, and at that time a close ally of Viktor Yushchenko (visible on the poster in the background, in a photo taken before his face was pockmarked as a result of dioxin poisoning). Later their alliance would turn to bitter rivalry.

The demonstrators were indeed far from passive. Some, led by Pora, were able to encircle the main government building and even Kuchma's dacha. The authorities knew that there would be mass resistance and bloodshed if they moved against the Maidan. They were sufficiently uncertain about the demonstrators' 'reserve tactics': the demonstrators could blockade the steep access roads to the Maidan with cars, and could put in the front line the militia who had defected. Regime soft-liners like Kuchma clearly baulked at the amount of violence that would be necessary. Later claims that arms had been stockpiled by the opposition near the Maidan seem to have been bravado.[26]

The carnival in the Maidan helped contribute to the decline of the fear factor. As he zigzagged from a harder to a softer line through 2004, fewer people thought that Kuchma would actually use force against demonstrators; and fewer thought that his strong-arm Chief of Staff Viktor Medvedchuk had the power to order the use of force on his own—although both were still possibilities. Ironically, Kuchma made a self-fulfilling prophecy in private in 2001, when he disparaged the protests of the time by saying, 'I can see only a few hundred pre-paid students. If I see 200,000 people demanding my resignation, I will resign.'[27]

In 2004 Kuchma was anxious about his image in the West. Ukraine's new model oligarchs (Viktor Pinchuk, Rinat Akhmetov) didn't want to risk their future business plans. Kuchma had used violence before, in 2001; but the propaganda and *provocateur* aspects of his defeat of the campaign to oust him had been more important. Scores of Pora activists were arrested in October 2004, but the early release of many on what was reported to be Kuchma's personal order, gave growing confidence to the opposition.[28] Kuchma had put a lot of effort into repairing his image since the Gongadze scandal broke in 2000; and, whether deluded or not, looked forward to an elder statesman role in retirement. He had a foundation to preside over, and a career as an author to promote, with several ghost-written books appearing in his last years.[29] Attempts to intimidate the opposition before November were real enough, but half-hearted. After a raid at least one NGO received apologies from officers: 'It's a political thing.'[30]

According to Potekhin:

> [the] preceding political crisis of 2001 ... produced a clash within the regime. Combined with the perceived likelihood of regime change, this made some people in the security forces and other pillars of [state] support hedge their bets. As a result, when they realized that change was close, they either switched sides, or at least played both.[31]

---

[26] Wilson, *Ukraine's Orange Revolution*, 135.

[27] Kuchma was in conversation with first president Kravchuk, as reported to the author by Pavlenko, 30 Oct. 2006.

[28] Author's interview with Kaskiv.

[29] Most prominently, Leonid Kuchma, *Ukraïna—ne Rosiia* (Moscow: Vremia, 2003).

[30] Author's interview with Kohut.

[31] Email from Potekhin to the author, 24 Jan. 2007.

The elite was split. There was no consensus behind a hard line. Even particular institutions were split, especially the security forces.[32] One faction in the SBU was even supplying the Yushchenko camp with information.

Just as importantly, Yushchenko was consistently reluctant to go beyond the immediate issues of electoral fraud, and of course his own poisoning.[33] Backdoor contacts allegedly produced an agreement that Our Ukraine would refrain from mass demonstrations if Yushchenko were allowed to win the first round. This led to the first disagreements with Pora. More generally, Yushchenko was temperamentally disinclined to all types of direct action. His business supporters didn't want revolution. Even Tymoshenko calmed the crowds on at least one occasion.

Pora wanted revolution, but Pora was never the prime moving force. At best, they occupied the bridgehead in those crucial early hours. In general, the division of labour was clear: 'sponsors sponsored, Pora did the physical work, and Yushchenko's headquarters coordinated' it all.[34] But the crowds made the difference. Even the 'professional revolutionaries' found it easier to operate behind their cloak. More exactly therefore:

> Black Pora did most of the physical work. Yellow Pora concentrated on PR, and was in closer touch with Yushchenko's headquarters, who consequently felt they were coordinating everything. However, their inability to coordinate became obvious when Our Ukraine wanted to get election fraud evidence to the Supreme Court. Basically, they failed, and the civic campaigners had to help out.[35]

The Kiev factor was also crucial. 'The Yushchenko side won the capital, in all of its layers of social life.'[36] Even on the official figures, the vote for Yushchenko in Kiev city in the second round was an impressive 74.7 per cent. The key levers of government were in Kiev, beyond the direct control of Yanukovych and his supporters from Donets'k in eastern Ukraine. When institutions made key decisions, such as when the Supreme Court ordered government newspapers not to print the fraudulent results on 24 November (which would have made them official) and when it finally condemned the election fraud on 3 December, they did so with one eye on the local crowd. Following the Tiananmen Square principle, 'outsider' forces from Crimea were present in Kiev, but 'felt themselves in a hostile environment. They were aware their Kiev colleagues would not help them',[37] if they

---

[32] Anika Locke Binnendijk and Ivan Marović, 'Power and Persuasion: Nonviolent Strategies to Influence State Security Forces in Serbia (2000) and Ukraine (2004)', *Communist and Post-Communist Studies*, 39, no. 3 (Sep. 2006), 411–29. For the debate on the role of the SBU, see C. V. Chivers, 'Back Channels: How Top Spies in Ukraine Changed the Nation's Path', *New York Times*, 17 Jan. 2005, versus Taras Kuzio, 'Did Ukraine's Security Services Really Prevent Bloodshed during the Orange Revolution?', *Eurasia Daily Monitor*, 2, no. 16, 24 Jan. 2005.

[33] Yushchenko had been diagnosed with dioxin poisoning after a secret dinner with the leaders of the Security Services of Ukraine on 5 September 2004, which the authorities attempted to blame on a 'hangover', 'herpes', botched 'botox' or self-inflicted stunt.

[34] Author's interview with Pavlenko.

[35] Email to the author from Dmytro Potekhin, 31 Jan. 2007.

[36] Author's interview with Pavlenko.

[37] Author's interview with Pavlenko.

were ordered against the crowds. Rumours about the presence of Russian Special Forces were never substantiated.

A violent crackdown by the authorities was possible, but never probable, in the first days of the protest. It was, however, seriously contemplated on the night of Sunday 28 November 2004, one week into the Orange Revolution.[38] Medvedchuk and/or Interior Minister Mykola Bilokon allegedly gave an order to move troops, but the upper and middle ranks quietly rebelled, delaying implementation and seeking confirmation. A flurry of nervous phone calls and leaks meant that the opposition was instantly informed. When Kuchma was telephoned for a clear 'yes' or 'no', he said 'no' after he was overwhelmed by pressure from all sides: from the US and UK ambassadors and from Colin Powell, from Ihor Smeshko, head of the SBU, and from leading oligarchs like Viktor Pinchuk.[39]

## The role of external actors and norms

Foreign funding was an issue for some early critics of the Orange Revolution,[40] although their arguments—the amount of money, foreign financing of the key exit poll, accusations of partiality, hints at, or the assumption of, additional covert measures—have so far proved chimerical.[41] As one expert aptly put it, 'the whole Maidan was an indigenous project, in terms of leadership, style, model and money'[42]—with the important exception of Boris Berezovskii's alleged support, which did great damage to Yushchenko's image when it was revealed in 2005 (1990s oligarchs like Berezovskii being just as unpopular in Ukraine as in Russia).[43] Seminars for youth activists had been run as early as 2002–3, supported by the Alfred Moser Foundation (Netherlands), the Westminster Foundation (UK), and the Fund for European Education (Poland).[44] The main US foundations—National Endowment for Democracy (NED), International Republican Institute (IRI), Eurasia, Freedom House, and George Soros's Renaissance Foundation—were all very active in Ukraine, as were Ukrainian-specific groups like

[38] See Chivers, 'Back Channels', and Kuzio, 'Did Ukraine's Security Services Really Prevent Bloodshed?', n. 32 above; and Konrad Schuller, 'Der Befehl wurde nicht befolgt', *Frankfurter Allgemeine Zeitung*, 20 Dec. 2004, translated as 'The Command was not Obeyed' in *The Ukraine List*, no. 318, 20 Dec. 2004.

[39] Olexiy Solohubenko, 'How Ukraine Verged on "Civil War"', *BBC News*, 22 Nov. 2005.

[40] Jonathan Steele, 'Ukraine's Postmodern Coup d'état', *The Guardian*, 26 Nov. 2004; Steele, 'Not a Good Way to Start a Democracy', ibid., 31 Dec. 2004; Ian Traynor, 'US Campaign Behind the Turmoil in Kiev', idem, 26 Nov. 2004; Nick Paton Walsh, 'Inquiry Sought into Claims of US Funding', idem, 13 Dec. 2004.

[41] Richard Youngs, 'Ukraine' in Ted Piccone and Richard Youngs (eds.), *Strategies for Democratic Change: Assessing the Global Response* (Washington, DC: Democracy Coalition Project, 2006), 97–121; Wilson, *Ukraine's Orange Revolution*, 183–9.

[42] Author's interview with Haran'.

[43] Oleg Varfolomeyev, 'Did Berezovsky Finance Ukraine's Orange Revolution?', *Eurasia Daily Monitor*, 2, no. 173, 19 Sep. 2005.

[44] Oleksandr Solantai, 'Pravda pro PORU ochyma zseredyny', available at www.pravda.com.ua/archive/2005/april/15/3.shtml.

the Polish-American-Ukrainian Cooperation Institute (PAUCI). The US State Department spent $US34.11 million on democracy assistance in 2004, mainly channelled through USAID.[45] Timothy Garton Ash and Timothy Snyder have estimated overall Western assistance at nearer $US100 million.[46] Crucially, no evidence yet exists of any extra covert payments.

Pora's own version of events is that:

> The [i.e. their] campaign's initial funding was supplied by Pora founders. These funds were directed to organizing activities, information support and printing of materials. Training of activists was supported by small grants provided by the German Marshall Fund of the United States, Freedom House and the Canadian International Development Agency (in the overall amount of approx. $130,000). It is worth noting, thus, that Pora, unlike its counterparts in Serbia and Georgia, received only minimal financial support from the international community.[47]

Znayu records a $US650,000 grant from the US-Ukraine Foundation, plus an extra $US350,000 for the third round, and $US50,000 from Freedom House.[48] Most of this went on setting up a toll-free helpline and on distribution of ten million leaflets (see above).

Learning from other colour revolution groups was obviously important. Help came mainly on an individual level from Belarus and Georgia; links were strongest with Serbia and Slovakia. Otpor's Aleksandar Marić helped run seminars for Ukrainian activists in Yugoslavia, though his return visits to Ukraine were eventually disrupted when he was denied re-entry in October 2004. Marić claimed that, 'we trained them [Ukrainian youth activists] in how to set up an organization, how to open local chapters, how to create a "brand", how to create a logo, symbols, and key messages.'[49] Pora would reject the idea of such comprehensive tutelage, but accept that some particular points were finessed.[50] Considerable help for Pora also came from Slovak organizations, whose experience in humbling Vladimír Mečiar in 1998 with an NGO-based civic rights and bring-out-the-vote campaign was arguably more relevant to Ukraine, and from Pavol Demeš, the Slovak director for central and eastern Europe for America's German Marshall Fund.

Mostly though, foreign influence was indirect, and only helped to push the key actors in directions they were moving anyway. There were tensions, however. The

[45] See www.state.gov/p/eur/rls/fs/36503.htm, report dated 13 Sept. 2004, these figures are therefore provisional. Joel Brinkley, 'Dollars for Democracy? US Aid to Ukraine Challenged', *New York Times*, 21 Dec. 2004, quotes $US97 million in the fiscal year that ended on 31 Oct. 2004, including approximately $US28 million for democracy-building projects.

[46] Timothy Garton Ash and Timothy Snyder, 'The Orange Revolution', *The New York Review of Books*, 28 Apr. 2005.

[47] Kaskiv et al., 'Pora—Vanguard of Democracy', available at http://pora.org.ua/eng/content/view/2985/325/.

[48] 'Making Revolution: Q&A with Dmytro Potekhin', *The Kyiv Post*, 24 Feb. 2005.

[49] Jeremy Bransten, 'Ukraine: Part Homegrown Uprising, Part Imported Production?', www.rferl.org/featuresarticle/2004/12/BE8E5D97-7EAF-404E-8E91-E21723FF74B6.html; John Simpson and Marcus Tanner, 'Serb Activists Helped Inspire Ukrainian Protests', 26 Nov. 2004, www.iwpr.net/index.pl?archive/bcr3/bcr3_200411_530_1_eng.txt.

[50] Author's interview with Kaskiv.

Renaissance Fund deemed some of Kaskiv's original plans too political, especially the intention to hand out 'information packs' into which pro-Yushchenko material could easily have been inserted. 'Soros didn't want to be seen to be funding partisans.'[51] On the other hand, 'although the Znayu core group was sure that it would take more than an information campaign to get rid of the ancien regime', it rejected suggestions by US funders that it run a 'negative campaign with a specific "Stop Corruption" logo'.[52]

Diplomatic pressure encouraged elite 'fence-sitting' before the election. It was also crucial on 28 November—the one occasion when elements in the regime were clearly tempted to use force. At the same time as there was resistance to the use of force within the army and SBU, Western diplomats redoubled their efforts, using political contacts and urging business leaders to put private pressure on political leaders. Ukrainian business in 2004 was much more vulnerable to this kind of pressure than its counterparts in Belarus in 2006. Because of minimal privatization, Belarus has no real 'oligarchs'. Nor do Ukrainian oligarchs enjoy the easy money their Russian counterparts make from oil and gas. Even in 2004 there were signs that Ukrainian oligarchs were more dependent on the rules of international finance, as they sought capital to modernize the assets they had acquired. As foreign investment, foreign lending, and public share issuing all took off in 2005–6, arguably they made the right call as capitalists during the Orange Revolution.

The Polish-led EU intervention—including the round-table negotiations that began five days into the protests, which were led by Polish president Aleksander Kwaśniewski—also worked to deter violence, on both a political and an economic level. Ukrainian elites on both sides had more contacts, and more common language, with Poland's post-communist leaders than with others in the West. East Ukrainian oligarchs had big investment plans in Poland.

Election observers made a huge moral difference. The Organization for Security and Cooperation in Europe (OSCE), the Council of Europe, the European Parliament, Freedom House, the NATO Parliamentary Assembly, and Ukrainian diaspora organizations in the US and Canada collectively sent many thousands of observers. The OSCE Office for Democratic Institutions and Human Rights (ODIHR) and the Parliamentary Assembly of the Council of Europe (PACE) reports were particularly damning and important, because Ukraine attached so much importance to continuing membership of the outer ring of the European 'club'. After 2004, Russia would lead a campaign for the 'de-internationalization' of post-Soviet space.

Russia's role in assisting the Yanukovych campaign has been well documented,[53] although its one-sided and heavy-handed approach was only decided

---

[51] Author's interview with Kohut.

[52] Author's interview with Potekhin.

[53] Nikolai Petrov and Andrei Ryabov, 'Russia's Role in the Orange Revolution', in Michael McFaul and Anders Åslund (eds.), *Revolution in Orange: The Origins of Ukraine's Democratic Breakthrough* (Washington DC: Carnegie Endowment for International Peace, 2006), 145–64; Wilson, *Ukraine's Orange Revolution*, 93–5, 118, & 174–6.

**Figure 20.3** A round table again—and international mediators. The round table at which Ukraine's two rival presidential candidates met on 26 November 2004, for the first time since the disputed vote. From left to right: Ukrainian opposition leader and presidential candidate Viktor Yushchenko, Polish president Aleksander Kwaśniewski, outgoing Ukrainian president Leonid Kuchma, Lithuanian president Valdas Adamkus, European Union foreign policy chief Javier Solana, and Ukrainian prime minister and presidential candidate Viktor Yanukovich. The role of international mediators was crucial here, notably that of the Polish president, who himself had participated in the Polish round-table negotiations of 1989.

relatively late, in September 2004. Russia's methods were noticeably different, however. If the West concentrated on funding due process and NGOs, albeit within a broader 'soft power' context,[54] Russia preferred 'political technology', grand gestures, and big money. The first involved the covert methodology and dirty tricks of the Yanukovych campaign, in which many Russian 'technologists' played a leading role. So-called political technology included black PR against Yushchenko, covert funding of 'technical candidates' to split his vote, and the ballot-rigging techniques that provoked the eventual protest. The second involved symbolic and substantive moves to shore up the Russophile element in the Yanukovych camp: the promise of dual citizenship, VAT concessions on oil exports to Ukraine, easier working conditions for Ukrainian citizens in Russia and so on. The third involved lining up Russian corporations in Yanukovych's support. Any spillage of monies coming from the West was therefore dwarfed by the alleged $US300 million spent on the Russian side.

Judging the success of the three methods would require judging how close Yanukovych was to success without them. Several activists have claimed that Russia's clumsy bias helped mobilize Yushchenko's supporters, shifted some neutrals towards them, and fuelled overconfidence on the side of the authorities.[55] During the Orange Revolution itself, however, Russia was mostly shocked into passivity, but there is some evidence of private pressure that did little to encourage a peaceful solution. When Kuchma met Putin at Moscow's Vnukovo

[54] Michael McFaul, 'Ukraine Imports Democracy: External Influences on the Orange Revolution', *International Security*, 32, no. 2 (Fall 2007), 45–83.

[55] Author's interview with Kohut and author's exchange of emails with Potekhin, 24 Jan. 2007.

airport on 2 December, Putin's alleged comment to 'put your cattle back in the barn' was leaked by Kuchma's aides.

## Negotiation, away from the Maidan

The crowd made the revolution in its first week. In fact, given later disappointments, it is this active agency of the mass public that is the main reason for continuing to insist that, in its initial phase at least, the Orange Revolution was truly revolutionary. With time, however, more thoughtful members of the opposition worried about holding the line. According to Potekhin, 'after five or six days people were tired. The risks of an upset were greater. There were reports of clashes in the suburbs, which were not necessarily believed, but risked becoming a self-fulfilling prophecy. The longer the stand-off, the greater the risks of a clash. That's why negotiations were needed. Otherwise, it was just too tense. The terms of the negotiations were another matter, however.'[56] There was also a justifiable fear that the Maidan wouldn't hold the attention of the world's media forever. The opposite point of view was represented by Pora, who argued that Yushchenko shouldn't even sit at the same table as people who should be in jail. 'It legitimized them—whatever the outcome of the negotiations',[57] and shifted power away from the Maidan, helping the gradual return of 'corridor politics' (*kul'uarna polityka*,[58] meaning politics not just behind closed doors, but outside of official offices, producing agreements that are never written down).

Nevertheless, there were many forms that a pact could have taken. It was far from clear that Yushchenko needed to cede most of the fruits of victory by agreeing to a radical constitutional reform that would take away much of his power after 1 January 2006, especially as the reform was so similar to that originally proposed by Medvedchuk before the election, when he had attempted to deprive any incoming president of much of his or her power. Kuchma was the main obstructive force this time, insisting on bracketing together the constitutional reform with the reform of the election commission and the electoral law that was deemed necessary to ensure a clean 'third round'. Many activists have said they would have stayed in the Maidan almost indefinitely—which in any case they did until the end of January, albeit in circumstances that were considerably less tense. Yushchenko could have called Kuchma's bluff, but he wasn't temperamentally inclined to do so. As even the real results in the second round had been so close, and the mood in eastern Ukraine was so volatile, it was quite rightly felt that a third round had to be held soon to give a Yushchenko presidency real legitimacy.

However, there was so much negotiation 'in the corridors', that all sorts of other deals have been alleged.[59] Tymoshenko became prime minister because of a

---

[56] Author's interview with Potekhin.       [57] Author's interview with Kaskiv.
[58] Author's interview with Kohut.

[59] See Marcin Bosacki and Marcin Wojciechowski, 'Behind the Scenes of the Ukrainian Revolution', *Gazeta Wyborcza*, 3 Apr. 2005, as translated by Maciej Mark Karpinski for *The Ukraine List*, no. 354, 15 July 2005, available at www.ukrainianstudies.uottawa.ca/ukraine_list/ukl354_11.html.

secret deal. Yushchenko's main campaign financier Petro Poroshenko became head of the National Security and Defence Council after private reassurances. He and others soon became involved in business scams that were uncomfortably similar to the ones that had run in the Kuchma era.[60] Most controversially, there was allegedly a private amnesty for those involved in the election fraud and the broader crimes of the Kuchma era. Yushchenko shocked many supporters by agreeing to a public amnesty with Yanukovych in September 2005,[61] by which time the policy seemed to operate in practice anyway. This agreement was supposedly protected by the return of do-nothing Procurator Sviatoslav Piskun, on a dubious legal technicality, two days after the 'package agreement', on 10 December 2004. In June 2005 a tape was released on which Piskun supposedly promised to be a 'great friend' to leading oligarchs, 'like family' and that 'everything will be normal' after his appointment.[62]

## CONCLUSION

What difference did non-violent civil resistance ultimately make? It prevented an immediate declaration of a Yanukovych victory based on fraudulent results. It provided the foot-soldiers for key tasks that Our Ukraine couldn't accomplish; not just Pora acting as the vanguard of the Maidan, but also in practical areas like gathering evidence for the Supreme Court. Non-violence prevented bloodshed, which briefly seemed possible on 28 November. It brought the old order close to revolutionary collapse.

Ultimately, this was not what the key politicians wanted, Yushchenko especially. The civil resistance movement was unable to prevent the shift to negotiation and compromise, in part because it overlapped with the political organizers of the Maidan. The Ukrainian case shows that negotiation can achieve the original aims of civil resistance, but it can also frustrate them. One great paradox, however, is that the civic movement and opposition avant-garde would never have been in the position it was without Yushchenko, who led the reinvention of opposition electoral politics between 1999 and 2004. Ukrainian voters wanted a moderate. Tymoshenko or the leaders of Pora were at this time simply unelectable. Yushchenko's great achievement was actually to be elected. His great weakness was to defuse the forces that helped propel him to power.

The Orange Revolution was indeed an 'electoral revolution', yet its effects were largely electoral rather than revolutionary. Viktor Yushchenko became the presi-

---

[60] On the RosUkrEnergo affair, see the report 'It's a Gas: Funny Business in the Turkmen-Ukraine Gas Trade', at www.globalwitness.org/reports/show.php/en.00088.html.

[61] This deal was to secure the necessary votes in parliament to push through Yurii Yekhanurov as prime minister, after Yushchenko sacked Tymoshenko after only seven months.

[62] Koshiv, *Gongadze*, 221.

dent of Ukraine, but the potentially broader impact of the protests of November and December 2004 was blunted. Not only did Yushchenko lose many powers on 1 January 2006, but the Orange parties contrived to argue amongst themselves and allow Yanukovych's Party of Regions back into office after parliamentary elections in March 2006. A very non-revolutionary revolution has had paradoxical effects.

# 21

# The Moment of the Monks: Burma, 2007

*Christina Fink*

The case of Burma's September 2007 demonstrations in the context of civil resistance and power politics is important: it shows that even if large, popularly supported civil resistance movements can be organized, they are not always successful, at least in the short term. This is particularly true when the government in power is a military regime and sufficient international pressure is lacking. In such an unforgiving political environment as Burma's where the regime forbids public displays of discontent, and political prisoners are incarcerated for years at a time, the challenges of devising and carrying out a successful civil resistance movement are daunting. In other countries, activists can learn from their mistakes, refine their strategies, and try again. In Burma (renamed Myanmar by the regime in 1989), many people have only one, or at most, two chances.

As noted in other chapters in this book, the international context can also shape the way that domestic power holders perceive their options in dealing with a civil resistance movement. In the case of Burma, its growing economic engagement with other countries potentially made it more vulnerable to international censure. However, because China and India, the two regional powers with the greatest influence over Burma, were not willing to exert any significant pressure on the regime, it was easier for the generals to crack down. The UN Security Council discussed the Burmese events, but with China and Russia holding veto power, it was not able to take serious action, and the visit of a UN special envoy during the crackdown achieved no tangible results. The regime felt confident it could carry out its plans unhindered while activists and ordinary citizens felt abandoned in their moment of need.

Yet, as other chapters in this book have also highlighted, despite the failure of a civil resistance movement to achieve immediate success, there may be both concrete and psychological impacts that affect the balance of power in the years to come. In the case of Burma, the use of violence against the monks awakened the political sentiments of the public and greatly damaged the regime's claims to moral legitimacy. *reason*

I thank Peter Carey, Małgorzata Gorska, and Win Min for their valuable comments and suggestions on earlier drafts of this chapter.

This chapter will address the interplay between the September 2007 civil resistance movement, Burma's military regime, and international actors, in particular Burma's largest neighbours and the UN. In addition, it will consider why the monks took the initiative and how the impact of the movement should be assessed. The varying degrees of commitment to non-violence, the role of new technologies, and the particularities of Burma's situation, where a struggle for ethnic autonomy has also been taking place, will also be touched on.

*content of essay*

## OVERVIEW OF THE 2007 DEMONSTRATIONS

In mid-August 2007, people in Burma were shocked to learn that the regime had suddenly removed fuel subsidies, resulting in massive price increases for diesel and compressed natural gas. Transportation and food prices skyrocketed with devastating effect, particularly for the urban poor: some people could literally no longer afford to go to work.

The 88 Generation Students' Group—comprised of former political prisoners who had led the 1988 pro-democracy demonstrations—initiated marches in Rangoon, Burma's largest city, and called for the regime to rescind the price increase. Worried that the number of marchers would grow, the authorities quickly arrested all the leaders of the Group that they could find.

Following that, a small network of politically educated monks decided that it was incumbent on them to keep the demonstrations going. They and ordinary monks were acutely aware of the suffering of the people because monks go out daily to receive offerings of food from the laity. More and more people could no longer properly feed themselves or the monks. This was also upsetting because offering food to monks is the primary form of merit-making in Theravada Buddhist practice.

On 5 September, hundreds of monks appeared in the streets of Pakkoku, a town known for its monastic education centres, chanting the *metta sutta* of loving kindness towards all beings. Thousands of cheering residents came out to show their support. The local authorities responded by firing over the monks' heads and beating monks, some of whom they had tied to poles. To physically assault a monk is one of the greatest sins in Buddhism: this incident sparked mass indignation and helped the movement grow far more quickly than it would have otherwise.

Five days later, the network of monks proclaimed the formation of the All Burma Monks Alliance (ABMA) and demanded that the regime apologize to the monks, reduce the prices of fuel and other basic commodities, release all political prisoners, and begin a dialogue with the democratic movement for national reconciliation.[1] The statement also threatened that if the regime did not comply

---

[1] Announcement of All Burma Monks Alliance: 12th Waning Day of Wagaung, 1369 BE, Sunday, Letter No. 1/2007.

by 17 September, the monks would initiate a religious boycott, refusing to receive offerings from the military and their families or to perform religious rites for them.[2] When the regime ignored their demands, the monks began the boycott and took to the streets. News of the events in Pakkoku and the ABMA's statements spread throughout the monastic and lay communities via exile radio broadcasts and word of mouth. Small groups of monks began organizing, with or without the permission of their abbots.

*[handwritten margin note: ✓ religious boycott]*

During the first few days of the 'Saffron Revolution', the monks (and later nuns) marched alone.[3] However, some people were so moved by the monks' efforts on their behalf that they begged to be allowed to participate. In a spirit of compromise, it was agreed that lay people could form human chains on either side of the monks' columns as they walked through the streets, holding their religious flags and upturned alms bowls and chanting the *metta sutta*. Similar demonstrations took place in several other cities and towns, with many by-standers clapping and crying. Taken aback by the speed with which the demon-strations were gaining momentum and not sure how to proceed, the regime initially reacted with caution. Plain-clothed intelligence officers videotaped the demonstrations, but no one was arrested.

In the meantime, to broaden the movement and push for political reform, the ABMA made a formal alliance with other lay activists, including leading 88 Generation Students' Group activists in hiding, and issued a statement on 21 September urging the people to join the monks in order to 'banish the evil regime'.[4] On 22 September, several hundred monks, surrounded by lay people, proceeded through police barriers to pro-democracy leader Aung San Suu Kyi's house in University Avenue, Rangoon, where she was being kept under house arrest. She came to the gate with tears in her eyes. News of this moment, which spread through the international and Burmese exile media, electrified the popu-lation and led to yet more people joining the marches. Starting on 24 September, famous entertainers publicly demonstrated their support, and the monks allowed democracy activists to walk in the middle of their processions, holding their political flags aloft. As many as 100,000 people were in the streets in Rangoon, with thousands more marching in other towns.

The regime had had enough. On the evening of 24 September, the state-controlled monastic council urged all monks to stay out of secular affairs. On the 25th, the authorities in Rangoon and Mandalay declared a night-time curfew and warned the monks to get off the streets. The next morning, the crackdown began, with *Tatmadaw* (Burma Army) soldiers and riot police using tear gas, rubber and live bullets, beatings, and mass arrests to crush the demonstrations.

---

[2] Termed *Patta Nikkujjana Kamma* in Pali, this practice originated during the Buddha's lifetime and is symbolized by an upturned alms bowl.

[3] In fact, many monks in Burma wear crimson-coloured robes.

[4] People's Alliance Formation Committee, 'Statement of the People's Alliance Formation Commit-tee to the Entire Clergy and the People of the Whole Country', 21 Sept. 2007.

**Figure 21.1** Demonstration for compassion. A march of some 20,000 Buddhist monks and citizens in Rangoon, 23 September 2007. The monks were chanting Buddhist verses calling for loving kindness in an effort to compel the Burmese generals to do something to alleviate their citizens' suffering. Many of the monks believed that they could march calling for loving kindness without being punished because this was a religious march rather than a more overtly political protest.

Some units of the Union Solidarity Development Association (USDA), a mass organization created in 1993 to support the military regime, and the more recently formed *Swan Arr Shin* (Masters of Force) militia, helped carry out the crackdown. During the night, soldiers and riot police raided monasteries, beating monks and dragging them away to detention centres. Angry groups of youth gathered in the streets for a few more days, but with no leadership and troops everywhere, they found it impossible to continue. Afterwards, the regime acknowledged fifteen people had been killed, including a Japanese video reporter. However, the UN Special Rapporteur on Human Rights for Burma stated that this figure 'may greatly underestimate the reality'.[5] More deaths occurred in the temporary detention centres and prisons to which as many as 4,000 people were taken. Many monks were forcibly disrobed.

Throughout the demonstrations, citizen reporters and bloggers sent out photos, eyewitness accounts, and videotapes over the internet. Governments and leading figures around the world urged the regime to handle the peaceful

[5] Paolo Sergio Pinheiro, *Report of the Special Rapporteur on the Situation of Human Rights in Myanmar*, UN doc. A/HR/6/14 of 7 Dec. 2007, 10.

demonstrators with restraint, although China and India claimed that it was Burma's internal affair. The regime went ahead with its plans. Many eyewitness accounts indicate that some soldiers and police offered gestures of respect to the monks during the early days of the demonstrations, but when the troops were ordered to beat and shoot the demonstrators, they did so without mercy.

*why did troops follow orders of the regime in this instance?*

## FACTORS BEHIND THE MONKS' DECISION
## TO TAKE THE INITIATIVE

Burma gained independence (and left the Commonwealth) in 1948. A federal, democratic government was established, but most powers remained with the central government. The military's dissatisfaction with party politics and with Prime Minister U Nu's willingness to consider ceding more power to the ethnic minority states led General Ne Win to stage a coup in March 1962. Subsequently, several ethnic nationalist armies waged war with the *Tatmadaw* in the mountainous regions ringing the plains, but central Burma remained largely quiescent. Throughout more than forty years of military rule, only two large-scale episodes of civil resistance have taken place, in 1988 and in 2007, although smaller student and worker-led protests broke out at other times.[6] In 2007, as in 1988, a long, steady economic decline followed by a severe economic shock was the precipitating factor for the demonstrations. At a deeper level, the problem was the regime's lack of concern for the well-being of its citizens. The health and education sectors had been grossly neglected while the regime invested huge sums of money in building a new capital in the jungle and upgrading its military arsenal. Many abbots felt compelled to establish orphanages, schools for poor children, and even health-treatment programmes, including for HIV-AIDS, in the grounds of their monasteries. Frustrated as the people and monks were with the deteriorating situation in the country, the vast majority felt too afraid to take action.

*resistance does not come out of thin air - just waiting for the time to mobilize*

   In both 1988 and 2007, it was an act of unacceptable violence by the authorities (against students in 1988 and monks in 2007) which led people momentarily to put their fear aside and take action. In both cases, small networks of activists, many with connections to an older generation of activists, had been waiting for a spark which they could use to mobilize the population. In Burma, as in so many countries, students have generally taken the lead. In both 1988 and 2007, students organized the initial protests, with monks joining later to fill the gaps and lend their moral authority. In 1988, monks jointly led demonstrations with students and other local activists in the second largest city, Mandalay, and in small towns, although they did not play a large role in the former capital, Rangoon (renamed

---

[6] For an overview of contemporary political issues in Burma, see David I. Steinberg, *Burma: The State of Myanmar* (Washington DC: Georgetown University Press, 2001). For an engaging historical account, see Thant Myint-U, *The River of Lost Footsteps: Histories of Burma* (New York: Farrar, Straus, & Giroux, 2006).

**Figure 21.2** Lay demonstrators highlight economic concerns. Supporters of the Buddhist monks march down a street in Rangoon, 25 September 2007, despite stern warnings from Myanmar's junta against the anti-government protests. It was another day of large-scale public defiance against the generals and their iron grip on the country. The marchers just behind the young men holding the banner are holding flags from the outlawed All Burma Federation of Students Unions. This organization has re-emerged with each new generation of student activists and traces its history to the independence struggle.

Yangon in 1989). In 2007, once most of the 88 Generation Students' Group leaders had been arrested, more politically aware monks decided to step in. A large number of urban-based monks, mostly ranging in age from 20 to 45, joined them.

Few, if any, Burmese monks knew about monks' involvement in civil resistance movements in other countries, but all knew of the historical role Burmese monks had played in domestic civil resistance movements from the colonial period onwards. Protection of the Buddhist faith and concern for the suffering of the people had always been the primary motivations. Most of the monks who participated in the 2007 demonstrations were from monastic education centres, where they either taught or studied. Some of the organizers had spent years in prison for their involvement in the 1988 demonstrations or in the 1990 religious boycott of the military. The boycott was declared after the military used violence against monks and students who organized a public commemoration on the second anniversary of the 1988 demonstrations in Mandalay. While in prison, some of the monks developed friendships with leading 88 Generation activists. Other young monk leaders had learned about human rights, democracy, and non-violent resistance movements through activist contacts or self-study. Several of the monks who became leaders on the street had no political background except for occasionally listening to BBC and Burmese exile radio broadcasts. Yet even ordinary monks were drawn in. As one monk put it, 'health, education, religion, and politics are all connected. You can't separate them.'[7]

Frustration over the country's political deadlock also prompted the activists and monks to act. After crushing the 1988 nationwide demonstrations, the regime sought to appease the people by holding a parliamentary election in 1990. However, when Aung San Suu Kyi's National League for Democracy (NLD) trounced the regime's party, the generals refused to transfer power. Claiming that a new constitution had to be written first, the regime organized a tightly controlled National Convention to write the principles for the constitution. This process took fourteen years, from 1993–2007. To fend off international criticism, the regime asserted it was moving toward democracy at a pace that was right for Burma, but the generals had no intention of stepping down. Throughout most of this period, Aung San Suu Kyi was kept under house arrest. Meanwhile, the authorities set about systematically imprisoning leading NLD strategists and intimidating members into resigning. The remaining NLD leaders focused on maintaining the legal status of the party and were reluctant to engage in activism on the streets. In 2007 though, many NLD youth and district members decided to take an active role in the demonstrations, even before the monks joined in.

### REASONS FOR THE SHORT-TERM FAILURE OF THE DEMONSTRATIONS

The demonstrators failed to achieve their goals for a number of reasons: the inadequate strategic planning of the demonstrations, the lengths to which the regime was prepared to go to remain in power, and the lack of a more robust

---

[7] Interview, 28 Jan. 2008.

international response. The strategic planning of the movement was hampered all along by the authorities' extensive surveillance capabilities which made it difficult for the organizers to meet. In addition, the organizers themselves were stunned by how quickly the demonstrations gained momentum and had not prepared sufficiently. To use the language of Gene Sharp, the 2007 movement was not able to remove all or even most of the 'pillars of support' for the regime. The movement was able to draw in a large number of monks, whose acquiescence in receiving alms from the military in the past bestowed some legitimacy on the regime. However, the State Monastic Council (*Sangha Maha Nayaka*) and most leading abbots did not publicly endorse the ABMA, although many privately indicated their tacit support. Only a small number of civil servants participated. Thus, the normal functioning of the state was not paralysed. More importantly, despite reports of commanders who did not want to shoot the monks, no commander openly split from the army.

As the demonstrations grew, the organizers differed in opinion regarding whether to allow the public and political groups to join in or whether to direct the civilians to engage first in less risky civil disobedience activities at their homes. With many activists and people eager to join the monks, the organizers agreed to call for mass participation. In hindsight, it appears that this, along with including political demands from the beginning, may have been a tactical mistake. Had they initially focused only on the apology for the authorities' brutality in Pakkoku and the price hikes, and insisted on only religious people on the streets, the regime might have waited a bit longer before cracking down. The organizers might have had more time to organize a non-cooperation campaign among the civil service and the military and to work out their end-game strategy. In fact, civil servants, soldiers, and low to mid-level officers have been poorly paid and mistreated. If there had been a specific campaign targeting the military and dealing with their particular concerns, perhaps at least the divisions created in the military would have run deeper.

Nonetheless, it is not easy to persuade the civil service and members of the military to demonstrate their support before it is clear that an opposition movement will win. Should the movement fail, civil servants would lose their jobs and members of the armed forces would be sentenced to life in prison or even death for having committed treason. Yet, it seems that only by drawing in a powerful faction from the military can a civil resistance movement in Burma ultimately succeed.

While there may have been divisions among the top generals regarding the handling of the economy and the use of force against monks, they remained united in their desire to stay in power. Aware of the fate of some other deposed leaders, such as the Ceauşescus in Romania, they are determined to ensure their and their families' security. At the same time, the top military leaders seem genuinely to believe that it is their duty and right to govern. Since the late 1950s, the military leadership has regarded the military as the one truly patriotic institution which can safeguard the interests of the state. In conjunction with this, Mary Callahan has argued, the generals consider Burmese citizens as 'objects of distrust and potential enemies'.[8] In ubiquitous public billboards, the *Tatmadaw* refers to itself as the father and mother of the people, in a country where obedience to superiors is the norm. Thus, Than Shwe, the top general and decision-maker, treated the peaceful marches as insubordination.

The regime's claim that only the *Tatmadaw* can hold the country together has found some support in the international community. Some Asian governments in particular seem to have taken the threat of anarchy seriously, and this, along with their economic interests in Burma, has contributed to their adopting a more equivocal stance toward the regime than most Western countries. Many would argue that the regime's refusal to consider the ethnic groups' demands has exacerbated the ethnic conflict, and that the establishment of a genuine democratic, federal union, as the ethnic political parties and armed groups have called for, would lead to peace. Nevertheless, Chinese and other Asian leaders, particularly from authoritarian states, have voiced doubts about the ability of Aung San Suu Kyi and an elected government to prevent the eruption of ethnic violence.

Moreover, China worries that an NLD-led government would be closely allied to the US and far less amenable to working with the Chinese than the military regime has been. In particular, China wants to ensure that its numerous energy-related projects in Burma are not jeopardized in the future. Still, China has been unhappy with the regime's gross mishandling of the economy, which has reduced the potential for Chinese investment and created the conditions for civil unrest. China seems to believe that stability in Burma could best be achieved by moving forward with the regime's roadmap, which calls for elections, but based on a constitution which ensures continued military dominance in politics.

Nevertheless, China's position in the world has been changing, and as it has sought recognition as a global statesman, it has had to consider carefully how to balance its interests and its image. In 2007, China came under significant pressure from the West and the UN Secretary-General to use its leverage over Burma to help bring about a process of national reconciliation. China vetoed a UN Security Council resolution condemning the Burmese regime's human rights abuses in January 2007, in part, because this could set a precedent for investigations into China's human rights situation. However, when Ban Ki-moon, the UN Secretary-General, decided to send his representative to Burma during the crackdown, Chinese authorities played a key role in persuading Burma's generals to allow the visit.[9] Days later, China voiced its opposition to the idea of a binding UN Security Council resolution on Burma, but it did acquiesce in a much softer presidential statement from the Security Council calling for talks between the regime, Aung San Suu Kyi, and the ethnic groups, with UN involvement.[10]

---

[8] Mary Callahan, *Making Enemies: War and State Building in Burma* (Ithaca, NY: Cornell University Press, 2003), 221.

[9] Lalit K. Jha, 'International Pressure Building on Burma', *Irrawaddy* (Thailand), 28 Sept. 2007. Mr Gambari was allowed to meet Aung San Suu Kyi but could not visit sites where the violence occurred.

[10] 'Statement by the President of the Security Council', UN doc. S/PRST/2007/37 of 11 Oct. 2007.

Like China, India's need for fossil fuels has grown rapidly, and it sees Burma as an important supplier. The Indian oil minister was in Burma signing oil and gas exploration contracts during the height of the demonstrations, and India refrained from criticizing the regime's crackdown, saying only that it wished 'all sides would resolve their issues peacefully'.[11] In the past decade, the military regime cleverly took advantage of the competition between India and China for Burma's resources, playing one off against the other. China has provided the *Tatmadaw* with over a billion dollars worth of military equipment, and India has also supplied arms in recent years. After the crackdown, the US and the EU imposed further economic sanctions targeting the regime and its cronies, but the generals clearly feel confident that China and India will continue to do business with Burma.

The United Nations has taken notice of Burma's problems but has not been able to take effective action. Year after year, the UN General Assembly and the Commission on Human Rights, reorganized in 2006 as the Human Rights Council, issued annual resolutions on Burma urging the release of political prisoners and political dialogue with all stakeholders, but the Burmese authorities have responded with indifference. For four years, the regime denied a visa to Paulo Sergio Pinheiro, the UN-appointed special rapporteur on human rights in Burma, making it impossible for him to carry out his work. During the crackdown, UN Special Envoy, Ibrahim Gambari went to Burma to urge the regime to stop the violence and begin talks with Aung San Suu Kyi. At that point, many Burmese hoped that Gambari could make the generals listen.[12] Sr General Than Shwe agreed to appoint a liaison minister to meet with Aung San Suu Kyi, but in the ensuing months no substantive discussions took place. When the UN Security Council put out a non-binding presidential statement on Burma following the crackdown, it was significant for those seeking to broaden the mandate of the Security Council, but it was not a threat to the regime. In February 2008, the regime announced it would hold a referendum on the new constitution in May and an election in 2010. General Than Shwe clearly had no intention of engaging in political dialogue or working with the UN.

The UN Security Council has the means to make a difference in Burma. It could, for example, impose an arms embargo, but that cannot happen until China agrees. Persuading China to change its position is crucial to enabling the Security Council to be able to do more. Stronger measures from the Security Council and indications that China would not back the regime indefinitely could help facilitate the emergence of a faction in the military that might feel more vulnerable and therefore see political reform as in its interest.

---

[11] Mungpi, 'At Last India Voices Concerns over Burma Turmoil', *Mizzima News* (India), 26 Sept. 2007.

[12] Aung Hla Tun, 'UN Peace Envoy meets Detained Leader', *Reuters*, 30 Sept. 2007.

**Figure 21.3** UN involvement achieves little. From left to right, UN Special Envoy Ibrahim Gambari poses with Myanmar's Senior General Than Shwe, Vice-Senior General Maung Aye, General Thura Shwe Mann, and Acting Prime Minister Lieutenant General Thein Sein after a meeting in Myanmar's administrative capital Naypyidaw, 2 October 2007. Gambari also met with Myanmar's pro-democracy leader Aung San Suu Kyi. His mission failed to halt the bloody crackdown on anti-government protests.

## IMPACTS OF THE MOVEMENT

While the movement did not succeed in realizing its demands, it was not without achievements. For many of the demonstrators, pulling off such a large-scale protest in such a repressive environment was something to be celebrated. The daily marches were well organized, with logistics handled very professionally. Individual monks volunteered on the spot to plan and lead the marches. Once lay people joined in, the leading monks took steps to ensure that the demonstrations

*success w/ planning + executing mvmt actions*

remained non-violent. Students, health professionals, and others also quickly organized support services for the marchers, providing water, face masks, and medical treatment as necessary. All of this made it difficult for the regime to claim there was anarchy on the streets.

In addition, a number of groups, ranging from monks to entertainers, were able to come together, with those involved in the strategic planning managing to keep a low profile. The reorganization of the military intelligence branch a few years earlier may have also made it harder for the new officers to identify the leading monks. As a result, the authorities could not immediately arrest the leaders, and this made it difficult for them to stop the movement without having to resort to temple raids and widespread arrests.

The decision to use violence against the monks enraged the population, horrified the international community, and created problems within the military. Maung Aye, the second highest ranking general in the regime, reportedly disagreed with Than Shwe's decision to involve the USDA and *Swan Arr Shin* in the crackdown; and he and some middle-ranking officers also felt that less brutal means could have been used and were upset that the image of the military had been tarnished.[13] After the crackdown, Maung Aye distanced himself from Than Shwe, while some military families faced social sanctions from their communities, with other people not wanting to associate with them. Sources close to the military suggest that the military's morale was weakened by the crackdown. Whether this can be exploited by a resurgent movement remains to be seen.

The success most touted by the movement's participants was that they were able to demonstrate to people outside Burma the depth of their desire for change. *reason* The haunting images of the peacefully marching monks being beaten and hauled away drew unprecedented international attention to Burma. Activists hoped this would translate into a broader international consensus on the need to do more for Burma.

A new generation of student and youth activists was born out of the demonstrations, giving rise to hopes that they could carry on, even if many older leaders were in prison. The positive impacts of the 2007 movement may help set the stage for a more successful civil resistance movement in the future, although it is also true that some people seriously doubt whether a civil resistance movement alone can bring about change.


## POSSIBILITIES FOR A FUTURE CIVIL DISOBEDIENCE MOVEMENT

Will the movement be revived and if so, how? Many activists involved in the 2007 demonstrations were determined to re-ignite the movement. Yet the regime was

---

[13] Interview, 23 Jan. 2008.

equally determined to prevent opposition protests. People were filled with hatred for the regime but they were also terrified by the violence they witnessed and by the ongoing arrests.[14] In some cases, family members were detained and held hostage in an attempt to force activists to turn themselves in.[15] Over fifty monasteries were raided during the crackdown, and thousands of monks were ordered to return to their villages and towns.[16] As of early 2008, almost all of the leaders of the 2007 demonstrations were in prison, in exile in neighbouring countries, or in hiding. Surveillance of internet cafes and monasteries was stepped up, and Maggin Monastery, one of the main organizing centres for the demonstrations, was shut down. As a result, many Burmese citizens wondered where the leadership for a new round of civil disobedience would come from.

Still, small groups of activists sought to revive the movement. In late 2007, student groups such as 'Generation Wave' distributed posters and pamphlets with messages such as 'Change New Government' and 'Freedom From Fear' and encouraged people to tie pieces of monks' robes on their clothing as a symbol of their solidarity with the monks.[17] Meanwhile, some monks continued to refuse alms or passed them on to poor people, and numbers of young monks decided to boycott the 2008 government-sponsored religious exams. Some well-known preaching monks and abbots dared to criticize the regime in widely attended religious talks, recordings of which were distributed around the country. Meanwhile, NLD members continued to hold weekly prayers for the release of Aung San Suu Kyi and other political prisoners. Poster campaigns calling for political dialogue were also initiated in two ethnic minority states, Kachin State and Arakan State.

Although by early 2008 these small-scale activities had not led to a bigger movement, Sr General Than Shwe appears to have been worried enough to make the February 2008 announcement about a referendum on the constitution in May 2008 and an election for a new government in 2010. As in 1988, the regime sought to divert people's attention away from the crackdown by giving them the hope that the upcoming elections could lead to some improvements; and China had pressured the regime to hold the referendum before the August 2008 Olympics in Beijing, so that Burma would not become an issue there. The All Burma Monks Association and the 88 Generation Students' Group both denounced the regime's plans, while others doubted the voting would be free and fair. Activists found it difficult to organize boycott campaigns, as this was explicitly forbidden by the

---

[14] According to Amnesty International, 'Myanmar: Arrests Increasing Four Months On', 25 Jan. 2008, over 700 people arrested in connection with the 2007 demonstrations were still in prison, along with over 1,100 political prisoners incarcerated earlier.

[15] Human Rights Watch, *Crackdown: Repression of the 2007 Popular Protests in Burma*, Dec. 2007, documents many cases, 87–8.

[16] 'Monasteries Raided Since September 26', *Assistance Association of Political Prisoners Burma* (Thailand), www.aappb.org.

[17] Ko Dee 'Sporadic Movements Defying Junta', *Mizzima News*, 7 Nov. 2007; Ko Dee, 'Activists Group Urge People to Revive "Saffron Revolution"', *Mizzima News*, 27 Nov. 2007.

regime. The referendum was marred by reports of intimidation, but the regime announced that over 90% of voters approved the constitution.

## NON-VIOLENCE AS A MORAL PRINCIPLE

For Theravada Buddhist monks, a non-violent approach to problem-solving is the only one permitted by the monastic code. Monks are instructed to ensure that each word they speak and each action they take does no harm to others, so as to move toward greater moral perfection in this life and the next. More than that, monks in Burma believe in the power of good words and good deeds to bring about a positive reaction in others. The chanting of the *metta sutta* is meant to give rise to feelings of loving kindness on the part of the listeners as well as the chanters. Thus, the monks could be termed as engaging in satyagraha in the style of Gandhi, trying to transform the cruel and indifferent regime into a more caring and responsive one. While many of the monks sincerely hoped that their peaceful chanting would awaken in the generals a sense of responsibility for the citizens' well-being, the older and more politically experienced monks knew from the beginning that the authorities could react with force as they had done in the past. Some abbots originally hesitated to let their young monks join the protests because of concerns for their security. However, as the demonstrations grew in size, the monks and lay people alike began to lose their fear. When troops began pouring into Rangoon on 25 September, people realized a crackdown was imminent. However, many expected tear gas and water cannons, not ruthless beating and live bullets.[18]

During the demonstrations, some lay people wanted to bring sticks or stones to use if they were attacked, but the monks forbad it. Indeed, some monks initially opposed allowing lay people to join the demonstrations because they thought lay people might not be able to control their emotions if provoked. Moreover, it would be harder to prevent *agents provocateurs* from joining in and stirring up trouble. The monks worked hard to ensure that the demonstrations stayed peaceful and orderly even when the crackdown loomed.

Aung San Suu Kyi has also insisted on non-violence for moral rather than tactical reasons. As a practising Buddhist who has also been deeply inspired by Gandhi, she has argued that 'united action by a people armed merely with the principles of justice and non-violence can achieve far greater results than the vast institutions of a state that is not upheld by the consent of the populace'.[19] Many demonstrators also intentionally used non-violent methods as a way to communicate their dignity

[18] Interview, 4 Feb. 2008.

[19] Aung San Suu Kyi, Thakore Prize Acceptance Speech, 2 Oct. 1995. For a detailed explanation of Aung San Suu Kyi's philosophy of non-violence see Gustaaf Houtman, *Mental Culture in Burmese Crisis Politics* (Tokyo: Institute for the Study of Languages and Cultures of Asia and Africa, 1999), part IV.

and set themselves apart from the authorities whose deliberate use of force has had such a demeaning effect. Nevertheless, after the authorities cracked down with shocking brutality, many of the dispirited participants, including some monks, began to doubt whether a non-violent approach alone could be effective. Some suggested that military means were also needed, at a minimum, to protect unarmed demonstrators. Others advocated a more systematically organized armed struggle. In reality, very few acted on those impulses in the months following the demonstrations, because of the failures of past armed movements in Burma to achieve their aims, the lack of international support for an armed movement, and the difficulties of operating in such a repressive environment. Nevertheless, some small groups may organize secretly and carry out small-scale operations.

Few in Burma want to take up arms. Instead, they want the international community to do more. While grateful for the significant media and diplomatic interest in Burma during the crisis, many Burmese were extremely dissatisfied with the level of international involvement. This neither prevented the military from using violence nor protected people from subsequent arrests and imprisonment. As one monk in exile put it, 'I want to say this to the UN Security Council: How many people have to die for democracy and human rights?'[20] This was echoed by U Gambira, one of the organizers of the monks' movement, just days before he was arrested. 'To the six billion people of the world, to those who are sympathetic to the suffering of the Burmese people, please help us to be free from this evil system.'[21] Many activists and ordinary people alike would welcome armed intervention by the US or by UN forces. As a prominent editor in Burma declared, 'We need air strikes.'[22]

## THE ROLE OF NEW TECHNOLOGIES

The 1988 demonstrations had been far bigger in scale than the 2007 demonstrations, but the world did not see them. In 2007, a constant stream of footage, photos, and eyewitness accounts came out in real time, stunning the world and compelling people to pay attention. Although a cell phone cost over US$1,000 in Burma, and few people could afford internet access fees, activists and self-appointed citizen reporters were able to use both to great advantage. Images and comments were sent to the BBC and CNN via email, while Burmese bloggers and exile Burmese media outlets constantly updated their websites with pictures, news, and personal accounts. Although the leading monk and student activists were in hiding, they managed to use cell phones to conduct live interviews with

[20] *Burma: After the Crackdown*, BBC documentary, Nov. 2007.
[21] 'Burmese Monks' Leader Speaks From Hiding', *Radio Free Asia* (Washington DC), 18 Oct. 2007.
[22] 'Apocalypse Naypyidaw', *Irrawaddy*, 22 Nov. 2007.

reporters abroad and to email out statements and appeals to the UN, China, and the Association of Southeast Asian Nations, of which Burma is a member. Many restaurants, hotels, and wealthier homes had satellite TV hook ups, making it possible for people to watch their demonstrations and world leaders' reactions on international news stations and the Democratic Voice of Burma, an exile TV and radio station. Almost all the images came from Rangoon, as people had less access to new technologies in other cities and towns. Still the impact of what did get out was enormous. The speed and ease of cell phone and email communication facilitated consultation among several of the leading activists. As in 1988, radios were also a crucial source of information, with people listening not only to find out what had happened that day but what was planned for the next day.

During the crackdown, the authorities sought to thwart the use of these technologies. Cyber cafes were shut, popular blog sites blocked, internet connections slowed down dramatically, and cell phone lines disconnected. However, the authorities also benefited from the new technologies, in particular by using the images produced by themselves and others to identify and hunt down those who participated in the demonstrations.

## CONCLUSION

In Burma there are two political struggles, one for the restoration of democracy and one for ethnic nationality rights. Burma's political crisis can only be solved if both are dealt with. This means that for a civil disobedience movement to succeed *HUGE* there has to be a significant degree of ethnic minority participation. Ethnic organizations include non-violent political parties, armed groups that have made ceasefires with the regime, and armed groups that are still fighting. Some members of the ethnic political parties affiliated with the NLD joined the demonstrations, and some leaders of the armed groups which were still fighting announced their support for the demonstrations but took no further actions. The ceasefire groups largely kept silent, worried that their participation could lead to reprisals from the regime. Ethnic civilian participation in the movement was also uneven. The regime has sought to keep the democracy movement and the ethnic nationalities' movements apart, but the two must work more closely together if both are to achieve their aims.

The case of Burma suggests that civil resistance movements will not always be successful in the short or even medium term. A firmly entrenched authoritarian government used to exercising virtually absolute power will not bend easily, and a number of factors may need to come together at the same time to bring about change. While the Burmese military regime lost legitimacy as a result of the indiscriminate use of violence against the demonstrators, the movement was not able to create significant fissures in the government forces, or to inhibit their use of violence. Difficulties of coordination and the complexities of uniting the ethnic and pro-democracy struggles were two significant internal factors that hampered the movement. Equally important was the lack of effective action from the international community despite the high degree of attention Burma received in the media and from the UN Security Council. The Burmese military regime is not invincible, but for a domestic non-violent movement to effect change, it may need to be almost perfectly executed and strongly supported by members of the international community.

mvmt's
- execution
- international support

# 22

# A Century of Civil Resistance: Some Lessons and Questions

*Timothy Garton Ash*

It is just over a hundred years since a young Indian lawyer called Mohandas Gandhi launched, in South Africa, his first attempts at what we now call civil resistance. Across these hundred years, civil resistance has become an increasingly important feature of world politics. Most of the events covered in this book date from the period since the 1960s—and they keep on coming. How far what happened in Tibet in the spring of 2008 can be described as civil resistance it is hard to say, but at least on the part of Buddhist monks the protests do seem to have included a significant element of non-violent action. By the time you read this, there may well be other episodes on other continents, crying out for more scrupulous and penetrating comparative study than even the best news media can provide.

Whatever the future holds, we must surely agree with Kenneth Boulding that historians have so far paid too little attention to what he aptly characterizes as 'the rise of organized non-violence as an instrument of social and political change'.[1] As Boulding points out, most human activity throughout most of human history has been what he calls 'unviolent', but the new and developing phenomenon to be studied is organized, purposive non-violent action.

Were you to ask anyone to draw up a short list of what they consider to be the most inspiring leaders, movements, and moments over the last hundred years, it's a fair bet that list would include some featured in this book: Mohandas (now more generally known as Mahatma, that is 'great soul') Gandhi, Martin Luther King, Václav Havel, Lech Wałęsa, Nelson Mandela, Mikhail Gorbachev, Aung San Suu Kyi, the civil rights movement in the United States, Solidarity in Poland, 'people power' in the Philippines, assorted velvet and colour revolutions—to name but a few. That list would contain not only some of the most inspiring, but also some of the most tragic: one thinks, for example, of the crushing of the 'moment of the monks' by the Burmese military in 2007, the subject of our last case study in this volume. For by no means all these movements and moments ended in success, at least so far as contemporaries could see.

---

[1] Kenneth E. Boulding 'Nonviolence and Power in the Twentieth Century,' in Stephen Zunes et al., *Nonviolent Social Movements: A Geographical Perspective* (Oxford: Blackwell, 1999), 9.

In this chapter I do not pretend to offer a comprehensive conclusion to what is, itself, only a beginning. Instead, I merely tease out a few of the lessons that seem to emerge from these studies, as well as from others that have preceded them, and highlight some of the many open questions that remain.

## THE POWER OF THE POWERLESS?

Many people casually associate civil resistance with morality, religion, goodness or even goody-goodiness. Nice, moral but impotent: that would be a common enough verdict from the man or woman on the street—unless, of course, he or she had participated, on the street, in one of these peaceful mass actions. Like several earlier writers on this subject, our authors separately but almost unanimously arrive at a different conclusion. The choice of non-violence, we find them arguing again and again, was more pragmatic than principled, and often less unequivocal than is generally assumed. Even Gandhi countenanced the use of armed force in some circumstances. Only a very few of the leading actors in these histories are true pacifists, like the Theravada Buddhists of Burma, according to Christina Fink, and, it seems to me, Pope John Paul II—offering an imitation of Christ rare enough among Christians.[2]

While pragmatic, political choices of non-violence predominate, it would be worth studying in more depth the significance of religion, and of ideologies, cultures, and value systems more broadly, in the adoption or rejection, and subsequent trajectory, of non-violent action. Stanley Hauerwas and others have made an eloquent case for active Christian non-violence, based on the New Testament.[3] European and colonial history tells a rather different story. The native inhabitants of the Americas would have been very surprised to hear—in the moments before they were shot—that Christianity is a religion of non-violence. And reflecting on Europe's own wars of religion, Montesquieu observed that 'no kingdom has ever existed with as many civil wars as occur in the kingdom of Christ'.[4]

Islam is currently associated in many people's minds with violence, while others insist it is 'a religion of peace'. It would be interesting to explore empirically what part the religion of Islam, and the faith-based political ideology of Islamism, have played in individual and group choices of non-violent as against violent action, for example in the first Palestinian intifada.[5] Ervand Abrahamian's chapter on Iran has some suggestive reflections on the connections between vox dei

[2] For this assessment, see Timothy Garton Ash, *History of the Present: Essays, Sketches and Despatches from Europe in the 1990s* (London: Penguin, 2000), 347–52.

[3] Stanley Hauerwas, *Performing the Faith: Bonhoeffer and the Practice of Nonviolence* (London: SPCK, 2004).

[4] Montesquieu, *Persian Letters* (Oxford: Oxford University Press, 2008), 39.

[5] For some suggestive comments in this connection, see Mary Elizabeth King, *A Quiet Revolution: The First Palestinian Intifada and Nonviolent Resistance* (New York: Nation Books, 2007).

©AFP/Stringer/Getty Images

**Figure 22.1** An appeal to loving kindness. This beautiful photograph shows Buddhist nuns taking part in a procession in Rangoon on 25 September 2007, despite stern warnings from Burma's ruling junta against the anti-government protests. It is unusual for nuns to come onto the streets in this way—unlike the monks, who routinely walk out to collect contributions of food—and the crowd show their appreciation. The military regime subsequently crushed protests that Western journalists were perhaps too quick to label the 'saffron revolution'. Whether they will be adjudged a failure in the long run, only time will tell.

and vox populi in the Shiite context of Iran. Doctrinal and sectarian differences between Sunni and Shia, sufi, takfiri, wahhabi or deobandi, would need to be examined. Merle Goldman suggests in her chapter on China that the Confucian tradition of 'moral remonstrance' with the rulers was (perhaps unsurprisingly) more important than Gandhi in the Tiananmen movement of 1989. Buddhism clearly does have a central message of non-violence, articulated most eloquently by the fourteenth Dalai Lama. The Burmese protests of 2007 began when monks went on the streets of Pakkoku chanting the *metta sutta* of loving kindness towards all human beings. They were repaid for their loving kindness by being beaten and tied to poles.[6] Is it a mere accident of geopolitical circumstance that, so far, the history of Buddhist civil resistance has largely been—at least in terms of

---

[6] See Christina Fink, Ch. 21 above.

worldly, political outcomes—a history of failure? A partial exception would be the Buddhist-led protests in South Vietnam in 1963. However, as Adam Roberts points out, it took a military coup, with heavy US involvement, to depose the government that the monks wished to change.

This takes us to an important point, already highlighted in the introductory chapter. In many politically successful cases of civil resistance, non-violence and violence have been intertwined. The connections are of many different kinds. In Portugal and Serbia, for example, the success of civil resistance followed bloody, failed wars prosecuted by the regimes that were then non-violently challenged and eventually toppled. In Northern Ireland, as Richard English shows, it went the other way: what began as civil resistance descended into civil war. In Kosovo, too, the guerrilla (or, according to an initial US government assessment, terrorist) actions of the Kosovo Liberation Army (KLA) emerged as a response to the perceived failure of a campaign of civil resistance. In South Africa, the non-violent struggle of the African National Congress (ANC) was accompanied from the early 1960s by the 'armed struggle' of Umkhonto we Sizwe. Many campaigners against apartheid regarded these not as opposites or mutually exclusive alternatives but as two arms of the same body politic—the armed and the unarmed arm, so to speak. We do well to remember that, even as a political prisoner, Nelson Mandela refused to denounce and renounce the armed struggle.

What is more, historians—properly concerned with what actually was rather than what should have been—may conclude that it was precisely the combination of unarmed and armed struggle, of Sinn Fein and Irish Republican Army (IRA), of Archbishop Desmond Tutu and what Tom Lodge calls the 'armed propaganda' of Umkhonto we Sizwe, of Ibrahim Rugova's non-violent League for a Democratic Kosovo and the Kosovo Liberation Army, that achieved the desired result. They did so, however, always only in a larger context, with factors such as the state of the economy and the involvement of external actors contributing to the result.

That said, non-violent action is itself a significant and distinctive form of power, often underrated in political science, political theory, and the study of international relations. In fact, the record of civil resistance invites us to refine our understanding of power itself. Three dimensions of power are now widely acknowledged in the study of international relations: 'hard power', meaning the possession, use or threatened use of military force and other forms of direct coercion; economic power; and 'soft power', seminally defined by Joseph Nye as 'the ability to get what you want through attraction rather than coercion or payments'.[7] Civil resistance might loosely be referred to as a form of 'soft power', but it does not really fit Nye's definition or the broader context in which he and others use the term.

Its power draws rather on a strategic insight, itself going back at least to the *Discourse on Voluntary Servitude* of the sixteenth-century French thinker Etienne de la Boétie, about the inability of even the most well-armed despot to rule

---

[7] Quoted already by Adam Roberts (Ch. 1 above, 6) from Joseph S. Nye, *Soft Power: The Means to Success in World Politics* (New York: Public Affairs, 2004), x.

without a minimum degree of cooperation from the ruled. As Gandhi put it, no clapping is possible without two hands, no quarrel without two people, and no state without two entities: the rulers and the ruled.[8] Non-violent action is therefore about depriving the power-holders of the deepest sources of their power, outflanking their more visible coercive instruments. Gene Sharp has described it as 'political jiu-jitsu'. To achieve this effect, it deploys what Václav Havel, as a dissident writer under communism, famously called the 'power of the powerless'.[9] When it works, it exposes what one might call 'the powerlessness of the powerful'—something that Havel himself would come to experience as president of a now free Czech Republic.

Civil resistance does not merely interact with power politics, traditionally conceived. It has changed the very nature of power politics in our time. It challenges a still widespread assumption that military or coercive action ('hard power') is the most effective and certain way of achieving change both within and between states.[10] Reflecting on Gandhi's famous march to the sea, to make salt in defiance of a British law, an Indian scholar suggests that we might pose the power question thus: can you dethrone the King-Emperor by boiling seawater in a kettle?[11] The answer from a century's experience of non-violent action would seem to be 'yes, given the right combination of strategy, circumstances, time and luck, you sometimes, eventually, can'. Among other things, this book is about what those combinations are. It offers no simple lessons. History never does.

## RE-DEFINING REVOLUTION

The kind of power generated by civil resistance—'people power', to use the catchy Filipino English coinage—would usually and plausibly be contrasted with the use of force. Force without violence, or at least the threat of violence, sounds like whisky without alcohol.[12] But what about non-violent revolution? The published

---

[8] From a text of 1916, quoted in Judith Brown (ed.), *Mahatma Gandhi: The Essential Writings* (Oxford: Oxford University Press, 2008), 313.

[9] A helpful edition (edited by John Keane and introduced by Steven Lukes) is Václav Havel et al., *The Power of the Powerless: Citizens against the State in Central-eastern Europe* (London: Hutchinson, 1985).

[10] On the basis of a dataset of 323 violent and non-violent resistance campaigns between 1900 and 2006, Maria Stephan and Erica Chenoweth argue that 'major nonviolent campaigns have achieved success 53 per cent of the time, compared with 26 per cent for violent resistance campaigns'. 'Why Civil Resistance Works: The Strategic Logic of Nonviolent Political Conflict', *International Security*, 32, no. 4 (Spring 2008), 7–40. See below for some questions about what constitutes success.

[11] In the 2000 television documentary version of *A Force More Powerful* (see www.aforcemorepo-werful.org), produced and written by Steve York, the Gandhi biographer B. R. Nanda summarized the way British officials underestimated the possible impact of the salt march in these words: 'You can't dethrone the King-Emperor by boiling seawater in a kettle.' I have reformulated this striking phrase as a question.

[12] See the entry for 'force' in the Index to Rupert Smith, *The Utility of Force: The Art of War in the Modern World* (London: Allen Lane, 2005): 'force *see* military force'.

version of the historian A. J. P. Taylor's 1978 lectures on revolutions begins with the statement that 'there have been violent political upheavals as long as there have been political communities' and goes on to argue that the French Revolution originated revolution 'in the modern sense'.[13] Clearly he regarded 'violent political upheaval' as a defining feature of revolution. Chairman Mao agreed. 'Revolution', he famously observed, 'is not a dinner party.'[14] In a survey of European revolutions from 1492 to 1992, published in 1993, Charles Tilly argues that 'whatever else they involve, revolutions include forcible transfers of power over states'.[15] The first definition of 'forcible' in the Oxford English Dictionary is 'done by force; involving the use of force or violence'. Yet Tilly includes what happened in central Europe in 1989—almost entirely without violence—in his account of European revolutions.

This is something that people wrestled with at the time. I remember a moment in the Magic Lantern theatre in Prague in November 1989, during the internal debates (which I was privileged to witness) among the leaders of what was already being called Czechoslovakia's 'Velvet Revolution', when one Czech dissident queried whether they should call it a revolution at all, suggesting that 'in our linguistic context "revolution" has a clear sub-text of violence'.[16] This is perhaps why outside observers most easily recognized what happened in Romania, with the accompanying violence in the streets and summary execution of Nicolae Ceaușescu, as a revolution—although in fact, its immediate outcome (the transfer of power from one set of communists to another) was in substance one of the least revolutionary of them all. And this is why observers generally feel the need to qualify these new-style, non-violent transfers of power over states with an adjective: self-limiting, evolutionary, carnation, velvet, singing, rose, orange, negotiated, electoral, peaceful, or even non-revolutionary revolution.

In this sense, civil resistance, with the people acting en masse but peacefully, whether on the streets, in strikes and sit-ins, or in other kinds of demonstration, has helped redefine revolution since the 1960s. It has done so, however, in a complex interplay with at least two other elements that keep recurring in our studies: elections and negotiations. It's no accident that what is arguably the first of these new-style revolutions in Europe, the 'Revolution of the Carnations' in Portugal in 1974, is held to have begun what Samuel Huntington called the third wave of democratization, while some scholars suggest that 1989 began a fourth wave. Sometimes the mass action is to kick-start a negotiation which culminates in an election (Poland 1988/9, South Africa to 1994). Mass mobilization may go towards voter registration (Chile, for the 1988 plebiscite) and it may occur to protect—one might even say, enforce—what is believed to be the true result of a

---

[13] See his *Revolutions and Revolutionaries* (Oxford: Oxford University Press, 1981), 17.

[14] This comment from Mao's 1927 *Investigation into the Peasant Question in Hunan* is quoted by Rana Mitter in his *Modern China: A Very Short Introduction* (Oxford: Oxford University Press, 2008), 56.

[15] Charles Tilly, *European Revolutions, 1492–1992* (Oxford: Blackwell, 1993), 5.

[16] Timothy Garton Ash, *The Magic Lantern: The Revolution of '89 Witnessed in Warsaw, Budapest, Berlin and Prague*, 2nd edn. (New York: Vintage, 1999), 113.

falsified or 'stolen' election (Serbia 2000, Georgia 2003). This may, however, only be achieved through negotiation, supported by mass action, leading to another election (Ukraine 2004). Sequencing and permutations vary, but the ingredients recur.

Domestic and international election monitors, unofficial vote counts and exit polls, independent and international media to disseminate the results: these, too, increasingly belong to the repertoire of new-style revolution. Often, the outcome of the peaceful–electoral–negotiated revolution is a disappointment to revolutionary expectations. Thus, for example, Aleksander Smolar describes how, more than fifteen years after the event, Polish politics continued to be plagued by furious right-wing accusations of a 'betrayal' of Polish national interests by Solidarity leaders at the round-table negotiations of 1989. Sometimes, as Andrew Wilson indicates in the case of Ukraine, the outcome of the negotiation not only disappoints the more radical civil resisters but even brings in to question the applicability of the term revolution—for was there really a lasting transfer of power over the state?[17] There is surely a warning here about the instant branding of such events as 'the [insert colour or catchy label] revolution', by opposition activists, political consultants, and, not least, domestic and foreign journalists. There is a real question whether, in the case of the 2005 'Tulip Revolution' in Kyrgyzstan and 'Cedar Revolution' in Lebanon, the contents matched the label on the bottle.

Nonetheless there are sufficient substantial instances, with durable outcomes, for us to assert that civil resistance has assisted at the birth of a new genre of revolution, qualitatively different from the Jacobin–Bolshevik model of 1789 and 1917.

## THE INDIVIDUAL AND THE PEOPLE

Peaceful revolutions, like the violent ones of old, are distinguished by the eruption of very large numbers of people—call them, according to taste, the masses, the people, the crowd, or the citizens—into public spaces, and hence onto history's stage. They are those exceptional moments when, to adapt Karl Marx, the people make their own history; or at least, feel that they do. The sheer numbers involved are extraordinary. One must enter an immediate caveat here: all numbers are estimates, and sometimes poetic estimates, exaggerated by protest movements for dramatic effect. A curious folk belief about journalists is that they have a special, magical ability to count the numbers of crowds. They don't. They're just guessing, like everyone else. Yet photographs help to confirm the fantastic scale of these moments.

---

[17] In the case of Ukraine, one could argue that, even if the old guard returned, there was, at least, a step change in the way power was exercised in the state. But it may need a longer historical perspective to confirm that judgement.

©Sharok Hatami/Rex Features

**Figure 22.2** The power of numbers. The vast turnout to welcome Ayatollah Khomeini to Tehran on his return from exile is vividly captured in this photograph from 1 February 1979, and soon overwhelmed the vestiges of the old regime. Compare the photograph (on page 130) of Pope John Paul II's return to his native Poland a few months later in the same year; but the consequences were very different, in both the short and the long term.

The crowd that turned out to welcome Ayatollah Khomeini back to Iran in February 1979 has been estimated at two million. When Pope John Paul II returned to his native land in the summer of that same year, crowds of up to two million joined him to sing 'return to us, O Lord, a free fatherland', in a manifestation of mass solidarity that prefigured the birth of Solidarity. Mark Beissinger suggests that the number of people participating in the Baltic Way human chain of August 1989 approximated the entire able-bodied adult population of the Baltic states. For a few hours, the nation was the crowd and the crowd was the nation. Howard Clark records that in 1990 nearly half the adult population of Kosovo signed a petition to the United Nations 'For democracy, against violence'. In Kiev, during the 'Orange Revolution' of 2004, they lost count at 500,000. ('If I see 200,000 people, I will resign,' President Leonid Kuchma had said, faced with an earlier, much smaller demo. Well . . . ) There is strength in these numbers, and there is safety. Such mass gatherings break through the barrier of fear which, as Gandhi saw, is the essential bulwark of all non-democratic regimes. Here is 'people power' in its most elemental form—not the theatrical impresario's proverbial 'bums on seats' but bodies on squares. I remember a Ukrainian academic telling me during the Orange Revolution that, while normally he hoped people would turn to him for his mind, here, on Kiev's Independence Square, his contribution was simply to be another body.

In these movements and moments, social actors who are not usually thought to 'make history' emerge to do so. 'Ordinary people' do extraordinary things. Students, being more impatient, fearless, and perhaps more idealistic than their elders—who have families and jobs to worry about, and may remember what it is like to be defeated—are often found to play a vanguard role, whether in China, Burma, or Czechoslovakia. If violent action has traditionally been a man's business, women often come to the fore in non-violent action, and in opposition to further violence. One thinks immediately of the Mothers of the Plaza de Mayo in Argentina. Merle Goldman gives a moving account of a less well-known example: the Tiananmen mothers' movement, formed by the mothers of those killed on Tiananmen Square in June 1989. Ivan Vejvoda adds the remarkable story of a Serbian movement of *grandparents*, formed to defend their grandchildren, who were active in the Otpor youth protest movement. Grannies of the world, unite!

One of the keys to effective mass social action is the forging of alliances between social groups that are usually separate from, if not indifferent or even hostile to each other. As Aleksander Smolar explains, in Poland in 1968, students and intellectuals protested while workers barely lifted a finger to help them; in 1970, workers protested while students and intellectuals barely lifted a finger; in 1976, they started coming together, with the formation of a Workers' Defence Committee (KOR) that soon significantly renamed itself the Committee for Social Self-Organization-'KOR'. In Poland's Solidarity movement, you then had a grand alliance of workers, intelligentsia, and peasant farmers, together with important elements in the Catholic Church. In China in 1989, there was a coming-together of students and workers, with the support of some entrepreneurs. In Burma in 2007, it was students and monks—and then 'ordinary people' coming out to protect the monks.

What is the glue that holds hundreds of thousands of diverse individuals together in such moments? First of all, to be sure, a common enemy: some abhorrent 'them'. The magical solidarity does not usually long outlast the disappearance of the common enemy. But there also needs to be an identity of 'us'. In Poland, there was a conscious attempt to build that collective identity around the notion of 'society'—a self-organizing society in which worker, student, and intellectual, Christian and Jew, socialist and conservative, all had their place. In more traditional language of the left, this was the familiar concept of 'the people'. Yet very often we find that the glue was also national—or a mix of national, ethnic, and religious. Solidarity's 'society' was at the same time the nation uniting against alien rule—'żeby Polska była polską', they sang, 'so that Poland should be Polish'—and for some that meant specifically a Catholic nation. East Germany in 1989 furnishes the classic example of a transition between the two forms of 'we': the crowds in Leipzig started chanting 'Wir sind das Volk' (we are the people) and gradually switched to 'Wir sind ein Volk' (we are one nation). Mark Beissinger makes this point very strongly, suggesting that while the recent history of the Balkans shows how 'ethnic passions' can lead to war, that of the Baltics shows how they can be mobilized in non-violent struggle.

In his book *The Crowd in the French Revolution*, the historian George Rudé pioneered the study of the revolutionary crowd. As well as highlighting the exceptional role of women (including the legendary fishwives marching on Versailles) he contrasted two archetypical ways of characterizing the crowd: Hippolyte Taine's despicable *canaille*, the rabble or mob, and Jules Michelet's noble *le peuple*, the people. By the early nineteenth century, Rudé concluded, a new type of revolutionary crowd was beginning to emerge.[18] In the early twenty-first century, we need new studies of the crowd in these new-style revolutions. Their sociology cries out to be understood better, as do their group dynamics. This is, let it be said at once, difficult to do. You cannot interview 500,000 people. Even if you could, memory rewrites history.

I have spent many hours of my life standing in revolutionary crowds, on freezing squares from Warsaw in 1980 to Prague in 1989 to Kiev in 2004, and they remain gloriously mysterious. What is it that sways them one way or another? Who is it that comes up with the chants that erupt, apparently spontaneously, as the crowd speaks back to the speaker as if it were itself one person? Who, as we stood on Wenceslas Square in Prague in 1989, had the idea of taking his (or was it her?) key ring out of his (or her) pocket, holding it up and rattling the keys like a Chinese bell? (Within minutes, some 300,000 people were doing the same, producing a sound that I shall never forget.) Sometimes we do know the answer: in Ukraine and Georgia, student and opposition groups sat around beforehand, devising such japes, occasionally advised by activists from an earlier revolution. More often we don't. Perhaps even the person who really started it does not know.

What is clear, however, is the importance of individual leaders on the platform. One should not idealize the new-style revolutionary crowd. This book contains all too many cases where it turned violent; *le peuple* became, indeed, *canaille*. Tom Lodge reminds us that an estimated 16,000 people died in the last five years of South Africa's freedom struggle, many of them in ethno-political conflict between the United Democratic Front/African National Congress (UDF/ANC) and the Zulu Inkatha movement. In Lhasa in 2008, peaceful protests in defence of Buddhist monks rapidly degenerated into race riots against Han Chinese and Hui Muslims.[19] Non-violence is not the natural default setting of angry young men inflamed with ethnic passions.

Leaders are needed to keep them exercising unnatural restraint, often using some of those same strong national, ethnic, and religious emotions to that effect. A Polish opposition activist describes how, in the early days of the strike in the Lenin shipyard in Gdańsk in August 1980, Lech Wałęsa and his colleagues struck

---

[18] George Rudé, *The Crowd in the French Revolution* (Oxford: Oxford University Press, 1959).
[19] See Robert Barnett, 'Thunder from Tibet', *New York Review of Books*, 29 May 2008.

©Dinodia Photo Library

**Figure 22.3** Individuals matter. Mohandas Gandhi as a young man, before he become the 'Mahatma'. Informed by his early experience of organizing protest in South Africa, he developed seminal elements of both the theory and the practice of civil resistance. Over the next century, these spread both through his personal example and through his writings.

up the national anthem so an unruly crowd of strikers would stop and stand to attention, rather than marching out through the gates, inviting police reprisals and possible bloodshed, as had happened in 1970. As this activist recalled, they got the strikers singing 'March, march Dąbrowski' (the refrain of the Polish national anthem) precisely so they would *not* march.[20] Over the next decade, I watched many times how Wałęsa used this technique. Faced with a crowd that was getting turbulent, he would strike up the national anthem to calm it. The patriotic catharsis.

Gandhi, Nelson Mandela, Václav Havel, Desmond Tutu, Aung San Suu Kyi, Ricardo Lagos—all were tested in such moments, and all were criticized for choosing the path of negotiation and compromise over violent triumphalism. Again and again, our case studies emphasize the importance of individual leaders in determining the course of events, for good or ill. Henry Kissinger told Mario Soares in Portugal that he was 'doomed' to become a Kerensky—the Menshevik loser in the Russian revolution of 1917. But in Portugal, Kerensky won, Lenin lost.[21] In Iran, however, as Ervand Abrahamian shows, the Islamic Kerensky,

[20] Jerzy Borowczak in the 2000 television documentary version of *A Force More Powerful*.
[21] Kenneth Maxwell records Kissinger acknowledging as much in a subsequent private conversation with Soares: '... what you have done surprised me', he told Soares in 1976, according to a recently

Ayatollah Kazem Shariatmadari, with his moderate programme of a return to the 1906 constitution, lost out to Ayatollah Ruhollah Khomeini, the Islamic Lenin. But leadership on the side of the existing power-holders is vital too. Non-violent transitions depend also on the restraint, and the political skills, of those whom the German writer Hans Magnus Enzensberger has called the 'heroes of retreat': Mikhail Gorbachev, archetypally, but also F. W. de Klerk in South Africa and Eduard Shevardnadze twice, as Soviet foreign minister in the late 1980s and as Georgian president in 2003.

Civil resistance thus illustrates—and its outcomes can depend upon—the interaction between two kinds of historical actor, both of which are less import-ant in the normal, everyday politics of consolidated liberal democracies. On the one hand, there are very large numbers of individual people acting collectively, directly, publicly, and unpredictably; on the other, there are great or less great individuals who, here more than ever, can play a decisive role in human history.


## POP ART AND STRATEGIC DRAMATURGY

The history of civil resistance is also art history. The logos, flags, symbols, improvised posters, street performances, music, slogans, and graffiti of these movements are more genuinely Pop Art than Pop Art ever was. It's somehow appropriate that the Civil Disobedience Committee in Georgia was also known as the Art Committee—*Artcom*, for short—because of the large number of artists, screen-writers, and directors in its leadership. The choice of colour, logo, setting, slogan—Orange in Ukraine, the white on black '*Gotov je*' ('He's finished') in Serbia—is often made with some sort of expert involvement. The experts are not just artists, PR men, and 'political technologists' of opposition. Ayatollahs, Buddhist abbots, and Christian priests take a hand. (After all, it was the Catholic Church which invented propaganda.) But there are also elements of genuine, spontaneous, popular creativity, like the hand-made posters I saw in central Europe in 1989 saying 'the heart of Europe beats for freedom' (Prague) and 'what big teeth you have, granny' (over a sketch of the big-toothed last commun-ist leader of East Germany, Egon Krenz); or the graffito I spied on a wall in East Berlin saying 'only today is the war really over'. And no artist composed the beautiful picture that adorns the cover of this book: Burmese monks in their crimson and saffron robes, swishing and chanting through the rain, protected on either side by a polychrome populace.

declassified American note, 'I must admit this. I don't often make mistakes of judgement.' (Ch. 9, above, 161.) As Zita Seabra, then a leader of the Portuguese Communist Party, made very clear at the Oxford conference, the hope of many Portuguese communists was precisely that Soares would be a Kerensky, and that the 'February revolution' of April 1974 would be followed by an 'October revolution' later that year.

Freedom of expression—recovered, or fully enjoyed for the first time—is of the essence in such moments. As Alexander Solzhenitsyn and Václav Havel both argued, the freedom to say what you want, to challenge a regime of organized lying with 'one word of truth', is both a symptom and a cause of political change. When people 'speak truth to power' they are themselves empowered. They shift the power balance simply by saying words in public. At best, these are pentecostal moments, when ordinary men and women speak as if inspired.

Above all, this is theatre. You need your stage, your set, your script, and your actors. As Judith Brown argues, Gandhi perfectly understood that he was engaged in political theatre. So have many of his successors. This culminated—almost to the point of parody—in the Velvet Revolution in Prague. Its leader, Václav Havel, was a playwright; its headquarters was the Magic Lantern theatre; its press conferences were held on the stage of that theatre. On Wenceslas Square, from the balcony of the newspaper *Svobodné Slovo* (The Free Word), Havel directed and starred in a performance with 300,000 extras. Cry your eyes out, Cecil B. de Mille. For a few days, the frontier between life and art almost disappeared.

But this is theatre with a difference. Its objective is not to entertain, to inspire fear and pity, or to cause some moral reaction in its audience. Here, these effects

© Peter Turnley/Corbis

**Figure 22.4** Political theatre. On the stage of the Magic Lantern theatre in Prague, the headquarters of the Velvet Revolution, on 24 November 1989, Václav Havel (right), playwright and hero of '89, and Alexander Dubček (2nd from right), the hero of '68, toast the resignation of the ruling politburo. The author of this chapter had the unforgettable experience of being there.

are all means to another end: social and political change. So what is needed is, in Doug McAdam's striking phrase, 'strategic dramaturgy'.[22] Clausewitz meets Shakespeare. Successful directors will have a clear sense of the many different audiences for the play—the protesters on the streets, the people who have stayed at home, the rulers (and the different factions and interest groups among them), international public opinion, foreign governments, international organizations— and of what they wish to achieve with each audience in every act. This book illustrates the difference between three levels of civil resistance as political theatre: protest without dramaturgy, dramaturgy without strategy, and strategic dramaturgy. Even the last will not always succeed, given the wrong circumstances, but it stands a better chance than the other two.

## INTERNATIONAL CONTEXT AND EXTERNAL INTERVENTION

Our case studies are mainly within the framework of a single state—although not always within a single nation, a dissonance that has sometimes, as in Kosovo and Northern Ireland, been among the main sources of popular grievance. A job that remains to be done is to examine transnational movements, networks and impacts of civil resistance. Yet even in these state-framed chapters we find rich evidence of influences across borders. Sometimes these influences are surprising: for example, the 1982 Hollywood film *Gandhi*, starring Ben Kingsley, being shown in a Chinese village in 2005. Sometimes they are wholly unintended. Kieran Williams argues that the extensive treatment in the Czechoslovak communist media of both the US civil rights movement and the May '68 protests in Paris, while intended to illustrate the oppressive evils of imperialist capitalism, actually inspired Czechoslovak civil resistance against Soviet communist invasion.

Almost every author emphasizes the importance of the international context. Some point to specific elements of deliberate external intervention, although this is by no means always present. Sometimes it is precisely the lack of intervention that is decisive. In Burma in 2007, for example, one could argue that it was the failure of China, India, and the country's partners in the Association of Southeast Asian Nations (ASEAN) to intervene more effectively which condemned the civil resistance movement to defeat. It was not so much that the governments of China and India supported the Burmese generals; just that they did not stop them. The scope of international context is thus much broader than that of deliberate external intervention.

---

[22] Doug McAdam in Doug McAdam, John D. McCarthy, and Mayer N. Zald (eds.), *Comparative Perspectives on Social Movements: Political Opportunities, Mobilizing Structures, and Cultural Framings* (Cambridge: Cambridge University Press, 1996).

From the late 1940s to the early 1990s, that broader international context was what Odd Arne Westad has called the 'Global Cold War'.[23] Cross-influences between the Cold War 'West' and 'East' are manifold, complex and fascinating. Drawing on the work of Mary Dudziak, Doug McAdam shows how international criticism of racial segregation in the United States—especially from the Soviet bloc and the decolonized 'third world'—fed into what eventually became Washington's official responsiveness to the US civil rights movement. How could the US claim to be the champion of human rights abroad while trampling on them at home?[24] As Kenneth Maxwell indicates, Portugal in 1974–5 was the theatre for a complex quadrille of Cold War politics, with the Nixon and Ford administrations in Washington fearing communist takeover in Portugal, Brezhnev's politburo in Moscow divided over how far to support an attempt at communist takeover in Portugal, and the two superpowers playing a hidden game, also involving Cuba, for supremacy in the former Portuguese colonies of Angola and Mozambique.

There were double standards on the part of both superpowers. The United States, for example, supported martial law in the Philippines under Ferdinand Marcos but denounced it in Poland under Wojciech Jaruzelski. Yet one superpower influence that emerges very strongly from these pages is something of an exception to that rule. This is the Carter administration's human rights policy. Clearly this was applied with more acerbity in the Soviet sphere. In alliance with local dissidents in countries such as Poland and Czechoslovakia, it gave Europe's fledgling 'Helsinki process' its human rights cutting edge. Yet it also challenged the conduct of 'friendly dictators' in Chile, Iran, and the Philippines. In Iran, illustrating once again the law of unintended consequences, the Carter human rights policy contributed to the fall of the Shah, the triumph of Ayatollah Khomeini, and thus to the emergence of an Islamist regime which has plagued the United States for the last thirty years.

The forces of international economics and finance played an important role, especially when they were the subject of political linkages. The hard currency indebtedness of several east-central European states in the 1980s, including Poland and East Germany, contributed significantly to those regimes' weariness and weakness, prompting the historian Fritz Stern to recall Mirabeau's pre-1789 observation that 'the nation's deficit is the nation's treasure'.[25] It is sometimes argued that 'sanctions don't work', but Poland and South Africa are two cases where they did contribute to the eventual, relatively peaceful transition to democracy. South Africa illustrates a final, intriguing Cold War connection. Tom Lodge shows how the fall of the Berlin Wall encouraged F. W. de Klerk to release

---

[23] Odd Arne Westad, *The Global Cold War: Third World Interventions and the Making of Our Times* (Cambridge: Cambridge University Press, 2005).

[24] In an old Soviet bloc joke the apocryphal 'Radio Yerevan' is asked by a Soviet worker how many years an average American worker has to work and save before he is in a position to buy his first car. After a long silence, the answer comes back: 'but they kill negroes'.

[25] Quoted in Garton Ash, *The Magic Lantern*, 135.

Nelson Mandela from prison and open negotiations with the ANC. Soviet support for an ANC armed struggle was no longer to be feared.[26]

One way and another, few historians would doubt that civil resistance made a significant contribution to the largely peaceful ending of the Cold War. Since the end of the Cold War, and with the continued rise of non-Western powers, the structure of international politics has become more complex: no longer bipolar, it has variously been claimed to be unipolar, multipolar, and no-polar. In this new setting, indeed as part of the debate about defining it, controversy has focused on real or alleged attempts by Western powers to foment civil resistance (or 'colour revolution') in what other powers regard as their 'backyards', be it Ukraine, Georgia and Belarus for Russia or Burma for China.

Such allegations of subversion or 'interference in internal affairs' are nothing new. Nor are the real activities which may or may not be present.[27] For example, Western financial help did flow to Solidarity in Poland, especially in its years of underground activity between 1982 and 1988.This does not mean the West and its agents created Solidarity; they emphatically did not. They were as surprised as anyone by its emergence. But they helped to keep it going when it was down and nearly out. One of the more striking examples of external intervention to support democratic opposition and civil resistance—striking also because so far from the stereotype of American anti-Russian and anti-communist subversion—is the major role played by West Germany's Christian Democrats, and other German party foundations, in supporting the democratic opposition in Pinochet's Chile. German party foundations also played an important role in the end of right-wing authoritarian regimes in Spain and Portugal.

Nonetheless, it seems fair to say that over the last two decades, as the experience stock of civil resistance has grown, so has the amount of explicit knowledge transfer, up to and including financial support and training activities which dictators would call 'subversion'. This has been greatly facilitated by new media, to the extent that regimes allow them to operate. The clearest example in our set of case studies is Georgia. Stephen Jones describes how Georgian opposition activists learned deliberately, intensely, and directly from Serbian colleagues who had been involved in toppling Milošević. He quotes Ivane Merabishvili, the organizational genius of Georgia's 'Rose Revolution', observing with self-evident hyperbole: 'all the demonstrators knew the tactics of the revolution in Belgrade by heart because they showed...the film on their revolution. Everyone knew what to do. This was a copy of that revolution, only louder.'[28]

---

[26] Ch. 13 above, 144–61. The fear of Soviet support for ANC armed struggle, though very exaggerated, was not pure paranoia: see Westad, *Global Cold War*, 215–16.

[27] The mere presence of such charges is not an accurate indicator of the presence of such activities. In a presentation for a panel discussion on 'The European Way of Civil Resistance' organized by the Oxford University Project on Civil Resistance and Power Politics at St Antony's College, Oxford, on 23 May 2008, Alex Pravda documented baseless Soviet claims about Western masterminding of the Prague Spring and of subsequent civil resistance to Soviet occupation. Sometimes there is smoke without fire.

[28] Jones, Ch. 19 above, 324.

In fact, one can discern an international learning chain running through a series of neo-authoritarian regimes in newly formed post-communist states, where the leader was toppled and a more democratic—or at least, less undemocratic—government was installed, with the help of a more or less salient element of civil resistance: Slovakia 1998, Croatia 1999/2000, Serbia 2000, Georgia 2003, Ukraine 2004. However, as Andrew Wilson points out in his chapter on Ukraine, the external interventions came from both sides—pro-revolutionary and counter-revolutionary. It is not just the protagonists of peaceful change who can learn from history. The Putin administration in Moscow did so too, establishing a special department to counter the spread of colour revolution. Pavol Demeš argues that one reason why civil resistance has (at this writing) failed to achieve the desired result in Belarus, despite a major push around the presidential elections in 2006, is that Alexander Lukashenko has learned lessons from the toppling of his post-communist, neo-authoritarian peers: Vladimir Mečiar in Slovakia, Franjo Tudjman in Croatia, Slobodan Milošević in Serbia, Eduard Shevardnadze in Georgia, and Leonid Kuchma in Ukraine.[29]

Much remains to be explored about this whole complex of external interventions by state and non-state actors, cross-border influences, funding, transnational advocacy and knowledge transfer, including the role of new and international media. The evidence is, however, difficult to collect, partly because of the sheer multiplicity of often small-scale actors on all sides, partly because some of them do not wish fully to reveal what they are doing at the time—and then either deny or exaggerate it afterwards.

Besides that difficult but necessary empirical enquiry, there could also be a normative exercise. In recent years there has been an extensive and sophisticated discussion of the circumstances in which military intervention may be justified— the debate about 'humanitarian intervention' and the 'responsibility to protect', or R2P—but almost none about the norms for non-military intervention in the affairs of other states. What is and is not legitimate? Might it be possible to elaborate a 'right to promote' civil resistance, democracy or respect for human rights, even a 'responsibility to promote'—a second R2P? But would this not be regarded in many parts of the world as a kind of Western neo-colonialism in liberal internationalist guise? Might not non-democratic rulers draw on other, more 'Westphalian' principles in international law and practice to articulate a countervailing R2P—a 'right to prevent'?

## FOUR DICHOTOMIES AND AN AGENDA

An old truth: the more you know, the less you know. Or perhaps more accurately: the better you understand how much there is still to understand. Some of the

---

[29] I owe this insight to a presentation by Pavol Demeš at a panel discussion on 'The European Way of Civil Resistance' organized by the Oxford University Project on Civil Resistance and Power Politics at St Antony's College, Oxford, on 23 May 2008.

most fundamental questions raised by the studies in this book can be organized around four necessarily simplifying dichotomies:

- agency/structure
- ends/means
- success/failure
- analysis/prescription

The relationship between agency and structure is a hardy perennial of all historical enquiry and has been a recurrent theme here. To what extent do the choices made by historical actors—in this case, the protagonists but also the antagonists of non-violent action—determine the outcome? To what extent are outcomes dictated by circumstances and conditions, from physical geography, through economic, political, and military structures, to the international context? In the literature, one finds both the voluntarist and the determinist tendencies. The truth, as Doug McAdam and others have argued, is that both agency and structure matter. They also interact. Skilful strategy by the proponents of change can over time create new structures of opportunity. Skilful strategy by defenders of the status quo can close down opportunities that were there before. It is the combination of good strategic dramaturgy and a favourable structure of opportunity that produces the probability, though never the certainty, of significant change.

The classic Jacobin–Bolshevik position was that 'the end justifies the means'. 'What base act would you not commit, to | eradicate baseness?' asked the young Leninist Bertolt Brecht, and exhorted his readers to 'Sink into filth | embrace the butcher, but | change the world: it needs it!'[30] Civil resistance challenges both the moral and the political claims of that position. Morally, Gandhi argued that there was ultimately no distinction between ends and means. As Judith Brown summarizes his view: the right means produce moral ends, while bad means inevitably produce immoral ends.[31] You cannot lie your way through to the truth.

But this is not just a moral argument. Politically, too, the means you adopt will determine—or at least, very significantly influence—the end at which you arrive. This is a point made most eloquently by the Polish dissident intellectual and Solidarity activist Adam Michnik in a letter from prison written in 1985. 'Taught by history,' Michnik writes, 'we suspect that by using force to storm the existing Bastilles we shall unwittingly build new ones.' And he goes on to warn that 'historical awareness of the possible consequences of revolutionary violence must be etched into any programme of struggle for freedom. The experience of being corrupted by terror must be imprinted upon the consciousness of everyone who belongs to a freedom movement.'[32] It is therefore best to start as you mean to go on.

---

[30] Bertolt Brecht, *Die Massnahme*, translation and context in Timothy Garton Ash, *The Uses of Adversity* (London: Penguin, 1999), 29.

[31] Brown, Ch. 3 above, 47.

[32] Adam Michnik, *Letters from Prison and Other Essays* (Berkeley: University of California Press, 1985), 86–87.

Statistically, the prevalence of non-violent means correlates significantly with successful transitions to consolidated liberal democracy.[33] Of course one has to beware the correlation/cause fallacy, and look for other significant variables. It may be, for example, that the kinds of society that adopt non-violent means are the kinds of society that are also more likely, and better equipped, to consolidate liberal democracy. Non-violent action and the consolidation of liberal democracy might both be symptoms of deeper underlying causes, rather than the former being a cause of the latter. The correlation remains striking.

This, in turn, goes to the question of success or failure. In one of the last texts Gandhi published, he wrote of the 'unconquerable non-violence of the strong'. The editors entitled his article '*Ahimsa* [non-violence] never fails'.[34] Three weeks later he was assassinated by a fanatic, while horrendous internecine violence between Muslims, Hindus and Sikhs raged all around. How are we to understand what were almost his last published words? Moral success, despite apparent political failure? Long-term political success, against short-term political failure? Sixty years after Gandhi's violent death, it does not seem empty rhetoric to talk of 'the power of Gandhi's example'.

One point to emerge from the historical record of those sixty years is that the timescale for success of non-violent action can be long. This raises the question of how far the final victory can be attributed to the non-violent struggle, as opposed to other factors—which may include elements of armed struggle and changing external circumstances. (Recall our earlier observation about the frequency with which non-violent and violent action are in practice intertwined.) It was extra-ordinary to see Alexander Dubček, the hero of Czechoslovakia's 1968, standing with Václav Havel, the hero of Czechoslovakia's 1989, on the balcony in Wenceslas Square, while the crowd chanted 'Dubček-Havel, Dubček-Havel'; but in what sense can we meaningfully say that the Prague Spring triumphed in '89?[35] That claim can more plausibly be made where there is a continuous history of organized non-violent struggle, as with Solidarity in Poland.

What, anyway, is the yardstick of success? As the Polish poet Zbigniew Herbert observed in another context, 'simple questions | require such complicated an-swers'.[36] A relatively neutral and historically sensitive definition of success might be 'to achieve the goals that non-violent protagonists set themselves': self-rule for India, ending racial segregation in the US, ending apartheid in South Africa, ending communist rule in central Europe, independence for Kosovo, and so on.

---

[33] See the data and analysis in Adrian Karatnycky and Peter Ackerman, *How Freedom is Won: From Civic Resistance to Durable Democracy* (New York: Freedom House, 2005).

[34] '*Ahimsa* never fails', *Harijan*, 11 Jan. 1948, in Brown (ed.), *Mahatma Gandhi: The Essential Writings*, 373.

[35] As Alex Pravda has noted (see n. 27 above) the larger influence would seem to have been not on Czech or Slovak protagonists but on Soviet policymakers around Gorbachev, several of whom had been in Prague in 1968 and were deeply influenced by the Prague Spring. Their helpful illusion was that 'socialism with a human face' could still be achieved in 1989.

[36] 'The Return of Mr Cogito', in Zbigniew Herbert, *The Collected Poems: 1956–1998* (London: Ecco, 2008).

This assessment is more complicated than it might appear at first glance, since different non-violent actors had different goals and individual non-violent actors sometimes had multiple ones. Often outcomes are ambiguous: what looks like failure in the short term may appear as success in the longer term, or vice versa.

If we define success as 'to achieve consolidated liberal democracy' we are applying a normative assumption which by no means all protagonists of non-violent action shared. That seems to me legitimate—so long as we are explicit about the nature of the exercise. Here we are measuring achievement and outcomes *ex post facto*, by standards that seem to us valuable, but may not have been so important to those who made the change at the time, or to those who are still working for change in other places.

This takes us to a final dichotomy: analysis and prescription. Most of the contributors to this book probably share a preference for democracy over dictatorship, and for non-violent action over the use of force—that is, for not killing people rather than killing them. Most would probably regard it as legitimate to offer non-violent activists lessons, or at least a body of distilled experience, from past examples of civil resistance. Moreover, in our lives as citizens we may wish to contribute directly to that prescriptive and political purpose. But I must emphasize again that this has not been our purpose in this academic and analytical project.

Here the task we have set ourselves is the classical one of unprejudiced enquiry into the nature and causes of things, *rerum cognoscere causas*, respecting, so far as humanly possible, Tacitus's injunction to write without bias or anger, *sine ira ac studio*. The end of this enquiry is knowledge—nothing more, nothing less. If our findings are helpful to those who wish to use the methods of non-violent action to achieve goals we personally share, that will give us pleasure. If dictators wish to draw on such findings to learn how to foil such efforts, that will cause us pain. But the knowledge gained, such as it is, is freely available for all to use as they see fit.

Much, however, still remains to be learned. Even within its own self-imposed limits, this book, along with other studies, has merely made a beginning in the description and analysis of what has actually been. It covers only some of the cases that might qualify for treatment under our definitions, and does so only briefly in each case. One of our authors wrote to us suggesting a much larger project to produce a set of carefully researched comparative monographs, addressing the initial questions, and others that have emerged in the course of this enquiry, on the basis of all the available evidence in each case. We hope someone will take up this challenge.

Because many of the events chronicled here are recent, and participants still alive, there is a reservoir of oral history waiting to be tapped. Oral history is particularly important when dealing with underground and popular movements whose development is, for reasons at once of conspiracy and chaos, not usually documented as the work of governments is. Meanwhile, as official papers are opened after the usual thirty years, or sooner due to a change of regime, they can yield new insights into the way states react to such challenges. Nothing would give us greater pleasure than to see this volume ultimately render itself redundant.

# Index

Compiled by Rohan Bolton

Note: *f* following a page number denotes a figure/photograph, *n* denotes a footnote (with the number where necessary).

*Index*